DISCRIMINATION LAW

LᴺHD

(EMPL)
Con
Std

DISCRIMINATION LAW

SECOND EDITION

BY

MICHAEL CONNOLLY

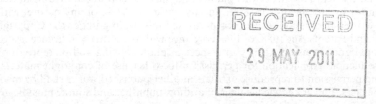

SWEET & MAXWELL

 THOMSON REUTERS

Published in 2011 by Sweet & Maxwell,
100 Avenue Road, London NW3 3PF
part of Thomson Reuters (Professional) UK Limited
(Registered in England & Wales, Company No 1679046.
Registered Office and address for service:
Aldgate House, 33 Aldgate High Street, London EC3N 1DL)

Typeset by YHT, London
Printed in Great Britain by TJ International, Padstow, Cornwall

*For further information on our products and services, visit
www.sweetandmaxwell.co.uk

No natural forests were destroyed to make this product;
only farmed timber was used and re-planted.

A CIP catalogue record for this book is available from the British Library.

ISBN 978-0-414-04606-1

Thomson Reuters and the Thomson Reuters logo
are trademarks of Thomson Reuters.
Sweet & Maxwell ® is a registered trademark
of Thomson Reuters (Professional) UK Limited.

Crown copyright material is reproduced with the permission
of the Controller of HMSO and the Queen's Printer for Scotland.

PREFACE

The last edition of this book appeared in 2006. The long wait for this edition was due to the long wait for the Equality Act 2010, which began with the Government's Discrimination Law Review, launched back in February 2005.

The Equality Act 2010 streamlined the vast array of disjointed legislation enacted over the years, mostly in reaction to decisions and Directives made at European level. The Act also introduced some new notions, such as (limited) positive action and a (limited) right for equal pay claimants to rely on hypothetical comparisons. Generally, the Act has enhanced the protection against discrimination. The Act and these new developments are explored within, as are the harmonised and extended Public Sector Equality Duties. Other innovations in the Act have not been brought into force. This rather curious situation can be explained by the political background. The Act was drafted and passed under the Labour Government in April 2010, but with the main parts not due in force until after the May general election. This returned the Coalition Government, which had less enthusiasm towards the more ambitious provisions, such as the "Public sector duty regarding socio-economic inequalities" and the duty on large employers to publish "gender pay gap information". Hence, these provisions are unlikely to come into force in the foreseeable future, if at all. At the time of writing, the Coalition Government was "still considering" whether to bring into force the concept of "dual discrimination", and so that concept is discussed in this edition.

In the meantime, the European Court of Justice has been busy, especially in the field of age discrimination, and the European Court on Human Rights has been developing discrimination law under the European Convention on Human Rights. These developments there are included within.

As before, I have included comparative material, especially from the United States. The US Civil Rights Act 1964 was the forerunner of much of the discrimination law in Great Britain and Europe, and the US Federal courts have decades of experience dealing with many issues arising here fore the first time. Hence, these materials can help "fill the gaps".

I hope once again to present the law as a tool of compassion to help redress the failings in our societies, and not simply as a highbrow philosophical concept.

I have tried to state the law as it stood on January 1, 2010.

Michael Connolly
January 2010

CONTENTS

vii

TABLE OF CASES

TABLE OF STATUTES

TABLE OF STATUTORY INSTRUMENTS

CHAPTER 1

THEORIES OF DISCRIMINATION LAW

1. THE MEANING OF DISCRIMINATION

For the general public, an easily-received legal definition of discrimination is different treatment motivated by prejudice or hostility.[1] For practitioners of discrimination law, this is too simplistic. The lawyer knows that discrimination must include, at the least, behaviour that has an unintended adverse effect on a protected group (normally indirect discrimination), say a customary length of residence requirement to work in local services. Meanwhile the judiciary, aware of this professional opinion, are conscious of the public's perception when defining discrimination. Hence, in *Khan v Chief Constable of West Yorkshire*,[2] Lord Woolf M.R. (as he then was) stated: "To regard a person as acting unlawfully when he had not been motivated either consciously or unconsciously by any discriminatory motive is hardly likely to assist the objective of promoting harmonious racial relations." In *Nagarajan v London Regional Transport*,[3] Lord Browne-Wilkinson dissented: "To introduce something akin to strict liability into the Acts which will lead to individuals being stamped as racially discriminatory ... where these

1–001

---

[1] Alexander argues strongly not all discrimination should be unlawful, even where it is immoral. "For example, a person who, in choosing a spouse ... excludes members of a particular race solely because of a bias, may be acting within her moral rights even if she is acting immorally." L. Alexander, "What makes wrongful discrimination wrong? Biases, preferences, stereotypes and proxies" (1992) 141 Penns UL Rev 149, p.201.
[2] [2000] I.C.R. 1169 (CA), [14]. Discussed, Ch.7, para.7–008.
[3] [2000] 1 A.C. 501 (HL), at 510. Discussed, Ch.7, para.7–007.

1

matters were not consciously in their minds when they acted is unlikely to recommend the legislation to the public as being fair and proper protection for the minorities that they are seeking to protect."

The use of public understanding as an interpretive tool is clearly controversial, but for some, public understanding is "crucial in a democracy ... and necessary for the enactment and enforcement of civil rights law".[4] Whatever the merits of that view, the reality is that the legal definition of discrimination will be, to some degree, influenced by the public's understanding of discrimination. So it cannot be ignored in the following discussion.

Even as a simplistic notion of prejudice, discrimination can be attributed with several meanings. Sunstein considers that it encompasses three types of mistake.[5] The first is an incorrect view that people in certain groups possess characteristics.[6] The second is a belief that many members of a group have certain characteristics when in fact only a few of them do. Here, the error is an extremely over-broad generalisation. The third mistake is a reliance on fairly accurate group-based generalisations when more accurate (and not especially costly) classifying devices are available. Thus even where a group predominantly possesses a particular characteristic, it is possible to identify the relevant individuals, rather than treat the group as a whole. An example arose in *Bohon-Mitchell v Common Professional Examination Board*,[7] where those with degrees from outside the British Isles were presumed to be unfamiliar with the British way of life. For Rutherglen, the typical liberal understanding of discrimination is "doubly paradoxical".[8] It appreciates unintentional discrimination, yet at the same time endorses positive action programmes which expressly account for protected characteristics, such as sex or race.

1–002   A new more subtle and challenging definition of *racial* discrimination was brought into the public's consciousness in 1999 by the Macpherson Report (the inquiry into the police response to the murder of the black teenager, Stephen Lawrence). The Report drew together many explanations of the phrase *institutional racism* to produce a widely accepted definition. After making the point that overt racism was not at issue in the inquiry, it identified "unwitting", and "unconscious", racism. The Report then noted the *effect* of actions and police culture as areas for attention: the problem lies not

---

[4] G. Rutherglen, "Discrimination and its discontents" (1995) 81 Virginia L Rev 117, pp.127–128.

[5] C. Sunstein, "Three civil rights fallacies" (1991) 79 California L Rev 751, pp.752–753.

[6] M.O. McGowan, "Engendered Differences", SSRN ELibrary 1361196 (2009), suggests that for gender: "We have created difference and inequality despite our sameness, partly because of our irresistible cognitive urge to categorize people on the basis of sex and the systematic errors in judgments that result from that categorization".

[7] [1978] I.R.L.R. 525 (IT). See further, para.6–039.

[8] G. Rutherglen, "Discrimination and its discontents" (1995) 81 Virginia L Rev 117, pp.127–28.

with individual officers, but with the organisation. The Macpherson Report defined institutional racism as:

> "The collective failure of an organisation to provide an appropriate and professional service to people because of their colour, culture, or ethnic origin. It can be seen or detected in processes, attitudes and behaviour which amount to discrimination through unwitting prejudice, ignorance, thoughtlessness and racist stereotyping which disadvantage minority ethnic people."[9]

Discrimination can also be characterised under principles of either *harm* or *unfairness*.[10] The harm principle rests on a strong connection between the stigma and denied opportunity of the different treatment, and social historical factors, such as the forms of second-class citizenship experienced typically (but not exclusively) by some racial groups and women. The stigma, degradation and humiliation of slavery (and the more recent racial segregation) is revived with every modern-day act of racial discrimination. Well into the 20th century, women were legal second-class citizens. They were inferior in marriage, where their legal existence was suspended, domestic violence condoned, and rape lawful. They were denied the vote, and suffered inferior job opportunities, prospects and pay.[11] Consequently, every act of sex discrimination may be seen and felt as an act championing the old arrangements. Two consequences flow from this analysis. The first is that the discriminator is easily stamped as the wrongdoer, which it makes it harder to justify outlawing unintentional (usually indirect) discrimination which, as *Griggs v Duke Power*[12] illustrates, is necessary to redress the problems associated with second-class citizenship. The second consequence is that arguments for discrimination law to include other groups appear less convincing than those for sex and race.[13] Take, for instance, the latest addition to the British statute book, age discrimination. The ECJ has produced several judgments unusually tolerant of age discrimination.[14] The Canadian Supreme Court is more tolerant of age discrimination because it is based on neither feelings of hostility nor intolerance.[15] A study of age discrimination law in the United States revealed that the chief beneficiaries were middle-class white males.[16]

---

[9] The Stephen Lawrence Inquiry, Report of an Inquiry by Sir William Macpherson, advised by Tom Cook, The Right Reverend Dr John Sentamu, Dr Richard Stone. February 1999. Presented to Parliament by the Home Secretary. Cm 4262-I, London: TSO, at paras 6.1–6.34.

[10] See J. Gardner, "Liberals and unlawful discrimination" (1989) 9 OJLS 1, pp.2–8.

[11] See S. Fredman, *Women and the Law* (Oxford: Clarendon Press, 1997), Ch.2.

[12] (1971) 401 US 424. See Ch.6, para.6–001.

[13] See further below para.1–008.

[14] See Ch.8, paras 8–071 et seq.

[15] *McKinney v University of Guelph* [1990] 3 SCR 229, at 297. The US Supreme Court takes a similar line, see Ch.2, para.2–018.

[16] See G. Rutherglen, "From race to age: the expanding scope of employment discrimination law" (1995) 24 *Journal of Legal Studies* 491, at 495.

1–003   The fairness principle relies on a much weaker link between social history and discriminatory practices. History informs us that decision-making based on irrational factors such as race and sex is inherently *unfair*. This view is easier to reconcile with the law of indirect discrimination, as less, or no, blame need be attached to the discriminator. It also makes it easier to explain the inclusion of other grounds (such as age) within the anti-discrimination legal framework. Its weakness is that it risks treating "all non-meritocratic preferences as being on all fours with slavery"[17] and "opens up the possibility of white male legal actions which exploit the vulnerability of any legal recognition of race or gender difference ...".[18] The fairness principle is also harder to reconcile with positive action programmes, which inherently discriminate against a dominant but protected group, typically white males. Preferences for women or minority racial groups repeat the same wrong that caused their subjugation in the first place. Positive action is easier to reconcile with the harm principle because here the "wrongs" are not comparable. One is to subjugate a class of persons, the other is to redress subjugation.

2. The Aims of the Law

1–004   Assuming that discrimination is either harmful or unfair, or both, the next question is what should be the aim of legal intervention. The single aspiration upon which all interested parties appear to agree is the achievement of "equality". This word appears in discrimination legislation and Human Rights instruments the world over. But it is not free of debate. First, after examination, one learns that its most distinctive feature is its "shifting meaning".[19] Rather like a politician seeking a broad mandate, it reflects whatever meaning the observer wishes it to have. The second problem is that although equality is "virtue word"[20] and as such difficult to criticise, once it is given a firm meaning, it becomes clear that equality is not necessarily a good thing. What follows is a discussion of various models and ideals of equality within discrimination law.

(1) Formal Equality

1–005   Equality has been the underpinning principle of modern anti-discrimination law, beginning in the United States with the Civil

[17] See J. Gardner, "Liberals and unlawful discrimination" (1989) 9 OJLS 1, p.8.
[18] N. Lacey, "From individual to group", in B. Hepple, and E. Szyszczak (eds), *Discrimination: The Limits of Law* (London: Mansell, 1992), p.104.
[19] P. Westen, *Speaking of Equality* (Princeton: Princeton University Press, 1990), p.xviii.
[20] ibid.

Rights Act 1964. The primary goal of that Act was redressing the historic inequalities suffered by the United States' African-American population. The Act made it unlawful to "discriminate" because of such individual's race, colour, religion, sex or national origin.[21] From this, the US Supreme Court developed the disparate treatment (or direct discrimination) model.[22] The logical consequence is that those obligated by the Act must practice same—or *equal*—treatment. Britain too, adopted this model, with, for example, the 1976 Race Relations Act providing that direct discrimination was treating someone "less favourably" on racial grounds, with the obvious and intended meaning that, on racial grounds, persons should be treated equally.

These models of equality are symmetrical, meaning that the law protects whites as well as blacks, men as well as women, and so on and so forth. In their simplest form, these models represent *formal* equality, that like should be treated as like.[23] (The notable exception here is disability discrimination law, which insists upon *different* treatment.)[24] There a number of problems associated with formal equality.

The first problem is that equal treatment is not necessarily virtuous. At its most general, equal treatment is a consequence of the rule of law, by which laws must be enforced equally. But this does not prevent discriminatory laws, such as apartheid, being enacted and enforced equally.[25] A law of equal treatment is a step removed from unequal laws, but its enforcement can have counter-productive or unequal results. In his comment on the French law of vagrancy and theft, Anatole France mocked: "The law, in its majestic equality, forbids the rich as well as the poor to sleep under bridges, to beg in the streets, and to steal bread."[26] In this context, Westen notes the equal treatment handed out in Hitler's concentration camps.[27] The point is that equal treatment can amount to equally *bad* treatment.

In one infamous US case, after a court ordered a Mississippi city to abandon its racial segregation policy for its swimming pools (four white-only, one black-only), the city administration responded by closing down all its pools instead. This act did not offend the US

1–006

---

[21] e.g. Title VII, s.703(a), codified as 42 USC s.2000e-2.

[22] See e.g. *McDonnell Douglas Corp v Green* 411 US 792 (1973).

[23] This can be traced back to Aristotle in *Nicomachean Ethics,* V.3.

[24] See generally, Ch.13, para.13–001. Hugh Collins identified three "deviations" from a simple equal treatment principle. First, different *treatment* is required in some cases, e.g. pregnancy and disability. Second, equal treatment is not permitted where it causes unjustifiable indirect discrimination. Third, affirmative action. See H. Collins, "Discrimination, Equality and Social inclusion" (2003) 66 M.L.R. 16, at 16–17.

[25] See J. Jowell, "Is Equality a Constitutional Principle?" (1994) 47 *Current Legal Problems* (Pt 2, Collected Papers) 1, pp.4–91.

[26] Anatole France, *Le Lys Rouge* (*The Red Lily*), 1894, quoted in John Bartlett, *Familiar Quotations*, 14th rev. edn (Boston: Little Brown, 1968), p.802a.

[27] P. Westen, *Speaking of Equality* (Princeton: Princeton University Press, 1990), p.xvii.

constitutional right to equality.[28] In the context of sex discrimination law, employers have defended claims by arguing (successfully) that they treated the claimant and her comparator equally *badly*. This has arisen in the field of sexual harassment, where homophobic abuse of a lesbian was not actionable because a male homosexual would have been equally abused.[29] Similarly, men and women in a factory were treated equally by the display of pornographic pictures of women.[30] In the field of pregnancy, British courts have compared the pregnant woman with a "sick man", allowing employers to prevail if they can show that they would dismiss any worker who took a certain amount of time off work for illness.[31] The irony here is that the worse the treatment, the more likely it is that he will be believed. Some industries employing predominantly female or minority workers, may pay poverty wages.[32] In all these cases the solution has been asymmetrical law, requiring no comparator, such as free-standing laws against sexual harassment and pregnancy discrimination, and the National Minimum Wage Act 1998.

Workers also may be "equally" victimised for bringing discrimination claims so long as all workers are treated that way, whatever the nature of their claim. Under this meaning of equality, such workers can be denied a reference,[33] or a transfer, or a grievance hearing.[34]

1–007 The second problem centres on the need of the equal treatment model for a comparator. A claimant cannot insist that she has been treated unequally until she produces a person who would have been treated more favourably. There are technical and philosophical problems associated with the comparator-driven approach. Technical problems arise because this model does not allow for differences between the groups. This most notable case here is pregnancy discrimination. A claimant cannot produce a pregnant male comparator.[35] Similarly, in cases involving religion, claimants will often be seeking *different*, rather than equal treatment. For instance, there is no obviously suitable comparator for a Muslin worker requesting Friday afternoons off work to attend a Mosque. This problem has been recognised overtly in the United States. In *EEOC v Ithaca Industries*[36] the employer was obliged to accommodate a worker's

---

[28] *Palmer v Thompson* 403 US 217 (1971).
[29] *Pearce v Governing Body of Mayfield Secondary School* [2003] UKHL 34. See further, paras 4–002 and 5–023.
[30] *Stewart v Cleveland Guest Ltd* [1996] I.C.R. 535 (EAT). See further, Ch.5 para.5–023.
[31] *Hayes v Malleable Working Men's Club and Institute* [1985] I.C.R. 703 (EAT). This approach was effectively overruled by the ECJ. See further, Ch.4, para.4–040.
[32] See the discussion on real or hypothetical comparators, Ch.9, para.9–005.
[33] *Khan v Chief Constable of West Yorkshire* [2002] 1 W.L.R. 1947 (HL). See further, Ch.7, para.7–008.
[34] *Corneleus v University College Swansea* [1987] I.R.L.R. 141 (CA); *US v New York City Transit Authority* 97 F 3d 672 (2nd Cir. 1996). See further Ch.7, para.7–008.
[35] See, Ch.4, para.4–040.
[36] 849 F 2d 116 (4th Cir. 1988), certiorari denied, 488 US 924 (1988).

refusal to work on a Sunday for a religious reason, by enquiring if fellow workers would cover that shift. This was because, for cases of religious discrimination, the legislation's equality theory is not disparate treatment or disparate impact, but "reasonable accommodation".[37] This theory was reconciled with a notion of equality: "We are convinced that [the legislation] ... has the primary secular effect of preserving the *equal* employment opportunities of those employees whose moral scruples conflict with work rules ...".[38]

The philosophical objection is that the comparator, when found, "far from being an abstract individual, is in fact white, male, Christian, able-bodied, and heterosexual".[39] Hence, this approach provides only *"equality in terms of a norm set by men"* leaving women with the right only to aspire to be the same as men.[40] Similarly, Townsend-Smith feared that the law could be used to reinforce male-based values, such as an ability to work longer hours, have unbroken and long service, aggression or dynamism. "[I]t is important to see how deep-rooted is the notion of merit in our society, and that merit has historically been determined in male terms. The danger is that the law will accept male definitions of what is meritorious in employment, and that this will not correspond with the desires or best interests of many or most women."[41] Likewise, equipment and machinery in the workplace can have gender connotations: "In a training workshop ... it is impossible to get a teenage lad to wipe the floor with a mop, though he may be persuaded to sweep it with a broom."[42]

Similarly, Lacey argues that, for women, formal equality does not go far enough as "it has little bite in view of the disadvantages which women suffer in private areas such as family life, untouched by the sex discrimination legislation".[43] The problem, she argues, is formal equality conceptualises the problem as *sex discrimination* rather than *discrimination against women*, rendering "invisible the real social problem". This objection applies to other grounds as well as gender. A benign quality, such as being socially reserved, can be used as a

---

[37] In 1972, an amendment to Title VII, s.701(j) (codified in 42 USC s.2000e(j)) was enacted with the stated purpose to protect Sabbath observers whose employers fail to adjust work schedules to fit their needs. "The Act thus requires that an employer, short of undue hardship, make reasonable accommodations to the religious needs of its employees", ibid. at 118 (Judge Hall).

[38] ibid. at 119 (Judge Hall). Emphasis supplied.

[39] S. Fredman, *Discrimination Law*, (Oxford: OUP, 2001), p.9.

[40] See T. Ward, "Beyond sex equality: the limits of sex equality in the new Europe", in T. Hervey and D. O'Keeffe (eds), *Sex Equality Law in the European Union* (Chichester: John Wiley, 1996), p.370.

[41] R. Townshend-Smith, *Sex Discrimination in Employment: Law, Practice and Policy* (London: Sweet & Maxwell, 1989) pp.25–26. See *Price Waterhouse v Hopkins* 490 US 228 (Sup Ct 1989) where the job required aggressiveness. Discussed, Ch.4, para.4–033.

[42] C. Cockburn, *In The Way of Women: Men's Resistance to Sex Equality in Organisations* (Basingstoke: Macmillan, 1991), p.38.

[43] N. Lacey, "Legislation against sex discrimination: questions from a feminist perspective" (1986) 14 JLS 411, pp.413–417.

reason not to hire, even though this quality is characteristic of Indian Hindus of the Brahmin caste.[44]

The third problem is that in principle, equal treatment prevents *more* favourable treatment, and so prevents positive action. It is naive to believe that positive action is not necessary to redress the effects of past discrimination, which is a major reason for the legislation in the first place. Yet it clashes with the basic notion of equal treatment, especially in the mind of the public. Positive action plans are only permissible as an exception to the equal treatment model.[45]

1–008   The fourth problem with the equal treatment model is that it suggests that *everyone* is entitled to it, rather than just those groups specified in dedicated legislation. On the face of it, this should not be a problem. But dedicated legislation confining *equal* treatment to just *some* groups can ferment discontent and resentment by those not formally protected. And many other groups, whose political power is not so strong, are as likely to be need of equal treatment as many covered by the legislation. Further, it is difficult to construct arguments to deny equal treatment to any individual, whether idiosyncratic or conventional. There is ample evidence that anyone feeling aggrieved will feel entitled to equal treatment. Men,[46] atheists,[47] whites[48] and white racists,[49] have readily used the symmetry of the equal treatment model to redress their own grievances. In the UK, before the introduction of dedicated religious discrimination legislation, religious groups argued that they, by coincidence, were also racial groups, and so fell within the protection of the Race Relations Act 1976.[50] Many on low wages have tried obtaining a "fair" wage using equal pay law.[51]

In a relatively short time, the world has moved from a "norm" of treating races and women differently, to specifying religion, disability, sexual orientation, gender reassignment and age (in addition to race and gender) as deserving of equal treatment. People generally may

[44] See *Kapoor v Monash University* (2001) VSCA 0247, 4 VR 483 (Supreme Court of Victoria, Australia).

[45] Positive, or affirmative, action, is discussed in Ch.11.

[46] *Jepson and Dyas-Elliott v The Labour Party* [1996] I.R.L.R. 116 (IT). Cases brought by male claimants under equal pay legislation have been instrumental in the restructuring of pension plans. See e.g. *Barber v Guardian Royal Exchange* C Case-262/88; [1990] I.R.L.R. 240 (ECJ).

[47] *EEOC v Townley Engineering* 859 F 2d 610 (9th Cir. 1988). The employer made "a covenant with God" that the company would be a "would be a Christian, faith-operated business" and insisted that employees attend a weekly devotional service. It was held that this was religious discrimination against an atheist.

[48] See e.g. *McDonald v Santa Fe Trail Transportation Co* 427 US 273 (Sup. Ct 1976); *Carter v Gallagher* 452 F 2d 315 (8th Cir. 1971) cert denied 406 US 950 (1972).

[49] *Redfearn v Serco* [2006] EWCA 659 (see further Ch.4, para.4–026). There are numerous examples in the US of the Ku Klux Klan invoking equality law. See e.g. *New York ex rel Bryant v Zimmerman (No.2)* 278 US 63.

[50] *Mandla v Dowell Lee* [1983] A.C. 548 (HL) (Sikhs recognised as race); *Crown Suppliers v Dawkins* [1993] I.C.R. 517 (CA) (Rastafarians denied recognition). Discussed, Ch.3, para.3–009.

[51] See e.g. *Strathclyde Regional Council v Wallace* [1988] 2 W.L.R. 259 (HL); *Glasgow CC v Marshall* [2000] 1 W.L.R. 333 (HL). Discussed Ch.9, para.9–030.

feel entitled to equal treatment because there is little evidence of any single fundamental principle dictating which groups should be singled out. The reasons for inclusion appear to be more capricious than principled.

One explanation is that these groups operated successful political campaigns. Some are embedded in the respective nation's consciousness. President Kennedy was moved by Martin Luther King's "I have a dream" speech to promote the Civil Rights Act of 1964.[52] In the UK, the daughter of the Minister for Disabled People drew huge public support by leading a campaign that embarrassed a reluctant government to introduce the Disability Discrimination Act 1995.[53] But not all groups obtained protection principally through their own political campaigns. The EU's Race Directive was partly, at least, the result of the politicians' fear of Europe's far-right fascists exploiting the enlargement from 15 to 25 nations.[54] The EU's equal pay law was enshrined in the original Treaty of Rome at the insistence of the French: as France was the only country with an equal pay law at the time, French *employers* (not workers or feminist groups) campaigned for its inclusion in the Treaty to avoid unfair competition from other member states.[55] Gender was introduced into the Civil Rights Act 1964 as a wrecking amendment, the proposer believing that Congress would never vote for it.[56]

Thus, the reasons why particular groups have been singled out for **1–009** dedicated anti-discrimination legislation are many and varied. On the other hand, a sense of a principle can be detected from attempts to apply the "equality" rubric contained in human rights or constitutional instruments. The Supreme Court of Canada centres its approach on "human dignity". The US Supreme Court identifies

---

[52] See J. Greenya, "Rites of Passage: The Civil Rights Act of 1964", *Washington Lawyer* March/April 2000 (*www.dcbar.org*, search for "Rites of Passage"); C. Whalen and B. Whalen, *The Longest Debate: a Legislative History of the Civil Rights Act* (Washington, DC: Seven Locks Press, 1985).

[53] Respectively, Victoria and Nicholas Scott. See *The Times* May 12, 1994 and May 21, 1994; *The Independent* May 12, 1994.

[54] In its proposal, the European Commission stated: "[T]he [Race] Directive will provide a solid basis for the enlargement of the European Union, which must be founded on the full and effective respect of human rights. The process of enlargement will bring into the EU new and different cultures and ethnic minorities. To avoid social strains in both existing and new Member States and to create a common Community of respect and tolerance for racial and ethnic diversity, it is essential to put in place a common European framework for the fight against racism", COM/99/0566 final—CNS 99/0253, at p.4, para.[6].

[55] "What is particularly striking about what we know of the debates and manoeuvres which produced Article 119 is the level of abstraction at which they took place. At no time are the interests of women considered even obliquely or the issues of social justice raised. The distance from the reality of work or any real struggle seems complete. However, the potential for a stronger implementation of equal pay was embedded in the history of the article and, paradoxically, in the history of the EC itself. It took activist women to realise these possibilities—and switch the debate from one of economic rationality to a demand for rights", C. Hoskyns, *Integrating Gender* (London: Verso, 1996), at p.57.

[56] The proposer was the 80-year-old segregationist Democrat Howard Smith of Virginia. See Greenya, above n.52.

"suspect", "non-suspect", and "residual" classes of persons. The jurisprudence of the European Court of Human Rights is less developed, with a tentative notion of "personal characteristics", but often a simple difference in treatment is enough.[57]

A fifth objection to the equal treatment model is its characteristic of "equality as consistency". Its like-for-like nature is too rigid to address to all forms of inequality.[58] The equal treatment model starts from the position that the claimant and comparator are in the same position, say a woman and man doing work of equal value. Of course they are not like-for-like when the woman is doing work of less value. Yet, theoretically at least, the formal equality dictates that she may be paid 30 per cent less even though her work is only 20 per cent less value. Conversely, a woman doing work of *more* value is only entitled to the same pay. She cannot claim proportionally more money than him.[59] But this problem is less to do with principle and more to do with the restriction in the equal pay legislation that allows only a real (i.e. not hypothetical) comparator. Once this restriction is disregarded, claims like this can succeed under the equal treatment principle.[60]

The last objection is that formal equality can be used as a facade for bigotry. In 1896, in *Plessy v Ferguson*[61] the US Supreme Court held that "separate but equal" segregation in streetcars did not breach the constitutional right to equal protection of the laws. "We consider the underlying fallacy of the plaintiff's argument to consist in the assumption that the enforced separation of the two races stamps the colored race with a badge of inferiority. If this be so, it is not by reason of anything found in the act, but solely because the colored race chooses to put that construction upon it." In other words, the Court considered that once formal equality had been achieved, how people felt about the result was their problem.

(2) Substantive Equality[62]

1–010 These limitations of formal equality have led to moves towards substantive equality. Perhaps the most dramatic shift occurred with the US Supreme Court's change of heart towards the racial segregation policies of the southern States. Some 60 years after *Plessy v*

---

[57] These approaches are considered further in Ch.2, para.2–010.
[58] See S. Fredman, *Discrimination Law* (Oxford: OUP, 2001), p.10.
[59] *Evesham v North Hertfordshire Health Authority* [2000] I.C.R. 612 (CA). See further Ch.9, para.9–008.
[60] See *County of Washington v Gunther* 452 US 161 (Sup. Ct 1981). See further Ch.9, para.9–008.
[61] 163 US 537, at 551 (1896).
[62] See C. Barnard and B. Hepple, "Substantive equality", (2000) 59(3) CLJ 562; For a discussion of EC discrimination law as a substantive rights, or anti-discrimination, model, see M. Barbera, "Not the Same? The Judicial Role in the New Community Anti-Discrimination Law Context" (2002) 31 ILJ 82; For a Canadian perspective, see C.D. Bavis, "*Vriend v Alberta, Law v Canada, Ontario v M and H*: the latest steps on the winding path to substantive equality", 37 Alberta L Rev 683.

Fergusan (above), the US Supreme Court in *Brown v Board of Education*[63] ruled that segregation in education was inherently unequal and unconstitutional. And so substantive equality demands that social justice and equality is meaningful and real to disadvantaged groups. The shift has been recognised expressly by Canadian Supreme Court Justice (now Chief Justice) Beverly McLachlin:

"It is the belief that if equality is to be realized, we must move beyond formal legalism to measures that will make a practical difference in the lives of members of groups that have been traditionally subject to the tactics of subordination. ... The use of the law to promote substantive equality, the phase we presently find ourselves in, takes two forms. The first is legislated programs whereby government, social and economic institutions are encouraged or, in some cases, required, to include people of under-represented groups. The second is the judicial concept of substantive equality, developed by the courts ...".[64]

Substantive equality suggests that responsibility for discrimination rests not just with the wrongdoer in court, but the dominant group as a whole which has benefited from society's structuring on racial, gender, and other grounds. This means that the dominant group should bear the cost of change.[65] It arises for example, when "innocent" whites and males lose out to apparently lesser-qualified minorities or women in positive action programmes in employment, education, or housing. Substantive equality also suggests that the State has a role. If it does nothing it is perpetuating discrimination. Thus it has a positive duty to intervene.[66]

Two particular theories are aligned with substantive equality: *equality of opportunity* and equality *of results*. Lustgarten described these two notions thus:

"In its purest or most extreme form the first accepts that discrimination has been abolished when all formal and deliberate barriers against blacks have been dismantled. Its concern stops with determining whether the factor of race has caused an individual to suffer adverse treatment. At the furthest point at the other end of the spectrum the unalloyed fair-share approach is concerned only with equality of result, measured in terms of

---

[63] 347 US 483 (1954).
[64] B. McLachlin, "The evolution of equality" (1996) 54 Advocate 563, citing *Andrews v Law Society of British Columbia* [1989] 1 S.C.R. 143.
[65] See S. Fredman, *Discrimination Law* (Oxford: OUP, 2001), p.129.
[66] ibid.

proportionality. Its inherent logic leads to the adoption of quotas as a remedy once a finding of discrimination is made."[67]

1–011 The shift from formal equality to equality of opportunity was articulated by Wasserstrom, who suggested that that in a sea of inequalities, it seems pointless, philosophically and practically, to redress just one. As formal equality seeks to reward individual merit (rather than group status), it is the most qualified who deserve the most benefits. Yet, the distribution of these qualifications is dictated by factors beyond the control of the individual, such as the home environment, socio-economic class of parents, and the quality of the schools attended. "Since individuals do not deserve having had any of these things vis-à-vis other individuals, they do not, for the most part, deserve their qualifications. And since they do not deserve their abilities they do not in any strong sense deserve to be admitted because of their abilities . . .".[68] Thus, there can only be true equality if the competitors in a race begin from the same starting point.[69] Lacey's criticism of formal equality (above, para.1–007) can be just as relevant here. If the race is one designed by white men, and is one in which they naturally prevail, even an equality of opportunity model fails to address the true problem.[70] Regardless of the merits of that opinion, it is undeniable that equality of opportunity cannot guarantee that society's benefits will be evenly distributed. The *equality of results* approach rests on the patent injustice of unevenly distributed benefits. At the least, this a measure by which the equality of opportunity model can be tested. But even this approach may fall short of expectation: "as one might have suspected from its American antecedents the fair-share approach is in no way compatible with great inequalities of income, wealth and social resources: it merely requires that blacks fit into the existing patterns of inequality in the same proportions as whites."[71]

The pragmatic view of all this is that the undefined slogan *equal opportunities* was able to unite diverse political groups to support anti-discrimination legislation. "How many liberal supporters of the current legislation, for example, would have been content to reflect on the implications of a thorough-going commitment to equality of

---

[67] L. Lustgarten, *Legal Control of Racial Discrimination* (London: Macmillan Press, 1980), pp.6–7; see also L. Mayhew, *Law and Equal Opportunity* (Cambridge, MA: Harvard Uuniversity Press, 1968), pp.59–74.

[68] R. Wasserstrom,, "Racism, sexism and preferential treatment: an approach to the topics" (1977) 24 UCLA L Rev 581, pp.619–20.

[69] K. O'Donovan and E. Szyszczak, *Equality and Sex Discrimination Law* (Oxford: Blackwells, 1988), pp.4–5; S. Fredman, *Discrimination Law* (Oxford: OUP, 2001), p.14.

[70] S. Fredman, *Discrimination Law* (Oxford: OUP, 2001), pp.128–129.

[71] L. Lustgarten, *Legal Control of Racial Discrimination* (London: Macmillan Press, 1980), pp.6–7.

opportunity in terms of socialisation of childrearing or even genetic engineering?"[72]

(3) Equality, Pluralism and Compassion

Wasserstrom[73] has presented three alternative goals of "equality" law. **1–012** The first is the *assimilationist* model. Here, in a non-racist society, a person's race is the "functional equivalent" of their eye colour. This is less easy to present in respect to sex, disability and religion, where there are accepted differences that characterise these groups. The second is diversity. Here genuine differences, say between religions, are a "positive good". It would be a worse society if everyone were a member of one religion. The third is tolerance. Here, there is nothing intrinsically positive about diversity, but tolerance outweighs the evils of achieving homogeneity.

The second and third of these goals align with current policy in North America and the European Union. But slogans commonly by governments in search of these goals, such as *different but equal* and *equality and diversity*[74] are paradoxical, giving the law the delicate task of achieving both equality and diversity. Wasserstrom suggests that this may be achieved with celebration or tolerance. Of course, in reality a dose of both is required. It suggests that the key is psychological, or emotional, rather than formal. Human rights law generally originates, partly at least, from human compassion, or the milk of human kindness. People generally have a sense of compassion, especially for the underdog. This appears at odds with the resistance by ordinary (so presumably decent) people to much discrimination law, especially positive action programmes[75] and the truism that anti-discrimination laws are enacted to combat prejudices in mainstream society. The comments by Lords Woolf and Browne-Wilkinson at the beginning of this chapter (above, para.1–001) reveal that the general public's perception is important in defining the law. But in complex societies where so much disadvantage is invisible to an uninformed public, this is no more useful than asking for a jury's opinion after providing it with newspapers instead of the evidence. The notion falls well short of an ideal. This implies that there is a duty on politicians and the judiciary to educate the public in the real

---

[72] N. Lacey, "Legislation against sex discrimination: questions from a feminist perspective" (1986) 14 JLS 411, p.414.

[73] R. Wasserstrom, "Racism, sexism and preferential treatment: an approach to the topics" (1977) 24 UCLA L Rev 581, pp.585–589.

[74] Government documents on discrimination law have employed this phrase, e.g. "Equality and Diversity: Age Matters. Age Consultation" (2003); "Equality and Diversity: Updating the Sex Discrimination Act" (2003).

[75] In the 2004 general election, in a core Labour constituency, Peter Law resigned from the Labour Party in protest at the selection of a candidate from an all-women short-list. He stood as an independent and overturned the Labour majority of 19,000 votes, winning with a majority of 9,000 (*The Times*, April 6, 2004). In 2006 the Labour Party issued an apology to the electorate "for getting it wrong" (*The Independent*, May 8, 2006).

disadvantages that exist in their society, so triggering their innate human compassion. The neglect of this duty is perhaps most sadly apparent with immigration and asylum. Mainstream politicians commonly and quite comfortably inform the public of problems associated with asylum seekers[76] but rarely explain a traumatic story behind any plea for sanctuary. Similarly, politicians shamelessly express "populist" but pernicious opinions on minority groups such as Gypsies and Travellers.[77] This breeds cynicism rather than compassion, which in turn feeds into the legal interpretations, as Lords Woolf and Browne-Wilkinson have confirmed.

The judiciary can take a lead as well. For the law to be structured around human compassion is not as fanciful as it first seems. As noted above, the Canadian Supreme Court has developed its human rights jurisprudence around the theme of "human dignity".[78] The US Supreme Court identifies groups for constitutional protection against discrimination by factors such as a history of purposeful and invidious discrimination, based on prejudice or inaccurate stereotypes, against a class without political power.[79] These observations about the state of groups in society are as loaded with compassion as they are with intellectual rigour. This attempt at defining legally the underdog shows that positive human emotions can be identified and realised in law.

---

[76] There are countless examples. In 2002, the Home Secretary, David Blunkett, observed that the children of asylum seekers were "swamping" some schools (*The Times*, April 25, 2002). In 1972 it was observed that the Government's "ambivalent" policy was to proclaim racism wrong while declaring that Britain was too small to absorb any more immigrants: "Understandably, few people have grasped the distinction. The more obvious conclusion that has generally been drawn is that if coloured immigration presents a threat to Britain's well-being, so does the coloured minority living in Britain", A. Lester, and G. Bindman, *Race and Law* (Harmondsworth: Penguin, 1972), p.13.

[77] See Royce Turner, "Gypsies and British Parliamentary language: an analysis" (2002) 12 *Romani Studies*, pp.1–34, who summarises that they are portrayed in Parliament as: "dishonest, criminal, dirty". For an account of the Coalition's "offensive" on Gypsies and travellers, see J. Grayson, "Playing the Gypsy 'race card'" (2010) Institute of Race Relations June 4, 2010, *http://www.irr.org.uk/2010/june/ha000020.html* (accessed January 1, 2011).

[78] For a discussion of dignity in English law, see D. Feldman, "Human dignity as a legal value", Pt I [1999] PL 682, Pt II [200] PL 61. For a discussion on the role that dignity can play in discrimination law, see G. Moon and R. Allen, "Dignity discourse in discrimination law: a better route to equality?" (2006) 6 E.H.R.L.R. 610.

[79] Accordingly racial groups are afforded more protection than age groups (see further, Ch.2, para.2–017). The Supreme Court has not refined the matter much further though, as, somewhat perversely, whites are afforded the same equal protection as other racial groups: *Adarand Constructors v Pena* 515 US 200 (1995).

CHAPTER 2

THE SOURCES OF ANTI-DISCRIMINATION LAW

INTRODUCTION

The principal UK dedicated discrimination and equality legislation is   **2–001**
contained in the Equality Act 2010, although the Equality Act 2006,
so far as it established the Equality and Human Rights Commission,
remains in force. There are several dedicated discrimination Treaty
Articles and Directives at EU level, covering much the same ground
as the Equality Act 2010. A further dimension to discrimination law
has been brought about by the Human Rights Act 1998, which
incorporated the European Convention on Human Rights into
domestic law. The Convention demands that the rights within it must
be secured without discrimination. The judiciary also has a part to
play. There is the role of the common law in combating discrimination, which has developed very little, if at all. There is also the
interpretation of the legislation, which has proved to be particularly
important in the development of discrimination law.

The Equality Act 2006 s.14, empowers the Equality and Human
Rights Commission to issue Codes of Practice. It is not compulsory

to follow a Code of Practice, but a failure to follow a Code may be taken into account in proceedings.[1]

1. UK LEGISLATION

2–002   The Equality Act 2010 was passed on April 8, 2010, although it was intended it should come into force in stages, beginning in October 2010. However, in May 2010 a new Coalition Government came into office and was less enthusiastic about some of the more ambitious provisions which, the Government announced, it was "considering" or abandoning altogether. The result is that the vast majority of the Act came into force on October 1, 2010,[2] with the public sector single equality duty[3] and positive action in recruitment and promotion (employment) both due in force in April 2011.[4] The Government abandoned the public sector socio-economic duty, and the gender pay gap reporting duty for large employers. By January 2011, the Government was "considering": Dual discrimination; Duty to make reasonable adjustments to common parts of leasehold and commonhold premises; Provisions relating to auxiliary aids in schools; Diversity reporting by political parties; Provisions about taxi accessibility; Prohibition on age discrimination in services and public functions; civil partnerships on religious premises.[5]

The two main purposes of the Act were to harmonise discrimination law, and to "strengthen the law to support progress on equality".[6] The first purpose was necessary because Britain's discrimination legislation had developed piecemeal into a bewildering range of heavily amended statutes and statutory instruments.[7] The principal domestic legislation consisted of the Race Relations Act 1976 (RRA 1976), Sex Discrimination Act 1975 (SDA 1975), which included gender reassignment, Equal Pay Act 1970, and the Disability Discrimination Act 1995 (DDA 1995). This "scheme" covered discrimination in employment and other fields, such as the provision of goods, facilities and services, education, housing and premises, and public body functions. In addition (deriving from EC law), for *employment*, there were statutory instruments covering Religion or

---

[1] EA 2006 s.15(4).
[2] SI 2010/2317.
[3] "Equality Act 2010: The public sector Equality Duty" (2010) JN402461, Ch.4. *http:// www.equalities.gov.uk/pdf/402461_GEO_EqualityAct2010ThePublicSectorEqualityDuty_acc.pdf* (accessed December 23, 2010).
[4] For details of planned implementation, see *www.equalities.gov.uk/PDF/DLRConsultation.pdf* (accessed January 1, 2011).
[5] ibid.
[6] Equality Bill 2009, Explanatory Note 10.
[7] See S. Fredman, "Equality: a new generation?" (2001) 30 ILJ 145.

Belief, Sexual Orientation, and Age.[8] Subsequently, coverage to other fields was extended to religion or belief and sexual orientation.[9]

In the meantime, European Community law was developing with ECJ decisions and Directives. Successive Governments chose to implement these changes under their powers given by the European Communities Act 1972, which meant that the implementations could go no further than the European law in question. Some parts of the pre-existing domestic legislation (RRA 1976, SDA 1975, DDA 1995) remained unreformed by these changes and this created two classes of domestic law. The differences could be subdivided into definitions, procedural rules, and fields covered. The Directives provided a different (broader) definition of indirect discrimination, and new dedicated definitions of harassment and sexual harassment. The Race Directive 2000/43/EC covered discrimination only on the grounds of "racial or ethnic origin", while the coverage of RRA 1976 extended to "colour" and "nationality". Second, the Directives provided a procedural difference, mandating a shifting burden of proof, which was new to domestic practice. Third, unlike their domestic counterparts, the Directives' coverage for sex and disability discrimination was limited to employment matters. The essential story here is the failure to amend domestic legislation universally, when implementing EC law. This left a "residual" class of claims, which had to be decided under the unreformed law, and a multitude of anomalies.

By the year 2000, it was estimated that there were at least 30 **2–003** relevant Acts, 38 Statutory Instruments, 11 codes of practice, and 12 EC Directives and Recommendations directly relevant to discrimination,[10] and within sex discrimination law alone, 15 differences between EC and domestic law.[11] The following examples show how tortuous the statutory "scheme" became. Sexual harassment was made specifically unlawful in employment matters, but this was not extended to other fields. So claims for sexual harassment in the supply for goods or services, for instance, had to be pleaded as direct sex discrimination, a more technical and sometimes impossible task. A tribunal entertaining a claim for direct race discrimination, based on ethnicity and nationality, would have to divide the hearing

---

[8] Respectively, Employment Equality (Religion or Belief) Regulations 2003, SI 2003/1660; Employment Equality (Sexual Orientation) Regulations 2003, SI 2003/1661; Employment Equality (Age) Regulations 2006, SI 2003/1031.

[9] Respectively, Pt 2 of the Equality Act 2006, the Equality Act (Sexual Orientation) Regulations 2007, SI 2007/1263.

[10] B. Hepple, M. Coussey and T. Choudhury, *Equality: A New Framework Report of the Independent Review of the Enforcement of UK Anti-Discrimination legislation* (Oxford: Hart, 2000), at para.[2.1]. See also J. Harrington, "Making Sense of Equality Law: A Review of the Hepple Report" (2001) 64 (issue 5) M.L.R. 757, and S. McKay, "Proposing a New Framework to Combat Discrimination" (2001) 30 ILJ 133.

[11] ibid. para.2.6.

procedurally.[12] The formalised burden of proof rules applied to the ethnicity aspect, while the residual rules applied to the nationality aspect. Similarly, there are different definitions of indirect discrimination depending upon whether the claim was based on nationality, colour (residual definition) or racial or ethnic origins (EC derived definition). Under the DDA 1995, the definitions of discrimination differ, depending upon whether the claim fell within employment matters, or the one of the other fields, such as the supply of services, or education.

There were, however, reservations about moving to a single equality statute. The now defunct Commission for Racial Equality argued that a single equality statute would blur the focus on specific types of discrimination, with a general concept of equality unable to achieve the "sharp impact" necessary to tackle institutional racism.[13]

The need for reform outweighed these doubts and in 2005, the Government embarked upon a wide-reaching discrimination law review to achieve a clearer and more streamlined framework.[14] Thus, the first purpose of the Equality Act 2010 was to harmonise this disparate body of law concerning discrimination claims. In general, whether existing law fell short of Community law, or vice versa, the Act "levelled up".

2–004   The Equality Act's other main purpose was to step beyond to individualistic discrimination model and launch a range of collective solutions to inequality, such as (limited) positive action, extending (and harmonising) public sector equality duties, and providing collective remedies for individual employment claims.[15] Prior to the 2010 Act, the Equality Act 2006 established the Commission for Equality and Human Rights, a new single strategic enforcement body which absorbed the three existing bodies (Equal Opportunities and Disability Rights Commissions, Commission for Racial Equality), and had powers and duties regarding the other strands of discrimination (age, religion or belief, and sexual orientation). In addition, the Commission has human rights within its remit, which has a general prohibition against discrimination in the securing of those rights.[16]

---

[12] See *Okonu v G4S Security Services* [2008] I.C.R. 598 (EAT), [23], cf. *Abbey National v Chagger* [2009] I.C.R. 624(EAT), [32]–[35], appeal dismissed on other grounds [2010] I.C.R. 397 (CA).

[13] Hepple et al. (above, n.10), para.2.10.

[14] *www.equalities.gov.uk/PDF/DLRConsultation.pdf* (accessed January 1, 2011).

[15] See respectively, Ch.11, para.11–008; Ch.10; Ch.12, para.12–034.

[16] See below, para.2–006.

2. EUROPEAN COMMUNITY LAW

Beginning with the Treaty of Rome in 1957, Community law has   **2–005**
addressed two "orthodox" grounds of discrimination, nationality and
equal pay. The relevant articles are now contained in the Treaty of
the Functioning of the European Union (TFEU). First, nationality
discrimination is outlawed generally ("Within the scope of application of the Treaties"),[17] and specifically in employment by a prohibition of "discrimination based on nationality between workers of the
Member States".[18] This prohibition flows from the principle of free
movement of workers inherent to the ambition of creating a common
market.[19] Second, the Treaty of Rome provided for equal pay
between men and women.[20] This is now provided by art.157 TFEU
(ex 141 TEC) and has been the basis of the more comprehensive
prohibitions on gender discrimination in employment and vocational
training, now consolidated into the "Recast" Directive 2006/54/EC.

More recently, and more generally, art.19 TFEU[21] provides the
power to "combat discrimination based on sex, racial or ethnic origins, religion or belief, disability, age or sexual orientation." Article
19 has great potential, especially as it is not limited to employment
matters. Apart from the Recast Directive, art.19 is the basis for all the
equality Directives and Commission Proposals outlined below.

The main Directives flowing from either art.157 or art.19 TFEU
are as follows. For *employment and vocational training*, discrimination on the ground of sex, including gender reassignment and equal
pay is addressed by the "Recast" Directive 2006/54/EC; for race, by
the Race Directive 2000/43/EC, and for religion or belief, sexual
orientation, disability and age, by the "Framework" Directive 2000/
78/EC.

In fields beyond employment, racial discrimination is outlawed by
the Race Directive, covering social protection, including social
security and healthcare; social advantages; education; and access to
and supply of goods and other services which are available to the
public, including housing. Sex discrimination is outlawed by the
Goods and Services Sex Discrimination Directive 2004/113/EC covering the supply of goods and services, but it does not apply to the

---

[17] art.18 TFEU (ex 12 TEC).
[18] art.45 TFEU (ex 39 TEC).
[19] See e.g. *Ingetraut Scholz* v *Opera Universitaria di Cagliari* Case C-419/92 [1994] E.C.R. 1-
507.
[20] See now, art.157 TFEU (ex 141 TEC).
[21] Ex art.13 TEC. Introduced by the Treaty of Amsterdam, May 1, 1999.

"content of media and advertising nor to education".[22] Although not expressed, the supply of services should include housing, and has been presumed as such by the Commission.[23] The European Commission has proposed a parallel Directive for the remaining strands of religion, sexual orientation, age, and disability, covering the same activities as the Race Directive.[24]

3. THE HUMAN RIGHTS ACT 1998[25]

2–006 The Human Rights Act 1998 incorporated the European Convention on Human Rights (ECHR) into domestic law, coming into force on October 2, 2000.[26] At the time, it served as a "safety net" to catch many discrimination cases that fell through the rather haphazard coverage of the dedicated discrimination legislation. Since then, the protected characteristics and activities covered by dedicated legislation have grown into a fairly comprehensive scheme, cumulating with the Equality Act 2010. This would seem to reduce the scope of the Human Rights Act in domestic discrimination law. Nonetheless, case law is developing the grounds of discrimination covered by the ECHR beyond the protected characteristics stipulated in the domestic and EU dedicated discrimination legislation, and so the Convention is still the only instrument to provide a remedy to many cases of discrimination.[27]

The Human Rights Act brings into domestic law a model of "higher" law familiar to most western democracies, by which the state and its "ordinary" laws must comply. The United States' Equal Protection Clause of the 14th and 5th Amendments provides a

---

[22] art.3(3). Recital 11 of the preamble refers to art.50 TEC (now art.57 TFEU) for the definition of services, as those: "normally provided for remuneration, in so far as they are not governed by the provisions relating to freedom of movement for goods, capital and persons. 'Services' shall in particular include: (a) activities of an industrial character; (b) activities of a commercial character; (c) activities of craftsmen; (d) activities of the professions." For a definition of goods, the preamble refers the free movement of goods provisions of the TEC, which have been interpreted to cover anything capable of money valuation and of being the object of commercial transactions (*Commission v Italy* (case 7/68)).

[23] See COM(2008) 426 final, pp 1–2. Such documents can be found at the Register for Official Documents *ec.europa.eu/transparency/regdoc/registre.cfm?CL=en*.

[24] ibid.

[25] See N. Foster, "The European Court of Justice and the European Convention for the Protection of Human Rights" (1987) 8 Human Rights L.J. 245; Y. Aras, "The ECHR and non-discrimination" (1998) 7 *Amicus Curiae*, the Journal of the Society for Advanced Legal Studies 6. Generally, B. Clarke (ed.), *Challenging Racism* (London: Lawrence & Wishart, 2003, in association with the Discrimination Law Association, ILPA, CRE and 1990 Trust); K. Ewing, "The Human Rights Act and Labour Law" (1998) 27 ILJ 275.

[26] SI 2000/1851.

[27] For the advantages of using the Convention for discrimination claims, see C. Ferguson, "Running Ahead of Strasbourg: Indirect Discrimination and Article 14 ECHR" (2008) JR 71, [20]–[25].

constitutional guarantee of equal protection of the laws, so (respectively) state or federal discriminatory laws may be challenged as unconstitutional. Similarly, Canada enjoys the Charter of Rights and Freedoms, by which national and provincial laws must comply. The matter is more complex in the UK, because of the absence of a formal written constitution and with it a system that facilitates "higher" law. Thus, while the Human Rights Act encourages the State, including the courts, to comply with the Convention, where legislation cannot be reconciled with a Convention right, it cannot be struck down by the courts. Note that, although the Convention, and the Court of Human Rights (ECtHR or "the Strasbourg court"), are separate from European Community law, the European Court of Justice (ECJ) will respect the Convention's principles,[28] and so Convention principles can find their way into UK law via Community law.

What follows is a discussion of how the Convention deals with discrimination, and how its incorporation may modify and compliment existing discrimination law.

(1) Discrimination and the European Convention on Human Rights

(a) The Claim Must Fall within a Convention Right
The Convention gives no free-standing right against discrimination.[29]   **2–007**
Article 14 provides merely that the rights and freedoms in the Convention must be "secured" without discrimination. The free-standing, or *substantive*, rights given by the Convention are: to Life (art.2), against Torture (3) and Slavery (4); to Liberty (5); a Fair Trial (6); No Punishment Without Law (7); to Respect for Family and Private Life, Home and Correspondence (8); to Freedom of Thought, Conscience and Religion (9); to Freedom of Expression (10) and Assembly and Association (11); to Marry (12); to Peaceful Enjoyment of One's Possessions (1st Protocol, art.1); to Education (P1, A2), to Free Elections (P1, A3).

---

[28] See e.g. *R. v Kirk* (Case 63/83) [1984] 2 E.C.R. 2689; *Johnston v Chief Constable of the Royal Ulster Constabulary* (Case 222/84) [1986] E.C.R. 1651. Grosz, Beatson and Duffy, *Human Rights: The 1998 Act and the European Convention*, (London: Sweet and Maxwell, 2000) pp.11–15, [1.18]–[1.23]). See generally, J. Steiner and L. Woods, *Textbook on EC Law*, 10th edn (Oxford: OUP, 2009), p.141, [6.4].

[29] The 12th Protocol provides a free-standing right against discrimination, but not yet been ratified. (To follow its progress, see *http://www.conventions.coe.int/Treaty/Commun/Que VoulezVous.asp?NT=177&CM=8&DF=31/08/2010&CL=ENG* [Accessed August 31, 2010].) For a discussion of the protocol see G. Moon (2000) 1 E.H.R.L.R. 49; J. Schokkenbroek, "Towards a stronger European protection against discrimination: the preparation of a new additional protocol to the ECHR" and J. Cooper, "Applying equality and non-discrimination rights through the Human Rights Act 1998", both in *Race Discrimination* (Oxford: Hart, 2000); and V. Khaliq, "Protocol 12 to the ECHR: a step forward or a step too far?" [2001] P.L. 457; R. Wintemute, "Filling the Article 14 'gap': Government ratification and judicial control of Protocol No.12 ECHR: Part 2" [2004] 5 E.H.R.L.R. 484.

The first thing to note is that in some instances, a discriminatory practice may violate a substantive article, irrespective of art.14. In *Vogt v Germany*,[30] the dismissal of a schoolteacher for her membership of the Communist Party was held to violate art.11. In *Goodwin v UK*,[31] the State's refusal to give legal recognition to a transsexual's acquired sex violated art.8. So here, discrimination based on political belief or gender reassignment was resolved without recourse to art.14.

There is no need to prove a *breach* of a substantive right for claims of discrimination. Were it otherwise, art.14 would serve no useful purpose, being redundant or, at best, duplicative. Indeed, when the Court, entertaining a discrimination claim, finds a violation of the substantive article, normally it declines to discuss the art.14 claim.[32] Accordingly, it is normal practice for the Court only to consider art.14 when a substantive article, although *engaged*, is *not* breached.[33]

2–008   To engage a substantive article, the general rule is that the activity must fall within the "ambit" of one of the rights. This brings art.14 into play. In *Petrovic v Austria*,[34] the State paid parental leave allowance to mothers, but not fathers. A father challenged this rule under the Convention, for discriminating on the ground of sex. He relied on art.8 in combination with art.14. The Court held that although art.8 imposed no obligation upon States to give financial assistance to parents, the allowance fell within the ambit of art.8 and so art.14 was engaged. The Court's reasoning was that art.14 comes into play whenever "the subject-matter of the disadvantage ... constitutes one of the modalities of the exercise of a right guaranteed" or the measures complained of are "linked to the exercise of a right guaranteed". And so, by granting parental leave allowance "States are able to demonstrate their respect for family life within the meaning of art.8".[35] This suggests two paths to engaging a substantive article: "modalities" and "link". The meaning of both of these expressions is not readily obvious, and indeed, they have been applied "flexibly"[36] by the ECtHR.

This flexible approach is exemplified in *Adami v Malta*.[37] Here, the preponderance of men chosen for compulsory jury service was challenged, under art.4 (forced labour) in combination with art.14. It

---

[30] (App. No.17851/91) (1996) 21 E.H.R.R. 205.
[31] (App. No.28957/95) (2002) 35 E.H.R.R. 18.
[32] e.g. *Vogt v Germany* (App. No.17851/91) (1996) 21 E.H.R.R. 205; *Goodwin v UK* (App. No.28957/95) (2002) 35 E.H.R.R. 18; *Dudgeon v UK* (App. No.7525/76 (1982) 4 E.H.R.R. 149; *Smith & Grady v UK* (App. Nos 33985/96 and 33986/96) (2000) 29 E.H.R.R. 493. *Cf Sibabras v Lithuania* (App. No.55480/2000) (2006) 42 E.H.R.R. 6, [41], [50], [63] and *SL v Austria* (App. No.45330/99) (2003) 37 E.H.R.R. 39, [28], [47].
[33] cf. the odd reasoning in *Gypsy Council v UK* (App. No.66336/01) where a ban on a Gypsy horse fair was justified under art.11, and so apparently did not invoke art.14. See also *Sidabras* (2006) 42 E.H.R.R. 6.
[34] (1998) 33 E.H.R.R. 307.
[35] ibid. [27]–[29].
[36] *M. v Secretary of State for Work and Pensions* [2006] 2 A.C. 91 (HL), [14] (Lord Nicholls).
[37] (App. No.17209/02), (2007) 44 E.H.R.R. 3.

might be thought strange that jury service could be described as "forced labour", and indeed, art.4 contains a qualification that the term "forced or compulsory labour" shall not include "any work or service which forms part of normal civic obligations". Yet, with two pieces of imaginative logic, the ECtHR found that jury service fell within the ambit of art.4. First, the Court accepted that jury service falls within this qualification, but considered the qualification "is not intended to 'limit' the *exercise* of the right ... but to 'delimit' the very *content* of that right".[38] In other words, there is an "exception to the exception".[39] Second, as the jury selection was discriminatory, it was "abnormal", and so not covered by the qualification of *normal* civic obligations.[40] This logic is rather fragile, as it is considering art.14 before art.4 is triggered and effectively using art.14 to engage a substantive article. In his concurring Opinion, Judge Bratza criticised the "delimit" logic and held that the *ambit* of a substantive article is "significantly wider" than its *scope*, and so art.4 encompassed jury service.[41] Meanwhile Judge Garlicki, also concurring, criticised the "delimit" logic because he feared it would make it "very difficult to establish"[42] a link with art.4. In other words, even this imaginative approach was not liberal enough.

It follows that the Court's flexible approach has created a seemingly haphazard body of discrimination case law. This is highlighted by the range of admissible employment complaints,[43] which stand out because the Convention is neither designed nor expressed to provide employment rights.[44] In *Thlimmenos v Greece*,[45] the Court held a refusal to admit the applicant as a chartered accountant, because of his criminal conviction for failing to wear military uniform for religious reasons (being a Jehovah's Witness), was disproportionate under arts 9 and 14. Other discriminatory employment practices could engage arts 10 or 11 (political beliefs),[46] or art.8 concerning either gender identity[47] or sexual orientation,[48] or less obviously, an exclusion from a profession or career, as this can

---

[38] ibid. [44], citing *Schmidt v Germany* (App No 13580/88) (1994), [22]. Emphasis supplied.

[39] ibid. P.72 [0–113], (Judge Garlicki, concurring).

[40] ibid. [45], citing *Van der Mussele v Belgium* (App. No.8919/80) [43].

[41] ibid. P.71, [0–17].

[42] ibid. p.72 [0–114].

[43] See R. Wintemute, "'Within the ambit': how big is the 'gap' in Article 14 European Convention on Human Rights? Part 1" [2004] 4 E.H.R.L.R. 366, esp. at 369–372.

[44] The ECHR is aimed at political and civil rights. Social and economic rights (including employment rights) are provided by its lesser known companion, the Charter of Social Rights. The Charter is beyond the competence of the ECtHR: *Rudenko v Ukraine* (App. No.19441/03) (ECtHR) July 12, 2007, [18]; *Kucherenko v Ukraine* (App. No.27347/02) (ECtHR) December 15, 2005, [28].

[45] (App. No.34369/97) (2001) 31 E.H.R.R. 15, [41]

[46] See *Vogt v Germany* (App. No.17851/91) (1996), above, para.2–007.

[47] *Goodwin v UK* (App. No.28957/95) (2002) 35 E.H.R.R. 18.

[48] *Dudgeon v UK* (App. No.7525/76 (1982) 4 E.H.R.R. 149; *Smith & Grady v UK* (App. Nos 33985/96 and 33986/96) (2000) 29 E.H.R.R. 493.

violate one's private life because of its effect on the person's ability develop human relationships at work or to earn a living.[49]

Those cases illustrate the uncertainties surrounding the "ambit test". In *M v Secretary of State for Work and Pensions*, Lord Nicholls tried to explain the cases thus:

> "... the approach to be distilled from the Strasbourg jurisprudence is that the more seriously and directly the discriminatory provision or conduct impinges upon the values underlying the particular substantive article, the more readily will it be regarded as within the ambit of that article; and vice versa. In other words, the ECtHR makes in each case what in English law is often called a 'value judgment' ".[50]

A "value judgment" should be "made by reference to the circumstances prevailing when the issue has to be decided" and "not the position when the legislation was enacted or came into force."[51]

What can be said with more certainty is as follows. For "modalities", it would seem that "Article 14 is engaged whenever the subject matter of the disadvantage comprises one of the ways a state gives effect to a Convention right."[52] This explains this aspect of *Petrovic*, which shows that if a State chooses to provide rights or freedoms beyond its Convention obligations, but within the ambit of a substantive article, it must comply with art.14 when doing so.[53]

The meaning of "link" has been debated at some length. In the Court of Appeal in *Mendoza v Ghaidan*,[54] Buxton L.J. cited Grosz, Beatson and Duffy, which concluded that "even the most tenuous link with another provision in the Convention will suffice for art.14 to enter into play".[55] Some judges have doubted this opinion. For instance, in *R. (Erskine) v London Borough of Lambeth*,[56] Mitting J. suggested "it overstates the effect of the Strasbourg case law."[57] And

---

[49] See e.g. *Sidabras v Lithuania* (App. No.55480/2000) (2006) 42 E.H.R.R. 6, where a ban on ex-KGB officers from working in the civil service and other professions engaged art.8 and violated art.14.

[50] [2006] 2 A.C. 91 (HL), [14].

[51] *Wilson v First County Trust (No.2)* [2004] 1 A.C. 816 (HL), [62] (Lord Nicholls). See also the "Living Tree/Framer's Intent" debate, below, para.2–030.

[52] [2006] 2 A.C. 91 (HL) [16].

[53] See also *Stec v UK* (App. No.65731/01)(2006) 43 E.H.R.R. 43, where the Court held that a non-contributory state benefit (Reduced Earnings Allowance) fell within the ambit of Protocol 1, art.2 (Right to Possessions). Followed by *R. (RJM) v Sec. of State for Work and Pensions* [2009] 1 A.C. 311 (HL).

[54] [2002] 4 All E.R. 1162, affirmed *Godin-Mendoza v Ghaidan* [2004] UKHL 30, although the HL offered no opinion on this particular opinion, at [12].

[55] Grosz, Beatson and Duffy, *Human Rights: The 1998 Act and the European Convention* (London: Sweet and Maxwell, 2000), p.327, [C14–10].

[56] [2003] EWHC 2479 (Admin).

[57] ibid. [21]–[22].

in *R. (Douglas) v North Tyneside Metropolitan Borough Council,*[58] Scott Baker L.J. commented:

"For my part I do not read Buxton, L.J. as seeking to extend the ambit of the test as set out in Petrovic's case. The bottom line is that the measures of which complaint is made have to be linked to the exercise of the right guaranteed."[59]

More recently, the House of Lords, in *M. v Secretary of State for Work and Pensions,*[60] emphatically rejected the "tenuous link" rubric. In his concurring Opinion in *Adami v Malta,*[61] Judge Bratza accepted that the "tenuous link" doctrine "may be seen as going too far".[62]

The difference between "link" (per Scott Baker L.J.) and "tenuous **2–009** link" (per Grosz et al.) is perhaps illustrated in *Douglas*, where it was claimed that the refusal of student loans to over-55 year olds amounted to age discrimination, under art.2 of the 1st Protocol (Right to Education) combined with art.14. The Court of Appeal held that student funding was "one stage removed"[63] from the right to education. This is a convenient rubric, with the attraction of apparent certainty, but its logic is questionable. In *Petrovic*, the Court stated that parental leave allowance showed the state's "respect for family life". It is impossible to escape the similarity to student loans demonstrating the state's respect for education.

A similar distinction was relied on in *M*, where the claim centred on the calculations by the Child Support Agency for contributions by absent parents. The scheme treated absent parents who were married more favourably than absent parents living together in a same-sex relationship, with the result that the claimant had to make higher contributions. The House of Lords held that art.8 was not engaged, distinguishing *Petrovic* on the basis that there was no adverse impact against her in her family life with her own children, only against her in her same-sex relationship, which did not engage art.8.[64]

These cases suggest that there is divergence of approach between the British and European Courts, with the British approach appearing more restrictive. However, it seems that where a case before a domestic court is on all fours with a Strasbourg decision, that decision will be followed.[65]

[58] [2004] 1 All E.R. 709 (CA).
[59] ibid. [54].
[60] [2006] 2 A.C. 91 (HL).
[61] (App. No.17209/02), (2007) 44 E.H.R.R. 3 (ECtHR)
[62] ibid. p.71 [0–17].
[63] [2004] 1 All E.R. 709, at [57] and [60], CA. Distinguished in *S v Special Educational Needs and Disability Tribunal* [2005] EWHC 196 (Admin) where the funding extended beyond the mere facilitating of education to its nature and quality, at [35].
[64] [2006] 2 W.L.R. 637, [17]–[18], [85]–[87], and [124].
[65] See *R. (RJM) v Secretary of State for Work and Pensions* [2009] 1 A.C. 311 (HL), [34]–[23]; *R. (Clift) v Secretary of State Home Dept* [2007] 1 A.C. 484 (HL), [28] (Lord Bingham).

(b) Grounds of Discrimination Covered by the ECHR

(i) The Strasbourg approach

2–010   Article 14 provides that the Convention rights must be "secured" without discrimination "on any ground such as sex, race, colour, language, religion, political or other opinion, national or social origin, association with a national minority, property, birth or other status". Not only are the specific examples far wider than current domestic or European discrimination legislation, it is clear that the use of the phrases *such as* and *or other status* (a fortiori the French version *toute autre situation*)[66] opens art.14 to more grounds than those listed. Among other things, this non-exhaustive formula allows for changing values, and discrimination that was once acceptable may become unacceptable.[67] The basis for identifying other grounds for protection under art.14 is vague. In an early case, *Kjeldsen v Denmark*,[68] the Court stated that art.14 prohibits discrimination based on a "personal characteristic ('status') by which persons or groups of persons are distinguishable from each other."[69] This is somewhat narrow to be taken as a definitive interpretation, as art.14 itself lists "property" as a protected ground. The ECtHR has since entertained art.14 claims from groups as wide-ranging as owners of non-residential buildings (distinct from residential), owners of pit bull terriers (distinct from other breeds of dog), small landowners (distinct from large landowners), coastal (distinct from open sea) fishermen, foreign residence, and previous employment by the KGB.[70] This led Brooke L.J. to comment that *Kjeldsen* has been "superseded" by later cases.[71] More conventionally, the ECtHR has recognised sexual orientation, marital status, illegitimacy, trade union status, military rank, and conscientious objection[72] as falling within this residual category.

---

[66] "or any other situation". Noted in *Carson v UK* (App. No.42184/05) (2010) 51 E.H.R.R. 13, [70]; see also *RMJ v Secretary of State for Work and Pensions* [2009] 1 A.C. 311 (HL), [39].

[67] See the maturing attitude to gender reassignment in *Sheffield & Horsham v UK* (1998) 27 E.H.R.R. 347 and *Goodwin v UK* (2002) 35 E.H.R.R 18, and more generally, (below para.2–030) the "living tree" school of interpretation.

[68] (1976) 1 E.H.R.R. 711.

[69] ibid. [56].

[70] Respectively, *Spadea v Italy* (1996) 21 E.H.R.R. 482, at paras 42–46; *Bullock v UK* (1996) 21 E.H.R.R. CD 85, at para.5; *Chassagnou v France* (2000) 7 B.H.R.C. 151, at paras 86–95; *Posti and Rahko v Finland* (2002) 37 E.H.R.R. 158, at paras 79–87; *Darby v Sweden* (App. No.11581/85) (1990) E.H.R.R. 774; *Sidabras v Lithuania* (App. No.55480/2000) (2006) 42 E.H.R.R. 6.

[71] *Wandsworth LBC v Michalak* [2003] 1 W.L.R. 617 (CA), [33].

[72] Respectively, *Salgueiro v Portugal* (2001) 31 E.H.R.R. 47; *Wessels-Bergervoet v The Netherlands* (2004) 38 E.H.R.R. 793 (incl. *unmarried*: *PM v UK* (App No.(6638/03) (2006) 42 E.H.R.R. 45, [27]); *Sahin v Germany* [2003] 2 FLR 671, [94] (incl. different treatment of *parents* of children born out of wedlock: *Zaunegger v Germany* (App. No.22028/04) (2010) 50 E.H.R.R. 38, [51]); *Swedish Engine Drivers Union v Sweden* (1976) 1 E.H.R.R. 617; *Engel v NL* (1979–80) 1 E.H.R.R. 647, [72] ("house arrest" for commissioned officers, jail for other servicemen); *De Jong, Baljet and Van den Brink v The Netherlands (No.1)* (1986) 8 E.H.R.R. 20.

(ii) The British approach

Until recently, the British courts—especially the House of Lords— **2–011**
took a more technical approach. This produced a narrower interpretation of art.14, which excluded, for example, those charged but
not convicted of a criminal offence, those who have commenced legal
proceedings, the "hunting community", employees working abroad,
and those serving intermediate prison sentences.[73] This more restrictive approach was facilitated by three principles.

First, several Law Lords have suggested that art.14 is not entirely
open-ended, or infinite. The reasoning was provided by Lord Steyn:

> "[T]he proscribed grounds in article 14 cannot be unlimited,
> otherwise the wording of article 14 referring to 'other status'
> beyond the well-established proscribed grounds, including things
> *such as* sex, race or colour, would be unnecessary. It would then
> preclude discrimination on any ground. That is plainly not the
> meaning of article 14".[74]

The suggestion here is that to be recognised, the ground of discrimination must be analogous to one of the listed characteristics,
such as sex or race. This significantly reduces the reach of art.14 and
invokes a key debate: whether to focus on the phrase *such as* and
confine recognition to closely analogous grounds which may arise as
social values develop;[75] or treat art.14 as completely open ended and
recognise *any* difference of treatment between persons in analogous
situations. Baroness Hale, in particular, has championed the restrictive stance, contrasting the United States' 14th Amendment, providing equal protection of the law, which is "completely open-ended"
and so "instantly . . . different" from art.14.[76] She likens art.14 to the

---

[73] Respectively, *R. (S) v Chief Constable of the South Yorkshire Police* [2004] UKHL 39, at
[48]–[51]; *R. (Hooper) v Secretary of State for Work and Pensions* [2005] UKHL 29, [65]; *R.
(Countryside Alliance & others) v Attorney General* [2008] 1 A.C. 719 (HL) [24], [64], [130],
[145]; *Botham v Ministry of Defence* UKEAT/0503/04/DM,[21] (reversed on other grounds,
[2006] 1 All E.R. 823, HL); *R. (Clift) v Secretary of State Home Dept.* [2007] 1 A.C. 484
(HL) (distinguished from short or life sentences). In *R. (Carson) v Secretary of State for
Work and Pensions* [2005] UKHL 37, the defendant conceded that "residence abroad" fell
within art.14 ([52] and [95]), although Lord Hoffman considered it was a personal characteristic, at [13].

[74] *R. (S) v Chief Constable of South Yorkshire Police* [2004] 1 W.L.R. 2196, [48], emphasis
supplied (and relied upon by the Court of Appeal in *R. (RJM) v Secretary of State for Work
and Pensions* [2007] 1 W.L.R. 3067 (CA), [38], reversed [2009] 1 A.C. 311 (HL); see further
below). See also: *AL (Serbia) v Secretary of State for the Home Dept* [2008] UKHL 42, [26]
(Baroness Hale). *R. (Clift) v Secretary of State Home Dept* [2007] 1 A.C. 484 (HL), [27]
(Lord Bingham), [43] (Lord Hope), [61] (Baroness Hale).

[75] Obvious examples are sexual orientation (*Salgueiro da Silva Mouta v Portugal* (1999) 31
E.H.R.R. 1055), and gender reassignment: *Sheffield & Horsham v UK* (1998) 27 E.H.R.R.
347, cf. *Goodwin v UK* (2002) 35 E.H.R.R 18.

[76] *AL (Serbia) v Secretary of State for the Home Dept* [2008] UKHL 42, [21] & [31]. cf. *Carson*
[2005] UKHL 37, [15], where Lord Hoffman observes that "the Strasbourg court has given
[art.14] a wide interpretation, approaching that of the 14th Amendment".

Canadian Charter of Rights and Freedoms, which focuses on human dignity,[77] and so confines art.14 to "offensive" discrimination.[78] (The US and Canadian approaches are considered below.)

This second principle (underpinned by the first), is an adherence to the *Kjeldsen* "personal characteristic" doctrine (see above, para.2–010) to the exclusion of all other ECtHR jurisprudence. This occurred most notably in *Clift v Secretary of State for the Home Office*,[79] where a prisoner serving an "intermediate" sentence—of over 15 years, but not life—challenged the practice that only his "intermediate" group were subject to the Home Secretary's veto on parole. The House of Lords invoked the ECtHR decision in *Gerger v Turkey*,[80] where more restrictive parole entitlement for convicted terrorists did not engage art.14 because: "the distinction is made not between different groups of people, but between different types of offence, according to the legislature's view of their gravity".[81] Consequently, for Baroness Hale: "The real reason for the distinction is not a personal characteristic of the offender but what the offender has done".[82] This confidence in the decision was not shared by the rest of the House. Lord Bingham (with whom Lords Hope, Carswell and Brown specifically agreed) found it "difficult to apply so elusive a test" and observed that Clift did not complain of the sentence, but the denial of parole.[83] This makes the case one step removed from *Gerger*. He went on to say that a prisoner serving a life sentence would have an "acquired status" (e.g. a religion or political opinion) as a "lifer", and found it hard to see why someone in Clift's group should be differently regarded.[84] Despite these doubts, Lord Bingham yielded to a lack of Strasburg authority on the point and so found that Clift had no status for the purposes of art.14.

2–012   The third principle is that it is not for domestic courts to break new ground in Convention jurisprudence. In *Clift*, despite the doubts expressed by the majority, it found against Clift because "a domestic court should hesitate to apply the Convention in a manner not … explicitly or impliedly authorised by the Strasbourg jurisprudence".[85] Lord Hope added:

---

[77] *Law v Canada* [1999] 1 S.C.R. 497 (SCC). The "human dignity" approach has been revised because it was "an abstract and subjective notion that [can be] confusing and difficult to apply … [and] an *additional* burden on equality claimants, rather than the philosophical enhancement it was intended to be": *R. v Kapp* [2008] 2 S.C.R. 483 (SCC) [19]–[24].

[78] *R. (Clift) v Secretary of State Home Dept* [2007] 1 A.C. 484 (HL) [57]–[58], quoting Karen Reid, *A Practitioner's Guide to the European Convention on Human Rights*, 2nd edn (London: Sweet & Maxwell, 2004), pp.261–262.

[79] [2006] 1 A.C. 484 (HL).

[80] (App. No.24919/94) July 8, 1999.

[81] ibid. [69].

[82] [2006] 1 A.C. 484 (HL), [62]. See also Lord Hope agreeing with this point, [49].

[83] ibid. [28]. Lord Hope [47], noted that the Order granting the Home Secretary's veto was made after the sentence was passed on Clift.

[84] ibid. See also Lord Hope at [46].

[85] ibid. [28].

"[T]he duty of national courts is to keep pace with the Strasbourg jurisprudence as it evolves over time. A measure of self-restraint is needed, lest we stretch our own jurisprudence beyond that which is shared by all the states parties to the Convention".[86]

The effect of this cautious approach is to render automatically inadmissible discrimination claims not yet decided upon by the ECtHR, unless of course, the claimant has the resources, time and energy, to go all the way to Strasbourg. A scenario rather defeating the point of the Human Rights Act 1998, which was intended to "bring rights home".[87]

These three principles combined to lead the Court of Appeal, in *R. (RJM) v Secretary of State for Work and Pensions*,[88] to find that "homelessness" was not a ground of discrimination recognised by art.14. This was because homelessness: (1) was not analogous to those grounds listed in art.14; (2) was not—especially if by choice—a personal characteristic (the "key point"); and (3) had not been recognised by the ECtHR.[89] As we shall see (below), this "status" aspect of the case was reversed by the House of Lords.

In *Clift*, Baroness Hale attempted to reconcile these discrepancies between the Strasbourg and the British (technical) approaches. She noted that for the most part, the ECtHR identifies discrimination by looking for different treatment of someone in "an analogous situation", and then seeing if the treatment was justified. The ECtHR, she observed, usually addresses these two issues without considering separately the "status" point. This explains the wide range of grounds entertained by the ECtHR (mentioned above, para.2–010), apparently recognising non-residential property owners, pit bull terrier owners, small landowners, coastal fishermen, foreign residence, and previous KGB employment. For Baroness Hale, it seems, as the "status" issue was not separately considered, these cases do not supplement nor disturb the "personal characteristics" doctrine adopted from *Kjeldsen*.[90] "More instructive", Baroness Hale continues, are the cases where the discrimination was held to fall outside of art.14's proscribed grounds, such as *Gerger v Turkey*.[91]

---

[86] ibid. [49].
[87] The White Paper preceding the Human Rights Act was entitled *Rights Brought Home: The Human Rights Bill* (Cm 3782, 1997). In the preface, the Prime Minister wrote: "It will give people in the United Kingdom opportunities to enforce their rights under the European Convention in British courts rather than having to incur the cost and delay of taking a case to the European Human Rights Commission and Court in Strasbourg. It will enhance the awareness of human rights in our society."
[88] [2007] 1 W.L.R. 3067.
[89] ibid. respectively [38], [46], [37].
[90] [2006] 1 A.C. 484, [54]. Lord Neuberger dubbed this a "holistic" or "'broad brush" approach: *R. (RJM) v Secretary of State for Work and Pensions* [2009] 1 A.C. 311 (HL), [39].
[91] ibid. [57]. See above.

2–013   The problem with this analysis is that it does not explain why the ECtHR addressed the "status" issue in some cases but not others. Why would the Court dismiss some applications on the relatively simple ground of status, and yet go to the trouble of exploring the "analogous situation" and justification points in others? The obvious explanation is that in these cases the Court tacitly recognised the applicant's status (or discovered it using the "analogous situation" test). It also suggests that domestic courts could perhaps take the same approach. Moreover, Baroness Hale's analysis fails to explain the *successful* claims, one on grounds of property, one on residence, and one on previous KGB employment,[92] none of which readily fall into the *Kjeldsen* "personal characteristic" principle, while the "KGB case" clearly relates to something the applicant has done, more than who he is, upsetting Baroness Hale's logic for the *Clift* decision. Consequently, in 2010, the ECtHR overturned the *Clift* decision. In doing so, it read the *Kjeldsen* doctrine to cover personal characteristics, *or* status "by which persons or groups of persons are distinguishable from one another."[93] Thus, "intermediate prisoner" was a status for the purposes of art.14. *Gerger* was distinguished on the difference between a type of crime and a length of sentence, which can reflect factors other than the type or gravity of the crime, such as the prisoner's risk to the public.[94]

More recently, one can detect a softening in the approach of the British courts. First, on the "limited" or "analogous grounds" principle, some two years after *Clift*, the House of Lords in *RJM*[95] moved their emphasis away from art.14's phrase *or other status* towards the French language version,[96] which translates as *or any other situation*, suggesting "a rather wider scope than 'or other status'".[97] Combined with the wide range of scenarios recognised by the ECtHR, this suggests that art.14 reaches way beyond grounds analogous to those listed, even if it is not "completely open-ended".

Second, although the "personal characteristics" doctrine has not been abandoned, there are signs that it is being relaxed. Subsequent speeches have echoed the *Clift* majority's less trenchant view of the doctrine. In *RJM* Lord Walker stated:

---

[92] Respectively, *Chassagnou v France* (2000) 7 BHRC 151, at §§86–95; *Darby v Sweden* (App. No.11581/85) (1990) E.H.R.R. 774; *Sidabras v Lithuania* (App. No.55480/2000) (2006) 42 E.H.R.R. 6.

[93] *Clift v UK* (App. No.7205/07), [55].

[94] ibid. [61]

[95] [2009] 1 A.C. 311 (HL).

[96] "ou toute autre situation". See also *Clift v UK* (App. No.7205/07), [55] (ECtHR). cf. *Belgian Linguistic Case* (A/6) (1979–1980) 1 E.H.R.R. 252, [I B 10], where the ECtHR preferred the narrower English phrase *without discrimination* (in art.14) to the French *without distinction of any kind* (sans distinction aucune).

[97] [2009] 1 A.C. 311 (HL), [39] (Lord Neuberger, giving the leading speech).

"'Personal characteristics' is not a precise expression and ... a binary approach to its meaning is unhelpful. ... Other acquired characteristics ... are more concerned with what people do, or with what happens to them, than with who they are; but they may still come within article 14."[98]

Given the ECtHR's reversal of *Clift* and with it Baroness Hale's reading of *Gerger v Turkey* (above), this must be considered to represent the proper approach for British courts.

The third principle was completely abandoned by the House of Lords in *RJM*, who held that homelessness fell within art.14, with the absence of ECtHR case law on the point being an "entirely neutral" factor.[99]

2–014

It seems now that domestic courts will acknowledge that art.14 is not confined to analogous grounds, that the "personal characteristics" doctrine can be applied more generously, and they are free to recognise grounds not yet litigated in the ECtHR. For the ECtHR, it seems it will continue to entertain art.14 claims using its "analogous situation" and justification tests, and only in exceptional cases pose separately the "status" question.

(iii) The Canadian and United States's approaches
As noted above,[100] Baroness Hale compared and contrasted art.14 with parallel legislation in Canada and the United States. The approaches in these jurisdictions are worth exploring to better understand the possibilities and/or limits of art.14.

2–015

To appreciate the grounds covered by Canadian Charter of Rights and Freedoms, it is necessary to look at its discrimination provisions in the round. First, note that, by s.1, all rights provided by the Charter are "subject only to such reasonable limits prescribed by law as can be demonstrably justified." Section 15 of the Charter provides a twofold formula for discrimination:

> (1) Every individual is equal before and under the law and has the right to the equal protection and equal benefit of the law without discrimination and, in particular, without discrimination based on race, national or ethnic origin, colour, religion, sex, age or mental or physical disability.

---

[98] ibid. [5].
[99] ibid. [47] (Lord Neuberger). See also *In re G* [2009] 1 A.C. 173 (HL), [119] where Baroness Hale held that English courts in some cases should "go further" than the Strasbourg Court would do. See also below para.2–030 statutory interpretation.
[100] See para.2–011. *Clift v Secretary of State for the Home Office* [2006] 1 A.C. 484 (HL) [57]–[58]. See also: *AL (Serbia) v Secretary of State for the Home Dept* [2008] UKHL 42, [21], [26]; *M. v Secretary of State for Work and Pensions* [2006] 2 A.C. 91 (HL), [103]; *R. (Carson) v Secretary of State for Work and Pensions* [2005] UKHL 37, [10] (Lord Hoffman).

(2) Subsection (1) does not preclude any law, program or activity that has as its object the amelioration of conditions of disadvantaged individuals or groups including those that are disadvantaged because of race, national or ethnic origin, colour, religion, sex, age or mental or physical disability.

Rather like ECHR, art.14, the grounds covered are expressed with a non-exhaustive list, leaving it to case law to recognise other grounds. Some guidance for this task is implicit in the twofold nature of s.15. Subsection (1) is aimed at *preventing* discrimination, while subsection (2) *facilitates* positive discrimination for disadvantaged individuals or groups. This signals that the purpose of s.15 is to achieve substantive—rather than formal—equality,[101] and immediately disassociates s.15 from the comparator-driven, symmetrical, and "sterile" doctrine of treating likes alike.[102] This asymmetrical approach suggests that "discrimination" in s.15 means "perpetuating disadvantage and stereotyping"[103] and so confined to groups easily recognised as suffering a disadvantage. In this sense, it is narrower than ECHR art.14.

With this philosophy in mind, we can now turn to the questions posed by courts when answering a s.15(1) discrimination claim:

(1) Does the (challenged) law create a distinction based on an enumerated or analogous ground?

(2) Does the distinction create a disadvantage by perpetuating prejudice or stereotyping?[104]

2–016 Here, the discrimination must be on a ground "enumerated" in s.15 (race, national or ethnic origin, etc.), or on an "analogous ground". But, it can be seen from questions (1) and (2) that that the tasks of identifying an "analogous ground" and that of identifying discrimination are somewhat interlinked: if the discrimination must perpetuate stereotyping or prejudice, the group itself must somehow be associated with stereotyping or prejudice. This means that isolating the first question is a rather artificial exercise. Nonetheless, to get a case off the ground, it must be done. The Canadian Supreme Court's guidance to this question suggested that the starting point was s.15's *enumerated* grounds:

---

[101] On substantive and formal equality, see Ch.1, paras 1–005 et seq.
[102] *R. v Kapp* [2008] 2 S.C.R. 483 (SCC), [15]; see also *Andrews v Law Society* [1989] 1 S.C.R. 143 (SCC), 165.
[103] ibid. [24].
[104] ibid. [17]. See also *Hutterian Brethren of Wilson Colony v Alberta* 310 D.L.R. (4th) 193 (SCC) [106].

"[W]hat these grounds have in common is the fact that they often serve as the basis for stereotypical decisions made not on the basis of merit but on the basis of a personal characteristic that is immutable or changeable only at unacceptable cost to personal identity".[105]

This suggests that analogous grounds should be "based on characteristics that we cannot change or that the government has no legitimate interest in expecting us to change". This translates as "immutable, like race, or constructively immutable, like religion".[106] Grounds recognised within this guidance include: citizenship,[107] sexual orientation,[108] children (immutable) and adults (constructively immutable) adopted into a recognised aboriginal tribe,[109] members of an aboriginal tribe living "off-reserve".[110]

Grounds not recognised include: independently funded election candidates (as opposed to party funded),[111] prisoners,[112] beggars,[113] "poverty",[114] place of work,[115] police officers,[116] school employees or school teachers,[117] health care workers,[118] taxpayers (as opposed to tax collectors),[119] place of residence of "average Canadians",[120] and those not with a disability.[121]

It is notable that many of these groups not recognised could be defined by *what they do* rather than *who they are*.[122] This is resonant of Baroness Hale's now obsolete restrictive approach to ECHR art.14

---

[105] *Corbière v Canada* [1999] 2 S.C.R. 203 (SCC), [13].
[106] ibid.
[107] *Law Society of British Columbia v Andrews* [1989] 1 S.C.R. 143.
[108] See e.g. *Egan v Canada* [1995] 2 S.C.R. 513; *M v H* [1999] 2 S.C.R. 3.
[109] *Grismer v Squamish Indian Band* 2006 FC 1088, [46]. Applicants were adopted as adults and were denied the advantages afforded to "natural born" members of the Squamish Nation, however the distinction was held to be justified under s.1 in this case.
[110] *Corbière v Canada* [1999] 2 S.C.R. 203 (SCC), [6], [15] and [62]. The Court stressed that the decision should be confined to its facts. It does not apply to place of residence per se: see *Archibald v Canada* [2000] 4 F.C. 479 (Fed CA), [23].
[111] *R. v Nunziata* [2005] O.N.C.J. 292 (Ontario Court of Justice), [24]–[26].
[112] *Sauvé v Canada* [2002] 3 S.C.R. 519 (SCC), [195], obiter, per Gontier, J., dissenting (the majority did not consider the point).
[113] *R. v Banks* (2007) 275 D.L.R. (4th) 640.
[114] *Re Affordable Energy Coalition* (2009) 307 D.L.R. (4th) 293.
[115] *R. v Hy & Zel's Supermarket Drug Store* (2005) 257 D.L.R. (4th) 651 (Ontario CA), [34]–[36].
[116] *Delisle v Attorney General of Canada* [1999] 2 S.C.R. 989 (SCC) [43]–[44] (Royal Canadian Mounted Police).
[117] *Baier v Alberta* [2007] 2 S.C.R. 673 (SCC), [43].
[118] *Health Services & Support-Facilities Subsector Bargaining Assn v British Columbia* [2007] 2 S.C.R. 391.
[119] *Lessard v Québec* [2007] R.J.Q. 999, [69]. Here, those appealing their tax bill were not allowed representation, unlike the tax collector.
[120] *Chippewas of Nawash First Nation v Canada* 2002 F.C.A. 485 (Fed CA), [40].
[121] *Clyke v Nova Scotia* [2005] NSCA 3(NS CA).
[122] See in particular, *Health Services & Support-Facilities Subsector Bargaining Assn v British Columbia* [2007] 2 S.C.R. 391 (SCC), [165] where the Supreme Court observed: "The differential and adverse effects of the legislation on some groups of workers relate essentially to the type of work they do, and not to the persons they are".

in *Clift*.[123] More generally, these cases demonstrate the rather limited scope of grounds covered by the Canadian Charter of Rights in comparison to ECHR art.14.

2–017   In the USA the Equal Protection Clause of the Fourteenth or Fifth Amendments provides a constitutional guarantee of equal protection of the laws.[124] Unlike the ECHR, or the Canadian Charter, no list of grounds is provided; it is completely open-ended. The method of classifying those who qualify for protection is quite different. The US Supreme Court has identified three classes of protected groups under the Clause: suspect class; quasi-suspect class; and a residual, "normal", class. Suspect classes are entitled to strict scrutiny of the challenged law. These means that such a law will survive only if it is suitably tailored to serve a compelling state or Government interest.[125] Quasi-suspect classes are entitled to intermediate—or "heightened" scrutiny. Challenged laws will survive this scrutiny if they are "substantially related" to a legitimate State, or Government, interest.[126] Laws that discriminate against a residual class will be subjected to "normal" or "rational" scrutiny, which means they must be "rationally related to a legitimate state interest."[127]

In deciding if a group qualifies as a suspect class, a court will normally consider three factors. The first is a history of purposeful discrimination.[128] Second, the discrimination embodies a gross unfairness that it is "invidious." Considerations here could be a class trait that bears no relation to ability to perform or contribute to society, or that the class has been saddled with unique disabilities because of prejudice or inaccurate stereotypes, or that the trait defining the class is immutable. Third, the group lacks the political power necessary to obtain redress from the political branches of government. The factors necessary to qualify as a quasi-suspect group are less concrete. It has been suggested that a history of past discrimination is relevant,[129] or where the characteristic, beyond the individual's control, bears "no relation to the individual's ability to

---

[123] Above para.2–011, p.28.

[124] The equal protection component of the Fifth Amendment imposes precisely the same constitutional requirements on the federal government as the equal protection clause of the Fourteenth Amendment imposes on state governments: *Weinberger v Wiesenfeld* 420 US 636, at 638 n2 (Sup Ct 1975).

[125] *McLaughlin v Florida* 379 US 184, at 192 (Sup Ct 1964); *Graham v Richardson* 403 US 365 (Sup Ct 1971). The Equal Protection Clause is used also to attack affirmative action programmes: see further Ch.13.

[126] *Mills v Habluetzel*, 456 US 91, at 99 (Sup Ct 1982).

[127] *City of Cleburne, Texas v Cleburne Living Center* 473 US 432, at 446 (Sup Ct 1985).

[128] See, e.g. *City of Cleburne, Texas v Cleburne Living Center* 473 US 432, 441 (Sup Ct 1985); *Massachusetts Board of Retirement v Murgia* 427 US 307, 313 (Sup Ct 1976).

[129] See *Watkins v US Army* 875 F 2d 699, 712 n4 (9th Cir. 1989) (Norris, J. concurring in the decision on different grounds).

participate in and contribute to society".[130] It has been held that groups defined by race, alienage (non- citizenship), national origin,[131] are suspect classes while gender and illegitimacy[132] are quasi-suspect classes.

The open-ended nature of the Equal Protection Clause means that the residual class can entertain a virtually infinite range of grounds. Courts have questioned the rationality of distinctions of wealth,[133] homelessness,[134] illegitimacy,[135] and a ban on a sitting judge from standing for political office and the corresponding temporary restriction on the voters' choice of candidate.[136] Courts have placed some more recognisable grounds of discrimination—age, disability and sexual orientation—into the residual class.

On age, the Supreme Court noted that (unlike racial groups) this group has not experienced a "history of purposeful unequal treatment or been subjected to unique disabilities on the basis of stereotyped characteristics not truly indicative of their abilities."[137]   **2–018**

On disability, the Supreme Court stated that (1) the range of legislation addressing issues of disability show there is no continuing prejudice; and (2) this also shows that this group is not politically powerless; and (3) the range of disabilities undermines the value of the "immutability theory" in this context:

> "... classifications based on physical disability and intelligence are typically accepted as legitimate. ... The explanation ... is that *those* characteristics ... are often relevant to legitimate purposes. At that point there's not much left of the immutability theory, is there?"[138]

On sexual orientation, in the absence of a definitive Supreme Court ruling, various Circuits of the United States have not ventured to

---

[130] *City of Cleburne, Texas v Cleburne Living Center* 473 US 432, 441 (Sup Ct 1985) (White J.), citing *Mathews v Lucas* 427 US 495, 505 (Sup Ct 1976).

[131] "These factors are so seldom relevant to the achievement of any legitimate state interest that laws grounded in such considerations are deemed to reflect prejudice and antipathy—a view that those in the burdened class are not as worthy or deserving as others" ibid. at 440.

[132] Respectively, *United States v Virginia* 518 US 515 (1996); *Mathews v Lucas* 427 US 495, 505 (Sup Ct 1976).

[133] *Shaffer v Board of School Directors of Albert Gallatin Area* 687 F 2d 718, 721–722 (3rd Cir 1982), cf. *Worthy v Michigan*, ibid. 811.

[134] *Joel v City of Orlando* 232 F 3d 1353, 1357 (11th Cir 2000), cert denied 532 US 978 (Sup Ct 2001).

[135] *Trimble v Gordon* 430 U.S. 762 (Sup Ct 1977).

[136] *Worthy v Michigan* 142 F. Supp. 2d 806 (ED Mich 2000).

[137] *Massachusetts Board of Retirement v Murgia*, 427 US 307, 313 (Sup Ct 1976).

[138] *City of Cleburne, Texas v Cleburne Living Center* 473 US 432 (Sup Ct 1985), 442–446 citing, at 443, J.H. Ely, *Democracy and Distrust* (Cambridge, MA: Harvard University Press, 1980), at p.150.

afford it more than a residual status.[139] The opportunity was passed up by Supreme Court in *Romer v Evans*,[140] where Colorado legislation preventing any laws designed to protect homosexuals, was struck down as "irrational", failing "even this conventional inquiry".[141] As such the Supreme Court had no need to apply a higher level of scrutiny and so avoided the question of status. Apart from the absence of precedent, the rationale of the Circuit Courts appears to be (1) although homosexuality has suffered a history of discrimination; (2) it is not an immutable characteristic: "it is behavioral and hence is fundamentally different from traits such as race, gender, or alienage"; and (3) "homosexuals are not without political power; they have the ability to and do 'attract the attention of the lawmakers' ".[142] The weakness of this rationale is that with a slight change of emphasis, points (2) and (3) could just as easily be answered the other way. For instance: (2) sexual orientation bears no relation to ability to perform or contribute to society, and has been saddled with unique disabilities because of prejudice or inaccurate stereotypes, and is immutable in the sense that the characteristic was so central to a person's identity that it would be abhorrent for a government to penalise a person for refusing to change; and (3) the fact of historic underrepresentation and victimisation by political bodies is itself strong evidence that they lack the political power necessary to ensure fair treatment.[143]

2–019   This approach, of course, is in stark contrast to that of the European Court of Human Rights, which demands the highest level of scrutiny for discrimination on the ground of sexual orientation.[144] It could be argued, especially in light of *Romer v Evans* (above) that as sexual orientation discrimination is inherently irrational, the lower status afforded by the US courts should not matter much.[145] This is true to an extent, but it did not prevent discrimination in military

---

[139] See e.g. *Scarbrough v Morgan County Bd of Edu* 470 F 3d 250, 261(6th Cir 2006) (noting homosexuality is not suspect classification in the 6th Circuit); *Citizens for Equal Protection v Bruning* 455 F 3d 859, 856 (8th Cir 2006) (noting Supreme Court has never held that sexual orientation is a suspect classification for equal protection purposes); *Johnson v Johnson* 385 F 3d 503, 532 (5th Cir 2004) (noting neither Supreme Court nor 5th Circuit has recognised sexual orientation as a suspect classification); *Lofton v Secretary of Dept of Children & Family Service* 358 F 3d 804, 818, n 16 (11th Cir 2004) (noting that all circuits that have addressed the issue have held that homosexuals are not a suspect class).

[140] 517 US 620 (1996).

[141] ibid. 632. The minority assumed the whole Court considered sexual orientation to be a residual class, ibid. 640, n.1.

[142] *High Tech Gays v Defense Indus. Sec. Clearance Office* 895 F 2d 563, at 573–574 (9th Cir 1990), citing *City of Cleburne, Texas v Cleburne Living Center* 473 US 432, at 446 (Sup Ct 1985).

[143] Taken from the detailed reasoning in the concurring opinion of Norris J. in *Watkins v US Army* 875 F 2d 699 (9th Cir 1989) 724–728. The majority did not address the issue, deciding the case on other grounds.

[144] See below, para.2–021.

[145] e.g. *Price-Cornelison v Brooks* 524 F.3d 1103 (10th Cir 2008) (sheriff's refusal to deal with same-sex domestic violence "irrational").

under the now-repealed "Don't Ask, Don't Tell" policy,[146] devised in the Clinton years as a compromise to the previous ban on homosexuality. This policy banned only those *openly* homosexual from serving in the military, which was been held to be "rational" under equal Protection scrutiny.[147] It would seem that unless the Supreme Court addresses the issue with a more progressive attitude, sexual orientation will remain a residual class.

(c) The Definition of Discrimination under the ECHR
In order to establish discrimination under art.14, the applicant has to show treatment different to another person in an analogous situation, or a failure "to treat differently persons whose situations are significantly different."[148] These two phrases correspond to direct and indirect discrimination, although the Court has been slow in developing indirect discrimination.

2–020

For indirect discrimination, the breakthrough came in the 2008 case, *DH v Czech Republic.*[149] Here, primary school children who performed poorly in intelligence tests were placed in a special school for those with mental deficiencies. Statistics showed that in one district a Roma child was 27 times more likely to be placed in a special school. The end result of this facially neutral policy was that over half of Roma and just 1.8 per cent of non-Roma children were placed in these special schools. Until this case, the Court had acknowledged the concept of indirect discrimination,[150] but had declared that it would not entertain cases based on statistical evidence.[151] However, the Court cited a number of authorities including the US seminal case

---

[146] 10 USCS § 654. See Kenji Yosino, "Assimilationist Bias in Equal Protection: The Visibility Presumption and the Case of 'Don't Ask, Don't Tell'" (1998–99) 108 Yale L.J. 485; N. Bamforth and D. Richards, *Patriarchal Religion, Sexuality and Gender: A Critique of New Natural Law* (New York: Cambridge University Press, 2008), Ch 6. Due for repeal under the Obama administration—Congress website: *http://thomas.loc.gov/cgi-bin/bdquery/D?d111:1:. /temp/~bdfh2E::\\home\LegislativeData.php?n = BSS;c = 111* July 5, 2010.

[147] e.g. *Witt v Dept of Air Force* 527 F 3d 806, 821 (9th Cir 2008) (Canby J.'s dissent holds sexual orientation is a "suspect" class, 823–826); *Thomasson v Perry* 80 F 3d 915, 928 (4th Cir 1996) (military personnel who engage in, or have a propensity to engage in, homosexual acts are not a suspect class). But note, the DODT attracts heightened scrutiny under the Due Process Clause of the 5th Amendment; *Witt* ibid. 813–821, following *Lawrence v Texas* 539 US 558 (Sup Ct 2003).

[148] *Thlimmenos v Greece* (2001) 31 E.H.R.R. 14, [44]. See above, para.2–008, p.23.

[149] (App. No.57325/00) (2008) 47 E.H.R.R. 3. Contrast the lame approach in *Gypsy Council v UK* (App. No.66336/01) where the Court held that a ban on a Gypsy horse fair did not discriminate because "It prevented any persons attending the horse fair irrespective of their origin."

[150] *Thlimmenos v Greece* (2001) 31 E.H.R.R. 14, [44]. See also *Hugh Jordan v UK* (App. No.24746/94) (2001) 37 E.H.R.R. 2, [154].

[151] See *Hugh Jordan v UK* (App. No.24746/94) (2001) 37 E.H.R.R. 2, [151]–[155], where, between 1969 and 1994, of 357 persons killed by the security forces in Northern Ireland, the overwhelming majority were nationalist/Catholic, with just four corresponding convictions. The Court refused to recognise a case of indirect discrimination based on statistics: "[T]he Court does not consider that statistics can in themselves disclose a practice which could be classified as discriminatory within the meaning of Article 14" ([154]).

Griggs v Duke Power,[152] Baroness Hale's definition of discrimination,[153] as well as European Community and United Nations materials. Accordingly, the Court reasoned that: "to guarantee those concerned the effective protection of their rights, less strict evidential rules should apply in cases of alleged indirect discrimination".[154] And so now, in line with other jurisdictions, the Court will accept statistics as proof of a prima face case of indirect discrimination.[155] The decision also confirmed that there could be liability for indirect discrimination even if the defendant had no discriminatory intent.[156] The significance of this judgment was articulated by one commentator:

> "The effect of this is that governments, when formulating social, economic and administrative policies and laws, are going to have be aware of the fact that, even if they are not deliberately setting out to discriminate through a policy or approach, if that is the result then they may still face challenges on the basis of indirect discrimination".[157]

The State defendant has the burden to "objectively and reasonably justify" the challenged discriminatory measure. In contrast to most discrimination schemes, direct discrimination is potentially justifiable. To understand this process it is better to divide it, loosely, into two categories. First, the discriminatory measure must pursue a legitimate aim and have reasonable relationship of proportionality between the means employed and the aim sought to be realised.[158] Second, the Court can afford defendant States a "margin of appreciation".

2–021   First, in some cases, the Court subjects the defence to "intensive" scrutiny, demanding "very weighty reasons" to justify discrimination. There is no hard and fast rule as to when this should occur, but one emerging theme is that these cases can be distinguished by the *ground* of the discrimination. The Court has demanded very weighty reasons in cases of discrimination on grounds of sex, sexual orientation, birth out of wedlock (including different treatment of unmarried parents),

---

[152] 401 US 424, 429–432 (Sup Ct 1971). See para.6–001.
[153] (App. No.57325/00) (2008) 47 E.H.R.R. 3, [105]. *R. (European Roma Rights Centre) v Immigration Officer, Prague Airport* [2004] UKHL 55, [73]–[91].
[154] ibid. [186]. See also *Hoogendijk v Netherlands* (App. No.58641/00) (2005) 40 E.H.R.R. SE22 189, at para.207; and *Adami v Malta* (App. No.17209/02) (2007) 44 E.H.R.R. 3, [77]–[78].
[155] ibid. [188].
[156] ibid. [184].
[157] G. Hobcraft, "Roma children and education in the Czech Republic: DH v Czech Republic: opening the door to indirect discrimination findings in Strasbourg?" [2008] 2 E.H.R.L.R. 245, 260.
[158] *Belgian Linguistic Case* (A/6) (1979–1980) 1 E.H.R.R. 252, [I B 10]; *Karner v Austria* (2003) 2 FLR 623, [37]. See also A. Baker, "Proportionality and employment discrimination in the UK" (2008) 37(4) ILJ 305.

marital status, and nationality.[159] Without saying as much, the Court appears to be dividing cases into "suspect" and "non-suspect" classes, loosely corresponding to the classifications made by the US Supreme Court (above).[160] This certainly is the view of some senior British judges.[161] This suggests that disability, religion, and age will be treated less seriously, or as "non-suspect" classes, but these questions are not settled. In *Carson*, Lord Walker considered that religion,[162] but not age,[163] belonged to the "most sensitive", or suspect class, although in *AL (Serbia)*, Lord Brown assumed age *was* a suspect ground.[164] Further, bearing in mind that the Court treats the Convention as a "living instrument",[165] these classifications are liable to change as society's values change. A recent example is *Zaunegger v Germany*,[166] where a father challenged the inferior parental rights afforded to, inter alia, unmarried parents. In finding a violation of art.14, the Court took into consideration the "evolving European context in this sphere and the growing number of unmarried parents".

An example of the Court's intensive scrutiny of a "suspect" class can be seen in *Karner v Austria*.[167] The applicant lived with his partner in a same-sex relationship in his partner's apartment. After his partner died (designating Karner as his heir), the landlord sought possession relying on the Austrian Rent Act, which provided rights of succession only for family members. The Austrian Government argued that the provision in the Rent Act was for the protection of "the traditional family unit". The Court held that while the protection of the family could be a weighty and legitimate reason, it had not been shown that the exclusion of same-sex relationships from the benefit of the Rent Act was necessary for that aim.

A second principle that may arise in the justification process is the "margin of appreciation", which varies according to the

---

[159] Respectively *Ünal Tekeli v Turkey* [2005] 1 FCR 663, [53]; *Karner v Austria* (2003) 2 F.L.R. 623, [37]; *Sahin v Germany* [2003] 2 F.L.R. 671, [94] (*Zaunegger v Germany* (App No 22028/04) (2010) 50 E.H.R.R. 38, [51]); *Wessels-Bergervoet v The Netherlands* (2004) 38 E.H.R.R. 793, [49]; and *Koua Poirrez v France* (2005) 40 E.H.R.R. 34, [46].

[160] See also, O. De Schutter, "The Prohibition of Discrimination under European Human Rights Law: Relevance for the EU", ISBN 92-894-9171-X (EN), pp.14–15 *http:// www.migpolgroup.com/public/docs/41.ProhibitionofDiscriminationunderHumanRtsLaw_EN_ 02.05.pdf* (accessed July 7, 2010).

[161] e.g. *AL (Serbia) v Secretary of State for the Home Dept* [2008] UKHL 42, [30]–[31] (Baroness Hale), [53] (Lord Brown); *R. (Carson) v Secretary of State for Work and Pensions* [2005] UKHL 37, [15]–[17] (Lord Hoffman), [55]–[57] (Lord Walker); *R. (RJM) v Secretary of State for Work and Pensions* [2009] 1 A.C. 311 (HL) [5] (Lord Walker), [14] (Lord Mance).

[162] ibid. [58], citing *Hoffman v Austria* (App. No.12875/87) (1994) 17 E.H.R.R. 293, [36].

[163] ibid. [60].

[164] ibid. [53].

[165] *Goodwin v UK* (2002) 35 E.H.R.R 18, [74]–[75] (see further, Ch.3, para.3–024).

[166] (App. No.22028/04) (2010) 50 E.H.R.R. 38, [60].

[167] (2003) 2 F.L.R. 623. Followed in *Godin-Mendoza v Ghaidan* [2004] UKHL 30.

circumstances, the subject-matter and its background.[168] This cuts right through suspect/non-suspect dichotomy, and so, for instance, a wide margin may be afforded even in a case of sex discrimination, a so-called suspect ground.[169] As such, any certainty created by the suspect/non-suspect dichotomy is somewhat undermined by this doctrine. However, the case law provides some guiding principles. A wide margin may be given to general measures of social and economic policy.[170] And it seems that where there is no common value or practice across Contracting States, it is more likely that the Court will afford a defendant State a wide margin of appreciation. For instance, in *Petrovic v Austria*,[171] the Austrian Government was afforded a wide margin of appreciation when paying only women parental leave allowances, because, at the time, there was no common standard in this field: the majority of the Contracting States did not provide parental leave allowances. Likewise, in *Schalk v Austria*,[172] the Court noted the absence of a consensus among Contracting States towards legal recognition of same-sex couples (another "suspect" category), and so "States must also enjoy a margin of appreciation in the timing of the introduction of legislative changes".[173] On the other hand, the Court has observed:

> "... an emerging international consensus amongst the contracting states ... recognising the special needs of minorities and an obligation to protect their security, identity and lifestyle, not only for the purpose of safeguarding the interests of the minorities themselves but to preserve a cultural diversity of value to the whole community".[174]

The recognition of these common values meant a State could not justify practices that resulted in the majority of Roma children being placed in special schools for the mentally retarded.[175]

Finally, note that as direct discrimination can be justified, the Court is able to sanction positive action schemes, which would otherwise be held directly discriminatory.[176]

---

[168] *Ünal Tekeli v Turkey* [2005] 1 FCR 663, [52]; *Handyside v UK* (1979–80) 1 E.H.R.R. 737, [48]. For a thorough discussion, see Y. Arai-Takahashi, *The Margin of Appreciation Doctrine and the Principle of Proportionality in the Jurisprudence of the ECHR* (Oxford: Intersentia, 2001).

[169] *Petrovic v Austria* (1998) 33 E.H.R.R. 307. See I. Radacic, "Gender equality jurisprudence of the European Court of Human Rights" (2008) 19(4) E.J.I.L. 841.

[170] *Stec v UK* (App. No.65731/01) (2006) 43 E.H.R.R. 43, [52].

[171] ibid. [38]–39].

[172] (App. No.30141/04) (2010).

[173] ibid. [105].

[174] *DH v Czech Republic* (App. No.57325/00) (2008) 47 E.H.R.R. 3, [181], citing *Chapman v UK* (App. No.27238/94) (2001) 33 E.H.R.R. 18, [93]. See [2008] 2 E.H.R.L.R. 245.

[175] ibid.

[176] See Ch.12 and also C. Van de Heyning, "Is it still a sin to kill a mockingbird?" [2008] 3 E.H.R.L.R. 376.

(2) Liability of Private Parties under the Human Rights Act 1998

Principally, the Convention binds only the State, and it is only the   **2–022**
State that can be sued ("vertical effect"). However, there is a grey area
where disputes between private parties may involve Convention
rights ("horizontal effect"). Article 1 obliges States to "secure for
everyone within their jurisdiction the rights and freedoms defined in
... the Convention". So, a state can be liable for a breach arising
from a dispute between private parties. In *Young, James & Webster v
UK*[177] the Court held that the State could be liable under art.11
(freedom of association) by legalising the dismissal (by a state or
private employer) of workers who refused to join a (closed-shop)
trade union.

The Human Rights Act 1998 (HRA 1998) attempts to confine
liability to "public authorities", or anyone carrying out public functions. Section 6(1) of the Act provides that a "public authority" must
act compatibly with the Convention rights. However, "public
authority" includes "any person certain of whose functions are
functions of a public nature" (s.6(3)(b)). Section 6(5) qualifies this,
excluding acts by private parties where the nature of the act is private.
Thus, the drafters envisaged two classes of "public authority". First,
"core" public authorities, which will be liable for Convention breaches, whether the act was public or private. Obvious examples would
be the police, local councils and Government departments. Second,
"hybrid" authorities, which may be a private party carrying out some
public functions; these bodies can be liable for Convention breaches,
but only (1) when carrying out public functions, and (2) if the nature
of the particular act is not private.

The HRA 1998 does not provide the certainty of a list of public
bodies,[178] handing a significant interpretive role to the courts. Guidance can be drawn from two House of Lords cases. For the first
question, courts should take a "generous"[179] multi-factor, case-by-
case approach. Relevant factors are the extent to which in carrying
out the relevant function the body is (a) publicly funded, (b) exercising statutory powers, (c) taking the place of central government or
local authorities, or (d) providing a public service.[180] The House of
Lords has also identified three factors generally which should carry
little, if any, weight: (a) the fact that the function is one which is
carried out by a public body does not mean that it is a public function

---

[177] (1981) 4 E.H.R.R. 38.
[178] Contrast the Equality Act 2010.
[179] *Aston Cantlow v Wallbank* [2004] 1 A.C. 546 (HL), [11] (Lord Nicholls), *YL v Birmingham
CC* [2008] A.C. 95, (HL), [4] (Lord Bingham), [91] (Lord Mance).
[180] ibid. [12] (Lord Nicholls).

when carried out by a potentially hybrid body;[181] (b) that the functions are subject to detailed statutory regulation;[182] (c) it is only of
limited significance that the function will be subject to the principles
of judicial review; the question under s.6 is different from the principles of administrative law.[183]

2–023   A finding that the body was carrying out a public function can be
vitiated if the particular act in question was of a private nature. This
is the second question. Here, it is harder to detect any clear guidelines. In *R. (Weaver) v London and Quadrant Housing Trust*,[184] Elias
L.J. ventured these "tentative propositions": (a) the source of the
power will be a relevant factor; (b) that will not be decisive, however,
since the nature of the activities in issue is also important; (c) the
character of an act is likely to "take its colour from" the character of
the function of which it forms part; and so it is likely that if the
function was of a public nature, then so too was the act.[185]

Elias L.J. drew these propositions from two House of Lords cases.
The first was *Aston Cantlow v Wallbank*.[186] The background here was
a civil obligation of a land-owner to repair a church belonging to a
parochial church council. The land-owner invoked the Human Rights
Act (Peaceful Enjoyment of Possessions: 1st Protocol, art.1), and so
the question was whether the church council was a core public
authority. A majority held it was not, seemingly because the act in
question (enforcement of the repair) was clearly a private act.[187]

The second case was *YL v Birmingham City Council*.[188] Here, acting
under its statutory duty, a local authority had placed the applicant in
a care home, which in this case was private. This created a tenancy
agreement between the care home and the applicant, although the
authority contributed to her rent. When the care home tried to evict
the applicant, she invoked the Human Rights Act (relying on ECHR
art.8). The question was whether the care home was a hybrid
authority. A bare majority found that it was not. There was a distinction between the *arrangements* for the applicant's care (a public
function carried out by the local authority), and the *provision* of it, a
private function carried out by the care home.[189] The eviction was

---

[181] *YL v Birmingham CC* [2008] A.C. 95 (HL), [30]–[31].
[182] "Otherwise, for example, companies providing financial services, running restaurants, or
manufacturing hazardous materials, would ipso facto be susceptible to be within the ambit
of section 6(1)": *YL v Birmingham CC* [2008] A.C. 95 (HL), [134] (Lord Neuberger).
[183] *Aston Cantlow v Wallbank* [2004] 1 A.C. 546 (HL), [52] (Lord Hope), cited with approval by
Lord Mance in *YL v Birmingham CC* [2008] A.C. 95, (HL) [87].
[184] [2010] 1 W.L.R. 363 (CA).
[185] ibid. [41].
[186] [2004] 1 A.C. 546.
[187] ibid. [16], [64], [90].
[188] [2008] A.C. 95 (HL). See S. Palmer, "Public functions and private services: a gap in human
rights protection" (2008) 6(3/4) I.J.C.L. 585; A. Williams, "*YL v Birmingham City Council*:
contracting out and 'functions of a public nature' "(2008) 4 E.H.R.L.R. 524.
[189] ibid. [115] (Lord Mance), [168]–[169] (Lord Neuberger).

based on "contractual provision in a private law agreement" which "could not be thought to be anything other than private".[190]

In both of these cases the powers being exercised (repair of church/ **2–024** termination of tenancy) were private legal rights by source and in nature (Elias L.J.'s propositions (a) and (b)). In *Aston Cantlow*, the private nature of the act seemed to indicate that the church council was not a public authority, while in *YL*, the converse was true: the care home's obvious private status indicated that the act was private in nature (Elias L.J.'s proposition (c)). Elias L.J.'s analysis ties together (or "blurs")[191] the questions of "functions of a public nature" and "private act" (respectively ss.6(3)(b) and 6(5)). As Lord Collins said in *Weaver*: "[I]t is not easy to imagine circumstances where an act could be of a public nature where it is not done in pursuance . . . of public functions".[192] Accordingly, a majority in *Weaver* held that the act of evicting a tenant by a "registered social landlord" was "so bound up with"[193] its public function of providing social housing, the eviction was a public act.

The approach in *YL* is in marked contrast to that of the European Court of Human Rights towards education. In *Costello-Roberts v UK*[194] the Strasbourg Court made clear "that the State cannot absolve itself from responsibility by delegating its obligations to private bodies or individuals." Further, "in the United Kingdom, independent schools co-exist with a system of public education. The fundamental right of everyone to education is a right guaranteed equally to pupils in State and independent schools, no distinction being made between the two."[195] The implication is that education is governmental in character and that private schools are bound by the Human Rights Act. This logic cannot extend fully to the provision of housing (ECHR art.8 provides only the right to respect for a person's home, not a right to obtain one),[196] but it should apply to the eviction of persons from homes provided by the State, or by someone on behalf of the State, such as social housing or care homes. And where a State chooses to provide something beyond its Convention obligations, but which falls within the ambit of a Convention right, it must be provided without discrimination.[197]

---

[190] ibid. [34] (Lord Scott).
[191] cf. Rix L.J.'s dissent, in *Weaver* [2010] 1 W.L.R. 363 (CA), [151]. See J. Leslie, "Approaches to Section 6 HRA: Lessons from *Weaver v London and Quadrant Housing Trust*" [2009] JR 327, [14]–[17].
[192] [2010] 1 W.L.R. 363 (CA), [100].
[193] ibid. [76].
[194] (1993) 25 E.H.R.R. 112.
[195] ibid. at [27].
[196] *X v Germany* (1956) 1 YB 202.
[197] *Petrovic v Austria* (1998) 33 E.H.R.R. 307; *Stec v UK* (App. No.65731/01) (2006) 43 E.H.R.R. 43; *R. (RJM) v Secretary of State for Work and Pensions* [2009] 1 A.C. 311 (HL) (various state benefits fell within A1, P2, "possessions").

In the event, the controversial *YL* decision was reversed by Parliament, and care homes are now bound by the Human Rights Act.[198] But the broader principles remain, which suggest that the State, when contracting out its functions, very often can simultaneously extinguish any relevant Convention obligations. Parliament's reversal of *YL* could be read as a criticism of the *reasoning* of *YL*, and this may have influenced the Supreme Court to refuse permission to appeal the *Weaver* decision.[199] The combination of these events may encourage courts to bring a more liberal approach to this matter.

Notwithstanding HRA 1998 s.6, private parties, when exercising *private* functions, may find themselves bound by Convention rights. This is because the courts must observe the Convention when applying and developing the common law and interpreting statutes. Each is discussed below.

4. THE COMMON LAW

(1) Before the Human Rights Act

2–025   The common law has not developed a sophisticated principle of equality or non-discrimination. This may be the result of it being reactive in nature and its tradition of freedom of contract.[200] The general attitude of the common law towards specific cases of equality and discrimination was epitomised by the House of Lords in *Roberts v Hopwood*[201] where Poplar Borough Council embarked upon an equal pay policy for its lowest paid workers. The policy was struck down by the House of Lords on the ground that the Council had been misguided "by some eccentric principles of socialistic philanthropy, or by a feminist ambition to secure the equality of the sexes in the matter of wages in the world of labour." In *Scala Ballroom v Ratcliffe*[202] the Court of Appeal observed that a "colour bar" was a policy that the owners of a ballroom "were entitled to adopt in their own business interests".[203] The introduction of discrimination legislation paradoxically reinforced this position, allowing the common law, in deference to Parliament, to wash its hands of discrimination issues

---

[198] Health and Social Care Act 2008 s.145(1).

[199] UKSC 2009/0072 (November 5, 2009) (Lord Hope, Lady Hale, Lord Brown, none of whom were party to the majority decision in *YL*) *www.supremecourt.gov.uk/docs/pta-0910-1002.pdf*. In light of Parliament's reversal of *YL*, and other matters, Lord Pannick QC "expects" the issue to return to the Supreme Court at some time: "Functions of a Public Nature" [2009] JR 109, [16].

[200] St John A. Robilliard, "Should Parliament enact a Religious Discrimination Act" [1978] Public Law 379, at 380.

[201] [1925] A.C. 578, HL at 599.

[202] [1958] 3 All E.R. 220.

[203] ibid. at 221, but the Court refused an injunction to prevent the musician's union from boycotting the ballroom.

whenever the facts fell outside of an activity prescribed by the legislation. So even where there was patent sex discrimination[204] or indirect sex discrimination[205] by the immigration authorities, and the activity fell outside the discrimination legislation, the courts considered themselves powerless to act: "sex discrimination of itself is not unlawful. It is unlawful only in circumstances prescribed by the [Sex discrimination Act]."[206]

From time to time, it has been suggested that the common law carries some form of equality principle. In *Short v Poole Corporation*,[207] the Court of Appeal suggested that the courts could strike down as ultra vires any decision made by a public body made on "alien and irrelevant grounds", such as a teacher being dismissed "because she had red hair, or for some equally frivolous or foolish reason." Any hope inferred from this pronouncement was immediately crushed when the Court upheld a decision to dismiss a teacher because she was married.

More recently, Lord Hoffman has hinted that there exists an equality principle in the common law of a more substantive nature. In *Matadeen v Pointu*[208] he said "that treating like cases alike and unlike cases differently is a general axiom of rational behaviour", and thus irrational discrimination was subject to judicial review, a remedy against public bodies.[209] In *Arthur J Hall v Simons*,[210] he invoked a "fundamental principle of justice which requires that people should be treated equally and like cases treated alike", as one of his reasons for holding that advocates, like any other professional, should enjoy no immunity from professional negligence claims, a private law matter. Lord Steyn has written that there is a "constitutional principle of equality developed domestically by English courts" which is wider than the "relatively weak" art.14 of the ECHR.[211] However, arguments (based on these comments) that there exists at common law a general tenet against discrimination have so far found little favour in the courts' decision-making, either being rejected or sidelined: Lord Hoffman's comments do no more than pronounce that irrational discrimination (like any irrational behaviour by a public body) was subject to judicial review in public law;[212] and any principle

---

[204] *R. v Entry Clearance Officer Bombay ex p Amin* [1983] 2 A.C. 818 (HL).

[205] *Bernstein v Immigration Appeal Tribunal and Department of Employment* [1988] 3 CMLR 445 (CA).

[206] ibid. [41] (Mann L.J.).

[207] [1926] Ch 66, 91.

[208] [1999] 1 A.C. 98, delivering the opinion of the Privy Council.

[209] ibid. at 109, but Lord Hoffman also highlighted the difficulties of a general principle of non-discrimination, in contrast to specified enumerated grounds, such as sex and race.

[210] [2000] 3 All E.R. 673 (HL), 689.

[211] Lord Steyn, "Democracy through law" [2002] (6) E.H.R.L.R. 723, 731–732.

[212] Under the *Wednesbury* ([1948] 1 K.B. 223) principle; see *R. (Association of British Civilian Internees: Far East Region) v Secretary of State for Defence* [2003] EWCA Civ 473, [83]–[86] (also overruling *Gurung v Ministry of Defence* [2004] EWCA Civ 1863 so far as it held (at [29]) that discrimination on the ground of birthplace was irrational).

of equality does not add much, if anything, to a claimant's Convention Rights under the Human Rights Act.[213]

There are some ancient duties placed by the common law upon the likes of innkeepers, common carriers and some monopoly enterprises such as ports and harbours, to accept all travellers and others who are "in a fit and reasonable condition to be received."[214] A rare (if not only) example of one of these "ancient duties" coinciding racial discrimination arose in *Constantine v Imperial Hotels*.[215] Here, a black West Indian cricketer (and later a member of the Race Relations Board) was refused accommodation for fear of upsetting white American soldiers. The Kings Bench Division awarded Constantine nominal damages for the breach of the innkeepers' duty to receive all travellers.

(2) The Common Law and the Human Rights Act 1998

2–026   As seen above, HRA 1998 s.6 provides that a public authority must act compatibly with Convention rights. According to s.6(3)(a) a public authority includes the courts and tribunals. This appears to broaden the scope of s.6, but also creates some uncertainty as to just how far a court can develop the common law to accord with Convention rights. The particular question here is whether under s.6(3)(a) the courts should: (a) do nothing with the common law (and simply entertain s.6 "public authority" cases,[216] and comply with the Convention when acting within their judicial sphere);[217] or (b) merely develop existing common law to accord with Convention rights; or (c) create new common law actions to accord with Convention rights. The question is particularly relevant to how far the common law can be used to enforce Convention rights against private parties for purely private acts (in other words, claims falling outside of s.6).

The question was first debated around the "vertical/horizontal effect" dichotomy (equating to state/private party liability), but with a more subtle analysis, employing a further distinction between two types of horizontal effect: direct and indirect. With *direct* horizontal effect, private parties are bound by Convention rights and so can be sued for a violation (equating to (c), above). With *indirect* horizontal effect, a private party may be bound by a convention right, but only

---

[213] *R. (Montana) v Secretary of State for the Home Department* [2001] 1 WLR 552 CA, at § 15.
[214] See J. Jowell, "Is Equality a Constitutional Principle?" (1994) 47 *Current Legal Problems* (Part 2, Collected Papers) 1, p.91.
[215] [1944] 1 K.B. 693.
[216] Using s.7's enforcement mechanism. Courts have a further duty to interpret legislation, so far as possible, to comply with the Convention.
[217] R. Clayton, *The Law of Human Rights,* (Oxford: OUP, 2000), at p.225, para.5.76.

via some indirect mechanism, for example, a pre-existing common law obligation developed to accord with Convention rights (equating to (b), above).[218] When the Human Rights Bill was going through Parliament, the Government anticipated it would have indirect, but not direct, horizontal effect.[219]

The most notable Convention right embraced by the common law is art.8's right to privacy, at least so far as it protects invasions of privacy. In *Campbell v MGM Ltd*[220] the House of Lords held that a famous model had a right to privacy from a newspaper when attending a Narcotics Anonymous meeting. This extended the existing doctrine of breach of confidence, which had once required a relationship between the parties "importing an obligation of confidence".[221] Thus, the House developed the existing law into a more general law of privacy, which more fully reflected art.8.[222] This was presented as a development of the law which began before the HRA 1998,[223] with Baroness Hale (echoing the Canadian approach, below, para.2–027) cautioning that: "[T]he courts will not invent a new cause of action to cover types of activity which were not previously covered...".[224] However, in successive claims of invasions of privacy, courts have gradually given up on this posture. In *Mosley v News Groups Newspapers*,[225] the cause of action for an invasion of privacy was stated to be breach of confidence and/or infringement of the art.8 right to privacy. In *Murray v Express Newspapers*,[226] the claim was presented as a breach of the art.8 right to privacy. From *Campbell* to

---

[218] For a summary of these arguments, see Thomas D.C. Bennett, "Horizontality's new horizons—re-examining horizontal effect: privacy, defamation and the Human Rights Act: Part 1" (2010) 21(3) Ent. L.R. 96; or R. Clayton, *The Law of Human Rights,* (Oxford: OUP, 2000) at p.225, para.576 et seq.

[219] The Lord Chancellor stated: "[I]t is right as a matter of principle for the courts to have the duty of acting compatibly with the convention not only in cases involving other public authorities but also in developing the common law in deciding cases between individuals. ... In my view the courts may not act as legislators and grant new remedies for infringement of convention rights unless the common law itself enables them to develop new rights or remedies" (HL Deb cols 783–785 (Nov 24, 1997)).

[220] [2004] 2 A.C. 457 (HL).

[221] *Coco v Clark Ltd* [1968] F.S.R. 415 (Ch.D.), 419–421. Traditionally, this has been treated as an equitable doctrine, "the cousin of trust" (ibid. 419). More recently, the distinction is rarely mentioned and courts simply talk of the "tort of breach of confidence". See e.g. *McKennitt v Ash* [2006] EWCA Civ 1714, [8].

[222] Dubbed "misuse of private information" by Lord Nicholls: [2004] 2 A.C. 457 (HL), [11], [14], and [34]. See G. Phillipson, "Transforming breach of confidence? Towards a common law right of privacy under the Human Rights Act" (2003) 66 M.L.R. 726.

[223] See e.g. [2004] 2 A.C. 457 (HL), [14] (Lord Nicholls), [47] (Lord Hoffman), [85] (Lord Hope) relying on *A-G v Observer* [1990] 1 A.C. 109, 281.

[224] [2004] 2 A.C. 457 (HL), [133]. See also *Wainwright v Home Office* [2004] 2 A.C. 406 (HL). For a collection of essays on this issue in a variety of countries, see *The Constitution in Private Relations: Expanding Constitutionalism*, edited by András Sajó and Renáta Uitz (Eleven International Publishing, 2005); reviewed by S. Gardbaum, "Where the (State) Action Is" (2006) 4(4) I.J.C.L. 760.

[225] [2008] EWHC 1777 (QB), [3]. (Exposé by newspaper of sadomasochistic activities in private by claimant and other consenting adults.)

[226] [2009] Ch. 481 (CA), [2]. (Press photograph taken in public of famous author's (J.K. Rowling) infant son.)

Murray, claims based upon an invasion of privacy have morphed from a development of the common law into a bald assertion of a Convention right, leaving the common law behind, giving art.8's *privacy* aspect full (direct) horizontal effect. Elsewhere though, the House of Lords has resisted the influence of Convention rights. For instance, unlike the right to *privacy*, art.8's companion right *to the home* has been confined to public authority defendants.[227] So it cannot even be said that that some *articles* have been given full horizontal effect. In actions against the police, domestic courts have preserved a distinction between tort and art.6.[228]

2–027   These cases show that the courts will enforce *some* Convention rights, but not others. And, in particular, the privacy cases show that it is quite impossible (and so perhaps, pointless) to categorise them in terms of the Convention's horizontal effect. In *Campbell*, it is arguable that the existing law of confidence was already liberated (no horizontal effect), or that the Law Lords *developed* the existing law (*indirect* horizontal effect), or that they created a new cause of action (*direct* horizontal effect).[229] *Murray* suggests that the existing law of confidence has been bypassed and the cause of action for privacy is provided by the HRA 1998. In other areas, the private parties are not being burdened with Convention obligations, be it via the common law or by the simple enforcement of a Convention right. The cases show that "there is a great deal of discretion in the hands of the judges to decide whether or not the common law will be developed in accordance with Convention rights ...".[230] Thus, it is impossible to provide a sweeping statement about the effect of HRA 1998 s.6.

The approach taken by the Canadian Charter of Rights and Freedoms is more cautious than the HRA 1998, but for that perhaps, it is more certain. Section 32(1) of the Charter states that the Charter applies to the national and provincial governments and legislatures, but *not* to the courts. Accordingly, the Canadian Supreme Court has stated that although courts should "develop the principles of the common law in a manner consistent with the fundamental values enshrined in the Constitution", it cannot be said "that one private party owes a constitutional duty to another."[231]

And so, in the context of discrimination in the UK, the "great deal of discretion" in the hands of the judges makes it *possible* for them to

---

[227] See *YL v Birmingham CC* [2008] A.C. 95 (HL), above para.2–023.

[228] *Van Colle v Chief Constable of Herts. Police* [2008] UKHL 50; [2009] 1 A.C. 225 at [82] (Lord Hope), [138] (Lord Brown), cf. [58] (Lord Bingham, dissenting). See the analysis of M. Arden, "Human rights and civil wrongs: tort law under the spotlight" [2010] PL 140.

[229] Bennett argues the *decision* created a new cause of action, despite the reasoning given in the speeches: (2010) 21(3) Ent. L.R. 96, 100. Subsequent cases support this.

[230] M. Arden [2010] PL 140, 154. Even so, the Strasbourg Court may hold a State liable for not protecting an individual's Convention rights where a private party has infringed a right—see e.g. *Young, James & Webster v UK* (1981) 4 E.H.R.R. 38 and *Costello-Roberts v UK* (1993) 25 E.H.R.R. 112 (see further above para.2–022).

[231] *Retail, Wholesale and Department Store Union v Dolphin Delivery Ltd* [1986] 2 S.C.R. 573, at 593.

develop existing, or create new, causes of action. If the courts needed some common law for purchase, there are the ancient common law duties (see above, para.2–025) which could be used—in a similar way that the law of confidence was used in *Campbell*—in the areas of the provision of goods, facilities and services, housing and education. As things stood before the HRA 1998, these duties could be imposed upon hoteliers, and perhaps even a yacht club, who refuse admission, or membership, on irrational (including discriminatory) grounds. Under the HRA 1998, the courts could develop these duties to prevent discrimination on the wider grounds of art.14, in education (1st Protocol, art.2), housing (art.8), and employment (various articles).[232] For goods, facilities and services, the courts may consider themselves limited by *Botta v Italy*,[233] where the European Court of Human Rights held that art.8 did not extend to a purely social right outside the workplace (disabled access to a beach) concerning "interpersonal relations of such a broad and indeterminate scope" that there is "no conceivable link" between the State and a person's private life. It is arguable that this one sweeping statement rules out any coverage by art.8 of the private provision of goods, facilities, or services. However, there is nothing to prevent the courts going beyond the Strasbourg case law here. The Convention is a "living instrument", and as such, the Government suggested that the HRA 1998 enabled our judges to contribute to the "dynamic and evolving interpretation of the Convention."[234]

5. JUDICIAL STATUTORY INTERPRETATION

Although the common law has failed to develop substantive principles of equality and non-discrimination, the judiciary has played a significant part in the development of discrimination law when interpreting the legislation.[235] There are many theories of statutory interpretation, from "framer's intent" to "living tree", from "literal" to "purposive". Most domestic and ECJ cases fall into the literal/purposive dichotomy, while the European Court of Human Rights prefers to treat the Convention as living tree, or "living instrument".

2–028

For English judges the literal rule of interpretation has its roots in the constitutional settlement of 1689. Article 9 of the Bill of Rights 1689 proclaimed that "... the freedom of speech and debates or proceedings in Parlyament ought not to be impeached or questioned

---

[232] See para.2–027, above.
[233] (App. No.21439/93) (1998) 26 E.H.R.R. 241, [35].
[234] *Rights Brought Home: the Human Rights Bill* (Cm 3782) (1997), at para.2.5.
[235] See M. Barbera, "Not the Same? The Judicial Role in the New Community Anti-Discrimination Law Context" (2002) 31 ILJ 82.

in any court or place out of Parlyament." By the Victorian era the deference afforded to statutory words by the judiciary amounted to a rule of interpretation that would do no more than give the words their literal meaning.[236] The consequence is that a judge cannot go behind the face of the statute to discover its meaning and purpose, even if the result frustrates its purpose. In *Perera v Civil Service Commission*,[237] a job specification stated that applicants with British nationality, a good command of English and experience in the UK would be at an "advantage". The Race Relations Act 1976 at the time prohibited "requirements or conditions" that had a disproportionate impact on a racial group. The Court of Appeal held that as the specification was a "mere preference" and not an absolute bar to the job, it was not a "requirement" and so fell outside the Act. This meant that employers could relegate all their requirements to "mere preferences" and evade the legislation. (The phrase "requirement or condition" has since been replaced with "provision, criterion or practice" to rectify this problem.)

A consequence of the literal rule was ever more complex Acts of Parliament with torturous formulas to cover every imagined scenario within the statutes' purpose.[238] More recently, a shift from this position could be detected. Some judges began to reject the literal approach and gave words their "natural" and "ordinary" meaning.[239] But this was not universal. Another development came in *Pepper v Hart*[240] where the House of Lords ruled that in cases of ambiguity a court could look to Parliamentary debates to resolve the meaning of a statute. But this is an exceptional, rather than normal, practice. As shown in *Perera,* ambiguity is not normally the problem.

2–029   A third development undermining the literal rule is the increasing need for judges to interpret the legislation of the European Community. Community law is entrenched in the "purposive" school of interpretation. Legislation pronounces general principles for the judiciary to develop and apply. This has been the practice of the European Court of Justice. Britain's obligations under EU membership require the judges to give Community legislation and its domestic counterparts a purposive interpretation. Further,

---

[236] See Lord Bramwell, *Hill v E & W India Dock Co* (1884) 9 A.C. 448 (HL), at 464–465 and later Lord Loreburn L.C., *London & India Docks v Thames Steam & Lighterage* [1909] A.C. 15 (HL), at 19, and Lord Atkinson, *Vacher & Sons v London Soc. of Compositors* [1913] A.C. 107 (HL), at 121–122.

[237] [1980] I.C.R. 699 (CA). The classic case of the literal rule frustrating the purpose of the statute is *Fisher v Bell* [1961] 1 Q.B. 394.

[238] Lord Diplock remarked—in *Fothergill v Monarch Airlines* [1980] 3 WLR 209, at 222—that "the current style of legislative draftsmanship" was an "unhappy legacy of this judicial attitude."

[239] See e.g. *Fothergill v Monarch Airlines* [1980] 3 W.L.R. 209 (HL), and *Brutus v Cozens* [1973] A.C. 854, HL.

[240] [1983] 1 All E.R. 42 (HL).

Community law requires that domestic legislation is interpreted, so far as possible, to conform to Community law.[241] In *Falkirk Council v Whyte*[242] a job specification that "management training and supervisory experience" was "desirable" adversely affected women. The Sex Discrimination Act 1975 (like the Race Relations Act) prohibited only "requirements or conditions" that had an adverse impact on women. This case differed from *Perera* because at the time sex discrimination law was governed ultimately by the Community law (the Equal Treatment Directive 76/207/EEC). This enabled the EAT to interpret the phrase "requirement or condition" according to the purpose of the legislation: "In many ways this was a classic situation of indirect sex discrimination, with mostly women in basic grade posts, and mostly men in promoted management posts—a vivid example of what the Act and its forerunners in the United States set out to eliminate".[243] Again, this approach is not universal practice. On occasion the courts have used the literal rule when applying European law[244] and elsewhere English judges still employ the literal rule as their basic tool of statutory interpretation.

A fourth development that may change the judges' approach to statutory interpretation, at least so far as human rights are concerned, was the passing of the Human Rights Act 1998, which came into force in October 2000. This Act introduced the European Convention on Human Rights (ECHR) into domestic law. Section 3 of the Human Rights Act provides: "So far as it is possible to do so, primary legislation and subordinate legislation must be read and given effect in a way which is compatible with the Convention rights". Failing this, by s.4, a court must issue a declaration of incompatibility. Domestic courts are obliged by HRA 1998 s.2, to take into account the case law of the European Court of Human Rights, which treats the Convention as a "living instrument" and rarely constrains itself to a literal approach. Thus, domestic courts ought to adopt this more expansive approach when interpreting the Act.[245] In the context of discrimination, this means that legislation falling within the ambit of one of the free-standing Convention rights must be interpreted, if possible, so that it does not have a discriminatory effect in violation of ECHR art.14. This makes it possible for parties to call upon Convention rights in a private dispute which is governed by legislation.

---

[241] *Marleasing SA v La Comercial Internacional de Alimentacion SA* Case C-106/89 [1990] E.C.R. 4135, at 4159.
[242] [1997] I.R.L.R. 560. For a Comment, see (1998) 27 ILJ 133. The classic case of a purposive interpretation of EC-derived law is *Litster v Forth Dry Dock & Engineering Co* [1990] 1 A.C. 546 (HL).
[243] ibid. at 562.
[244] See e.g. *Secretary of State v Spence* [1987] Q.B. 179 (CA), approved by Lord Oliver in *Litster Forth v Dry Dock & Engineering Co* [1990] 1 A.C. 546 (HL), at 577.
[245] See below, para.2–030.

2–030   In *Godin-Mendoza v Ghaidan*[246] the claimant and Mr Walwyn-Jones lived together in a same-sex relationship in Mr Walwyn-Jones' rented flat. When Mr Walwyn-Jones died, Mendoza claimed from the landlord a right to succeed the statutory tenancy under the Rent Act 1977, which provided (by Sch.1, para.2) that the surviving spouse of the original tenant shall succeed the tenancy. It defined "spouse" as "a person who was living with the original tenant as his or her wife or husband". The Court of Appeal held that "as his or her wife or husband" in para.2 should read to mean "as if they were his wife or husband".[247] The House of Lords upheld that decision, but it is notable that Lord Nicholls reasoned: "The precise form of words read in for this purpose is of no significance. It is their substantive effect which matters."[248] This tells us that courts should not be fettered by an impossibility of a grammatical solution and that s.3 goes further merely than resolving ambiguities in legislation. However, the interpretation should "go with the grain of the legislation"[249] and not be against a fundamental feature of it or amount to a decision better suited for Parliament, for instance, where recognising a male-to-female transsexual as female under the Matrimonial Causes Act 1973 "would have had exceedingly wide ramifications".[250]

An alternative analysis to the literal/purposive dichotomy was provided by Lord Browne-Wilkinson who argued that English judges, when interpreting statutes, merely "seek to ensure that the meritorious triumph and the dirty dogs lick their wounds."[251] The point is that the decision is made on moral grounds, but articulated on legal reasoning. That may explain why there appears to be no single approach: judges may have simply identified the "dirty dog" and then chosen the reasoning, be it literal, "ordinary", "natural" or purposive, as a matter of convenience to justify the decision. According to Lord Browne-Wilkinson, the Human Rights Act would change this in two ways. Judgments on the Act will be made *and* articulated on moral grounds, but this will no longer be the moral standpoint of the individual judge, but the code of morals developed, inter alia, by the European Court of Human Rights and the social and political realities of the day. This approach resembles the "living tree" school of interpretation,[252] which holds that legislation of constitutional nature should be read according to the values of the present day, as opposed to the time it was enacted, or the "framer's intent". The flaw in "framer's intent" school is illustrated in *Dred*

---

[246] [2004] 2 A.C. 557.
[247] [2003] 1 F.L.R. 468, [35].
[248] [2004] 2 A.C. 557, [35].
[249] ibid. [121] (Lord Rodger)
[250] ibid. [33] (Lord Nicholls), citing *Bellinger v Bellinger* [2003] UKHL 21.
[251] B. Markesinis, (ed.), *The Impact of the Human Rights Act on English Law* (Oxford: OUP, 1998), p.22.
[252] *Edwards v A-G of Canada* [1930] A.C. 124 (PC), at 136; see B. Wilson, "The Making of a Constitution" [1988] P.L. 370.

Scott v Sandford,[253] where the US Supreme Court denied a black man the right to sue because the Constitution, when drafted, recognised blacks only as "an inferior class of beings" and not US citizens. The Living Tree approach has become entrenched in the Strasbourg Court's reasoning:

> "The Court reiterates that the Convention is a living instrument which must be interpreted in the light of present-day conditions and that the increasingly high standard being required in the area of the protection of human rights and fundamental liberties correspondingly and inevitably requires greater firmness in assessing breaches of the fundamental values of democratic societies".[254]

And according to the White Paper introducing the Human Rights Act, British courts should follow this approach:

> "The Convention is often described as a 'living instrument' because it is interpreted by the European court in the light of present day conditions and therefore reflects changing social attitudes and the changes in the circumstances of society. In future our judges will be able to contribute to this dynamic and evolving interpretation of the Convention".[255]

In the context of discrimination, this approach was apparent in the Strasbourg Court's changing attitude towards transsexualism,[256] and the House of Lords when overturning a ban in Northern Ireland on unmarried couples' right to adopt.[257]

2–031 In sum, when interpreting domestic discrimination legislation which falls within the scope of Community law, the courts should take a purposive approach, and if possible, interpret domestic law to accord with Community law. When interpreting domestic legislation which falls outside Community law, courts *ought* to take a purposive approach (to avoid another "*Perera* problem"). Should the legislation fall within the scope of the Human Rights Act, courts should interpret it according to the Convention rights, with the approach shown by *Godin-Mendoza*.

---

[253] US 393 (Sup Ct 1857). For a fine example of the living tree/framer's intent dichotomy, see respectively the dissenting (Lord Scarman) and majority (Lord Denning and Orr L.J.) speeches in *Ahmed v ILEA* [1978] Q.B. 36 (CA).

[254] *Öcalan v Turkey* (App. No.46221/99) (2005) 41 E.H.R.R. 45, [163]. See also *Soering v UK* (1989) 11 E.H.R.R. 439, [102]; *V v UK* (2000) 30 E.H.R.R. 121, [72]; *Rantsev v Cyprus and Russia* (App. No.25965/04) (2010) 51 E.H.R.R. 1, [277].

[255] *Rights Brought Home: the Human Rights Bill* (Cm 3782) (1997), at para.2.5. Cited in *In re G* [2009] 1 A.C. 173 (HL), [119] (Baroness Hale), [52] (Lord Hope).

[256] *Sheffield & Horsham v UK* (1998) 27 E.H.R.R. 347; *Goodwin v UK* (2002) 35 E.H.R.R 18.

[257] *In re G* [2009] 1 A.C. 173 (HL), [119] (Baroness hale), [52] (Lord Hope).

CHAPTER 3

THE PROTECTED CHARACTERISTICS

INTRODUCTION

European Community legislation specifically covers sex (including **3–001** pregnancy and maternity, and gender reassignment),[1] racial and ethnic origin;[2] nationality;[3] and religion and belief, disability, age and sexual orientation.[4] Power to legislate for discrimination on these grounds is provided by Treaty of the Functioning of European Union (TFEU), art.19 (ex 13 TEC). The broader coverage of the European Convention on Human Rights is discussed in Chapter 2.[5]

The Equality Act 2010 s.4, lists the "protected characteristics" as: Race, Religion or Belief, Gender reassignment, Sexual orientation, Marriage and Civil Partnership, Age, Sex, Pregnancy and Maternity, and Disability. The definition of disability is discussed separately in

---

[1] Recast Directive 2006/54/EC.
[2] Race Directive 2000/43/EC.
[3] TFEU, art.45 (ex 39 TEC).
[4] "Framework" Directive 2000/78/EC.
[5] See para.2–007.

Chapter 13.[6] In addition, the Act proscribes "dual discrimination", although this yet to be brought into force.[7]

1. RACE

3–002   Section 9(1) of the Equality Act 2010, states that "Race" includes colour, nationality, and ethnic or national origins. Section 9(5) provides the power for a Government Minister to add "caste" to this list. The Race Directive 2000/43/EC is expressed to cover "racial or ethnic origin" (art.2(1)) and expressly excludes "nationality" (art.3(2)), which is covered elsewhere, for instance by TFEU art.45. Before considering each of these, it is helpful to understand how the definition works with sub-groups and overlaps.

Section 9(4) of the Equality Act 2010 provides: "The fact that a racial group comprises two or more distinct racial groups does not prevent it from constituting a particular racial group". As an example, the Explanatory Note to s.9 suggests that "Black Britons" form a racial group. This also prevents reducing each racial group to its smallest possible number. Thus, discrimination against "the Spanish" would be actionable, even though that group comprises Basques, Catalans, and so on. It is implicit in s.9(4) that this logic can be inversed. In *Ealing LBC v Race Relations Board*[8] Lord Simon suggested that within Great Britain, Scots, Welsh and English could each be defined by national origins. On this basis "sub-groups" such as Catalans, Basques, Walloons (Belgiums of French origin), Sicilians, Bretons and the Cornish are definable by national or ethnic origins, and discrimination against any one of these sub-groups is actionable.

Lord Simon's example also suggests that sub-groups can still exist even if they overlap, as the English, Welsh and Scottish certainly overlap. This should also be the case with further sub-groups, such as the Cornish. This was confirmed by the Supreme Court in *R (A) v Governing Body of JFS*,[9] which held that an Orthodox Jewish school's discrimination against a Masorti Jew was actionable, despite no evidence that Orthodox and Masorti Jews (as opposed to Jews generally) had distinct ethnic origins.[10]

The fluidity of identifying sub-groups was illustrated in the US case *Walker v Secretary of the Treasury*,[11] where a predominantly dark-

---

[6] See p.388.
[7] See Ch.2, para.2–002.
[8] [1972] A.C. 342 (HL), 363–364, applied in *Northern Joint Police Board v Power* [1997] I.R.L.R. 610 (EAT).
[9] [2010] 2 W.L.R. 153. For a Comment, see (2010) 39 ILJ 183.
[10] See especially, ibid. [86] (Lord Mance).
[11] 713 F Supp 403 (ND Ga 1989) and 742 F Supp 670 (ND Ga 1990).

skinned black workforce discriminated against a light-skinned black colleague. The Court found that Ms Walker's direct discrimination claim based solely on her colour ("light-skinned black" being a sub-group of, and overlapping with, "black") could succeed under the Civil Rights Act 1964.

(1) The Meaning of "Race"

Modern opinion is that there is no scientific definition of race which could serve any purpose under discrimination legislation.[12] In *Mandla v Dowell Lee*,[13] the Court of Appeal offered some ultimately doomed technical discussions on the meaning of "ethnic origins". This approach was rejected by the House of Lords, with Lord Fraser stating it would be "absurd" to depend upon scientific proof of distinctive biological characteristics (assuming they exist) of a person. First, the "practical difficulties of such proof would be prohibitive", and second, "within the human race, there are very few, if any, distinctions which are scientifically recognised as racial."[14] Lord Fraser approved the following comments of Lord Simon in *Ealing LBC v CRE*:[15]

3–003

> "... 'racial' is not a term or art, either legal or ... scientific. I apprehend that anthropologists would dispute how far the word 'race' is biologically at all relevant to the species amusingly called homo sapiens."

This tells us how *not* to define "race". On what is now Equality Act 2010 s.9(1), Lord Simon said the language was "rubbery and elusive", because the concept of race was drafted in its popular sense "to leave no loophole for evasion."[16] Thus, the definitions of race in s.9(1) should be used in their "popular" sense with a purposive approach, to avoid loopholes. This was demonstrated in *Mandla*, where the House of Lords defined "ethnic origins" as a cultural, rather than a strict racial, question (see further below, para.3–008). Accordingly, courts have recognised "African" and "Asian" as racial grounds.[17] Given its purposive approach to interpretation, the ECJ is likely to take the same approach. To avoid any doubt, Recital (6) to the Race Directive's (2000/43/EC) preamble states:

---

[12] See e.g.: J. Solomos, *Race and Racism in Britain*, 2nd edn (London: Macmillan, 1993), pp.8–9, 183–85, 193; R. Miles, *Racism* (London: Routledge, 1989), p.119; J. Solomos and L. Back, *Racism and Society* (London: Macmillan, 1996), pp.210, 216.

[13] [1983] Q.B. 1, at 10–15 (Lord Denning M.R.), 15–16 (Oliver L.J.) and 22–24 (Kerr L.J.). [1983] A.C. 548 (HL). See further below, para.3–008.

[14] [1983] A.C. 548, 561.

[15] [1972] A.C. 342 (HL), see also below, "(4) National origins", para.3–007.

[16] ibid. 362 (HL).

[17] e.g. *R. v White* [2001] 1 W.L.R. 1352 (CA), [17] (for the Crime and Disorder Act 1998 s.28); *Abbey National v Chagger* [2009] I.C.R. 624 (EAT), [30].

> "The European Union rejects theories which attempt to determine the existence of separate human races. The use of the term 'racial origin' in this Directive does not imply an acceptance of such theories."

3–004　In the United States, there has been much litigation over the definition of race, but ultimately, the courts rejected the scientific approach. In *Saint Francis College v Al-Khazraji*,[18] a case brought under the general equality provision (s.1981) of the Civil Rights Act 1866, the Supreme Court rejected an argument that modern scientific theory placed humans into three major racial groups: Caucasoid, Mongoloid, and Negroid. White J. noted that when passing the Civil Rights Act 1866, Congress referred to the Scandinavian, Chinese, Latin, Spanish, Anglo-Saxon, Jewish, Mexican, black, Mongolian, Gypsy, and German races. He concluded that:

> "Congress intended to protect from discrimination identifiable classes of persons who are subjected to intentional discrimination solely because of their ancestry or ethnic characteristics. Such discrimination is racial discrimination ... whether or not it would be classified as racial in terms of modern scientific theory. ... It is clear ... that a distinctive physiognomy is not essential ...".[19]

(2) Colour

3–005　Although "colour" is included in the Equality Act 2010, it is absent from the Race Directive 2000/43/EC. Ordinarily, this should not present a problem because given the Equality Act's generally broad coverage, there will be few, if any, cases relying solely on the Directive. In any case, most cases involving discrimination on the ground of colour could be pleaded just as effectively as being on the ground of "ethnic origin". In *Abbey National v Chagger*[20] the EAT held that: "claimants who formulate their claim on the basis of 'colour discrimination' will inevitably in fact be complaining, whether or not they appreciate it, of discrimination on the ground of race and ethnic origin...". However, discrimination *purely* on the ground of colour

---

[18] 481 US 604 (Sup Ct 1987). For a full review of this and other cases on the issue see *Sandhu v Lockheed Missiles* 26 Cal App 4th 846 (1994).

[19] 481 US 604 (1987), 610 fn.4, and 612–613. The argument that there were only three racial groups for the purposes of the legislation was rejected for another reason by a lower court (3rd Circuit) in this case. It found that the strict "three race" approach would lead to anomalies: "while a white would be able to claim anti-white discrimination under the statute ... a Mexican-American or an Indian would be unable to make out a claim, unless they contended they were unfairly treated by virtue of being Caucasians" (784 F 2d 505, at 520).

[20] [2009] I.C.R. 624 (EAT), [33] (appeal dismissed on other grounds [2010] I.C.R. 397 (CA)). Followed in *Milton Keynes General Hospital NHS Trust v Maruziva* (2009) UKEAT/0003/09/DM, [7].

has arisen in the United States (see *Walker v Secretary of the Treasury*, above, para.3–002).

(3) Nationality

This category was introduced into the legislation as a result of the **3–006** House of Lords' decision in *Ealing LBC v CRE*,[21] a case on the 1968 Race Relations Act, which prohibited discrimination on the ground of *national origin*, but not *nationality*. The House of Lords held that a Polish national, whom the Council had refused to put on its housing list, had no claim under the 1968 Act. The Explanatory Note (50) to the Equality Act 2010 s.9, confirms that "Nationality includes being a British, Australian or Swiss citizen".

There is an overlap with Community law here, which has a general principle of free movement of persons. Consequently, nationality discrimination is outlawed generally ("Within the scope of application of the Treaties"),[22] and specifically in employment by a prohibition of "discrimination based on nationality between workers of the Member States".[23] The principal purpose is to secure free movement, rather than to outlaw irrational discrimination.[24] As such, these provisions can have a narrower application than the Equality Act. They do not cover discrimination within a Member State against a national of that State.[25] Neither should they cover, for example, discrimination in England against a Welsh person. However, such discrimination should be covered by the Equality Act 2010, under national or ethnic origins (see below). The Race Directive 2000/43/EC does not cover claims of nationality discrimination per se, as art.3(2) expressly excludes "a difference of treatment based on nationality".

(4) National Origins

There are a number of situations where a claim under "national **3–007** origins", may succeed where a claim under "nationality" would not. For instance, where a nation no longer exists, or at least no longer

---

[21] [1972] A.C. 342, see also below, "(4) National origins", para.3–007.
[22] TFEU art.18 (ex 12 TEC).
[23] TFEU art.45 (ex 39 TEC).
[24] See C. Barnard, "British jobs for British workers": the Lindsey Oil Refinery dispute and the future of local labour clauses in an integrated EU market" (2009) 38(3) ILJ 245; S. O'Leary, "Equal treatment and EU citizens: A new chapter on cross-border educational mobility and access to student financial assistance" (2009) 34(4) E.L. Rev. 612; G. de Búrca, "The role of Equality in European Community Law" in A. Dashwood, and S. O'Leary, *The Principle of Equal Treatment in European Community Law* (London: Sweet and Maxwell, 1997).
[25] *Morsen* and *Jhanjan* Joined Cases 35, 36/82 [1982] E.C.R. 3723 (ECJ) [11]–[18]. See also *R. v Saunders* Case 175/78 [1979] E.C.R. 1129 (ECJ), [10]–[12]; *Re Bignell's Application* [1997] NI 36 (NICA).

exists as a nation state (e.g. Scotland).[26] In *Ealing LBC v Race Relations Board*[27] Lord Simon suggested that within Great Britain, Scots, Welsh and English could each be defined by national origins.[28] In *Northern Joint Police Board v Power*[29] the EAT held that an Englishman could claim that he was discriminated against in Scotland on the ground of his national origin. On this basis Walloons (Belgiums of French origin), Catalans, Basques, Sicilians, Bretons and Cornish should have a claim under "national origins", or if not, under "ethnic origins" (considered below).

(5) Ethnic Origins

3–008   The benchmark case on the definition of ethnic origins is *Mandla v Dowell Lee*.[30] Only Lord Fraser and Lord Templeman gave speeches. Lord Fraser's guidance contained two "essential" and five further "relevant" characteristics. The essential characteristics were: (1) a long shared history, of which the group is conscious as distinguishing it from other groups, and the memory of which it keeps alive; (2) a cultural tradition of its own, including family and social customs and manners, often but not necessarily associated with religious observance. The further "relevant" characteristics were: (1) either a common geographical origin, or descent from a small number of common ancestors; (2) a common language, not necessarily peculiar to the group; (3) a common literature peculiar to the group; (4) a common religion different from that of neighbouring groups or from the general community surrounding it; (5) being a minority or being an oppressed or a dominant group within a larger community, for example a conquered people and their conquerors might both be ethnic groups (say, the inhabitants and Normans of England shortly after the Norman conquest).[31]

Lord Templeman spoke of (a) group descent, (b) geographical origin and (c) group history, as features to recognise a group by ethnic origins.[32] Lords Brandon and Roskill concurred with the speeches of both Lord Fraser and Lord Templeman while Lord Edmund-Davies restricted himself to concurring in the decision. On

---

[26] On the specific issue of "national" minorities within the UK, see M. MacEwen, "Racial grounds: a definition of identity" (1998) 3 IJDL 51.
[27] [1972] A.C. 342 (HL).
[28] ibid. 363–364.
[29] [1997] I.R.L.R. 610, EAT. See also *BBC Scotland v Souster* [2001] I.R.L.R. 150 CS (English); and *Griffiths v Reading University Students Union* (1996) unreported, Case No.16476/96, see 31 DCLD 3 (Welsh); *Caylon v Wardle* (2010) UKEAT/535/09/SM (French city firm prefer French over English candidate).
[30] [1983] A.C. 548 (HL).
[31] ibid. 560–563.
[32] ibid. 569E.

the face of it, this is rather confusing,[33] as the criteria proposed in each speech differ. Only "group history" was stated by Lord Fraser to be an "essential" characteristic. "Group descent" and "geographical origin", said Lord Fraser, were merely "relevant" characteristics. In practice Lord Fraser's test has become fashionable and it is the one usually applied nowadays.

Lord Fraser was influenced by the New Zealand Court of Appeal in *King-Ansell v Police*,[34] and in particular, this extract:

"... a group is identifiable in terms of its ethnic origins if it is a segment of the population distinguished from others by a sufficient combination of shared customs, beliefs, traditions and characteristics derived from a common or presumed common past, even if not drawn from what in biological terms is a common racial stock. It is that combination which gives them an historically determined social identity in their own eyes and in the eyes of those outside the group. They have a distinct social identity based not simply on group cohesion and solidarity but also on their belief as to their historical antecedents."[35]

Accordingly, Lord Fraser thought that converts could be included, for example, "persons who marry into the group", and apostates (those who renounce a belief or allegiance) could be excluded. He concluded "it is possible for a person to fall into a particular racial group either by birth or by adherence... ".[36]

This combines to show that the question is more cultural than it is technical, scientific or biological. As such, the House unanimously held that Sikhs formed a racial group because of their ethnic origins, which comprised: a distinctive and self-conscious community, a history going back to the 15th century, a written language (which a small proportion of Sikhs can read but which can be read by a much higher proportion of Sikhs than Hindus), being at one time politically supreme in the Punjab. It did not matter they are not biologically distinguishable from the other peoples living in the Punjab.

3–009

Under Lord Fraser's guidance, it has been held that Jews,[37] but not

---

[33] For criticisms of *Mandla* see G.T. Pagone, "The Lawyer's Hunt for Snarks, Religion and Races" [1984] CLJ 218 and H. Benyon and N. Love, "*Mandla* and the Meaning of 'Racial Group'" (1984) 100 LQR 120.

[34] [1979] 2 N.Z.L.R. 531.

[35] ibid. 543 (Richardson J.).

[36] [1983] A.C. 548 (HL), 563. Cf. Lord Templeman, 569. In the Canadian case *Grismer v Squamish Indian Band* 2006 FC 1088, [46], those adopted as adults into the Squamish Nation were recognised under the Charter of Fundamental Freedoms for a discrimination claim.

[37] *R. (A) v Governing Body of JFS* [2010] 2 W.L.R. 153 (SC). See also *King-Ansell v Police* [1979] 2 N.Z.L.R. 531, approved in *Mandla v Dowell Lee* [1983] A.C. 548 (HL), at 562. It was the Government's intention that persons of the Jewish faith be protected under the Race Relations Act 1965. In a debate on that Act the Home Secretary stated that the word "ethnic" would "undoubtedly" include Jews (711 HC Deb 3 May 1965 cols 932–933).

Rastafarians,[38] fall within the definition of ethnic origins. In the latter case, the Court of Appeal concluded Rastafarians did not have a long enough shared or group history (about 60 years' at the time), although it failed to suggest how many years were required to qualify. This case was heard before the specific outlawing of religion or belief discrimination in 2003,[39] and so nowadays, a victim of religious discrimination, such as a Rastafarian, should have little trouble being recognised for protection (see further below, para.3–014).

Lord Fraser's guidelines on the meaning of ethnic origins also show that the characteristics of race and religion are not always mutually exclusive for legal purposes. In *R. (A) v Governing Body of JFS*,[40] the Jewish Free School's admissions policy gave preference to children recognised as Orthodox Jewish by the Office of the Chief Rabbi (OCR), which required that the child's mother be Jewish either by matrilineal descent or by conversion under the OCR doctrine. A boy was refused admission because his Italian (previously Roman Catholic) mother was a Masorti Jew convert, a denomination not recognised by the OCR. He was unable to complain of *religious* discrimination because "faith schools" enjoy an exemption from religious discrimination in their admissions.[41] Faith schools enjoy no such exception from *racial* discrimination, and the boy complained of direct racial discrimination. A 5–4 majority of the Supreme Court found that the admissions policy directly discriminated on racial grounds. Lord Phillips held that it was "racial, and in any event, ethnic". Lord Kerr said there can be "mixed ethnic origins that do not fall neatly into one group or category" and so the claimant also could define his ethnic origins as a half-Italian Masorti Jew. Similarly, Lord Clarke found that identifying the ground of treatment was not an either/or question (either religion *or* ethnic). So it was possible to discriminate on both religious and ethnic grounds. Lord Mance said the boy was at a disadvantage because of his descent. And Lady Hale held that "M was rejected because of his mother's ethnic origins, which were Italian and Roman Catholic".[42]

3–010 Although these conclusions appear to vary a little, they are united in emphasising the flexibility permitted in identifying a racial group. It seems that each and every denomination of Judaism can amount to a *racial* group. In the context of this religion/ethnic debate, this could prove problematic. The race discrimination legislation was not enacted to prevent religious discrimination, a point emphasised by

---

[38] *Crown Suppliers v Dawkins* [1993] I.C.R. 517 (CA), 526.
[39] SI 2003/1660. Now replaced by the Equality Act 2010.
[40] [2010] 2 W.L.R. 153 (SC).
[41] Equality Act 2006 s.50 (now Equality Act 2010 Sch.11, para.5). The European Convention on Human Rights provides the right of parents to ensure education and teaching in conformity with their own religions and philosophical convictions (1st Protocol, art.2). See further below para.3–019.
[42] [2010] 2 W.L.R. 153, respectively, [42] (Lord Phillips); [108–109] (Lord Kerr); [127]–[129] (Lord Clarke); [89] (Lord Mance); [66] (Lady Hale).

the two speeches in *Mandla*,[43] which both emphasised that Sikhs were more than just a religion.[44] The *JFS* majority's emphasis on flexibility led them to go further than required to resolve the case. Their speeches suggested Orthodox, Masorti, Reform or Liberal Jewish denominations could each be defined by *Mandla* ethnic origins, when all that was required was to identify the preference for matrilineal lineage to those addressed by Moses at Mount Sinai. This clearly contains a racial element and as such this case could have been brought *anyone* who could not comply (not just Masorti Jews). Thus, there was no need to introduce such religious flexibility into the *Mandla* test. The problem is that it is now difficult for any organisation (e.g. schools, employers) to take advantage of the potentially more liberal exceptions provided in the *religious* discrimination provisions,[45] say, by stipulating that applicants are of a certain religion, because this *religious* preference may also amount to a *racial* one, and so leave the organisation open to a racial discrimination claim. It also makes it difficult, if not impossible, for Parliament to draft an exception for Jewish (or other faith) organisations, because religion and ethnic origins have now become, in legal language anyway, virtually inseparable.[46]

(a) Romanies, the Roma and Travellers
The European Court of Human Rights, in claims of discrimination against Roma people, has noted an "international consensus ... recognising the special needs of minorities and an obligation to protect their security, identity and lifestyle, not only for the purpose of safeguarding the interests of the minorities themselves but to preserve a cultural diversity of value to the whole community".[47] A local example of this "consensus" was the Government planning guidance for English local authorities, *Planning for gipsy and traveller caravan sites* (Circular 01/2006), which stated:

3–011

> "5. Gypsies and Travellers are believed to experience the worst health and education status of any disadvantaged group in England. Research has consistently confirmed the link between the lack of good quality sites for gypsies and travellers and poor health and education."

---

[43] [1983] A.C. 548 (HL), 562, 568.
[44] ibid. 563–565, 569.
[45] See Ch.8, para.8–056.
[46] For a case comment, see (2010) 39(2) ILJ 183.
[47] *DH v Czech Republic* (App. No.57325/00) (2008) 47 E.H.R.R. 3, [181], citing *Chapman v UK* (App. No.27238/94) (2001) 33 E.H.R.R. 18, [93]. See [2008] 2 E.H.R.L.R. 245.

That relates to planning law, where local authorities are bound by their Equality Duty[48] and the Human Rights Act 1998. The groups covered by this Circular are relatively wide:

> "15. Persons of nomadic habit of life whatever their race or origin, including such persons who on grounds only of their own or their family's or dependants' educational or health needs or old age have ceased to travel temporarily or permanently, but excluding members of an organised group of travelling show people or circus people travelling together as such."

This "consensus" could be tested as the Coalition Government announced in 2010 that it would replace this Circular and adopt a "light touch" approach, "encouraging" the provision of sites and (ironically) giving local authorities "stronger planning enforcement powers". This may, or may not, not involve narrowing the coverage.[49]

3–012   For claims of racial discrimination under the Race Relations Act 1976 (now Equality Act 2010), the courts have taken a narrower view. In *Commission for Racial Equality v Dutton*,[50] the Court of Appeal found that "Gypsies" fell within Lord Fraser's criteria from *Mandla*, recognising this ethnic group as having a common descent from Northern India and some distinctive customs, but did not include "travelling" in this analysis, which indicates that those Romanies who are no longer nomadic are included. More recently, "Irish Travellers" and the Roma from mainland Europe have been accepted as racial groups.[51]

Limits were expressed in *Dutton*. Nicholls L.J. identified a wider group of nomadic people who could not be identified by "ethnic origins": "didicois, mumpers, peace people, new age travellers, hippies, tinkers, hawkers, self-styled 'anarchists', and others".[52] Some of these groups may be recognised for planning purposes (see above) and/or under ECHR art.14, thus, via the Human Rights Act 1998, obliging the State (including the courts) not to discriminate under the Convention's principal rights.[53] In addition to planning, this could

---

[48] See Ch.10.
[49] See *http://www.communities.gov.uk/planningandbuilding/travellers/* (accessed January 1, 2011).
[50] [1989] Q.B. 783 (CA).
[51] Respectively, *Baker v Secretary of State for Communities and Local Government* [2008] EWCA Civ 141, [28]; *R (European Roma Rights Centre) v Immigration Officer at Prague Airport* [2005] 2 A.C. 1, [1] , [32], [34], [36], [38], [79] (Czech nationals of Romani ethnic origin).
[52] [1989] 1 Q.B. 783, 796.
[53] See Ch.2, para.2–006.

involve laws preventing travellers from parking up temporarily on private or public land, and/or any disproportionate punishments.[54]

The difference between the definitions in *Dutton* and the Government Circular had the potential to cause problems. When making a planning complaint, claimants may well cite the Equality Duty and the Human Rights Act 1998 thus bringing into court two definitions of traveller. In practice, the courts have adopted the Government Circular definition.[55] Much will turn now on the new Circular.

(b) Language

A particular issue is whether a racial group can be defined by language.[56] The matter arose in *Gwynedd County Council v Jones*,[57] where the council required job applicants to speak Welsh. Two Welsh complainants—who spoke English only—brought a claim of discrimination on grounds of their ethnic origins. The EAT held that it was "wrong in law" to define a racial group by a language factor alone and that even if it was a question of fact, such a finding would be "wholly unreasonable". Sir Ralph Kilner Brown noted: "We cannot believe that, for example, a Mrs Jones from Holyhead who speaks Welsh as well as English is to be regarded as belonging to a different racial group from her dear friend, a Mrs Thomas from Colwyn Bay who speaks only English."[58] The ratio decidendi of *Jones* is that direct discrimination against English-only-speaking Welsh persons is not unlawful under the Race Relations Act 1976. However, the decision, and the statement that language alone could not be used to define a racial group, implied that Welsh speakers did not form a racial group. This analysis has been criticised by one commentator who suggested (Scottish) Gaels at least, fell within the definition of ethnic origins.[59] Another problem is the insistence that racial groups must be distinct from each other, in order to be recognised. That

3–013

---

[54] In *Massey v Secretary of State for the Communities* [2008] EWHC 3353 (Admin), "new travellers" (persons who wished to engage upon a nomadic life for the first time) were not recognised for planning law purposes, although the Human Rights Act 1998 was not cited. For successful Roma claims in the ECtHR, see *Muñoz Díaz v Spain* (App. No.49151/07) (2010) 50 E.H.R.R. 49 (refusal to recognise Roma marriage breached art.14 and P.1, art. 1); *DH v Czech Republic* (App. No.57325/00) (2008) 47 E.H.R.R. 3 (discussed Ch.2, para.2–020).

[55] See e.g. *Baker v Secretary of State for Communities and Local Government* [2008] EWCA Civ 141, where *Dutton* was not cited at all.

[56] See W. McLeod, "Autochthonous language communities and the Race Relations Act", *Web of Current Legal Issues* [1998] 1 Web JCCI-htm. See also for the USA, I. Locke-Steven, "Language discrimination and English-only rules in the workplace: the case for legislative amendment of Title VII", (1996) 27 Texas Tech Law Rev pp.33–72. A claim of "accent" discrimination has been upheld as direct racial discrimination by an ET. See *The Times* November 28, 2007.

[57] [1986] I.C.R. 833 (EAT). For an unsatisfactory case, where an insistence that staff in a Welsh restaurant speak English was held to be direct racial discrimination, see *Cowell (T/A The Stables) v Williams (No.2)* (2010) EAT/0904/97, esp. [13].

[58] ibid. 834.

[59] See McLeod, above n.56.

notion was dispelled by the Supreme Court in the *JFS* case.[60] There remains an anomaly with the *Jones* decision. An English woman resident in Wales, who could not comply with a Welsh language requirement, could bring a claim of *indirect* discrimination based her national origin.[61] A considerably smaller proportion of English than Welsh could comply with the requirement. To build on the imagery of Sir Ralf Kilner Brown, of two non-Welsh speaking neighbours, only Mrs Smith enjoys the protection of the Act. Mrs Jones can be discriminated against because she is Welsh.

2. RELIGION OR BELIEF

3–014   Until 2003, there was no express protection for religious discrimination in Great Britain.[62] There has been, since 1976, legislation against discrimination on grounds of "religious or political opinion" in Northern Ireland.[63] Otherwise, the position for religious groups was capricious. As noted above, religious groups could claim under the Race Relations Act 1976 (RRA 1976) only if their religion coincided with a racial group by its "ethnic origins", as defined by Lord Fraser's *Mandla* criteria.[64] By this, Sikhs[65] and Jews[66] would qualify, but not Rastafarians.[67] The difficulty for Muslims qualifying under the *Mandla* criteria was summarised in *Nyazi v Rymans Ltd*:[68] "Muslims include people of many nations and colours, who speak many languages and whose only common denominator is religion and religious culture." However, it was possible for a Muslim to claim indirect discrimination under the RRA 1976 where the religion is predominant in the claimant's nation of origin. So for example, Muslims of Pakistani origin could define themselves by national

---

[60] [2010] 2 W.L.R. 153. See above para.3–009, p.62.

[61] See above, (4) "National Origins". Of course, such a requirement would be lawful if it were justified. For the ease of justifying language requirements in see *Groener v Minister of Education* Case 397/87 [1989] 2 E.C.R. 3967 ECJ. See F. Palermo, "The use of minority languages: recent developments in EC law and judgments of the ECJ" (2001) Maastricht J. 8, 299.

[62] See generally, B. Hepple and T. Choudhury (2001) "Tackling Religious Discrimination: Practical Implications for Policy-makers and Legislators" Home Office Series 221. London: Home Office; P. Cumper, "The Protection of Religious Rights under Section 13 of the Human Rights Act 1998" [2002] PL 254; C. Evans, *Freedom of Religion under the ECHR* (Oxford: OUP, 2001), Ch.4.

[63] Fair Employment (Northern Ireland) Act 1976. See now, Fair Employment (Northern Ireland) Order 1998 SI 1998/3162.

[64] *Mandla v Dowell Lee* [1983] A.C. 548 HL, see above "1 (5) Ethnic Origins", para.3–008.

[65] ibid.

[66] *R (A) v Governing Body of JFS* [2010] 2 W.L.R. 153 (SC). See also *King-Ansell v Police* [1979] 2 NZLR 531, approved in *Mandla v Dowell Lee* [1983] A.C. 548 (HL) at 562.

[67] *Crown Suppliers v Dawkins* [1993] E.C.R. 517 CA. See above "1(5) Ethnic Origins" para.3–008.

[68] EAT/6/88 (Unreported).

origin. Any discrimination against Muslims is also likely to discriminate, indirectly, against Pakistanis.[69]

Dedicated legislation came first with the Employment Equality **3–015** (Religion or Belief) Regulations 2003 covering employment, and then Part 2 of the Equality Act 2006, which extended the coverage to the provision of goods, facilities and services, premises and education, and also to public authorities. These two pieces of legislation have been replaced by the Equality Act 2010, which defines "religion or belief" in a similar way, and so the case law on the preceding legislation provides useful guidance.

Religion or belief discrimination coincides with the "freedom of thought, conscience and religion" provided by art.9 of the European Convention on Human Rights. And so courts are bound to interpret the Equality Act 2010 in accordance with art.9, which plays a major role in these cases.[70]

(1) Religion and Religious Belief

Section 10(1) of the Equality Act 2010 includes "any religion" for **3–016** protection. Explanatory Note 53 suggests that this includes "The Baha'i faith, Buddhism, Christianity, Hinduism, Islam, Jainism, Judaism, Rastafarianism, Sikhism and Zoroastrianism". The same Note confirms that sects or denominations should be recognised. Thus, for example, Protestants and Catholics (Christians), Sunnis or Shias (Muslims), are protected beliefs despite each also belonging to the "parent" religion. Section 10(1) includes a "lack of religion", thus including agnostics.

For the purposes of ECHR art. 9, some further guidance was provided by Lord Nicholls in *R. (Williamson) v Secretary of State for Employment*:[71]

> "[R]eligious belief is intensely personal and can easily vary from one individual to another. Each individual is at liberty to hold his own religious beliefs, however irrational or inconsistent they may seem to some, however surprising ...".

This means that "emphatically, it is not for the court ... to judge its 'validity' by some objective standard". A court should scrutinise a

---

[69] See, for example, *Hussain v Midland Cosmetics Sales*, EAT/915/00 ("Pakistani Muslims"); and *JH Walker v Hussain* [1996] I.C.R. 291 EAT ("Asian Muslims").
[70] HRA 1998 s.3. See also Equality Act 2006, Explanatory Note 170, and e.g. *Eweida v BA* [2009] I.C.R. 303 (EAT), [27] (Elias J.), affirmed [2010] I.C.R. 890 (CA).
[71] [2006] 2 A.C. 246 (HL), [22].

person's claimed religious belief only to ensure good faith and that it is "neither fictitious, nor capricious, and that it is not an artifice."[72]

(2) "Belief"

3–017   As well as its religious dimension, art.9 provides "a precious asset for atheists, agnostics, sceptics and the unconcerned". The pluralism inherent in a democratic society, "which has been dearly won over the centuries, depends on it."[73]

In this spirit, s.10(2) of the Equality Act 2010 includes "any religious or philosophical belief" and a "lack of belief" for protection. Guidance on the meaning of this was provided in *Grainger v Nicholson*:[74] (1) The belief must be genuinely held. (2) It must be a belief and not an opinion or viewpoint based on the present state of information available. In *McClintock v Department of Constitutional Affairs*,[75] a Magistrate sitting on the family panel refused to handle adoption cases for same-sex couples because on the evidence he considered it was not in the best interests of the child; if the evidence changed, so to would his viewpoint. This was not a philosophical view or religion in which he actually believed. (3) It must be a belief as to a weighty and substantial aspect of human life and behaviour. (4) It must attain a certain level of cogency, seriousness, cohesion and importance (it should have a similar status or cogency to a religious belief). (5) It must be worthy of respect in a democratic society, be not incompatible with human dignity and not conflict with the fundamental rights of others.[76] In this context, note that ECHR art.17 provides that the Convention cannot be used to abuse its rights and freedoms. In addition, a belief can be a "one-off", held by just one person, and it need not "allude to a fully-fledged system of thought" or govern "the entirety of the person's life".[77]

Political philosophies can be included, such as Socialism, Marxism,

---

[72] ibid. [22], citing *Syndicat Northcrest v Amselem* (2004) 241 D.L.R. (4th) 1 (Sup Ct of Canada), [52]–[54] (Iacobucci J.). See e.g. *X v UK* (App. No.7291/75) (1977) 11 DR 55, where the (European Human Rights) Commission found no evidence of the existence of the claimed "Wicca" religion.
[73] *Kokkinakis v Greece* (1993) 17 E.H.R.R. 418 (ECtHR), [31].
[74] [2010] I.R.L.R. 4 (EAT), [24]–[28].
[75] [2008] I.R.L.R. 29 (EAT), [45].
[76] [2010] I.R.L.R. 4 (EAT), [28], citing *R. (Williamson) v Secretary of State for Employment* [2006] 2 A.C. 246 (HL) [23], and *Campbell and Cosans v UK* (1982) 4 E.H.R.R. 283, [36].
[77] ibid. citing *Arrowsmith v UK* (1978) 3 E.H.R.R 218 [69] (pacifism), and *H v UK* (1993) E.H.R.R. CD 44 (veganism).

Communism or free-market capitalism.[78] Odious political beliefs, such as fascism, will not be protected because of point (5), above.[79]

A philosophical belief which is based on science might be protected. For instance, "Darwinism must plainly be capable of being a philosophical belief, albeit that it may be based entirely on scientific conclusions (not all of which may be uncontroversial)." Accordingly, a belief in climate change (that mankind was heading towards catastrophic climate change and everyone was under a moral duty to lead their lives in a manner to prevent or mitigate that catastrophe) was protected.[80]

(3) Manifestations of Beliefs—ECHR

Article 9(1), ECHR also preserves a freedom to *manifest* ones religion   **3–018**
or belief "in worship, teaching, practice and observance". However, art.9(2) provides that this freedom is:

> "... subject only to such limitations as are prescribed by law and are necessary in a democratic society in the interests of public safety, for the protection of public order, health or morals, or for the protection of the rights and freedoms of others".

This provides a form of justification defence for interferences with the freedom. In theory, a court should determine first whether the manifestation falls within art.9(1) and second, if it does, whether the interference was justified under art.9(2).[81] In practice, the Court tends to focus on justification.[82] And so, in claims that fail, it is sometimes difficult to tell if the manifestation actually engaged art.9(1). Nonetheless, *recognition* and *justification* will be considered in turn.

---

[78] ibid. [28]. In the US case, *American Postal Workers Union v Postmaster General* 781 F 2d 772 (9th Cir 1986), two window clerks refused to handle draft (conscription) papers on the grounds that their religion prohibited them from doing anything to facilitate war. Their employer's refusal to accommodate was held to be religious discrimination under the Civil Rights Act 1964.

[79] The US Supreme Court has observed that an asserted belief might be "so bizarre, so clearly nonreligious in motivation, as not to be entitled to protection ..." (*Thomas v Review Board of Indiana Employment Security Div* 450 US 707, at 715 (1981), a case under the Free Exercise Clause). In *Bellamy v Mason's Stores* 508 F 2d 504, at 505 (4th Cir 1974) affirming 368 F Supp 1025, at 1026 (ED Va 1973), it was held that the Ku Klux Klan was not a religion under the Civil Rights Act 1964: "[T]he proclaimed racist and anti-semitic ideology ... takes on a ... narrow, temporal and political character inconsistent with the meaning of 'religion'".

[80] *Grainger v Nicholson* [2010] I.R.L.R. 4 (EAT), [30].

[81] See e.g. *Skugar v Russia* (App. No.40010/04) (2009, Admissibility decision).

[82] "In the majority of cases, the court has avoided making any express determination as to whether the subject matter comes within the scope of article 9. In other cases, the court has either assumed the existence of a religious belief without question, or has found against the existence of a manifestation of religious belief without determining whether there was a religion in issue" (Clayton and Tomlinson, *The Law of Human Rights* (Oxford: OUP, 2000), p.971, para.14.40.)

(a) Article 9(1)—Recognising the Manifestation

3–019 Article 9(1), especially with the words *practice* and *observance*, is rather open ended and vulnerable to an extremely broad interpretation. There is all the difference between the practices of getting married in church, and throwing rice at church weddings.[83] Naturally, the courts have placed limits on what manifestations will engage art.9. Convention jurisprudence maintains that "Article 9 does not protect every act motivated or inspired by a religion or belief"[84] and that the manifestation must be "intimately linked" to the belief.[85] And so, in *Pichon and Sajous v France*,[86] the ECtHR did not recognise the manifestation of the religious belief of two pharmacists who refused to sell the contraception pill, because they were still free to "manifest those beliefs in many ways outside the professional sphere".[87]

That said, courts have recognised practices beyond mere worship and ceremony. *R. (Williamson) v Secretary of State for Employment*,[88] concerned a challenge to a ban on corporal punishment in schools. The House of Lords recognised—for art.9—a Christian *adherence to* corporal punishment of school children ("spare the rod and spoil the child"). In *Skugar v Russia*[89] the ECtHR recognised a Christian's "sincere" rejection of a tax reference number because it was the "forerunner of the mark of the Antichrist" as told in the Bible, despite evidence to the contrary from the Russian Orthodox Church.

(b) Article 9(2)—Justifying Interferences under the ECHR

3–020 It is of course likely that the more peripheral the manifestation, the more likely it is that an interference could be justified.[90] Hence, the interferences in *Williamson* and *Skugar* were each found to be justified. It seems, where a person could avoid a restriction, that

---

[83] *Employment Division, Department of Human Resources of Oregon v Smith* (1990) 494 US 872 (US Sup Ct, 1990), 888, n.4 (Scalia J.).

[84] *Kalac v Turkey* (1997) 27 E.H.R.R. 552, [27].

[85] *A v UK* (App. No.10295/82) (1983) 6 EHRR 558, (Commission decision), [1], cited in *R.(Williamson) v Secretary of State for Employment* [2006] 2 A.C. 246 (HL) [32] (Lord Nicholls).

[86] App. No.49853/99 (2001) (Admissibility decision).

[87] See also *A v UK* (App. No.10295/82) (1983) 6 EHRR 558 (Commission decision) (pacifist's request that 40 per cent of her taxes be diverted from weapons and defence expenditure to other peaceful purposes, was not a manifestation of her belief); *Porter v UK* (2003) 37 E.H.R.R. CD8 (Conservative politician's use of public funds for political purposes not a manifestation of her political or other beliefs); *Arrowsmith v UK* (1981) 3 E.H.R.R. 218 (Commission decision) (pacifist's distribution of leaflets dissuading soldiers from serving in Northern Ireland not a manifestation).

[88] [2006] 2 A.C. 246 (HL), [22]. In *Lautsi v Italy* (App. No.30814/06) [2010] 50 E.H.R.R. 42 the second section of the Court of Human Rights recognised a parent's right to raise her children according to secular principles and held that the display of crucifixes throughout her children's school violated this right. An appeal was heard by the Grand Chamber on June 30, 2010, but as of January 1, 2011, no decision had been published.

[89] (App. No.40010/04) (2009, Admissibility decision).

[90] *Eweida v BA* [2009] I.C.R. 303 (EAT), [31] (Elias J.), affirmed [2010] I.C.R. 890 (CA).

restriction may be justified. In *Kalac v Turkey*,[91] the ECtHR held that the applicant had "accepted" the restrictions on his religious practices by joining a military which must be loyal to the expressly secular state. In *Şahin v Turkey*[92] a university's ban on the wearing of Islamic headscarves, although engaging art.9(1), was justified. The principle was taken further in *R. (Begum) v Denbigh High School Governors*,[93] where a 3–2 majority of the House of Lords held that a school-uniform ban on the jilbab[94] did not engage art.9 because a pupil could choose another school. This finding meant that the school was under no obligation to justify its ban, although a unanimous House found it was justified in any case.

(4) Manifestation of Beliefs—Equality Act 2010

The structure of art.9 means that any interference with this freedom, including *direct* discrimination, is potentially justifiable. The position under the Equality Act 2010 is slightly different. Generally, only *indirect* discrimination can be justified, although there are some specific exceptions for direct discrimination, such as the "occupational requirement" defence in employment cases.[95] This leaves domestic courts with a problem. If they recognise manifestations in claims of direct discrimination they will have less room to manoeuvre than art.9 affords.

3–021

The difficulty arises from the logic that where an apparently neutral practice coincides with a person's recognised manifestation of their religion or belief, a finding of direct discrimination must inevitably follow.[96] In *Azmi v Kirklees MBC*,[97] a teacher was instructed to remove the veil, which she felt compelled to wear by her Muslim religion. Whether this instruction is facially discriminatory (direct discrimination) or facially neutral (indirect discrimination) depends upon how her religious belief and manifestation is defined for protection. Wearing of the veil is undoubtedly a religious "observance" for art.9,[98] and so should be a protected manifestation of her belief. As such, the instruction is facially discriminatory: the protected characteristic is the face covering and the ground of the treatment is the face covering. Most cases under the domestic legislation have evaded this problem by failing to define precisely the claimant's

---

[91] (1997) 27 E.H.R.R. 552, [28].
[92] (App. No.44774/98) (2007) 44 E.H.R.R. 5, (ECtHR), [78].
[93] [2007] 1 A.C. 100. See also *R. (X) v Headteachers and Governors of Y School* [2007] EWHC 298 (QBD), [101].
[94] A long coat-like garment which effectively conceals the shape of the female body.
[95] See Ch.8, para.8–057.
[96] cf. *McFarlane v Relate Avon Limited* [2010] I.R.L.R. 196 (EAT), [18] (Underhill J.).
[97] [2007] I.R.L.R. 484 (EAT).
[98] *R. (X) v Headteachers and Governors of Y School* [2007] EWHC 298 (QBD), [101] (Niqab veil); *Sahin v Turkey* (App. No.44774/98) (2007) 44 E.H.R.R. 5, (ECtHR), [78] (Islamic headscarf), *R. (Watkins-Singh) v Aberdare Girls' High School Governors* [2008] EWHC 1865 (Admin) ("Kara", a steel bangle).

protected characteristic and focusing on the ground of the treatment. And so, in *Azmi*, the EAT held that instruction to a Muslim teacher to remove the veil did not directly discriminate because the comparator was a teacher who covered her face for a non-religious reason. Likewise, in *Islington LBC v Ladele*,[99] a Christian registrar who refused to conduct civil partnerships was compared to a registrar who similarly refused, but for non-religious reasons. Upon this test, the claimants were treated equally to how their comparators would have been treated. Some cases have even skipped the comparison, identifying the "ground" of the treatment. If the evidence shows that the reason for the treatment was the manifestation of the belief, rather than the belief itself, "the question of how to define the comparator becomes academic."[100]

3–022   The seemingly plausible logic of these cases disguises the fact that only the *belief*, and not the *manifestation*, has been recognised. As such, virtually all claims of direct discrimination based on a manifestation would fail. But these *decisions* do not necessarily contradict ECHR art.9, which of course, by art.9(2) permits some interferences with manifestations of religious beliefs. In most cases, the treatment can be challenged as being indirectly discriminatory, thus placing a burden on the defendant to objectively justify the treatment. This more closely follows the structure of art.9. But there is a limited type of case where this will not happen. Where someone holds a "one-off" belief "however irrational or inconsistent" (see *Williamson*, above para.3–016), a claim indirect discrimination will fail at the first stage, because it has been held that the legislation demands *group* (rather than individual) disadvantage. In *Eweida v British Airways*,[101] a ban on visible jewellery for cabin crew adversely affected a Christian who insisted on displaying a small cross. This ban did not raise a prima facie case of indirect discrimination because it affected only the claimant. Although in *Eweida*, it was not clear whether the display of the cross was a protected manifestation, the case shows that it is possible that a person with a protected manifestation would receive no protection from domestic or EC discrimination law.

What then, is the proper approach? In addition to the "narrow" approach in *Azmi* and *Ladele*, there are (at least) two further possibilities.

---

[99] *Islington LBC v Ladele* [2009] I.C.R. 387 (EAT) [39], affirmed [2010] 1 W.L.R. 955 (CA), [64].

[100] *Chondol v Liverpool CC* (2009) UKEAT/0298/08/JOJ, [23] (Christian social worker "foisting" his beliefs on service users), citing *Shamoon v RUC* [2003] I.C.R. 337 (HL), [7]–[11] (Lord Nicholls) (see further, Ch.6). See also *Islington LBC v Ladele* [2009] I.C.R. 387 (EAT), [38] (Elias J.) affirmed [2010] 1 W.L.R. 955 (CA).

[101] [2010] I.C.R. 890 (CA), [12]–[17]. In the US case, *Wilson v United States West Communications* 58 F 3d 1337, a Roman Catholic worker made a religious vow to wear an anti-abortion button displaying a colour photograph of a foetus and two anti-abortion slogans. Although the evidence showed that the wearing of the badge was within the vow, the *displaying* of it was not, and so outside of the meaning of "religion".

An "intermediate" approach is to include *some* manifestations as "protected characteristics", in line with ECHR case law, so including only those manifestations "intimately linked" to the belief.[102] This will of course, call for a degree of value judgment, something not favoured by the House of Lords in *Williamson* (above, para.3–016). A wider interpretation is to take the Equality Act 2010 beyond art.9, and assume that virtually all (genuine) manifestations are protected characteristics.

With either approach, the defendant is left with virtually no **3–023** defence. For instance, in employment cases, the Equality Act 2010 (Sch.9), permits a defence to direct discrimination where there is a requirement to have a particular protected characteristic, which does not help the employer requiring the worker *not* to have the characteristic (such as the veil). And even if such a defence were available (seemingly available under the Framework Directive 2000/78/EC, see also para.8–046) in some cases at least, it would be more difficult to prove a requirement than it would to prove objective justification. In *Ladele*, for instance, the council justified its treatment in pursuit of its equality and diversity policy and its legal obligation to provide services without discrimination.[103] It would have proved more difficult for the council to show that conducting civil partnerships was determining and *necessary* to do the job, when say, there were enough other registrars to cover these ceremonies.[104] This may explain the narrow approach taken in *Azmi* and *Ladele*.

Lucy Vickers anticipated these difficulties and suggested an alternative legislative model based on the "reasonable adjustments" duty under disability discrimination law.[105] The logic behind this is that the *manifestations* of a belief resemble (legally) the *effects* of a disability. For instance, a requirement for a fast typing speed does not directly target those with arthritis, but the effects of the disease. In such cases, employers are obliged to make reasonable adjustments (such as supplying an adapted keyboard). In the United States, religious discrimination employment law is centred on a similar "reasonable accommodation" model, placing a duty on employers to accommodate the religious needs of their workers, unless this would cause "undue hardship". Some examples are given in Chapter 6, para.6–054.

---

[102] *A v UK* (App. No.10295/82) (1983) 6 EHRR 558, (Commission decision), [1]. See above, para.3–020.

[103] Under the Equality Act (Sexual Orientation) Regulations 2007/1263 reg.3. See now, Equality Act 2010 s.29.

[104] See e.g. *Etam Plc v Rowan* [1989] I.R.L.R. 150 (EAT), holding that a "women-only" policy was not an occupational requirement to work in a ladies' fashion store when 16 other (female) employees could cover fitting room duties.

[105] L. Vickers, *Religious freedom, religious discrimination and the workplace* (Oxford, Portland, OR: Hart, 2008), pp.129–130. On the "reasonable adjustment" duty, see See Ch.13 para.13–039.

3. GENDER REASSIGNMENT

3–024 Two cases addressed two major equality issues for transsexuals. The first issue is the lack of legal recognition of a person's acquired sex. Some of the problems associated with this were highlighted in *Goodwin v United Kingdom*[106] where a male-to-female transsexual: suffered abuse at work; had to undergo special procedures for her National Insurance contributions and her state pension; had to make special appointments to attend the DSS, as transsexuals' files were marked "sensitive"; feared (reasonably) that her present employer could learn about her past identity through her National Insurance number, and discriminate as a result; (unlike other women) she had to wait until she was 65 before she could claim her state pension and free bus pass; and she had to declare her birth sex when applying for life insurance, mortgages, private pensions or car insurance, which led her not to pursue these possibilities to her advantage.

The European Court of Human Rights held that the State's refusal to give legal recognition to a transsexual's acquired sex violated art.8 (private life). Consequently, Parliament passed the Gender Recognition Act 2004 by which transsexuals can apply for legal recognition of their acquired sex if (1) they have or have had gender dysphoria, and (2) have lived in the acquired gender for two years prior to the application, and (3) intend to live permanently in the acquired gender.[107] Surgery and/or hormone treatment is not essential for recognition.

The second issue was discrimination against transsexuals. This was (first) recognised by the ECJ in *P v S and Cornwall County Council*,[108] where it was held that the dismissal of a worker because he intended to undergo gender reassignment amounted to *sex* discrimination. This accounts for the inclusion of gender reassignment as a protected characteristic in the current sex discrimination (Recast) Directive 2006/54/EC. The Equality Act 2010, s.7(1) provides:

> "A person has the protected characteristic of gender reassignment if the person is proposing to undergo, is undergoing or has undergone a process (or part of a process) for the purpose of reassigning the person's sex by changing physiological or other attributes of sex."

This extends the previous provisions in the Sex Discrimination Act 1975 as it no longer requires the person to be under medical

---

[106] [2002] E.H.R.R. 447, [60]–[63].
[107] Gender Recognition Act 2004 s.2.
[108] Case C-13/94 E.C.R. I-2143, [1996] I.C.R. 795.

supervision. It now includes, for instance, a female-to-male trans-sexual who successfully "passes" as a man without medical intervention.[109]

4. SEXUAL ORIENTATION

Section 12 of the Equality Act 2010 provides that the Act covers homosexual, heterosexual and bisexual persons.   **3–025**

5. MARITAL AND CIVIL PARTNERSHIP STATUS

The Equality Act 2010 s.8 includes for protection a person's marital status or civil partnership.[110] There are two significant features to definition. First, it is limited effectively[111] to employment matters only. Second, s.8 is drafted to protect only those in a civil partnership or marriage, and not those, for example, who are engaged to be married, divorced, or who have had their civil partnership dissolved, or who are just single.   **3–026**

Article 2(1) of the Equal Treatment Directive 76/207/EEC pro-hibited sex discrimination *by reference in particular to marital or family status*. In some senses, this appears broader than s.8, as it could cover those intending to marry and divorcees. However, this phrase was dropped from the Recast Directive 2006/54/EC.[112] And so the limits in s.8 cannot be challenged under that Directive.

---

[109] Equality Act 2010 Explanatory Note 43.

[110] See M. Bell, "Employment law consequences of the Civil Partnership Act 2004" (2006) ILJ 179.

[111] It is excluded from all other areas, save "schools", where it is not impossible but unlikely to be an issue.

[112] No reason for this is evident in the Directive's legislative history. See S. Koukoulis-Spilio-topoulos, "The Amended Equal Treatment Directive 2002/73: an Expression of Constitu-tional Principles/Fundamental Rights" (2005) 12 *Maastricht Journal* 327, 337–347, 357–358, who argues that the phrase reflected the principle of family and parental protection and so should be restored, citing *Busch v Klinikum Neustadt GmbH & Co Betriebs-KG*, Case C-320/01, [2003] E.C.R. I-2041 (pregnancy and parental leave discrimination).

6. AGE

3–027   Age discrimination was included in the Framework Directive 2000/
78/EC,[113] and implemented in the UK in October 2006.[114] So there is
some case law, EU and domestic, for guidance. Age is now included
as a protected characteristic in the Equality Act 2010 s.5. Defining an
age group in some cases is rather more nebulous than defining, say,
race or sex. Much depends on the nature and/or the effect of the
challenged practice. For instance, a groups defined as "over 50s" or
simply "21-year-olds", are easily distinguished from "people in their
40s". However, these last two groups form another group of those
"under 50".[115]

The coverage is limited to Services and Public Functions (but not
those under 18),[116] Employment, and Further and Higher education.
Also note that, unlike the other protected characteristics in the
Equality Act, direct age discrimination carries an objective justification defence.

Prior to this legislation coming into force, experience in other
jurisdictions suggests that age discrimination carries far less stigma.[117]
Thus, employers may be given more leeway when trying to justify any
prima facie discrimination. This generally has proved to be the case in
the ECJ, where with some exceptions, it has afforded states and
employers a broad margin of discretion in justifying some blatant
ageist practices. Domestic courts have followed this lead.[118]

7. PREGNANCY AND MATERNITY

3–028   Pregnancy discrimination, for seemingly obvious reasons, has been
treated as a form of sex discrimination. The technical barriers to this
approach (men cannot get pregnant, so a logical comparison is
impossible) were overcome, crudely, in *Dekker*,[119] when the ECJ
pronounced that as only women become pregnant, discrimination on

---

[113] SI 2006/1031. See generally, H. Meenan, "Age equality after the Employment Directive"
(2003) 10(1) *Maastricht Journal of European and Comparative Law* 9.
[114] SI 2006/1031.
[115] Equality Act 2010, Explanatory Note 37.
[116] Equality Act 2010 s.28(1)(a).
[117] See, in Canada, for instance, *Gosselin v Quebec (Attorney General)* [2002] 4 SCR 429, [68].
See also *Large v Stratford* [1995] 3 SCR 733; *McKinney v University of Guelph* [1990] 3 SCR
229. In the USA, *Massachusetts Board of Retirement v Murgia*, 427 US 307, 313 (Sup Ct
1976). See further, Ch.2.
[118] See further, Ch.8 para.8–068.
[119] *Dekker v Stichting Vormingscentrum voor Jonge Volwassen (VJV-Centrum) Plus* Case C-
177/88, [1990] E.C.R. I-3941.

the ground of pregnancy and maternity is direct sex discrimination. No comparison with a man is necessary. The EU model still operates on this basis,[120] while domestic law has singled out pregnancy and maternity discrimination as distinct causes of action. This is discussed in more detail in Chapter 4, paras 4–040 et seq.

Unfavourable treatment because of IVF treatment is not in itself pregnancy discrimination. The rationale behind this is legal certainty: a fertilised ova could be frozen for years before being placed in the woman's uterus. Thus, where a woman's ova are fertilised, but not yet transferred to her uterus, she is not protected from pregnancy discrimination.[121] However, it may amount to *sex* discrimination to treat a woman less favourably because of her IVF treatment during the (limited) advanced period between the follicular puncture and the immediate transfer of the in vitro fertilised ova into the uterus.[122]

8. DUAL DISCRIMINATION[123]

The Equality Act 2010 s.14, breaks new ground by outlawing "dual **3–029** discrimination", although, at the time of writing, it was yet to be brought into force.[124] It makes unlawful discrimination based on a combination of the protected characteristics of: age, disability, gender reassignment, race, religion or belief, sex or sexual orientation. The theory behind this is that where, for example, an employer fails to appoint a black woman because it considers black woman to perform certain tasks poorly, the employer would not be able to escape liability (for race or sex discrimination) by pointing to a similarly qualified black man and white woman who were appointed. Likewise, a Muslim man could be stereotyped as a terrorist and be refused entry to a bus. Claims of either religious or sex discrimination could falter because non-Muslim men and Muslim women were permitted entry.[125]

---

[120] See Recast Directive 2006/54/EC, Preamble, Recital (23).
[121] *Mayr v Bäckerei und Konditorei Gerhard Flöckner OHG* Case C-506/06 [2008] 2 C.M.L.R. 27 (ECJ), [53]. Applied, *Sahota v Home Office* [2010] I.C.R. 772 (EAT).
[122] ibid. [52].
[123] See generally: G. Moon, "Multiple discrimination—problems compounded or solutions found?" (2006) 3(2) *Justice Journal* 86.
[124] See *http://www.equalities.gov.uk/equality_act_2010.aspx* (accessed January 1, 2011).
[125] Equality Act 2010, Explanatory Note 68. For a "dual" claim of sex and race discrimination by a single (female) parent of Vincentian origin, see *Ministry of Defence v DeBique* [2010] I.R.L.R. 471 (EAT).

CHAPTER 4

DIRECT DISCRIMINATION

1. INTRODUCTION TO THE LEGISLATION

In its simplest form, direct discrimination arises when a defendant **4–001** expressly links the victim's protected characteristic (say, sex, or race) with his less favourable treatment of her. For instance, a job advertisement may read: "Librarians wanted, no women need apply." As

79

we shall see, most cases are more subtle than that. It may be contrasted with *indirect* discrimination, where an apparently neutral practice has a disproportionate impact on the protected group. The advert above could be reworded: "Librarians wanted, applicants must be over six foot tall." This is not direct discrimination; but because it has broadly the same effect, it will be scrutinised, this time as *indirect* discrimination. Unlike indirect discrimination, there is no general defence to direct discrimination (except for age),[1] only specific exceptions for a particular field, such as employment, or the provision of goods, facilities, or services.[2] The definitions of direct discrimination across the legislation are broadly the same, although there are some differences, which will be highlighted in this chapter when appropriate.

For direct discrimination, the EC equality Directives use this formula, adapted here for sex discrimination:

Recast Directive 2006/54/EC

Article 2

"(1)(a) 'direct discrimination': where one person is treated less favourably on grounds of sex than another is, has been or would be treated in a comparable situation...".

The formulas for other grounds are substantially the same, as is the domestic formula which (save for pregnancy cases),[3] uses this single formula:

Equality Act 2010

13 Direct discrimination

"(1) A person (A) discriminates against another (B) if, because of a protected characteristic, A treats B less favourably than A treats or would treat others."

These formulas have in common have two broad elements: (a) "treats less favourably" and (b) "*because of* (or *on grounds of*) a protected characteristic."

---

[1] See Ch.8, para.8–064. For a discussion on whether direct discrimination generally should be justifiable see J. Bowers, and E. Moran, "Justification in Direct Discrimination Law: Breaking the taboo" (2002) 31 ILJ 307. For a response see T. Gill, and K. Monaghan, "Justification in Direct Sex Discrimination Law: Taboo Upheld" (2003) 32 ILJ 115.

[2] The employment defences are considered in Ch.8, paras 8–018 et seq.

[3] See below, para.4–043.

2. LESS FAVOURABLE TREATMENT

(1) "Less Favourably"

(a) What is "Less" Favourably?
The treatment must be *less* favourable, rather than unfavourable. In **4–002**
Macdonald v Advocate General for Scotland,[4] the Royal Air Force had
a policy of interrogating, humiliating and then dismissing both male
and female homosexuals. The claim of sex discrimination[5] failed
because although the treatment for males and females was, in some
respects, necessarily different, it was *equal* treatment, albeit equally
bad.

Although *different* treatment is not in itself actionable, it is enough
that the victim perceived—reasonably—that she had been treated less
favourably. The key is that there must be some reasonable ground for
that perception. In *R. v Birmingham City Council, ex parte EOC*,[6] the
council provided more grammar school places for boys than for girls.
It argued that the girls had not been treated *less* favourably because
there was no evidence that grammar schools were better than the
other schools. The House of Lords rejected this argument, holding
that as the girls were denied a choice—which they, reasonably,
valued—they had been treated less favourably than the boys.[7] In *Gill
v El Vino*[8] only men were served at the bar of a wine bar. Women
were asked to be seated and given table service. The Court of Appeal
held that although table service provided an adequate (if not superior) alternative, women were treated less favourably because, unlike
the men, they were denied a choice. In *Chief Constable of West
Yorkshire v Khan* (a case of victimisation)[9] the House of Lords held
that an employer's refusal to give a reference amounted to less
favourable treatment, even though that reference would have been
negative and *lessened* the candidate's chances. The candidate, reasonably, would have preferred to have the reference. It is not enough
that the claimant simply considered, without reason, that she was
treated less favourably. In *Burrett v West Birmingham HA*,[10] a female
nurse complained that she had to wear headgear, while male nurses

---

[4] [2003] UKHL 34.
[5] The case was argued as sex discrimination because it pre-dated the Employment Equality
(Sexual Orientation) Regulations 2003.
[6] [1989] A.C. 1155 (CA and HL).
[7] ibid. 1193. See also *R. v Secretary of State for Education and Science, ex parte Keating, The
Times* December 3, 1985 (council to run single-sex school for girls held to be treating boys
less favourably).
[8] [1983] Q.B. 425, CA.
[9] [2002] 1 W.L.R. 1947. Discussed Ch.7, para.7–008, p.211.
[10] [1994] I.R.L.R. 7 EAT. This does not mean that all dress codes necessarily treat men and
women equally. See below, para.4–035. The decision on the facts is not above criticism, see
n.174 below, and accompanying text.

did not. The EAT held that as both male and female nurses were bound to wear respective uniforms (jacket with epaulettes for men, headgear for women) the claimant could not, reasonably, claim to have been treated *less* favourably.

4–003   The Court of Appeal struggled with this issue in *Simon v Brimham Associates*.[11] At a job interview, Mr Simon was asked to disclose his religion. He refused. The interviewer then explained that the job was with an Arab company and stated "If, for instance, you were of the Jewish faith, it might preclude your selection for the job". Mr Simon ended the interview there and then and made a claim for direct discrimination. It was held that as all applicants were asked about their religion, the interviewer had treated Mr Simon no less favourably than he would treat any other applicant. This narrow interpretation carries a serious flaw. The question was not facially neutral. It is not the law that employers may state to all candidates, that they do not employ, for example, immigrants, homosexuals or Roman Catholics.[12] Further, what if this employer stated in its job advertisement that "Jews might be precluded"? It is hard to imagine a more blatant (and offensive) case of direct discrimination. The advertisement, like the interviewer's statement, is made to all. In either case, the result is the same; Jews are not welcome to apply. In either case it is absurd to say that all those who read, or hear, the statement are being treated equally. Quite clearly, Jews are being treated less favourably than non-Jews. Alternatively, if, as the decision suggests, the practice was neutral, Simon could have argued a claim of *indirect* discrimination.

4–004   Finally, note that the ECJ has held that an employer who declared he would not hire immigrants was liable for direct discrimination.[13] This means that where, for instance, a job advertisement, states "no Roma need apply", a Roma man simply *deterred* from applying by the advertisement could bring a claim of direct discrimination.[14]

(2) The Comparison

4–005   The direct discrimination formula demands *less* favourable treatment, and this supposes a comparison between how the claimant was treated and how a person without the protected characteristic, in the same circumstances, was, or would have been, treated.[15] The phrase "or would treat", in the statutory definition (above, para.4–001) makes it clear that the comparator may be a hypothetical person. It does not matter if the discriminator shares the protected

---

[11] [1987] I.C.R. 596, CA. See also below para.4–024.
[12] See, Case C-54/07 *Feryn* [2008] ECR I-05187 (ECJ).
[13] ibid.
[14] See EA 2010, Explanatory Note 63.
[15] See A. McColgan, "Cracking the comparator problem: discrimination, 'equal' treatment and the role of comparisons" [2006] 6 E.H.R.L.R. 650.

characteristic(s) of the victim, so, for example, a gay man can be liable for refusing to hire gay men.[16]

(a) Relevant Circumstances

Equality Act 2010   4–006

23 Comparison by reference to circumstances

(1) On a comparison of cases for the purposes of [direct, combined,[17] and indirect, discrimination] there must be no material difference between the circumstances relating to each case.

This means, in other words, the comparison must be "like-with-like", the only difference between the two being the protected characteristic e.g. sex, race, etc.

Section 23 substantially reproduces the rubric in the previous legislation,[18] which was discussed at length by the House of Lords in *Shamoon v Chief Constable of the RUC*.[19] Here, a superintendent relieved Inspector Joan Shamoon of her appraisal duties in response to complaints by officers. She brought claim of sex discrimination,[20] using as comparators two male inspectors, who had not been relieved of their appraisal duties. Her difficulty was that no complaints had been made against these inspectors, and she had not proved that she had been treated less favourably than a male inspector would have been, had he been the subject of similar complaints. On these relatively straightforward facts the House dismissed her claim, but stressed she had failed on *both* elements, (*less favourable treatment* and *because of sex*). In doing so the House went further than necessary to resolve the case before it, by insisting that the relevant circumstances must not be altered for both elements. This was based on an interpretation of the equivalent of the Equality Act 2010 s.23(1) (above), that, according to the House, applies to the definition of direct discrimination (s.13(1)), *as a whole*.

This interpretation is problematic because often it will mean incorporating irrelevant facts into the comparison, making it an unduly complicated and clumsy exercise. It leaves tribunals with an

---

[16] EA 2010 s.24. See also *R. (E) v Governing Body of JFS* [2009] UKSC 15, [152(i)], and in the United States, *Ross v Douglas County, Nebraska* 234 F 3d 391 (8th Cir.2000) where a black supervisor called a black worker "black boy" and "nigger".

[17] At the time of writing, combined (or dual) discrimination had yet to be brought into force. See *http://www.equalities.gov.uk/equality_act_2010.aspx* (accessed January 1, 2011).

[18] e.g. RRA 1975 s.3(4): "A comparison of the case of a person of a particular racial group with that of a person not of that group . . . must be such that the relevant circumstances in the one case are the same, or not materially different, from the other."

[19] [2003] I.C.R. 337 (HL).

[20] Under the Sex Discrimination (Northern Ireland) Order 1976, which, for this purpose, is materially the same as the EA 2010.

unpalatable choice. They incorporate merely the circumstances "relevant" for the comparison, and risk omitting evidence crucial to the second element, "because of". The alternative, to retain that crucial evidence for the second element, is to incorporate it into the first element and embark upon a clumsy, complicated and artificial exercise of making the comparison with irrelevant factors. This is illustrated using a classic example of direct discrimination, *King v Great Britain-China Centre*.[21] Ms King, who was Chinese but educated in Britain, applied for a post at the China Centre, an organisation established to foster closer ties with China. She met the requirements of fluent spoken Chinese and a personal knowledge of China. A white English person was appointed. The background circumstances were that none of the five Chinese applicants made the short list of eight white candidates, and that no Chinese person had ever been employed in the centre. The Court of Appeal held that the industrial tribunal was entitled to draw the conclusion that King was discriminated against because she did not come from the "same, essentially British, academic background" as the existing staff. If the tribunal had heard the case after *Shamoon*, it would be obliged to incorporate those two background factors into the comparison, when they are irrelevant to the question of less favourable treatment. A simple comparison between King and the equally qualified successful (white) candidate was all that was necessary. The short-listing and employment history are irrelevant to the question of whether King was treated *less* favourably, although, of course, they are relevant for the second question of the identifying the reason for the treatment. This interpretation is consistent with the legislation which demands that the relevant circumstances be materially the same in each case for the "comparison", but makes no such demand for identifying the reason for the treatment. It is true that the reason for the treatment may be identified by a comparison in some instances (such as *Shamoon*), but for the majority of cases the ground of the treatment will be identified from a variety of circumstantial evidence (as in *King*).

4–007   The problem is aggravated by the House of Lords' suggestion that the second question ("because of") is subjective, with Lord Roger expressing the logical conclusion of this view, that the relevant circumstances should be those that were taken into account by the defendant.[22] This unduly restricts the circumstances that can be included when asking if the treatment was less favourable. Suppose a variation on *Shamoon*: the complaints against her were based on sex—male officers did not like being appraised by a female superior—but neutral on their face. As the superintendent was unaware that the complaints were based on sex, he could not have taken this into

---

[21] [1992] I.C.R. 516 (CA).
[22] [2003] I.C.R. 337, [134].

consideration,[23] and so it would be excluded from the comparison. This would mislead a tribunal to the perverse conclusion that the claimant had not been treated less favourably than a man would have been, when she lost her appraisal duties because she was a woman. It is better, simpler, and consistent with the legislation, to keep the comparison discrete from the second element, "because of". The principal goal of the comparison is to see if there had been *less* favourable treatment. The comparison then may, or may not, be used, in the second question to help establish whether the treatment was on a protected ground.

The *Shamoon* approach would also cause a problem in mixed ground cases, where there is both a discriminatory and benign reason for the treatment (e.g. black job applicant rejected because of race and poor employment record). The rule is that there is liability even if discrimination was just *one* of the reasons for the treatment.[24] If the comparator is endowed with *all* the circumstances (i.e. white, *with* a poor employment record) the result would be misleading, because the comparator would have been treated in exactly the same way.[25] A simple comparison between the rejected black candidate and the successful white candidate would be enough to establish that there was less favourable treatment. It is perfectly legitimate to use an "imperfect" comparator (see immediately below). The reason for the treatment should be a matter for the (second) "because of" question.

(b) The Usefulness of the Imperfect Comparator
Sometimes a real comparator may imperfect, because the circumstances are not in every respect the same. Where a tribunal is considering all the possible evidence, the defendant's actual treatment of a real but imperfect comparator may nonetheless be evidence from which a court may infer how the hypothetical comparator would have been treated.[26]

4–008

(c) The "Compulsory" Comparison
There is mixed authority over whether a comparison must be made in every case. The Explanatory Note (91) to s.23 states that "The treatment of the claimant *must* be compared with that of an actual or a hypothetical person—the comparator..." (emphasis supplied). In

4–009

---

[23] Known in the US as the "cat's paw" theory, discussed below, para.4–022.

[24] *Owen and Briggs v James* [1982] I.C.R. 618 (CA). See below, para.4–014.

[25] See *Islington LBC v Ladele* [2009] I.C.R. 387 (EAT), [39] (Elias J.), affirmed on other grounds [2010] 1 W.L.R. 955 (CA). See further Ch.3, para.3–021. See also *Chondol v Liverpool CC* (2009) UKEAT/0298/08/JOJ, [23].

[26] *Carter v Ahsan* [2008] 1 A.C. 696 (HL), [36] (Lord Hoffman).

Glasgow CC v Zafar,[27] an industrial tribunal held that the employer's dismissal procedure had been so seriously defective, it constituted unreasonable treatment, and that such unreasonable treatment amounted to less favourable treatment on racial grounds. The House of Lords held that this approach was defective because there had been no comparison with the treatment that would have been afforded to a worker of another race, in the same circumstances. The tribunal wrongly focused on the *reasonableness* of the employer's treatment of the worker, and *not* whether that treatment included racial discrimination. In fact, the only comparison made was with another *employer*, which is irrelevant. This is not to state that a tribunal cannot infer from the defendant's unreasonable behaviour that he would have treated a comparator more favourably.[28] *Zafar* was followed by the Court of Appeal in *Marks & Spencer v Martins*,[29] where an employment tribunal decision was reversed because it was based on the defendant's racial "bias", rather than a consideration of how a white person would have been treated: the "compulsory comparison". Elsewhere, senior judges have spoken of a "necessary" or "required" comparison,[30] and a united House of Lords in *Carter v Ahsan*[31] agreed that, "The test for discrimination involves a comparison between the treatment of the complainant and another person...". Elsewhere, Lord Hobhouse has stated: "The comparison test must be satisfied and dicta which state or suggest the contrary are wrong."[32]

Nonetheless, there are suggestions to the contrary of high standing. In *Shamoon v Chief Constable of the RUC*,[33] Lord Nicholls suggested that in some cases a comparison cannot be made without first deciding the "reason why" the claimant was treated so.[34] And if this reason is based on a prohibited characteristic (such as race, sex, etc.), then a tribunal can "avoid arid and confusing disputes about the identification of the appropriate comparator".[35] This may be correct, but it carries two dangers. First, it sends out mixed messages to a variety of first instance tribunals (often sitting with lay members) on how to approach the often difficult question of identifying direct

---

[27] [1998] I.C.R. 120 (HL). See further Ch.12, para.12–007.

[28] Of course, in the circumstances of a particular case unreasonable treatment may be evidence of discrimination such as to call for an explanation from the defendant: see *Bahl v Law Society* [2004] I.R.L.R. 799, [100]–[101] (Peter Gibson L.J.).

[29] [1998] I.C.R. 1005 (CA), p.1019.

[30] *Macdonald v Advocate General for Scotland* [2003] UKHL 34, [106], [109], [110] (Lord Hobhouse), [153] (Lord Roger). Lord Nicholls resolved the case without resorting to a comparison ([5]–[7]). Lord Scott agreed with Lord Rodger *and* Lord Nicholls.

[31] [2008] 1 A.C. 696 [36] (Lord Hoffman gave the single speech).

[32] *Macdonald v Advocate General for Scotland* [2003] UKHL 34, [110].

[33] [2003] I.C.R. 337 (HL). For the facts, see above para.4–006. See also *Macdonald v Advocate General for Scotland* [2003] UKHL 34, [5]–[7] (Lord Nicholls); *Islington LBC v Ladele* [2009] I.C.R. 387 (EAT), [37]–[39] (Elias J.).

[34] This point is debatable, see above, para.4–006.

[35] ibid. [11].

discrimination. Second, it risks being taken a step further, or mis-interpreted, so that in cases where the reason appears *not* dis-criminatory, a tribunal will also ignore the comparison. In the context of religious discrimination, Elias J. did just that, holding that where the reason for the treatment was benign, "the question of how to define the comparator becomes academic."[36]

(d) Other Problems with the Comparison

It is important that the circumstances of the comparator are not   **4–010** tainted with discrimination on the ground in question, as this can sabotage a good claim. This is illustrated in *Re Equal Opportunities Commission for Northern Ireland's Application*.[37] In Northern Ireland, the Department of Education allocated non-fee paying grammar school places equally to boys and to girls: each group received 27 per cent of the places. That discriminated against the girls because they performed better in the entrance exam. Consequently 422 boys were awarded places, even though they had achieved lower marks than a group of 555 girls, who were not awarded places. This was held, in a prior case, to be unlawful sex discrimination. However, the Depart-ment refused to withdraw the boys' offers out of "fairness" because, unlike the girls, the boys had not had their hopes raised. The EOC challenged this refusal as being discriminatory. The Department argued that the treatment (the refusal) was based, not upon sex, but on "fairness". Hutton L.C.J. held that it was incorrect to include the "fairness" aspect in the circumstances of the comparators (the 422 boys), as the situation leading to the "fairness argument" was itself caused by sex discrimination. Thus the comparators should remain in the same circumstances as in the prior case (boys offered a place with a lower mark than the claimant girls) and the 555 girls should be awarded places instead of the boys.

It can be misleading to change the *defendant's* circumstances for the comparison. In *Grieg v Community Industry*,[38] Ms Grieg was refused a job with an all-male decorating team because otherwise it would have "created an imbalance to the composition of the team". The employer defended a sex discrimination claim by arguing that the comparator should be a man refused a job with an *all-women* team. The EAT held that the comparator's circumstances should not include a different job. The correct comparator was a man applying for the *same* job. The "relevant circumstances" would not be the same if the job were changed. In *Smyth v Croft Inns*,[39] a case of religious discrimination in Northern Ireland, an employer showed no concern

---

[36] *Chondol v Liverpool CC* (2009) UKEAT/0298/08/JOJ [23]. See further Ch.3, n.100.
[37] [1989] I.R.L.R. 64 (NI High Court). A case brought on the Sex Discrimination (Northern Ireland) Order 1976.
[38] [1979] I.C.R. 356, EAT.
[39] [1996] I.R.L.R. 84 (NICA).

for a Catholic barman in a Protestant area when he was threatened. The employer's argument that it would have showed an equal lack of concern for a threatened Protestant barman in a *Catholic* area was rejected. The claimant should be compared to a Protestant barman in the same *Protestant* pub. Again, the employer wanted to change the circumstances of the *job*.

Complications again arise in the comparison where the discrimination is on a prohibited ground of a third party.[40] In *Showboat Entertainment Centre v Owens*,[41] Mr Owens, who is white, was sacked for refusing to obey an order to exclude black youths from an amusement arcade. The EAT held that the comparator should be a man having all the same characteristics as the complainant except his "attitude" to race,[42] or, as the case may be, to another protected characteristic.

(e) The Comparison and Gender Reassignment—Work Cases Only

4–011 For discrimination on the ground of gender reassignment, Equality Act 2010 s.16(2), provides in relation to a worker's absence, that the worker must not be treated less favourably than if the "absence was because of sickness or injury, or [the] . . . absence was for some other reason and it is not reasonable for the [worker] to be treated less favourably."

This is aimed at the situation where the worker is taking time off work in relation to undergoing gender reassignment. It invites a comparison with the employer's sick leave practice, or other practices in relation to absences. It is designed to avoid the comparison used in the analogous situation of pregnancy, where a pregnant woman is *not* normally compared to a sick man (see below, paras 4–040 and 4–044).

(f) The Comparison and Marriage or Civil Partnership

4–012 For discrimination on the ground of marriage, the logical comparison is with an unmarried person *of the same sex* as the complainant, so that the provision applies, for instance, even to a wholly female, or wholly male, workforce. Thus, it is no defence for an employer to treat all married employees equally badly; if it treats married workers less favourably than unmarried ones, then the employer is liable. This applies with the same logic to civil partnership status.

---

[40] Discussed below, para.4–026.
[41] [1984] 1 All E.R. 836, see also below, para.4–026'.
[42] ibid. at 842 c–g (Browne-Wilkinson J.). Applied, *Weathersfield v Sargent* [1999] I.C.R. 425 (CA), where a worker who resigned rather than implement a racist instruction was compared to a hypothetical worker who was prepared to go along with it.

(g) The Comparison and Sexual Orientation

For the purposes of direct, combined,[43] and indirect discrimination, **4–013** Equality Act 2010 s.23(3) provides that where the protected characteristic is sexual orientation, being a civil partner or married is not a material difference between the circumstances relating to each case. The Explanatory Note (92) states that this "enables a civil partner who is treated less favourably than a married person in similar circumstances to bring a claim for sexual orientation discrimination." For instance, a small hotel may welcome married couples but not couples in a civil partnership. The hotel cannot avoid liability for direct sexual orientation discrimination by pointing a material difference ("being married") between the victims and their comparators. The only difference would be the sexual orientation of those admitted and those barred.[43a]

3. "BECAUSE OF" A PROTECTED CHARACTERISTIC

(1) Mixed Ground Cases

In some cases the defendant would have acted on discriminatory and **4–014** non-discriminatory grounds. In *Owen and Briggs v James*[44] a firm of solicitors refused to employ a black applicant, Ms James. A partner in the firm stated to the successful candidate: "I cannot understand why an English employer would want to take on a coloured girl when English girls are available." However, race was not the only factor in the decision to reject the applicant. Other reasons were Ms James' lack of employment in the previous three years, and her "unsatisfactory demeanour" at the interview. The firm argued that it was not liable because the rejection of Ms James was not solely motivated by race. The Court of Appeal ruled that for liability, it was sufficient that race was an "important" or "substantial"[45] factor in the decision, and so Ms James' claim for discrimination succeeded. However, the rule announced was quite restrictive because it excluded claims where the discriminatory factor was less than substantial. The rule has been expanded more recently, under the influence of various European discrimination Directives, some of which[46] mandate that there should

---

[43] At the time of writing, combined (or dual) discrimination had yet to be brought into force. See *http://www.equalities.gov.uk/equality_act_2010.aspx* (accessed January 1, 2011).

[43a] See *Hall and Preddy v Bull* (2011) Bristol County Court January 18, 2011. Available at *www.Judiciary.gov.uk*.

[44] [1982] I.C.R. 618 (CA).

[45] ibid. respectively, [22] and [35]–[36].

[46] A notable exception is the Race Directive 2000/43/EC, and the phrase was dropped when the ETD 76/207/EEC was redrafted as the Recast Directive 2006/54/EC. It remains in the Framework Directive 2000/78/EC, Directive 79/7 (sex discrimination in social security) and is written into the recent Directive 2010/41/EU (sex discrimination and the self-employed).

be "no discrimination *whatsoever*" on the protected grounds (emphasis supplied). In *Igen v Wong*[47] the Court of Appeal stated that only if "the treatment was in no sense whatsoever" on the protected ground would the defendant escape liability, but qualified this when stating: "We find it hard to believe that the principle of equal treatment would be breached by the merely trivial."[48] Whether this goes far enough to comply with the Directives is questionable, and may lead to all manner of complex disputes. Of course, as the trier of fact, a court of first instance is entitled to find that the discriminatory element was so trivial that it played no part in the treatment. But once it is found that the discriminatory element, no matter how trivial, was a reason for of the treatment, a finding of discrimination becomes irresistible, especially if the case is governed by a Directive's demand for no discrimination *whatsoever*. Note though, that compensation may be reduced in accordance with the chances that the same decision would have been made even without the discriminatory element.[49]

(2) Discriminatory Motive and the *But For* Test

4–015   It is not enough that a person has a protected characteristic and was treated less favourably than a person without that characteristic. The statutory formula requires that the victim was treated less favourably *because of* a protected characteristic. The words "because of" replaced the phrase used in previous legislation "on grounds of". The Explanatory Note (61) to the Equality Act 2010 s.13 stated that this "does not change the legal meaning of the definition". It was merely "designed to make it more accessible to the ordinary user of the Act."

However, the legal meaning of the definition has been the subject of much controversial judicial debate. At one time, courts were urged to discover the reason for the treatment by asking if the defendant would have treated the claimant so *but for* the protected characteristic. The point of this "objective and not subjective"[50] approach was to avoid questions of defendants' discriminatory intent, or "benign motive". Otherwise it would be a good defence for a defendant to

---

[47] *Igen (formally Leeds Careers Guidance) v Wong* [2005] I.C.R. 931.
[48] ibid. [37]. In some employment cases where the claimant has to prove, in addition, that she suffered a "detriment", the Court of Appeal has recognised the de minimis principle: *Jiad v Byford* [2003] I.R.L.R. 232, [34] and [43]. See further, Ch.8. The US Supreme Court, in *Price Waterhouse v Hopkins* 490 US 228 (1989) suggested that an employer may avoid liability with an "affirmative defense" of showing that it would have made the same decision absent the discriminatory factor. Congress reversed this by legislating that liability can be established where discrimination was "a motivating factor for any employment practice, even though other factors also motivated the practice" (42 USC s.2000e-2(m)). However, where the employer makes out an "affirmative defense", the remedies are restricted to declarations, injunctions and costs (42 USC s.2000e-5(g)(2)(B)).
[49] *Chagger v Abbey National* [2010] I.R.L.R. 47, (CA) [55]–[60]. See further, Ch.12, para.12–025.
[50] *Nagarajan v LRT* [2000] 1 A.C. 501 (HL), at 511 (Lord Nicholls).

show that he discriminated against a protected group not because of a hostile intent, but (for example) because of customer preference, or to save money, or avoid controversy.[51] In *R v Birmingham City Council, ex parte EOC*,[52] there was a general trend over a number of years to move away from (selective) grammar schools towards (non-selective) comprehensive schools. Small pockets of resistance ensured that a few remained, the majority of which were boys' schools. So the Council found itself in the position of having more grammar school places for boys than for girls. The EOC challenged the Council for discriminating against girls. The Council argued that, for liability, there had to be an *intention* or *motive* to discriminate on the ground of sex, which was absent here. A unanimous House of Lords rejected that argument, stating the council offered fewer places to girls *because of* their sex.

A year or so after the *Birmingham* grammar schools case, in *James v Eastleigh Borough Council*,[53] only a bare majority held this line. Here, the Council's municipal swimming baths admitted free-of-charge persons "of pensionable age". In the United Kingdom at the time, men reached pensionable age at 65 and women at 60.[54] So when Mr and Mrs James, each aged 61, visited the baths, Mrs James was admitted free while Mr James was required to pay. Mr James complained that he was receiving less favourable treatment on the ground of his sex. The Council argued that the policy was motivated by a wish to help pensioners, and not by sex. The Court of Appeal agreed with the Council, but a majority of the House of Lords reversed, promoting the *but for* test.[55]

However, this was followed by several judicial statements suggesting a more subjective approach: that for liability, a defendant must have acted with a discriminatory motive. First, comments arose in two cases on the parallel phrase *by reason that* in the victimisation provisions of the discrimination legislation.[56] In *Nagarajan v LRT*,[57] Lord Nicholls suggested: "Save in obvious cases, answering the crucial question will call for some consideration of the mental processes of the alleged discriminator."[58] In his dissent, Lord Browne-Wilkinson went further and considered that the courts should not introduce:

4–016

---

[51] *R. v Birmingham City Council, ex parte Equal Opportunities Commission* [1989] 1 A.C. 1156 (HL), 1194, citing *R. v Commission for Racial Equality ex parte Westminster City Council* [1985] I.C.R. 827 (CA), below n.83.

[52] ibid.

[53] [1990] 2 A.C. 751, HL.

[54] The Coalition Government plans to equalise the state pension age at 66 by April 2020. *http://www.direct.gov.uk/en/Pensionsandretirementplanning/StatePension/DG_183754* (accessed January 1, 2011).

[55] [1990] 2 A.C. 751, at 774B–C.

[56] See now, Equality Act 2010 s.27, which, in line with the change to the definition of direct discrimination, replaced this phrase with "because".

[57] [2000] 1 A.C. 501 (HL). Discussed below, Ch.7 at para.7–007.

[58] ibid. 511.

"... something akin to strict liability ... which will lead to individuals being stamped as racially discriminatory ... where these matters were not consciously in their minds."[59]

In *Khan v Chief Constable of West Yorkshire*, Lord Woolf M.R. commented:

"To regard a person as acting unlawfully when he had not been motivated either consciously or unconsciously by any discriminatory motive is hardly likely to assist the objective of promoting harmonious racial relations."[60]

On appeal, the House of Lords appeared to agree by holding that the question was "subjective" and found the employer was not liable for victimisation because the employer had acted "honestly and reasonably",[61] a benign motive defence if ever there was one. A year or so later, in *Shamoon v Chief Constable of the RUC*[62] (a claim for direct sex discrimination), neither the *but for* test, *James v Eastleigh*, nor the *Birmingham* grammar schools case were mentioned during five lengthy speeches. Instead, the Law Lords asked *why* the claimant was treated so. What few other comments were made on the issue suggested that tribunals should look for a discriminatory motive,[63] and that the relevant circumstances for the comparison should be those that the *defendant* took into account,[64] again pointing to a subjective approach.

4–017   More recently, in *R. (E) v Governing Body of JFS*,[65] a majority of the Supreme Court ruled emphatically against a benign motive defence. In this case, the Jewish Free School's admissions policy gave preference to children recognised as Orthodox Jewish by the Office of the Chief Rabbi (OCR), which required that the child's mother be Jewish either by matrilineal descent or by conversion under the OCR doctrine. The claimant's son was refused admission because he did not meet these requirements. His Italian mother was a Masorti Jew convert, a denomination not recognised by the OCR. He brought a claim of *racial* discrimination, as faith schools enjoy an exemption from *religious* discrimination in their admissions.[66] It was held that

[59] ibid. 510.
[60] [2000] I.C.R. 1169 (CA), [14]. In spite of this opinion, Lord Woolf felt bound by *James* and the *Birmingham* grammar school case to apply the *but for* test and decide for the claimant. But this dictum was vindicated by the reversal of his decision by the House of Lords: [2001] UKHL 48. Discussed below, Ch.7, para.7–008, p.211.
[61] [2001] UKHL 48, [29], [77].
[62] [2003] I.C.R. 337 (HL). The facts are set out above, para.4–006.
[63] ibid. [55] (Lord Hope), [116] (Lord Scott). See also *Azmi v Kirklees MBC* [2007] I.R.L.R. 484 (EAT), [75] (Wilkie J.): "there was in any event no evidence of any motivation to discriminate on the grounds of religious belief."
[64] ibid. [134] (Lord Roger).
[65] [2009] UKSC 15. See (2010) 39(2) ILJ 183.
[66] Equality Act 2006 s.50, see now Equality Act 2010 Sch.11, para.5.

being Orthodox Jewish was a racial requirement. The school then argued that although its policy disadvantaged non-Orthodox applicants, nonetheless, as this policy was religiously ("benignly") motivated, the ground for rejection was religious and not racial. A 5–4 majority rejected this defence and found the school liable for direct racial discrimination. As Lord Clarke observed:

"... a person who honestly believed, as the Dutch Reformed Church of South Africa until recently believed, that God had made black people inferior and had destined them to live separately from whites, would be able to discriminate openly against them without breaking the law."[67]

However, the majority were not so emphatic about the status of the *but for* test. They tried to reconcile it with the subjective approach by identifying two types of direct discrimination.[68] There are "obvious" cases, where the reason for the treatment is patently racial (or on another protected characteristic). Presumably, an example would be "No Blacks need apply". In these cases, there is no need to enquire into the defendant's motive, no matter how worthy it might be.

Second, there are "less obvious" cases. Lord Phillips provided a **4–018** vivid example: A shopkeeper says to a fat black man, "I do not serve people like you."[69] A more realistic example was provided by Lady Hale, where in job applications, the patent criterion is "that elusive quality known as 'merit.'" In such cases it is necessary to assess the motive of the defendant to ascertain the ground of the treatment, respectively whether it was obesity or colour, or merit or race. The racial bias may even be subconscious, to be discovered by proper inferences from the evidence.[70]

Although little was said about the actual application of the *but for* test (Lord Phillips said he did not find the test "helpful"),[71] it was not expressly overruled. The focus was on what a test was intended to *avoid*, which was a benign motive defence. The majority agreed that motive was relevant only for the "less obvious" cases, but only to discover the ground of the treatment. If the ground of the treatment is unlawful, a benign motive cannot prevent liability. Hence, for the majority, in this "obvious" case, the school's religious motive did not preclude liability.

In addition to this current lack of judicial enthusiasm, the *but for* test carries other weaknesses. First, it has been suggested that it is not

---

[67] [2009] UKSC 15, [150].
[68] [2009] UKSC 15, [21]–[23] (Lord Phillips), [62]–[64] (Lady Hale), [78] (Lord Mance), [114]–[117] (Lord Kerr), [132] (Lord Clarke).
[69] ibid. [21].
[70] ibid. [64].
[71] ibid. [16].

suitable for "background" cases.[72] In *Seide v Gillette Industries*[73] a
worker was moved to a different department to escape anti-Semitic
harassment. In his new department, he fell out (for non-racial reasons) with his colleagues and was disciplined. Again, *but for* the prior
anti-Semitic harassment, the worker would not have been in the
situation where he was disciplined. It was held, however, that he was
not disciplined on racial grounds.

4–019   Second, the *but for* test is unsuitable for mixed ground cases.[74] In
these cases, where there are both discriminatory and non-discriminatory reasons for the treatment, the test is of no use. Its theoretical weakness was explained by the US Supreme Court in *Price
Waterhouse v Hopkins*:[75]

> "Suppose two physical forces act upon and move an object, and
> suppose that either force acting alone would have moved the
> object. As the [*but for* test] would have it, *neither* physical force
> was a 'cause' of the motion unless we can show that but for one
> or both of them, the object would not have moved; apparently
> both forces were simply 'in the air' unless we can identify at least
> one of them as a but-for cause of the object's movement. ...
> Events that are causally overdetermined, in other words, may
> not have any 'cause' at all. This cannot be so."[76]

Its practical weakness is that it could lead a tribunal into far too
much speculation as to the proportion, or weight, of the various
factors which led to the treatment, as well as what might have been,
but for the protected ground. If it were applied in the *Owen and Briggs
v James* case[77] (which predated the *but for* test), the tribunal would
have been drawn into the position of deciding—or speculating—
whether Ms James still would have been rejected simply because of
her three years of unemployment and/or her "unsatisfactory
demeanour".

---

[72] See *Amnesty International v Ahmed* [2009] I.C.R. 1450 (EAT), [37] (Underhill J.).
[73] [1980] I.R.L.R. 427 (EAT). Less helpfully, (in *Ahmed*, ibid.) Underhill J. also cited the
controversial decision in *Martin v Lancehawk* UKEAT/0525/03, where a (female) worker
was dismissed following the breakdown of her relationship with her (male) managing
director. The *but for* test was not used and so the worker lost her sex discrimination claim.
See also *B v A* [2007] I.R.L.R. 576 (EAT). cf. *Chamberlain Solicitors v Emokpae* [2004]
I.R.L.R. 592 (EAT). See S. Middlemiss, "A licence to discard? Failed sexual relationships in
the workplace and sex discrimination" (2007) 78 Emp. L.B. 2 (Westlaw).
[74] Described above, para.4–014.
[75] 490 US 228 (1989).
[76] 490 US 228, at 241 (1989) (Brennan J.). This was a criticism of the conservative minority's
dissent, which was using the but for test to *restrict* the application of the legislation.
[77] [1982] I.C.R. 618 (CA). See above, para.4–014. Note though, a tribunal may still be in a
position of assessing the chances of the same decision being made absent discrimination for
the less critical task of calculating damages: *Chagger v Abbey National* [2010] I.R.L.R. 47,
(CA) [55]–[60]. See further, Ch.12, para.12–025.

(a) The Correct Approach

With these weaknesses and the apparent judicial indifference, the *but* **4–020** *for* test seems effectively dead, or at best marginal. What then, is the correct approach? The *JFS* majority favoured (in all but "obvious" cases) an enquiry into the defendant's "mental processes", but only to establish the ground of the treatment. Once that was established, any motive (however benign) of the defendant was irrelevant.[78] This "quasi-subjective" test may appear as no more than an exercise in semantics. It may be helpful to test its practical value against a number of concrete examples.

1. *The defendant treated badly a person with a protected characteristic.* Without more, these cases will fail under any subjective approach (or under the *but for* test) because, without more, there is no discriminatory element to the defendant's act.[79]

2. *"Obvious Cases". The defendant acted out of prejudice towards the protected group.* A blatant example would be a "No Blacks" notice. A more likely one would be an employer who states: "I cannot understand why an English employer would want to take on a coloured girl when English girls are available."[80] This category includes stereotyping where the reason for discrimination is explicit.[81] In this category of "obvious" cases, there is no need to enquire into the defendant's motive at all.

3. *"Benign Motive."* These cases resemble category 2 (above), as the defendant is aware of the discriminatory effect of his action. The difference is that discrimination is not his principal motive. Examples include "customer preference" (where an employer discriminates to please its customers,[82] or other third parties;[83] impermissible affirmative action

---

[78] For this, the *JFS* majority relied heavily on Lord Nicholls' speech in *Nagarajan v LRT* [2000] 1 A.C. 501 (HL), 511–513.
[79] *Glasgow CC v Zafar* [1998] I.C.R. 120 (HL), above, para.4–009.
[80] See *Owen and Briggs v James* [1982] I.C.R. 618 (CA), see above, at para.4–014.
[81] e.g. *Alexander v Home Office* [1988] 2 All E.R. 118 (CA). See below, para.4–033.
[82] See the US case, *Diaz v Pan Am* 442 F 2d 385 (5th Cir. 1971), certiorari denied, 404 US 950 (1971) (preference for (female) air stewardesses); and *Chaney v Plainfield Healthcare* 612 F.3d 908 (7th Cir. 2010) where a care home acceded to patient's preference for a white nurse.
[83] *R. v Commission for Racial Equality ex parte Westminster City Council* [1985] I.C.R. 827 (CA). (Local authority dismissed black worker because of pressure from workforce.)

programmes;[84] acts of chivalry;[85] acting to benefit pensioners;[86] a refusal to hire to ensure employer's neutrality,[87] or to protect from harassment in the workplace,[88] or from violence;[89] preferences informed by religious doctrine.[90] This category also includes the situation where the discrimination arises from an "accident of history", where there is no motive, such as the *Birmingham Grammar Schools* case.[91]

As these cases, like category 1 (above), are "obvious", there should be no enquiry into the defendant's "mental processes",[92] and since confirmation by the *JFS* decision, any benign motive (or absence of a hostile discriminatory one) is irrelevant. Thus, there will be liability in these cases. The exception would be where the benign motive coincides with a specific defence provided by the legislation in any particular field of application (e.g. employment, education, provision of goods, facilities and services). An obvious example would be employing only men to play male roles in a dramatic performance, the motive being authenticity, the specific defence being the Occupational Requirement.[93]

This accords with the case law in the United States, which insists upon a discriminatory motive for liability for direct discrimination (or "disparate treatment"), but rejects "benign motive" defences. For instance, a union was liable for disparate treatment of its black members for failing to challenge their employer's discriminatory practices, even though the union's stance was not motivated by racial prejudice, but in deference to its white membership, and/or to gain favour with the employer to achieve other goals.[94]

---

[84] e.g. *Jepson and Dyas-Elliott v The Labour Party* [1996] I.R.L.R. 116 (IT) (an attempt to balance the representation of the sexes in Parliament amounted to direct discrimination. Reversed by legislation: Equality Act 2010 s.104 (originally SDA 1975 s.42A), which is due to lapse in 2030). See also *ACAS v Taylor* (1997) EAT/788/97 (policy of choosing women predominantly for interview for 31 posts, because only 17 per cent of SEOs at ACAS were female, was direct discrimination). See generally, Ch.11, para.11–002.

[85] *Ministry of Defence v Jeremiah* [1980] Q.B. 87 (CA). (Women not required to work in dirty part of factory.)

[86] *James v Eastleigh BC* [1990] 2 A.C. 751 (HL).

[87] *Amnesty International v Ahmed* [2009] I.C.R. 1450 (EAT). (Preference for case-workers *not* to be a national of the country under investigation.)

[88] *Grieg v Community Industry* [1979] I.C.R. 356, EAT. (Woman denied work with all-male decorating team.)

[89] *Amnesty International v Ahmed* [2009] I.C.R. 1450 (EAT).

[90] *R. (E) v Governing Body of JFS* [2009] UKSC 15.

[91] *R. v Birmingham City Council, ex parte EOC* [1989] 1 A.C. 1156 (HL). See above, para.4–015, p.91.

[92] *Nagarajan v LRT* [2000] 1 A.C. 501 (HL), 511 (Lord Nicholls). Discussed below, Ch.7, at para.7–007.

[93] EA 2010, Sch.9, para.1. See Ch.8, paras 8–018–8–020. For (unsuccessful) arguments that a "benign" motive constituted a Bona Fide Occupation Requirement defence under the US legislation, see *United Automobile Workers v Johnson Controls* 499 US 187 (1991) and *Diaz v Pan Am* 442 F 2d 385 (5th Cir.1971), certiorari denied, 404 US 950 (1971).

[94] *Goodman v Lukens Steel* 482 US 656 (Sup. Ct 1987).

Similarly, an employer was held to carry the requisite discriminatory motive when refusing to hire fertile women on health grounds.[95] The Supreme Court stated that: "[D]isparate treatment ... does not depend on *why* the employer discriminates but rather on the explicit terms of the discrimination. ... The beneficence of an employer's purpose does not undermine the conclusion that an explicit gender-based policy is sex discrimination."[96] Customer preference cases are likewise treated as carrying the requisite discriminatory intent.[97] In affirmative action cases the Supreme Court has been more forthright, stating that "racial discrimination based on benign prejudice is just as noxious as discrimination inspired by malicious prejudice."[98]

4. *The defendant acts upon discriminatory factors, of which he ought to be aware, but is not.* It has been observed that it is unusual to find direct evidence of discrimination, and that few defendants would even admit to themselves that they had discriminated, instead assuming that the claimant "would not have fitted in". Thus, tribunals should make "proper inferences" from the primary facts.[99] This was approved by the House of Lords in *Glasgow CC v Zafar*,[100] where Lord Browne-Wilkinson added: "those who discriminate on the grounds of race or gender do not in general advertise their prejudices: indeed, they may not even be aware of them."　　　**4–021**

An example of this form of discrimination arose in *King v China Centre-Great Britain*.[101] This category includes stereotyping where the reason for discrimination is *not* explicit.[102]

Here, the defendant does not have the protected ground in his mind, which points to no liability under a fully- or quasi-subjective subjective approach (although there is liability under the *but for* test). The difficulty with this conclusion is

---

[95] *United Automobile Workers v Johnson Controls* 499 US 187 (Sup. Ct 1991). (Holding that decisions about the welfare of future children should be left to the parents.)

[96] ibid. at 199–200 (Blackmun J.), emphasis supplied.

[97] *Diaz v Pan Am* 442 F 2d 385 (5th Cir.1971), certiorari denied, 404 US 950 (1971). (Preference for (female) air stewardesses.)

[98] *Adarand Constructors v Pena* 515 US 200, at 241 (1995), a constitutional challenge under the equal protection clause of the Fifth Amendment. (Five per cent per annum of all government contracts should be awarded to certified small business concerns owned and controlled by socially and economically disadvantaged individuals.)

[99] *King v Great Britain-China Centre* [1992] I.C.R. 513 (CA), at 518 (Neill J.). See above, para.4–006, p.84, and further, Ch.12, para.12–008.

[100] [1998] I.C.R. 120 (HL), at 126. See further above, para.4–009 and on proving discrimination, Ch.12, para.12–007.

[101] [1992] I.C.R. 513 (CA), at 518 (Neill J.). See above, para.4–006, and further, Ch.12, para.12–008.

[102] e.g. *Price Waterhouse v Hopkins* 490 US 228 (Sup Ct 1989). See below, para.4–033.

that excludes a classic direct discrimination claim and is at odds with the policy of the legislation. As the US Supreme Court stated in the context of sex discrimination:

> "An employer who objects to aggressiveness in women but whose positions require this trait places women in an intolerable and impermissible catch 22: out of a job if they behave aggressively and out of a job if they do not."[103]

Further, it is most unlikely that those judges promoting the fully subjective approach intended to overrule a line of cases specifically approved by their most persistent advocate, Lord Browne-Wilkinson.[104] In *King*, liability was established by inferences made from the circumstances. Theoretically, the only way to reconcile these cases with the "mental processes" approach is with a rather artificial and semantic notion that the defendant holds the discriminatory factors in his mind, even though he is unaware that those factors are discriminatory.

4–022   5.   *"Cat's Paw" theory: the defendant acts upon discriminatory factors of which he is* not *aware.* Here an employer treats a worker less favourably in response to discriminatorily motivated, but facially neutral, acts by other workers. The *Shamoon* variation (offered above)[105] is an example of this, where male workers complain about a female supervisor because they do not like being subordinate to a woman, resulting in the supervisor being disciplined. Here, there were no discriminatory factors in the employer's mind when acting. In the US, some courts have developed an "imputed intent" or "cat's paw" theory for cases like this. In *Shager v Upjohn*,[106] Shager's supervisor (aged 38) was hostile to Shager (aged 53) because of his age. The supervisor influenced the hiring committee, who were unaware of Shager's age, to dismiss Shager, who was replaced with a younger worker. It was held that the committee had acted as a conduit—or "cat's paw"—for the supervisor's prejudice, and so the

---

[103] ibid. at 251 (Brennan J.).
[104] Respectively, in *Zafar v Glasgow CC* [1998] I.C.R. 120 (HL), at 126; and dissenting in *Nagarajan v LRT* [2000] 1 A.C. 501 (HL), at 510: "stereotypes provide no excuse for what would otherwise be racially discriminatory."
[105] See para.4–007.
[106] 913 F 2d 398 (7th Cir. 1990); see also *Poland v Chertoff* 494 F.3d 1174, at 1182 (9th Cir. 2007) (rejecting the metaphor as a narrow causation rule), *Russell v McKinney Hosp* 235 3 F 3d 219, at 227 (5th Cir 2000); *Griffin v Washington Convention Centre* 142 F 3d 1308, at 1312 (DC Cir. 1998); *Burlington Ind v Ellerth* 524 US 742, at 762 (Sup. Ct 1998). cf. *Hill v Lockheed Martin* 354 F.3d 277 (4th Cir. 2004). See generally, T. Davies, "Beyond the cat's paw: an argument for adopting a 'substantially influences' standard for Title VII and ADAE liability 2, (2007) 6 Pierce L. Rev. 247.

employer was liable for direct age discrimination. The features of this theory are that the prejudiced subordinate has influence over the decision-maker and so "poisons the well"[107] from which that decision-maker draws his knowledge.

It is yet to be seen if this theory takes hold in the UK, although in *Williams v YKK*,[108] Elias J. suggested obiter that an unprejudiced manager's decision may be affected or tainted by a report made by a prejudiced supervisor.

The "mental processes" test is not yet developed enough to offer a clear answer for these cases. On the one hand, it could short-circuit the Cat's Paw theory. It is arguable that a factor tainted with discrimination influenced the decision-maker to act, and so was part of his mental processes when so doing. As such, the ground of the treatment was discriminatory. This view makes it unnecessary to resort to Cat's Paw theory. On the other hand, as the discriminatory aspect was neither consciously nor unconsciously in his mind, it is equally arguable that it played no part in the decision-maker's mental processes. Here, Cat's Paw theory is required to impute the discriminatory factor into the decision-maker's act. If analysed as imputed intent, or a variation of vicarious liability, Cat's Paw theory is not such a big leap to be unthinkable, and it would serve the policy of the legislation.

6. *Honest, but mistaken, belief.* Where the treatment of a person   **4–023** of a protected group is for an entirely non-discriminatory reason (such as dismissal for theft, or non-recruitment for lack of necessary qualifications) there is no liability. However, similar cases arise where there is evidence of discrimination, and the defendant held an honest, but *mistaken*, belief that he acted for a separate non-discriminatory reason. This is illustrated by two US cases. In *Pesterfield v TVA*,[109] a worker's doctor wrote to the employer stating that the worker had a psychological disorder, but was fit to return to work. The employer misinterpreted the second part of this letter, and thinking he was *unfit* for work, refused to take the worker back. The worker's claim for disability discrimination failed because the employer had acted honestly, albeit mistakenly, for a non-discriminatory reason. In *McKnight v Kimberly Clark*,[110] a worker was dismissed because of an allegation of a sexual assault. There was evidence that the allegation was unfounded, and of hostility in the workplace

---

[107] *Sarate v Loop Transfer Inc* US Dist LEXIS 13170, at 12 (ND Ill 1997).
[108] EAT/0408/01 AM (November 22, 2002), [23]. See *www.employmentappeals.gov.uk*.
[109] 941 F 2d 437, at 443–444 (6th Cir 1991).
[110] 149 F 3d 1125, at 1129 (10th Cir 1998).

to older workers, although the allegation was not motivated by age. The claim for age discrimination failed, because even if the (sexual assault) allegation were untrue, the employer had acted upon an honest mistake. The US Circuits are divided on whether the employer's belief needs to be honest *and* reasonable, or merely honest.[111] The difference between this category and the "cat's paw" cases (above) is that the non-discriminatory reason is not tainted, or "poisoned", with discrimination.

For the purpose of this discussion, these cases are clearer than they appear. Discrimination played no part in the employers' mental processes, not even tainting the decision. Likewise, under the *but for* test, it could not be said in *Pesterfield's* case (where the letter and the protected characteristic were closely tied), that *but for* Pesterfield's disability, he would have been retained.[112] The evidence suggested that even with his disability, he was "fit for work" and would have been retained. In *McKnight's* case it could not be said that he was dismissed *because of* his age, or *but for* his age he would not have been dismissed.

4–024   7. *"Are you Jewish?"*: *the defendant is unaware that the claimant belongs to a protected group, but nonetheless treats the claimant less favourably because of a protected characteristic.* This category differs from the "honest mistake" cases (above) because the mistake here is not realising that the claimant had a protected characteristic. However, the defendant holds the protected characteristic in his mind. In *Simon v Brimham Associates*,[113] Mr Simon, who is Jewish, attended an interview with a firm of job consultants. When asked, he refused to disclose his religion. The interviewer then explained that the job was with an Arab company and those of "the Jewish faith" would not be selected. Mr Simon ended the interview there and then and claimed that he had been discriminated against. The industrial tribunal held that for there to be discrimination, it must be shown that the discriminator was aware of the claimant's race. The Court of Appeal disagreed in part, stating that it was a question of fact in each case and that such knowledge could be a factor. It agreed with the industrial tribunal that there had not been

---

[111] See the discussion in *Smith v Chrysler* 155 F 3d 799 (6th Cir 1998) and R. Michaels, "Legitimate reasons for firing: must they be reasonable?" (2003) 71 Fordham L Rev 2643.

[112] Under the UK's Equality Act 2010 s.15 ("discrimination arising from disability") there may be a case to answer, although there is a justification defence. See Ch.13, para.13–024.

[113] [1987] I.C.R. 596 (CA). See also above, para.4–003. The case was brought as racial discrimination because it predated the introduction of Religious discrimination legislation in 2003. For a similar case in the US, where the practice was held to be unlawful direct discrimination, see *Abrams v Baylor College of Medicine* 805 F.2d 528 (5th Cir 1986).

discrimination in this case. With respect to the Court of Appeal, its focus on the interview led it into a rather pointless discussion on whether this "treatment" was on the ground of Mr Simon's religion. The primary fact here is that the defendant would not employ Jews, and it is this treatment that should have been the focus of the discussion. The interview is merely evidence of the "no-Jews" policy. Once that is recognised, it is clear that this is an "obvious" case requiring no inquiry into the mental processes of the defendant.

In any case, *Simon* must now be considered bad law following the ECJ decision in *Feryn*,[114] where it was held that an employer who announced he would not employ immigrants could be liable for direct (racial) discrimination. The mischief indentified by the ECJ is the dissuasive effect of this conduct; it did not matter that there was no identifiable victim to bring a claim.[115] Accordingly, the Explanatory Note (63) to the Equality Act 2010 s.13 (direct discrimination) provides an example of a patently discriminatory job advertisement which is unlawful merely because it would deter victims from applying. If a discriminatory statement to no one in particular can amount to direct discrimination, then a fortiori so should the same statement when made directly to all applicants, some of whom may be identifiable victims.

These examples show that the mental processes test is perhaps easier to apply than put into words. The one ambiguity is lies with the "Cat's Paw" cases, which may require an imputed intent. On the other hand, the *but for* test raises problems with mixed-ground and "background" cases. The better view is to stay true to the purpose and wording of the legislation, and ask simply, if the treatment was because of the protected characteristic. This question can resolve, correctly and relatively simply, all seven of the categories listed above (liability in all but categories one and six). There is no need to venture into new notions and different language to express and resolve this question.

(3) Where the Victim has no Protected Characteristic

The definition of direct discrimination in the Equality Act 2010 s.13 **4–025** states that the less favourable treatment should be "because of *a* protected characteristic" (emphasis supplied). It does not state "because of *his* protected characteristic". This drafting detail (the omission of the possessive adjective, *his* (or *her*)) means that the

---

[114] Case C-54/07 [2008] ECR I-05187.
[115] ibid. [25].

victim does not have to possess a protected characteristic.[116] This facilitates three types of claim: (a) third party discrimination, (b) perceived discrimination, and (c) (arguably) discrimination where nobody's protected characteristic is in question.

(a) Third Party Discrimination

4–026   "Third party discrimination" itself covers (at least) two scenarios: instructions to discriminate, and "association discrimination". In *Showboat Entertainment Centre Ltd v Owens*,[117] a white manager of an amusement centre was instructed by his employer to refuse admission to black youths. He declined to obey this order and was dismissed. The EAT held that the instruction (plainly amounting to racial discrimination against black youths) constituted racial discrimination against the (white) manager.

This broad definition produced an unintended consequence in *Redfearn v Serco (t/a West Yorkshire Transport Service)*,[118] where a driver, whose passengers were 70–80 per cent Asian, was dismissed for being a member of the British National Party (an all-white racist political party). The EAT held that as he was dismissed for his racial views, he was dismissed on racial grounds. The Court of Appeal reversed, but more on policy grounds than a logical interpretation of the legislation. The policy objection, according to Mummery L.J., was that the logical conclusion of Redfearn's argument was that an employer dismissing a worker for serious racial harassment would be treating him less favourably "on racial grounds", which was not the purpose of the legislation.[119] This reasoning has force, but there is a difference between conduct at work and publicly held views which are not manifested at work. On the matter of strict interpretation, Mummery L.J. found that Redfearn was *not* dismissed on racial grounds. Instead, it was:

> "... on the ground of a particular non-racial characteristic shared by him with a tiny proportion of the white population, that is membership of ... a political party like the BNP."[120]

He added, perhaps needlessly, that an employer could "apply the same approach to a member of a similar political party, which confined its membership to black people".[121] This is a fragile distinction

---

[116] This does not apply to work cases where the characteristic is marriage or civil partnership: s.13(4).

[117] [1984] 1 All E.R. 836 EAT. See also above, para.4–010. Approved in *Weathersfield (t/a Van & Truck Rentals) v Sargent* [1999] I.C.R. 425 (CA). (White woman resigned after instruction not to hire vehicles to "coloured and Asians".)

[118] [2006] I.R.L.R 623 (CA). See also *HM Prison v Potter* (2006) UKEAT/0457/06/DM.

[119] ibid. [43].

[120] ibid. [49].

[121] ibid. [49].

from *Showboat v Owens*, and would come under further strain should a black worker be dismissed for being a member of an innocuous association, for instance, a Caribbean arts club.

The logic behind this decision was doubted by a differently constituted Court of Appeal. Although, it accepted *Redfearn* as good law and correct in policy terms, both Laws and Sedley L.JJ. shared "unease" with its reasoning. Laws L.J. found it "difficult to see" that the reason for Redfearn's dismissal was anything other than the race of most of Serco's customers and many of its employees.[122]

These doubts should not be used validate racial discrimination **4–027** claims rooted in BNP (or similar) membership. Public policy is a well-established tool of statutory interpretation in English law. It would be against public policy principle for anti-discrimination legislation to come to a person's aid *because* he was a racist, just as it would for an inheritance statute to favour a son who murdered his mother:

> "The principle ... must be so far regarded in the construction of Acts of Parliament that general words which might include cases obnoxious to the principle must be read and construed as subject to it".[123]

Thus, technical qualms with *Redfearn* should in no way cast doubt over its correctness. Of course, European-derived *purposive* interpretation would provide the same result, which reinforces the correctness of *Redfearn*.[124]

"Association discrimination" occurs against someone for their association with a person with a protected characteristic. Examples would include an employer refusing to hire a white woman because her husband is black,[125] or much older than her, or that her son is gay. In *Coleman v Attridge Law*,[126] upon return from maternity leave after giving birth to a baby with several disabilities, a legal secretary was refused flexible working (unlike others returning from maternity leave), and subjected to insulting remarks about her baby's disabilities. The ECJ upheld her claim for direct discrimination (and harassment), on the ground of her baby's disability.

---

[122] *English v Thomas Sanderson Blinds* [2009] I.C.R. 543, respectively, [20] (Laws L.J.), [41] (Sedley L.J.). See further below, para.4–029.

[123] *Re Sigsworth* [1935] Ch. 89 (Ch) 92.

[124] Redfearn has taken his case to the ECtHR (App. No.47335/06), complaining under arts 9 (Freedom of thought, conscience, and religion, 10 (Expression), 11 (Assembly), 13 (Effective remedy) and 14 (Discrimination).

[125] See *Wilson v TB Steelwork* (1978) COIT 706/44 (See IDS Employment Law Handbook 48 (1990) p.9) IT.

[126] Case C-303/06 [1998] 3 C.M.L.R. 27 (ECJ). For harassment on the ground of another's religion, see *Saini v All Saints Haque Centre* [2009] I.R.L.R. 74 (EAT).

(b) Perceived Discrimination

4–028 It can happen that a defendant discriminates against a person because he thinks, or perceives, incorrectly, that the person belongs to a protected group. For instance, an employer may reject a job application from a white man, wrongly thinking he is black, because of his African-sounding name.[127] Equally, a publican may refuse to admit a two straight men, wrongly perceiving them to be gay. There would be liability for direct discrimination in such cases. It does not matter that the victim had no protected characteristic.

(c) Where Nobody's Protected Characteristic is in Question

4–029 The concept of perceived discrimination (above) was taken a step further by the case of *English v Sanderson*,[128] a case of *harassment* on the ground of sexual orientation under the old Sexual Orientation Regulations 2003.[129] Here, Mr English was harassed by colleagues using sexual innuendo[130] suggesting he was homosexual. This conduct was rooted, apparently, in two things: he lived in Brighton (a well known centre of the gay scene) and had attended boarding school. What made this case unusual was not that Mr English is heterosexual, but because his tormentors neither assumed nor perceived Mr English to be gay, *and* that Mr English was aware throughout that his tormentors never mistook him for being homosexual. The Court of Appeal, by a 2–1 majority, found that the mockery amounted to unlawful harassment on grounds of sexual orientation.

Quite clearly, the phrase "on grounds of sexual orientation" or *because of* sexual orientation, lends itself to cover the scenario where the harassment (or less favourable treatment) was unrelated to any person's sexual orientation. As Sedley L.J. observed, the distance between perceived harassment and harassing a man as if he were gay when he is not "is barely perceptible".[131] However, policy considerations were prevalent in the speeches. This was to protect homosexual (or bisexual) workers from being "outed" by a systematic campaign of abuse. In such a pernicious scenario, the worker would have to suffer in silence unless or until he "came out".[132] As such, this decision helps preserve the dignity of workers that discrimination law is supposed to enshrine.

---

[127] Equality Act 2010, Explanatory Note 63.

[128] [2008] EWCA 1421. See "The multiple definitions of harassment and Direct Discrimination: a 'Pandora's Attic'" (2009) 10 IJDL, 101–108.

[129] Sexual Orientation (Employment Equality) Regulations SI 2003/1661, reg.5(1).

[130] On this basis, it seems that the claim could have succeeded more conventionally if *sexual* harassment was pleaded.

[131] [2008] EWCA 1421, [38].

[132] ibid. [39] (Sedley L.J.), [47] (Collins L.J.).

Of course, the logic applies equally to other protected characteristics.[133] Collins L.J. envisaged it would cover the scenario where:

"... an employee is repeatedly and offensively called a Paki or a Jew-boy even when he is not of Asian or Jewish origin, and even when his tormentors do not believe that he is".[134]

Nothing in the Equality Act 2010 sought to upset the *English* decision, and so it remains good law. The question is whether the logic applies to *discrimination*.

The harassment provisions in force at the time of *English v San-* **4–030** *derson* employed the phrase *on the ground of* (sexual orientation, race, etc.). The same phrase was used for the direct discrimination provisions. This was changed under the Equality Act 2010 to *because of*, which is intended to have the same meaning.[135]

This tempts a conclusion that the logic of *English* applies equally to direct discrimination. An employer says when firing a worker, "Look son, I know you're not Pakistani, but you look like you are, and that's been putting my customers off"; or, "*I* know you're not gay, but your effeminate manner gives that impression, and the punters do not like it." Alternatively, suppose a homophobic (or racist) employer fires a worker to prevent the worker informing the workforce of his homophobia (or racism), which the worker overheard by chance.

In any of these scenarios, no particular person's protected characteristic is involved, and the employer is under no mistake about the protected characteristic of the worker. But as the reason for the treatment was race or sexual orientation (as the case may be), it would seem that on the logic of *English*, these employers ought to be liable for direct discrimination. However, there is an important difference between direct discrimination and harassment. Direct discrimination normally requires a comparison. As such, it is difficult to envisage a comparator in these scenarios. Even in cases of perceived discrimination, a comparator can be identified as a person not wrongly perceived as having the protected characteristic by the defendant, thus making it straightforward to compare how this person would have been treated. But in these scenarios, it is difficult to create a comparator for the purpose of seeing how the defendant would have treated him. A person without the protected characteristic in question would be no different from the victim. This leads to the delicate conclusion that the comparator should be a person without the characteristic that led to the treatment, that is, a worker who would not be mistaken for a Pakistani, or a gay man, or a worker without knowledge of his employer's prejudices. Although

---

[133] This does not apply to work cases where the characteristic is marriage or civil partnership: EA 2010 s.13(4).
[134] [2008] EWCA 1421, [48].
[135] Explanatory Note 61.

these are not protected characteristics, they are *material differences* required by the comparison (EA 2010 s.23). Alternatively, the comparison may be bypassed using the suggestion of Lord Nicholls, in *Shamoon v Chief Constable of the RUC*,[136] that where a prohibited reason (such as race, sexual orientation, etc.) for the treatment is identifiable, a tribunal can "avoid arid and confusing disputes about the identification of the appropriate comparator".[137]

(4) Distinguishing Direct and Indirect Discrimination

4–031   In the *JFS* case,[138] Lady Hale observed that "Direct and indirect discrimination are mutually exclusive. You cannot have both at once." In that case, the minority analysed the facts as indirect discrimination.[139] The minority's view was based in the notion that as the challenged policy admitted pupils through the "convert route", it did not exclude *all* those not "racially Jewish", and so it could not be said to directly discriminate. This missed the point. The "convert rule" was merely the hurdle faced by those not racially Jewish. It was not the challenged rule. The challenged rule was the one that demanded that those not racially Jewish have to pass the "convert test". A claim should not be dispatched automatically to the indirect discrimination provisions just because only some of a claimant's protected group were disadvantaged by the challenged practice. Hence, in the majority, Lady Hale said:

> "M was rejected because of his mother's ethnic origins. ... The fact that the OCR would have overlooked his mother's Italian origins, had she converted to Judaism in a procedure which they would recognise, makes no difference to this fundamental fact."[140]

Lord Mance made the same point: "[A]n organisation which admitted all men but only women graduates would be engaged in direct discrimination on the grounds of sex".[141]

---

[136] [2003] I.C.R. 337 (HL). See above, para.4–009, and for the facts, para.4–006. See also *Islington LBC v Ladele* [2009] I.C.R. 387 (EAT), [37]–[39] (Elias J.).
[137] ibid. [11].
[138] [2009] UKSC 15, citing Mummery L.J. in *Elias v Secretary of State for Defence* [2006] 1 W.L.R. 3213, [117]. The facts of *JFS* are set out above, para.4–017.
[139] With Lords Hope and Rodger holding that the School could not justify the admissions policy.
[140] ibid. [66].
[141] ibid. [89].

4. DIRECT DISCRIMINATION AND STEREOTYPING

(1) Stereotyping and Less Favourable Treatment
It must not be assumed that stereotyping alone is enough for liability. **4–032**
It must operate to treat the claimant *less* favourably than the com-
parator. It is possible, theoretically at least, for a defendant to ste-
reotype both claimant and comparator, and thus treat them equally.
This is illustrated vividly in the dress code cases, discussed below.[142]

(2) Stereotyping on the Protected Ground
Less favourable treatment based upon a stereotype can be unlawful **4–033**
where the stereotype relates to a protected characteristic. In *Alex-*
ander v Home Office[143] a prisoner was refused (preferable) work in the
prison kitchen. The prison assessment stated:

"He displays the usual traits associated with people of his ethnic
background being arrogant, suspicious of staff, anti-authority,
devious and possessing a very large chip on his shoulder ... that
seems too common in most coloured inmates."[144]

The trial judge held that the prisoner had been treated not as an
individual, but as a racial stereotype, a decision upheld on appeal.
Other examples of racial stereotyping amounting to direct discrimination include: a refusal to hire a hall for a Pakistani wedding,
because of problems over payment from previous Asian hirers;[145] a
garage refusing to re-spray a car for a black person because the
proprietor thought that black people always haggled over the price;[146]
and a ban on West Indians from the Hammersmith Palais, following
a brawl involving some black youths. In this last case, the judge
stated that the licensee "... has to bring his judgment to bear upon
the individuals as such as distinct from being of a particular colour,
race or ethnic origin."[147]
    Although these were race discrimination cases, the principle applies
to other protected grounds. The leading US case is *Price Waterhouse*
v Hopkins[148] where Ann Hopkins, a successful senior manager was

---

[142] See below para.4–035.
[143] [1988] 2 All E.R. 118 (CA).
[144] ibid. at 120h.
[145] *Hussain v Canklow Community Centre* CRE Report 1980, p.85, Leeds County Court.
[146] *Race Relations Board v Botley Motor Vehicle Repairs* CRE Report 1977, p.118, Westminster
    County Court.
[147] *Race Relations Board v Mecca Ltd (Hammersmith Palais)* RRB Report 1974 p.39, West-
    minster County Court (Judge Ruttle).
[148] 490 US 228 (1989).

refused a partnership, a position that required aggressiveness. However, partners were on record describing her as "overly aggressive" and "macho", and one advised her to "walk more femininely, talk more femininely, dress more femininely, wear make-up, have her hair styled, and wear jewelry."[149] The US Supreme Court held that that stereotyping such as this could be evidence that the refusal was based on sex.

However, stereotyping a person on the ground of their age appears to more acceptable. In *Peterson*[150] the ECJ suggested that the compulsory retirement of dentists at 68 years was justifiable because "performance of dentists declines from that age".[151] In *Wolf*[152] the ECJ accepted an age restriction on the recruitment of fire-fighters because "very few officials over 45 years of age have sufficient physical capacity to perform the fire-fighting part of their activities."[153]

4–034   Claims will encounter a technical problem where defendants have stereotyped *some*, but not all, of the protected group, because of an additional factor. An example would be a refusal to recruit women with young children, on the assumption that they are unreliable. The protected characteristic is sex; the additional factor is having young children. Defendants may argue that as they have made assumptions about only *some* women, the refusal to hire only those women was not based on sex. However, the approach taken by the courts is to include the additional factor in the comparison, and so defeat the argument. In *Horsey v Dyfed CC*,[154] Mrs Horsey was obliged by her job with a county council in Wales to take a course at any British University, and then return to work for at least two years. She chose the University of Kent so that she could reside with her husband, who had just obtained work in nearby London. The Council refused her request, assuming that she would not return to work in Wales, preferring to be with her husband. The EAT held this was discrimination because the refusal was based on a stereotype that women follow their husbands' jobs, and not vice versa. Browne-Wilkinson J. stated: "In our view ... the tribunal has to compare the treatment of Mrs Horsey with the treatment which would have been afforded to a

---

[149] ibid. at 235.
[150] Case C-341/08 *Peterson v Berufungsausschuss fur Zahnarzte fur den Bezirk Westfalen-Lippe* [2010] 2 C.M.L.R. 830.
[151] This justification was rejected only because it only applied to public sector dentists.
[152] Case C-229/08 *Wolf v Stadt Frankfurt Am Main* [2010] I.R.L.R 224.
[153] ibid. [41]. cf. *Commonwealth v Human Rights & Equal Opportunity Commission (Bradley)* 60 ALD 157 (1999, Fed. Ct of Aus), [41]: physical fitness requirement could not be allowed to "have the effect of damning individuals over 28 years by reference to a stereotypical characteristic (less physical fitness) of their age group." Another discriminatory stereotype was a lack of ability "to fit in" to military life after too many years being "independent" in civilian life).
[154] [1982] I.C.R. 755 (EAT).

married man."[155] The evidence that the council would have treated a man differently was its assumption that Mr Horsey would refuse to follow his wife back to Wales.[156] In *Hurley v Mustoe*[157] the employer dismissed Mrs Hurley, who had four young children, because in his experience women with young children were unreliable. Again, this was held to be less favourable treatment. In *Skyrail v Coleman*[158] a female worker became engaged to a worker at a rival travel agents. The two employers, both of whom were worried about the leaking of confidential information, got together and decided that the female worker should be dismissed after the marriage, on the basis that she was not the "breadwinner". The Court of Appeal held that:

"... the dismissal of a woman based on an assumption that men are more likely than women to be the primary supporters of their spouses and children can amount to discrimination...".[159]

In the United States, this approach has been conceptualised as "sex-plus" theory, where the sex of the claimant, plus a factor, is the cause of the less favourable treatment.[160]

Finally, note that employers refusing to employ women for physically demanding jobs on the assumption that women were unable, or less able, to perform this work will directly discriminate.[161] Such an employer should instead identify the physical demands and specify the requirements in the job description. If the specification has a disproportionate impact on women, it may be challenged as *indirect* discrimination, giving the employer the opportunity to justify the specification. So it is essential that the employer can show that the need for the requirements is legitimate, and the requirements are appropriate and necessary to meet that need.[162]

---

[155] ibid. at 761.
[156] In fact, the council had overlooked that Mr Horsey had in the past twice followed his wife's job.
[157] [1981] I.C.R. 490 (EAT).
[158] [1981] I.C.R. 864 (CA).
[159] ibid. at 871.
[160] See *Phillips v Martin Marietta Corp* 400 US 542 (1971), where an employer hired fathers with pre-school age children, but rejected mothers with pre-school age children. Otherwise, it hired workers of either sex, without discrimination. The Supreme Court found this could amount to direct discrimination despite the employer showing that 75–80 per cent of recruits were women. The unlawful discrimination was based on sex *plus* the factor of being the parent of a young child.
[161] Equality Act 2010, Explanatory Note 63.
[162] See *FM Thorn v Meggit Engineering Ltd* [1976] I.R.L.R. 241 (IT). In the US Supreme Court case, *Dothard v Rawlinson* 433 US 321 (1977), height and weight requirements designed to measure strength were used in the recruitment of prison officers, but excluded 41 per cent of women in contrast to under one per cent of men. The employer had no evidence that the requirements were related to job performance, and so the claim of indirect discrimination succeeded. On indirect discrimination, see Ch.6.

5. DRESS CODES FOR MEN AND WOMEN AT WORK

4–035   Challenges to dress codes that treat male and female workers differently have been treated as special cases. The judiciary seems reluctant to interfere with a business's choice of image, although bound by the statutory formula (requiring *less* favourable treatment) to compare the treatment afforded to each sex by a dress code. Courts have managed to give employers a large measure of discretion by taking a "package" approach to the comparison. Appearance codes are compared as a package, and not on an item-by-item basis. In *Smith v Safeway*,[163] a delicatessen assistant was dismissed because his pony-tail became too long to be contained under his hat. The rule for male employees insisted on: "Tidy hair not below shirt collar length. No unconventional hair styles or colouring." For women, the parallel provision stated: "Shoulder-length hair must be clipped back. No unconventional hair styles or colouring." The rule was not based on hygiene. Of course, Mr Smith's objection was that only women could keep long hair. But the Court of Appeal compared the hair codes as a whole (tidiness, styling, colouring, as well as length) and ruled that that as the code applied conventional standards even-handedly, Safeway did not treat Mr Smith less favourably.[164]

A similar approach is taken in the United States.[165] Only if the requirements, taken as a whole, place an "unequal burden" upon one of the sexes, will it be challengeable. In *Jespersen v Harrah's Operating Company*,[166] a casino required staff to be "well groomed, appealing to the eye, be firm and body toned, and be comfortable with maintaining this look while wearing the specified uniform", and in addition, women had to wear stockings and coloured nail polish, and wear their hair "teased, curled, or styled", while men were barred from wearing makeup or coloured nail polish, and were required to keep short haircuts and neatly trimmed fingernails. Ms Jespersen's complaint that having to wear make-up was discriminatory was rejected as the code placed an equal burden on men and women.

This "package" approach is open to criticism on two fronts. First, technically, it is questionable. It is unlikely in other cases of direct

---

[163] [1996] I.C.R. 868.

[164] The only UK exception to this approach appears to be *McConomy v Croft Inns* [1992] I.R.L.R. 561 where the High Court of Northern Ireland held that a ban by a bar on male customers wearing earrings was unlawful sex discrimination, under the equivalent of EA 2010 s.29. Although the bar operated a "smart" dress code for both sexes, the court did not adopt a "package" approach. The case pre-dates *Smith v Safeway*, and perhaps more significantly, was not an employment complaint, suggesting that for dress codes, the courts may be more generous to employers than to service-providers.

[165] On US dress codes see, K. Bartlett, "Only girls wear barrettes" 92 Mich. L. Rev. 2541; K. Klare, "Power/Dressing: Regulation of employee appearance" 26 New Eng L Rev 1395.

[166] 392 F 3d 1076 (9th Cir. 2004).

discrimination that the courts would entertain it. If say, in *Gill v El Vino*,[167] the wine bar served only men at the bar, but gave *only* women table service, Ms Gill's claim of sex discrimination still would have succeeded. She was deprived of a choice which she, reasonably, valued. Similarly, if a sports centre offered free swimming only to women, but free badminton only to men, a man could claim direct discrimination: that men get free badminton is no consolation to man who wishes to swim.[168] It is also a striking departure from the established approach to equal pay claims, where pay and benefits must be compared on an item-by-item basis, and *not* as a package. It is no defence to say that a women does just as well as her male comparator because although her pay is less, her dinner breaks are longer.[169] There is, of course, a distinction between these examples and the dress code cases, where relevant differences between men and women may be a factor for appearances. But differences between men and women have not prevented the ECJ, albeit via a torturous route, from concluding that pregnancy discrimination *is* sex discrimination.[170] An item-by-item approach for dress codes need not lead to absurd results, such as compulsory cross-dressing. For instance, a code requiring men to wear a smart shirt and trousers, and women to wear a smart blouse and skirt, may be treating them *differently*, but could not be said to be treating men *less favourably* than women.

The second criticism of the package approach has facilitated the entrenchment of gender stereotypes. In addition to *Smith v Safeway*, two examples illustrate this. In *Schmidt v Austicks Bookshops Ltd*[171] the claimant was required to wear a skirt at work, and while serving the public, to wear overalls. The only restriction on men was a ban on tee-shirts. The EAT dismissed the overalls complaint as too trivial to amount to a "detriment",[172] and held (on the skirt issue) that Schmidt had been treated no less favourably than male workers. In *Cootes v John Lewis Plc*,[173] female sales staff were required to wear a uniform of a polyester blue suit with a green blouse, while male equivalents had to wear a dark suit and tie. The EAT held that the codes treated the sexes even-handedly, despite Ms Cootes' arguments that: (1) she objected to the polyester; (2) the male suits marked men out as more senior; and (3) the uniform marked her out in public (commuting and at lunchtimes) as a member of the sales staff.

4–036

---

[167] [1983] Q.B. 425 (CA). See above, para.4–002.
[168] This point was made by R. Wintemute: see "Recognising new kinds of direct sex discrimination: transsexualism, sexual orientation and dress codes" (1997) 60 M.L.R. 334, pp.354–355.
[169] See *Hayward v Cammell Laird (No. 2)* [1988] A.C. 894 (HL) (discussed below, Ch.9, para.9–045).
[170] *Webb v EMO Cargo* Case C-32/93, [1994] ECR I-3567, ECJ. (discussed below, para.4–045)
[171] [1978] I.C.R. 85 (EAT).
[172] Under what is now EA 2010 s.39(2)(d). See Ch.8, para.8–013.
[173] EAT/1414/00, (Transcript) February 27, 2001.

It is clear in both these cases that the codes treated women less favourably than the men. Tribunals avoid this seemingly obvious result by applying *Smith v Safeway's* test: did the code apply conventional standards even-handedly? Exchange the word "conventional" for "stereotypical" and the test is debunked. At their heart, these decisions are based on stereotypes of men and women in the workplace. One commentator noted: "*Schmidt* permits employers to reinforce, through dress codes, the very stereotypes of 'male' (serious, responsible, mature) and 'female' (decorative handmaidens) which disadvantage women at work."[174] Further, allowing employers this amount of discretion is, in many cases, pandering to customer preference, a notion ordinarily rejected in direct discrimination.[175] Some courts in the United States have held codes based on stereotypes to amount to direct discrimination. In *Carroll v Talman Federal Savings and Loan Association of Chicago*[176] female staff were obliged to wear a uniform, while equivalent males only had to wear customary business attire, which could be a suit, a sport jacket and trousers, or even a "leisure suit", as long as it was worn with a shirt and tie. The court held that this different treatment was demeaning to women because it suggested that the men were more senior. Moreover, the code suggested that only men were able to choose suitable business attire, which was an "offensive stereotype".[177] Similarly, in *Frank v United Airlines*,[178] a policy of subjecting women to more onerous weight requirements than men was held to be a discriminatory appearance code. Accordingly, the Court in *Jespersen* (above) suggested that if an appearance code imposed an unequal burden on women because of the expense and time in buying and applying make-up, it could be unlawful.[179]

---

[174] A. McColgan, *Discrimination Law* (Oxford: Hart, 2005), p.483. See also *Burrett v West Birmingham HA* (EAT/1414/00 (Transcript) February 27, 2001) where a female nurse complained (unsuccessfully) that a rule that female nurses wear headgear, while male nurses wear a jacket with epaulettes, stereotyped the sexes.

[175] See *R. v Birmingham CC ex p EOC* [1989] 1 A.C. 1155, per Lord Goff, at 1194, discussed above, para.4–015.

[176] 604 F 2d 1028 (7th Cir. 1979), certiorari denied 445 US 929 (1980).

[177] ibid. at 1033. In fact, the employer argued: "the selection of ... clothing on the part of women is not a matter of business judgment. It is a matter of taste, a matter of what the other women are wearing, what fashion is currently. When we get into that realm ... problems develop. Somehow, the women who have excellent business judgment somehow follow the fashion, and the slit-skirt fashion which is currently prevalent. ... They tend to follow those (fashions) and they don't seem to equate that with a matter of business judgment" (ibid.).

[178] 216 F 3d 845 (9th Cir 2000).

[179] Ms Jesperson produced academic evidence of the expense to women of the make-up requirement, but no evidence of the expense to men of their requirements, so no comparison could be made: 392 F 3d 1076, at 1081 (9th Cir 2004).

In both the UK and US, challenges by men required to keep their **4–037** hair short have repeatedly failed.[180] Although the British courts characterise such a requirement as imposing no more than "conventional" standards, they are just another stereotype, this time, that men with long hair—but not women—do not appear either authoritative, smart, presentable, or hygienic, as the case may be. Further, by adhering to the "conventional standards" rubric, courts are, at best, applying a purely objective test, which is a departure from the usual approach, which is to ask whether the *claimant*, reasonably, perceived the treatment as less favourable.[181] Unlike most dress codes, short hair is an appearance that the worker must take home with him into his private and social life.[182] Just as a person reasonably may value a poor job reference,[183] a grammar school place[184] or service at the bar,[185] he may, just as reasonably (at the least) value his choice of appearance in his private and social life.

In dress code cases, the approach should be to make an item-by-item comparison, and ask whether a particular sex has been treated *less* favourably (rather than just differently). Consideration should be given to the complainant's reasonably held perception, and exclude unnecessary complications of conventions and stereotypes. This approach will not lead to absurdities (such as men being required to wear skirts or blouses), nor will it inhibit employers from presenting a particular image of their choice, so long as it is not based on gender stereotypes.

---

[180] See *Smith v Safeway* [1995] I.C.R. 472 (CA) (above); *Fuller v Mastercare Service & Distribution* (2001) EAT/0707/00; *Dansie v Commissioner of Police for the Metropolis* (2009) UKEAT/0234/09. See also *Department of Work & Pensions v Thompson* [2004] I.R.L.R. 348 (EAT (men required to collar and tie not discriminatory). In the US, see *Willingham v Macon Telegraph Publishing Co* 507 F 2d 1084 (5th Cir 1975) (hair length not immutable); *Harper v Blockbuster* 139 F 3d 1385 (11th Cir 1998) certiorari denied 525 US 1000 (1998), and the cases cited within.

[181] See "What is 'Less' Favourably" above, para.4–002.

[182] Quaere is such an interpretation of the equality legislation is an interference with a man's private life and thus incompatible with the ECHR, either under art.8 alone (right to a private life), or in combination with art.14 (rights must be secured without discrimination)? cf. *Kara v UK* (1998) 27 EHRR CD 272, where a claim that a "cross-dressing" ban breached arts 8, 10 and 14 was ruled inadmissible by the Commission. On the ECHR and discrimination, see Ch.2, para.2–007.

[183] *Chief Constable of West Yorkshire v Khan* [2002] 1 W.L.R. 1947 (HL). See Ch.7, para.7–008, p.211.

[184] *R. v Birmingham City Council ex parte EOC* [1989] A.C. 1155 (CA and HL). See para.4–015, above.

[185] *Gill v El Vino* [1983] Q.B. 425 (CA). See para.4–002.

6. DIRECT DISCRIMINATION AND SEGREGATION—RACE ONLY

4-038   Section 13(5) of the Equality Act 2010 (EA 2010) provides that for race only, less favourable treatment includes "segregating" a person from others. In the White Paper preceding the Race Relations Act 1976 (RRA 1976), *Racial Discrimination*, the Government adopted the observation of the Race Relations Board that:

> "[F]or a time segregation may represent a form of accommodation acceptable to all, but if it hardens into patterns, tensions and conflicts will occur when pressures to change that pattern arise."[186]

The inspiration for this is was the US Supreme Court's seminal decision in *Brown v Board of Education*,[187] holding that "separate but equal" segregated schooling was unconstitutional. Thus, s.13(5) ensures that it is no defence that, say, separate workplace canteen facilities for Asians and whites are of equal quality.

4-039   In *Pel Ltd v Modgill*,[188]a paint shop in a factory was staffed solely by Asians. This was the result of the vacancies being filled by friends or relatives of the Asians through word of mouth; the personnel department did no recruiting. The paint spray work was the dirtiest in the factory and the Asians complained of segregation under the similar provision in the RRA 1976. The EAT held that in the absence of policy to segregate, there was no unlawful segregation under the Act. In effect, the EAT is holding that to fall within the statutory definition, there must be a *positive* act of segregation by the defendant. In this case, the employer merely *acquiesced* in the segregation. As well as being contrary to the sentiment expressed in the White Paper, this interpretation of the Act carries technical problems. On the face of it, the word employed by the Act "segregating" is a verb, suggesting that there must be some positive act by the defendant. However, s.78 provided that for the purposes of the RRA 1976, an act included a deliberate omission (see now EA 2010 s.202(2)).[189] And clearly, in this case, segregation arose as a result of the employer's deliberate omissions. The simple "non-intervention" of the personnel office is a powerful weapon in the workplace.[190]

Note that all parties in this case referred to the job of working in the paint shop as "the dirtiest in the factory". That should not matter

---

[186] Cmnd.6234 [62].
[187] 347 US 483 (1954). See also Ch.1, para.1–010.
[188] *FTATU v Modgill; Pel Ltd v Modgill* [1980] I.R.L.R. 142 (EAT).
[189] cf. *R v Cleveland CC ex p. CRE* [1993] 1 F.C.R. 597 (CA), at 606.
[190] For the difficulties of analysing cases of large scale "passive" segregation, see the US case *Wards Cove v Atonio* 490 US 642 (1989), discussed in Ch.6, para.6–010.

when segregating, *in itself*, amounts to less favourable treatment. The Equality Act 2010 uses the same verb *segregating*, although the Explanatory Note (62) states that "racial segregation is always discriminatory", again suggesting that segregation, however caused, should be unlawful.

Since the *Pel* decision, a new, broader, definition of indirect discrimination has emerged. Under it, where the word-of-mouth hiring puts a protected group at a disadvantage, it might be challengeable, although the employer would have an objective justification defence. Word-of-mouth hiring as indirect discrimination is discussed in Chapter 6, at para.6–013.

7. DIRECT DISCRIMINATION AND PREGNANCY

(1) History

Pregnancy discrimination law has its roots in *sex* discrimination law.   **4–040**
At first sight, this appears logical. But it carries technical barriers. The equal treatment model, being symmetrical, demands a comparison between the treatment given to the woman, and that which would have been given to a man in the same circumstances. Of course, as men do not get pregnant, this comparison is impossible for pregnancy cases. Back in 1980, the EAT in *Turley v Alders Department Stores Ltd*,[191] held that a claim of sex discrimination on the ground of pregnancy must inevitably fail, for want of a comparator.[192] Next, in 1985, the EAT in *Hayes v Malleable Working Men's Club and Institute*[193] used a "sick man" as a comparator. Apart from the obvious absurdity of this proposition, it carries practical problems. Employers could escape liability by showing that they treated their sick male workers equally *badly*, for instance, with a policy of dismissing any worker after four weeks' absence. This defence becomes truly poisonous to discrimination law if used by typical sweatshop employers with an all-female workforce. These workers cannot bring a real comparator into court, only a hypothetical one. A tribunal would have the somewhat dubious task of deciding how a sweatshop employer might treat male workers; the evidence being how badly it treats its female workers.

---

[191] [1980] I.C.R. 6.
[192] In the US Supreme Court a majority held that a distinction "between pregnant and non-pregnant persons" was not one based on sex, as there were "nonpregnant" women (*General Electric v Gilbert* 429 US 125 (1976), 134–135). The position remedied by the (non-symmetrical) Pregnancy Discrimination Act 1978, which amended s.701, Title VII with a new sub-section (k) (USC §2000e(k)).
[193] [1985] I.C.R. 703.

The law was salvaged in 1991 by the ECJ in *Dekker*.[194] It held that as only women become pregnant, discrimination on the ground of pregnancy is direct sex discrimination. No comparison with a man is necessary. This rather crude approach ignores the niceties of symmetry, but achieves the purpose of the legislation.

(2) The Current Law

4–041 The position is complex. Legislation provides some absolute (or specific) rights for pregnant women, such as maternity leave. These rights are enforceable without recourse to discrimination provisions. So in any case of pregnancy, there may be a mix of absolute and discrimination rights in play. The range of legislation providing these rights includes the Recast Directive 2006/54/EC, the Equality Act 2010, the Pregnant Workers Directive 92/85/EC, the Employment Rights Act 1996 (ERA 1996), ss.47C and 99, and the Maternity and Parental Leave Regulations 1999.[195]

(3) Specific Protection for Workers

4–042 The Pregnant Workers Directive 92/85/EEC provides a right to at least 14 weeks maternity leave, including a compulsory two weeks.[196] The domestic legislation goes further, providing Ordinary (26 weeks, including two weeks Compulsory), and Additional (a further 26 weeks) maternity leave.[197] Inherent in the maternity leave rights is a right to return to the same job (or a suitable alternative) on terms no less favourable than before, and to benefit from any improvement in working conditions to which she would have been entitled during her absence.[198]

An employer's abuse of these rights may lead to a discrimination claim (see below, Recast Directive, art.2(2)(c)). However, a parallel cause of action is provided for employment claims by the Employment Rights Act 1996. Section 99 stipulates that if the principal reason for a dismissal is pregnancy, childbirth, or maternity leave, the dismissal is automatically unfair.[199] The philosophy behind this strict approach is provided in the Preamble to the Pregnant Workers Directive:

[194] *Dekker v Stichting Vormingscentrum voor Jonge Volwassen (VJV-Centrum) Plus* Case C-177/88, [1990] ECR I-3941.
[195] SI 1999/3312.
[196] Article 8.
[197] ERA 1996, respectively ss.71(3), 72, and 73 (details provided by SI 1999/3312, regs 7(1), 8, 7(4)). There are qualifying conditions, especially on notification: SI 1999/3312, reg.4.
[198] Recast Directive 2006/54/EC, art.15, ERA 1996 ss.71–73, SI 1999/3312, regs 18, 18A.
[199] Implementing art.10 of the Pregnant Workers Directive, which provides for no dismissal from the time of pregnancy to the end of maternity leave "save in exceptional circumstances not connected with their condition", and provided that the worker has informed her employer of her condition (art.2).

"[T]he risk of dismissal for reasons associated with their condition may have harmful effects on the physical and mental state of pregnant workers, workers who have recently given birth or who are breastfeeding".

As with sex discrimination claims, no qualifying period of employment is required: it applies from day one. Any detriment short of dismissal is made unlawful by s.47C.

These are specific *employment* rights. Damages for unfair dismissal, but not for a detriment short of a dismissal,[200] are capped, at the time of writing, to £68,400.[201]

(4) Discrimination

Article 2(2)(c) of the Recast Directive 2006/54/EC states that dis-   **4–043**
crimination includes "any less favourable treatment of a woman related to pregnancy or maternity leave within the meaning of [the Pregnant Workers] Directive 92/85/EEC". The Equality Act 2010 (EA 2010) provides separate definitions for "non-work" and "work" cases. For all non-work cases, s.17 outlaws unfavourable treatment because of the pregnancy, or (for a period of 26 weeks following the birth), because of the birth. For work cases, s.18 outlaws unfavourable treatment because of a woman's pregnancy, or a related illness, or her maternity leave. The difference between the European and domestic schemes is that the European scheme treats pregnancy discrimination as *sex* discrimination (for historic reasons, see above, para.4–040), whereas the domestic scheme provides separate causes of action for direct pregnancy discrimination.[202]

There are some notable features to pregnancy discrimination law. No comparison is required. It seems that there can be liability for treatment for a reason *related* to the pregnancy, such as a pregnancy-related illness. There are exceptions for health and safety reasons. Finally, there is a more pragmatic approach to the issue of maternity pay.

(a) No Comparator Required

The Equality Act definition requires *unfavourable*, rather than, *less*   **4–044**
favourable treatment. This dispenses with the need for a comparator. The reason for this was illustrated in the case of *Hardman v Mallon*

[200] ERA 1996 s.49(1)(b).
[201] ERA 1996 s.124(1). This was the figure on February 13, 2011: SI 2010/2926. It is normally adjusted each February in line with retail prices. For claims of sex discrimination by those dismissed by the armed forces for pregnancy see Ch.12, para.12–025.
[202] The Equality Act's indirect discrimination provisions do not cover pregnancy or maternity (s.19(3)), and so pregnancy-related indirect discrimination claims should be pleaded as indirect *sex* discrimination.

t/a Orchard Lodge Nursing Home.[203] In this case, Ms Hardman was a
Care Assistant, a job which involved heavy lifting (of patients). After
she became pregnant, her employer offered no risk assessment. It
merely offered her cleaning work instead. In response to her claim of
sex discrimination the employer argued that it had treated her no less
favourably than it would have treated a man, or a non-pregnant
woman. At the first stage, the employment tribunal agreed:

> "What, it appeared to us, we were being asked to do was to
> widen the definition of discrimination to encompass a failure of
> an employer to treat a woman *more* favourably than a man."[204]

On appeal, the EAT reversed, holding that in pregnancy cases a
comparison was not required. Following a High Court ruling that the
requirement for a comparator in pregnancy cases was incompatible
with EC law, the domestic legislation was amended,[205] and this was
carried over to the Equality Act 2010.

(b) Pregnancy or Unavailability?

4–045   In *Webb v EMOS Air Cargo (UK) Ltd*[206] the claimant—who was
hired on an indefinite basis, but initially to replace a worker on
maternity leave—was dismissed because *she* became pregnant a few
weeks into the job. The ECJ held that this was direct sex discrimination.[207] When the case returned to the UK, Lord Keith suggested that this left an exception whereby an employer could refuse to
hire pregnant women for a short-term fixed contract where she would
be unavailable for the duration of that contract.[208] However, the ECJ
went some way to denying that possibility in *Tele Danmark v Brandt-
Nielson.*[209] It ruled that it makes no difference whether the contract
was fixed or indefinite. "In either case the woman's inability to perform her contract of employment is due to pregnancy."[210] The
question for the ECJ was whether the woman's inability to perform a
substantial part of the contract made any difference. Unfortunately,
for the sake of clarity, the ECJ did not extend its answer beyond this
to the situation where a woman is unavailable to perform the *whole* of
the contract, because of her pregnancy. However, the ECJ

---

[203] [2002] I.R.L.R. 516 (EAT).
[204] ibid. cited at [13].
[205] *EOC v Secretary of State for Trade and Industry* [2007] I.C.R. 1234 (HC), [41]–[47]. Consequently, the SDA 1975 s.3A, was amended by SI 2008/656 reg.2.
[206] Case C-32/93 [1994] I.R.L.R. 482, ECJ.
[207] Thus in *Abbey National v Formoso* [1999] I.R.L.R. 222, the EAT held that a dismissal of a
woman unable to attend her disciplinary hearing because she was on maternity leave,
amounted to sex discrimination.
[208] *Webb v EMO Air Cargo (UK) Ltd (No.2)* [1995] I.R.L.R. 645 (HL), at 647–648.
[209] *Tele Danmark v HK (acting for Brandt-Nielson)* Case C-109/00, [2001] ECR I-6993 (ECJ).
[210] ibid. [31].

underpinned its ruling by noting that there were no exceptions for fixed-term contracts in the relevant legislation and that fixed-term contracts may be terminated, renewed or extended, thus resembling indefinite contracts.[211] This observation—that it is not possible to predict the length of an employment contract—suggests that there cannot be such an exception, but the question remains undecided.

In relation to the issue of availability, the ECJ has held that a woman is under no obligation to disclose her pregnancy at recruitment, even if she knows that she will not be able to perform a substantial part of the contract.[212] The ECJ took the same view where a woman requested an early return from parental leave, knowing that her (new) pregnancy would prevent her from performing her all her duties.[213] In these cases, according to the ECJ, dismissal is because of the pregnancy, and as such amounts to direct sex discrimination.

(c) Pregnancy or "Morality"?

Some employers may consider the *circumstances* of the pregnancy, rather than the pregnancy itself, as a reason to treat a worker adversely.[214] In *O'Neill v Governors of St Thomas More Roman Catholic School*[215] a school teacher of religious education and "personal relationships" became pregnant as the result of a relationship with a local Roman Catholic priest. When this became public, she was dismissed. The school argued that it was the paternity of the child and the adverse publicity that made her job untenable, and *not* her pregnancy per se; had the pregnancy occurred in other circumstances, she would not have been dismissed. The EAT rejected this argument, holding that the pregnancy was at least one effective cause of the dismissal. The EAT distinguished, but endorsed,[216] the decision in *Berrisford v Woodard Schools*[217] where a matron in an all-girls boarding school was dismissed upon becoming pregnant. The circumstances were that the employer initially congratulated her, but then discovered she had no intention of marrying, and so it dismissed her because of the "obvious manifestation of extra-marital sex" which went against the school's ethos. There was evidence that a male worker would have been dismissed for the same reason. The EAT found the school not liable for discrimination. The case predated *Webb*[218] and the consequent art.2(2)(c) (treatment *related* to the

4–046

---

[211] ibid. [32].
[212] *Tele Danmark v HK (acting for Brandt-Nielson)* Case C-109/00, [2001] ECR I-6993 (ECJ), [34].
[213] *Busch v Klinikum Neustadt GmbH* Case C-320/01, [2003] I-02041 (ECJ).
[214] For a case on pregnancy or "misconduct", see *Shomer v B and R Residential Lettings Ltd* [1992] I.R.L.R. 317 (CA).
[215] [1997] I.C.R. 33, EAT.
[216] ibid. [45]–[46].
[217] [1991] I.C.R. 564 (EAT).
[218] Above, para.4–045.

pregnancy), as well as removal of the need for a comparison. As such, if the case arose today, it might prove more difficult, if not impossible, for the employer to rely on such factors.

(d) Pregnancy or the Resulting Illness?

4–047   As noted above, art.2(2)(c) of the Recast Directive 2006/54/EC states that discrimination includes less favourable treatment *related* to a woman's pregnancy or maternity leave. This endorses the ECJ decision in *Brown v Rentokil*,[219] which held that dismissal for unavailability (caused by a pregnancy-related illness) during the pregnancy and any period of subsequent maternity leave, amounts to discrimination on the ground of pregnancy, and so amounts to direct sex discrimination.[220] On the other hand, if the pregnancy-related illness persists beyond the maternity leave, or if the illness during pregnancy or maternity is *not* pregnancy-related, then the treatment must be compared with the treatment that would have been afforded to a male comparator.[221] The Equality Act 2010 s.18(2)(b) outlaws unfavourable treatment *because of illness* suffered by the woman as a result of the pregnancy. The treatment must occur within the "protected period", which begins with the pregnancy and ends when the woman returns to work from her maternity leave.[222] This codifies *Brown v Rentokil*.

It follows from the reasoning in *Brown v Rentokil*, that any less favourable treatment short of dismissal (except in relation to pay),[223] during pregnancy or maternity leave, because of a pregnancy-related illness, should amount to sex discrimination. This is confirmed by the broad wording of art.2(2)(c).

(e) Health and Safety

4–048   The next issue is how far an employer may act to protect a pregnant, or breastfeeding, woman on health and safety grounds. Of course, the law here moves further away from the equal treatment model. It specifically *prohibits* employers from obliging these workers to do

---

[219] Case C-399/96 [1998] I.C.R. 790. For commentary see, M. Wynn, "Pregnancy Discrimination: Equality, Protection or Reconciliation?" (1999) 62 M.L.R. 435.

[220] ibid. [26].

[221] ibid. [26]–[27]. cf. AG Ruiz-Jarabo Colomer in *Mayr v Bäckerei und Konditorei Gerhard Flöckner OHG* Case C-506/06 [2008] 2 C.M.L.R. 27 (ECJ), [60]–[61]. In *Caledonia Bureau v Caffrey* [1998] I.C.R. 603, a Scottish EAT held that post-natal depression arising during maternity leave, but persisting beyond that, was an illness related to pregnancy, so that the dismissal amounted to sex discrimination on the ground of pregnancy. This decision went beyond the boundaries set by *Brown*, and the Pregnant Workers Directive, and now EA 2010 s.18(2)(b), as it goes beyond the "protected period".

[222] Or, if she is not entitled to maternity leave, two weeks after the pregnancy ended: EA 2010 s.18(6).

[223] See below, para.4–052.

certain tasks.[224] More generally, the Recast Directive art.28 expressly allows employers to derogate from the discrimination principle for "the protection of women, particularly as regards pregnancy and maternity". This includes the duties imposed by the Pregnant Workers Directive 92/85/EC, passed ostensively on health and safety grounds, which requires employers to assess the risks to these workers, and make temporary adjustments to their work or, if not feasible, move them to another job, or if that is not feasible, grant them leave.[225] A worker cannot be dismissed, or not appointed, because it would be unsafe or unhealthy for her to do her work while pregnant or breastfeeding.[226] Within that limit, the rubric is proportionality.

An employer may not derogate merely out of a public concern for women's safety. In *Johnston v RUC*,[227] the police force of Northern Ireland dismissed female police officers, to protect them from being assassination targets, even though both men and women were at risk. The ECJ held that the derogation must specifically be related to the "biological condition and the special relationship which exists between a woman and her child" which this was not.[228]

(f) Unfavourable Treatment because of Maternity Leave

Detriments which are not pay,[229] but are related to maternity leave will be challengeable as maternity leave discrimination (under EA 2010 s.18(3), or s.18(4)), or under the specific protection afforded by ERA 1996 ss.99 (dismissal) and 47C (other detriments).[230] This includes detriments flowing from the maternity leave that affect the pay *outside of the maternity leave period*. For instance, in *Land Brandenburg v Ursula*[231] the wage scale was decided by length of service. A woman was not upgraded on the wage scale because her employer failed to incorporate into this calculation her time off on

4–049

---

[224] Pregnant Workers Directive 92/85/EC art.6 (risk of specified exposure), art.7 (night work).

[225] ibid. arts 4 and 5. For the domestic equivalent, see Management of Health and Safety at Work Regulations 1999, SI 1999/3242, reg.16. Where there is no risk to a pregnant woman, there is no requirement for a risk assessment: *Madarassy v Nomura International* [2007] I.R.L.R. 246 (CA) [135]–[138], applied *O'Neill v Buckinghamshire CC* [2010] I.R.L.R. 384 (EAT).

[226] See *Silke-Karin Mahlburg v Land Mecklenburg-Vorpommern* Case C-207/98 (2000) ECR I-549 (ECJ).

[227] Case 222/84, [1987] 1 Q.B. 129 (ECJ).

[228] ibid. [44]. But the ECJ held it was possible to derogate under ETD 207/76, art 2(2) (now recast Directive, art.14(2)) in special circumstances in Northern Ireland at the time.

[229] See below, para.4–052.

[230] See above, para.4–041.

[231] Case C-284/02, [2004] ECR I-00000.

maternity leave. The ECJ treated this as a case of sex discrimination rather than equal pay, and found for the claimant. Likewise in *CNAVTS v Thibault*,[232] the ECJ held that to deprive a woman on maternity leave of her annual assessment, and the resulting possibility of promotion, amounted to sex discrimination.

(g) Pregnancy-Related Treatment

4–050   Article 2(2)(c) of the Recast Directive 2006/54/EC states that discrimination includes less favourable treatment *related* to a woman's pregnancy or maternity leave. This goes further than merely codifying *Brown v Rentokil*,[233] because it is not confined to illness. It is drafted so to cover treatment for a reason one step removed from the pregnancy.

The pregnancy discrimination provisions of the Equality Act 2010 use the phrase *because of*, and so appear narrower in scope than the parent Directive. For employment cases, there are other solutions. The Maternity and Parental Leave Regulations 1999, which expand upon the right for unfair dismissal, explain that the reason for dismissal is unfair if it is *connected with* pregnancy, childbirth or maternity leave,[234] while ERA 1996 s.47C outlaws detrimental treatment *related to* pregnancy, childbirth, and maternity leave. These more accurately reflect art.2(2)(c).

Another solution of more general application is for the courts to continue their unusually broad approach to pregnancy-related discrimination, as seen with pregnancy-related illness, unavailability or "morality" (each discussed above).[235]

Liability for treatment *related* to pregnancy resembles disability-related discrimination established by the Disability Discrimination Act 1995.[236] It suggests that that where the pregnancy is one step removed from the employer's act, the employer can be liable when, at the time of the treatment, it is unaware of the pregnancy. In a disability discrimination case, *Heinz v Kendrick*[237] the Lindsay, J. suggested obiter:

> "If a woman was, for example, sacked for repeatedly falling faint one morning over the machinery at which she worked or over

---

[232] *Caisse nationale d'assurance vieillesse des travailleurs salaries (CNAVTS) v Evelyne Thibault.* C-136/95, [1998] ECR I-2011, [1998] I.R.L.R. 399. In *Athis v Blue Coat School* [2005] All E.R. (D) 53 (Aug.), the EAT stated it could be discriminatory for a school not to inform a teacher on maternity leave that she could make representations regarding decisions about her performance-related pay.

[233] Above, para.4–047.

[234] SI 1999/3312, reg.20. Curiously, this phrase is not used for the parallel regulation on subjected to detriment: reg.19(2).

[235] Paragraphs 4–047, 4–045, and 4–046.

[236] Save that there is no justification defence. See now EA 2010 s.15. Discussed Ch.13, para.13–024.

[237] [2000] I.C.R. 491 (EAT), [24].

her food production line, would she not, objectively regarded, have been dismissed for 'a reason *connected with* her pregnancy' if she was able to demonstrate at the hearing that it had been her pregnancy that had made her faint, even if both she and the employer had thought at the time that she had fainted because she had been out clubbing too late the night before?"

Another scenario might be absenteeism because of a pregnancy 4–051 related illness, where the women may not be telling her employer of her pregnancy for fear of dismissal. In *Ramdoolar v Bycity Ltd*[238] a pregnant women was dismissed because she was unable to carry out routine tasks and occasionally was late for work. The employer was unaware that she was pregnant. The worker claimed for dismissal "connected to" her pregnancy using the Maternity and Parental Leave Regulations 1999 (above). The EAT declined to follow Lindsay J.'s opinion and held that for liability the employer has to know of the pregnancy. Further, obiter, an employer who was aware of the symptoms could not be fixed with liability even if he *ought* to have known she was pregnant (although an employer who *suspects* she was pregnant may be liable if he dismisses her to get her off the books before it is confirmed). This is going too far. It does not square even with the conventional view of direct discrimination, which holds that employers can be liable where they *ought* to have been aware that they were acting on discriminatory factors.[239] The decision, but not the obiter, accords with the later House of Lords' view that defendant must have known, or ought to have known, of the claimant's disability in order to be liable for disability-related discrimination (a view codified by EA 2010 s.15(2)).[240] Some of the rationale behind that view was that without knowledge of the disability at the time of the act, the defendant would be in no position to justify the challenged treatment.[241] Whatever the merits of that rationale, it cannot apply to pregnancy discrimination, because it carries no justification defence.

(5) Pregnancy, Pay and Benefits

As well as stipulating a right to maternity leave, the Pregnant 4–052 Workers Directive 92/85/EEC art.11 instructs Member States to establish a right to maternity pay to accompany the leave. The level of pay need only be the level of State sick pay in the Member State concerned. This is a minimum.[242] The ECJ has commented that the

---

[238] [2005] I.C.R. 368 (EAT) [23]–[24].
[239] See *King v Great Britain-China Centre* [1992] I.C.R. 516 (CA), above, para.4–006, p.84, and the discussion at para.4–021.
[240] *Lewisham LBC v Malcolm* [2008] 1 A.C. 1399. See further, below.
[241] ibid. [18] (Lord Bingham), [86] (Baroness Hale).
[242] See The Statutory Maternity Pay (General) Regulations 1986, SI 1986/1960.

level of maternity pay should not be set "so low as to undermine the purpose of maternity leave."[243] Employers may set conditions, such as 12 months' previous continuous employment (but no more). As with sick pay, employers are free to pay more than the legal minimum. Nonetheless, under the Pregnant Workers Directive, a pregnant woman may receive less pay than she would have done if she were not pregnant, either by comparison with her employer's sick pay or her normal salary.

The Equality Act 2010 s.73 introduces a "Maternity Equality Clause" into a woman's employment contract in three circumstances described in s.74. No comparator is required in these cases. The three circumstances are explained in the Explanatory Notes, which state that the clause will:

> "253. ... ensure that any pay increase a woman receives (or would have received if she had not been on maternity leave) is taken into account in the calculation of her maternity-related pay where her terms do not already provide for this.[244]

> 254. ... ensure that pay, including any bonus, is paid to the woman at the time she would have received it if she had not been on maternity leave.

> 255. ... provide for a woman's pay on her return to work following maternity leave to take account of any pay increase which she would have received if she had not been on statutory maternity leave."

Section 76 of the EA 2010 provides that the pregnancy and maternity *discrimination* provisions (EA 2010 ss.17 and 18) of the Act do not apply where a Maternity Clause operates.

4–053   Neither can maternity pay be challenged as discriminatory under the Equal Pay provisions. In *Gillespie v Northern Health and Social Services Board*,[245] women on maternity leave received full weekly pay for the first four weeks, nine-tenths for the next two weeks and then one-half for 12 weeks. The ECJ held that although maternity pay came within what is now art.157 TFEU (see Recast Directive 2006/54/EC art.4), this did not amount to discrimination because women on maternity leave were "in a special position which requires them to be afforded special protection, but which is not comparable either with that of a man or with that of a woman actually at work."[246]

The *Gillespie* ruling is essentially pragmatic. An alternative decision in effect would force employers to provide full pay, or at least their normal sick-pay (where it is above the State level), thus

---

[243] *Gillespie v Northern Health and Social Services Board* Case C-342/93, [1996] I.C.R. 498, [20].
[244] See *Alabaster v Woolwich Plc* Case C-147/02, [2004] ECR I-3101, below, para.4–054.
[245] Case C-342/93, [1996] I.C.R. 498, ECJ.
[246] ibid. [17].

rendering this part of the Pregnant Workers Directive redundant. As Advocate General Léger noted in *Gillespie*, to give full protection to pregnant women on maternity leave "would threaten to upset the balance of the entire social welfare system."[247] The theoretical weakness of this decision is illustrated in *Hoj Pedersen*,[248] where *before* maternity leave was due, a woman unavailable for work because of a pregnancy-related illness was given only half-pay, while other workers (this included women), absent for a non-pregnancy related illness, were given full pay. The ECJ held that this was discrimination on the ground of pregnancy, and so amounted to sex discrimination (under what is now art.157). This claim succeeded because, arising as it did before the maternity leave was due, it fell outside of the maternity leave and pay provisions of the Pregnant Workers Directive. Had the half-pay fallen within the maternity period, and thus the Pregnant Workers Directive, the claim would have failed.[249] Note though, that a comparison was required, and so this departs from the rule for *dismissals* for a pregnancy-related illness, which does not require a comparison with how a male worker would have been treated.[250]

The *Gillespie* ruling was applied in the following cases. In *Boyle v EOC*[251] the Civil Service paid the same amount for either sick pay or maternity pay, save that to qualify for maternity pay, the woman had to return to work for at least a month. Following the logic of *Gillespie,* the ECJ refused to compare the maternity pay with the sick pay, and held the condition did not amount to sex discrimination. In *Todd v Eastern Health and Social Services Board*[252] the Northern Ireland Court of Appeal held that *contractual* maternity pay, which was lower than the *contractual* sick pay, could not be challenged as discriminatory. In *Hoyland v ASDA*,[253] the EAT held that a bonus dependant on profits and attendance constituted "pay", and so (save for two weeks' compulsory maternity leave)[254] a women on maternity leave was not entitled to a bonus related to that period of absence.

The *Gillespie* ruling was sidestepped in *Alabaster v Woolwich Plc*,[255] **4-054** where the claimant's maternity pay was related to her salary. However, the formula pinned maternity pay to the salary some time before her leave began. Thus, a pay rise awarded after this time was not

---

[247] ibid. [48] (AG's Opinion).
[248] *Hoj Pedersen v Faellesforeningen for Danmarks Brugsforeninger and Dansk Tandlaegeforening* Case C-66/96, [1998] ECR I-7327, ECJ. See also In *North Western Health Board v McKenna* Case C-191/03, [2005] E.C.R. I-7631 (ECJ).
[249] ibid. [38]–[39].
[250] *Brown v Rentokil* Case C-399/96 [1998] I.C.R. 790 (ECJ), see above, para.4–047.
[251] Case C-411/96 1998 ECR I-6401.
[252] [1997] I.R.L.R. 410, NICA.
[253] [2005] I.C.R. 1235 (EAT), affirmed, [2006] CSIH 21.
[254] See now EA 2010 s.74(7)(b).
[255] Case C-147/02, [2004] ECR I-0000. Upon its return, the Court of Appeal implemented this ruling through the Equal Pay Act 1970, by disapplying the Act's requirement for a comparator: *Alabaster v Barclays Bank (No.2)* [2005] EWCA 508.

reflected in her maternity pay. The ECJ held that this *was* sex discrimination, under the equal pay provisions, as pregnant women did not receive the benefit of the pay rise, expressed in their maternity pay, because they were pregnant. The Court stated that so far as maternity pay is related to salary, any pay rise from the calculation date to the end of maternity leave must be reflected in the maternity pay.[256]

Detriments which are not pay but are related to maternity leave fall outside the *Gillespie* ruling, and should be challengeable as maternity leave discrimination (see above, para.4–049).

---

[256] ibid. [50].

CHAPTER 5

HARASSMENT AND OTHER UNLAWFUL ACTS

INTRODUCTION

This chapter covers legal *definitions* of harassment, while Chapter 8 **5–001** covers an employer's liability for harassment in the workplace.[1] It also rounds together other acts made unlawful by the legislation: "Instructing, Causing, or Inducing," or "Aiding", unlawful acts of discrimination, harassment, or victimisation.

---

[1] At para.8–008.

1. HARASSMENT—A BRIEF HISTORY

5–002   In both the UK and United States, the first major pieces of discrimination legislation[2] did not include a concept of harassment.
Consequently, courts developed the law of harassment as a form of
direct discrimination, and these developments took place in the
employment field.[3] The major problem with the direct discrimination
model in this context is the need for a comparison with how a person
without the protected characteristic would have been treated. This
means that the person who harassed all races, or both sexes, equally
badly, could escape liability. The symmetrical nature of direct discrimination legitimises arguments such as: "In this office both whites
and blacks get racial abuse". Claims of sexual harassment are the
most vulnerable, because conduct of a *sexual* nature, per se, was
beyond the scope of *sex* discrimination legislation. The US courts
were more imaginative than the British ones when faced with this
problem. It so happened that the first major US federal case to for-
mulise harassment as a form of direct discrimination was brought on
racial grounds. *Rogers v EEOC*[4] established that a "working environment heavily charged with discrimination" could discriminate
against a Hispanic worker. In 1980, the US enforcement agency, the
Equal Opportunities Employment Commission (EEOC), published
guidelines for sexual harassment, which included this definition:

> "Unwelcome sexual advances, requests for sexual favors, and
> other verbal or physical conduct of a sexual nature constitute
> sexual harassment when (1) submission to such conduct is made
> either explicitly or implicitly a term or condition of an indivi-
> dual's employment, (2) submission to or rejection of such con-
> duct by an individual is used as the basis for employment
> decisions affecting such individual, or (3) such conduct has the
> purpose or effect of unreasonably interfering with an individual's
> work performance or creating an intimidating, hostile, or
> offensive working environment."[5]

This definition, which the US Supreme Court adopted wholesale,[6] is
designed to cover two scenarios. First, where sexual favours are

---

[2] Sex Discrimination Act 1975 (UK), and Civil Rights Act 1964 (US). For a discussion of
harassment at common law, see D. Brodie, "Deterring harassment at common law" (2006)
36 ILJ 213.
[3] The publication of C. Mackinnon, *Sexual Harassment of Working Women* (New Haven, CT:
Yale UP, 1979) was a key development in the legal recognition of sexual harassment.
[4] 454 F 2d 234 (5th Cir 1971).
[5] Section 1604.11(a). (See *www.eeoc.gov*, and click on "sexual harassment", and then "The
regulations".)
[6] See e.g. *Meritor Savings Bank v Vinson* 477 US 57 (1986).

sought in return for employment advantages ("quid pro quo"). The second is where the conduct causes a hostile environment[7] (which is relevant to other unlawful grounds of harassment).

Nonetheless, problems persisted and eventually in Europe and the   **5–003** UK, dedicated statutory provisions outlawed employment harassment. They began with race, sexual orientation and religion or belief (from 2003), Disability (2004), sexual and sex harassment (2005), and age (2006).[8] The key to these statutory definitions was that there is no need for a comparison, thus moving away from the symmetrical model inherent in direct discrimination. Much of the language used in the US case law was incorporated into the statutory definitions. Hence, even though the US law is rooted in direct discrimination, it remains instructive for statutory harassment in Britain.

The Equality Act 2010 s.26 absorbed this range of coverage, and outlaws harassment on any of the protected characteristics, save for pregnancy and maternity, and marriage and civil partnership (s.26(5)). The coverage is broad, but not universal. In general, it covers:

- provision of services (s.29(3)) and public functions (29(6)), save for sexual orientation or religion or belief (29(8));

- management and disposal of premises (ss.33(3), 34(2), 35(2)), save for age (32(1)) and sexual orientation or religion or belief (33(6), 34(4), 35(4));

- work (s.40), including contract workers (41(2)), partnerships (44(3)), occupational pensions (61(2));

- ex-employees (s.108(2));

- schools (s.85(3)), save for gender reassignment, sexual orientation or religion or belief (85(10));

- further and higher education (s.91(5));

- associations (s.101(4)).

The Equality Act 2010 outlaws three types of harassment: harassment   **5–004** related to a protected characteristic, sexual harassment, and (if related to sex, gender reassignment, or of a sexual nature) less favourable treatment based on a person's rejection of, or submission to, unwanted conduct ("quid pro quo"). Where an act of harassment would also amount to direct discrimination, a direct discrimination

---

[7] Adopted from the analysis of C. Mackinnon, *Sexual Harassment of Working Women*, (New Haven, CT: Yale UP, 1979), at p.32.
[8] Respectively, RRA 1976 s.3A (in force July 19, 2003); EE (SO) Regs 2003 SI 2003/1661, reg.5 (December 1, 2003); EE(RB) Regs 2003, SI 2003/1660, reg.5 (December 2, 2003); DDA 1995 s.3B; SDA 1975 s.4A (October 1, 2005); EE (Age) Regs 2006, SI 2006/1031, reg.6 (October 1, 2006).

claim is barred because s.212(1) decrees that "detriment" (which is usually necessary for liability) does not include conduct which amounts to harassment.[9] In other words, harassment and direct discrimination are mutually exclusive.

2. DEFINITION OF HARASSMENT

(1) Harassment Related to a Protected Characteristic

5–005   **"26 Harassment**

(1) A person (A) harasses another (B) if—

(a) A engages in unwanted conduct related to a relevant protected characteristic, and
(b) the conduct has the purpose or effect of—
(i) violating B's dignity, or
(ii) creating an intimidating, hostile, degrading, humiliating or offensive environment ['hostile environment'] for B."

(a) "Related to"

5–006   The phrase *related to* replaces the phrase in previous harassment provisions *on the ground of*. The problem with the previous phrase was illustrated by the facts in *Kettle v Ward*.[10] Here, there was a history of enmity between a cleaner, Ms Ward, and her manager, Mr Gowens. On one occasion Ms Ward was in the women's toilets, waiting for someone to leave a cubicle. Her manager thought she was malingering and barged into the toilet, announcing: "You'll not hide in here". When Ms Ward asserted that he should not enter the women's toilet, he stated: "I can go anywhere in the factory." It was held that this was not *sex* discrimination because Mr Gowens would have done the same to a male cleaner in the male toilets.

Nonetheless, the first statutory formula, introduced into the Sex Discrimination Act 1975 (SDA 1975), would not resolve this issue either, because the conduct was not *on the ground of* sex. Following a legal challenge, the SDA 1975 version was amended with the phrase

---

[9] This does not apply where the harassment provision does not apply: s.212(5). See below, para.5–020, p.141.
[10] (2006) UKEATS/0016/06/MT (EAT). The case pre-dates any statutory harassment provision, but the facts illustrate the limitation with the subsequent statutory definition in the SDA 1975 s.4A. See also *B v A* (2007) EAT/0450/06.

related to sex to address this problem (and to comply with the parent Directive).[11] The Equality Act 2010 now employs this phrase for all the protected characteristics covered.

The formula is not restricted to *her* sex, or *his* race, or *his* sexual orientation, and so on. (There is no possessive adjective.) This facilitates claims of "third party" harassment (for instance, where an employer makes derogatory remarks about a worker's disabled baby),[12] and "perceived" harassment (where the harasser wrongly perceives the victim is Jewish, Muslim, gay, Pakistani, etc.), as well harassment where nobody's protected characteristic is in question.[13] These cases are discussed in Chapter 4, para.4–025. This accords with the purpose of the provisions. A woman, for instance, could find her working environment "offensive" or "hostile", or have her dignity violated, as male workers make derogatory remarks about women, even though their conduct is not directed at her, and irrespective of whether they are directed at anybody at all. Further, another *man* may find this environment hostile or offensive. Likewise, a white man may find racist comments create for him a hostile workplace.

(b) Same-Group Harassment

The statutory definition is broad enough to cover the situation where the harasser and the victim share the same protected characteristic and the conduct is related to that characteristic.[14] Some examples have emerged from the United States. In *Oncale v Sundowner Offshore Services*[15] the Supreme Court held that "male-to-male" *sexual* harassment could amount to sex discrimination, and suggested that for cases where the harassment is not sexual in nature, there could still be liability where, say, a female worker harasses a female colleague in sex-specific derogatory terms because of hostility towards the woman's presence in the workplace.[16] Accordingly, it can be unlawful harassment for a black supervisor to call a black worker "black boy" and "nigger".[17] So long as the conduct is related to a protected characteristic, the harasser's protected characteristic need not bar a claim.

5–007

---

[11] SI 2008/656, reg.3, following *EOC v Secretary of State for Trade and Industry* [2007] I.C.R. 1234 (HC Admin).

[12] See e.g. *Coleman v Attridge Law* Case C-303/06 [1998] 3 C.M.L.R. 27 (ECJ); *Saini v All Saints Haque Centre* [2009] I.R.L.R. 74 (EAT) (harassing worker on the ground his associate's religion).

[13] *English v Thomas Sanderson Blinds* [2008] EWCA 1421 (homophobic harassment of worker, where harassers knew worker was not gay).

[14] This is expressed for direct discrimination by EA 2010 (s.24). See also *R. (E) v Governing Body of JFS* [2009] UKSC 15, [152(i)].

[15] 523 US 75 (1998). See also the UK case *BHS v Walker* (2005) UKEAT/0001/05/TM, where "female-to-female" sexual harassment amounted to sex discrimination, although this was not an issue in the appeal.

[16] ibid. at 80.

[17] *Ross v Douglas County, Nebraska* 234 F 3d 391 (8th Cir 2000).

Of course, in other cases, the protected characteristic(s) of the harasser could be relevant. Where, say, two Pakistani workers exchange self-deprecating remarks about Pakistanis, their racial origin *may* be relevant to proving whether this violated somebody's dignity or created a hostile environment.

(c) Conduct

5–008 The conduct may take any form, such as oral, written, the displaying of pictures or symbols or even dressing up.[18] For harassment related to *sex*, it must be emphasised that this need not be *sexual* harassment, which is provided for separately.[19] The Government accompanied the introduction of statutory harassment in 2005 with these examples:[20]

> "(i) Male workers placing tools on a high shelf, out of the reach of the female workers.
>
> (ii) A manager makes humiliating and embarrassing remarks to a female subordinate and in one incident depicts her as 'brash', which a tribunal finds to be insensitive and to have gender undertones—it being more frequently applied to a woman than a man.
>
> (iii) In a predominantly female workplace, a male complains about the climate and culture, caused by, e.g. belittling remarks.
>
> (iv) Derogatory remarks relating to the person's gender, e.g. 'Don't worry your pretty little head about it'; 'she's not thinking straight today—it must be the time of the month'; and 'you're looking a bit fat—do you have a bun in the oven?'
>
> (v) A pregnant worker suffers derogatory comments, such as she will no longer be up to the job.
>
> (vi) A sole woman on a team is always asked to take notes and make the tea, because it's considered women's work."[21]

Other examples may include derogatory remarks about women's driving skills, emotional rationality, grasp of political affairs, or other gender (but not necessarily sexual) stereotypes.

---

[18] In the US case *Harris v International Paper* 765 F Supp 1509 (1991) *vacated in part* 765 F Supp 1529 (1991) the symbol "KKK" (representing the Ku Klux Klan) was written on the (black) victim's work materials, and colleagues dressed up in white clothes and pranced around the black victim to recall Ku Klux Klan events.

[19] See also the confusion between harassment on the ground of sexual orientation and sexual harassment evident in *English v Thomas Sanderson Blinds* [2008] EWCA 1421, especially [39] (Sedley L.J.).

[20] "Changes to Sex Discrimination Legislation in Great Britain: Explaining the Employment Equality (Sex Discrimination) Regulations 2005", 2005 (URN 05/1603), p.7.

[21] ibid. p.9.

(d) "Unwanted" Conduct

Issues of proof aside, the courts must decide precisely what is meant **5–009** by "unwanted." It could range from merely that the conduct was not invited, to a requirement that the claimant overtly expressed her aversion to such conduct. The only case history on this point relates to *sexual* harassment, which is discussed below (para.5–027). However, the Government issued some guidance in 2003 that observed, on the one hand, where a person is engaged in light-hearted banter and remarks on her own sexual orientation or religion, a colleague's repetition of those comments in the same context might not be considered as unwanted. On the other hand, a worker may "go along with" office banter to fit in. Indeed, the more offensive the banter, the more difficult it may become for a junior or minority worker to complain.[22]

(e) Purpose or Effect

The use of the word *or* gives this a particularly wide sweep, which has **5–010** been explained thus:

> "... a respondent may be held liable on the basis that the effect of his conduct has been to produce the proscribed consequences [violating dignity or hostile environment] even if that was not his purpose; and, conversely, that he may be liable if he acted for the purposes of producing the proscribed consequences but did not in fact do so...".[23]

This means that the elements should not be blurred. Where it is shown that the defendant's *purpose* was to violate the claimant's dignity or create a hostile environment, there is no need to show that it actually had that effect. A separate incident could be that irrespective of the defendant's purpose (or motive or intent, however benign), his conduct had the required *effect*. Thus:

> "Where factory or office banter creates an environment that (for example) violates the dignity of a gay employee or creates a degrading or humiliating environment for a female member of staff, then (subject to a successful deployment of the 'reasonably practicable' steps defence)[24] the scene is set for a successful complaint of harassment against the employer, even though that

---

[22] DTI explanatory notes on the EE(RB)R 2003 SI 2003/1660 and the EE(SO)R 2003 SI 2003/1661.

[23] *Richmond Pharmacology v Dhaliwal* (2009) I.C.R. 724 (EAT), [14] (Underhill J.). For a case where an employment tribunal mistakenly looked only for "purpose", see *Garret v Lidl Ltd* (2009) UKEAT/0541/08/ZT, [28].

[24] See Ch.8, para.8–101.

employer may have neither known nor approved of the behaviour in question."[25]

(f) The Required Effect

5–011   **"26 Harassment** ...

(4) In deciding whether conduct has the effect referred to in
subsection (1)(b) [violation of dignity or hostile environment],
each of the following must be taken into account—

(a) the perception of B;
(b) the other circumstances of the case;
(c) whether it is reasonable for the conduct to have that
effect."

(i) Violates dignity or creates a hostile environment

5–012 Section 26 goes further than the US definition, and indeed the EU
definition presented in the equality Directives, which require that the
conduct violates the person's dignity *and* creates a hostile environment.[26] The result is that a person who feels that his dignity was
violated can claim, even though there is no evidence of a hostile
environment. When the Bill was in the House of Lords, Lord Lester
(a well-known liberal and human rights lawyer), complained that this
would encourage "frivolous and crazy claims" by "thin-skinned
people whose dignity was being violated." This was because:

" 'Dignity' is not a legal rule. It is a value. To allow someone to
bring a claim on the basis of their dignity is a dangerous thing to
do. It is not saved by the requirement of reasonableness because
it still allows the claim to be brought."[27]

For a case brought on violation of dignity, see *Richmond Pharmacology v Dhaliwal*,[28] below, para.5–015.

(ii) Objective or subjective?

5–013 Section 26(4) mandates that the claimant must have perceived that
the conduct had the required effect ("subjective"), *and* that her

---

[25] *Harvey on Industrial Relations and Employment Law* (London: Butterworths, 2010), [425].
[26] For a challenge to this discrepancy in Northern Ireland, see *Re Christian Institute* [2008]
I.R.L.R. 36 (NIQB).
[27] *Hansard* HL (Equality Bill Committee), Vol.716, col.577 (January 13, 2010).
[28] (2009) I.C.R. 724 (EAT).

perception was reasonable ("objective"). Ultimately, the test is objective.[29] In *Richmond Pharmacology v Dhaliwal*, Underhill J. explained:

> "... if, for example, the tribunal believes that the claimant was unreasonably prone to take offence, then, even if she did genuinely feel her dignity to have been violated, there will have been no harassment within the meaning of the section."[30]

As a template, this is too simplistic. First, it suggests that a person "unreasonably prone to take offence" cannot be the victim of harassment. Quite plainly, such a person still could reasonably take offence at some conduct. In *Commissioner of Police of the Metropolis v Osinaike*,[31] a tribunal found the claimant was prone to take offence and read offensive conduct into innocuous events (evidenced by many unfounded claims), but nonetheless held it reasonable for her to have taken offence when her employer suggested she needed to see a psychiatrist.[32]

Second, Underhill J.'s comment appears straightforward when envisaging severe and overt incidents of harassment, or (at the other extreme) obviously hypersensitive claimants. But with more subtle— and no doubt common—forms of harassment, a lot will turn on the meaning ascribed to the word "reasonable". There are a number of options the courts could choose, presented here progressing from heavily objective to heavily subjective. This discussion relates purely to the objective/subjective debate.

5–014

1. The man on the Clapham omnibus

If courts were look at the situation from the point of view of the "man in the street", the law will fall short of its purpose of promoting diversity. A normal sensitivity of a black

---

[29] *Driskel v Peninsula Business Services* [2000] I.R.L.R. 151 (EAT) at 155 (Holland J.). The Government expressly endorsed this *Driskel* approach in the *pre-consultation* Explanatory Notes to the Regulations on Sexual Orientation and Religion or Belief, and the amendment regulations to the Disability Discrimination Act (e.g. Explanatory Notes to the *pre-consultation draft Disability Discrimination Act 1995 (Amendment) Regulations 2003*, [40]. It stated elsewhere that the "ultimate judgement is an objective assessment" ("Equality and Diversity: Updating the Sex Discrimination Act. Government Response to Consultation", 2005 (URN 05/1345) p.9, [3.17]). It has been held that this objective approach complies with the EC Directives: *EOC v Secretary of State for Trade and Industry* [2007] I.C.R. 1234 (HC Admin) [30]–[35]. For racial harassment, s.26(4)(c) does not reflect the recommendation of the Lawrence Inquiry to define a racist incident (criminal and non-criminal) as "any incident which is perceived to be racist by the victim or any other person." The Stephen Lawrence Inquiry, Report of an Inquiry by Sir William Macpherson, advised by Tom Cook, The Right Reverend Dr John Sentamu, Dr Richard Stone, February 1999. Presented to Parliament by the Home Secretary. Cm 4262-I, London: TSO, Ch.47, paras 12–13. See also Ch.1, para.1–002.

[30] [2009] I.C.R. 724 (EAT), [15].

[31] (2010) UKEAT/0373/09/SM. Decided under RRA 1976, s.3A.

[32] ibid. [38]. However, the EAT reversed on the basis that the comment was not on racial grounds.

person may appear to be a hypersensitivity to a white person. And so, judging a claimant's sensitivity by the standard of the average person is unlikely to account for the diverse range of characteristics expressly protected by the Equality Act 2010 and its harassment provisions. There is little merit in the law lecturing a black woman, with a history of discrimination and persistent "low level" racial abuse in her life, that she must be as robust as the "average white person" in the face of seemingly minor workplace racial slurs or "banter".

Of course, most tribunal panellists would consider themselves to be "the reasonable man in the street", and might endow the claimant with their own values. Here, liability could depend on, say, the race, sex, religion, age, or sexual orientation, as well as the experiences of, a tribunal panel, leading to a host of inconsistencies.

2. *Was it reasonable for the claimant to take offence?*
Here, the "reasonable" person is endowed with the protected characteristic in question, (e.g. by race, sex, sexual orientation, religion, disability) and the court asks if the average person with this protected characteristic (e.g. black, Indian, female, gay, wheelchair-bound) would have been similarly offended.

5–015   In *Richmond Pharmacology v Dhaliwal*,[33] the claimant, a British woman with ethnic Indian origin, resigned from her job, causing strained relations with her Medical Director. At a meeting, he told her: "We will probably bump into each other in future, unless you are married off in India." This was an "ill-judged remark" not intended to cause offence. Nonetheless, the comment—invoking a stereotype of Indian women and forced marriages—left the claimant "very upset". The EAT considered this a "borderline" case, but upheld a finding that the comment had violated the claimant's dignity. Underhill J. gave little guidance on the meaning of "reasonable", but the decision suggests that for the tribunal, the reasonable person was a British woman of Indian origin, and although not *all* such women would have taken offence, many would have, and so it was reasonable for such a person to have taken offence.

This resembles the approach taken in the United States, which has been explored in more detail. The starting point resembles s.26(4): "the objective severity of the harassment should be judged from the perspective of the reasonable

[33] (2009) I.C.R. 724 (EAT), [15]. Decided under RRA 1976 s.3A.

person in the plaintiff's position, considering all the circumstances."[34] In the context of racial harassment, its logic was explained thus: in a society ingrained with cultural stereotypes, blacks regularly face negative attitudes, often unconsciously held. As a result, even "an inadvertent racial slight unnoticed either by its white speaker or white bystanders will reverberate in the memory of its black victim." Accordingly, the trier of fact must "walk a mile in the victim's shoes" to understand the effects.[35] In the context of sex and sexual harassment, it was observed that the "sex-blind reasonable person standard tends to be male-biased" and that if only an objective view is considered, a court "would run the risk of reinforcing the prevailing level of discrimination."[36] For instance, "A male supervisor might believe ... that it is legitimate for him to tell a female subordinate that she has a 'great figure' or 'nice legs'."[37] Of course, the same logic applies to cases related to age, disability, gender reassignment, religion or belief, and sexual orientation.

3. *Was it unreasonable for the claimant to take offence?*
This may appear to be the same question as above, simply **5–016**
posed in the negative. But there is a difference of substance between to two. Here, *even if just one* of the average persons with the relevant protected characteristic would have been similarly offended, the claimant was not unreasonable in taking offence.

This is best illustrated by the established approach to the question of whether treatment is *less* favourable to establish direct discrimination. In *R. v Birmingham City Council, ex parte EOC*[38] the House of Lords held that it is enough that victims perceived—reasonably—that they had been treated less favourably, even in the face of objective evidence to the

---

[34] *Oncale v Sundowner Offshore Services* 523 US 75, at 81 (Sup Ct 1998).
[35] *Harris v International Paper* 765 F Supp 1509, at 1515–1516 (vacated on other grounds 765 F Supp 1529) (1991), citing: Lawrence, "The id, the ego, and equal protection: reckoning with unconscious racism", 39 Stan L Rev 317 (1987); Matsuda, "Public response to racist speech: considering the victim's story", 87 Mich L Rev 2320, 2326–2335 (1989); Williams, "Alchemical notes: reconstructing ideals from deconstructed rights", 22 Harv CR-CL L Rev 401, 406–413 (1987) (explaining why black and white apartment-seekers assume different perspectives on the formalities of renting an apartment).
[36] *Ellison v Brady* 924 F 2d 872, at 878-880 (9th Cir 1991), citing, Ehrenreich, "Pluralist Myths and powerless men: the ideology of reasonableness in sexual harassment law", 99 Yale LJ 1177, at 1207–1208 (1990) (men tend to view some forms of sexual harassment as "harmless social interactions to which only overly-sensitive women would object"); Abrams, "Gender discrimination and transformation of workplace norms", 42 Vand L Rev 1183, at 1203 (1989) (the characteristically male view depicts sexual harassment as comparatively harmless amusement).
[37] *Lipsett v University of Puerto Rice* 864 F 2d 881, at 898 (1st Cir, 1988).
[38] [1989] A.C. 1155 (HL). See Ch.4, para.4–015, p.91.

contrary. Thus, it was not unreasonable for victims to prefer grammar schools, even though the evidence was that children were no worse off in comprehensive schools. Accordingly, in *Gill v El Vino*,[39] it was reasonable for *a* woman to consider that bar service for men and waited table-service for women to be less favourable, because she was denied a choice, even though many women may have preferred that arrangement. In *Chief Constable of West Yorkshire v Khan*[40] it was reasonable for a job candidate to expect an employer's reference, even though it would have been negative and *lessened* his chances. Of course, most people in his position would have preferred that the reference was not provided.

4. *Unusual but not unreasonable*

5–017
Bearing in mind the defendant's purpose can be irrelevant, it might be reasonable for a person with particularly severe (undisclosed) personal circumstances to be offended by otherwise innocuous conduct. For instance, a woman with a history of sexual abuse my feel violated by an otherwise innocuous one-off comment, where a male work colleague refers to a newspaper story supportive of a man acquitted of rape. In such cases, the woman might be unusually prone to take offence, but not *unreasonably* so. As s.26(4)(b) mandates that other circumstances should be considered, a claimant's personal and hitherto undisclosed history would seem to be relevant. Here, the reasonable person should be endowed with the personal characteristic(s) *and* personal circumstances of the claimant.

These examples illustrate the difficulty of deciding how far defendants should be responsible for a modern environment free from bigotry and outdated stereotypes, and the individual (and sometimes undisclosed) sensitivities of their workers, pupils, students, tenants, customers, as the case may be. The courts will draw a line somewhere, either with some general guidance, or, more likely, on a case-by-case basis, using "common sense" and pragmatism under the shelter of the relatively elastic statutory element "reasonableness".

(iii) "The other circumstances of the case"

5–018
The circumstances may be particularly pertinent in one-off incidents of harassment.

---

[39] [1983] Q.B. 425 (CA). See Ch.4, para.4–002.
[40] [2002] 1 W.L.R. 1947 (HL). Discussed Ch.7, para.7–008, p.211 (a case on victimisation under the RRA 1976).

"Suppose that Y, a man, shouts and swears loudly at Z, a woman. He does so immediately after Z accidentally spills a cup of coffee over his clothing; and prior to this Y had never shouted or sworn at Z. ... The spilling of the coffee is not merely explanation; it is also part of the context in which the tribunal must decide whether there is a prima facie case of sexual harassment. And this is the case whether or not Y's conduct is thought to be reasonable."[41]

By contrast, in *Insitu Cleaning v Heads*[42] (a direct discrimination case), the company manager who was also the director's son, said to a much older female supervisor, "Hiya, big tits". The EAT stated that liability for one-off incidents was "a question of fact and degree." It noted that for a boss's son to make such a comment to a female worker nearly twice his age would cause distress, and this was compounded by his status and his aggressive, arrogant and dismissive attitude. In these circumstances, the defendant was found liable for direct sex discrimination.[43]

Other circumstances could include seemingly innocuous conduct, which forms part of a pattern of harassment and so becomes relevant. *Harvey's* offers two examples:

"An invitation to dinner is hardly harassment by itself, but may become so if persisted in, or accompanied by inducements that go beyond the limits of convention. An event showing sexual interest may not itself be unlawful, but it can be important in showing the existence of a continuing regime of harassment."[44]

Also, as noted above (para.5–017), any undisclosed personal circumstances of the claimant may be relevant.

There is much guidance in the United States on this matter: the **5–019** EEOC Guidelines for sexual harassment cases provide that the court should "look at the record as a whole and at the totality of the circumstances".[45] These may include: the frequency of the discriminatory conduct; its severity; whether it is physically threatening or humiliating, or a mere offensive utterance; and whether it unreasonably interferes with an employee's work performance.[46] Other factors such as the victim's provocative speech or dress may be used

---

[41] *Nazir v Aslam* (2010) UKEAT/0332/09/RN, [71] (Judge Richardson).
[42] [1995] I.R.L.R. 4 (EAT).
[43] ibid. [10]–[11].
[44] *Harvey on Industrial Relations and Employment Law* (London: Butterworths, 2010), [417].
[45] Section 1604.11(b). (See *www.eeoc.gov*, and click on "sexual harassment", and then "The regulations".) Approved by the Supreme Court in *Meritor Savings Bank v Vinson* 477 US 57, at 69 (1986).
[46] *Harris v Forklift Systems* 510 US 17, at 23 (Sup Ct 1993).

to show that the conduct of a sexual nature was welcome.[47] It also allows a court to consider the context of the conduct: a coach may smack a football player's buttocks as he heads on to the field, but should not do the same to the secretary (male or female) back at the office.[48]

Where the conduct is verbal, one US court quoted this saw of Oliver Wendell Holmes:

> "'[A] word is not a crystal, transparent and unchanged' but 'is the skin of a living thought and may vary greatly in color and content according to the circumstances and the time in which it is used'."[49]

Thus, there may be liability where a white supervisor uses code words such as "another one", "one of them" and "poor people" when referring to black workers.[50]

(iv) Competing rights—free speech and freedom to manifest religion

5–020 **Equality Act 2010**

Explanatory Note (99):

"In determining the effect of the unwanted conduct, courts and tribunals will continue to be required to balance competing rights on the facts of a particular case. For example this could include balancing the rights of freedom of expression (as set out in Article 10 of the European Convention on Human Rights) and of academic freedom against the right not to be offended in deciding whether a person has been harassed."

This highlights another factor to consider when deciding if the conduct had the required effect. We have seen that a person's right to express a view (related to a protected characteristic) may be tempered by another's sensitivity. Conversely, a person's sensitivity (related to a protected characteristic) may have to be tolerant of another's expressed view. The statutory word "reasonable" (26(4)(c)) is the legal vehicle for this "balancing" act.

The most obvious protected characteristics for concern here are religion and sexual orientation. For religion, the problem is that:

---

[47] ibid. at 69. See *Mclean v Satellite Technology* 673 F Supp 1458 (ED Mo 1987), below para.5–027, p.146.

[48] Per Scalia J., *Oncale v Sundowner Offshore Services* 523 US 75, at 81 (1998).

[49] *Towne v Eisner*, 245 US 418, at 425 (1918), cited in *Horney v Westfield Gage* 211 F Supp 2d 291, at 309 (2002). See also, R. Kennedy, *Nigger: The Strange Case of a Troublesome Word* (New York: Pantheon Books, 2002).

[50] *Aman v Cort Furniture* 85 F 3d 1074, at 1083 (3rd Cir 1996).

"One person's strong expression of religious belief is another religion's blasphemy."[51] Thus, by expressing one's religious beliefs, a person might offend another's religious belief. Further, some religions believe, and wish to express the view, that homosexuality is sinful,[52] and would look for their right to do so under ECHR art.9 (freedom of religion). Of course, such conduct could amount to sexual orientation harassment. These situations may present particularly difficult balancing acts.

In some cases that will not be necessary. It might be that because of this difficulty the Act disapplies the harassment provisions for religion or belief and sexual orientation, in the areas of the provision of services, premises, and schools.[53] The government defended this position by stating that harassment in these areas—such as school bullying—could be covered by the direct discrimination provisions.[54]

(v) When does the conduct become unlawful?
A tribunal must decide whether the conduct was serious enough to have the effect of violating a person's dignity or creating a hostile environment. In *Richmond Pharmacology v Dhaliwal*,[55] Underhill J. offered some general guidance:

5–021

> "We accept that not every racially slanted adverse comment or conduct may constitute the violation of a person's dignity. Dignity is not necessarily violated by things said or done which are trivial or transitory, particularly if it should have been clear that any offence was unintended. While it is very important that employers, and tribunals, are sensitive to the hurt that can be caused by racially offensive comments or conduct ... it is also important not to encourage a culture of hypersensitivity or the imposition of legal liability in respect of every unfortunate phrase."

This suggests a pragmatic rather than technical approach. For hostile environment claims in US employment discrimination cases, workers are expected to be somewhat robust, and this is governed with a relatively technical approach. The standard is that that the conduct

---

[51] House of Commons Public Bill Committee on the Equality Bill 2008–2009, 16th Sitting, [563] (Dr Harris).

[52] See *Re Christian Institute* [2008] I.R.L.R. 36 (NIQB). For a case where the claimant's religious views clashed with their employer's obligation not to discriminate on the ground of sexual orientation, see *Islington v Ladele* [2009] I.C.R. 387 (EAT), above, para.3–021.

[53] See para.5–004, above.

[54] *Hansard* HL (Equality Bill Committee), Vol.716, col.582 (January 13, 2010) (Baroness Thorton). EA 2010 s.212(5) disapplies the "mutually exclusive" rule in 212(1) ("detriment"), a provision so convoluted, Lord Lester thought it "hilarious" that anyone thought that the public would understand it: *Hansard* HL (Equality Bill Committee), Vol.716, col.584 (January 13, 2010).

[55] (2009) I.C.R. 724 (EAT), [15]. See further above, para.5–015.

must be "sufficiently severe or pervasive to alter the conditions of the victim's employment".[56] In practice, this "working conditions" standard has meant that two racial comments (interracial marriage was "disgusting"; blacks are "lynched" in this area) within a month did not create a hostile environment;[57] neither did one racial comment ("Nigger, you're suspended") in response to the claimant's persistent interruptions of a meeting.[58] Further, this law "does not reach genuine but innocuous differences in the ways men and women interact", and "requires neither asexuality nor androgyny in the workplace."[59] Moreover, it seems, that some "one-off" serious instances may not amount to sexual harassment: a male forcibly fondling a colleague's breast,[60] and a State governor making sexual advances to an employee, including stroking her leg and exposing himself to her.[61] On the other hand, victims do not have to show an "economic" or "tangible" loss,[62] and the environment need not be so hostile to affect the victim's mental or physical health.[63] Examples of working conditions being altered include six instances of harassing a Jew;[64] five to ten references to a worker as "nigger",[65] and a supervisor continually demeaning a worker before his colleagues because of the worker's professed religious views.[66]

5–022   British courts are most unlikely to adopt this "working-conditions" standard for a number of reasons. First, in the employment context, the US model is restricted to the working-conditions standard because it has been developed entirely from the statutory definition of discrimination, which must be related to "compensation, terms, conditions, or privileges of employment."[67] By contrast, the Equality Act 2010, by s.40(1), simply states that an employer must not harass employees or applicants.[68] Second, the UK legislation allows for damages for injury to feelings, whether or not compensation is due under any other head.[69]

---

[56] *Harris v Forklift Systems* 510 US 17, at 21 (Sup. Ct 1993).
[57] *Logan v Kautex Textron* 259 F 3d 635, at 639 (7th Cir 2001).
[58] *Sanders v Village of Dixmoor* 178 F 3d 869, at 870 (7th Cir 1999).
[59] *Oncale v Sundowner Offshore Services* 523 US 75, at 81 (Sup Ct 1998).
[60] *Brooks v City of San Mateo* 229 F 3d 917 (9th Cir 2000). However, the court suggested a one-off incident by a workplace *superior*, rather than a colleague, might be severe enough to be actionable (at 927 n.9).
[61] *Jones v Clinton* 990 F Supp 657 (ED Ark 1998), appeal dismissed 161 F 3d 528 (8th Cir 1998).
[62] *Meritor Savings Bank v Vinson* 477 US 57, at 64 (Sup Ct 1986).
[63] *Terry v Ashcroft* 336 F 3d 128, at 148 (2nd Cir 2003).
[64] *Shanoff v Illinois Department of Human Services* 258 F 3d 696, at 698–699 (7th Cir 2001).
[65] *Rodgers v Western Southern Life Ins* 12 F 3d 668, at 673 (7th Cir 1993).
[66] *Compston v Borden* 424 F Supp 157, at 160–161 (SD Ohio 1976).
[67] Civil Rights Act 1964, Title VII, s.703(a) (codified as 42 USC s.2000e-2).
[68] In other fields, similar, phrasing is used e.g.: Provision of Services (s.29(3); Pensions (s.61(2); Schools (60(2); and Further and Higher Education (91(5)).
[69] EA 2010 s.119(4).

(2) Sexual Harassment

(a) A Brief History

Before dedicated provisions for sexual harassment were first intro-   **5–023**
duced in 2005,[70] claims of sexual harassment had to be couched as
direct sex discrimination. This necessitated a comparison with how a
man was, or would have been, treated. This comparison was a major
obstacle, where the distinction between sexual conduct and conduct
based on a person's gender become vital. The House of Lords made
this point emphatically in the joint case of *Pearce v Governing Body of
Mayfield Secondary School* and *Macdonald v A-G for Scotland.*[71] In
Pearce, the claimant, a lesbian, was regularly called "lesbian",
"dyke", "lesbian shit", "lemon", "lezzie" or "lez". She went off sick
for a second time and took early retirement. Her claim of sexual
harassment, argued as sex discrimination, failed. The House of Lords
compared the claimant to a homosexual male and concluded that the
comparator would have suffered a "comparable campaign," albeit
using different language. In *Macdonald,* both male and female military staff were subjected to abusive and demeaning interrogation
about their sex lives. The decision in this case was made all the easier
by the existence of a real comparator, and so, inevitably, the House
found that there was no discrimination on the ground of the claimant's sex. Accordingly, in *Brumfitt v Ministry of Defence,*[72] a military training officer used sexual, offensive and obscene language
directed at both male and female participants. Although Ms Brumfitt
found the conduct "offensive and humiliating to her as a woman", it
was held that the conduct was not on the ground of sex, and so her
claim, couched again as direct sex discrimination, failed. This logic
was taken to an absurd conclusion in *Stewart v Cleveland Guest
(Engineering)*[73] where the EAT found no error of law in an industrial
tribunal's decision that the display of naked female pin-ups in a
factory where the prevalent (male) attitude treated women as sex
objects, treated both male and female workers equally, and so did not
amount to sex discrimination.

(b) The Legislation

Nowadays, section 26(2) of the Equality Act 2010 provides that a   **5–024**
person sexually harasses another if he "engages in unwanted conduct
of a sexual nature" that (as with s.26(1)), has the purpose *or* effect of
violating the victim's dignity *or* creating a hostile environment. The
second limb (*purpose or effect*) is discussed above and applies here

---

[70] See above, n.8.
[71] [2003] I.C.R. 937 (HL).
[72] [2005] I.R.L.R. 4 (EAT).
[73] [1996] I.C.R. 535. Contrast the approach in the US cases of *Horney v Westfield Gage* 211 F
Supp 2d 291 (2002) and *Robinson v Jacksonville Shipyards* F Supp 1486 (MD Fla 1991).

similarly (see para.5–010). The elements to discuss here are *conduct of a sexual nature* and *unwanted*.

(c) "Conduct of a Sexual Nature"

5–025   This removes the obstacle to many sexual harassment claims under the old direct discrimination route. There is no need to show that the conduct was related to the victim's sex, only that it was sexual. Thus it is no defence that that the sexual conduct treats male and female, gay and straight (or should it occur, Christian and Muslim, old and young) claimants equally badly. This effectively reverses the House of Lords decisions in *Pearce* and *Macdonald*, as well as *Brumfitt* and *Stewart* (above).

The conduct may take any form, such as oral, written, or the displaying of pictures.[74] When first introducing the concept of sexual harassment (into the SDA 1975), in 2005, the Government provided the following examples of sexual harassment.[75]

(i)   A provincial newspaper provides short unpaid work experience placements for journalism students of local colleges. The editor wishes to run a feature on a dispute between residents and a strip club. He wants to send a female work experience student with the photographer to take pictures inside the club during its opening hours. The student makes it clear that she feels very uncomfortable with the idea of this, but the editor says it will be good experience and insists that she accompany the photographer, despite her objections. The student reluctantly agrees, but finds the experience distressing and humiliating. In such a case, a tribunal is likely to find that sexual harassment has occurred.

(ii) A barmaid in a pub is subjected to unwelcome sexual overtures, inappropriate physical behaviour by her boss and is offered money for sex.

(iii) A colleague making derogatory sexual comments to the claimant and making sexual remarks to other service users about the claimant.

5–026   (iv) On three occasions, male colleagues working in the same room as the claimant downloaded pornographic images on to a computer screen. Viewed objectively, the behaviour complained of clearly had potential to cause affront to a female employee working in close proximity to the men and

---

[74] See the US case, *Horney v Westfield Gage* 211 F Supp 2d 291 (2002) (pictures of naked and semi-naked women displayed in workplace).

[75] "Changes to Sex Discrimination Legislation in Great Britain: Explaining the Employment Equality (Sex Discrimination) Regulations 2005", 2005 (URN 05/1603), p.10.

was thus to be regarded as degrading or offensive to her as a woman. The fact that the claimant did not complain to her employer was irrelevant, given the obviously detrimental effect that the behaviour had in undermining her dignity at work.

(v) A model subjected to repeated unwanted sexual advances from X who was employed by the same company and was responsible for engaging models for photographic shoots for advertising purposes. The model claimed that during a shoot, X came to her hotel room and attempted to kiss her. The model rebuffed her advances. X also sent the model text messages and invited her to visit a sex shop.

(vi) A city worker (of either gender) required to go on team outings to strip clubs.

(d) "Unwanted" Conduct and the "Welcomeness Defence"

The claimant must prove that the conduct was "unwanted". It has **5–027** been argued that this element is unnecessary: conduct that violates dignity, or creates a hostile environment, without more, amounts to harassment.[76] On the other hand, this element is necessary to "ensure that sexual harassment charges do not become the tool by which one party to a consensual relationship may punish the other."[77]

Although the issue of whether conduct is unwelcome has been discussed under the old discriminatory harassment cases, it was not an element for liability, but rather one of the circumstances that may decide whether there was discrimination. In a case under the new definition, the EAT showed itself unsympathetic to an "welcomeness defence". In *Munchkins Restaurant v Karmazyn*[78] a manager constantly talked about sex to the waitresses. On occasions one of waitresses would initiate the sex-talk herself, but only "to keep the peace", as it diverted the manager from making intrusive questions about the waitresses' sex lives.[79] The waitresses tolerated his conduct for several months, until the assistant manager, who acted as a "buffer" between the manager and the waitresses, left the restaurant. After this, the waitresses resigned, claiming sexual harassment. The employment tribunal accepted the waitresses' reasons for tolerating

---

[76] C.J. Wood, "'Inviting sexual harassment': The absurdity of the welcomeness requirement in sexual harassment law", 38 Brandeis LJ 423 (1999–2000). See also M.M. Jackson, "Confronting 'Unwelcomeness' From the Outside: Using Case Theory to Tell the Stories of Sexually-Harassed Women" (2007) 14 Cardozo Jo. of Law & Gender 61, who states that (at 61) "Implying welcomeness through an examination of plaintiff's conduct intimidates and embarrasses the plaintiff and typically plays to traditional sex roles and stereotypes."

[77] Brief for the EEOC as Amicus Curiae, in *Meritor Savings Bank v Vinson* 477 US 57 (1986), (No.84-1979).

[78] (2010) UKEAT/359/09/LA. Discussed, [13]–[25].

[79] ibid. [16].

the manager's conduct for so long and for initiating the sex-talk, and rejected the employer's argument that the conduct was not "unwanted". The EAT upheld this finding.

Unwanted, (or *unwelcomeness*) is also an element for sexual harassment in the United States. The extensive case law there is instructive. The rule is that the "conduct must be unwelcome in the sense that the employee did not solicit or incite it, and ... that the employee regarded the conduct as undesirable or offensive".[80] This approach, as far as possible under the element, favours the claimant. No express, or even implied, gesture showing an aversion to the conduct is required.

However, what amounts to "soliciting" has been the subject of some controversy in the United States, following comments by the Supreme Court in *Meritor Savings Bank v Vinson*,[81] where Rehnquist J. stated that a claimant's sexually provocative speech or dress is "obviously relevant" as a matter of law in determining whether she found particular sexual advances unwelcome.[82] In *Mclean v Satellite Technology*[83] the claimant "displayed her body through semi-nude photos or by lifting her skirt to show her supervisor an absence of undergarments" and made salacious comments to colleagues, customers and competitors. It was held that, because of her "character" she may have welcomed any alleged sexual advances made to her by a superior. Thus, her claim of sexual harassment failed. This suggests that there is a "welcomed conduct" defence, which has been criticised as implying sexual attraction is a motive for harassment, ignoring that harassment is often a manifestation of power, stereotyping female sexual conduct, and being evocative of attempts in rape cases to blame the victim for the crime.[84]

5–028   *Meritor* also established an important principle regarding the claimant's behaviour. In that case Ms Vinson alleged that her supervisor fondled her in front of other employers, and had followed her into the women's lavatory and exposed himself to her. During this period, it was contended, she had voluntary sexual intercourse with him some 40 to 50 times. The District Court held that voluntary nature of the sexual relationship showed that Ms Vinson welcomed the supervisor's conduct at work. The Supreme Court held that this approach was mistaken: "The correct inquiry is whether respondent by her conduct indicated that the alleged sexual advances were unwelcome, not whether her actual participation in sexual intercourse

---

[80] *Henson v City of Dundee* 683 F 2d 897, at 903 (11th Cir 1982).
[81] 477 US 57 (1986).
[82] ibid. at 69.
[83] 673 F Supp 1458 (ED Mo 1987).
[84] C.A. Bull, "The implications of admitting evidence of a sexual harassment plaintiff's speech and dress in the aftermath of *Meritor Savings Bank v Vinson*", (1993) 41 UCLA L Rev 117, at 119.

was voluntary."[85] In other words, consent to a sexual relationship does not amount to consent to sexual harassment at work.

By the same principle, a woman who takes part in sexual banter,[86] or appears to enjoy it,[87] or uses foul language,[88] does not necessarily welcome sexually explicit comments. In an opinion relevant to all this behaviour (and echoed in *Munchkins* (above)), Posner J., in *Galloway v General Motors*[89] stated that the use of foul language:

"... may be defensive; may be playful rather than hostile or intimidating; may be colored by tone or body language; [or] ... may be done in a placating, conciliatory, or concessive manner in an effort to improve relations with hostile or threatening coworkers."

(e) Purpose or Effect
See above, para.5–010.   **5–029**

(f) The Required Effect
See above, para.5–011.   **5–030**

(g) Same-Sex Harassment
It does not matter if the harasser and the victim are both men, or   **5–031**
both women. See above, para.5–007.

(3) Consequences of Rejecting or Submitting to Unwanted Conduct ("Quid Pro Quo")
For sex, gender reassignment, and sexual harassment only, there is a   **5–032**
third provision. The Equality Act 2010 s.26(3) provides that a person (or another) harasses the victim by engaging in "unwanted conduct of a sexual nature or that is related to gender reassignment or sex" and because of her "rejection of or submission to the conduct", the person treats her less favourably than he would treat her had she not rejected or submitted to the conduct. As with the other two forms of harassment, the conduct must have the purpose or effect of violating her dignity or creating a hostile environment.

The usefulness of this provision is for the situation where, for instance, a person who rejects a sexual advance suffers retaliation,

---

[85] 477 US 57, at 68 (1986).
[86] *Van Jelgerhuis v Mercury Finance* 940 F Supp 1344, at 1361 (SD Ind 1996).
[87] *Carr v Allison Gas Turbine* 32 F 3d 1007, at 1011 (7th Cir 1994).
[88] *Horney v Westfield Cage* 211 F Supp 2d 291, at 309 (D Mass 2002).
[89] 78 F 3d 1164, at 1167 (7th Cir 1996), (abrogated on other grounds, *Nat Rail Passenger Corp v Morgan*, 536 US 101, at 105–107).

which does not necessarily amount harassment or sex discrimination, such as a denial of an expected pay rise or a promotion. The retaliation will be actionable under this provision. The phrase "submission to or rejection of" is lifted from the US EEOC Code of Federal Regulations.[90]

If favouritism based upon the granting of sexual favours is widespread in a workplace, those women (say) not approached would find it difficult to establish a claim under this sub-section. Nonetheless, they may be able to establish a hostile environment claim under s.26(2) (sexual harassment) because "in these circumstances, a message is implicitly conveyed that the managers view women as 'sexual playthings,' thereby creating an atmosphere that is demeaning to women."[91] Arguably, this also causes an offensive atmosphere for men, who may also have a claim under s.26(2).

3. Other Unlawful Acts

(1) Instructing, Causing or Inducing Unlawful Acts

5–033   Section 111 of the Equality Act 2010 makes it unlawful for a person to instruct, cause or (directly or indirectly) induce someone to discriminate against, harass or victimise another person, or to attempt to do so. The person giving the instruction must be "in a relationship with the recipient of the instruction in which discrimination, harassment or victimisation is prohibited."[92]

As well as the Equality and Human Rights Commission, the recipient of the instruction may bring a claim, although the recipient must have suffered a detriment. It does not matter if the instruction was not implemented. This codifies *Weathersfield v Sargent*,[93] where a worker who resigned rather than implement a racist instruction won her claim for direct discrimination. Likewise, provided he has suffered a detriment, the intended victim may bring a claim.

The Explanatory Notes (367) offer this example:

> "A GP instructs his receptionist not to register anyone with an Asian name. The receptionist would have a claim against the GP if subjected to a detriment for not doing so. A potential patient would also have a claim against the GP if she discovered the

---

[90] C.F.R §1604.11(a)(2). See generally, *EEOC.Gov*, click on "sexual harassment", then "Policy & Guidance". For US "quid pro quo" examples, see *Miller v Bank of America* 600 F.2d 211, 20 (9th Cir 1979) (claimant fired when she refused to cooperate with her supervisor's sexual advances); *Barnes v Costle* 561 F.2d 983 (DC Cir 1977) (claimant's job abolished after she refused to submit to her supervisor's sexual advances).

[91] EEOC Policy Guidance, N-915.048, ibid.

[92] EA 2010, Explanatory Note 365.

[93] [1998] I.C.R. 198 (EAT).

instruction had been given and was put off applying to register. The receptionist's claim against the GP would be brought before the employment tribunal as it relates to employment, while the potential patient's claim would be brought in the county court as it relates to services."

(2) Aiding Unlawful Acts

Section 112 of the Equality Act 2010 provides that a person who "knowingly" aids another person to do an act of unlawful discrimination will be treated as if he did the act himself, unless he relied, reasonably, on a statement[94] by the primary discriminator that the act was lawful. The Explanatory Notes (371) offer this example:

5–034

> "On finding out that a new tenant is gay, a landlord discriminates against him by refusing him access to certain facilities, claiming that they are not part of the tenancy agreement. Another tenant knows this to be false but joins in with the landlord in refusing the new tenant access to the facilities in question. The new tenant can bring a discrimination claim against both the landlord and the tenant who helped him."

It does not matter that the party who aids was in fact the "prime mover" of the discriminatory act. Thus, in *Anyanwu v South Bank Student Union*,[95] where the university made allegations against student union employees, which ultimately led to their allegedly discriminatory dismissal, the university could be liable for aiding the union's act.

---

[94] It is an offence knowingly or recklessly to make a false or materially misleading statement (s.112(3)).
[95] [2001] I.C.R. 391 (HL). Decided under the former RRA 1976 s.33.

CHAPTER 6

INDIRECT DISCRIMINATION

INTRODUCTION

"Librarians required: no women need apply". This job specification **6–001**
expressly, or directly, discriminates against women. Much the same

effect could be achieved by rewording it to read: "Librarians required: applicants must be over six feet tall". This indirectly discriminates against women (as well as some racial groups) because of its adverse impact on the group. This rather simple example shows that a law against direct discrimination is not enough to achieve the aims of discrimination law.

The modern concept of indirect discrimination originates from the US case *Griggs v Duke Power*.[1] Duke Power's station in North Carolina was divided into five departments: Labour, Coal Handling, Operations, Maintenance, and Laboratory and Test. Work in the Labour Department was the dirtiest and lowest paid. A high school diploma and/or the passing of an intelligence test was necessary to gain employment in, or promotion to, any of the four other Departments. Duke Power employed 95 workers at the Station, 14 of whom were black; these 14 were employed in the Labour Department. They sued Duke Power under the Civil Rights Act 1964, Title VII, which prohibited, inter alia, classifying an employee in any way which would adversely affect his status as an employee, because of his race, colour, religion, sex or national origin. Statistics revealed that 34 per cent of whites completed high school, in contrast to 12 per cent of blacks. Research showed that 58 per cent of whites, in contrast to six per cent of blacks, passed the Intelligence Tests used by Duke Power. Duke Power showed they had not *intended* that the requirements would discriminate, but failed to show that the requirements were related to job performance. A unanimous Supreme Court found Duke Power liable, based on the following reasoning, given in the famous speech of Burger C.J. who invokes Aesop's fable of the stork and the fox:

6–002
"Congress has now provided that tests or criteria for employment or promotion may not provide equality of opportunity merely in the sense of the fabled offer of milk to the stork and the fox. On the contrary, Congress has now required that the posture and condition of the jobseeker be taken into account. It has—to resort again to the fable—provided that the vessel in which the milk is proffered be one all seekers can use.

The Act proscribes not only overt discrimination but also practices that are fair in form but discriminatory in operation. The touchstone is business necessity. If an employment practice which operates to exclude [black people] cannot be shown to be related to job performance, the practice is prohibited ...

Congress directed the thrust of the Act to the *consequences* of employment practices, not simply the motivation. More than

[1] 401 US 424 (1971). For an argument that *Griggs* was wrongly decided, see M. Gold, "Griggs' folly: An essay on the theory, problems and origin of the adverse impact definition of employment discrimination and a recommendation for reform", 7 Indus Rel L J 429 (1985).

that, Congress has placed on the employer the burden of showing that any given requirement must have a manifest relationship to the employment in question."[2]

This speech established that indirect discrimination is based upon two broad limbs: the prima facie case and justification. First, the claimant must show that an apparently neutral practice has led to an adverse impact on a protected group, for example, where a high school diploma is a condition of employment and a larger proportion of whites than blacks complete high school. Second, the burden shifts to the defendant to justify the practice by showing it was *necessary* to achieve a (non-discriminatory) goal, for instance, by showing that a high school diploma was necessary to perform the job. Indirect discrimination is also known as *disparate impact* (especially in the US), *adverse impact*, and *adverse effect*.

1. THEORETICAL BASIS OF INDIRECT DISCRIMINATION LAW

Although the Supreme Court in *Griggs v Duke Power*[3] provided the foundation of the modern law of indirect discrimination, the Court was less clear about its precise theoretical basis.[4] Of course, many have been offered. From time to time, there have been suggestions that purpose of indirect discrimination is to prevent unscrupulous employers from evading the conventional direct discrimination law, simply by introducing an apparently neutral practice as a pretext.[5] This "pretext theory" carries an ingredient of discriminatory intent for liability. There has been more confusion than necessary on this issue. In 1988, in the Court of Appeal, Staughton L.J. suggested that neutral criteria that adversely affect a racial group, should not arouse liability if they were invoked upon a whim. Without discriminatory intent, he said, the definition of indirect discrimination would have "an extraordinarily wide and capricious effect".[6] More generally, in 1999, in the House of Lords, Lord Browne-Wilkinson stated courts should not introduce "something akin to strict liability ... which will lead to individuals being stamped as racially discriminatory ... where these matters were not consciously in their minds."[7] In 2000, the Master of the Rolls (and later Lord Chief Justice), Lord Woolf

6–003

---

[2] ibid. at pp. 429–432.
[3] 401 US 424 (1971).
[4] B. Landsberg, "Race and the Rehnquist Court" 66 Tul L Rev 1267, at 1281 (1992).
[5] G. Rutherglen, "Disparate impact under Title VII: an objective theory of discrimination" (1987) 73 Virginia L Rev 1297, pp.1310–1311.
[6] *Meer v London Borough of Tower Hamlets* [1988] I.R.L.R 399 (CA), at 403.
[7] Dissenting in *Nagarajan v LRT* [2000] 1 A.C. 501 (HL), at 510. Discussed below, Ch.7, para.7–007.

commented: "To regard a person as acting unlawfully when he had not been motivated either consciously or unconsciously by any discriminatory motive is hardly likely to assist the objective of promoting harmonious racial relations."[8] These statements overlook the express rejection in *Griggs* of discriminatory intent as an element and incorrectly portray the British position. Nothing in the UK statutes has suggested that discriminatory intent is necessary for liability for indirect discrimination. Indeed, for the purpose of remedies, the legislation has always distinguished between intentional and unintentional discrimination.[9]

This shows that indirect discrimination has potential beyond pretext cases. In *Griggs,* Burger C.J. said that the legislation was concerned with the consequences of employment practices, suggesting a societal or ethical dimension. The most extreme expression of this purpose is to allocate benefits (such as jobs) in proportion to group membership in the general population, regardless of merit. This could be achieved only by quotas. Among other things, this has been labelled a "pure disparate impact model".[10] The image of hiring purely by quota is politically and judicially unthinkable nowadays. In one of the most controversial discrimination cases in the United States, the Supreme Court rejected a claim of indirect discrimination by native Alaskan and Phillipino workers at an Alaskan salmon cannery factory who found themselves predominantly in the worst jobs, which carried lowest pay, separate dining facilities and accommodation, and which, according to a dissenting Justice, resembled a plantation economy.[11] Yet the claimants could not show that this scenario was caused by any particular recruitment practice, and a majority rejected the claim, because otherwise employers would be forced to hire by quota. The mere mention of the "Q" word, it seems, was justification enough for the decision, such is its evocative power. In addition, there is a legal objection to quotas and most positive action programmes, as they offend the equality principle, which is symmetrical in nature, and so protects whites as well as blacks, men as well as women, and so on.[12] The US Supreme Court's attitude is trenchant:

---

[8] *Chief Constable of West Yorkshire v Khan* [2000] I.C.R. 1169, (CA) at para.4, discussed below, Ch.7, para.7–008, p.211.

[9] See now, EA 2010 s.124(4). And previously: SDA 1975 s.65; RRA 1976 s.57; Sexual Orientation Regulations 2003 reg.30; Religion or Belief Regulations 2003 reg.30; Age Regulations 2006 reg.38. In *Draehmpaehl v Urania Immobilien Service ohg* Case-180/95 [1997] I.R.L.R 538, the ECJ held that damages could not be withheld because the discrimination was unintentional. See also *Orphanos v Queen Mary College* [1985] A.C. 761 (HL).

[10] See S. Willborn, "The disparate impact model of discrimination: theory and limits" (1985) 34 American UL Rev 799, pp.801–803; M. Carvin, "Disparate Impact Claims Under the New Title VII" 68 Notre Dame Law Rev 1153, who calls this a "pure" standard (at 1154); L. Lustgarten, *Legal Control of Racial Discrimination* (London: Macmillan Press, 1980) who names this "unalloyed" in contrast to the "compromised" statutory theory (at p.54).

[11] *Wards Cove Packing Co v Atonio* 490 US 642, at 663 (1989) (Stevens J.).

[12] On positive action, see, see Ch.11, para.11–002.

"[G]overnment-sponsored racial discrimination based on benign prejudice is just as noxious as discrimination inspired by malicious prejudice. In each instance, it is racial discrimination, plain and simple."[13] Less trenchant, but equally effective, was the decision of a British industrial tribunal to declare unlawful, as discriminating against men, the Labour Party's policy of all-women short lists for parliamentary candidates, despite the gross under-representation of women, seen (or heard!) in the Westminster Parliament.[14] Thus, politically and legally quotas are out of the question, whether or not indirect discrimination theory encompasses them.

There is a more inherent reason why indirect discrimination does **6–004** not encompass quotas, and that is its element of justification. The Court in *Griggs* stated that employers would not be liable if they showed that their practice was job-related. In *AMAE v State of California*[15] Afro-American, Hispanic and Asian groups established that higher proportions of their groups, compared to whites, failed schoolteacher entrance exams. Without more, the "pure" model would bring them success. With that in mind the school governors would have long since abolished the exams and hired by quota. Instead, the element of justification allowed them to show that the exams were necessary for the job. The element of justification means that indirect discrimination theory does not envisage quotas. With this in mind, it is arguable that in fact, the justification element completes a "pure" model of indirect discrimination (rather than compromising it), by identifying the cause(s) of any adverse impact.

In any case, the existing model lies somewhere between the extremes of the discriminatory-intent and quota models. Theories within this scope include "functional equivalency". This goes beyond the pretext theory, because it covers unintentional discrimination. Its premise is that the purpose of indirect discrimination law is to prohibit practices, adopted without discriminatory intent, that have the functionally equivalent effect as intentional discrimination. Hence, the law addresses not only formal recruitment criteria (as in *Griggs*), but informal or subjective decision-making that, say, perpetuates an imbalanced workforce profile.[16] This reveals that indirect discrimination is more concerned with the *effects* of any behaviour, rather than the nature of the behaviour itself.[17] Thus, there is liability

---

[13] *Adarand Constructors v Pena* 515 US 200, at 241 (1995) (Thomas J.) The Court struck down a policy that 5 per cent per annum of all government contracts should be awarded to certified small business concerns owned and controlled by socially and economically disadvantaged individuals.

[14] *Jepson and Dyas-Elliott v The Labour Party* [1996] I.R.L.R 116, IT. Effectively reversed by statute. See further, Ch.11, para.11–012.

[15] 231 F 3d 572 (9th Cir 2000).

[16] See e.g. O'Connor J. in *Watson v Fort Worth Bank* 487 US 977, at 987 (Sup Ct 1988). "Subjective decision making" is discussed below, para.6–009.

[17] Fredman argues that the law does not aim to achieve equality of results, rather, it focuses on a disproportionate effect merely to "diagnose" a discriminatory act. See S. Fredman, "Equality: a new generation" (2001) 30 ILJ 145, at 162.

even for "innocent" causes (such as an accident of history, or unforeseen consequences) of an adverse effect, unless they are justified, say, as work-related and proportionate. Another dimension is that indirect discrimination is more group-orientated, benefiting protected groups even where some of the group were unaffected by a particular discriminatory practice (for instance, in *Griggs*, black applicants with a high school diploma).[18]

Elsewhere, indirect discrimination theory in employment matters is seen as an economic tool, equating discriminatory decision-making with inefficient decision-making.[19] This chapter will show, especially with the case law, that there is no consensus on the precise theory of indirect discrimination law.

2. History of Indirect Discrimination Legislation

6–005 The British indirect discrimination legislation has its origins in the US Civil Rights Act of 1964 and the Supreme Court's landmark decision in *Griggs v Duke Power Co*, set out above.[20] The Civil Rights Act 1964 contained many Titles outlawing discrimination in such areas as voting rights, public accommodation, facilities and education, and federally assisted programmes. Title VII covered employment. The Act contained no specific definition of *indirect* discrimination, but the Supreme Court recognised indirect discrimination and developed the "disparate impact" theory to outlaw it.[21] The inclusion of indirect discrimination in Britain's legislation is a direct result of the Home Secretary's (the late Roy Jenkins) discovery of *Griggs* while on a trip to the United States. Mr Jenkins, upon his return, introduced clause 1(1)(*b*) (defining and outlawing *indirect* discrimination) in a late amendment to the 1975 Sex Discrimination Bill. That explains why the White Paper[22] that preceded the Bill contained no indication of

[18] Note that the definition of indirect discrimination in both the equality Directives and the EA 2010 refer to *persons* being put at a disadvantage.

[19] See, e.g. P. Caldwell, "Reaffirming the disproportionate effects standard liability in Title VII Litigation" 46 U Pitt L Rev 555 (1985); S. Greenberger, "A Productivity approach to Disparate Impact and the Civil Rights Act of 1991" 72 Oregon Law Rev 253 (1993). cf. R. Epstein, *Forbidden Grounds: The Case Against Employment Discrimination Laws* (Cambridge: Harvard University Press, 1992), esp. pp.226–229.

[20] 401 US 424 (1971). See para.6–001, p.152.

[21] In the years that followed, the Supreme Court developed the disparate impact theory in accordance with the basic tenets of *Griggs*. However, in the late 1980s this was checked by judicial and political divisions. The Supreme Court upset many well-established principles of the theory. Most notable was the bare-majority decision in *Wards Cove Packing Co v Atonio* 490 US 642 (1989) which followed the plurality decision in *Watson v Fort Worth Bank & Trust* 487 US 977 (1988). In response Congress passed the Civil Rights Act 1991. Although this statute re-established some of the earlier principles, it also codified some parts of the *Wards Cove* decision. See further below, para.6–001.

[22] *Equality for Women* Cmnd 5724, 1974, London: HMSO.

the Government's understanding of, and policy towards, indirect discrimination. In fact, the average Parliamentarian of the day had no understanding of the concept of indirect discrimination. The Conservative Opposition objected to the amendment because:

> "...we do not know what it means. Secondly we do not think the Government knows what it means; and, thirdly, if we did know what it meant, we do not think that we would like it, but we cannot be sure."[23]

Nonetheless, the Government added a formula defining indirect discrimination to the Bill and that became law. A year later Parliament used the same formula in the Race Relations Act 1976. This time the respective White Paper on Race Relations[24] included *some* indication of the Government's aims in introducing indirect discrimination laws. It stated that *direct* discrimination laws alone could not address the "practices and procedures which have a discriminatory effect" and "practices which are fair in a formal sense but discriminatory in their operation and effect". But that was all. And so, from its inception in Britain, the legislators offered very little guidance about their aims and ambitions for indirect discrimination law. Consequently, a large amount of the meaning has been developed by Community Law developments and—not always competently, it must be said—by domestic case law.

When the *Griggs* two-limbed theory of indirect discrimination[25]   **6–006** was introduced into British legislation, (i.e. Sex Discrimination Act 1975 and Race Relations Act 1976) some detail was added. There were seven elements contained in the British statutory scheme (six belonging to the first limb). During the 1980s and 1990s, while the judges were wrestling with the statutory formula, the ECJ was developing a concept of indirect discrimination from the basic tenets of equal treatment enshrined Community legislation. In time, tension developed between Community and British law where the British definition was narrower, or given a narrower interpretation, than its EC counterpart. This began with the Equal Pay Act 1970[26] and then the Sex Discrimination Act 1975.[27] Eventually a series of Directives forced the broader definition into domestic law, but only in areas of EC competence. The new definition took effect in the Sex

---

[23] Ian Gilmour, Standing Committee B (April 22, 1975), col.36.

[24] *Racial Discrimination* Cmnd 6234, 1975, London: HMSO.

[25] Prima facie case and justification. See above, para.6–002.

[26] See *Enderby v Frenchay HA* [1991] I.C.R. 382 EAT and [1994] I.C.R. 112 (CA) and ECJ, below paras 6–024 and 6–038.

[27] See *Falkirk Council v Whyte* [1997] I.R.L.R 560, and Comment (1998) 27 ILJ 133.

Discrimination Act on October 12, 2001, but only for employment matters,[28] and in the Race Relations Act in July 2003 in all fields, but only for discrimination on the grounds of race or ethnic or national origins (not colour or nationality). Consequently there remained a class of residual cases that fell outside the scope of the parent Directives (which were mainly confined to employment discrimination). The Sexual Orientation, Religion or Belief, and Age Regulations contained the new definition from their outset.

Now, the Equality Act 2010 brings the EC-derived definition in one singular formula. What follows is an account of the elements of indirect discrimination.

3. THE ELEMENTS OF INDIRECT DISCRIMINATION

6–007   **Equality Act 2010**

19 Indirect discrimination

(1) A person (A) discriminates against another (B) if A applies to B a provision, criterion or practice which is discriminatory in relation to a relevant protected characteristic of B's.

(2) For the purposes of subsection (1), a provision, criterion or practice is discriminatory in relation to a relevant protected characteristic of B's if—

(a) A applies, or would apply, it to persons with whom B does not share the characteristic,

(b) it puts, or would put, persons with whom B shares the characteristic at a particular disadvantage when compared with persons with whom B does not share it,

(c) it puts, or would put, B at that disadvantage, and

(d) A cannot show it to be a proportionate means of achieving a legitimate aim.

The formula consists of the following elements: (1) an apparently neutral[29] provision, criterion or practice, (2) which puts, or would put, (3) the claimant and the claimant's group at a "particular disadvantage", and (4) cannot be justified (para.(d)). As with *Griggs*, the

---

[28] This was achieved by the Burden of Proof Directive 97/80/EC. This definition was further amended on October 1, 2005 by art.2, Equal Treatment Amendment Directive, 2002/73/EC. It was extended to the provision of goods and services by General Sex Equality Directive 2004/113/EC. See further, Ch.2, para.2–005.

[29] Paragraphs (a) and (b) combine to require that the provision, criterion or practice (PCP) applies to persons irrespective of whether they share the claimant's protected characteristic. If the PCP is not facially neutral, it could be challenged as direct discrimination, even if it affects only some persons with the claimant's protected characteristic: see Ch.4, para.4–031.

first three complete the claimant's prima facie case, after which the burden shifts to the defendant to justify the challenged practice. Identifying a *protected group* is covered in Chapter 3, and disadvantage to the *claimant* (para.(c)) requires no further discussion, because it is merely to ensure a claimant has locus standi (a right to sue).[30]

What follows is a discussion of the elements in a slightly rearranged order, starting with (1) the "provision, criterion or practice", (2) proving the particular disadvantage, (3) causation, and (4) justification.

(1) Provision, Criterion or Practice

A broad range of requirements can be attacked as indirectly discriminating against a protected group. For instance, maximum age requirements may adversely affect women,[31] and nepotistic requirements for membership in associations or trade unions may adversely affect or exclude certain racial groups.[32] The relatively new statutory phrase *provision, criterion or practice* (replacing *requirement or condition*, beginning in 2001) significantly broadened the reach of indirect discrimination law in the UK. British case law on the new formula is still thin, so cases from the United States (where since its inception in 1964, the legislation used the phrase "employment *practice*") are particularly instructive. The new formula should cover not just strict requirements, but also mere *preferences*, such as job criteria stating that local experience, or management experience, or British nationality, is "desirable".[33] It should also cover the situation where points are awarded to candidates fulfilling each of a number of criteria, such as experience in a certain country, in line with the approach taken by the ECJ.[34] Accordingly, the new definition reverses the effect of *Brook v Haringey LB*,[35] that a last-in-first-out selection procedure (that adversely affected women) was not a "requirement" for the purpose of the old definition because it was not the sole criterion.

6–008

The new definition has the potential to encompass two other practices: subjective decision making and word-of-mouth recruitment and promotion.

---

[30] See e.g. 893 *Hansard* HC 1491-2 June 18, 1975.
[31] See e.g. *Price v Civil Service Commission (No.2)* [1978] I.R.L.R, IT 3; *Jones v University of Manchester* [1993] I.C.R. 474 (CA).
[32] See below, para.6–031.
[33] See respectively, *Meer v London Borough of Tower Hamlets* [1988] I.R.L.R 399 (CA); *Falkirk Council v Whyte* [1997] I.R.L.R 560 (EAT); *Perera v CSC* [1983] I.C.R. 428 (CA).
[34] *Ingetraut Scholz v Opera Universitaria di Cagliari* Case C-419/92 [1994] ECR 1-507 (if the German candidate had experience *in Italy* (rather than Germany) she would have amassed enough credit to have been chosen).
[35] [1992] I.R.L.R 478 (EAT), followed *Hall v Shorts Missile Systems* [1996] NI 214 (NICA).

(a) Subjective Decision Making

6–009 This takes many forms. For instance, the final decision for job candidates who meet the minimum requirements may be a subjective evaluation of the candidates' previous work and potential. This may disfavour those groups who have suffered discrimination in the past, indeed, it may perpetuate it.[36] This can occur in recruitment, promotion and redundancy. In the US case *Caron v Scott Paper*,[37] the plaintiffs were allowed to challenge a redundancy procedure as adversely affecting older workers. Workers were evaluated using six subjective factors and one objective factor. The subjective factors used were: job skills; leading change skills; interpersonal skills; self-management; performance; and versatility. The only objective factor was length of service. The US Supreme Court, in *Watson v Fort Worth Bank*,[38] confirmed that the indirect discrimination theory developed in *Griggs* (see above)[39] could apply to "an employer's undisciplined system of subjective decision making", although it noted that where some personal qualities, for example, common sense, good judgment, originality, ambition, loyalty and tact, cannot be measured accurately by objective testing, the decision-making may be easier to justify.[40] It is maybe more difficult to justify other subjective recruitment practices, such as delegation to managers or supervisors who simply favour those "whose face fits", or who "go on gut reactions" to the applicants;[41] or advertising in areas that happen to be predominantly white.[42]

In many cases, there is mixture of these practices. Here are two examples from US case law. In *Rowe v General Motors*,[43] the following promotion/transfer procedure was identified:

(1) The foreman's recommendation was the indispensable single most important factor in the promotion process.

(2) Foremen were given no written instructions for the qualifications or qualities necessary for promotion.

(3) Those standards which were determined to be controlling were vague and subjective.

---

[36] See E. Bartholet, "Application of Title VII to jobs in high places" (1982) 95 Harv L Rev 947, pp 955–58, 978–80.

[37] 834 F Supp 33 (D Me 1993). See also *Graffam v Scott Paper* 870 F Supp 389, at 395 (D Me 1994) affirmed 60 F 3d 809 (1st Cir 1995), and *District Council 37 v New York City Department of Parks* 113 F 3d 347, at 351 (2nd Cir 1997) (subjective choice of job titles for redundancy may adversely affect those aged over 40).

[38] 487 US 977 (1988).

[39] At para.6–001, p.152.

[40] 487 US 977 (1988), at 999.

[41] *Green v US Steel* 570 F Supp 254, 269 (ED Pa 1983), certiorari denied 498 US 814.

[42] *US v City of Warren, Michigan* 138 F 3d 1083 (6th Cir 1998).

[43] 457 F 2d 348, at 358–359 (5th Cir 1972).

(4) Hourly employees were not notified of promotion opportunities nor were they notified of the qualifications necessary to get jobs.

(5) There were no safeguards in the procedure designed to avert discriminatory practices.

It was held that this "procedure" amounted to a discriminatory employment practice which discriminated against blacks, who predominantly occupied the "Hourly" jobs. Similarly, in *Montana Rail Link v Byard*[44] it was held that the following amounted to a discriminatory employment practice:

(1) The impression made on the interviewers by the applicants **6–010** was the single most important factor in the hiring process, although the applicants were not told of this.

(2) Those responsible for making hiring decisions followed no written instructions as to the qualifications necessary for hiring.

(3) The standards which were determined to be controlling were vague and subjective.

(4) The applicants were not properly informed, and indeed may have been misled about the qualifications necessary to get jobs and about the procedures they had to follow to be hired.

(5) There were no safeguards in the hiring procedure designed to avert discriminatory practice.

(6) A "word of mouth" recruitment campaign was instigated by the employer.

(7) Interviews for some applicants were no more than "informal chats".

(8) Some applicants were hired without an interview.

There comes a point where an employer's decision-making becomes so informal that it is impossible to pinpoint any specific criterion that causes an adverse impact. This is frustrating for claimants where statistics reveal a significant disparity in the workforce. Whether such situations are challengeable under indirect discrimination law has been the subject of fierce debate in the United States. It was triggered by the case of *Wards Cove Packing Co v Atonio*.[45] Wards Cove ran salmon canneries in Alaska. Three practices were identified. It

---

[44] 260 Mont 331, at 352 (1993). Decided under the Montana Human Rights Act under Title VII disparate impact principles.
[45] 490 US 642 (Sup Ct 1989).

recruited its skilled workers using its offices in Washington and Oregon. Second, there was no promotion from the unskilled to the skilled positions; all skilled jobs were filled solely through the Washington and Oregon offices (many unskilled workers testified that they possessed the necessary skills to fill some of the skilled jobs). Third, the skilled and unskilled workers were accommodated in separate dormitories and mess halls. The statistics showed that the skilled workers were mainly white and the unskilled ones mainly Filipino or native Alaskan. A class of non-white unskilled workers brought a case of indirect discrimination, heavily based on the statistics.

6–011   A bare majority of the Supreme Court rejected the claim, holding that it was necessary to isolate each specific employment practice and show it caused a disparity, something the claimants could not do. The reasoning of the majority was clear, with White J. stating that an alternative result would mean that any employer with a racially imbalanced workforce could be "haled into court" to justify to the situation.[46] This would force employers to adopt quotas. The decision caused uproar and confusion. Congress acted to clarify the law and passed s.105 of the Civil Rights Act 1991, which endorsed *Wards Cove* by providing that complainants must show that "each particular challenged employment practice causes a disparate impact ..." but qualified it by stating that where the decision making process is not capable of separation for analysis, it may be treated as one employment practice. The Act provided an example: in *Dothard v Rawlinson*,[47] height and weight requirements designed to measure strength were used in the recruitment of prison officers but discriminated against women. According to the exception, these requirements could not be separated for analysis and so could be taken as a whole when linking them to the adverse impact.

Section 105 appears to restore matters to the pre-*Wards Cove* position, emphasising that there must be a causal link between the practice, or groups of practices, and the disparity. In a case following the 1991 Act, *Butler v Home Depot*,[48] statistics showed that over a four-year period, women made up just 6.4 per cent of the new recruits, whereas women made up some 36–39 per cent of the labour market qualified for the jobs. The employer's recruitment policy consisted of delegating decisions to store managers who based their decisions on their own subjective judgments, with virtually no written criteria. It was held that the recruitment practices were not capable of separation and could be analysed as a whole. It was then relatively easy for the claimants to show that the practice caused the disparity and establish a prima facie case.[49]

[46] ibid. at 652.
[47] 433 US 321 (Sup Ct 1977). See also below, paras 6–033 and 6–047.
[48] No C-94-4335 SI, C-95-2182 SI, (ND Cal. August 29, 1997).
[49] ibid. at 47–48.

The position in the US now appears to be that where a decision-making process is so vague that it is impossible to pinpoint a specific criterion causing a disparate impact, the process may be treated as a whole, making proof of causation much more straightforward. This should not lead to the adoption of quotas, as feared in *Wards Cove*. First, any significant imbalance should alert the employer that something is wrong. An investigation will identify a cause, which should be eradicated, refined or justified. If the employers in say, *Butler v Home Depot*, had taken that action, there would have been no litigation. Second, if instead the employer panics and adopts quotas, it will face *direct* discrimination claims from those intentionally disadvantaged under the quotas.[50]

This American experience suggests that the statutory phrase *provision, criterion or practice* can be interpreted to cover even the most vague decision making processes, where they can be combined to show that, as a whole, they cause a disparate impact. However, *Wards Cove*, and the subsequent Congressional reform, make it clear that some offending practice must be identified. No case can be brought on statistics alone. Again, the reason behind this is the fear that such claims would force employers into adopting quotas. As noted above, this would not necessarily be the case. Further, an absolute bar on such claims may prove unjust in rare cases. Take the following example. A factory in a predominantly black area employs a predominantly white workforce. The jobs are low-skilled, making it unlikely that the cause of the disparity is a skills shortage among the local black population. The employer uses a heavily disguised recruitment process, which claimants are unable to identify. Here, the recognition of a claim based on statistics would, at the least, force the employer to expose its recruitment policy to scrutiny. The key to recognising a prima facie case in these circumstances is making an inference from the statistics that the employer is using a discriminatory employment practice.[51]

6–012

(b) Word-of-Mouth Recruitment

Like some subjective decision making, word-of-mouth recruitment (or promotion) has a tendency to perpetuate an imbalanced workforce or membership (be it predominantly male, or white, or Protestant, Muslim, and so on), and so should fall within the purpose of the legislation. This is a live issue in employment, as many employers use "employee referral schemes" to recruit. These provide incentives

6–013

---

[50] In the US, intentional discrimination will attract higher damages. See *Ricci v De Stefano* (2009) 129 S.Ct 2658, below, para.6–046. For permitted positive action, see Ch.11, below.

[51] The ECJ is taking this line in equal pay claims when there is a disparity in wages and the pay structure is not transparent. See further Ch.9.

for existing workers to introduce new recruits. These can fill a skills gap or save costs of expensive recruitment agency fees.[52] The issue may also arise in club, association or trade union membership.[53] To date, there are no British cases deciding this issue under the new formula, although in *Coker v Lord Chancellor*[54] the Court of Appeal observed obiter:

> "It is possible that a recruitment exercise conducted by word of mouth, by personal recommendation or by other informal recruitment method will constitute indirect discrimination."

The Code of Practice for sex discrimination in employment suggests that where it precludes members of one sex from applying, word-of-mouth recruitment should be "avoided".[55] When word-of-mouth recruitment or promotion forms part of a decision making process, and this process is analysed as a whole (see above), it becomes subject to scrutiny, albeit only in a loose sense. This should be incentive enough for employers and others to at least monitor their effect and/ or build in safeguards. However, where the word-of-mouth recruitment or promotion is the only process, it is less clear if it is challengeable as indirect discrimination. In the United States, in the absence of a Supreme Court ruling on the matter, the courts are divided. Some Circuits recognise word-of-mouth recruitment as an employment practice,[56] others do not.[57] The reason given for rejecting such claims is that "passive reliance on employee word-of-mouth recruiting" is not "affirmative" enough to amount to an employer's *practice*.[58] However, there seems to be no reason or principle why an employer's acquiescence in a discriminatory practice by its workers

---

[52] See e.g. case study of Xansa in "Recruitment, Retention and Turnover", Annual Survey Report 2006 CIPD (London 2006), 10.

[53] *Handsworth Horticultural Institute Ltd v CRE* (unreported) Birmingham County Court; see "Ruled Out", F Invest 1992, ISBN 1 85442 0887 (all-white social club in area of just 40 per cent white population required that new members were sponsored by two members and approved by committee); and the US case, *Local 53, Asbestos Workers v Vogler* 407 F 2d 1047 (5th Cir 1969), (membership of trade union restricted to sons or close relatives of existing members, who were predominantly white).

[54] [2002] I.C.R. 321, [57].

[55] Originally issued by the Equal Opportunities Commission. See now *equalityhumanrights.com*, click on "gender Equality", then "Codes of Practice relating to gender equality legislation". Word-of-mouth hiring was challenged, unsuccessfully, as a form of racial segregation in *Pel Ltd v Modgill* [1980] I.R.L.R 142 (EAT), discussed above, Ch.4, para.4–039. The CRE Code of Practice (in force April 6, 2006) made no mention of word-of-mouth recruitment and neither does the EHRC Draft Code of Practice on Employment.

[56] *United States v Georgia Power* 474 F 2d 906, at 925–926 (5th Cir 1973) noting that word-of-mouth hiring created a "built in headwind" isolating blacks from the "web of information" regarding job openings.

[57] *EEOC v Chicago Miniature Lamp Works* 947 F 2d 292 (7th Cir 1991). This division has not proved critical in the US, because an employer who *ought* to have known that its word-of-mouth recruitment policy had a discriminatory effect, can be liable for intentional *direct* discrimination, the word-of-mouth recruitment being a mere pretext: *Domingo v New England Fish Company* 727 F 2d 1429 at 1435-36 (9th Cir 1984).

[58] See e.g. ibid. at 298–299.

should escape the law. On general tort principles, an omission amounts to an act. Indeed, in the US the Supreme Court has held that inaction by an employer, who did not do more than rely on the subjective judgment of supervisors in recruitment, can be challenged under indirect discrimination law.[59] Similarly, the British legislation stipulates that for the purpose of the legislation, an act includes a deliberate omission or a failure to do something.[60] Accordingly, word-of-mouth recruitment or promotion, even where the defendant has merely acquiesced in it, should be challengeable under the new statutory phrase *provision, criterion or practice* where it causes a disparate impact on a protected group.

(2) Proving a Particular Disadvantage

The only guidance in the Equality Act 2010 is provided by s.23(1):   **6–014**

"On a comparison of cases for the purposes of [indirect, discrimination] there must be no material difference between the circumstances relating to each case."

Upon this rubric, case law has developed a method of analysing a pool comprising persons whose circumstances are materially the same, save the protected characteristic. The pool is analysed to see if the protected group has been put at a particular disadvantage. The analysis is measuring the impact of the provision, criterion or practice on the claimant's group by comparing this with the impact on the others in the pool. Some methods of analysis will dictate the content of the pool, so Parts (a) and (b)(i), below, especially need to be digested as one.

(a) Choosing the Pool

(i) General principles

The first—and often the most difficult—task, is choosing the appro-   **6–015** priate pool.

"... one of the striking things about both the race and sex discrimination legislation is that, contrary to early expectations, three decades of litigation have failed to produce any universal formula for locating the correct pool, driving tribunals and courts alike to the conclusion that there is none."[61]

---

[59] *Watson v Fort Worth Bank* 487 US 977 (1988), see above para.6–009.
[60] EA 2010 s.212(2) and (3).
[61] *Grundy v British Airways* [2008] I.R.L.R. 74 (CA), [27] (Sedley L.J.).

Consequently, within the following (sometimes rather loose) principles, claims should be approached on a case-by-case basis.

The pool consists of a set of persons in the same circumstances as the claimant, save for the challenged factor, which should be irrelevant. In *Rolls Royce v Unite*,[62] the challenged practice was credit for long service in a redundancy selection procedure: those with longer service were less likely to be made redundant. The majority of the Court of Appeal accepted this indirectly discriminated on the ground of age (against younger workers). In his dissent, Aikens L.J. compared a group of older workers (50–55) with younger ones (40–45), but then presumed that each group had completed the same length of service, with the inevitable conclusion that the criterion did not adversely affect the younger group.[63] The mistake, of course, was including length of service (the challenged criterion) in the comparison as a "relevant circumstance".

In *Jones v University of Manchester*,[64] the job requirement was to be a graduate aged 27–35. The claimant argued that the age requirement indirectly discriminated against women. She argued that the pool should comprise graduates who had obtained their degree as mature students, i.e. aged at least 25. This was rejected as the age factor should be disregarded. The correct pool was *all* graduates. (Then the proportion of female graduates within the age requirement was compared with the proportion of male graduates within the age requirement.)

6–016   In another sex discrimination case, *Allonby v Accrington & Rossendale College*,[65] where part-time lecturers were dismissed and rehired through an agency on inferior terms, the part-time factor was disregarded providing a pool of *all* the College's teaching staff. (The comparison was between the proportions of female full-timers and male full-timers (i.e. those not dismissed), which was 21 and 38 per cent respectively.) In *McCausland v Dungannon DC*[66] the claim was that a job requirement to be an existing member of staff indirectly discriminated against Catholics. The other (unchallenged) requirement was a "standard occupational classification" (SOC) of 1, 2 or 3. The pool consisted of anyone from the whole Northern Ireland workforce with a SOC 1, 2 or 3. (The comparison was between the proportions of Catholics and Protestants from the pool who could comply with the requirement to be an existing member of staff.)

This approach was thrown into doubt by the majority's pronouncements in the House of Lords case *Rutherford v Secretary of*

---

[62] [2010] I.C.R. 1 (CA). The practice was justified, see below, para.6–021.
[63] ibid. [142].
[64] [1993] I.C.R. 474 (CA).
[65] [2001] I.C.R. 1189 (CA), see further below, para.6–041.
[66] [1993] I.R.L.R 583 (NICA). See further below, para.6–026. Heard under the Fair Employment (Northern Ireland) Act 1989, (outlawing discrimination on grounds of religious belief or political opinion).

State for Trade and Industry (No.2).[67] In this case, predating the specific age discrimination legislation first introduced by the Age Regulations 2006, Mr Rutherford was dismissed at the age of 67. By s.109 of the Employment Rights Act 1996, those over 65 could not claim for unfair dismissal. Mr Rutherford argued that s.109 adversely affected men and so was contrary to EC sex discrimination law. The majority compared men and women over 65 who were in work, and concluded that there was no adverse impact *at all*, because s.109 treated these workers equally, irrespective of sex. Notable in this methodology is the inclusion of the challenged factor (age) in deciding the pool. This seems to have come about because the majority struggled to equate an age limit with a condition, such as that for two-years' service for unfair dismissal rights in *Seymour-Smith*.[68] The claimant's case was relatively simple: that as men have a greater tendency to work beyond 65, they are disproportionately affected by s.109. Disregard the age factor and the pool (crudely) is the nation's entire workforce,[69] with the comparison between the proportions of men and women who cannot meet the condition (to be under 65). In the event, as the minority found, this did not show a significant enough difference to suggest that that s.109 adversely affected men.[70] The majority's approach compared only those in the disadvantaged group, with the inevitable result of no adverse impact. Indeed, the impact was *precisely* the same on men and women, a sure sign that there is something wrong with the test. The chances of a neutral requirement having precisely the same impact on two such large groups are low.

Rutherford has been taken by some to mean that the pool should be narrowest possible, which has produced a counter-argument advocating the widest possible pool. This rather polarised debate arose in *BMA v Chaudhary*.[71] Here, the challenged practice was a bar by the BMA to financially supporting racial discrimination claims by its members. While the claimant argued for a pool comprising its total membership, the BMA asserted the other extreme, that it should consist of only those few members wanting to bring racial discrimination claims. The Court of Appeal, obiter, applied *Rutherford* and agreed with the BMA. As everyone in that group was disadvantaged (as in *Rutherford*), the claim had to fail.

6–017

---

[67] [2006] I.C.R. 785 (HL).

[68] See below para.6–027. In *Rutherford*, Lord Scott said: "But where the provision in question does not constitute a condition for obtaining a benefit that some employees are able to satisfy and some are not but imposes a disadvantage on those who remain in employment after a specified age, the situation produced presents a rather different picture" (ibid. at para.15). Contrast *Price v Civil Service Commission* [1978] I.C.R. 27, below, para.6–018.

[69] Conceivably this could be refined with factors such as the (then) two-year qualification period for unfair dismissal and unemployed persons who wish to work. But this would make no difference to the outcome.

[70] Lord Nicholls and Lord Walker affirming [2002] I.C.R. 123 (EAT) and [2004] EWCA Civ 1186).

[71] [2007] I.R.L.R. 800 (CA).

6–018   Some sense was restored in *Grundy v British Airways*,[72] where
Sedley L.J., notably, neutralised this debate. He stated that the
guiding principle is that provided by what is now EA 2010 s.23(1):
like should be compared with like. Within this, the pool:

> "... needs to include, but not be limited to, those affected by the
> term of which complaint is made, which can be expected to
> include both people who can and people who cannot comply
> with it."

Further, "the pool must be one which suitably tests the particular
discrimination complained of".[73]

Using the old case of *Price v Civil Service Commission*,[74] he offered
two extreme examples to defuse notion that one or the other is correct. In *Price* the employer stipulated an age limit of 17–27. This was
challenged as adversely affecting women.[75] The employer argued for a
pool comprising the nation's entire workforce. Such a pool would
"empty the issue of reality", Sedley L.J. observed. On the other
extreme a pool of only those over 27 "would have assumed the
legitimacy of the very rule that was in issue."[76] The correct pool
(actually used in that case) was those men and women who were
qualified for civil service employment. Accordingly, the correct pool
for *Chaudhary* suggested Sedley L.J., was those members seeking
support for legal claims.[77]

On *Rutherford* directly, the whole court in *Grundy* considered that
that the ratio of *Rutherford* was not clear.[78] If *Rutherford* were taken
to provide a universal rule, Sedley L.J. added, "it is hard to see how
indirect discrimination claims could ever succeed."[79] These comments
and the general guidance should, one would hope, effectively confine
Rutherford to its own facts.

6–019   However, more recently, a differently constituted Court of Appeal
felt bound to apply it, doing little harm to the case before it, but
resurrecting *Rutherford* as an apparently universal rule. In *Somerset
CC v Pike*[80] teachers returning to work *part-time* could not make
pension contributions, unlike their *full-time* counterparts. The claimant argued that this indirectly discriminated against women. The
employment tribunal decided upon a pool comprising *all* teachers.

---

[72] [2008] I.R.L.R. 74 (CA).
[73] ibid. [33].
[74] [1978] I.C.R. 27 (EAT). See further below, para.6–025.
[75] The case pre-dated the dedicated Age Discrimination legislation.
[76] [2008] I.R.L.R. 74 (CA) [32].
[77] ibid. [30].
[78] ibid. [23] (Sedley L.J.), [43]–[46] (Carnwath L.J.), [47] (Waller L.J.). See also the similar
   unanimous opinion in *BMA v Chaudhary* [2007] I.R.L.R. 800 (CA), [193], [200] (Mummery,
   Maurice Kay L.JJ., Smith L.J.).
[79] ibid. [27].
[80] [2010] I.C.R. 46 (CA). Maurice Kay, Lloyd L.JJ., Sir Simon Tuckey.

Applying *Rutherford*, the Court of Appeal reversed, as this was "bringing into the equation people who have no interest in the advantage or disadvantage in question".[81] The correct pool was those teachers returning to work. This showed an adverse impact on women, as the part-timers were predominantly female by comparison to the full-timers. Although the Court cited *Rutherford* in coming to its decision, this was not necessary. The difference between this pool and *Rutherford's* is that here the challenged factor (part-time) was not a boundary to the pool, unlike in *Rutherford*, where the challenged factor (age) was. If *Rutherford* were applied strictly, the pool would consist of only *part-time* returning teachers. A pointless and doomed comparison would follow.

Other principles around selecting the pool are less contentious. Section 23(1) should not be used to include factors of defendant's objective justification. In *Spicer v Government of Spain*[82] a Spanish state school based in London paid teachers seconded from the Spanish civil service (all Spanish) more than teachers recruited in England (some English, some Spanish). The claim was for indirect discrimination on the ground of nationality, under the RRA 1976. The employer argued that the secondees should not be in the pool, as they were paid more because they were Spanish civil servants, and so their relevant circumstances differed from the other teachers. The Court of Appeal rejected this argument, holding that the correct pool consisted of all the teachers at the school. This is undoubtedly correct. Effectively, the employer was arguing that those favoured by the challenged practice should be excluded from the pool. As the Court of Appeal noted, if that were allowed, no claim of indirect discrimination could succeed.[83] The question of *why* the secondees were paid more was relevant only to the objective justification defence.

The pool can be dictated by the facts. For example, a dismissal selection procedure (the challenged practice) may dictate that the pool is the entire workforce, as in *Allonby* (above, para.6–016). This is commonly so in employment cases when the challenged practice applies only to existing workers, so making the logical pool the whole (or perhaps a class) of the workforce. Sometimes, where national legislation is being challenged as discriminatory (contrary to EU discrimination law), the pool is drawn from the entire population. In *R. v Secretary of State for Employment, ex parte Seymour-Smith*,[84] the extension of the qualification period for Unfair Dismissal rights to two years was challenged as indirectly discriminating against women,

---

[81] ibid. [18], citing *Rutherford (No.2)* [2006] I.C.R. 785 (HL), [82] (Baroness Hale).
[82] [2005] I.C.R. 213.
[83] ibid. [28].
[84] [2000] I.C.R. 244 (HL).

who are more transient in the workforce than men.[85] The pool chosen
was the UK's total workforce.

6–020   Choosing a pool can be complex and less certain in other cases.
This is especially so in recruitment. To compare the success rate of
male and female, or black and white, or Catholic or Protestant,
applicants is attractive because it measures precisely the impact of the
challenged practice. However, this may be misleading as it omits
persons deterred from applying in the first place. It does not account
for those deterred by say, an employer's reputation for nepotism or
discrimination, or a discriminatory factor in the job description, such
an unnecessary academic qualification or minimum height requirement. It may also be distorted where an employer has promoted
enthusiastically its equal opportunities policy so that a disproportionately high number of minorities or women apply. If the
pool is not restricted to applicants, a geographical pool may be used.
Here, there are a number of factors to consider. In job recruitment,
for instance, an appropriate labour market must be chosen, identifying those otherwise qualified for the job (see *McCausland v Dungannon DC*, below, para.6–026). In sex discrimination cases, normally
women and men with any given qualifications are evenly distributed
throughout the nation, so any statistics are unlikely to be distorted by
a limited or extended geographical pool. However, other protected
groups, especially racial groups, are less likely to be evenly distributed. Other factors may be incorporated to measure more accurately the impact on the claimant's group. The nature of the job may
be important. People will relocate readily for many jobs (academics
for instance), suggesting the pool could be geographically wide,
perhaps the whole nation. Where the job is likely to be taken only by
local people, the pool becomes geographically smaller, although
perhaps denser. This may be especially so for low-skilled jobs, where
potential applicants are unlikely to relocate or commute over long
distances, while at the same time, there is likely to be a large proportion of qualified persons in the locality. Parallel or similar arguments may apply in other fields, such as membership of associations,
or access to services or education.

(ii) The pool and age discrimination

6–021 There is a school of thought in the United States that it is inappropriate to analyse a facially neutral practice for indirect age discrimination, because unlike other forms of discrimination, there are
no historical prejudices and lingering effects of prior discrimination;
all older workers were once younger and able to make choices about

---

[85] It was reduced to one year where the effective date of termination is after June 1, 1999:
Unfair Dismissal and Statement of Reasons for Dismissal (Variation of Qualifying Period)
Order 1999, SI 1999/1436.

their education, training, and jobs, free from age discrimination.[86] However, after some doubts, the Supreme Court ruled (by a 5 to 3 majority) that age is a ground subject to indirect discrimination analysis, although with a modified defence.[87]

Irrespective of any conceptual doubts, the Framework Directive 2000/78/EC included age in its definition of indirect discrimination (art.2(2)(b)), and this is implemented in the Equality Act 2010. It applies the general principle of group disadvantage to the characteristic of age. This throws up the problem of assembling a distinctive age group. Such groups will not be as obvious, or tangible, as other groups, such as sex, race, religion, and so on. This is not an impossible task, but it is likely to be more difficult and less precise.

This difficulty was not helped by the judgment in *Chief Constable of West Yorkshire v Homer*,[88] where a new requirement of a law degree for top grade legal advisors was challenged. The claimant, who was 61, complained that he would be unable to complete the degree (part-time) before retirement, and so the requirement disadvantaged older workers. The employment tribunal, with an apparently easy logic held that the requirement put workers aged 60–65 at a particular disadvantage. The Court of Appeal disagreed:

> "... it was not the appellant's age but the temporal proximity of his intended retirement that stood in his way and prevented him from obtaining a law degree ...".[89]

This Delphic statement is distinguishing age from retirement and attributing the claimant's disadvantage to his impending retirement, rather than his employer's new requirement. In a case of indirect discrimination, this is a meaningless distinction, rather like attributing the disadvantage in *Griggs*[90] to the school system. Indirect discrimination is more concerned with of *effect* of the challenged practice, rather than the cause(s) of the disadvantage, which will often be multiple. As one commentator observed: "This adds a judge-made requirement to show causation to the statutory definition of

---

[86] See comment of Kennedy J. in *Hazen Paper Co v Biggins* 507 US 604, at 618 (Sup Ct 1993), citing P.S. Krop (1982) "Age Discrimination and the Disparate Impact Doctrine" 34 Stan L Rev 837, at 854. See also, E.H. Pontz (1995) "Comment, What A Difference The ADEA Makes: Why Disparate Impact Theory Should Not Apply To The Age Discrimination In Employment Act" 74 NC L. Rev. 299-300. Contrast *Lorillard v Pons* 434 US 575, at 584 (Sup Ct 1978).

[87] *Smith v City of Jackson* 544 US 228 (Sup Ct 2005). A similar result was achieved by the Federal Court of Australia using that nation's adoption of the ILO Discrimination (Employment and Occupation) Convention CIII (1958): *Commonwealth of Australia v Human Rights & Equal Opportunity Commission (Hamilton)* (2000) 63 ALD 641, at [27]–[45].

[88] [2010] I.R.L.R 619 (CA).

[89] ibid. [619] (Maurice Kay L.J.).

[90] See above, para.6–001, p.152.

indirect discrimination."[91] The better approach would have been to keep the law as clear as possible, recognise the obvious negative effect of the requirement on those approaching retirement, and control the outcome with the justification defence (the EAT suggested that the employer could have relaxed the requirement for older workers without impeding its legitimate aims).[92]

More conventionally, in *Rolls Royce v Unite*,[93] it was held that credit for long service in a redundancy selection procedure adversely affected younger workers "as a group" (but was justified as promoting loyalty and workforce stability).

6–022 In the US case *Caron v Scott Paper*,[94] the plaintiffs challenged a redundancy procedure by which they were evaluated by a team of co-workers using seven factors: job skills; leading change skills; interpersonal skills; self-management; performance; versatility; and length of service (the only objective factor). The comparison was made between the victim's group (those over 50) and the others (those 40–50). This revealed that the redundancy process retained 61.5 per cent of the victim's group and 91.5 per cent of the others, which is clearly significant enough to raise a prima facie case. The apparent precision of the statistics is deceptive, as they were based on the somewhat arbitrary—and imprecise—selection of the groups. Selecting age groups by decade appears neat and tidy, but is no more logical than selecting a group aged, say, 53–61, and comparing it with a younger group of 44–52. This should not detract from the decision though. In some cases at least, using somewhat arbitrary and imprecise groups will be the only way to get a case off the ground and fulfil the purpose of the legislation.

Other examples of practices that could adversely affect certain age groups could be a bar on "overqualified" job applicants (likely to disadvantage older applicants),[95] or incremental pay scales (likely to disadvantage younger workers).

(b) The Particular Disadvantage

6–023 This section discusses (i) the range of analytical methods, (ii) the use of negative and positive figures, (iii) the scenario of appointing from a circle of family, friends or acquaintances, and (iv) group disadvantage.

[91] M. Rubenstein, I.R.L.R Highlights July 2010.
[92] [2009] I.C.R. 223 (EAT), [46] (Elias J.).
[93] [2010] I.C.R. 1 (CA). See also above, para.6–015.
[94] 834 F Supp 33 (D Me 1993).
[95] See *Noonan v Accountancy Connections* (2004) DEC-E2004-42 (Equality Tribunal, Ire). See *www.equalitytribunal.ie*.

(i) Choosing the appropriate analytical model

Two preliminary points need to be made. First, it may feel intuitively **6–024** wrong to find discrimination where both the disadvantaged and advantaged groups contain a majority of those with the protected characteristic. For instance, in *Grundy v British Airways*,[96] one category (60 per cent female) of cabin crew was paid more than another (90 per cent female). In *Enderby v Frenchay Health Authority*[97] speech therapists (98 per cent female) were paid more than pharmacists (63 per cent female). What mattered here (given that each was doing like work or work of equal value) is that women were disproportionally affected by the pay policies.

Second, the provision, criterion or practice is being challenged for its disproportionate impact on the claimant's group. Hence, it is better to compare *proportions*, not numbers. Take this simple example. A shopkeeper refuses to serve men with beards. It is obvious that in a district predominately populated by Sikhs, that the rule will adversely affect Sikhs, whether by number or proportion. But now imagine an area where just a few Sikhs reside, a comparison of Sikhs and non-Sikhs *by number* will probably show *fewer* Sikhs than non-Sikhs were barred from the shop. This comparison misses the point. It does not reveal the impact on Sikhs as a group. A comparison by *proportions* would show that Sikhs are more likely than non-Sikhs to wear beards. This shows that the shopkeeper's rule had a disproportionate impact on Sikhs. Accordingly, in *Grundy* (above), out of a total of about 8,000 female workers, just 43 were disadvantaged by the challenged practice, and so far *more* women *benefited* from the challenged practice. Yet (as seen above), the practice still fell disproportionately on female workers. Of course, there will come a point where the disparity in numbers is so great, and comparison of proportions may be statistically insignificant (see, e.g. below, para.6–029, "Probability of Chance").

The statutory definition of indirect discrimination (EA 2010 s.19) requires that the claimant's group was put at a "particular disadvantage". This rubric is broad enough to accommodate a range of analytical methods. There are five established models[98] available: (a) intrinsically liable; (b) considerable difference; (c) small but persistent difference; (d) the four-fifths rule; and (e) the probability of chance.

---

[96] [2008] I.R.L.R. 74 (CA). See above, para.6–018.
[97] [1991] 1 CMLR 626 (EAT); Case C-127/92, [1994] I.C.R. 112 (ECJ). See further below, para.6–038.
[98] See T. Sugrue and W. Fairley, "A case of unexamined assumptions: the use and misuse of the statistical analysis of *Castenada/Hazlewood* in discrimination legislation" (1983) 24 Boston College L Rev 925; M. Garaud, "Legal standards and statistical proof in Title VII litigation: in search of a coherent disparate impact model" (1990) 139 Penns UL Rev 455, p 474.

(a) Intrinsically liable

6–025   The new definition of indirect discrimination was not intended to
mandate that statistical proof was the only method of proving a case.
In the absence of available statistics, it is enough if the challenged
practice is intrinsically liable to adversely affect a protected group.
The draft Race Directive referred to *O'Flynn v Chief Adjudication
Officer*[99] as its model for indirect discrimination.[100] In *O'Flynn* the UK
Government granted means-tested social security payments for funeral expenses incurred by all workers (including migrant workers),
but only if the burial or cremation took place in the UK. An Irish
national brought an action of discrimination on the ground of
nationality (under Regulation 1612/68 art.7(2)), arguing that the
restriction infringed the Community principle of free movement of
workers by indirectly discriminating against migrant workers. The
Government argued that there was no statistical evidence that the
rule adversely affected foreign nationals in the UK. The ECJ held
that it was not necessary to prove that the restriction did in practice
adversely affect migrant workers. It was sufficient that it was
"intrinsically liable" to have such an effect. In cases such as the
present, it was above all the migrant worker who may, on the death
of a member of the family, have to arrange for burial in another
Member State, in view of the links which the members of such a
family generally maintain with their State of origin.[101] Thus, where
the challenged practice by its nature, or intrinsically, is liable to
adversely affect a protected group, a prime facie case is made out.
This approach was adopted by the Court of Appeal in *Secretary of
State for Work and Pensions v Bobezes*[102] where child allowance
payments were withheld from a migrant worker because his child
spent time with its grandparents in Portugal. Citing *O'Flynn*, Lord
Slynn noted that "It was enough in cases of discrimination based on
nationality that the effect of the provision is 'essentially' 'intrinsically'
'susceptible by its very nature' 'by its own nature' liable to be discriminatory."[103] It was disappointing that Lord Slynn restricted these
comments to nationality discrimination. There is no reason why it
should not apply to any ground, especially where there is an absence
of statistics, or their use would escalate the costs of litigation beyond
the reach of many claimants, or for that matter, defendants (such as
small employers). Measures disadvantaging part-time workers
intrinsically discriminate against women; uniform requirements of
hats, or skirts, intrinsically discriminate against some racial groups.

---

[99] Case C-237/94, [1996] ECR I-2617 (ECJ). See also Case C-212/06 *Government of the French
Community v Flemish Government* [2008] ECR I-1683 (ECJ), [73].
[100] COM (1999) 566 Final 1999/0253 (CNS)/0655) p.6, n.8.
[101] Case C-237/94, [1996] ECR I-2617 (ECJ), [20]-[22].
[102] [2005] 3 All E.R. 497 (CA). Applied in *R (Elias) v Secretary of State for Defence* [2005]
I.R.L.R. 788 (HC Admin), affirmed [2006] 1 W.L.R. 3213 (CA).
[103] ibid. [24].

The sense in this approach was shown in *London Underground Ltd v Edwards (No.2)*,[104] where the claim was that a new rostering system would adversely affect single parents. The tribunal was happy to conclude that that it was "common knowledge" that more women than men were single parents. In *Price v Civil Service Commission*,[105] where an age limit of 17–27 adversely affected women because of family responsibilities, the EAT based its finding of adverse impact on "Knowledge and experience".[106]

(b) Considerable difference

Where statistics are appropriate, there are a number of models available. A fairly conventional model, of comparing the proportions of the positive figures for a considerable difference, is illustrated in *McCausland v Dungannon DC*.[107] The claim was that a job requirement for a chief works manager to be an existing worker in local government, indirectly discriminated against Catholics. The other (unchallenged) requirement was a "standard occupational classification" (SOC) of 1, 2 or 3. The pool chosen was the whole Northern Ireland workforce with the SOC 1, 2 or 3. The number of SOC 1, 2 or 3 workers in Northern Ireland consisted of 28,159 Catholics and 50,170 Protestants. The number of SOC 1, 2 or 3 workers in local government consisted of 423 Catholics and 1,039 Protestants. The comparison was between the proportion of Catholics, and the proportion of Protestants, who could comply with the requirement to be in local government. The proportions were 1.5 per cent and 2.1 per cent respectively. The ratio reveals a considerable difference. The Catholic percentage (1.5) is just 71 per cent of the Protestant percentage (2.1). Hence (roughly) for every ten Protestants who qualified, there were seven Catholics, (a ratio of 10:7).

6–026

(c) Small but persistent difference

This variation was made by the ECJ in *R. v Secretary of State for Employment, ex parte Seymour-Smith*.[108] Domestic legislation extended the qualification period for Unfair Dismissal rights from one to two years.[109] Ms Seymour-Smith challenged this as being contrary

6–027

---

[104] [1997] I.R.L.R 157 (EAT). See further below, para.6–044.
[105] [1978] I.C.R. 27 (EAT). See further above, para.6–018.
[106] ibid. at 32.
[107] [1993] I.R.L.R 583 (NICA). Heard under the Fair Employment (Northern Ireland) Act 1989, (outlawing discrimination on grounds of religious belief or political opinion).
[108] Case C-167/97, [1999] I.C.R. 447. See M. Connolly, "Commentary, *R v Secretary of State for Employment, ex parte Seymour-Smith*" [2000] 05/2 Jo Civ Lib 212, pp.217–219.
[109] The Unfair Dismissal (Variation of Qualifying Period) Order 1985, SI 1985/782. It has since been reduced to one year where the effective date of termination is after June 1, 1999: Unfair Dismissal and Statement of Reasons for Dismissal (Variation of Qualifying Period) Order 1999, SI 1999/1436.

to art.119 TEC (now art.157 TFEU), because it discriminated against women, who are more transient in the workforce than men. Both sides accepted the Annual Labour Force Surveys from 1985 to 1991 (when Ms Seymour-Smith was dismissed) as evidence of the impact of the two-year requirement. These are surveys of the UK's total workforce. They reveal that in 1985, for example, the total workforce in the UK was 18.73 million. If the two-year requirement were neutral in its effect, some 8.48 million men and 5.44 million women would have qualified under the two-year rule. However, the survey revealed that, in fact, only 5.07 million women qualified. So some 370,000 women were adversely affected. That was the situation expressed as *numbers*. The disparity was eight-and-a-half percentage points. That means, roughly, for every ten men who qualified for Unfair Dismissal rights, only nine women did so. That figure remained roughly constant until 1991. In a nutshell, the problem was whether a "small" difference, constant over a number of years, was enough to show a prima facie case of sex discrimination. The ECJ held that case could be brought where "the statistical evidence revealed a lesser but persistent and relatively constant disparity over a long period."[110]

(d) Four-fifths rule

6–028   An alternative is to compare the success rates of candidates. Guidelines issued by the US Equal Employment Opportunity Commission state that an inference of adverse impact should not be made unless the rate of recruitment of the victim's group is less than four-fifths (or 80 per cent) of the rate at which the group with the highest rate is selected.[111] In *Bushey v New York State Civil Service Commission*[112] a written examination was used for the post of Captain in State prisons. Two hundred and forty three whites and 32 non-whites took the test. One hundred and nineteen (49 per cent) of the whites and 8 (25 per cent) of the non-whites, passed the test. As the pass rate for non-whites was approximately 50 per cent that of whites, a prima facie case was made out.

(e) Probability of chance

6–029   A variation on the four-fifths rule is the "probability of chance" model, again used in the United States. Here, unless a disparity in the test results occurs by chance, an adverse impact can be inferred. In the US case, *Bridgeport Guardians v City of Bridgeport*,[113] tests used in

---

[110] Case C-167/97, [1999] I.C.R. 447, [61].
[111] 29 C.F.R. 1607.4(D) (1978) revised 1 July 2000. See *www.eeoc.gov*, click "Laws, Regulations", click "Regulations", scroll down to 1607.
[112] 733 F 2d 220 (2nd Cir 1984), certiorari denied, 469 US 1117 (1985).
[113] 933 F 2d 1140 (2nd Cir 1991).

the promotion of police officers to the rank of sergeant were challenged. One hundred and seventy persons applied for 19 posts. The results were as follows:

Race of candidate	Number taking exam	Number passing	Per cent passing	Highest rank
White	115	78	68%	1–19
Black	27	8	30%	20
Hispanic	28	13	46%	22

Two things can be seen from these results. First, a substantially lower proportion of non-whites passed the test. Second, that each of the 19 best performers was white. And so the 19 vacancies were filled by whites. Statistical analysis was presented which showed that the disparity between the whites' and blacks' results would occur by chance once in 10,000 times and the disparity between the whites' and Hispanics' would occur twice in 10,000. The Court relied on the "rule of thumb" that anything less than one in twenty could not be put down to chance, and held that the statistics raised an inference adverse impact.

Courts in the United States are not bound by these models and are at liberty to reject a statistical model. In *Bushey* (see above) the category of non-whites included four Hispanics, two of whom passed the test. Thus, their pass rate (50 per cent) was comparable to that of the whites. It was held that in the case of the Hispanics, no prima facie case could be made out. In *New York City Transit Authority v Beazer*,[114] the employers refused to employ anyone enrolled in a drug rehabilitation programme. The plaintiffs produced evidence that of those in public rehabilitation, 63 per cent were black or Hispanic. This statistic was rejected because it did not account for those in *private* rehabilitation, and further, there was no evidence of how many of those in rehabilitation were otherwise qualified for the job. In *Connecticut v Teal*[115] a two-stage entrance test was used. The first screened out 46 per cent of the black applicants, but only 20 per cent of the white ones. However, 22.9 per cent of the initial black applicants passed the second test, compared to just 13.5 per cent for the white applicants. The employer argued a "bottom line" defence, that ultimately, the testing had not adversely affected the black applicants. The US Supreme Court rejected this argument, and held that the focus should be on the initial screening test (which was discriminatory).

---

[114] 440 US 568 (Sup Ct 1979).
[115] 457 US 440, at 452 (1982).

(ii) Positive or negative figures?

6–030 The original statutory formula, dating back to the 1975 Sex Discrimination Act, mandated a comparison between those groups who
"can comply" with the challenged requirement. This meant a comparison of positive figures. The modern statutory formula requires
that the provision, criterion or practice "puts" the protected group
"at a particular disadvantage", which suggests a comparison of the
negative figures, but is open enough to permit the use of positive
figures as well. In some cases, this choice of comparison can affect the
outcome.

This is illustrated in *Grundy v British Airways*.[116] Cabin Crew (CC)
were given incremental pay rises, unlike their counterparts, Supple-
mentary Cabin Crew (SCC), even though the actual work was the
same. One issue was whether this arrangement adversely affected
women.[117] In 2002, for instance, there were about 12,000 CC, of
whom 8,000 were female, and just 42 SCC (of whom 39 were female).
The employment tribunal compared the proportions of females and
males from both CC and SCC (all cabin crew) advantaged by the
arrangement and found that 99.53 per cent of the women and 99.93
per cent of men benefited. This difference was insignificant. The tribunal then compared the negative figures (those disadvantaged by the
arrangement) of men and women (i.e. 42 female/3 male) and found a
significant difference: the female/male ratio of those disadvantaged
was a significant 14:1 (there were 14 times as many women not in
receipt of incremental pay rises), while the overall ratio of male to
female cabin crew was 2:1 (there were only twice as many women as
men working as cabin crew). The Court of Appeal upheld this finding, despite BA arguing that the tribunal should have focused on the
"big picture" advantaged figures.[118] This case could be explained
more simply: as the SSC comprised a significantly higher proportion
of women than the CC, there was a prima facie case of sex
discrimination.

This case illustrates that where there are large numbers involved
but those adversely affected by the challenged practice (the disadvantaged group) are relatively small in number, the choice of
comparison could be critical.

---

[116] [2008] I.R.L.R. 74 (CA).
[117] This was an equal pay claim, where the issue was whether, once the claimant had identified a
male comparator on more pay but doing like work, the difference was caused by sex discrimination. See ibid. [25], [35] (Sedley L.J.).
[118] See also *Seymour-Smith* [2000] I.C.R. 244 (HL) where a comparison of negative figures
produced a different picture (although not result). In 1985, for example, 22.6% of women
could *not* meet the two-year requirement. The figure for men was 31%. Thus for every ten
women disadvantaged, there were only seven men, compared to the 10:9 ratio produced by
the positive figures.

(iii) Appointing from within a circle of family, friends or personal acquaintances

In *Coker v Lord Chancellor*,[119] the Lord Chancellor appointed a white   **6–031**
male (Gary Hart) as his special advisor. The requirements were inter
alia, a commitment to New Labour, knowledge of politics and the
law, and to be of "sufficiently high quality". The post was never
advertised, and the Lord Chancellor had not looked outside his circle
of acquaintances when making the appointment. An employment
tribunal[120] upheld Ms Coker's claim of indirect discrimination, finding that the Lord Chancellor had applied a requirement that the
successful candidate must be personally known to him. As this class
of persons were predominantly white males, it indirectly discriminated on the grounds of sex and race. However, the EAT and
the Court of Appeal found for the Lord Chancellor. Assuming the
pool consisted of all the persons qualified for the job, save being
personally known to the Lord Chancellor, the Court of Appeal reasoned that there can only be a disparate impact if a significant proportion of the pool could comply with the requirement:

> "... whatever the proportions of men and women or racial
> groups in the pool, the requirement excluded the lot of them,
> except Mr Hart. Plainly it can have had no *disproportionate*
> effect on the different groupings within the pool."[121]

Thus, the practice of appointing from within a circle of family,
friends, or personal acquaintances is unlikely to amount to indirect
discrimination. This reasoning is rather fragile, and cannot disguise a
rather blatant case of nepotism, the antithesis of equal opportunities.
There is no reason why the proportion of qualifiers should be "significant" (by which the Court of Appeal appeared to mean "large").
The legislation required that the proportion of qualifiers from the
claimant's group was "considerably smaller" than the proportion of
qualifiers from the comparator's group. In *McCausland v Dungannon
DC*[122] the court compared a small proportion of Protestant qualifiers—
2.1 per cent—with an even smaller proportion of Catholic
qualifiers—1.5 per cent. Thus Catholic qualifiers were 71 per cent of
Protestant qualifiers, and it was held that the Catholic proportion
was considerably smaller than the Protestant proportion. If the pool
consisted of those qualified for the post, save for being personally
known to the Lord Chancellor, it might contain, say, 50 persons, half
of whom were women. The proportion of male qualifiers (comprising
the single successful candidate, Mr Hart) would have been one in 25
(4 per cent), while the proportion of female qualifiers would have

---

[119] [2002] I.C.R. 321 (CA). See A. Morris, "Embodying the Law", (2003) 11(1) Fem. L.S. 45.
[120] [1999] I.R.L.R. 396.
[121] [2002] I.C.R. 321, [40]. Emphasis original.
[122] [1993] I.R.L.R. 583 (NICA). See further, above, para.6–026.

been zero.[123] This is a significantly greater disparity than that in *McCausland*. Further, (as noted above, para.6–030) the definition of indirect discrimination no longer requires a comparison of those *advantaged* by the challenged practice and hence can no longer be used to the support the notion that the practice must favour a "significant proportion" of the pool.

If the *Coker* decision was rooted in a policy to permit small family-businesses to recruit from within, then a more logical vehicle for this the objective justification defence. Reasons of trust, loyalty, and availability are legitimate aims in that context. As such, where it discriminates, less justifiable nepotism can be outlawed.

(iv) Where only one person is put at a disadvantage

6–032 The statutory formula is aimed at, and confined to, group disadvantage. In *Eweida v British Airways*[124] the Court of Appeal held that indirect discrimination does not operate to prevent a practice that disadvantages just one individual (a person whose religious belief obliged her to display a crucifix). This is confirmed by EA 2010 s.19(1)(b), and the equality Directives, which demand that the challenged practice puts *persons* with whom the claimant shares the characteristic at a particular disadvantage.

(3) "Puts or Would Put"—Causation

6–033 The first thing to note is that the phrase "or would put" (in EA 2010 s.19(2) (b) *and* (c))[125] signals that an action can be brought simply where persons in the claimant's group, as well as the claimant himself, are merely *deterred* from, say, applying for, a job, a promotion, or a club or union membership, or from using a service.

The statutory definition requires that the challenged practice "puts" the claimant's group "at a particular disadvantage". This

---

[123] Even under the old definition, a claim can succeed if the proportion of the claimant's group who can comply is zero. In *Greencroft Social Club v Mullen* [1985] I.C.R. 796, only members were entitled to a disciplinary hearing. Women were not admitted as members, so the proportion of women who were entitled to the disciplinary hearing was zero. The EAT found that the disciplinary hearing rule adversely affected women. In his commentaries to *Coker* in the I.R.L.R., Michael Rubenstein noted, "The prohibition of discrimination in selection arrangements—a concept which lies at the heart of discrimination law—can be circumvented by the simple expedient of not having any selection arrangements" ([2001] I.R.L.R. 116, at 115) and "[T]he Court of Appeal seems to be answering the wrong question of whether it was indirectly discriminatory to appoint Mr Hart rather than whether the tribunal was right to find the arrangements for selection were indirectly discriminatory. The applicants were not challenging the appointment of Mr Hart as such—the reduction of the 'elite pool ... to a single man'. They were challenging the selection arrangements whereby the potential candidates were confined to an 'elite pool'. The statutes rightly treats these as separate and distinct causes of action" ([2002] I.R.L.R., at 3).

[124] [2010] I.C.R. 890 (CA), [15]–[19]. See further, Ch.3, para.3–022. For Comment, see L. Vickers, "Indirect discrimination and individual belief", Ecc. L.J. 2009, 11(2), 197.

[125] See above, para.6–007.

causative element demands a connection between the challenged practice and the claimant's group.

Where there are tangible challenged practices, causation is unlikely to be an issue. It goes without saying that, for instance, entrance exams, last-in-first-out selection for redundancy, or length of service benefits, will have a tangible impact on those who respectively, fail the exam, are selected for redundancy, or who have shorter service. In such cases the issue will be whether that impact falls disproportionately upon a protected group, which is a separate matter. There is little domestic and Community case law on this issue, save in the field of equal pay.[126] In the US case, *Dothard v Rawlinson*,[127] minimum height and weight requirements combined with statistics showing the likely impact of such a measure on women was enough, without more, to prove a causal link between the two. This was because the practices were clearly defined and the disparity so great that it would offend common sense to come to any other conclusion.[128] In *O'Flynn v Chief Adjudication Officer*[129] the ECJ went further, holding that a requirement that burials or cremations took place in the United Kingdom (to qualify for funeral expenses) was "intrinsically liable" to adversely affect migrant workers. No statistics were necessary.

Where the challenged practice is not so tangible, such as vague   **6–034** subjective employment practices,[130] statistics are likely to play an important part in the claim. It is when the practices are vague that causation will be an issue. Once again, the experience in the United States offers some guidance on how the law may develop here.

A connection between a practice and the victim's group became an express and detailed element of the US scheme following the *Wards Cove* decision.[131] Congress codified this requirement by legislating that a plaintiff must link any disparate impact to a specific practice. In cases of subjective decision-making, there may be an identified suspect practice (e.g. nepotism in recruitment) and evidence of some racial disparity (e.g. among successful applicants), yet no tangible link between the two. The question is in what circumstances, if at all, can proof of the practice and disparity without more be used to prove a causal link between the two. The US courts have held that "Statistical evidence may be probative where it reveals a disparity so great that it cannot be accounted for by chance"[132] and "statistical disparities must be sufficiently substantial that they raise ... an inference

---

[126] See Ch.9 para.9–030.
[127] 433 US 321 (Sup Ct 1977).
[128] National statistics showed that the requirements would exclude over 40% of the female population but less than 1% of the male population. The main issue was whether the employer could justify the requirements.
[129] Case C-237/94, [1996] ECR I-2617 (ECJ). See further above para.6–025.
[130] See above, para.6–009.
[131] ibid.
[132] *Bridgeport Guardians v City of Bridgeport* 933 F 2d 1140, at 1146 (2nd Cir 1991).

of causation."[133] The loose term *sufficiently substantial* alludes to the courts' practice of not adhering to a particular formula when deciding whether there has been a disparate impact. There is nothing more precise than that.

It would seem from *Bushey v New York State Civil Service Commission*[134] and *Bridgeport Guardians*[135] that where the "four-fifths" or "probability of chance" formulas are used,[136] an inference of causation will be made from a simple finding of an adverse impact. There are other cases where causation was proved without these formulas. For instance, in *Butler v Home Depot*[137] the claimants presented statistics that showed a 20 per cent disparity between the women in the qualified labour market and those within the workforce. The Court held simply that the statistical evidence was "of a *kind* and *degree* from which causation may reasonably be inferred."[138] From this, it would seem that even if the disparity falls below 20 per cent, it is at least *conceivable* that a court may find that there is causation, should it find that disparity to be "sufficiently substantial".

(4) The Defence of Objective Justification

6–035 Once the claimant has established a prima facie case, the burden shifts to the defendant to "objectively justify" the provision, criterion or practice. For instance, an employer requiring candidates to have a certain physical strength (which adversely affected women) would have to show that the requirement was necessary to perform the job.[139] If it does so, there is no liability.

This section is sub-divided into two discussions. First, there is an attempt to establish the precise meaning of the defence, and second, some examples of the defence in practice.

(a) The Meaning of the Justification Defence[140]

6–036 There are three issues to explore here. First, the differences between the EC and British definitions, second, the "alternative practice" doctrine, and third, where the defence itself is based upon discrimination.

The new generation of discrimination Directives state that a defendant may "objectively justify" the challenged provision, criterion or practice by showing a *legitimate aim*, and that *the means of*

---

[133] *Watson v Fort Worth Bank* 487 US 977, at 995 (Sup Ct 1988).
[134] 733 F 2d 220 (2nd Cir 1984), certiorari denied, 469 US 1117 (1985). See above, para.6–028.
[135] 933 F 2d 1140, at 1146. See above, para.6–029.
[136] See above para.6–028.
[137] C-94-4335 SI, C952182 SI, (N.D. Cal. Aug. 29, 1997). See above, para.6–011.
[138] ibid. at 49. Emphasis supplied.
[139] See e.g. *Dothard v Rawlinson* 433 US 321 (1977), see below, para.6–047.
[140] See R. Townshend-Smith, "Justifying indirect discrimination in English and American law: how stringent should the test be?" (1995) 1 IJDL 103.

achieving that aim are appropriate and necessary. This formula codifies ECJ case law, especially *Bilka-Kaufhaus v Weber von Hartz*.[141]
The test has been transposed into the domestic legislation, including
the Equality Act 2010, as "a proportionate means of achieving a
legitimate aim" (s.19(2)(d)).

(i) Domestic and EC definitions contrasted
A short history is required to understand the relationship between the   **6–037**
domestic and EU definitions. The original British discrimination
legislation used the rather open-ended phrase, "justifiable irrespective
of sex [or race]".[142]

In the early years, tribunals (influenced by US case law, upon
which this formula was based),[143] equated this with "necessity", in
other words, the challenged practice had to be no more than necessary to achieve the aim. For example, in *Steel v Union of Post Office
Workers*,[144] Phillips J., President of the EAT, said that the practice
must be inter alia "genuine and necessary". In 1982, however, the
Court of Appeal in *Ojutiku v Manpower Services Commission*[145]
contrasted "necessity" with the statutory word *justifiable*; Kerr L.J.
stated that "justifiable ... clearly applies a lower standard than ...
necessary".[146] Eveleigh L.J. considered it to mean "something ...
acceptable to right-thinking people as sound and tolerable."[147] Following this, Balcombe L.J., in *Hampson v Department of Education*,[148]
created the "*Hampson* (balancing) test," which weighs the discriminatory effect of the challenged practice against the reasonable
needs of the *employer*.[149]

In the meantime, the ECJ was developing a differently formulated
justification test. This three-part test required employers to show a
legitimate aim, and that the means of achieving that aim were
appropriate and *necessary*. This became known as the "*Bilka* test",[150]
which itself is rooted in the Community law principle of proportionality.[151] The means of achieving the legitimate aim must be
appropriate, meaning at the least, that there must be a causal

---

[141] Case 170/84, [1987] I.C.R. 110, (discussed below, para.6–037).
[142] SDA 1975 s.1(1)(b); RRA 1976 s.1(1)(b).
[143] Described above para.6–005.
[144] [1978] I.C.R. 181 (EAT), at 187.
[145] [1982] I.C.R. 661 (CA). In Parliament, the Government resisted amendments to the Sex
Discrimination Bill that would have replaced "justifiable" with "necessary". Lord Harris
stated that where a body offered reduced fares for pensioners, the policy might be justifiable,
but not necessary (362 HL Deb 14 July 1975 cols 10116–17).
[146] ibid. at 670.
[147] ibid. at 668.
[148] [1989] I.C.R. 179 (CA).
[149] *Hampson v Department of Education* [1989] I.C.R. 179 (CA), at 196F.
[150] Case 170/84 *Bilka-Kaufhaus v Weber von Hartz*, [1987] I.C.R. 110, (discussed further below,
para.9–034).
[151] See the *Cassis de Dijon* case, C-120/78 (*Rewe-Zentral AG v Bundesmonopolverwaltung für
Branntwein*) [1979] ECR 649.

connection between the aim and the method employed to achieve it, and that the means must not be tainted with discrimination.[152] "Necessity" encapsulates two elements. The defence should not succeed where there exists a less discriminatory alternative. In addition, a court may have to balance any discriminatory effect of the challenged practice against the benefits of achieving the legitimate aim. It was codified in the equality Directives.

Gradually, a new EC-derived definition of indirect discrimination found its way into the British legislation,[153] with the justification defence stated as being a "proportionate means of achieving a legitimate aim", which remains the format used in the Equality Act 2010.

6–038 As the influence of EC law grew, domestic courts were forced to reconcile the *Hampson* test with the EC model, which they felt able to do by holding that the *Hampson* balancing test reflected the EU's model of proportionality.[154]

This, in substance, was a fiction. Although both models require a legitimate (or genuine) aim, there is a difference between requiring that the challenged practice goes no further than necessary to achieve the aim and requiring a balance of interests.[155] (See the three examples below.) Accordingly, in 2005 the Court of Appeal "reformulated" the test model to mean "*reasonably* necessary".[156] This did not mean that a defendant could justify a measure simply by showing it was one of "a band of reasonable responses which a reasonable defendant (e.g. an employer) would adopt";[157] tribunals should consider "fairly obvious alternatives".[158] But, in contrast to the strict necessity test, defendants were not bound to show that the practice was the only possible one available.[159]

This language of compromise puts an unnecessary judicial gloss on the statutory words. "Proportionate" and "necessary" do not mean *nearly* proportionate, or *reasonably* necessary. A strict approach does not mean that businesses would be forced to spend great sums for a marginal reduction in a discriminatory impact: economic reasons are acceptable as a legitimate aims.[160] Further, this gloss over-complicates

---

[152] See "Defences based on discrimination", below, para.6–041.
[153] Starting with the RRA 1976 s.1(1A) (inserted by SI 2003/1626 reg.3, in force July 19, 2003), and in the SDA 1975 s.1(2)(b) (substituted by SI 2005/2467 reg.3, in force on October 1, 2005).
[154] See e.g. *Barry v Midland Bank* [1999] I.C.R. 859 (HL), at 870; *Hardys v Lax* [2005] I.C.R. 1565 (CA), [32].
[155] See M. Connolly, "Discrimination Law: Justification, Alternative Measures and Defences Based on Sex" (2001) 30 ILJ 311.
[156] *Hardys v Lax* [2005] I.C.R. 1565 (CA), [32]; *Cadman v Health and Safety Executive* [2004] EWCA 1317 (CA), [30]–[31], citing *Barry v Midland Bank* [1999] I.C.R. 319 (CA), at 336. Approved *Ladele v Islington LB* [2010] I.R.L.R 211 (CA) [47]–[48] (Lord Neuberger M.R.). For a view that it is "impossible" to gauge the seriousness of the discriminatory effect under the *Hampson* test, see *British Airways v Grundy (No.2)* [2008] I.R.L.R. 815 (CA), [4].
[157] *Hardys v Lax* [2005] I.C.R. 1565 (CA), [31]–[32].
[158] *Allonby v Accrington and Rossendale College* [2001] I.C.R. 1189 (CA), [28].
[159] *Hardys v Lax* [2005] I.C.R. 1565 (CA) [32].
[160] See e.g. *Bilka* Case 170/84, [1987] ICR 110 (ECJ), [36].

the matter, and provides defendants a leeway to discriminate, thus upsetting the legislative policy and indirect discrimination theory, which is to find the least discriminatory way to achieve the legitimate aim.

Three examples highlight the difference between "necessary" and "reasonably necessary". In *Enderby v Frenchay Health Authority*[161] the defendant Health Authority was trying to justify a difference in pay between speech therapists (98 per cent female) and pharmacists (63 per cent female). The pharmacists were paid about 40 per cent more than the speech therapists. As women were overrepresented in the lower paid group the Health Authority were obliged to justify the difference. It argued that market forces caused the difference. But the evidence was that only an extra 10 per cent pay was needed to recruit a sufficient number of pharmacists. Thus, there existed a less discriminatory alternative of paying the pharmacists a 10 per cent premium. The EAT applied the *Hampson* test and weighed the 40 per cent difference in pay against the need for sufficient pharmacists. Given that stark choice, the EAT held that the difference in pay was justified. Under the "reasonably necessary" test, where employers are not bound to use the least discriminatory practice available, the same result would be likely. But the ECJ held that the pay difference could only be justified to the proportion that market forces required (10 per cent). The existence of the less discriminatory alternative meant that the practice (a 40 per cent pay difference) could not be justified. For the ECJ, proportionality meant *no more than* necessary.

Second, there is an early British case of discrimination under the old Race Relations Act 1976, predating *Hampson*. In *Bohon-Mitchell v Common Professional Examination Board*[162] the defendant's policy was that persons with a degree in a subject other than law were required to take a course in academic law to qualify to take the Bar finals. This was normally a 12-month course. However, those with a non-British or non-Irish degree were required to complete a 21-month course. In 1978 Ms Bohon-Mitchell, who had been living in England (except for one year) since 1972 and was married to an Englishman, applied to take her Bar Finals. When she was informed that, as an American graduate, she would have to sit the 21-month course, she complained of discrimination on grounds of nationality or national origin. The defendant tried to justify that requirement on the ground that barristers needed a wide knowledge of the English way of life, and the simplest way of identifying those without such experience was by their degrees. The industrial tribunal held that the requirement to sit a 21-month course was not justified because it was not *necessary* to achieve the aim. Instead, each candidate's familiarity

6–039

---

[161] [1991] 1 CMLR 626, at 663 and 668, EAT; Case C-127/92, [1994] I.C.R. 112, ECJ.
[162] [1978] I.R.L.R 525 (IT).

with the English way of life could be assessed on a case by case basis.[163] If the tribunal had applied the *Hampson* test, or asked if the policy was reasonably necessary, it may well have concluded that the requirement was justified. The evidence was that just eight out of 191 applicants with a non-law degree had overseas degrees. Probably fewer than that eight had been resident in Britain and were therefore "familiar with the English way of life". In any case the discriminatory effect was relatively minor. If this discriminatory effect were weighed against the inconvenience of changing the system, a court may well find that defendant's administrative needs justified the practice. In other words discrimination could be allowed to continue because that would be more convenient for the defendant.

Finally, take a hypothetical example of entrance exams that are not updated. Here the tests might adversely affect a minority group, say recent immigrants, simply because white candidates are more familiar with the test through their links with the predominantly white workforce. In other respects, the test may be a valid indicator of job performance. It is arguable that the tests are reasonably necessary because they remain a genuine indicator of job performance. But if the inquiry asked if there was a less discriminatory method of achieving the aim (predicting job performance), it would it find the tests unjustified, because there exists a less discriminatory alternative (regular updating).

(ii) The US alternative practice doctrine

6–040 In the United States, the Supreme Court developed the alternative practice doctrine. Should a prima facie case be met with a proper business necessity defence, the plaintiff may still win by proposing an alternative business practice which has a less discriminatory effect. This has since been recognised in the Civil Rights Act 1991.[164] The rubric generally used was set in *Albermarle Paper Co v Moody*[165] where the Court stated that the alternative should "also serve the employer's legitimate interest in 'efficient and trustworthy workmanship'".[166]

An example of a successful demonstration of an alternative practice can be seen in *Bridgeport Guardians v City of Bridgeport*[167] where tests used in the promotion of police officers to the rank of sergeant were challenged. One hundred and seventy persons applied for 19 posts and the results showed that the tests had a disparate impact on

---

[163] ibid. [29].
[164] Section 105, codified as 42 USC s.2000e2(k)(1), which also provides that the alternative practice doctrine should be applied according to pre-*Wards Cove* principles (see above, para.6–010).
[165] 422 US 405 (1975).
[166] ibid. at 425 citing *McDonnell Douglas Corp v Green* 411 US 792, at 802 (Sup Ct 1973).
[167] 933 F 2d 1140 (2nd Cir 1991). See also above, para.6–029.

blacks and Hispanics, with only 30 per cent and 46 per cent respectively passing in comparison with 68 per cent of whites. But the real impact was worse than that because the 19 best performers were selected, leaving *no* minorities with promotion. The employer successfully justified the tests as a reliable and accurate predictor of job performance. However, what the results table[168] did not reveal was that, of all those passing, the marks were extremely close. The plaintiffs put forward evidence that the difference between a few marks was insignificant. Accordingly the plaintiffs suggested that the marks should be banded: that is, marks within, say, 8 per cent of each other, placed in a single band. Then the successful candidates could be selected from those bands, using other (non-discriminatory) factors to decide. In this way the best performers were selected without a disparate impact. The Court found that the use of banding would alleviate the disparate racial effect of the examination without imposing any significant burden on the defendants while serving their legitimate interests.[169]

The doctrine has not been adopted by the EC or British schemes. However, a *strict* test of proportionality should achieve the same result. If a claimant can identify a less discriminatory alternative means of achieving the same (legitimate) aim, the justification defence should fail for being disproportionate. This is unlikely to happen in domestic cases. As noted above, domestic courts have stated that although tribunals should consider "fairly obvious alternatives",[170] a strict test should not be applied, and that defendants are not bound to show that the challenged practice was the only possible one available.[171]

(iii) Defences based upon discrimination

It is implicit in the *Bilka* test that the justification must not be related to the ground of discrimination in question. In *Jenkins v Kingsgate*[172] the ECJ stated the factors used as a defence should be objectively justified and be "in no way related to any discrimination based on sex". This was expressed in the original Sex Discrimination Act 1975 and Race Relations Act 1976 ("justifiable irrespective of sex/race"), but was not restated in the new domestic definitions, including the Equality Act 2010. However, it should come under the general expressed principle of proportionality, and it is inconceivable that the new definitions, based upon EC law, differ in substance in this matter. The issue is likely to arise where employers respond to a law giving

6–041

---

[168] ibid. at 1143. The results table is set out above, para.6–029.

[169] ibid. at 1145 and 1148.

[170] *Allonby v Accrington and Rossendale College* [2001] I.C.R. 1189 (CA), [28].

[171] *Hardys v Lax* [2005] I.C.R. 1565 (CA) [32]. See above, para.6–038.

[172] Case 96/80 [1981] I.C.R. 592, [11]. See below, para.9–035. See also *Bilka* [1986] 2 CMLR 701, [37].

rights to a protected group, by manoeuvring that group into a position where those rights are not applicable.

This appeared to be the case in *Allonby v Accrington & Rossendale College*.[173] Accrington & Rossendale College employed 341 part-time lecturers on successive one-year contracts. In 1996 legislation came into force obliging employers to afford part-time workers equal benefits to those given to full-time workers.[174] The purpose of the legislation was to prevent indirect sex discrimination, as part-time workers are predominantly women. Faced with the extra expense the College responded by dismissing all its part-time lecturers and re-employing them as sub-contractors, through an agency. Consequently the part-timers were paid less and lost a series of benefits (e.g. sick pay). Ms Allonby, a part-time lecturer, brought several actions against the College, including one for indirect sex discrimination, as the dismissals fell disproportionately upon women (who made up two-thirds of the part-time lecturers, but only one-half of the full-time lecturers). On appeal, Ms Allonby argued that the College had failed to justify the dismissals because, inter alia, although the primary aim was to save money, they were rooted in the legislation designed to prevent discrimination against women. The Court of Appeal allowed her appeal chiefly because the tribunal failed to consider any "fairly obvious" alternatives or apply an "objective balance" (*Hampson*) test. On this failure Sedley L.J. said that: "In particular there is no recognition [by the tribunal] that if the aim of the dismissal was itself discriminatory ... it could never afford justification."[175] But the judge said no more than that on the issue.

Ms Allonby cited *R. v Secretary of State, ex parte Equal Opportunities Commission* and *R. v Secretary of State, ex parte Seymour-Smith*.[176] In *ex parte EOC* Lord Keith held that existing Regulations affording inferior benefits to part-time workers constituted a "gross breach of the principle of equal pay and could not be possibly regarded as a suitable means of achieving an increase in part-time employment."[177] In *Seymour-Smith*, when giving a ruling on justification, the ECJ stated that a Government measure "cannot have the effect of frustrating the implementation of a fundamental principle of Community law such as that of equal pay...".[178]

6–042   Those cases concerned Government measures made in pursuance of a social policy, where a Government is allowed a "broad margin of discretion".[179] No such discretion is afforded in ordinary employment cases and so the College should be under a stricter duty to justify. The

[173] [2001] I.C.R. 1189 (CA). For Comment, see (2001) 30 ILJ 311.
[174] Although not specified by the EAT or the CA this was presumably the Employment Protection (Part-Time Employees) Regulations 1995, SI 1995/31, see now SI 2000/1551.
[175] [2001] I.C.R. 1189, [29].
[176] Respectively [1995] 1 AC 1 (HL); [1999] I.C.R. 447 (ECJ).
[177] ibid. at 30.
[178] [1999] I.C.R. 447, [75]. Discussed below, at para.6–050.
[179] See e.g. *Seymour-Smith*, ibid, [74], and below, para.6–048.

express aim of the College's arrangement was to give (predominantly female) part-time lecturers fewer benefits and less pay, which appears also to be a "gross breach of the principle of equal pay" and accordingly should never be justified. On this point alone Ms Allonby should have prevailed.[180]

There lies in such cases a related line of argument. The dismissals of a predominantly female group were inspired by Regulations passed to provide equal benefits to women. It is at least arguable that the requirement is "so closely related" to sex that it should not be justifiable. In *Orphanos v Queen Mary College*[181] the plaintiff challenged a requirement to be ordinarily resident within the European Community for three years, so to be exempt from full overseas student fees. The immediate goal of the requirement was to curtail public expenditure on education. The House of Lords held that the requirement was "so closely related" to nationality that it could not be justified and amounted to indirect racial discrimination.[182] Similarly, in *R. (Elias) v Secretary of State for Defence*,[183] it was held that a requirement to be born in the UK, or have a parent or grandparent born in the UK, to qualify for a £10,000 "debt of honour" for imprisonment in Hong Kong by the Japanese in World War 2, was so closely related to nationality that it could not be justified:

> "A stringent standard of scrutiny of the claimed justification is appropriate because the discrimination, though indirect in form, is so closely related in substance to the direct form of discrimination on grounds of national origins, which can never be justified."[184]

Orphanos and *Elias* show that where the defence is "closely related to", (rather than based upon), a protected characteristic, the standard of justification imposed will be correspondingly strict.

(b) Examples of the Defence

(i) Part-time workers and family responsibilities
Quite separately from the sex discrimination provisions of the   **6–043**
Equality Act 2010, dedicated legislation has been passed to protect part-time workers. The Part-time Workers (Prevention of Less

---

[180] The justification issue was remitted to an employment tribunal for a further hearing, while other issues were referred to the ECJ: Case C-256/01 [2004] I.C.R. 1328.
[181] [1985] A.C. 761 (HL).
[182] ibid. at 772–773.
[183] [2006] 1 W.L.R. 3213 (CA), [86]–[90].
[184] ibid. [161]–[162], citing *Orphanos v QMC* [1985] A.C. 761 (HL).

Favourable Treatment) Regulations 2000[185] provide that less favourable treatment of a part-time worker is unlawful unless "objectively justified".[186] These Regulations protect those who are already working part-time. They extend to the situation where a full-time worker switches, or returns to, part-time work (a typical move by expectant and new mothers).[187]

It is now firmly established that less favourable treatment of part-time workers adversely affects women, who are more likely than men to working part-time. Thus, less favourable treatment of part-time workers will usually require justification under *sex* discrimination law.

An employer refusing a request by a woman to switch to part-time or flexible hours is likely to indirectly discriminate against women, unless the refusal is justified. In *Home Office v Holmes*[188] the EAT rejected the employer's argument that a refusal was justified simply because the bulk of British industry, and its civil service, was organised around full-time working. An employer has to justify the refusal on the particular circumstances of the claimant's job. This was the case in *Greater Glasgow Health Board v Carey*,[189] where a health visitor asked to switch to a two-and-a-half, or three-day week. Her employer refused and instead offered her five half-days per week. This was because the nature of the work was not task orientated, but on a personal contact basis with patients; personal discussions with patients and personal observations were not all apt to put on record. This meant that it was important that each health visitor was available for patients and other agencies, such as doctors and social workers, every day of the week. The EAT held that the refusal was justified.

6–044   The justification may be also economic, where a switch to part-time by, say, a manager, would inevitably mean that the post becomes shared. This may involve a duplication of many tasks, such as interviews and meetings, and extra time spent communicating and record keeping. Such an employer would argue that job-sharing here would make the business less competitive.[190]

---

[185] SI 2000/1551, implementing Directive 97/81/EC. For a commentary concluding that the protections given by the regulations are too few and too narrow, see A. McColgan, "Missing the Point? The Part-time Workers (Prevention of Less Favourable Treatment) Regulations 2000 (SI 2000, No. 1551)" (2000) 29 ILJ 260. See, also, M. Schmidt, "The right to part-time work under German law: progress in or a boomerang for equal employment opportunities?" (2001) 30 ILJ 335. ERA 1996 s.80F gives rights to qualified employees to request time off for caring for children and certain adults.

[186] Justification of inferior pay for part-time workers is discussed in Ch.9 under "Economic Reasons", para.9–035.

[187] SI 2000/1551, regs 3, 4.

[188] [1984] I.C.R. 678.

[189] [1987] I.R.L.R 484 (EAT).

[190] See *Hardys v Lax* [2005] I.C.R. 1565 (CA), where such an argument failed mainly because the tribunal considered the employer's evidence was "exaggerated" (at [40]–[49]).

Those cases involved a switch from full-time to part-time work. It is possible to challenge a requirement to change the pattern of work. In *London Underground v Edwards (No.2)*[191] the employer implemented a new flexible shift pattern, where duties were to begin at 4.45 a.m. Ms Edwards, a single mother with a young child, had been working daytime hours so to be at home mornings and evenings. She objected to the new shift pattern and requested to continue working her daytime shifts. Her employer refused and she resigned, claiming indirect discrimination. On the issue of justification, the evidence was that the employer could have accommodated her request without damaging its business plan, and that the employer originally was willing to accommodate her request but changed its mind following pressure from the predominantly male workforce. Accordingly, the EAT held that the refusal was not justified.

Logically, if employers can be liable for denying a switch from full- to part-time work, or for forcing inflexible hours upon staff, they should equally be vulnerable when refusing to *hire* on a part-time or flexible basis.

(ii) Testing and educational qualifications[192]

Using tests or qualifications for employment decisions such as recruitment, promotion or redeployment has the merit of being objective, but tests carry the risk of operating as "built in headwinds"[193] against minority groups and women. They can adversely affect any of those groups, for, say, cultural or historic reasons. In *Griggs v Duke Power*,[194] the requirement to pass an intelligence test (or have a high school diploma), adversely affected blacks because of the history of segregated education. Tests for promotion may favour those with long work experience and so disfavour women, who generally would have entered the workplace more recently.[195] Such tests must be justified as necessary for the job. The Code of Practice for Employment advises employers that tests should be professionally validated. In particular, the tests should correspond to the job

6–045

---

[191] [1997] I.R.L.R 157. The decision was upheld by the Court of Appeal [1998] I.R.L.R 364, but there was no appeal on the justification issue. On the issue of the refusal having an adverse impact on women, see above, para.6–025, p.175.

[192] See also the discussion on causation, above, para.6–033, and the alternative practice doctrine, above para.6–040. See R. Wood, "Psychometrics should make assessment fairer" (1996) 67 EOR 27; M. Pearn, R. Kandola and R. Mottram, *Selection Tests and Sex Bias: the Impact of Selection Testing on the Employment Opportunities of Men and Women* (Manchester: EOC, 1987); *Towards Fair Selection: a Survey of Test Practice and Thirteen Case Studies* (London: Commission for Racial Equality, 1993).

[193] *Griggs v Duke Power* 401 US 424, at 432 (Sup Ct 1971). See further, above, para.6–001, p.152.

[194] ibid.

[195] See *R. v London Borough of Hammersmith and Fulham ex parte Nalgo* [1991] I.R.L.R 249 (QBD).

requirements and special care must be taken where there are candidates whose first language is not English.[196]

In UK and Community law, there is no general legal requirement that tests are validated, but of course validation will greatly improve the chance of justifying them. As with other challenged practices, employers must show that the tests meet the *Bilka* standard. Equally, qualifications which have only a vague relationship to the job (as in *Griggs*), or which overstate the true requirement ("excellent English" when good English is appropriate) are unlikely to be an appropriate and proportionate means of achieving a legitimate aim.

In the United States, courts will demand that challenged tests are validated "by professionally acceptable methods, to be predictive of or significantly correlated with important elements of work behaviour".[197] There, the courts afford "great deference"[198] to the Equal Employment Opportunity Commission's Uniform Guidelines, which classifies three types of test. "Content validity" tests replicate major tasks required by the job, such as typing speed for a computer operator. "Criterion" or "predictive validity" tests use empirical data to predict work job performance and potential. Third, "Construct validity" demonstrates which candidates have identifiable characteristics which have been determined to be important for successful job performance. Accordingly, general intelligence tests, such as those used in *Griggs*, are unlikely to be justified.

6–046   Where a test produces results favouring, say, whites, an employer may be tempted to withdraw the results and start again, for fear of an indirect discrimination claim by the disfavoured racial group, say, blacks. The danger now is that the otherwise successful white candidates, denied a job or a promotion, may sue for *direct* discrimination. In *Ricci v DeStefano*,[199] the US Supreme Court held that such an employer would be liable unless it had a "strong basis in evidence"[200] for its fear of an indirect discrimination claim, and that the test results alone was not strong enough. The test in that case was extensively well-prepared, job-related, and necessary. There was no lesser-discriminatory alternative test.[201]

The lesson for employers (and others, such as some schools) is that where they use validated or otherwise well-founded tests, they should stand by the results, no matter what the outcome in a one-off

---

[196] EHRC Draft Code of Practice on Employment, paras 16–52 to 16–53. The Code refers employers to the British Psychological Society and its Psychological Testing Centre, at *www.psychtesting.org.uk*.

[197] *Albermarle Paper v Moody* 422 US 405, at 431 (Sup Ct 1975), citing the Uniform Guidance issued by the EEOC, 29 C.F.R. 1607. See *www.eeoc.gov* and click on "Laws, Regulations", the "Regulations", scroll down to "1607".

[198] ibid.

[199] (2009) 129 S. Ct. 2658.

[200] ibid. at 2664, 2675–2676.

[201] ibid. 2678.

scenario. The loophole may be—in the United States at least—where an equally valid, but less discriminatory, alternative is found to exist.[202]

(iii) Physical and health and safety justifications
It is unlawful (as direct discrimination) to exclude *all* women from a job on the basis that few will be able to meet a strength or stamina requirement.[203] Employers must instead impose a standard common to both male and female applicants, and (assuming it would it adversely affect women or another protected group) justify it. The most well known US case on this matter is *Dothard v Rawlinson*,[204] where minimum height and weight requirements for employment as a prison guard were not justified because the employer produced no evidence that the requirements were related to the goal that prison officers needed to be physically strong. Instead, the Supreme Court noted, the employer could have used specific strength tests.[205]

6–047

In *Singh v British Rail Engineering Ltd*,[206] the employer introduced a requirement that workers wear "bump caps" when working under raised railway carriages. This requirement indirectly discriminated against Sikhs (orthodox Sikh men being obliged to wear a turban) but was held to be justified. This was a relatively early case in the life of Britain's discrimination law, and the result might not be the same today. Certainly, under the *Bilka* rubric, the employer's arguments were less than watertight. The first ground was the fear of civil and criminal liability, should a worker not wearing a bump cap be injured. But as it had supplied and recommended the wearing of the caps, the risk of civil liability was extremely low, in the face of a worker's refusal. Further, British Rail could not specify the criminal risk. Employers should be obliged under the *Bilka* standard to be more specific than pronouncing a vague unsubstantiated risk. The second ground was that making an exception for Sikh workers would cause the other workers to disobey the requirement. This amounts to imposing a discriminatory requirement out of fear of the reaction of the workers to what they perceive as special treatment for a racial minority. It parallels cases where employers directly discriminate because of pressure from the workforce, which is no defence.[207] In the context of justifying indirect discrimination, this cannot be accepted as a legitimate aim. A Sikh man cannot be blamed for management's

---

[202] See "The alternative practice doctrine", above, para.6–040.
[203] EA 2010 s.13, and Explanatory Note 63.
[204] 433 US 321 (1977), see further above paras 6–011 and 6–033.
[205] ibid. at 331–332.
[206] [1986] I.C.R. 22 (EAT). Followed in *Dhanjal v British Steel*, (unreported) EAT/66/94. Sikhs wearing turbans enjoy statutory exemptions from wearing safety helmets on construction sites (Employment Act 1989 s.11) and crash helmets on motorcycles (Road Traffic Act 1988 s.16).
[207] See *R v CRE ex parte Westminster CC* [1985] I.C.R. 827 (CA).

failure to supervise properly its workforce. The legitimate aim in this
case was safety. The proper question was whether the requirement to
wear a bump cap (instead of a turban enveloping his unshorn hair)
was necessary in pursuit of that aim. One contribution to that issue
was made by Mr Singh, when he pointed out that Sikh men were not
obliged to wear helmets when fighting (for Britain) in the two world
wars, or when employed as policemen.

An even less convincing justification was accepted in *Singh v
Rowntree Mackintosh*,[208] where a ban on beards (again indirectly
discriminating against Sikhs) in a confectionery factory to reduce the
risk of contamination by facial hair was held to be justified, despite
evidence that the "no beards" policy was not adopted in their other
factories, that "moustaches and side-whiskers" were not banned, and
that there existed an alternative of beard-masks.

More recently, however, in *R. (Watkins-Singh) v The Governing
Body of Aberdare Girls' High School*,[209] the High Court held that a
school's ban on wearing a Kara bracelet (favoured by Sikhs) was not
justified. The school's "health and safety" argument (one of three
defences) was neutralised by the claimant agreeing to remove or cover
it for sports and PE.

(iv) Social policy justifications

6–048 A social policy justification is used normally by Governments
defending a domestic measure against superior Community discrimination law, but it may be used by "social partners",[210] and it
should be possible for a private party defendant to justify a social
aim, or for a tribunal to summons the relevant government minister
to justify the challenged legislation.

Where a defence is based on social policy, the *Bilka* test is modified.
Defendants must still show that the practice reflects a necessary aim
of its social policy and is suitable and necessary for achieving that
aim, but at the same time, they are afforded a broad margin of discretion in choosing the appropriate means to achieve that policy. But
the margin of discretion is not so broad to have the effect of frustrating the implementation of the fundamental principle of equal
treatment. Mere generalisations will not suffice.[211]

---

[208] [1979] I.C.R. 554 (EAT). See also *Panesar v Nestle* [1980] I.R.L.R 60 (EAT), leave to appeal
refused [1980] I.R.L.R. 64 (CA).
[209] *The Queen on the application of Sarika Angel Watkins-Singh (A child acting by Sanita
Kumari Singh, her Mother and Litigation Friend) v The Governing Body of Aberdare Girls'
High School* [2008] EWHC 1865 (Admin).
[210] e.g. trade unions and employer's representatives, typically when agreeing discriminatory
provisions in collective agreements. See e.g. Case C-411/05 *Palacios*, discussed Ch.8, para.8–
071.
[211] Case C-167/97 *Seymour-Smith* [1999] I.C.R. 447 (ECJ), [69]–[77] (Sex discrimination. See
further paras 6–027 and 6–050); Case C-208/05 *ITC Innovative Technology Center GmbH v
Bundesagentur für Arbeit* [2007] E.C.R. I-181 (ECJ), [40]–[41] (Nationality discrimination).

It has been suggested that the raft of equality Directives coming into force since 2000, which effectively codify the *Bilka* test, will trigger a stricter test, so that a social policy defence no longer enjoys the broad margin of discretion.[212] These Directives do not apply to all grounds of discrimination prohibited by Community law, such as nationality, and if a stricter test were not applied in these areas as well, the result would be a dual standard. Since the new Directives came into force, beginning with the Burden of Proof Directive 97/80/ EC in 2001 (codifying the definition of indirect discrimination), the case law has been inconclusive. In *Nikoloudi*[213] (a sex discrimination case), the ECJ appeared to apply a stricter test, omitting to mention the broad margin of discretion. However, in a series of (direct) age discrimination cases, beginning a few months later with *Mangold v Helm*,[214] the ECJ affirmed the broad margin of discretion afforded to social policy justifications,[215] without reference to *Nikoloudi*.

Where a margin of discretion is appropriate, the cases show that encouraging more employment is a common and legitimate aim, that the more serious the adverse impact the stronger the justification needs to be, and that generally defendants should put forward some fairly detailed and objective evidence in support of their arguments.

Domestic measures disfavouring part-time workers, and thus adversely affecting women, appear to be the hardest to justify, mainly because the adverse effect is so well recognised and severe. In *R. v Secretary of State for Employment, ex parte Equal Opportunities Commission*,[216] the British Government's reason for restricting or excluding unfair dismissal and redundancy pay rights for part-time workers was no more than a statement asserting this would encourage employers to hire more part-time workers. As no objective evidence was produced to support this, the House of Lords held that the policy was not justified. In *Steinicke*,[217] German law for public sector workers provided that those over 55 could convert to part-time work, *if they had worked full-time for three of the five preceding years*. The German Government stated that the policy was for "budgetary reasons" and to encourage part-time work and save costs. The ECJ held

6–049

---

[212] See C. Barnard and B. Hepple, "Substantive equality" (2000) 59(3) CLR 562, at 575. For a brief description of legislative scheme, see Ch.2, para.2–002.

[213] *Nikoloudi v Organismos Tilepikoinonion Ellados AE* Case C-196/02 (2005), especially at [48], ECJ.

[214] Case C-144/04 [2006] I.R.L.R 143 (ECJ), [63]. See further below, Ch.8, para.8–066. Advocate-General Ruiz-Marabou Colomer also stated that Member States had a "broad discretion" with social policy in *Vergani v Agenzia delle Entrate, Ufficio di Arona* Case C-207-04, [52], (2005).

[215] Case C-411/05 *Palacios De La Villa v Cortefiel Servicios Sa* [2007] I.R.L.R 989, [68]. Case C-388/07 *R. (The Incorporated Trustees of the National Council on Ageing (Age Concern England)) v Secretary of State for Business, Enterprise and Regulatory Reform* [2009] 3 C.M.L.R. 4, [51]; Case C-45/09 *Rosenbladt* [2010] ECR 00, [41] (state), [69] (social partners "at a national level"). See further, Ch.8, para.8–071.

[216] [1995] 1 A.C. 1.

[217] *Steinicke v Bundesanstalt fur Arbeit* Case C-77/02, [2003] I.R.L.R 892, [61]–[69].

that the rule in fact discouraged part-time work, as it acted as a disincentive to enter part-time work in the first place. It added that if budgetary considerations were allowed to justify indirect discrimination, the principle of equal treatment would vary with the state of public finances. In *Rinner-Kuhn*[218] the German Government's justification for excluding those who worked up to ten hours per week from a right to sick pay from their employers, was that these workers were "not integrated in and connected with the undertaking in a way comparable with other workers". The ECJ rejected this as a "generalised statement" which did not amount to objective justification. However, in *Nolte*,[219] the challenge was to the exclusion of those who worked less than 15 hours per week ("minor employment") from the *State* sick pay scheme. Here, notably, the German Government advanced more detailed arguments: (i) the policy corresponded to a structural principle of the German social security scheme; (ii) the only way the foster the demand for minor employment was within this structure; and (iii) that otherwise there would be an increase in unlawful employment and circumventing devices (e.g. false self-employment). The ECJ held the policy was justified, noting the State's broad margin of discretion.

The next three domestic sex discrimination cases appear less consistent. In *Hockenjos v Secretary of State for Social Security*[220] an enhanced Jobseeker's Allowance ("JSA") was given to parents in receipt of Child Benefit, to account for the extra expense of child care. Where the parents were separated, the Child Benefit, and consequently the enhanced JSA, was paid to the "person responsible for the child", which was usually the mother. Consequently, Mr Hockenjos, a separated father, received only the lower amount of JSA, despite sharing a proportion of the child care duties. The Child Benefit link adversely affected men and Hockenjos challenged it at as contrary to Equal Treatment in Social Security Directive 79/7/EEC. The Government argued that the Child Benefit link was justified to "ensure consistency" and avoid the "obvious problems when two parents put forward conflicting claims of responsibility". The Court of Appeal stated that where a policy frustrates the fundamental principle of equal treatment, deference to its margin of discretion is no longer possible, and held that as the Government had not considered less discriminatory alternatives, the Child Benefit link was not justified.[221]

---

[218] *Rinner-Kuhn v FWW Spezial-Gebäudereinigung GmbH and Co KG* Case 171/88, [1989] I.R.L.R 493, at 496. See also *Nikoloudi v Organismos Tilepikoinonion Ellados AE* Case C-196/02, [52].

[219] *Nolte v Landesversicherungsanstalt Hannover* Case C-317/93, [1996] I.R.L.R 225.

[220] [2004] EWCA 1749 (Civ).

[221] ibid. [28], [44], [47] & [71] (Scott Baker L.J.) and [177] (Ward L.J. concurring).

Hockenjos was distinguished in a very similar case, *Humphreys v* **6–050** *Revenue and Customs Commissioners*.[222] Here, where parents were separated, this time, Child Tax Credit was paid to the parent having the main responsibility for the children. The father had the children for three days per week, and so the Tax Credit went to the mother. The father challenged this rule, this time under the European Convention of Human Rights,[223] as it indirectly discriminated against men. The Court of Appeal held that even where the discrimination was on a "core" ground, such as sex, when the matter involved social policy, the State had a broad margin of discretion, and all the more so when the discrimination was *indirect*.[224] The Court distinguished *Hockenjos*, because this rule was "not so stark", permitting parents to agree responsibility for each child, and the Tax Credit was directed at the child, unlike the Jobseeker's Allowance. So, no matter which parent got the payment, the child got the benefit. A less discriminatory alternative would have been to allocate the Tax Credit proportionately. But the Court held that the need for an easily applicable "bright lines" rule, administrative convenience, and saving costs, and the detailed analysis given to the rule by the defendant, justified the practice.[225] The obvious distinction here is that this case was decided under the separate regime of the Convention of Human Rights, but the Court played down that difference: "In the generality of cases we would not expect the differences to lead to materially different outcomes".[226]

A complete lack of detail in the defence did not seem to trouble the House of Lords when hearing *Seymour-Smith*[227] upon its return from the ECJ. Here, legislation which in 1985 extended the qualification period for Unfair Dismissal rights to two years' continuous employment,[228] was challenged as it adversely affected women, who are more transient in the workforce than men.[229] The Government's argument was that the legislation would encourage recruitment, although it offered no evidence that, after six years, it had made any impact. The House of Lords held that the Government had justified the legislation. Lord Nicholls cited the part of the ECJ's ruling on justification which omitted the word "necessary". That was enough for him to conclude that the burden on the Government was not "as

---

[222] [2010] EWCA 56 (Civ).
[223] Tax credits fall within ECHR, Protocol 1, art.1: *R (RJM) v Secretary of State for Work and Pensions* [2009] 1 A.C. 311 (HL). See further Ch.2, para.2–013. Child Tax Credits did not fall within the Directive 79/7/EEC.
[224] [2010] EWCA Civ 56, [50], citing *Stec v UK* (App No.65731/01) (2006) 43 E.H.R.R. 1017, [52].
[225] ibid. [51].
[226] ibid. [53]. The distinction was advanced by the defendant: [40]. For the ECtHR case law of the margin of appreciation, see Ch.2, para.2–021, p.39.
[227] [2000] I.C.R. 244. See above, paras. 6–019, p.169 and 6–027. For Comment, see [2000] 05/2 Jo Civ Lib 212.
[228] SI 1985/782.
[229] The statistics are set out above, para.6–027.

heavy as previously thought".[230] Read as a whole the ECJ's judgment
clearly envisaged that the measure must be "necessary" to achieve an
aim.[231] Even on Lord Nicholls' less stringent test, the decision was
surprising. After all, although the ECJ held that encouraging
recruitment was a legitimate aim, it observed that "Mere generalisations concerning the capacity of a specific measure to encourage
recruitment are not enough ...".[232] The decision might be explained
by the marginal adverse effect of the legislation (about 8 per cent less
women than men qualified for unfair dismissal rights). But on a
national scale, it meant that for no good reason, for some 14 years,
hundreds of thousands of British women worked without the protection of Unfair Dismissal rights.

(a) Private parties and social policy

6–051   As noted above, generally the defendant in these cases will be a
Member State, arguing that a domestic measure is compatible with
Community discrimination law. However, there is nothing in the
domestic or EC legislation that limits to this defence only to Governments. Accordingly, in *Hlozek v Roche Austria Gesellschaft
mbH*[233] Advocate-General Kokott stated that a private employer
should be able use this defence, and enjoy equally the broad margin
of discretion afforded to Member States. Some years earlier, in
Greater Manchester Police Authority v Lea,[234] the EAT held that there
had to be a link between the function of the employer and the
objective justification. Accordingly, the employer's policy of not
hiring those with occupational pensions (adversely affecting men) to
favour the unemployed was not justified, as the aim was not linked to
the employer's function. The EAT based its reasoning on the
Hampson balancing test, which requires that the discriminatory effect
of the challenged practice is balanced against the reasonable needs of
the *employer*.[235] Since *Lea*, the law has moved beyond the confines of
the *Hampson* test, and courts are free to consider a social policy as a
"legitimate aim". Thus, private parties should be able to use a social
policy as a defence, and *Lea* should not be followed.

Where a private defendant follows domestic legislation that
apparently contravenes the equal treatment principle in Community
law, a problem arises. The claimant is likely to be suing the defendant, but challenging the validity of the legislation, introduced by the
State in pursuit of a social policy. Unless the case proceeds by judicial

---

[230] [2000] I.C.R. 244, at 261.
[231] See e.g. [1999] I.C.R. 447, [65].
[232] ibid. [71] and [76].
[233] Case C-19/02, [2005] 1 CMLR 28 (ECJ), AG[57]-[58]. The case was decided by the Court on
    other grounds.
[234] [1990] I.R.L.R 372, EAT.
[235] See above, para.6–037.

review, the defendant may be in the position of defending State's social policy. Where the case progresses to the ECJ a Member State may make representations.[236] For domestic courts, the issue arose in *Harvest Town Circle Ltd v Rutherford (No.1)*.[237] In this case, pre-dating the age discrimination regulations of 2006, Mr Rutherford, aged 67, was dismissed. By s.109 of the Employment Rights Act 1996, those over 65 could not claim unfair dismissal. Mr Rutherford argued that s.109 adversely affected men and so was contrary to EC sex discrimination law. As Harvest Ltd produced no evidence to justify s.109, the tribunal concluded that the exclusion was not justified. The EAT held this to be an error of law. A tribunal could not come to a proper decision without hearing the Government's argument, and therefore it should invite or if necessary *summons* "against his will" the appropriate minister to put its case.[238]

(v) Religion or belief discrimination

For religion or belief discrimination in employment cases, different **6–052** considerations may apply to the application of the justification test. This is because it will be common for workers to seek *different*, rather than equal, treatment, typically, time off for religious observances and practices, or dispensation from an appearance rule (such as no beards, face coverings, jewellery, or mandatory skirts). Such problems normally arise from the defendant's facially neutral practices or provisions, and so are analysed as indirect discrimination. The nature of these problems more closely resembles claims under disability discrimination law which imposes a positive duty of "reasonable accommodation".[239] As the legislation provides no express duty of reasonable accommodation, these cases will be decided under the objective justification defence, which in some cases at least, may amount to the same thing.

JH Walker Ltd v Hussain[240] was heard under the old, and arguably less strict, test of justification.[241] In this case 18 workers were disciplined for taking a day off work to celebrate Eid, a Muslim holy day, in breach of a new rule that holidays could not be taken during the company's busiest time. The workers brought a claim of indirect racial discrimination (as the facts arose before the Religion of Belief

---

[236] See e.g. *Jenkins v Kingsgate*, C-98/80, [1981] E.C.R. 911, *Barber v Guardian Royal Exchange* Case C-262/88, [1990] E.C.R. I-1889.

[237] [2002] I.C.R. 123 (EAT).

[238] ibid. [28]–[29]. Harvest Ltd later became insolvent, leaving the Government liable for any unfair dismissal compensation payable, conveniently making it an interested party and a defendant in the proceedings. However, the House of Lords resolved the claim on basis that there was no adverse impact, and so justification was not required: *Rutherford v Secretary of State for Trade and Industry (No.2)* [2006] I.C.R. 785 (HL). Discussed, above para.6–016.

[239] Discussed below, para.13–039. See L. Vickers, *Religious freedom, religious discrimination and the workplace* (Oxford/Portland, OR: Hart, 2008), pp.129–130, arguing for such a defence.

[240] [1996] I.C.R. 291 (EAT), at 295–296. See also Ch.12, para.12–032.

[241] See above para.6–037.

Regulations 2003). The absence of half the production staff for a day caused a loss of profit, but this could have been reduced to a "minimum" had the employer made appropriate arrangements in advance and exploited the workers' willingness to put in extra hours. The tribunal weighed the competing interests and held that the rule was not justified.

In *Islington LBC v Ladele*,[242] the local authority employer refused the claimant's (religious-based) request not to conduct civil partnerships, believing them to be "contrary to God's law". The refusal was in deference to the authority's "Dignity for All" policy. This legitimate policy was for the benefit of residents and staff relations. At least two gay colleagues were offended by the claimant's request. Of course, strictly speaking, the claimant's request could have been accommodated, with others covering for the relatively few civil partnership ceremonies. But nature of the aim and the offence to the colleagues meant that the council's refusal to accommodate her request was proportionate.

6–053   In *Azmi v Kirklees MBC*,[243] the requirement for teaching staff not cover their face or wear clothing that unduly interfered with their ability to communicate with pupils adversely affected the claimant teaching assistant. Her Muslim religion obliged her to wear the veil when in the presence of adult males, in this case when assisting a male teacher in the classroom. Despite many suggestions for accommodating her practice (raise her voice, use a screen; remain with her back to any male teacher; remove the target group from the classroom; use more hand and body gestures; change the timetable so that she only taught with female teachers),[244] the EAT held that the requirement was legitimate and proportionate.

In *Mandla v Dowell Lee*[245] the school uniform for boys stipulated that a cap should be worn over short hair. Consequently, a Sikh pupil with unshorn hair and a turban was barred. The school's first justification was that the uniform minimised external differences between races and social classes, and discouraged "competitive fashions" among teenagers. Lord Fraser (with whom the House agreed) flatly rejected these reasons as insufficient to justify prima facie discrimination. The second justification on banning the turban was that it challenged the school's protected Christian image. This was rejected because it was not "irrespective" of the claimant's ethnic origins.[246]

---

[242] *Islington LBC v Ladele* [2010] 1 W.L.R. 955 (CA).
[243] [2007] I.R.L.R 484 (EAT).
[244] ibid. [67], [73].
[245] [1983] A.C. 548 (HL). See also, Ch.3, paras 3–003, 3–008.
[246] ibid. at 566–568.

In *Begum*,[247] the House of Lords stated obiter that a school-uniform ban on the "jilbab" (a long coat-like garment, worn by some Muslims, which effectively concealed the shape of the female body) was justified, under the European Convention on Human Rights. Curiously, *Mandla* was not cited. *Begum* was distinguished in another school uniform case, this time brought under the Race Relations Act 1976 and/or Equality Act 2006.[248] In *R. (Watkins-Singh) v The Governing Body of Aberdare Girls' High School*,[249] in deference to its strict uniform policy, a school refused to allow a Sikh pupil wear a Kara (a small metal bracelet, and an important Sikh practice). In addition to health and safety,[250] the school presented six reasons in justification: the pupil would "stand out"; the school uniform policy minimises wealth differences between pupils, and fosters a community spirit; the "floodgates" argument: other pupils would wish to wear "all manner of items"; the uniform prevents bullying; it is "very difficul" to explain the exception to other pupils; it would otherwise discriminate against other pupils. These were rejected, principally because the Kara was inexpensive and small, and only visible when not wearing long sleeves. *Begum* was distinguished on the basis that the Jilbab was "infinitely more visible than the Kara".[251] Again, the judgment failed to consider *Mandla*,[252] another case where the religious clothing was "infinitely more visible".

(a) Reasonable accommodation in the United States

As mentioned above, these cases resemble "reasonable accommodation" disability discrimination cases. In the United States, for religious discrimination in employment, the law is not centred on the "business necessity" defence,[253] but rather on a duty to "reasonably accommodate" a worker's "religious observance or practice without undue hardship on the conduct of the employer's business".[254] This places a positive duty on employers to take steps to accommodate the religious needs of their workers. For instance, an employer is obliged

6–054

---

[247] *R. (Begum) v Denbigh High School Governors* [2007] 1 A.C. 100 (HL). See also *R. (X) v Headteachers and Governors of Y School* [2007] EWHC 298 (QBD), [101].

[248] As Sikhs were recognised as a racial group (see Ch.3, para.3–008), the case could be brought under either racial or religious discrimination legislation. *Begum* arose before the Equality Act 2006 applied religious discrimination to schools.

[249] *The Queen on the application of Sarika Angel Watkins-Singh (A child acting by Sanita Kumari Singh, her Mother and Litigation Friend) v The Governing Body of Aberdare Girls' High School* [2008] EWHC 1865 (Admin). Decided under both RRA 1976 and Equality Act 2006.

[250] Which was rejected, see above, para.6–047, p.194.

[251] [2008] EWHC 1865 (Admin), [77].

[252] Save to confirm that Sikhs are a racial group under the RRA 1976.

[253] See above, para.6–002.

[254] Title VII, s.701(j), (codified in 42 USC s.2000e(j)). This amendment was inserted in 1972 with the stated purpose to protect Sabbath observers whose employers fail to adjust work schedules to fit their needs (see e.g. *EEOC v Ithaca Industries* 849 F 2d 116, at 118 (4th Cir 1988)).

to accommodate a worker's request to be absent on Sundays by inquiring if fellow workers would cover that shift.[255] In *Ansonia Board of Education v Phillbrook*,[256] the Supreme Court held that giving the right to unpaid leave plus three days paid leave, for religious holidays, was a reasonable accommodation. The "undue hardship" element affords the courts some flexibility to weigh the business needs against the accommodation sought. In *Trans World Airlines v Hardison*,[257] the Supreme Court held that the employer, which had pared its weekend staffing to a minimum and had asked for voluntary cover, was not obliged to pay premium rates to attract weekend staff nor upset its seniority system, to allow a worker Saturdays off for his Sabbath. It further stated that that any cost to the employer above de minimis was an undue hardship.[258]

(vi) Seniority, merit and bonus systems

6–055 These are covered in Chapter 9, paras 9–037 to 9–039.

---

[255] *EEOC v Ithaca Industries* 849 F 2d 116 (4th Cir 1988), certiorari denied, 488 US 924 (1988).
[256] 497 US 60 (1986).
[257] 432 US 63 (1977).
[258] ibid. at 84.

CHAPTER 7

VICTIMISATION

INTRODUCTION

It is not enough that the legislation proscribes direct and indirect   **7–001**
discrimination, and harassment. In addition, those who use the legislation, or assist others to do so, need protection against retaliation
for so doing. Indeed, "victimisation was as serious a mischief as direct
discrimination".[1] Accordingly, the legislation seeks to remove deterrents with the inclusion of provisions for victimisation, creating a
separate cause of action.[2]

The definition of victimisation in the Equality Act 2010 draws
together and largely replicates the previous provisions, save for one
major change. It is no longer necessary to prove that the defendant
treated the victim "less favourably", only that the defendant *subjects
him to a detriment*. This new phrase dispenses with the comparison,
and so technically, victimisation is no longer a form of
discrimination.[3]

---

[1] *Nagarajan v LRT* [2001] A.C. 502 (HL), [79] (Lord Steyn).
[2] The issue of discrimination after "the relationship has come to an end" is discussed in Ch.8
(victimising ex-workers) para.8–015.
[3] For problems with the comparison in victimisation, see *Aziz v Trinity Street Taxis Ltd* [1989]
Q.B. 463 (CA), overruling *Kirby v Manpower Services Commission* [1980] I.C.R. 420 (EAT).

Equality Act 2010

27 Victimisation

(1) A person (A) victimises another person (B) if A subjects B to a detriment because—

(a) B does a protected act, or
(b) A believes that B has done, or may do, a protected act.

(2) Each of the following is a protected act—

(a) bringing proceedings under this Act;
(b) giving evidence or information in connection with proceedings under this Act;
(c) doing any other thing for the purposes of or in connection with this Act;
(d) making an allegation (whether or not express) that A or another person has contravened this Act.

(3) Giving false evidence or information, or making a false allegation, is not a protected act if the evidence or information is given, or the allegation is made, in bad faith.

It is necessary to prove that (1) that the claimant has done a protected act, (2) the defendant subjected the claimant to a detriment (3) *because* the claimant did the protected act.

This also applies where the defendant believes the claimant has done, or may do, the protected act.

1. The Protected Acts

7–002   It is not necessary that the victim has done the protected act, as long as defendant believes she has done it, or will do it. Paragraph 27(1)(b) covers the situation where a defendant believes, by mistake, the victim has done the protected act. Section 27 also extends to the situation where, say, an employer believes a colleague of a claimant may give evidence in support of the principal complaint, and so the employer intimidates the friend, say, by postponing an expected promotion, in order to deter her.

Neither is it necessary that the victimiser is the same person as the "target" of the protected act. For example, where a person brings a racial discrimination claim against a shopkeeper for refusing to serve him, and the shopkeeper's brother, who happens to be the employer of the claimant, victimises him; or an employer rejects a job applicant because of previous actions of discrimination (even if unsuccessful) brought by the applicant against *another* employer. Conversely, the formula does not cover the scenario where the defendant victimises a friend or relative of the person doing the protected act, although this may be covered at EU level (see below, para.7–016).

Of the protected acts themselves, s.27(2)(a) covers those bringing a claim of discrimination. Paragraph (b) covers those giving evidence in a discrimination claim. The broadly worded para.(c) has been held to cover a job centre worker reporting that employers were encouraging the job centre to discriminate when supplying staff;[4] and the making of secret tape recordings in an attempt to establish discrimination by a taxi cab association.[5]

Paragraph (d) is worded more narrowly, requiring that the behaviour alleged actually was a breach of the Act. Apart from the most obvious cases, in practice, there will be very few protected acts falling under para.(d), as it has been held that the paragraph requires, as a prerequisite, proof of the breach. None of the other paragraphs require this, so long as the allegation was not made in bad faith and not false. In *Waters v Commissioner of Police of the Metropolis,*[6] Waters, a police officer, alleged that she was the victim of rape and buggery by a fellow officer while they were off duty. No action was taken against the alleged assailant. She testified that as a result of making the complaint she was aggressively treated, ostracised by colleagues and senior officers, transferred to civilian duties, denied proper time off, refused placements, told she should leave, subjected to pornography by colleagues, threatened with violence by her chief superintendent, and required to take a psychological analysis to verify she was fit for duty. Further, her complaints were not properly investigated and confidences were broken. The Court of Appeal rejected her claim of victimisation because the alleged assailant was acting outside the course of his employment, so she had not alleged that the Act had been breached.[7]

7–003

There is, of course, an obvious flaw in this logic. The Court of Appeal focused on whether the Act had been breached, instead of whether Waters had *alleged* such a contravention, which patently she had. The fact that she was mistaken is irrelevant, so long as it was not made in bad faith (s.27(3)), which it was not. In many cases, at the time of the original complaint, and right up to a final tribunal or court ruling, neither the victim nor victimiser will know whether the allegation contained a contravention of the Act. And so this unduly narrow interpretation of para.(d) does not seem to accord with the statutory wording nor serve its purpose. The solution, it seems, is to plead such cases under para.(c) ("doing any other thing ... in connection with this Act"). Had Waters pleaded this, the only question

[4] *Kirby v Manpower Services Commission* [1980] I.C.R. 420 (EAT).
[5] *Aziz v Trinity Street Taxis Ltd* [1989] Q.B. 463 (CA). See further below, para.7–008.
[6] [1997] I.C.R. 1073 (CA).
[7] Waters did not appeal against this aspect of the decision, but won her appeal on the basis that the management's response had been negligent: [2000] I.C.R. 1064 (HL).

would have been whether her principal allegation of rape and buggery was false and made in bad faith, rather than the more technical question of whether such conduct could amount to a breach of the Act.[8]

2. SUBJECTS TO A DETRIMENT

7–004 As noted above, this element replaces *treats less favourably*, and so dispenses with the need for a comparison. The policy behind this change is to bring the victimisation provisions into line with the growing number of victimisation provisions provided by Pt V of the Employment Rights Act 1996, which cover areas such as whistle blowing, jury service, health and safety, Sunday working, family leave and working time rights. This simplifies matters and as such is an improvement for both claimants and defendants. But the choice of wording brings problems.

The first problem is that this wording does not account for the "chilling effect" of a retaliatory act. This arises from the focus on what the claimant has *suffered*, rather than the defendant's *treatment*. Consider the following scenario:

> A worker wins a sexual harassment claim against her employer. Subsequently, she resigns and then some time later, applies for another job. Out of retaliation, her employer refuses to provide a reference. Nonetheless, she got the job because the new employer did not require a written reference. She now sues her former employer, this time for victimisation.[9]

In this scenario it appears that the claimant has suffered no detriment, even though her employer treated her unfavourably. This might appear to be a just outcome, until you consider the deterrent effect produced by the employer's refusal to provide a reference. Other workers minded to complain about discrimination or harassment now know they risk being refused a job reference at some future occasion. This is the "chilling effect". In the only ECJ judgment on victimisation, *Coote v Granada*,[10] the ECJ focused on the *deterrent* effect of an employer's act on workers. Here, Mrs Coote sued her employer following her dismissal for being pregnant. After those proceedings were settled, the employer refused to give her a reference

---

[8] See generally R. Townshend-Smith, (1996) 2 I.J.D.L. 137.
[9] See the US case, *Sparrow v Piedmont Health*, 593 F Supp 1107 (MDNC 1984).
[10] Case C-185/97, [1998] ECR-I 5199.

and Mrs Coote sued for victimisation. The ECJ held that ex-workers must be protected from victimisation, otherwise:

"Fear of such measures ... might deter workers who considered themselves the victims of discrimination from pursuing their claims ... and would consequently be liable seriously to jeopardise implementation of the aim pursued by the [Equal Treatment] Directive."[11]

The central issue was whether ex-workers were protected, but the underlying principle is that the purpose of the victimisation provisions is to outlaw deterrents to using the discrimination legislation. With this in mind, a more rational solution is for the claimant to prevail, with costs but little or no damages. This way, employers are put on notice that such retaliation will not be tolerated, and some fear of using the legislation is removed. To facilitate this outcome, this element should be replaced with "treats unfavourably".[12]

The second problem is that the focus on the claimant's suffering inevitably raises the question of whether it is judged objectively or subjectively. The phrase "subjecting him to any other detriment" was used in the employment provisions of the discrimination legislation since its inception,[13] and the case law on that element is less than certain.

In *Shamoon v Chief Constable of the Royal Ulster Constabulary*[14] **7–005** the House of Lords stated that the question was: "Is the treatment of such a kind that a reasonable worker would or might take the view that in all the circumstances it was to his detriment?" It was not necessary to demonstrate some physical or economic consequence.[15] But Lord Scott emphasised the subjective aspect, asserting that the question should be looked at from the victim's point of view, and it should suffice if that was a reasonable view to hold.[16] This is a slightly different question. Instead of asking how the average reasonable worker would have reacted, a tribunal should step into the *claimant's* shoes, and find against him only if his view was one that no other reasonable person in that position would take.

---

[11] ibid. [24].

[12] It would seem the drafters of EA 2010 s.27, were unaware of the significance of the phrasing, as Explanatory Note 100 explains victimisation where one person *treats* another *badly* rather than *subjects him to a detriment*.

[13] See RRA 1976 s.4(2); SDA 1975 s.6(2); DDA 1995 s.4(4); SI 2003/1660 (Religion or Belief), reg.6(2); SI 2003/1661 (Sexual Orientation), reg.6(2), SI 2006/1031 (Age) reg.6(2); Fair Employment and Treatment Order 1998 (NI) SI1998/3162, art.19. See now, EA 2010 s.39(2)(d).

[14] [2003] I.C.R. 337 (HL).

[15] ibid. [35] (Lord Hope, with whom agreed Lords Hutton, [91] Scott [104–105], and Roger [123]), citing *Ministry of Defence v Jeremiah* [1980] Q.B. 87 (CA), at 104.

[16] ibid. [105].

Lord Scott's opinion seems rooted in *Chief Constable of West Yorkshire v Khan*,[17] where (in a variation on the scenario above) the House of Lords held that an employer's refusal to give a job reference (in reaction to the candidate's existing discrimination claim) amounted to a detriment, even though, in the event, a reference would have been negative and *lessened* the candidate's chances. The candidate viewed the refusal as a detriment, and given his knowledge at the time, this was not unreasonable.[18] Most recently, however, in *St Helens BC v Derbyshire*,[19] the House of Lords reinterpreted *Khan*, stating that because the refusal of the reference did not reduce the candidate's chances, the refusal did *not* cause him a detriment.[20] This suggests, contrary to *Shamoon* (and, of course, the differently con-stituted House in *Khan* itself), that the matter is purely objective and turns on whether the claimant actually suffered tangible harm.

These three cases present three different meanings of *detriment*: first, the objective/subjective test in *Shamoon,* second, Lord Scott's variation on that (illustrated in *Khan*), and third, a purely objective test, apparent from *St Helens'* reinterpretation of *Khan*. As the opposing views of *Khan* demonstrate, the precise meaning afforded to *detriment* could be critical. Given that the legislation allows for an award of damages solely for injury to feelings,[21] the *St Helens'* version is unsupportable, as it is perfectly possible for a person to suffer injury to feelings without suffering tangible harm. Of the remaining two options, Lord Scott's version is preferable. This allows tribunals the power, to a degree at least, to control the chilling effect of victi-misation. This is supported by the ECJ's concern in *Coote v Granada* (above) for the deterrent effect of victimisation, which was taken by the House of Lords in *St Helens* to mean that the worker's per-spective should prevail.[22]

7–006   A third problem that may arise from this element again centres on previous interpretations of the parallel phrase "subjecting him to any other detriment". There is long-standing Court of Appeal authority that the de minimis principle applies to this.[23] However, as noted above, the provision for damages for injury to feelings[24] (which

---

[17] [2001] I.C.R. 1065.
[18] ibid. [53] (Lord Hoffman). Lord Nicholls [14] said simply there was a detriment because "Provision of a reference is a normal feature of employment". Lord Hutton [61] agreed with Lords Hoffman and Nicholls. Lord MacKay [37] assumed there was a detriment.
[19] [2007] I.C.R. 841. See below, para.7–009.
[20] ibid. [68] (Lord Neuberger, with whom the whole House agreed).
[21] EA 2010 s.119(4). Lord Hoffman in *Khan* said that this meant "detriment" should be given a "wide meaning": [2001] I.C.R. 1065, [53].
[22] [2007] I.C.R. 841 (HL), [24]–[27], [66].
[23] *Peake v Automotive Products* [1978] Q.B. 233, explained in *Ministry of Defence v Jeremiah* [1980] Q.B. 87, 98. See also *Jiad v Byford* [2003] I.R.L.R. 232 (CA) [21]: "Transitory hurt feelings may not (depending on the facts) suffice" for a detriment; and *Moyhing v Barts and London NHS Trust* [2006] I.R.L.R. 860 (EAT).
[24] EA 2010, s.119(4). In *Vento v Chief Constable West Yorkshire Police* [2002] I.C.R. 318 [65], the Court of Appeal stated that this included "less serious" cases, such as an "isolated or one-off occurrence", which suggests it could include at least some de minimis incidents.

legitimises claims where there was no economic or physical consequence), and the need to address any chilling effect, must cast some doubt over a generally applicable de minimis principle to victimisation cases.

3. "Because"

The third element in proving a case of victimisation centres on the   **7–007**
link between the protected act and the unfavourable treatment, or in the statutory language, subjecting the victim to a detriment must be *because* of victim did the protected act (or that the defendant believed he had done it, or may do it). The word *because* replaces the previous phrase *by reason that*. A similar amendment was made to the definition of direct discrimination, where it was not intended to change the legal meaning.[25] Generally, the same should apply here. Note, the phrase *by reason that* is used in the cases discussed below, which predate the Equality Act 2010.

This element is essential to prevent fanciful claims where a person who has performed a protected act is subjected to a detriment for an entirely separate reason, for instance, where a worker who has made a claim of sexual harassment is dismissed for theft. On the other hand, there only need be a causal link between the protected act and the detriment. In *Nagarajan v London Regional Transport*[26] the claimant, a man of Indian origin, was interviewed for a job with London Regional Transport (LRT), against whom he had in the past brought several complaints of racial discrimination. LRT did not offer Mr Nagarajan a job and he won his consequent claim of victimisation in the industrial tribunal, which based its decision on three findings. First, all three members of the interviewing panel were aware of the previous proceedings. Second, Mr Nagarajan was given one out of ten for "articulacy" [sic.] by the panel, despite him having been a transport information assistant for four months without complaint; the mark was "plainly ridiculous and unrealistically low", the tribunal found. Third, one of the panellists considered that Mr Nagarajan was "very anti-management". The tribunal concluded that the interviewers "were consciously or subconsciously influenced by the fact that the applicant had previously brought industrial tribunal proceedings against LRT".[27] LRT appealed on the basis that a defendant must be shown to have been "consciously motivated" by the protected act: as the tribunal failed to distinguish between

---

[25] Explanatory Note (61). The change was intended to make the definition "more accessible" to "ordinary users of the Act". See Ch.4, paras 4–015 et seq.

[26] [2001] A.C. 502 (HL).

[27] ibid. 516.

conscious and *subconscious* motivation, no case of *conscious* motivation had been made out. A majority of the House of Lords dismissed LRT's appeal,[28] following the "objective and not subjective",[29] or "straightforward",[30] approach, applied to the parallel element *on the ground of* in the definition of direct discrimination, in *EOC v Birmingham City Council*,[31] and again in *James v Eastleigh BC*,[32] where the House of Lords applied a *but for* test in order to avoid questions of the defendant's motivation. In *Nagarajan*, Lord Nicholls concluded "I can see no reason to apply a different approach to [victimisation]".[33] Thus, it seemed, the correct approach was to ask: "*but for* the protected act, would the claimant have been subjected to a detriment?" As we shall see, the *but for* test has fallen from favour and the matter has become more complex.

(1) The Demise of the *But For* Test and the "General Policy" Cases

7–008   In both direct discrimination and victimisation, the courts have drifted away from the *but for* test. In victimisation, this became apparent in a class of "general policy" cases. In these cases, the defendant subjects the victim to a detriment because he did the protected act, but the treatment was *irrespective of* discrimination ingredient of the protected act.[34] In the next three cases, *but for* the protected act, the defendant would not have treated the claimant unfavourably. Yet, in each, there was no liability.

In *Cornelius v University College of Swansea*,[35] the claimant issued sex discrimination proceedings. It was the employer's general policy to suspend the grievance procedure of any worker who issued proceedings. And so, in this case, the Court of Appeal held that the employer's suspension of Ms Cornelius' grievance procedure, did not amount to victimisation, because the employer would have treated *any* worker bringing *any* proceedings, in the same way. The Court noted that that the employer had acted *by reason* of the *existence*, rather than the *bringing*, of proceedings.

In *Aziz v Trinity Street Taxis*[36] the complainant was an Asian taxicab proprietor and a member of an association of taxicab operators. When the association required him to pay £1,000 to have a third taxi admitted to its radio system, he felt he was being unfairly

---

[28] Lords Nicholls, Steyn, Hutton and Hobhouse. Lord Browne-Wilkinson dissented.
[29] So described by Lord Bridge in *James v Eastleigh BC* [1990] A.C. 751, at 765.
[30] [2001] A.C. 502, at 521 (Lord Steyn).
[31] [1989] 1 A.C. 1156 (HL). Discussed Ch.4, para.4–015.
[32] [1990] A.C. 751 (HL). Discussed Ch.4, para.4–015.
[33] [2001] A.C. 502, at 512.
[34] For a more detailed exploration, see M. Connolly, "Rethinking Victimisation" (2009) 38 ILJ 149. A similar difficulty exists in the US. Contrast *EEOC v Board of Governors*, 957 F 2d 424 (7th Cir 1992) with *US v New York City Transit Authority* 97 F 3d 672 (2nd Cir 1996).
[35] [1987] I.R.L.R. 141. Discussed [2000] 29 ILJ 304.
[36] [1989] Q.B. 463 (CA).

treated on racial grounds. He secretly recorded conversations with other taxi drivers to gain evidence of racism, and made an unsuccessful complaint to a tribunal about the additional fee. The recordings were revealed during the hearing of that complaint. As a result, he was expelled from the association on the ground that the making of the recordings was an unjustified intrusion and a serious breach of the trust that had to exist between members. Aziz then sued for victimisation. The Court of Appeal held that the association was motivated by the breach of trust, not the racial discrimination claim *per se*, and so was not liable for victimisation.

In *Chief Constable of West Yorkshire v Khan*,[37] the employer, who refused to give a reference to a worker who had brought a discrimination claim, argued that he was acting on legal advice, so as not to prejudice its position at the trial. And so, it would refuse a reference to anyone with an existing claim, whatever its nature (discriminatory or other). The Court of Appeal[38] followed *Nagarajan* and found for the claimant, on the basis that *but for* Khan's outstanding proceedings, the Chief Constable would have given him a reference. A unanimous House of Lords reversed.[39] This decision, made within two-and-a-half years of *Nagarajan*, threw into doubt the precise meaning of the phrase *by reason that* (now, "because"). Clarity was not helped by the various interpretations of this element. Lord Nicholls said is not causative, while Lord Hoffman said that it was. Lord Hutton's position is unclear because he concurred with *both* Lord Nicholls and Lord Hoffman. Meanwhile Lord Scott said the phrase was one of "not strict causation".[40]

According to the whole House, the decision was supported by a **7–009** fine distinction, between the *bringing* and *existence* of proceedings. To this end Lords Nicholls, Hoffman and Scott drew support from *Cornelius v University College of Swansea* (above). This fine distinction shows a drift away from the straightforward approach adopted by the House of Lords in *Nagarajan*, where Lord Nicholls himself said "in the application of this legislation legalistic phrases, as well as subtle distinctions, are better avoided so far as possible".[41] This distinction becomes even less credible if one accepts that Sergeant Khan may have by-passed it by adding a second protected act to his pleadings, that he had "otherwise done anything under or by

---

[37] [2001] UKHL 48. See also above, para.7–005, p.208.
[38] [2000] I.C.R. 1169 (CA), [28].
[39] Contrast the US Federal District Court decision in *Sparrow v Piedmont Health* 593 F Supp 1107, at 1119 (MD NC 1984): liability where an employer refusing to give a reference for fear of creating evidence damaging to its defence of the discrimination charge.
[40] [2001] UKHL 48, respectively, at [29], [54] and [77]. For Comment, see (2002) 31 ILJ 161, at 166.
[41] [2000] A.C. 501, at 512.

reference to this Act".[42] As well as having *brought* proceedings, he was "otherwise" *maintaining* them in existence.

In coming to its decision, the House added another dimension, by observing that the employer had acted "reasonably and honestly"[43] and "in accordance with perfectly understandable advice",[44] and had not "singled out" a worker for less favourable treatment.[45] It is now possible to qualify the ratio as being that there is no liability for victimisation where the defendant acted, *reasonably and honestly*, by reason of the existence, and not the bringing, of proceedings.

The danger with the "honest and reasonable" approach was realised in *Derbyshire v St Helens Metropolitan Borough Council*,[46] where the Court of Appeal applied *Khan* to conduct that went beyond a "general policy". Here, 510 catering staff brought an equal pay claim. Most compromised, but 39 persisted. The council then wrote directly to every member of staff stating that should the claim succeed, the resulting cost was likely to cause mass redundancies. For the 39 litigants this effective threat was intimidating and likely to cause them fear of public odium and reproaches by colleagues; it induced pressure to "surrender" their claim.[47] In their consequent claim for victimisation, the Court of Appeal agreed that they had been treated less favourably (it was "usual" to correspond with their trade union or solicitors), but a majority, applying *Khan*, held that the council had acted "honestly and reasonably" in trying to settle the proceedings.[48] In effect, the majority held that even though the treatment was unfavourable, and out of the ordinary, so long as the employer acted honestly and reasonably, it did not matter that this treatment clearly was "because" the claimants were pursuing proceedings.

7–010 The House of Lords reversed,[49] but not without providing an illogical (re)interpretation of *Khan*. The majority stated that the *honest and reasonable* "defence" was simply another way of expressing that the worker had suffered no detriment: if the employer acted honestly and reasonably, it could not cause the worker a detriment,[50] which was not the case here (it seems that the detriment was caused by "going public", which, of course, was "unreasonable"). Only Baroness Hale was more trenchant, stating: "It would be better if the

---

[42] RRA 1976 s.2(1)(c). See now EA 2010 s.27(2)(c): "doing any other thing for the purposes of or in connection with this Act ...".
[43] [2001] UKHL 48, [31] (Lord Nicholls).
[44] ibid. [44] (Lord Mackay).
[45] ibid. [80] (Lord Scott).
[46] [2006] I.C.R. 90.
[47] ET Reasons, [4(d)], cited [2007] I.C.R. 841 (HL), [38].
[48] ibid. [58] (Parker L.J.), [78]–[82] (Lloyd L.J.). In addition, Parker L.J. used the distinction between the bringing and existence of proceedings ([53]).
[49] [2007] I.C.R. 841. Four of the five law lords gave speeches, with Lord Bingham agreeing with them all ([9]). Baroness Hale ([42]), Lord Carswell ([43]), and Lord Hope ([29]) agreed with Lord Neuberger.
[50] ibid. [68]. "Detriment" here was a requirement by the employment provisions of the legislation. See above, para.7–004, p.207, and more generally, Ch.8, paras 8–013 et seq.

[honest and reasonable] "defence" were laid to rest and the language of the legislation, construed in the light of the requirements of the Directives, applied."[51]

The flaw in the majority's logic is that in most cases an employer defending litigation *will* cause a detriment, no matter how "honestly and reasonably" it acts.[52] The denial of a grievance process or a job reference normally will cause a detriment. If a case came before the House precisely the same as *Khan*, save that the denial of the reference *did* cause the claimant harm (e.g. because it would have been positive), a court either would have to find for the claimant, leaving *Khan* marooned and fit to be distinguished to death, or find for the employer on the basis that it acted honestly and reasonably even though the claimant had been harmed. Thus, an honest and reasonable response by an employer normally cannot be equated with causing a worker no detriment.[53] Despite the opinions in *St Helens*, the deciding factor in *Khan* was the employer's reason, or motive, for acting, not the effect on the claimant, and the *honest and reasonable*, or "benign motive", defence survives.[54]

Once it is established that the decisions in *Cornelius*, *Aziz* and *Khan* turned on the employer's benign motive, it becomes easier to evaluate them. The first and most obvious problem for a benign motive defence is that it does not appear in the legislation.[55] This has been amplified by case law under the old parallel phrase *on grounds of* (race, sex, etc.) for direct discrimination, where the courts have steadfastly set themselves against the notion of a benign motive defence. The *but for* test decreed in *EOC v Birmingham City Council*,[56] and again in *James v Eastleigh BC*,[57] was expressly designed to avoid questions of the defendant's motive. This was adopted for the victimisation provisions in *Nagarajan*.[58] Although, more recently, the House of Lords has drifted away from the *but for* test, the Supreme

---

[51] ibid. [36].

[52] It also effectively overrules *Khan*, where a differently constituted House found that *Khan* had suffered a detriment. See above, para.7–005 and Michael Connolly, "Easy Case Makes Bad Law" (2007) 36 ILJ 364, 367–371.

[53] For a discussion of whether harm or detriment should be necessary for liability, see para.7–004.

[54] It was applied, post-*St Helens*, in *Bird v Sylvester* [2008] I.C.R. 208, [10], where the Court of Appeal also repeated the inaccurate equation that honest and reasonable conduct causes no detriment.

[55] In *Pothecary Witham Weld v Bullimore* [2010] I.C.R. 1008 (EAT) [18]–[19], Underhill J. suggested that *St Helens* and *Khan* were "of a very particular type" because the employer was defending litigation, and generally *Nagarajan* should be followed; and the "subtle" distinction between employer and litigant should be "eschewed". But this does not account for the fact that "particular types of case" are not identified in the legislation. See also, the US case, *EEOC v Board of Governors*, 957 F 2d 424, 428 (7th Cir 1992).

[56] [1989] 1 A.C. 1156 (HL), at 1194. Discussed Ch.4, para.4–015.

[57] [1990] A.C. 751 (HL), at 774B-C. Discussed Ch.4, para.4–015.

[58] *Nagarajan v LRT* [2001] A.C. 501 (HL). see above, para.7–007.

Court remains just as hostile to any notion of benign motive defence for direct discrimination.[59]

7–011   The only technical ground in support of a different approach to victimisation is that it is, plainly, a different cause of action. In *Khan*, Lord Hoffman first stated that the causal questions in the direct discrimination and victimisation provisions were "not identical".[60] This enabled him to distance the *but for* test from the victimisation cases.[61] However, this does not account for the absence of any benign motive defence in the legislation. Further, since then, the phrases *on grounds of* (direct discrimination) and *by reason that* (victimisation) have been harmonised, with the single "causative" element reduced to "because". This makes it harder distinguish the "causative" elements of direct discrimination and victimisation.

A more obvious difference between the formulas is that only direct discrimination carries specific *Genuine Occupational Requirement* defences (for employment discrimination), tempting a suggestion that courts should compensate for their absence in victimisation cases. But, if the legislature intended to validate victimisation where it would be rational, or financially prudent, or in "good faith", or otherwise, it would have expressed this.[62] This brings us back to the fundamental and technical objection to a benign motive defence in victimisation cases: none appears in the legislation. Distinguishing the victimisation from the direct discrimination provisions cannot validate implying such a defence.

That said, the upper courts' sympathy towards employers in these "general policy" cases cannot be swept aside. The problem is that with the "honest and reasonable" defence, they are using an unauthorised device to express that sympathy. It is also rather ill-defined and unpredictable, as the Court of Appeal's (split) decision and subsequent reversal, in *St Helens* illustrates. This suggests that if defendants are to be afforded some leeway, a new theory of victimisation is required.

(2) Alternative Theories

(a) Parallels with Indirect Discrimination

7–012   In these cases, the employer's defence of its policy to deny a reference or grievance process is two-fold. First, it wants to defend the principal case properly. Second, in doing so, it does not single out those who complain of discrimination. This second point suggests that the employer's act is neutral on its face, and so akin to *indirect*

---

[59] *R. (E) v Governing Body of JFS* [2009] UKSC 15. Discussed Ch.4, para.4–017.
[60] [2001] I.C.R. 1065, [56].
[61] ibid. [57].
[62] This point was made in the US case, *EEOC v Board of Governors* 957 F 2d 424, 427–428 (7th Cir 1992).

discrimination, which, of course, carries a general justification defence, which could accommodate an employer's benign motive.[63]

This attractive approach could be applied to *Cornelius, Aziz* and *Khan,* because general policies would affect all workers who litigated, not just those claiming discrimination. However, the analogy breaks down once it is appreciated that with conventional indirect discrimination cases there is a protected class identifiable by one single characteristic, be it sex, sexual orientation, religion or race, etc. This makes it a relatively straightforward task to distinguish a facially discriminatory practice from a facially neutral one.[64] By contrast, the protected persons in victimisation cases are identified by what they have done: the protected activity. In these "general policy" cases, the protected activity requires two factors to be identified: (1) issuing proceedings, (2) for discrimination.[65] The challenged practice, triggered by just "issuing proceedings", is *in part,* facially neutral and in part facially discriminatory. So an analogy with indirect discrimination is half right. Treating these cases as "direct" victimisation (which the legislation requires) omits the facially neutral aspect. But treating them as "indirect" victimisation omits the protected aspect. For victimisation, the distinction between direct and indirect discrimination becomes "fuzzy at the border"[66] and an analogy with indirect discrimination is not particularly rational or helpful.

(b) Parallels with Discrimination Arising from Disability

A more appropriate and useful analogy can be made with disability discrimination. Disability discrimination is prone to these "fuzzy border" cases because frequently apparently neutral policies are directed at a manifestation of a disability, rather than the disability itself. Examples include a restaurant's *no dogs* rule,[67] or a *no wheelchairs* rule.[68]

7–013

These examples compare with the "general policy" victimisation cases, where the employer's apparently neutral policy is directed at a manifestation of the worker's protected act (proceedings) rather than the nature of the act (discrimination or harassment). These cases are also on the fuzzy border between direct and indirect discrimination. They are in fact, victimisation *by proxy.* The solution for disability

---

[63] This logic was applied in the US case, *EEOC v Huber* 927 F 2d 1322 (5th Cir 1991).

[64] But see Lord Bridge in *James v Eastleigh BC* [1990] A.C. 751 (HL), 764, who held that as reference to "pensionable age" was "convenient shorthand" for sex discrimination. See also the US case, *International Union v Johnson Controls* 11 S Ct 1196, 1203–1204 (Sup Ct 1991).

[65] Alternatively, this could be (1) reporting wrongdoing of (2) unlawful discrimination; or (1) giving evidence in support of a colleague (2) in that colleague's discrimination claim; and so on.

[66] *McWright v Alexander* 982 F 2d 222, 228 (7th Cir 1992) (Cudahy J.).

[67] Minister of State for Social Security and Disabled People, 253 HC Official Report (6th series) col. 150, 24 Jan 1995. See also the US case, *Sullivan v Valllejo City Unified School District* 731 F Supp 947, 958 (ED Cal 1990) (school ban on service dogs).

[68] *McWright v Alexander* 982 F 2d 222, 228 (7th Cir 1992).

law is provided by an additional model of discrimination. The
Equality Act 2010 s.15 provides for "Discrimination arising from
disability", which carries a justification defence.[69] This embraces the
no dogs, or *no wheelchairs* type of rule, but absolves the defendant
who shows the rule was "a proportionate means of achieving a
legitimate aim". If adapted for victimisation—"victimisation by
proxy"—the manifestation of the protected act would be the issuing
of legal proceedings, which is the target of the employer's general
policy. But the as legal proceedings have arisen from the *discrimination* complaint, the defendant would have a case to answer,
which it could, if it could justify its practice.

The standard justification formula—used in equal pay and indirect
discrimination cases—requires the employer to show that the policy is
genuine (legitimate aim), appropriate and necessary (proportionate).[70] The formula requires the aim to be "irrespective" of the
protected ground, e.g. sex or race etc.[71] Here, because the prime facie
victimisation is related to a protected act, the defence cannot necessarily be "irrespective" of the protected act—by its nature, the aim
must be afforded more leeway than usual. Nevertheless, it should be
able to be applied with some coherence, as the "legitimate aim"
should be related to the "manifestation" of the protected act, such as
legal proceedings, whatever their nature. If the aim were related to
the nature of discrimination proceedings (e.g. sex or race etc.), then
there should be liability under conventional victimisation theory, or
even direct (e.g. sex or race) discrimination. The suspension of a
grievance process or denial of a reference, with the stated aim of
defending litigation, is likely to be genuine if it is no more than an
invocation of a general policy that applies across a range of cases, not
just discrimination ones. If it were invoked for the first time for a
discrimination case, it would be suspicious.

7–014   The response should be appropriate. This rules out underhand or
even illegal tactics (and so in part coincides with the *honest and
reasonable* test). The conclusion reached by the House of Lords in *St
Helens* accords with this analysis, as the employer acted inappro-
priately by "going public". Two US cases further illustrate inappropriate conduct. In *Berry v Stevenson Chevrolet*[72] the employer
formed a reasonable (but mistaken) suspicion of a worker's fraud,

---

[69] See further, Ch.13, paras 13–024 to 13–030. In the United States, under the federal Americans
with Disabilities Act 1990, courts developed this hybrid model: direct discrimination *by
proxy*, aimed at treatment "directed at an effect or manifestation of a handicap": *McWright v
Alexander* 982 F 2d 222, 228 (7th Cir 1992). It carries a justification defence: see EEOC 29
CFR s.1630.15 (available at *www.eeoc.gov*), and see e.g. *Ethridge v State of Alabama* 860 F
Supp 808, 817 (MD Ala 1993).
[70] The "*Bilka* test": Case 170/84 *Bilka-Kaufhaus v Weber von Hartz* [1987] E.C.R. 1607, [36]. See
Ch.6, para.6–019, p.169.
[71] Case 96/80 *Jenkins v Kingsgate* [1981] E.C.R. 911, [11]; Case 170/84 *Bilka-Kaufhaus v Weber
von Hartz* [1987] E.C.R. 1607, [37].
[72] 74 F 3d 980, 986 (10th Cir 1996).

but only reported it when the worker issued discrimination proceedings. In *Rochon v Gonzales*,[73] the FBI broke with policy by
refusing to investigate death threats against an agent because he had
complained of racial harassment.

The response should also be necessary to achieve the aim. An
employer cannot try to win at all costs. The indications from *Cornelius*, *Khan* and *St Helens*, are that the employer is permitted to do
what the courts consider is normal legal practice. A further consideration at the "necessity" stage is weighing the employer's needs
against the harm done, such as damage to the claimant, and/or the
deterrent effect on the claimant and others.

This provides a neat, technically sound solution that restores some
logic and certainty to the law. Its merit is that it would encompass *all*
genuine and proportionate reactions to litigation, even those
undreamt of, or not strictly related to defending the claim.[74] It would
allow the courts—legitimately—to evaluate each defence on its merits
according to known and predictable criteria.

(c) One or Two Causes of Action?

If victimisation by proxy were the only cause of action, every **7–015**
defendant would have a chance to justify its conduct, no matter how
pernicious the retaliation. Thus, it would be better to preserve the
original provision—"direct victimisation"—with the suggested
amendments,[75] accompanied by guidance, confining it to where the
unfavourable treatment was in response to the protected act, rather
than a manifestation of it.[76]

4. THIRD PARTY VICTIMISATION

"To retaliate against a man by hurting a member of his family is **7–016**
an ancient method of revenge, and is not unknown in the field of
labor relations".[77]

---

[73] 438 F 3d 1211, 1213 (DC Cir 2006).
[74] See the US case, *EEOC v Huber* 927 F 2d 1322 (5th Cir 1991), where the policy of withholding benefits from a class of workers who litigated was to protect the benefit's tax-exempt
status.
[75] i.e. Replace *subjects to a detriment* with *treats unfavourably*. See above, para.7–004, p.207.
[76] Such guidance was accompanied the introduction of direct disability discrimination into the
DDA 1995. It gave distinguishable examples of direct disability discrimination and disability-
related discrimination: Explanatory Notes to *the pre-consultation draft* Regulations (Disability Discrimination Act (Amendment) Regulations 2003 SI 2003/1673), [32].
[77] *NLRB v Advertisers Manufacturing Co* 823 F 2d 1086, 1088 (7th Cir 1987) (Posner C.J.). For
a more detailed exploration into this problem, see M. Connolly, "Victimising Third Parties:
The Equality Directives, the European Convention on Human Rights, and EU General
Principles" (2010) 35 E.L.Rev 822.

This particularly pernicious form of victimisation, designed to deter the worker from pursuing the claim, will also deter others from complaining, "the chilling effect". Yet, the Equality Act 2010 (or its predecessors) does not cover this form of "third party" victimisation. Consider the following scenarios. They have been grouped into three Classes.

A person issues discrimination proceedings against the defendant (the "protected act") and:

> *Class No.1: Same defendant—same place.* In retaliation, her employer fires the worker's fiancé (who worked for the same employer in the same workplace).
>
> Variations on this would be that the retaliation falls short of dismissal (e.g. rejecting a promotion application, giving a poor appraisal), or that the victim is the claimant's spouse, civil partner, relative, close friend, or even just a work colleague. (Or, if the defendant were a restaurateur, it bars her fiancé. And so on.)
>
> *No.2: Same defendant—different place.* As above, save that the fiancé worked for another company owned or managed by the same employer. (Or, the fiancé was barred from another restaurant owned by the same restaurateur.)
>
> *No.3: Different employer/proprietor.* As above, save that the fiancé worked for an undertaking owned or managed by a friend or relative of the employer, who fired him on the say-so of the employer, or out of tacit sympathy. (Or, the fiancé was barred from a restaurant owned or managed by a friend or relative of the principal restaurateur.)

7–017   The Equality Act 2010 does not cover these scenarios because it demands that the defendant subjects the claimant to a detriment because *the claimant* does a protected act. Thus, the third party victim is not protected. There are a number of alternative, but incomplete, solutions in these scenarios. For instance, if the victim were an employee, he might be able to sue for unfair dismissal. The main drawbacks here are that he would have to be a "qualifying" employee,[78] and there are limits on compensation.[79] An alternative is for the principal complainant to sue. After all, if she were a relative or loved one, she might suffer injury to feelings, because of the victim's suffering, and perhaps, if a spouse of a victim who was fired in retaliation, a loss of earnings to the household. This would be a partial remedy though, as the award is most unlikely to reflect the

---

[78] Among other things, this requires, at present, one year's continuous employment with the employer: ERA 1996 s.108(1).
[79] The cap for unfair dismissal claims stands at £68,400 on February 13, 2011: SI 2010/2926. It is normally adjusted each February in line with retail prices.

victim's actual loss, nor be "effective, proportionate, and dissuasive" as the equality Directives demand.[80]

The Race Directive's definition of victimisation is more broadly worded than the Equality Act 2010, requiring:

> ". . . measures as are necessary to protect individuals from any adverse treatment or adverse consequence as a reaction to a complaint or to proceedings aimed at enforcing compliance with the principle of equal treatment."[81]

The Framework Directive's definition is slightly narrower, requiring:

> ". . . measures as are necessary to protect employees against dismissal or other adverse treatment by the employer as a reaction to a complaint within the undertaking or to any legal proceedings aimed at enforcing compliance with the principle of equal treatment."[82]

The formula in the Recast Directive[83] is substantially the same as this. Unlike the Race Directive, these two Directives are confined to employment matters. The history of these formulas can be traced to *Coote v Granada*,[84] where the ECJ stated: **7–018**

> "Fear of such measures, where no legal remedy is available against them, might deter workers who considered themselves the victims of discrimination from pursuing their claims by judicial process, and would consequently be liable seriously to jeopardise implementation of the aim pursued by the Directive."[85]

The policy supporting the decision goes beyond the facts of *Coote*, and suggests that *any* retaliation that might deter workers from using the discrimination laws should be unlawful. The Court's opinion was itself rooted in the EC general policy of judicial protection. As victimising a friend or relative of the complainant would deter the complainant, and others, from enforcing EU law, *Coote* suggests that all three classes (above) should be covered.

---

[80] 2000/43/EC art.15; 2000/78/EC art.17. See also the slightly differently worded Gender Equality "Recast" Directive 2006/54, Recital (35), arts 18 and 25. These codified Case C-271/91 *Marshall v Southampton and South West Hampshire AHA (No. 2)* [1993] E.C.R. I-4367, [24]. On the same issue in the US, see *De Medina v Reinhardt* 444 F Supp 573 (DDC, 1978), 580: "[It] would produce absurd and unjust results . . . the 'make whole' purpose of [the Civil Rights Act 1964] would be frustrated."

[81] 2000/43/EC art.9.

[82] 2000/78/EC art.11.

[83] 2006/54/EC art.24.

[84] Case C-185/97, [1998] E.C.R. I-5199. See further, above, para.7–004.

[85] ibid. [24].

It is clear that those drafting the Directives did not envisage third party victimisation. It is equally clear that third party victimisation comes within the mischief identified by the ECJ. The Race Directive's formula is open enough to cover all three classes. It requires adverse treatment as a reaction to a discrimination complaint or proceedings. The Framework and Gender Directives share a common, but narrower, formula. This readily covers the first two scenarios, but there is room for doubt as to whether it covers action taken by *another* employer/proprietor (Class No.3). It would require a purposive interpretation for it to do so. This highlights that not only does the UK version fail to cover third party victimisation, in failing to do so, it falls short of the EC law. Reform is required.

CONCLUSION

7–019   The underlying shortcoming with the domestic law is that it does not account fully for the wider deterrent effect produced by an act of victimisation. The law at present has three particular shortcomings: first, the domestic provisions do not account fully for the chilling effect of victimisation; second, the maintenance by the Courts of a benign motive defence; and third, the absence of protection in the domestic formula for third party victims.

Consequently, reform is required. The expression *subjects to a detriment* should be replaced with *treats unfavourably*. A new cause of action, *victimisation by proxy*, carrying a justification defence, should be introduced, in order to control properly cases such as those arising from a general policy. This should accompany the existing definition. Finally, the domestic formula should be expressed to include third party victimisation.

CHAPTER 8

DISCRIMINATION AND WORK

INTRODUCTION

8–001 The definitions of employment, and of others falling within the Work provisions, and of unlawful acts within the field of work, are provided in Pt 5 of the Equality Act 2010. The employment-related exceptions are provided by Sch.9, while most of the other exceptions are provided by Schs 22 and 23. The liability of employers is governed by ss.109 and 110, while employer liability for harassment by third parties is provided by s.40.

1. DEFINITION OF EMPLOYMENT

8–002 Claimants using the employment provisions of the domestic discrimination legislation must be in employment at an establishment in Great Britain.

(1) Employment

The Equality Act 2010 Pt 5 covers "employment under a contract of   **8–003**
employment, a contract of apprenticeship or a contract personally to
do work", and includes Crown employment, House of Commons and
House of Lords staff (s.83). This, in substance replicates the previous
broad definition. It is intended to cover the self-employed, as well as
ordinary employees.[1] The definition is wider than that found in most
employment legislation, such as the law of unfair dismissal, which
covers only employees who work under a contract of employment.[2]
In *Quinnen v Hovells*,[3] Waite J. said that "those who engage, however
cursorily, the talents, skills or labour of the self-employed" must
ensure there is no discrimination in their appointment, terms or
dismissal.

The position of purely commercial contracts—where a sole trader
or practitioner, or partner of a firm, agrees to provide services—is less
certain. Here the requirements seem to be (a) a contractual relationship, (b) an obligation to carry out the work personally, which is
(c) the "dominant purpose" of the contract.[4] Each is discussed below.

(a) Contractual Relationship

An appointment that is not overtly contractual should not obscure   **8–004**
any underlying contractual nature to the arrangement. In *Percy v
Church of Scotland Board of National Mission*[5] the appointment of a
minister of the Church of Scotland to an "ecclesiastical office", in
other words, to act as a parish minister, was for a five-year term, with
a minimum stipend, a manse, holidays and travelling expenses. The
House of Lords held that holding an ecclesiastical office and the
existence of a contract to provide services were not mutually

---

[1] At EU level, there is no single definition of worker. For discrimination, it seems to be: "The
essential feature of an employment relationship ... is that for a certain period of time a
person performs services for and under the direction of another person in return for which he
receives remuneration" (*Lawrie-Blum v Land Baden-Wurttemberg* Case 66/85 [1986] E.C.R.
2121, [17] adopted by the Court in Case C-256-01 *Allonby* [2004] E.C.R. I-00873, [67] (equal
pay) and Case C-345/09 *van Delft* [2010] E.C.R. 0000 (free movement of workers). Applied
Perceval-Price v Department of Economic Development [2000] I.R.L.R. 380 (NICA) (sex
discrimination and equal pay). For a brief account of the varying views for just one Directive
(97/81/EC, part-time workers and discrimination), see *O'Brien v Department of Justice* [2010]
I.R.L.R. 883 (HL), which, because of the uncertainty, referred the question to ECJ (Case C-
393/10)).
[2] Employment Rights Act 1996 s.230(1).
[3] [1984] I.C.R. 525, at p.532, EAT.
[4] *Mirror Group Newspapers Ltd v Gunning* [1986] I.C.R. 145, at 151 (CA).
[5] [2005] UKHL 73.

exclusive, and the arrangement, which contained the ingredients for a contract, was contractual. Further, the fragmented arrangement of the Church, which made it difficult to pin down precisely who is the employer, should not stand in the way of otherwise well-founded claims.[6]

Consequently, in *Jivraj v Hashwani*,[7] arbitrators appointed under a commercial contract were covered because whatever the precise nature of the relationship, it is likely to be supported by a contract of some kind. On the other hand, in *X v Mid Sussex Citizens Advice Bureau*,[8] volunteers working for a charity were not covered because of the absence of any contractual relations underpinning the arrangement.

(b) To Carry Out the Work Personally

8–005 The obligation must be that the person to the contract carries out work personally. In *Patterson v Legal Services Commission*[9] a sole principal in a law firm (which employed several staff) claimed racial discrimination against the Legal Services Commission in relation to its awarding of a legal aid franchise. The Court of Appeal held that Ms Patterson was not employed by the Commission because she was not obliged to carry out any of the work—under the arrangement she was entitled to delegate all of the work to her staff.[10] Likewise, a motorcycle recovery driver, who contracted with a dealer to collect motorcycles using his own vehicle, but could delegate some or all of the work, was not "employed".[11] Neither was a sub-postmaster who was required to provide premises and ensure that the post-office work was carried out either by himself or his staff;[12] nor a taxi driver who supplied his own car and paid a taxi firm £75 per week for a radio and access to its customers, but was not obliged to take any work at all.[13]

---

[6] "Office-holders" are expressly included now (EA 2010 s.49) and so a minister of religion is protected either as an employee (if contractual) or an office-holder. See further below, para.8–094. But it seems, without a contractual relationship, they are office holders and as such, not employees for the ERA 1996 s.230 for the purpose of claiming unfair dismissal: *Reverend Allan J MacDonald v Free Presbyterian Church of Scotland* (2010) UKEATS/0034/09/BI. At the time of writing, an application for judicial review had been made, see [2010] CSOH 55.

[7] [2010] I.R.L.R. 797 (CA), [14], (for the Religion of Belief Regulations 2003 SI 2003/1660). See further, para.8–058, p.258.

[8] [2010] I.C.R. 423 (EAT) (for the DDA 1995).

[9] [2004] I.C.R. 312.

[10] The Commission was held to be a "qualifications body" for the purpose of RRA 1976 s.12 (now EA 2010 s.53). See below, para.8–099.

[11] *Hawkins v Darken (t/a Sawbridgeworth Motorcycles)* [2004] EWCA Civ 1755 (for the DDA 1995).

[12] *Tanna v Post Office* [1981] I.C.R. 374, EAT (for the RRA 1976).

[13] *Mingeley v Pennock* [2004] I.C.R. 727, CA (for the RRA 1976). Distinguished in *Khan v Premier Taxis* (2006) UKEAT/0322/06/LA, where there was prima facie evidence of "a working relationship", for the Religion or Belief Regulations 2003 SI 2003/1660).

(c) The Dominant Purpose
In *Loughran & Kelly v Northern Ireland Housing Executive*,[14] the **8–006**
housing executive invited applications from firms of solicitors to sit
on a panel to defend public liability claims, stating that from each
firm either one or two solicitors "would be mainly responsible for
carrying out panel work." It rejected the applications from Loughran, and from Kelly, who brought claims of discrimination under the
Fair Employment (Northern Ireland) Act 1976. The House of Lords,
by a bare majority in each case, held that claimants were "employed"
for the purposes of the Act. Loughran was a sole principal of his firm
and the majority held that the dominant purpose was work by him,
even though he may delegate some of it to an assistant solicitor and a
secretary. Kelly was a partner in a two-partner firm and while Lords
Steyn and Slynn found that *the partnership* was contracted to do most
of the work, Lord Griffiths found that just Kelly was responsible. So,
although Kelly prevailed, there was no majority to say that firms or
companies can come under the definition of "employment".

By contrast, in *Mirror Group Newspapers Ltd v Gunning*,[15] the
contract in question was to distribute a Sunday newspaper on terms
that the contractor would exercise "day-to-day supervision" of the
operation. The Court of Appeal held that the dominant purpose of
this contract was to distribute the newspapers, and the requirement of
day-to-day supervision was not enough to make it a contract of
employment under the Sex Discrimination Act 1975.

(2) Illegal Employment Contracts
The general rule is that the courts will not enforce an illegal contract, **8–007**
such as one operating to defraud the Inland Revenue. Accordingly,
the illegality of an employment contract will undermine a wrongful
dismissal claim (that is, for breach of contract).[16] However, in
Leighton v Michael and Charalambous[17] the EAT held that an
employee under an illegal contract was entitled to sue for sexual
harassment. In *Hall v Woolston Hall Leisure*,[18] the Court of Appeal
held that a victim of pregnancy discrimination should be compen-
sated fully, despite the discovery that her employer, with her compliance, had not been deducting tax and national insurance from her

---

[14] [1999] 1 A.C. 428.
[15] [1986] I.C.R. 145.
[16] *Napier v National Business Agency* [1951] 2 All E.R. 264, CA. The Court of Appeal, in
Hewcastle Catering v Ahmed and Elkanah [1991] I.R.L.R. 473, allowed a claim of *unfair*
dismissal to succeed, despite the claimant workers participating, but not profiting, in the
employer's tax fraud. The special circumstances were that the workers were sacked for giving
evidence against the employer regarding the fraud.
[17] [1995] I.C.R. 1091.
[18] [2001] I.C.R. 99.

wages. The reasoning was provided subsequently by Lord Roger in
Rhys-Harper v Relaxion Group:[19]

> "... the anti-discrimination Acts are not really concerned with
> employees' rights under their contracts of employment. So, for
> instance, where a contract of employment is tainted by illegality,
> an employee may nonetheless complain that her employer dis-
> criminated against her ... since [the domestic and EU dis-
> crimination legislation is] designed to provide effective relief in
> respect of discriminatory conduct 'rather than relief which
> reflects any contractual entitlement which may or may not
> exist'."

Note though, that policy may dictate that claim is barred. A tribunal
should:

> "... consider whether the applicant's claim arises out of or is so
> clearly connected or inextricably bound up or linked with the
> illegal conduct of the applicant that the court could not permit
> the applicant to recover compensation without appearing to
> condone that conduct."[20]

Thus, in *Vakante v Addey and Stanhope School Governing Body*,[21] it
was held that a claimant without a work permit who obtained his job
by deceit, could not claim for racial discrimination. *Hall* was distinguished because:

> "As for the illegal conduct here (a) it was that of Mr Vakante; (b)
> it was criminal; (c) it went far beyond the manner in which one
> party performed what was otherwise a lawful employment con-
> tract; (d) it went to the basic content of an employment situation;
> (e) the duty not to discriminate arises from an employment
> situation which, without a permit, was unlawful from top to
> bottom and from beginning to end."[22]

A less polarised approach was taken in *Blue Chip v Helbawi*,[23] where
the claimant, a foreign student, breached his work permit by sometimes working in excess of 20 hours per week. The EAT severed the
illegal parts of the contract, and held he could claim for the national
minimum wage for those weeks he had not overworked. This
approach may prove useful in discrimination cases, especially equal
pay claims.

[19] [2003] I.C.R. 867 (HL), [210].
[20] *Hall v Woolston Hall Leisure* [2001] I.C.R. 99 (CA), [42], see also, [46], [47], and [80].
[21] [2004] 4 All E.R. 1056 (CA).
[22] ibid. [34].
[23] [2009] I.R.L.R. 128 (EAT).

2. EMPLOYMENT: DISCRIMINATION, VICTIMISATION AND HARASSMENT

(1) Recruitment

Equality Act 2010 Section 39   8–008

39 (1) An employer (A) must not discriminate against [or victimise[24]] a person (B)—

    (a) in the arrangements A makes for deciding to whom to offer employment;

    (b) as to the terms on which A offers B employment;

    (c) by not offering B employment.

It also unlawful for an employer to harass a person "who has applied [to that employer] for employment".[25]

(a) Arrangements for Recruitment

Paragraph (a) covers all aspects of the recruitment process leading to   8–009
the appointment and the terms of that appointment. This will include
for example, the drawing up of the job specification, the taking up of
references and the short-listing process. In *Ministry of Defence v Fair
Employment Agency*,[26] it was held discriminatory to require a security
check only for the Roman Catholic candidate. An arbitration clause
in a commercial contract also forms part of the "arrangements" for
the recruitment of an arbitrator.[27]

The provisions do not refer to any particular person in the
recruitment process, but simply the arrangements made by the
employer. In *Brennan v JH Dewhurst Ltd*,[28] the defendant advertised
for a butcher's assistant, and appointed (in a non-discriminatory
manner) a local manager to carry out the "first-filter" interviews, the
final decision being with the district manager. The local manager
interviewed a female candidate in a discriminatory manner, making it
clear that he did not want a woman appointed. The EAT held that
the local manager's interview was part of the selection arrangements,
and so the defendant was liable. The employer could not disassociate
itself from the *effect* of its arrangement. Further, it did not matter
that in the event, no one was appointed to the post. This case also

---

[24] EA 2010 s.39(3).
[25] EA 2010 s.40(1)(b).
[26] [1988] 11 NIJB 75, NICA. (For the Fair Employment (NI) Act 1976, which outlawed discrimination on the ground of religion or political belief. See now Fair Employment (NI) Act 1989.)
[27] *Jivraj v Hashwani* [2010] I.R.L.R. 797 (CA), [23] (for the Religion of Belief Regulations 2003 SI 2003/1660). See further, para.8–058, p.258.
[28] [1984] I.C.R. 52 (EAT).

demonstrates that a discriminatory intent in the making of the arrangements is not necessary for liability.

Logically, advertising forms part of the "arrangements" for recruitment,[29] and is expressed to do so in the Explanatory Notes (63). Thus, a person deterred by a discriminatory advertisement could sue for discrimination. The previous legislation expressly prohibited discriminatory advertising, with the rider that those provisions were enforceable only by the relevant equality commissions. The absurd consequence was that advertisements could not be considered part of the employer's recruitment "arrangements", and so an individual could not complain about a job advertisement that discriminated against that individual.[30] The removal of the specific prohibition thus allows discriminatory advertisements to be attacked by affected individuals *and* the Equality and Human Rights Commission.

That said, the previous regime produced some useful and interesting pointers to future enforcement.[31] Obviously, employers should avoid any reference to protected characteristics in advertising, unless they relate to a Genuine Occupational Requirement, although care should be taken not to give the impression that the activity is unlawful (see below). Sexual, or other, connotations also should be avoided, such as waiter, salesgirl, postman or stewardess.[32] These suggest that one sex or another is preferred and may deter some applicants because of their sex.

The White Paper preceding the Race Relations Act 1976 explained as a matter of policy: "the public display of racial prejudices and preferences is inherently offensive and likely to encourage the spread of discriminatory attitudes and prejudices."[33] Hence, RRA 1976 s.29(1) outlawed advertisements which indicated, "or might reasonably be understood as indicating, an intention by a person to do an act of discrimination" *even if any subsequent act happens to be lawful*. This restriction no longer applies, but it will be interesting to see if the Equality and Human Rights Commission suggest that it should when, and if, it takes action (as it is empowered to do) against (apparent) discriminatory advertising. Of course, the sentiment expressed in the White Paper applies with more or less force, to the

---

[29] *Brindley v Tayside Health Board* [1976] I.R.L.R. 364 (IT).

[30] *Cardiff Women's Aid v Hartup* [1994] I.R.L.R. 390 (EAT).

[31] Sections 82, SDA 1975, and 78, RRA 1976, offered a common broad definition of an advertisement: "'Advertisement' includes every form of advertisement or notice, whether to the public or not, and whether in a newspaper or other publication, by television or radio, by display of notices, signs, labels, showcards or goods, by distribution of samples, circulars, catalogues, price lists or other material, by exhibition of pictures, models or films, or in any other way, and references to the publishing of advertisements shall be construed accordingly".

[32] SDA 1975 s.38(3). In *Equal Opportunities Commission v Robertson* [1980] I.R.L.R. 44 an industrial tribunal held that the words "craftsman", "ex-policeman or similar", "bloke", "manageress" each had sexual connotations, but "manager" and "carpenter/handyman" did not.

[33] Racial Discrimination Cmnd 6234, p.19.

other protected characteristics. For example, it would be offensive and spread discriminatory attitudes if a church organisation advertised for heterosexuals by stating "no gays need apply", even if the requirement were lawful.[34]

As well as facially discriminatory advertisements, it is conceivable that advertisements which indirectly discriminate are challengeable, such as job vacancies placed only in men's or women's magazines, or distributed only in predominantly white areas,[35] or displayed in part of the workplace frequented predominantly by men.

Word-of-mouth hiring should come within the "arrangements",[36] although this has not been tested in the courts.[37] It was accepted, obiter, in *Coker v Lord Chancellor*[38] that word-of-mouth hiring could amount to unlawful discrimination, although it was held in that case that creating a job for a member of the family, a friend or a personal acquaintance was not discriminatory. This logic prompted the comment: "The prohibition of discrimination in selection arrangements— a concept which lies at the heart of discrimination law—can be circumvented by the simple expedient of not having any selection arrangements."[39]

(b) The Terms Offered

The job offer must not be on discriminatory terms, such as lower pay   **8–010**
for a woman, a company car for a man, or a probationary period for a black person. For sex-, pregnancy- and maternity-discrimination, once the offer becomes part of the employment, the matter moves out of the employment regime, and into the Equal Pay regime of the Act (Pt 5, Ch.3). These are mutually exclusive (s.70). The relationship between these two regimes is explained in Chapter 9.[40]

(2) During Employment

Equality Act 2010 Section 39   **8–011**

(2) An employer (A) must not discriminate against [or victimise][41] an employee of A's (B)—

---

[34] e.g. under Sch.9 para.2. See below, para.8–030.
[35] See the US case, *US v City of Warren, Michigan* 138 F 3d 1083 (6th Cir 1998).
[36] Especially as the definition of indirect discrimination is now less restrictive: see Ch.6, paras 6–009 to 6–013.
[37] The US Circuits are divided on this issue: see *United States v Georgia Power* 474 F 2d 906, at 925–926 (7th Cir 1993) and *EEOC v Chicago Miniature Lamp Works* 947 F 2d 292 (7th Cir 1991). Discussed Ch.6, paras 6–009 to 6–013.
[38] [2002] I.C.R. 321 (CA), [57]. Discussed, Ch.6, para.6–031.
[39] Michael Rubenstein, commentary to *Coker* in the I.R.L.R., [2001] I.R.L.R. 116, at 115.
[40] At paras 9–002 et seq.
[41] EA 2010 s.39(4).

(a) as to B's terms of employment;
(b) in the way A affords B access, or by not affording B access, to opportunities for promotion, transfer or training or for receiving any other benefit, facility or service;
(c) by dismissing B;
(d) by subjecting B to any other detriment.

It is also unlawful for an employer to harass an employee,[42] and in certain circumstances the employer will be liable for harassment by a third party (e.g. a customer, client).[43]

(a) Discriminatory Dismissals

8–012   The Act confirms that dismissal (s.39(2)(c)) includes constructive dismissal, that is where the worker resigns because the employer's conduct, amounting to a serious breach of contract, entitles the innocent party to resign from the contract.[44] This codifies *Weathersfield Ltd (Trading As Van & Truck Rentals) v Sargent*,[45] where the Court of Appeal applied the established contract principles of acceptance of a repudiatory breach. Here Mrs Sargent, a white European, was appointed as a receptionist by the defendant. On her first day she was told not to hire out vehicles to "any coloured or Asians". She was stunned and a few days later resigned, without giving her reason. She brought a claim of racial discrimination, claiming constructive dismissal on the ground of race.[46] One issue was whether she could claim constructive dismissal without having given her reason for leaving. The Court of Appeal held that it was not necessary in law to state the reason for leaving and so found for Ms Sargent. "[T]he more outrageous or embarrassing are the instructions given to them, or suggestions made to them, the less likely they may be to argue the point there and then. ... Moreover, there is no suggestion in this case that the employers would have changed their policy had she asked them to do so."[47] However, the Court warned that when no reason was given at the time, it would be more difficult to show that the employer's conduct was the true reason for leaving.

Often, claims for discriminatory dismissal will overlap with unfair dismissal claims (provided by the Employment Rights Act 1996). But there are some important differences between unfair dismissal and discriminatory dismissal. The first is that for unfair dismissal only, there is a general one-year qualification period.[48] This applies equally

---

[42] EA 2010 s.40(1)(a).
[43] See below, para.8–103.
[44] EA 2010 s.39(7)(b).
[45] [1999] I.C.R. 425.
[46] It is possible to be discriminated against on the grounds of another's race: *Showboat v Owens* [1984] 1 W.L.R. 384 (EAT). See further, Ch.4, para.4–026.
[47] [1999] I.C.R. 425, at 433.
[48] ERA 1996 s.108(1). There are some exceptions to this rule.

to full- and part-time employees. Second, unfair dismissal compensation remains subject to a statutory maximum limit.[49] There is no cap on the compensation available for unlawful discrimination. Typically, this will benefit highly-paid workers,[50] or those whose career has been terminated by a discriminatory dismissal.[51] Third, the definition of an employee is much broader in the discrimination legislation, covering the self-employed. Unfair dismissal rights are available only to employees who work under a contract of employment. Fourth, unlike unfair dismissal, there is a right under discrimination law to damages for injured feelings.[52]

It is possible to combine the two allegations in a single case. As a matter of law, a discriminatory dismissal is not necessarily an unfair dismissal, although it would "need very special circumstances to justify a holding that an unlawfully discriminatory dismissal was a fair dismissal."[53] Thus a fair dismissal may have been discriminatory and vice versa.[54]

(b) Any Other Detriment

Should the facts not fall within any of the specified circumstances in s.39(2) (such as access to promotion, any other benefits, or dismissal) a claim may still succeed if the employee suffered "any other detriment" (s.39(2)(d)). In *Shamoon v Chief Constable of the Royal Ulster Constabulary*[55] the House of Lords stated the question was: "Is the treatment of such a kind that a reasonable worker would or might take the view that in all the circumstances it was to his detriment?" It was not necessary to demonstrate some physical or economic consequence.   **8–013**

---

[49] The cap for unfair dismissal claims stands at £68,400 on February 13, 2011: SI 2010/2926. It is normally adjusted each February in line with retail prices.

[50] In *BMA v Chaudhary (No.2)* (2004) UKEAT/1351/01/DA and UKEAT/0804/02/DA, the EAT upheld an award of £800,000 to a doctor whose career was damaged by racial discrimination (reversed on other grounds [2007] I.R.LR. 800 (CA)). In *Cheapside (formally Schroder Securities) v Bower* (2002) EAT/286/02, an employment tribunal awarded £1.4m to a city worker who was forced to resign because of sex discrimination (reported *The Times*, January 11, 2002, and noted EAT/678/01 (*see www.employmentappeals.gov.uk*)). See also *Caylon v Wardle* (2010) UKEAT/535/09/SM (over £300,000 awarded for discrimination by a French employer against worker of English origin). The cap was lifted in deference to EC law: see Ch.12, n.104.

[51] Such as those women dismissed form the armed forces for pregnancy. See, e.g. *Ministry of Defence v Cannock* [1994] I.C.R. 918, EAT; A. Arnull, "EC law and the dismissal of pregnant servicewomen" (1995) 24 ILJ 215. Discussed below, Ch.12 para.12–025.

[52] "An award of damages may include compensation for injured feelings (whether or not it includes compensation on any other basis)": EA 2010 s.119(4), which applies to employment tribunals via s.124(6). See *Vento v Chief Constable of West Yorkshire Police* [2003] I.C.R. 318 (CA). For unfair dismissal, see *Dunnachie v Kingston-upon-Hull City Council* [2004] UKHL 36.

[53] *Clarke v Eley (IMI) Kynoch Ltd* [1983] I.C.R. 165 (EAT), at 177 (Browne-Wilkinson J.).

[54] In *Claydon House v Bradbury* Unreported (2004) UKEAT/0315/04/MAA (Transcript) (available at *www.employmentappeals.gov.uk*), the claimant was dismissed for a fair reason (gross misconduct), although the reason for her "misconduct" (absenteeism) was a disability.

[55] [2003] I.C.R. 337, [35], citing *Ministry of Defence v Jeremiah* [1980] Q.B. 87 (CA), at 104.

In *Shamoon* a police inspector carried out as one of her duties appraisals of officers. Following complaints by officers, she was relieved of the appraisal duty. She brought a claim of sex discrimination.[56] The Northern Ireland Court of Appeal[57] held that Ms Shamoon had not suffered a detriment because she had no "right" to carry out appraisals and there was no accompanying loss of rank or financial loss. The House of Lords reversed, and held that the loss of the appraisal work was a detriment simply because it would reduce her standing among colleagues.[58]

In *Chief Constable of West Yorkshire v Khan*[59] the House of Lords held that an employer's refusal to give a reference amounted to a detriment, even though in the event a reference would have been negative and *lessened* the candidate's chances. The candidate, reasonably, would have preferred to have the reference.[60]

8–014 An unjustified sense of grievance cannot amount to "detriment". In *Barclays Bank Plc v Kapur (No.2)*,[61] workers were not given pension rights in respect to their previous service for their employer in Kenya, because they had been given a compensation package. As they were no worse off financially, the Court of Appeal held they had suffered no detriment. Less convincing is *Schmidt v Austicks Bookshops*,[62] where female, but not male, workers in a bookshop were required to wear overalls when in public areas. The EAT held that this was not serious enough to amount to a detriment. It is unlikely that this decision can survive the approach taken in *Shamoon*. A reasonable worker may well feel demeaned at having to wear overalls in public, which gives the impression that she is of a different status to her male colleagues.

There is some doubt as to precise meaning of this phrase, ranging from purely objective to highly subjective (from the claimant's perspective). This is discussed in Chapter 7. Many employer actions involving say, the suspension of a grievance procedure or transfer rights (as victimisation), or the withholding of a reference are more accurately characterised as a "benefit" under s.39(2)(b).[63] As such, claimants could avoid any uncertainties by pleading this instead of (or alternatively to) "any other detriment".

---

[56] Under the Sex Discrimination (Northern Ireland) Order 1976 art.8(2)(b), which is substantially the same as EA 2010 s.39(2)(b) (set out above).

[57] [2001] I.R.L.R. 520.

[58] [2003] I.C.R. 337, [37]. However, she lost appeal because she was treated no less favourably than a male inspector would have been in the same circumstances. See further Ch.4, para.4–006.

[59] [2001] I.C.R. 1065.

[60] This conclusion was doubted by the House in *St Helens v Derbyshire* [2007] I.C.R. 841. See further Ch.7, para.7–005, p.208.

[61] [1995] I.R.L.R. 87.

[62] [1978] I.C.R. 85, at 88.

[63] In *Khan*, Lord Mackay assumed a reference to be a "benefit": [2001] I.C.R. 1065, [38].

(3) Ex-Workers

Equality Act 2010   8–015

108 Relationships that have ended

(1) A person (A) must not discriminate against another (B) if—

    (a) the discrimination arises out of and is closely connected to a relationship which used to exist between them, and

    (b) conduct of a description constituting the discrimination would, if it occurred during the relationship, contravene this Act.

Section 108(2) applies the same rule (with the necessary changes) to harassment. And so s.108 outlaws discrimination and harassment by an employer against its former workers. It is expressly stated *not* to cover victimisation (s.108(7)). Yet most detrimental acts by former employers are likely to be retaliatory by nature,[64] for instance, refusing to provide a reference to an ex-worker because she had once sued for sexual harassment. This should not present a barrier to victimisation claims by former workers, as a brief history will illustrate.

The first point of note is the ECJ decision in 1999 in *Coote v Granada*.[65] Here, Mrs Coote sued her employer following her dismissal for being pregnant. Subsequently, and after those proceedings were dead, the employer refused to give her a reference and Mrs Coote sued again, this time for victimisation. An industrial tribunal ruled that s.6(2) of the Sex Discrimination Act 1975 ("It is unlawful for a person, in the case of a woman employed by him ... to discriminate against her") covered discrimination against persons *employed* by the defendant. As Mrs Coote no longer worked for Granada when it refused the reference, she was not protected by the Act. The ECJ disagreed, holding that it was:

"... necessary to ensure judicial protection for workers whose employer, after the employment relationship has ended, refuses to provide references as a reaction to legal proceedings [for discrimination]."[66]

As a result of *Coote*, the equality Directives specified that judicial   8–016
and/or administrative procedures should be available to those complaining of discrimination "even after the relationship in which the

---

[64] *Metropolitan Police Service v Shoebridge* [2004] I.C.R. 1690 (EAT), [13] (Burton J.).

[65] Case C-185/97, [1999] I.C.R. 100 (ECJ). See also, *Pothecary Witham Weld v Bullimore* [2010] I.C.R. 1008 (EAT) (employer provided reference mentioning ex-worker's discrimination claim).

[66] ibid. [28]. Following the ECJ's ruling, the EAT held that s.6(2) covered ex-workers: *Coote v Granada Hospitality Ltd (No.2)* [1999] I.C.R. 942.

discrimination is alleged to have occurred has ended".[67] Strictly speaking, this did not cover victimisation, which although outlawed by the Directives, is not expressed as a form of discrimination. Nonetheless, *Coote* remains good law. In the meantime, the House of Lords, in *Relaxion v Rhys-Harper*,[68] decided several post-employment victimisation cases in the wake of *Coote*, and set out some guidelines, providing a purposive interpretation of the domestic legislation (such as SDA s.6(2)) in accordance with *Coote*. In due course, the domestic legislation gradually was amended expressly to cover post-employment discrimination.[69] This was done under the influence of *Coote*, the Directives, and *Relaxion*. At this time, the domestic amendments included victimisation. This was because the legislation formulated victimisation as a form of discrimination (being less favourable treatment by reason that the victim had done a protected act). Under the Equality Act 2010, victimisation has been reformulated without the comparative element and so is no longer a form of discrimination.

The end result is a body of case law that is either: (1) post-*Coote* but pre-legislative amendments (*Relaxion*); or (2) post the relevant domestic amendment; or (3) (yet to be decided) cases on victimisation under the Equality Act 2010; these should follow *Relaxion* and *Coote*. It is strange that the drafter chose to exclude victimisation from s.108, although this more accurately reflects the structure of the equality Directives, it is a regression from the previous legislation. As we shall see, it should be possible to avoid anomalies by harmonising all three classes.

The first class is represented by *Relaxion*. The problem in that case was that SDA 1975 s.6(2) (above) did not naturally lend itself to covering ex-employees (covering a person *employed* by the employer), yet the ECJ in *Coote* had decided that the law should do so. The House of Lords heard several cases and gave five varying speeches. So it is not easy to discern a unanimous and straightforward principle. In general, the House held that s.6(2) related to conduct that had "substantive connection" with the prior employment relationship,[70]

---

[67] Race Directive 2000/43 art.7; Framework Directive 2000/74/EC art.9; Recast Directive 2006/54 art.17 (first appearing in Equal Treatment (Amendment) Directive 2002/73/EC art.1(5), and Rec.17, in force Oct 2005).

[68] [2003] I.C.R. 867.

[69] RRA 1976 s.27A (in force, July 19, 2003) SDA 1975 s.20A, (for discrimination July 19, 2003, for harassment October 1, 2005); Religion or Belief Regulations 2003 reg.21; Sexual Orientation Regulations 2003 reg.21; DDA 1995 s.16A (2003); Age Regulations 2006 reg.24 (October 2006).

[70] [2003] I.C.R. 867, [140] (Lord Hobhouse), [215] (Lord Roger).

or covered "all the benefits arising from that relationship", irrespective of whether that relationship had ended.[71]

The domestic amendments (the second class) were consolidated by   **8-017**
EA 2010 s.108 (set out above), which demands that the conduct
"arises out of and is closely connected to" the prior employment
relationship. This reflects the language of *Relaxion*, and so it should
not be difficult for the courts to harmonise the approaches in cases of
discrimination and harassment.[72]

The third class of victimisation cases under the Equality Act 2010
will fall back on the equivalent of SDA 1975 s.6(2), which is EA 2010
s.39(4), although the wording is slightly different: "An employer (A)
must not victimise an employee of A's". This appears as limiting as
SDA s.6(2). But under the shadow of *Coote*, courts should follow
Relaxion, and to give it an equally liberal interpretation.

The existing cases tell us the following. There is no set time limit,
although, of course, the longer the time between the employment and
conduct complained of, the more difficult it may be to show the
necessary connection. In some of the *Relaxion* cases the gap ranged
between 18 months, 22 months and 29 months.[73]

It does not matter if the conduct complained of differs from conduct that would arise when the person was employed. Indeed, much
conduct post-employment is likely to be different. In *Metropolitan
Police Service v Shoebridge*[74] it was alleged that the former employer
(the Metropolitan Police) made unsolicited detrimental remarks to
Shoebridge's current employer, which resulted in the current
employer dismissing him. (The remarks related to a sex discrimination claim brought by Shoebridge against the Metropolitan Police.)
Shoebridge's subsequent claim for victimisation was brought "post-
Coote but pre-legislative amendments". The EAT held that such
conduct could be victimisation *sufficiently connected* with the
employment relationship.

It would seem that for victimisation, the courts will demand evidence of an intention to deter or retaliate. In *Nicholls v Corin Tech*,[75]
Mr Nicholls was suing his former employer for disability discrimination. Outside the room where the hearing had taken place for

---

[71] ibid. [37] (Lord Nicholls). Thus, there is no liability where the act complained of does not
arise from the employment relationship, such as a refusal to implement an employment
tribunal's reinstatement order for which there was a free-standing remedy (under the
Employment Rights Act 1996 ss.112, 113, 114 and 117): ibid., in the case of *D'Souza*, [49]–
[53], [124]–[125], [159]–[160], [205] and [221]. But there can be liability where the employer
fails to honour an award of compensation: *Coutinho v Rank Nemo (DMS) Ltd* [2009] I.C.R.
1296 (CA).
[72] In *Metropolitan Police Service v Shoebridge* [2004] I.C.R. 1690 (EAT), [38] Underhill J. noted
that the domestic legislative codification of *Coote* (e.g. SDA s.20A) was "exactly in accord
with ... the majority decision ... in *Relaxion*".
[73] Respectively: *Angel v New Posibilities NHS Trust, Jones v 3M Healthcare Ltd, Kirker v
British Sugar* [2003] I.C.R. 867 (HL).
[74] [2004] I.C.R. 1690 (EAT), [30] (Underhill J.).
[75] (2008) UKEAT/0290/07/LA. See *employmentappeals.gov.uk*.

the day, it was alleged that the defendant and three others approached Mr Nicholls and one of them threatened him physical injury ("I
will give you a disability") if he maintained his claim. Mr Nicholls
then sued for victimisation. This was a "post-domestic amendment"
case. The EAT emphasised that the statutory formula required that
the conduct was "*closely* connected" to the employment relationship,
and by this, it seemed, the conduct had to be "intended or calculated
to deter Mr Nicholls from continuing with his proceedings", otherwise it was open for a tribunal to find no liability.[76]

3. EMPLOYMENT EXEMPTIONS

8–018   The Equality Act 2010 provides a range of defences, essentially to
direct discrimination. The main defence, common to all protected
characteristics, arises where the job *requires* a person with a particular
protected characteristic. This is provided by a single "Genuine
Occupational Requirement" (GOR) formula. Otherwise, the Act
provides more specific defences, some common to two or more protected characteristics. Finally, there are some general defences, such
as national security. After a discussion of the GOR defence, the
defences are set out below in the context of each protected
characteristic.

(1) Genuine Occupational Requirements—General Comments
8–019   The equality Directives allow for different treatment "based on a
characteristic related to" race, religion or belief, sex (including gender
reassignment), sexual orientation and age, where:

> "... by reason of the nature of the particular occupational
> activities concerned or of the context in which they are carried
> out, such a characteristic constitutes a genuine and determining
> occupational requirement, provided that the objective is legit-
> imate and the requirement is proportionate."[77]

The Equality Act 2010 by Sch.9, Pt 1, para.1, implements this formula, by providing an employer may enjoy an exemption:

---

[76] ibid. [14].
[77] Race Directive 2000/43/EC art.4; Framework Directive 2000/78/EC art.4(1); Recast
Directive 2006/54/EC art.14(2), which is slightly more limited, applying only to access to
employment and training.

"... by applying in relation to work a requirement to have a particular protected characteristic, if [it] shows that, having regard to the nature or context of the work—

(a) it is an occupational requirement,
(b) the application of the requirement is a proportionate means of achieving a legitimate aim, and
(c) the person to whom [it] applies the requirement does not meet it (or [it] has reasonable grounds for not being satisfied that the person meets it)".[78]

Schedule 9, para.1 applies to direct discrimination[79] in recruitment, access to promotion, transfer or training,[80] and (except for sex discrimination)[81] dismissal. This permits, for instance, the dismissal of workers recruited under a GOR who, say, convert to another religion, embark upon gender reassignment, or "come out" as gay. It is, of course, most unlikely that a worker could be dismissed using a race GOR save for cases solely based on nationality.

The presumable logic behind the restriction on dismissals for sex-related GORs is that persons do not change sex. But of course, they do. And so, a woman working under a GOR as, say, a women's refuge counsellor,[82] would become unsuitable for that job should she embark upon a sex change. Neither the Recast Directive (which conflates sex and gender reassignment discrimination) nor Sch.9 para.1 permit this person to be dismissed because he has become a man. If the employer expressed the GOR was to be a woman *and* not to be a transsexual, dismissal could be permissible under Sch.9, if not the Directive. **8–020**

The Directives stipulate that the protected characteristic "constitutes a genuine *and* determining occupational requirement". Schedule 9 reduces this to the single phrase "occupational requirement". Thus, tribunals should incorporate the Directive's more stringent word *determining* where appropriate.

Schedule 9, para.1 (and 2, see below, para.8–030) applies to a person who does not meet the requirement (to be e.g. male, heterosexual, white, Roman Catholic, young) *or* (save for sex) whom the employer is *reasonably satisfied* does not meet it. This means the exception can be invoked where the employer perceives (reasonably) that the person is homosexual, or transsexual, Moslem, aged, and so on, even if the employer is mistaken. It was held in *AMICUS v Secretary of State for Trade and Industry*[83] that this phrase was

---

[78] The words in parenthesis do not apply to sex discrimination: Sch.9 para.1(4).
[79] EA 2010 Sch.9, para.6(2).
[80] In this context, the words, "or for receiving any other benefit, facility or service" should be omitted from ss.39(2)(b), 44(2)(b), 45(2)(b), 49(6)(b) or 50(6)(b) (EA 2010, Sch.9 para.6(5)).
[81] EA 2010 Sch.9, para.6(6), following the similarly restrictive Recast Directive art.14(2).
[82] EHRC *Draft* Code of Practice on Employment, para.13.8.
[83] [2004] EWHC 860, [116].

compatible with the Framework Directive 2000/78/EC. The High Court endorsed the Government's argument that the basis of the phrase was to enable employers to reject a person who refused to disclose his sexual orientation, "without having to impinge on the applicant's privacy unnecessarily".[84] The obvious danger here is that employers will make stereotypical presumptions based on candidates' appearance and/or demeanour, the antithesis of discrimination law. Whatever its credibility in the context of sexual orientation requirements, the argument is irrelevant to other protected characteristics, especially race and religion, where mistakes can come about, say, by a white person's stereotyped perception of characteristics typical to any particular racial or religious group. Discrimination based on mistaken perceptions and stereotyping is unlawful direct discrimination under s.13[85] and it remains to be seen how the courts will approach tension between this phrase "reasonably satisfied" and s.13. Much will depend on the application of the word "reasonably": was the employer's perception reasonable by the standards of mainstream society, or by the standards of legislation intended to combat a prejudice of mainstream society? To minimise the danger, tribunals should opt for the latter.

(2) Gender, Pregnancy and Maternity

(a) Genuine Occupational Requirement

8–021　For sex discrimination, the Equality Act 2010 Sch.9, para.1, replaces the old regime of "Genuine Occupational Qualification" with "Genuine Occupational Requirement" (GOR). The GOQ exemptions comprised an exhaustive list of specific job requirements. Unlike Sch.9, the GOQ regime did not allow new exceptions to be developed by the courts under a general principle. Any job requirements suggested by the GOQs may still be imposed, so long as they comply with the GOR rubric. Indeed, some of the cases under the old (GOQ) regime help to indicate how Sch.9 might operate.

Under the old regime, a GOQ defence could be raised where only *some* of the job duties require a man or a woman.[86] However, the defence failed where other employees were "capable of carrying out the duties" and that it would be reasonable to employ them on such duties without undue inconvenience. This coincides with the proportionality principle in Sch.9 and means that is unlikely that an employer can reserve a job for, say, a woman, because one of the job's minor duties must be carried out by a woman, when there are

---

[84] ibid. [72].
[85] See Ch.4, paras 4–028 and 4–032, and generally Ch.5 on Harassment.
[86] SDA 1975 s.7(3). See *Tottenham Green Under Fives' Centre v Marshall* [1989] I.C.R. 214 (EAT) and *(No.2)* [1991] I.C.R. 320 (EAT), decided under the parallel provision under the old Race Relations Act s.5(3).

other female employees who could perform that duty.[87] The "other employees" must have existed at the time, and so, for example, where the employer was recruiting workers for a new all-women's health club which had not yet been opened, the GOQ exemption "to preserve decency or privacy" applied even though it might well fail once other employees had been hired.[88] However, if an employer used this as a tactic to avoid liability, say by recruiting senior staff first (say, all men) and then filling the remaining posts with a mix of men and women, it is unlikely that its claim could be considered "genuine" for Sch.9.

As noted above, a sex-based GOR cannot be used to dismiss a worker. This follows the old regime. However, where redundancies arise and a remaining job is revised, a GOR may used when selecting the person for the revised job. In *Timex v Hodgson*[89] a reorganisation reduced the need for three supervisors to one. Timex decided to retain the woman supervisor (and dismiss the two male ones) so that she could (i) deal with the personal and private problems of the female workers; (ii) accompany women to the first aid room, (iii) deal with the supply of sanitary towels in the women's lavatory and pills for period pains, and (iv) sometimes take urine samples from women who worked with toxic materials. The EAT held that "the correct analysis is that the employers discriminate against the man by selecting the woman to do the revised job, not in dismissing the man who is not selected for the revised job." Thus, this was a discriminatory omission to offer the man a job (permitted), rather than a dismissal of the man, and so the GOQ could apply.

What follows is a description of each GOQ exemption specified in the old regime, under the SDA 1975. These are included as illustrative only of circumstances where the new GORs might be applied. These represent the situations that Parliament envisaged when passing the original Act in 1975, and of course, may encourage employers to continue using them. Note that the statutory definitions use the terms "man" and "woman" interchangeably.

(i) Physiology and authenticity

The first specific GOQ under the old regime could apply where: **8–022**

"... the essential nature of the job calls for a man for reasons of physiology (excluding physical strength or stamina) or, in dramatic performances or other entertainment, for reasons of

---

[87] See e.g. *Etam Plc v Rowan* [1989] I.R.L.R. 150, EAT (16 other (female) employees in ladies' fashion store could cover fitting room duties). cf. *Lasertop Ltd v Webster* [1997] I.C.R. 828 (EAT) (unduly inconvenient for man selling membership of a women-only health club to hand over to a woman when showing potential customers the changing area).

[88] *Lasertop Ltd v Webster* [1997] I.C.R. 828 (EAT).

[89] [1982] I.C.R. 63 (EAT).

authenticity, so that the essential nature of the job would be materially different if carried out by a woman".[90]

The physiology exception would apply to wet-nursing and the sex industry. The authenticity exception had a potentially wide range, applying not only to "drama", but also to "entertainment". Of course, for dramatic authenticity, it would be permissible to cast female and male roles to their respective sexes. For entertainment, where the essence of the work is to entertain members of the opposite sex, such as a dance troupes to entertain at hen nights, or vice versa, it should be permissible to hire only men, or women, as the case may be.[91] Beyond that, cases may be harder to decide. In the US case, *Wilson v Southwest Airlines*,[92] an airline promoted its female cabin crews to attract male business travellers and accordingly hired only women. It was held that as the essence of an airline was safe travel, not entertainment, no "bona fide occupational qualification" (BFOQ)[93] could apply: "Sex does not become a BFOQ merely because an employer chooses to exploit female sexuality as a marketing tool, or to better insure profitability". Identifying the nature of the job will not always that straightforward. For instance, a restaurant or bar may employ all-female, or all-male,[94] serving staff, to accord with a theme.[95] Further, as Pannick has noted, "There is a thin but important line between sex as a GOQ where the essential nature of the job requires a woman, and the case where the job can more effectively be performed by a woman because of customer reaction."[96]

(ii) Privacy or decency

8–023 The second specific GOQ under the old regime could apply: "where the job needs to be held by a man to preserve privacy or decency" because either (i) it is likely to involve physical contact ... where men might reasonably object to its being carried out by a woman; or (ii) the holder of the job is likely to do his work in circumstances where men might reasonably object to the presence of a woman because

---

[90] SDA 1975 s.7(2)(a).
[91] In *Cropper v UK Express Ltd* (1992), unreported, (ET case no.25757/91; digested E.O.R. Dig. 1992, 12, 2–3) an employment tribunal held that sex was a GOQ for working on a telephone sex chat-line.
[92] 517 F Supp 292, at 303 (ND Tex 1981). See also *Diaz v Pam American Airlines* 442 F 2d 385 (5th Cir 1971) *certiorari denied* 404 US 950 (1971).
[93] The US Civil Rights Act 1964 equivalent of the GOR.
[94] See the *EEOC v Joe's Stone Crab* litigation (220 F 3d 1263 (11th Cir 2000)) where male serving staff were used to evoke an "Old World" ambiance.
[95] It was suggested in *Cross v Playboy Club*, Appeal No.773, Case No.CFS 22618-70 (New York Human Rights Appeal Board, 1971) that being female is a BFOQ to be a Playboy Bunny, female sexuality being reasonably necessary to perform the essential purpose of the job which is to entice and entertain male customers. Cited in *Wilson v Southwest Airlines* 517 F Supp 292, at 302 (ND Tex 1981).
[96] D. Pannick, *Sex Discrimination Law* (Oxford: OUP, 1985) p.238; *or* "When is Sex a Genuine Occupational Qualification?" (1983) 4(2) Oxford J. Legal Stud. 198, p.209.

they are in a state of undress or are using sanitary facilities.[97] (See also "communal accommodation", below.)

The "physical contact" exception will arise, say, where customers require measuring for clothing.[98] The second part of this *privacy or decency* defence arises where the jobholder is in a state of undress or is using sanitary facilities. In *Sisley v Britannia Security Systems Ltd*,[99] the EAT held that a jobholder's work encompassed "all matters reasonably incidental to it". Here the employer operated a security control station, described as a confined "building within a building". The (all-female) staff worked up to 12-hour shifts. The employer provided a folding bed and the staff were in the habit of sleeping during breaks in their underwear, so as not to crease their uniforms. The GOQ (to be a woman) defence succeeded here even though the "state of undress" was a matter merely incidental to the work. Under the new GOR regime, this requirement could fall within the "context" of the job, although it might be more difficult for the employer to show there were no other ways of accommodating men, such as providing a screen or dividing the room.[100]

(iii) Work in a private home

The third exception under the old regime arose where the job was   **8–024**
likely to involve the job holder working or living in a private home and "objection might reasonably be taken to allowing" a person of the opposite sex having the degree of physical or social contact with a person living in the home, or the knowledge of intimate details of such a person's life, which is likely because of the nature or the circumstances of the job.[101]

Under the new regime, this could cover, for instance, personal companions or nurses. It is not necessary that the employee works with the employer, so long as it is with a person in the home. The "intimate details" of that person surely must be confined to personal matters, and not those of a more general nature, such as financial or career matters.

(iv) Communal accommodation

The fourth exemption applied where it was impracticable for the job   **8–025**
holder to live elsewhere than in premises provided, which were

---

[97] SDA 1975 s.7(2)(b).
[98] See *Etam Plc v Rowan* [1989] I.R.L.R. 150, EAT. (Fitting room duties in women's fashion store could support a GOQ, but the defence failed because there were enough female staff to cover.)
[99] [1983] I.C.R. 628.
[100] The decision was criticised at the time for being incompatible with the Equal Treatment Directive: D. Pannick, *Sex Discrimination Law* (Oxford: OUP, 1985) p.250; *or* (1983) 4(2) Oxford J. Legal Stud. 198, p.218.
[101] SDA 1975 s.7(2)(ba).

normally occupied by persons of one sex and which did not have separate sleeping and sanitary facilities for the other sex.[102] It did not apply where workers might rest on the premises during a break in their duties.[103] This exception has been retained, in a different format, by the Equality Act 2010 Sch.23, para.3. It limits the coverage to communal accommodation, which is described as:

> "... residential accommodation which includes dormitories or other shared sleeping accommodation which for reasons of privacy should be used only by persons of the same sex."[104]

This includes:

> "(a) shared sleeping accommodation for men and for women;
> (b) ordinary sleeping accommodation;
> (c) residential accommodation all or part of which should be used only by persons of the same sex because of the nature of the sanitary facilities serving the accommodation."[105]

The exception relates to *admission to*, or a "benefit, facility or service" *linked to*, the accommodation, although for the purposes of "admission", it applies only if the accommodation is managed in a way that is "as fair as possible" to both men and women.[106]

Employers may restrict the accommodation to either men or women, but only if they make "arrangements as are reasonably practicable ... to compensate for" the refusal of admission or the linked benefit, facility or service.[107] Explanatory Note (1011) provides the following example:

> "At a worksite the only available sleeping accommodation is communal accommodation occupied by men. A woman employee who wishes to attend a training course at the worksite is refused permission because of the men-only accommodation. Her employer must make alternative arrangements to compensate her where reasonable, for example, by arranging alternative accommodation or an alternative course."

---

[102] SDA 1975 s.7(2)(c). In *Wallace v P and O Steam Navigation Co* (1979) (unreported, ET/31000/79) the claimant was refused a job as cinema projectionist on board a ship because the two cabins allocated to projectionists were in an all-male part of the ship. The tribunal found that although there was no suitable accommodation when she applied, it was reasonable to expect the respondents to adapt their premises to accommodate both sexes.

[103] In *Sisley* (above para.8–023), it was held that "live" meant to "dwell", rather than exist, and so the defence required actual residence rather than the use of rest facilities: [1983] I.C.R. 628 (EAT), p.635.

[104] EA 2010 Sch.23, para.3(5).

[105] ibid. para.3(6).

[106] ibid. para.3(2).

[107] ibid. para.3(8).

(v) Single-sex establishments

The next GOQ exemption applied where the job is in a single-sex **8–026** hospital or prison (or other establishment for persons requiring special supervision or attention) and it would not be reasonable having regard to the essential character of the establishment for a member of the opposite sex to do the job.[108] This applied equally to any part of a single-sex establishment. This GOQ exemption was criticised for being unnecessary, as the problems encountered in prisons and hospitals were catered for more specifically by other GOQ exemptions of either "privacy and decency", "single-sex accommodation" (both above), or "personal services" (below)). Under the new regime, these might be shown to be more a proportionate means to achieve a more precise aim.

The argument that inmates need to be dealt with by a person of their own sex (not for reasons of privacy, decency or personal services) "badly smells of the offensive sex stereotyping that the 1975 [Sex Discrimination] Act aims to eradicate".[109] In *Secretary of State for Scotland v Henley*[110] a woman's application to become the Assistant Prison Governor of an all-male prison was rejected on grounds that a woman could not cope with a riot and that the existing governor was a woman. The EAT rejected these arguments holding that the "riot" argument was purely hypothetical and based on a general assumption, and in any case, the employment of the female governor ruled out using the defence. By contrast, in the US case *Dothard v Rawlinson*,[111] the Supreme Court held that it was a BFOQ[112] to be a man to work as a guard "in contact positions" in an Alabama all-male prison which had no segregation and was characterised by "rampant violence" and "jungle atmosphere"; there was a likelihood of sexual assault upon women by sex offenders.

(vi) Personal services

The sixth GOQ exemption applied where the holder of the job pro- **8–027** vided individuals with personal services promoting their welfare or education, or similar personal services, and those services could most effectively be provided by a woman or a man.[113] Under the new regime, this might apply, for instance, to counsellor for rape victims.

---

[108] SDA 1975 s.7(2)(d).
[109] D. Pannick, *Sex Discrimination Law* (Oxford: OUP, 1985) p.256; *or* (1983) 4(2) Oxford J. Legal Stud. 198, p.223.
[110] Unreported, EAT/95/83 (1983).
[111] 433 US 321 (1977). The Court struck down the height and weight requirements for prison personnel. See further, Ch.6, para.6–047.
[112] The US Civil Rights Act 1964 equivalent of the GOR.
[113] SDA 1975 s.7(2)(e). For a discussion on the parallel GOQ in the RRA 1976, see below, para.8–045. For a transsexual person being excluded from providing personal services, see below, para.8–038.

(vii) Duties to be performed abroad by men or by women

8–028   The seventh GOQ exemption applied where a job involved the performance of some duties outside the UK[114] "in a country whose laws
or customs are such that the duties could not, or could not effectively,
be performed by a woman".[115] There were two criticisms of this
exemption.[116] First, in Parliament, the Government did not specify
which countries or which jobs were envisaged by this exception, and
so no one knew precisely what was being validated.[117] Second, it was
a concession to prejudice in other countries, which would not be
tolerated as an exemption to racial discrimination.[118] Such an
exemption under the new regime would have to argued as required by
the *context*, rather than the *nature*, of the job, and if courts were to
accept such a defence, it should only do so in deference to that
country's *laws*, and not its *customs*.

In the US case *Fernandez v Wynn Oil*,[119] the court rejected the
employer's defence that it was necessary to appoint a man to a post
that involved attracting business from Latin American clients who
"would react negatively to a woman vice-president of International
Operations". By contrast, in *Kern v Dynalectron*,[120] a Texan District
Court accepted a defence that only Muslims be hired to fly heli-
copters into Mecca. With notable understatement, the Court
observed:

> "This Court holds that Dynalectron has proven a factual basis
> for believing that *all* non-Moslems would be unable to perform
> this job safely. Specifically, non-Moslems flying into Mecca are,
> if caught, beheaded. ... Thus, the essence of Dynalectron's
> business would be undermined by the beheading of all the non-
> Moslem pilots based in Jeddah."

(viii) Married couples and civil partners

8–029   The SDA 1975 carried a GOQ exemption applying where the job was
one of two to be held by a married couple or by a couple who are civil

---

[114] The territorial application of the Equality Act 2010 has reverted to common law: see
Explanatory Note (15) and *Lawson v Serco* [2006] I.R.L.R 289 (HL).

[115] SDA 1975 s.7(2)(g).

[116] Discussed by D. Pannick, *Sex Discrimination Law*, (Oxford: OUP, 1985), pp 266–269; *or*
(1983) 4(2) Oxford J. Legal Stud. 198, p.231.

[117] The Government stated that this exception was "to deal with what one might call the Middle
East problem" (Standing Committee B, Fourth Sitting (1 May 1975) col.173) and gave Saudi
Arabia as an example (363 HL 984 (29 July 1975, Report Stage).

[118] See *Amnesty International v Ahmed* [2009] I.R.L.R. 884 (EAT), below, para.8–046.

[119] 653 F.2d 1273 (9th Cir 1981). See also, *Abrams v Baylor College of Medicine* 581 F Supp 570
(S.D. Tex 1984), affirmed in part 805 F.2d 528 (5th Cir. 1986); *American Jewish Congress v
Carter* 190 NYS 2d 218 (1959), affirmed on different grounds 199 NYS zd 157 (1960)
(Supreme Court of New York, Appellate Division) and 213 NYS 2d 60 (1961) (Court of
Appeals of New York); C. Sunstein "Three Civil Rights Fallacies", 79 Cal L. Rev 751, 760
(1991), observing that "economic" discrimination reinforces existing prejudice.

[120] 577 F.Supp 1196 (N.D. Tex), p.1200, affirmed F. 2d 810 (5th Cir 1984).

partners of each other. It was intended originally to cover jobs which require a husband and wife team, such as running a pub.[121]

Section 13(4) of the Equality Act 2010 (and its predecessor)[122] prohibits direct discrimination against those who *are* married or in a civil partnership, and not those who are single. This impliedly permits discrimination *in favour* of *individuals* who are married or in a civil partnership. And so, a sex-based GOR exemption would only be required where the requirement amounts to sex discrimination, where, say, a husband and wife team were required to carry out respective duties, such as caretaker and cleaner. Of course, discrimination law cannot facilitate such stereotyping. As such, the GOQ served no useful purpose,[123] and any arguments invoking it to justify such stereotyping under a sex-based GOR should be rejected.

(b) Gender, etc.—Organised Religions

The second exception (following on from the GOR) is the "religious **8–030** conscience" provision in Sch.9 para.2, which permits discrimination on the ground of sex, sexual orientation, gender reassignment, and of being married or in a civil partnership, by an employer[124] for the purposes of an organised religion. This exception applies to recruitment,[125] "opportunities and benefits" of employment, and dismissal.[126] In addition to imposing such requirements when recruiting, this means that an existing worker could be dismissed if, say, he undergoes gender reassignment, gets divorced, or "comes out" as gay. It applies also to qualifications bodies where the qualification is for the purpose of the exempted employment and the compliance or non-conflict principles are engaged.[127]

The discrimination must be for "requirements" applied "so as to comply with the doctrines of the religion" (the "compliance principle") or "because of the nature of the employment and the context in which it is carried out, so as to avoid conflicting with the strongly-held religious convictions of a significant number of the religion's followers" (the "non-conflict principle"). On the compliance principle, note the inconsistency. It does not apply to race, as racist (but not sexist or homophobic) religious doctrines are considered unacceptable.[128]

---

[121] The civil partnership exception was added in December 2005 (Civil Partnership Act 2004 s.251(4)).

[122] SDA 1975 s.3

[123] D. Pannick, *Sex Discrimination Law* 1985 (Oxford: OUP, 1985), p.270; *or* "When is Sex a Genuine Occupational Qualification?" (1983) 4(2) Oxford J. Legal Stud. 198, 233.

[124] This includes appointments to a personal or public office: Sch.9 para.2(7).

[125] EA 2010 s.39(1)(a) or (c), and for office holders: s.49(3)(a) or (c), s.50(3(a) or (c), s.51(1).

[126] EA 2010 s.39(2)(b) or (c), and for office holders: s.49(6)(b) or (c), 50 or (6)(b) or (c).

[127] See EA 2010 s.53.

[128] See e.g. *R. (E) v Governing Body of JFS* [2009] UKSC 15, [150]. See further, Ch.4, para.4–017.

Meanwhile, the non-conflict principle goes as far as permitting discrimination where the only objection comes from *some* of the congregation. So, for instance, even where a religion's doctrines and leaders have no objection to say—female, or homosexual, or divorced—clergy, discrimination may persist, or in some cases *commence,* lawfully, under this principle. When this exception was first introduced in relation to sexual orientation, the Government suggested that a legitimate aim here could be for a minister to have the confidence of the followers.[129] In most areas of discrimination law, as a matter of principle, "customer preference" is no defence.[130] It is hard to maintain in circumstances where the religion itself has no objection that the (contrary) view of the some of the congregation can amount to anything but prejudice. As such, this limb of the exception does not represent a legitimate aim. In *AMICUS v Secretary of State for Trade and Industry*[131] it was suggested that this limb would be "a far from easy test to satisfy in practice" and as such it was compatible with the equality Directive(s). But this misses the point. Once the test is satisfied, this limb legitimises prejudice unrelated to a religion's doctrines or leadership.

The phrase *organised religion* (as opposed to *religious organisation*) means this exemption is "intended to cover a very narrow range of employment", such as ministers of religion and a small number of lay posts, including those that exist to promote and represent religion.[132] It is not intended to be used by, say, a faith based-school when employing a teacher.[133] The exception only applies if *required* by the compliance or non-conflict principle. Accordingly, the Explanatory Notes (791) state a requirement must be *crucial* to the post. They suggest (793) that the exception would not apply to a church accountant, and it is unlikely to apply to a church youth worker who primarily organises sporting activities, but it may apply if the youth worker mainly teaches Bible classes.

(c) Gender, etc.—Armed Forces

8–031   By the Equality Act 2010 Sch.9, para.4, the armed forces may require that certain personnel are not female (or not transsexual), but only in arrangements for recruitment, refusals to appoint, and "opportunities and benefits".[134] This requirement applies only if employer shows that

---

[129] The *DTI* (not statutory) Explanatory notes to Employment Equality (Sexual Orientation) Regulations 2003 and the Employment Equality (Religion or Belief) Regulations 2003, para.96.

[130] See Ch.4, para.4–015.

[131] *AMICUS v Secretary of State for Trade and Industry* [2004] EWHC 860, [117] (on the previous version of this exemption).

[132] EA 2010, Explanatory Note 790.

[133] See *AMICUS v Secretary of State for Trade and Industry* [2004] EWHC 860, [116] (on the previous version of this exemption).

[134] See EA 2010, respectively, s.39(1)(a) or (c), or (2)(b).

the application is a proportionate means of "ensuring the combat effectiveness of the armed forces".

This exception reflects the ECJ case law on the matter. On the one hand, the ECJ has held that sex discrimination law does not apply to decisions of military organisation for internal and external security. On the other, in connection with employment, sex discrimination law cannot be "completely excluded". Hence, in *Dory v Germany*[135] it was held that the Equal Treatment Directive (now Recast Directive 2006/54/EC) had no application to a rule of voluntary military service for women and compulsory service for men. However, in *Kreil v Germany*[136] the ECJ held that a complete exclusion of women from military service breached the Directive.

Until *Johnston v Chief Constable of the Royal Ulster Constabulary*[137] was decided by the ECJ in 1986, the Sex Discrimination Act 1975 carried a blanket exemption for the armed forces. It was consequently modified with the "combat effectiveness" rubric (now Sch.9, para.4).[138] In *Sirdar v Secretary of State for Defence*[139] the Royal Marines did not permit women to serve in any capacity. Hence, Ms Sirdar was rejected when she applied to be a chef in the Marines. The ECJ found for the Ministry, accepting that the Marines were a small force, intended to be the first line of attack, and all members, including chefs, are required to serve as frontline commandos. The Court endorsed the "combat effectiveness" rubric, but only as far as it was necessary, with a margin of discretion, to guarantee public security.

(d) Non-Contractual Payments Related to Maternity Leave
The Equality Act 2010 Sch.9, para.17, replicates the relatively minor **8–032** exemption from equal pay liability to women on maternity leave, provided by ss.73 and 74 and the *Gillespie* ruling (discussed Chapter 4 para.4–053). This exemption is required in case any benefits were *non-contractual,* and so fell outside of the equal pay provisions.

(e) Gender, etc.—Insurance and Actuarial Calculations
The Equality Act 2010 Sch.9, para.20, permits "reasonable" reliance **8–033** on "actuarial or other data" suggesting different risks for men and women, and for maternity and pregnancy, in relation to "an annuity,

---

[135] Case C-186/02, [2003] 2 CMLR 26 (ECJ), [35].
[136] Case C-285/98 [2002] 1 CMLR 36, [25].
[137] Case 222/84 [1987] Q.B. 129, ECJ. See Ch.4, para.4–048, p.121.
[138] SI 1994/3276.
[139] Case C-273/97, [2000] I.C.R. 130, ECJ.

life insurance policy, accident insurance policy, or similar matter involving the assessment of risk".[140] Employers may also take advantage of this exception.

(f) Gender, etc.—Statutory Authority for the Protection of Women

8–034   The Equality Act 2010 Sch.22, para.2 permits different treatment based on sex, pregnancy or maternity, to comply with legislation for the protection of women in relation to pregnancy, maternity, or "any other circumstances giving rise to risks specifically affecting women." This exception is permitted by the Recast Directive 2006/54/EC, art.27(2). An Explanatory Note (990) gives two examples:

> "A care home cannot lawfully dismiss, but can lawfully suspend, a night-shift worker because she is pregnant and her GP has certified that she must not work nights."

> "It may be lawful for a road haulier to refuse to allow a woman lorry driver to transport chemicals that could harm women of child-bearing age."

(g) Gender, etc.—Educational Appointments

8–035   The Equality Act 2010 Sch.22, para.3 permits sex discrimination for certain posts in schools or institutions of further or higher education where a particular academic position must be held by a woman. This only applies where the governing instrument was made before January 16, 1990 (when the Employment Act 1989, s.5(3) came into force).

(h) National Security

8–036   The Equality Act 2010 s.192 provides a general defence for national security. See below, para.8–048.

(3) Gender Reassignment

8–037   An important preliminary point here is that once a person has obtained a Gender Recognition Certificate, that person's acquired sex is also their legal sex. Such persons should be able to participate in society without any discrimination related to their gender reassignment. The result is that a requirement *not* to be transsexual applied to

---

[140] See Case C-236/09 (2011) holding that this exception for services in Directive 2004/113/EC will expire on December 21, 2012.

a woman or man who in the past had gender reassignment would be extremely difficult to justify. Otherwise, requirements are likely to be temporary, existing whilst the person is, say, undergoing gender reassignment surgery.

(a) General Occupational Requirement
The general points relating to this exemption are discussed above, **8–038** para.8–019. The GOR applies to gender reassignment in the normal way, as well as permitting a job requirement *to be* transsexual, it includes a requirement *not* to be transsexual.[141]

One such instance arose in Canada, where the British Columbia Human Rights Code provides an exception for non-profit organisations with a primary purpose the promotion of the interests and welfare of an identifiable group. The exception allows them to operate "a preference to members of the identifiable group".[142] In *Vancouver Rape Relief Society v Nixon*,[143] the Society only engaged as counsellors women with a lifetime experience of "male oppression" and accordingly refused to appoint as a voluntary trainee a male-to-female transsexual person whose birth certificate had been amended to show that she was female. It was held that the refusal fell within the exception because there was "a rational connection between the preference and the [Society's] work".

(b) Organised Religions
The "religious conscience" provision in the Equality Act 2010 Sch.9, **8–039** para.2, permits discrimination on the ground of gender reassignment by an employer[144] for the purposes of an organised religion. This is not a "temporary" exemption, and so conceivably could be applied even to a person who has obtained a full gender recognition certificate under the Gender Recognition Act 2004. The general points relating to this exemption are discussed above, para.8–030.

---

[141] EA 2010 Sch.9, para.1(3).
[142] Human Rights Code (RSBC 1996, c 210) s 41: "If a charitable, philanthropic, educational, fraternal, religious or social organization or corporation that is not operated for profit has as a primary purpose the promotion of the interests and welfare of an identifiable group or class of persons characterized by a physical or mental disability or by a common race, religion, age, sex, marital status, political belief, colour, ancestry or place of origin, that organization or corporation must not be considered to be contravening this Code because it is granting a preference to members of the identifiable group or class of persons."
[143] [2006] BCD Civ J 8 (BC Court of Appeal), [58] and [77].
[144] This includes appointments to a personal or public office: Sch.9, para.2(7).

(c) Armed Forces

8–040 By the Equality Act 2010 Sch.9, para.4, the armed forces may require that certain personnel are not transsexual. The general points relating to the *armed forces* exemption are discussed above, para.8–031.

(d) Insurance and Actuarial Calculations

8–041 The Equality Act 2010 Sch.9, para.20, permits "reasonable" reliance on "actuarial or other data" suggesting different risks for transsexuals in relation to "an annuity, life insurance policy, accident insurance policy, or similar matter involving the assessment of risk".[145] Employers also are able to take advantage of this exception.

(e) Communal Accommodation

8–042 This exception, provided by the Equality Act 2010 Sch.23, para.3 permits discrimination on the ground of gender reassignment in the provision of communal accommodation, which is described above, para.8–025. Presumably, this exemption was intended to validate a refusal of accommodation to, say, a male-to-female transsexual who is planning to undergo, or is undergoing, reassignment, where the accommodation is occupied only by women. Employers may discriminate against transsexuals, but only if they make "arrangements as are reasonably practicable ... to compensate for" the refusal of admission or the linked benefit, facility or service.[146]

(f) National Security

8–043 The Equality Act 2010 s.192 provides a general defence for national security. See below, para.8–048.

(4) Race

(a) Genuine Occupational Requirement

8–044 The GOR defence provided by the Equality Act 2010 Sch.9, para.1, applies to racial discrimination in the normal way. The general points relating to this exemption are discussed above, para.8–019.

The old regime, under the Race Relations Act 1976, provided an exhaustive list of Genuine Occupational *Qualification* (GOQ) defences,[147] which could be invoked where only *some* of the job duties required a person with a particular racial characteristic.[148] However,

---

[145] For the EU aspect here, see n.140, above.
[146] EA 2010 Sch.23, para.3(8).
[147] RRA 1976 s.5(2)(a)–(d).
[148] RRA 1976 s.5(3). See *Tottenham Green Under Fives' Centre v Marshall* [1989] I.C.R. 214 (EAT) and *(No.2)* [1991] I.C.R. 320 (EAT).

the defence failed where other employees were capable of carrying out the duties and that it would be reasonable to employ them on such duties without undue inconvenience.[149] This coincides with the proportionality principle in Sch.9. The "other employees" must have existed at the time. Some of the cases under the old (GOQ) regime help to indicate how the GOR might operate, and so, what follows is a description of each GOQ exemption specified in the old regime.

(i) The race GOQ exemptions
The first three GOQ exemptions related to "authenticity" for (1) dramatic performances or entertainment, (2) modelling, and (3) catering in "a particular setting". This allowed the employment of a person of any race or nationality in all parts of the entertainment industry. Thus a theatre director may have decided that only a black person could convincingly play the part of Dr Martin Luther King, while a painter working on a scene from the Mahabharata may have asked an employment agency to send only Indian models.[150] The "catering" exception has been said to "have no contemporary relevance".[151] This defence is less likely to succeed under Sch.9.

8–045

The fourth GOQ exemption, provided, by RRA 1976 s.5(2)(d), applied where "the holder of the job provides persons of that racial group with personal services promoting their welfare, and those services can most effectively be provided by a person of that racial group."

A *personal services* defence is based essentially on "customer preference", a factor not normally permitted in discrimination law.[152] The service must be "personal". In *London Borough of Lambeth v Commission for Racial Equality*,[153] the council advertised two jobs in the housing benefit department, one for the assistant head and the other for group manager. The advertisement stated that candidates should be Afro-Caribbean or Asian. This was because more than half of the tenants dealt with by the department were of Afro-Caribbean or Asian origin. The Court of Appeal held that the *personal services* GOQ envisaged "direct contact between the giver and the recipient— mainly face-to-face or where there could be susceptibility in personal, physical contact."[154] Thus, it could not be used for management posts which had little contact with the public. The Court also noted that the

---

[149] RRA 1976 s.5(4). See *Etam Plc v Rowan* [1989] I.R.L.R. 150 (EAT), above, n.104.
[150] Examples from the CRE Code of Practice [London: CRE, 2005], ISBN 1 85442 570 6, Appendix 1, p.92, Example T.
[151] K. Monaghan, *Equality Law* (Oxford: OUP, 2007), p.472, para.8.38.
[152] See Ch.4, para.4–015. For a (US) case where nursing home acceded to patients' demands to be nursed by white staff see *Chaney v Plainfield Healthcare Center* 612 F.3d 908 (7th Cir 2010) (where a black nurse proved discrimination).
[153] [1990] I.C.R. 768.
[154] ibid. at 776.

provider of the service did not have to be from precisely the same ethnic or racial group as the recipient. What mattered was who could give the service "most effectively".[155] This suggests that in some cases where a particular skill is required (e.g. to speak Caribbean patois), the matter should be analysed as *indirect* discrimination, which the employer may be able justify.[156] The *Draft* Code of Practice suggests that for instance, where a local authority wishes to encourage Somalians to use health services (provided it has no existing suitable Somali workers) it may recruit a person of Somali origin to visit elderly people in their homes, as this worker requires a good knowledge of Somali culture.[157] This needs qualifying. The council would have show it was necessary that the worker was of Somali national origin, rather than merely having a good knowledge of Somali culture.

(ii) New scenarios under the GOR

8–046 As noted above, the GOR defence lends itself to new situations. One such scenario arose in *Amnesty International v Ahmed*,[158] a case decided under the old regime. Here, Amnesty, an international organisation that campaigns on behalf of "prisoners of conscience", advertised for a Researcher for Sudan. Ahmed, an existing worker of Sudanese origin, applied for the post, but her application failed in deference to Amnesty's conflict of interest policy, which generally barred Researchers from working in nations of their origin. Ahmed sued for direct racial discrimination. There were two reasons behind this policy. First, Amnesty feared for Ahmed's safety should she travel to Sudan or neighbouring Chad, because as a "northerner", she would be seen as hostile by rebels and the Government. Second, Amnesty's work is under close scrutiny and so its workers had to appear impartial. Of course, this defence did not coincide with any of the GOQs and was rejected.[159]

At first sight, it appears that the defence would (and should) succeed under the GOR. Under this defence, it would seem that if Amnesty could show is was necessary to exclude a candidate by her ethnic origins it would have a defence. The EAT observed, obiter, "... it is not difficult to conceive of cases where it would be indisputable that the national or ethnic origin of an employee would make it practically impossible for him or her to work effectively in a

---

[155] ibid. at 777.
[156] Although the requirement may be met by some white persons, it is likely to have an adverse impact on white persons. For justifying an adverse impact, see Ch.6, para.6–035.
[157] EHRC *Draft* Code of Practice on Employment, para.13.9.
[158] [2009] I.R.L.R. 884 (EAT).
[159] Although the GOR defence appeared in parallel in the RRA 1976 at the time, Amnesty did not plead it.

particular overseas country [leaving employers] ... in a highly invidious position."[160]

However, if the point *were* argued, it was noted that Amnesty would have faced two barriers. First, the domestic version of the GOR applies to "a requirement to have a particular protected characteristic".[161] It does not permit the inverse requirement, *not* to have a particular protected characteristic, which was Amnesty's requirement.[162] Curiously (and unusually) here, the domestic version was drafted in slightly narrower terms than the corresponding defence in its parent Race Directive 2000/43/EC, which permits "a difference of treatment *which is based on a characteristic related to racial or ethnic origin*".[163] The more general formula (italicised) in the Directive would permit an employer to state, for instance, "Candidates must not be of Sudanese origin". The problem for domestic tribunals could be overcome with a liberal reading of the domestic version, labelling the requirement positively: "to be any nationality except for Sudanese". The second barrier is the non-regression principle, discussed next.

(iii) The race GOR and the non-regression principle
The wording of the defence in both the Directive *and* the domestic version are wider than the pre-existing (GOQ) defences in the old regime, provided by the RRA 1976. The GOR is wider because (1) it applies to employment dismissals, (2) unlike the GOQs, it is non-exhaustive, and could allow a defence in a new factual situation (see *Amnesty v Ahmed*, above), (3) the occupational requirement can apply to a person whom the employer is "reasonably satisfied" does not meet it, and (iv) it applies to the *context* of the job, as well as the job itself. As such, the domestic GOR offends the non-regression principle expressed in art.6(2) of the Directive: "The implementation of this Directive shall under no circumstances constitute grounds for a reduction in the level of protection against discrimination already afforded by Member States in the fields covered by this Directive."[164]

8–047

---

[160] [2009] I.R.L.R. 884 (EAT), [58].
[161] The full GOR is set out above, para.8–019.
[162] Contrast Sch.9 para.1(3), extending the defence to cover requirements *not* to be a transsexual, or married, or a civil partner.
[163] art.4 (set out in full, above, para.8–019). (Emphasis supplied.)
[164] Noted, *Amnesty International v Ahmed* [2009] I.R.L.R. 884 (EAT), [59]. The non-regression principle in the Recast Directive 2006/54/EC is more generous, stating that it is: "without prejudice to the Member States' right to respond to changes in the situation by introducing laws, regulations and administrative provisions which differ from those in force on the notification of this Directive, provided that the provisions of this Directive are complied with".

(b) National Security

8–048 The Equality Act 2010 s.192 provides that:

> "A person does not contravene this Act only by doing, for the purpose of safeguarding national security, anything it is proportionate to do for that purpose."

At one time, RRA 1976 s.69(2)(b) provided that a certificate signed by a Government Minister was conclusive proof that an act was done for the purpose of national security. The Fair Employment (Northern Ireland) Act 1989 had a similar defence, which was condemned by European Court of Human Rights in *Tinnelly v UK*.[165] Here, at the time of the Northern Ireland "troubles", complaints by builders that they were refused public contracts because they were Roman Catholic were blocked by a ministerial certificate "on the ground of national security". No reasons were given. This was in breach of the Convention because it deprived the claimants of their right to "a fair and public hearing ... by an independent and impartial tribunal" under art.6 of the European Convention on Human Rights. As a result, the "ministerial certificate" can no longer be used. *Tinnelly* may now stand as a barrier to general statutory or Ministerial exclusions of certain nationalities and Muslims in deference to the contemporary "war of terror".

(c) Crown and Certain Public Bodies

8–049 The Equality Act 2010 Sch.22, para.5 provides that rules may be made in relation to employment in the service of the Crown, or certain prescribed public bodies,[166] or holding public office. The rules may restrict employment "to persons of a particular birth, nationality, descent or residence."

The Explanatory Notes (986–987) state that this allows restrictions on the employment of "foreign nationals in the civil, diplomatic, armed or security and intelligence services and by certain public bodies", and observes "People who are neither British, Commonwealth or Irish citizens nor British protected persons are generally prohibited from serving in the armed forces, with the notable exception of Ghurkhas."

---

[165] *Tinnelly & Sons Ltd & McElduff v UK* Cases 20390/92; 21322/93, (1998) 27 E.H.R.R. 249.
[166] See SI 1994/1986. Schedule 1 lists: Bank of England, Board of Trustees of the Armouries, British Council, House of Commons, House of Lords, Metropolitan Police Office, National Army Museum, National Audit Office, Natural Environment Research Council, United Kingdom Atomic Energy Authority. See (1994) 54 EOR 7.

(d) Nationality and Residence—Acts Authorised by Statute or the Executive

This exception, provided by Equality Act 2010 Sch.23, para.1, per-   **8–050**
mits Parliament or the Government to discriminate directly on the
ground of nationality and indirectly on the ground of race by
applying to a person a provision, criterion or practice which relates to
that person's place of ordinary residence; or "the length of time that
person has been present or resident in or outside the United Kingdom
or an area within it."

The Explanatory Notes (981) suggest three examples:

> "The points-based system which replaced the former work per-
> mit arrangements can discriminate on the basis of nationality in
> determining whether migrants from outside the European Eco-
> nomic Area and Switzerland should be given permission to work
> in the United Kingdom.
>
> The NHS can charge some people who are not ordinarily
> resident in the United Kingdom for hospital treatment they
> receive here.
>
> Overseas students at universities in England and Wales can be
> required to pay higher tuition fees than local students (there are
> no tuition fees in Scotland)."

(e) Training for Non-EEA Residents—Nationality Only

The Equality Act 2010 Sch.23 para.4 permits employers to provide   **8–051**
training for persons not ordinarily resident in the European Economic Area, if the employer "thinks" that the person does not intend
to exercise those skills in Great Britain as a result. The Explanatory
Notes (1003) suggest that the main purpose of this exemption "is to
enable people from developing countries to acquire vital skills which
may not be available in their country of residence". Thus:

> "It is not unlawful for a company specialising in sustainable
> irrigation that offers a training scheme in Great Britain for
> people who live in Mozambique, who then return home to put
> the skills learned into practice, to refuse to offer the same
> training to someone who lives in Great Britain."

(5) Sexual Orientation

(a) Genuine Occupational Requirement

8–052   The GOR defence provided by the Equality Act 2010 Sch.9 para.1 applies to sexual orientation in the normal way.[167] The general points relating to this exemption are discussed above, para.8–019.

An example offered for the preceding Sexual Orientation Regulations 2003[168] is the job of leadership of an organisation concerned with advising gay men and lesbians about their rights, or promoting those rights. Here, the job's credibility may require a gay or lesbian person. However, the post of *advising* people of these rights is unlikely to warrant a GOR.[169]

(b) Organised Religions

8–053   The "religious conscience" provision in the Equality Act 2010 Sch.9 para.2 permits discrimination on the ground of sexual orientation by an employer[170] for the purposes of an organised religion. The general points relating to this exemption are discussed above, para.8–030.

The requirement may be *related to* sexual orientation. This allows the employer to specify *behaviour*, related to sexual orientation. So, for instance, a church may employ a homosexual priest, but require that he must be celibate.[171]

(c) Benefits Dependent on Marital or Civil Partnership Status

8–054   The Equality Act 2010 Sch.9 para.18 is aimed at a "benefit, facility or service" provided by an employer which is dependant on married or civil partnership status. Before December 5, 2005 (the day that civil partnerships were established),[172] a benefit, such as a pension, could be payable to the spouse of worker after the worker's death. This would, of course, discriminate against gay or lesbian couples. The exception is preserved for benefits accruing before December 5, 2005.

Since that date, a benefit dependant on married or civil partnership status "to the exclusion of all other persons", could discriminate on the ground of sexual orientation. For example, a pension payable to surviving spouses or civil partners could indirectly discriminate on the ground of sexual orientation, depending on the respective

---

[167] See H. Oliver, "Sexual Orientation Discrimination: Perceptions, Definitions and Genuine Occupational Requirements" (2004) 33 ILJ 1.

[168] Employment Equality (Sexual Orientation) Regulations 2003, SI 2003/1661, reg.7.

[169] The *DTI* (not statutory) Explanatory notes to Employment Equality (Sexual Orientation) Regulations 2003 and the Employment Equality (Religion or Belief) Regulations 2003, para.75.

[170] This includes appointments to a personal or public office: Sch.9 para.2(7).

[171] Explanatory Note (739).

[172] Civil Partnership Act 2004 s.1.

proportions of gay and heterosexual couples who are not married or in a civil partnership. Schedule 9 para.18 permits this discrimination.

(d) National Security

The Equality Act 2010 s.192 provides a general defence for national security. See above, para.8–048.

8–055

(6) Religion or Belief

The Framework Directive 2000/78/EC provides two GORs for Religion or Belief. The first is for any employer and the second, provided by art.4(2), is only for employers with an ethos based on religion or belief. For this second GOR, the characteristic must be a requirement for the job, but not a *determining* (i.e. decisive) one, having regard to the organisation's ethos. This exception cannot be used to justify discrimination on any other ground save religion or belief. These two GORs are reproduced in the Equality Act 2010.

8–056

(a) Genuine Occupational Requirement[173]

The GOR defence provided by the Equality Act 2010 Sch.9 para.1, applies to religion or belief in the normal way. The general points relating to this exemption are discussed above, para.8–019.

8–057

(b) Employers with an Ethos Based on Religion or Belief

The Equality Act 2010 Sch.9 para.3 effectively replicates the standard GOR formula, this time for employers with "an ethos based on religion or belief" which requires a worker to be of a particular religion or belief. As with the standard GOR, it applies to direct discrimination in recruitment, access to promotion, transfer or training, and dismissal; it can be applied to a person who does not meet the requirement, *or* where the employer is "reasonably satisfied" the person does meet it. The general points (including these elements) relating to the GOR exemption are discussed above, para.8–019.

8–058

Note here the wide range of employers covered by this exception. It is not restricted to "religious organisations". An example of this exception could be a Christian hospice requiring its chief executive to be Christian, because of the role of leadership in relation to maintaining and developing the religious ethos. It is unlikely that the defence could be applied to a nurse in the hospice if the job did not go beyond the medical care of patients. Similarly, it could not be applied

---

[173] See generally, B. Hepple and T. Choudhury, "Tackling Religious Discrimination: Practical Implications for Policy-makers and Legislators" 2001, Home Office Series 221. London: Home Office; L. Vickers, "The *Draft* Employment Equality (Religion or Belief) Regulations" (2003) 32 ILJ 23.

to the job of a shop assistant in a bookshop with a religious ethos, merely on the preference of the employer or customers, if the job does not go beyond the normal duties for any bookshop assistant.[174]

Regard should be had to the employer's ethos, *and* the nature or context of the job. In *Jivraj v Hashwani*,[175] an arbitration clause in a commercial contract stipulated that: "All arbitrators shall be respected members of the Ismaili community [a Shiah sect] and holders of high office within the community". At first instance, the judge found that as one of the "more significant" Ismaili character-istics was an enthusiasm for dispute resolution, the clause fell within the exception[176] (para.3's predecessor under the Religion or Belief Regulations 2003).[177] The Court of appeal reversed, observing that the clause required disputes to be resolved according to English law and rules of natural justice. Thus, the Ismaili ethos, and nature of the arbitration, did not *require* an Ismailian. The Court added, obiter, had the clause required arbitration according to the principles of morality, justice and fairness of the Ismaili community (ex aequo et bono), the exception might have applied.[178]

(c) Educational Appointments

8–059 The Equality Act 2010 Sch.22 para.3 provides an exception from religious discrimination for certain posts in schools or further and higher education where the governing instrument (effective before January 16, 1990) requires the head teacher or principal to be of a particular religious order, or where the legislation or instrument which establishes a professorship requires the holder to be an ordained priest.

Paragraph 4 permits schools with a religious character or ethos ("faith schools") to discriminate for certain purposes within the School Standards and Framework Act 1998:

    (a) the dismissal of teachers because of failure to give religious education efficiently;[179]

    (b) applying religious considerations relating to the appointment of a head teacher, and the appointment, pay, or promotion of teachers;[180]

---

[174] DTI Explanatory Notes, above, n.169, at para.87. A requirement to have knowledge of say, Christian or Moslem literature, may have to be justified where it indirectly discriminates. For justification of indirect discrimination, see Ch.6, para.6–035.

[175] [2010] I.R.L.R. 797 (CA).

[176] [2009] EWHC 1364 (Comm), [45].

[177] SI 2003/1660, reg.7(3).

[178] [2010] I.R.L.R. 797, [29].

[179] School Standards and Framework Act 1998 s.58(6) or (7).

[180] ibid. s.60(4) and (5).

(c) applying preferences for certain teachers at independent schools of a religious character.[181]

(d) National Security
The Equality Act 2010 s.192 provides a general defence for national security. See above, para.8–048.

8–060

(e) Sikhs Wearing Turbans
A requirement to wear a safety helmet on a construction site is likely to adversely affect Sikhs, as many Sikh men wear turbans. The Employment Act 1989 s.11 permits Sikhs wearing turbans to work on construction sites without safety helmets. Others compelled to wear a safety helmet may allege that they were being treated less favourably because of religion. Section 12 of the 1989 Act provides that employers in this situation cannot be liable for direct discrimination.

8–061

(7) Age Defences
At EU level, the Framework Directive 2000/78/EC provides two defences for direct age discrimination. The first defence, provided by art.4(1), is the standard formula for a Genuine Occupational Requirement. Second, art.6(1) provides an extra defence allowing Member States to legislate for exceptions specific to age, providing that they are objectively and reasonably justified by a legitimate aim, and if the means of achieving that aim are appropriate and necessary. "Legitimate aims" may include employment policy, labour market and vocational training objectives. Article 6(1) provides a non-exhaustive list of three examples. The first allows the setting of special conditions for young people, older workers and persons with caring responsibilities in order to promote their vocational integration or ensure their protection. The second allows the fixing of minimum conditions of age, professional experience or seniority in service. The third allows the fixing of a maximum age for recruitment which is based on the training requirements of the post in question or the need for a reasonable period of employment before retirement.

The Equality Act 2010 applies the standard GOR in the normal way, but adds an objective justification defence to *direct* age discrimination, under the authority of art.6. In addition, there is a long list of specific exceptions.

8–062

---

[181] ibid. s.124A.

(a) Age—General Occupational Requirement

8–063   The GOR defence provided by the Equality Act 2010 Sch.9 para.1
applies to age in the normal way. The general points relating to this
exemption are discussed above, para.8–019. When introducing the
original Age Regulations in 2006, the Government suggested that
GOR exemptions would arise in "very few cases". One example given
was for acting jobs.[182]

(b) Age—Objective Justification

8–064   When the Age Regulations were introduced in 2006, the Government
opted to provide a standard objective justification defence (usually
reserved for indirect discrimination), for *direct* discrimination. Thus,
an employer may avoid liability by showing the treatment was "a
proportionate means of achieving a legitimate aim". This is reproduced in the Equality Act 2010 s.13(2).

This defence was challenged for going beyond the Framework
Directive 2000/78/EC, art.6(1), which appeared to permit only *specific* defences to direct discrimination (above, para.8–062). The ECJ
rejected the challenge and ruled that the defence was compatible, but
only as far as it fulfilled social policy aims, which were "distinguishable from purely individual reasons particular to the employer's
situation, such as cost reduction or improving competitiveness",
adding that such aims may be identified from the "general context" of
the specific section.[183] Back in the UK, the High Court confirmed that
the defence was compatible with the Directive, holding that the social
policy could be identified from the "context" of the explanatory notes
(to the Age Regulations 2006) and Government's "elaborate" and
publically available consultation process.[184] Further, any defect in the
defence as originally drafted could be cured by reading it down and in
light of the emerging ECJ case law.[185] The only caution (echoing the
ECJ's observation), was that there was a "clear distinction" between
a government's social policy and "individual business saying it is
cheaper to discriminate than to address the issues that the Directive
requires to be addressed".[186]

---

[182] "Equality and Diversity: Coming of Age" (July 2005), at para.4.2.8. DTI/Pub 7851/3k/07/
05/NP. URN 05/1171.
[183] Case C388/07 *R. (The Incorporated Trustees of the National Council on Ageing (Age Concern
England)) v Secretary of State for Business, Enterprise and Regulatory Reform* [2009] E.C.R.
I-1569 [45]–[46].
[184] [2009] I.C.R. 260 (HC Admin), [91]–[97].
[185] ibid. [96].
[186] ibid. [93].

(i) Age—objective justification and legitimate aims

The relevance of a social policy to a private employer's defence arose **8–065** in *Seldon v Clarkson, Wright & Jakes*.[187] Here, a partner in a firm of solicitors challenged the firm's compulsory retirement of partners aged 65. The firm's reasons were:[188]

(1) ensuring associates were given the opportunity of partnership after a reasonable period;

(2) facilitating the planning of the partnership and workforce across individual departments by having a realistic long-term expectation as to when vacancies will arise;

(3) limiting the need to expel partners by way of performance management, thus contributing to the congenial and supportive culture in the firm.

These reasons were challenged as fulfilling the firm's individual interests, rather than pursuing a social policy aim. The Court of Appeal held that the employer's aim did not have to be "limited strictly" to pursuit of the Government's social policy.[189] It was enough if they were "consistent" with it, which these were. In particular, reasons (1) and (2) ("dead men's shoes") coincided with the social policy of improving employment and promotion prospects of young people. Of the third "collegiality" reason, an aim "intended to produce a happy work place has to be within or consistent with the government's social policy justification ... my experience would tell me that it is a justification for having a cut-off age that people will be allowed to retire with dignity."[190] The Court went to hold that the retirement age was an appropriate and necessary way to achieve the aims.

Note that in *Woodcock v Cumbria Primary Care Trust*,[191] a case of direct age discrimination, the EAT suggested that costs alone could be a legitimate aim. In that case, a chief executive was made redundant for two reasons. First, to get him off the payroll before he reached 50, when he would have been entitled to early retirement, costing at least £500,000. The second reason was that his post had disappeared in a reorganisation some time previously, and he had been kept on for 12 months doing various temporary jobs. This second reason means the suggestion was obiter only.

---

[187] [2010] EWCA Civ 899.
[188] The specific "retirement" exemption (Sch.9 para.8) does not apply to partners, and so compulsory retirement must be objectively justified by the partnership.
[189] [2010] EWCA Civ 899, [14], [17].
[190] ibid. [20]–[23] (Waller L.J., giving judgment for the Court).
[191] (2010) UKEAT/0489/09/RN, [32].

(ii) Age—objective justification and proportionality

8-066 The EAT has held that an age-discriminatory policy (such as a retention and freezing of an age-dependant pay benefit for those receiving it before the benefit was abolished) cannot be automatically justified by the fact the policy was part of a collective agreement, nor that the employer's budget was "exhausted".[192] On the other hand, an employer wishing to cushion the impact of abolishing the benefit, was not "absolutely disentitled" to justify the policy even if it meant some continuing discrimination (against those who were not entitled because of their age).[193] This is in stark contrast to the unforgiving attitude towards such "cushioning" arrangements used where sex-discriminatory pay benefits are retained and frozen.[194]

This shows a marked lightness of touch towards age discrimination, in contrast to other protected characteristics,[195] and reflects the approach taken in other jurisdictions and (with some notable exceptions) the ECJ.[196]

The first age discrimination case to reach the ECJ was *Mangold v Helm*.[197] Here, German law exempted from regulation fixed-term employment contracts for any worker over 52. This relaxation of protective legislation was designed to encourage employers to recruit older workers. Its aim was to help older persons find jobs more easily. Of course, the more direct result of this measure was to remove safeguards for older workers, who could now be employed on temporary contracts for the rest of their working lives. The ECJ observed:

> "This significant body of workers, determined solely on the basis of age, is thus in danger, during a substantial part of its members' working life, of being excluded from the benefit of stable employment".[198]

The Court held that the policy could not be objectively justified because it went beyond what was appropriate and necessary to help *unemployed* older workers.

8-067 More recently, in *Swedex*,[199] the challenge was to a German rule that provided that periods of employment completed before the age of 25 were not to be taken into account in calculating a notice period.

---

[192] *Pulham v London Borough of Barking & Dagenham* [2010] I.R.L.R. 184 (EAT), [39]–[44].
[193] ibid. [27].
[194] *Redcar and Cleveland Borough Council v Bainbridge* [2008] I.R.L.R. 776 (CA). See further, Ch.9, para.9–040.
[195] See Ch.2, para.2–021.
[196] See, in Canada, for instance, *Gosselin v Quebec (Attorney General)* [2002] 4 SCR 429, [68]. See also *Large v Stratford* [1995] 3 SCR 733; *McKinney v University of Guelph* [1990] 3 SCR 229. In the US, *Massachusetts Board of Retirement v Murgia*, 427 US 307, 313 (Sup Ct 1976).
[197] Case C-144/04, [2006] 1 CMLR 43.
[198] ibid. [64].
[199] Case C-555/07 *Kucukdeveci v Swedex Gmbh* [2010] 2 C.M.L.R. 33.

The claimant, aged 28, was dismissed, with a notice period based on only three years' service. This was direct age discrimination. The ECJ held that the aim, of facilitating younger persons' recruitment by "increasing the flexibility of personnel management", tempered by the assessment that young workers generally reacted more easily and more rapidly to the loss of their jobs, was legitimate under art.6 as a labour market policy.[200] However, as the rule affected all workers who joined the undertaking before the age of 25, and as it affected young workers unequally (many, after extensive education and/or training, would not begin work until aged 25), it was not an appropriate means to achieve the aim.[201]

In *Wolf*,[202] the claimant, aged 31, was rejected as a firefighter, on the basis that "very few officials over 45 years of age have sufficient physical capacity to perform the fire-fighting part of their activities."[203] Hence, the maximum recruitment age of 30 was proportionate because, "the age at which an official is recruited determines the time during which he will be able to perform physically demanding tasks".[204] This approach, based on generalisations (if not stereotypes) instead of individual assessment is counter-intuitive to discrimination practitioners.[205] It shows a marked contrast to the orthodox strict approach of *Mangold* and *Swedex*. *Wolf* represents a lightness of touch taken by the ECJ in compulsory retirement cases (discussed below, para.8–071), and if a pattern could be discerned, it seems that the ECJ is willing to accept generalisations about older workers' abilities to perform at work, but otherwise it will apply the orthodox strict justification test.

(c) Age—Specific Exemptions

The employment-related specific exemptions are provided by Equality Act 2010 Sch.9 Pt 2, paras 7–16. Three further defences, related to the armed forces, statutory authority, and national security, follow.

8–068

(i) Default retirement age

It should be noted that the Coalition Government announced the phasing out this exception, beginning on April 6, 2011.[206] So the next

8–069

---

[200] ibid. [35]–[36].
[201] ibid. [38]–[42].
[202] Case C-229/08, [2010] I.R.L.R. 244 (ECJ).
[203] ibid. [41].
[204] ibid. [43].
[205] cf. *Commonwealth v Human Rights & Equal Opportunity Commission (Bradley)* (1999) 95 FCR 218 (Federal Court of Australia), [41]. In particular, the physical fitness requirement could not be allowed to "have the effect of damning individuals over 28 years by reference to a stereotypical characteristic (less physical fitness) of their age group" and their "ability to fit in" to military life. See further, below, para.8–082.
[206] Where the employer has notified the employee of retirement before April 6, the exception applies, but no compulsory retirements can take place after October 1, 2011.

two sections should be read with reference to the progress of that proposal.[207] The abolition of the exception means that employers will have to objectively justify a compulsory retirement (see para.8–065, above).

Schedule 9 para.8 provided a default retirement age for those aged 65[208] or over. This was an exemption for discrimination against those most vulnerable to it, and probably those who had had the highest expectation from age discrimination law. It permitted employers to dismiss workers who had reached 65, so long as they followed a complex procedure. Should employers agree to keep on a worker beyond 65, save for retirement, the general principle against age discrimination applied. So, for instance, discriminatory discipline, pay, harassment, and job classification would remain unlawful.

The exemption applied to a narrower class of workers than those normally covered by discrimination legislation, applying only to "employees" within the meaning of the Employment Rights Act 1996,[209] those in Crown employment, and House of Lords and House of Commons staff. To obtain exemption, the employer had to comply potentially with two procedures.[210] The first was compulsory. The employer had to give the worker at least six months notice of the retirement. However, the notice must be within one year of the retirement. The second procedure may have arisen because workers had a "right to request" not to be retired. If this right were exercised, the employer has a corresponding "duty to consider" the request. The employer must inform the worker of its decision, but there were no more demands than that: the employer need not give reasons for its decision. Hence, an employer could sit through a meeting to discuss the retirement with a closed mind and simply confirm his decision at the end.

(a) Compatibility

8–070 Upon its introduction, this sweeping exception to the general anti-discrimination principle was challenged for compatibility with the Framework Directive 2000/78/EC. The ECJ held merely that the default retirement age fell within the scope of the Directive and as it amounted to direct discrimination, it would have to be justified under

---

[207] *Phasing Out the Default Retirement Age: Government Response to Consultation* URN 11/536. This and related documents are at *http://www.bis.gov.uk/Consultations/retirement-age?cat = closedwithresponse* (accessed January 14 2011).
    Two government departments are dealing with this: *bis.gov.uk*; *dwp.gov.uk*.
[208] Or the employee's "normal retirement age" if higher: ERA 1996 s.98ZC.
[209] An individual who "works under . . . a contract of employment", ERA 1996 s.230(1).
[210] Employment Equality (Age) Regulations 2006 (SI 2006/1031), Sch.6 (this part of the regulations remained in force after the Equality Act 2010).

art.6(1) (set out above).[211] Upon return to the UK, the High Court held that is was justified, *but* had it been adopted in 2009 (it was introduced in 2006) and had the Government not brought forward a review of it to 2010,[212] it would have found the selection of age 65 would not have been proportionate.[213] This no doubt influenced the Coalition Government's decision to abolish the exception.

(b) Compulsory retirement in the ECJ and other jurisdictions[214]
Although the High Court decision was marginal, it echoes a similar   **8–071**
lax attitude to compulsory retirement elsewhere. In *Palacios de la Villa*,[215] a worker challenged a Spanish measure permitting compulsory retirement ages to be negotiated in collective agreements. The ECJ found that the aim of "checking unemployment" was a legitimate one.[216] This was generous because this measure could only *redistribute* unemployment from the young to the old. On proportionality, the Court stated:

> "It does not appear unreasonable for ... a Member State to take the view that a measure ... may be appropriate and necessary in order to achieve ... the promotion of full employment by facilitating access to the labour market."[217]

Further, the measure did not "unduly prejudice" workers of retirement age because compulsory retirement was subject to a worker being entitled to a "not unreasonable" retirement pension. "Moreover", it enabled trade unions and employers' organisations to agree "with considerable flexibility" a compulsory retirement mechanism that took account of the labour market concerned, and the specific features of the jobs in question.[218] Thus, the measure was justified, with a generous view of the social aim, and the deferral to what the *Member State* considered reasonable.

In *Petersen*,[219] German public sector dentists were forced to retire   **8–072**
at 68. The Government provided three reasons for justification:

---

[211] Case C388/07 R. (*The Incorporated Trustees of the National Council on Ageing (Age Concern England)*) v *Secretary of State for Business, Enterprise and Regulatory Reform* [2009] E.C.R. I-1569 [21]–[30], [63].

[212] The consultation for this was launched July 29, 2010, with a view of phasing it out from April 2011: *Phasing Out the Default Retirement Age* URN 10/1047.

[213] [2009] I.C.R. 260 (HC Admin), [128].

[214] See M. Sargeant, "The Default Retirement Age: Legitimate Aims and Disproportionate Means" (2010) 39 ILJ 244; M. Connolly, "Compulsory Retirement and Age Discrimination: a new deference to derogation?" (2008) 9 (3) I.J.D.L. 181.

[215] Case C-411/05, [2007] E.C.R. I8531 (ECJ).

[216] ibid. [52].

[217] ibid. [72].

[218] ibid. [73]–[74].

[219] Case C-341/08 *Petersen v Berufungsausschuss fur Zahnarzte fur den Bezirk Westfalen-Lippe* [2010] 2 C.M.L.R. 31 (ECJ).

(1) the protection of the health of patients as performance of dentists declines after a certain age;

(2) the distribution of employment opportunities among the generations;

(3) the maintenance of the financial balance of the German healthcare system.

The ECJ rejected the first reason, but *not* because of the generalising of the abilities of older practitioners. The reason failed to convince the Court solely because it did not apply to the private sector, and so lacked credibility. The other two reasons were accepted. The acceptance of the first reason per se fits a pattern of the ECJ being content with the use of generalisations to justify patent age discriminatory measures.

Further afield in Canada, the Supreme Court has taken an equally relaxed approach to forced retirement. In *McKinney v University of Guelph*[220] s.9(a) of the Ontario Human Rights Code 1981 went further than the British exemption by excluding those aged over 65 from *all* protection under the Code's age discrimination law. By a majority of five to two, the Canadian Supreme Court held that s.9 did not violate the non-discrimination tenet in s.15(1) of the Charter of Rights and Freedoms, principally on the basis that a general retirement age of 65 was necessary to preserve the stability and integrity of pension schemes.

It was noted in the dissent that compulsory retirement disproportionately hits the low paid (predominantly women in segregated occupations and ethnic minorities), who may be in greater need of continuing working beyond the age 65.[221]

A stricter approach is taken in the USA, by both the legislation and the courts. The Age Discrimination in Employment Act (ADEA) permits individual workers to waive their ADEA rights, although strict rules apply. This allows a worker to agree to retirement. A valid ADEA waiver must:

1. be in writing and be understandable;

2. specifically refer to ADEA rights or claims;

3. not waive rights or claims that may arise in the future;

4. be in exchange for valuable consideration;

5. advise the individual in writing to consult an attorney before signing the waiver; and

---

[220] [1990] 3 SCR 229 (Sup Ct of Canada).
[221] ibid. at 415–416. (Wilson J.).

6. provide the individual at least 21 days to consider the agreement and at least seven days to revoke the agreement after signing it.[222]

If an employer requests an ADEA waiver in connection with an "exit incentive programme or other employment termination program offered to a group or class of employees", more stringent rules apply. The time limit for consideration is extended to 45 days, while notice must be given of the "job titles and ages of all individuals eligible or selected for the program, and the ages of all individuals in the same job classification or organizational unit who are not eligible or selected for the program".[223] This transparency is designed to prevent an employer obtaining unconscionable waivers during a large scale lay-off, where workers would otherwise have no reason to suspect that age was a factor.[224] The US Supreme Court held in *Oubre v Entergy Operations*[225] that doctrines of equitable estoppel or affirmation of a voidable agreement cannot undermine these waiver conditions. If the agreement is defective, the worker may bring an ADEA claim, even where he does not return the consideration, such as a severance payment.

8–073

The ADEA provides much less scope for derogation from age discrimination than the Framework Directive. It does not permit direct discrimination to be objectively justified. Compulsory retirement is unlawful. And although *individuals* may agree to waive their age discrimination rights, by contrast to *Palacios de la Villa* it is not possible for these rights to be bargained away in a collective agreement.

(ii) Applicants at or approaching retirement age
A logical consequence of the default retirement age was that it should not be unlawful to refuse to hire a person who has reached 65 (or the employer's normal retirement age,[226] if higher), or who will reach it within six months. These exemptions were provided by Sch.9 para. 9, and applied only to the same classes of workers as para.8–069 (above), that is "employees" within the meaning of the Employment Rights Act 1996, those in Crown employment, and House of Lords and House of Commons staff. Of course, this exception should be abolished along with the default retirement age.

8–074

---

[222] 29 USC s.626(f)(1). The waiver provisions were added by the Older Workers Benefit Protection Act 1990. Extensive details and examples are provided by EEOC 29 CFR s.1625.22 (see *www.eeoc.gov*, click "Laws, Regulations", click "Regulations", scroll down to 1625).
[223] 29 USC s.626(f)(1).
[224] See the legislative history: S Rep No 101–263, 101st Cong 2d Sess 32 (1990) reprinted in 1990 USCCAN 1509, 1537-38.
[225] 522 US 422 (1998).
[226] According to ERA 1996 s.98ZH.

(iii) Benefits related to length of service

8–075		As noted above, art.6 of the Framework Directive (above, para.8–062) suggests an exemption allowing for the fixing of minimum conditions of age, professional experience or seniority in service. This covers pay and other benefits, such as a company car.

Schedule 9 para.10 EA 2010, provides a blanket exemption for length-of-service benefits relating to the first five years of service. Gaps in service are not counted for this purpose. So, for instance, a woman who after three years' service takes a year off, will return and begin her fourth year of service for the purpose of this exemption. After five years' service, a length-of-service benefit is exempted only if "it reasonably appears" to the employer that it "fulfils a business need" of the undertaking, (for example, by encouraging the loyalty or motivation, or rewarding the experience, of some or all of his workers).[227]

This exception does not apply to a "benefit, facility or service which may be provided only by virtue of a person's ceasing to work". Severance or redundancy payments linked to length of service are dealt with elsewhere, under para.13 (below). However, credit for long service in a redundancy selection procedure can amount to a "benefit" for this exception.[228]

At first sight, the five-year blanket exemption goes beyond anything contemplated by art.6. It allows most obviously, direct and indirect age discrimination, as well as indirect sex discrimination. However, in a sex discrimination challenge, the ECJ held that "rewarding experience ... which enables the worker to perform his duties better" is a legitimate objective, and that the "employer does not have to establish specifically that [a length of service criterion] ... is appropriate to attain that objective as regards a particular job", unless the worker proves the scheme is not an appropriate scheme to achieve the aim.[229] With this relaxed view in the field of sex discrimination, combined with the scope provided by art.6, it is most unlikely that the exemption in the field of age discrimination could be challenged for incompatibility.

(iv) Redundancy payments

8–076		There is a statutory scheme of minimum redundancy payments which is based on age and length of service.[230] The Government considers this to be compatible with art.6 of the Framework Directive.[231] The

---

[227] Explanatory Note (820).
[228] *Rolls Royce v Unite* [2010] I.C.R. 1 (CA) [103], [135], [140], [165].
[229] Case C-17/05 *Cadman v Health and Safety Executive*, [2006] I.C.R. 1623, [38]. A stricter line was taken by the Court of Appeal in *Wilson v Health and Safety Executive* [2010] I.C.R. 302. See further, Ch.9, para.9–039.
[230] ERA 1996 Pt IX.
[231] Explanatory Note (831).

exemption in Sch.9 para.13 EA 2010 applies to employers who make redundancy payments based on the statutory scheme but which are more generous than the statutory scheme requires.

Where a (discriminatory) contractual scheme is not based on the statutory one, it will have to be objectively justified under s.13(2) (see above, para.8–064). In *MacCulloch v Imperial Chemical Industries*,[232] the claimant was made redundant, aged 36, after eight years' service. She was paid 55 per cent of her gross annual salary, whereas an employee aged between 50 and 57 with 10 years' service would have received 175 per cent. The employment tribunal found this directly discriminated, but was justified. The EAT allowed the claimant's appeal as the employment tribunal focused on the broad aim of the scheme, overlooking the "very significant"[233] discriminatory effect on the claimant in comparison to her comparator.

An employer's redundancy payments scheme that limits payments as the worker approaches retirement age may have a legitimate aim, such as preventing the redundant person receiving a windfall (of a redundancy payment and a pension). Proportionality would depend on the circumstances, such as the nature of the respective redundancy and pension schemes.[234]

(v) National minimum wage

The National Minimum Wage Act provides two bands for younger workers (16–17 and 18–21). Accordingly, employers who base their pay structure on the national minimum wage are exempted by The Equality Act 2010 Sch.9 para.11 when paying lower wages to these younger persons.

8–077

(vi) Apprentices

The Equality Act 2010 Sch.9 para.12 enables an employer, which bases its pay structure on the national minimum wage, to pay an apprentice who is not entitled to the national minimum wage (any apprentice who is under 19 or in the first year of apprenticeship) less than an apprentice who is entitled to the national minimum wage.

8–078

(vii) Life assurance

The Equality Act 2010 Sch.9 para.14 applies if a worker takes early retirement because of ill health. An employer may provide that worker life assurance covers him (post-employment) until his normal retirement age, or if there is not one, at age 65. And so, for example:

8–079

---

[232] [2008] I.C.R. 1334 (EAT)
[233] ibid. [38].
[234] See *Loxley v BAE Systems Land Systems (Munitions & Ordnance) Ltd* [2008] I.C.R. 1348 (EAT); *Kraft Foods v Hastie* (2010) (UKEAT/0024/10/ZT).

"An employer who has no normal retirement age provides life assurance cover for an employee who has retired early due to ill health. If the employer then ceases to provide such cover when the employee reaches the age of 65, this is lawful."[235]

The Government considered that without this exemption employers might cease to offer life assurance at all.[236]

(viii) Child care

8–080   An employer may provide a crèche for employees' children aged two and under; or a holiday club open only to employees' children aged between five and nine.[237] Less favourable treatment of person because of their association with someone with a protected characteristic can amount to direct discrimination.[238] Accordingly, this employer could be accused of discriminating against workers because of their association with a child who does not fall within the specified age groups.

The Equality Act 2010 Sch.9 para.15 provides an exception in these circumstances where the child is under 17. Child care includes: (a) paying for some or all of the cost of the provision; (b) helping a parent of the child to find a suitable person to provide care for the child; (c) enabling a parent of the child to spend more time providing care for the child or otherwise assisting the parent with respect to the care that the parent provides for the child.[239]

(ix) Occupational pensions

8–081   The Directive covers occupational pension schemes and occupational invalidity benefits. Personal pension schemes are not covered, save where the employer contributes to one. Article 6(2) provides an exemption for the fixing of ages for entry or entitlement, and of age criteria in actuarial calculations (provided this does not result in sex discrimination). Under the Equality Act 2010 Sch.9 para.15, detailed regulations have been made of exempted age-related rules.[240]

(x) The armed forces

8–082   Article 3(4) of the Framework Directive 2000/78/EC expressly allows derogation from the age provisions for the armed forces. This has been taken up in Britain and the Equality Act 2010 Sch.9 para.4(3)

---

[235] Explanatory Note (837).
[236] ibid.
[237] ibid. (841)
[238] Case C-303/06 *Coleman v Attridge Law* [2008] E.C.R. I-5603 (ECJ). See Ch.4, para.4–027.
[239] EA 2010 Sch.9 para.15(3).
[240] Equality Act (Age Exceptions for Pension Schemes) Order 2010, SI 2010/2133.

provides a blanket exemption from age discrimination by the armed forces in relation to work.

This wholesale derogation seems unnecessary, as many age requirements are convenient shorthand for mental and physical fitness, which can be—and often are—independently measured. In an Australian case, the army required trainee pilots to be aged between 19 and 28. This age limit was based on the Army's "inherent requirements" for the job, which were stated to be: (i) an ability to be properly trained for the job of a military line pilot (including an ability to "unlearn" habits and skills acquired in civilian life, and the ability to adapt to the environment of military aviation); (ii) an ability to integrate into the Aviation Regiments; and (iii) an ability to maintain a high level of medical fitness for the duration of the six-year period of appointment. It was held that age was not "tightly connected" to these requirements and so the age limit was not justified. In particular, the physical fitness requirement could not be allowed to "have the effect of damning individuals over 28 years by reference to a stereotypical characteristic (less physical fitness) of their age group".[241] There seems to be no reason to exempt the armed forces in Great Britain from having to justify any age requirements as a Genuine Occupational Requirement in a similar way.

(xi) Statutory authority

The Equality Act 2010 Sch.22 para.1 provides that an employer may discriminate on the ground of age "pursuant to ... a requirement of an enactment". This permits employers, say, refuse to hire a driver of heavy goods vehicles because she is not old enough to hold the requisite specialist driving licence, as required by law.　　**8–083**

(xii) National security

The Equality Act 2010 s.192 provides a general defence for national security. See above, para.8–048.　　**8–084**

(8) Married and Civil Partnership Status

(a) General Occupational Requirement

The general points relating to this exemption are discussed above, para.8–019. It applies to married or civil partnership status in the normal way, and permits a job requirement that the person is, or *is not*, married or in a civil partnership.[242]　　**8–085**

---

[241] *Commonwealth v Human Rights & Equal Opportunity Commission (Bradley)* (1999) 95 FCR 218 Federal Court of Australia, [41]. See also *Commonwealth of Australia v Hamilton*, (2000) 63 ALD 641.

[242] EA 2010 Sch.9 para.1(3)(b).

(b) Organised Religions

8–086 The "religious conscience" provision in the Equality Act 2010 Sch.9 para.2 permits discrimination inter alia on the ground of being married or in a civil partnership, by an employer[243] for the purposes of an organised religion. The general points relating to this exemption are discussed above, para.8–030.

The exemption applies to: (1) a requirement not to be married or a civil partner; (2) a requirement not to be married to, or be the civil partner of, a person who has a living former spouse or civil partner; (3) a requirement relating to circumstances in which a marriage or civil partnership came to an end.[244] This extends to requirements, for instance, that a Catholic priest be a man *and* unmarried, or that a worker is not, or does not become, divorced.

This exception applies to recruitment,[245] "opportunities and benefits" of employment, and dismissal.[246] In addition to imposing such requirements when recruiting, this means that an existing worker could be dismissed if, say, he gets divorced. It applies also to qualifications bodies where the qualification is for the purpose of the exempted employment and the compliance or non-conflict principles are engaged.[247]

(c) Insurance and Actuarial Calculations

8–087 The Equality Act 2010 Sch.9 para.20 exempts marriage or civil partner discrimination by "reasonable" reliance on "actuarial or other data" suggesting different risks, in relation to "an annuity, life insurance policy, accident insurance policy, or similar matter involving the assessment of risk".[248] Employers also are able to take advantage of this exception.

(d) Benefits Dependent on Marital or Civil Partnership Status— Equality Act 2010 Schedule 9 Paragraph 18

8–088 This actually exempts discrimination related to sexual orientation. See above, para.8–054.

(e) National Security

8–089 The Equality Act 2010 s.192 provides a general defence for national security. See above, para.8–048.

---

[243] This includes appointments to a personal or public office: Sch.9 para.2(7).
[244] EA 2010 Sch.9 para.2(4)(c)–(e)
[245] EA 2010 s.39(1)(a) or (c), and for office holders: s49(3)(a) or (c), s.50(3(a) or (c), s.51(1).
[246] EA 2010 s.39(2)(b) or (c), and for office holders: s.49(6)(b) or (c), 50 or (6)(b) or (c).
[247] See EA 2010 s.53.
[248] For the ECJ attitude here, see *Neath v Hugh Steeper* Case C-152/91, [1994] I.C.R. 118 (ECJ) and n.140, above.

4. OTHER WORK-RELATED BODIES

(1) Contract Workers

The *employer* of contract workers is liable in the normal way. **8–090**
However, the Equality Act 2010 s.41 provides that workers supplied
to a "principal" in furtherance of a contract are protected from discrimination, harassment or victimisation by the principal. This would
cover, for instance, discrimination by a building company against an
electrician working for a sub-contractor, or discrimination by a
hospital against a nurse supplied by an agency. The GOR exemptions
apply as they would apply to employment.[249]

A contract worker may compare her treatment with that given to
another contract worker, or a person *employed by the principal*.[250] In
practice, this will not lead to a harmonising of the respective worker's
terms as normally most of the contract worker's terms will be set by
the employer. However, it may be that the principal treats its contract
workers differently, for example by providing inferior canteen or
washroom facilities, or by not providing professional indemnity
insurance or career development support.[251] If this difference in
treatment is also discriminatory (say where contract workers were
predominantly female, or black, in comparison to the employees) the
principal may be liable.

Section 41 should be afforded a broad interpretation. Identifying
the principal is a fact-sensitive task, so the cases have a more illustrative than precedential value.[252] What can be said is that a principal
is a person who makes work available for individuals or benefits from
their work. In *Harrods Ltd v Remick*[253] the employers had concessions
to sell goods in the Harrods department store. The employers
installed their own staff, who had to be approved by Harrods, and
wore the Harrods' uniform. Otherwise, the employer had control
over these staff. It was held that Harrods could be liable for racial
discrimination as a "principal". The definition was not limited to
situations where the principal had direct control over the work being
done. In *Leeds City Council v Woodhouse*,[254] the council set up an
"arm's length" subsidiary, the sole purpose of which was to do work
for the council. The subsidiary employed Woodhouse, and so the
council benefited from Woodhouse's work, even though it had no
control or influence over him. The Court of Appeal held that the
council could be liable for racial discrimination as a principal.

---

[249] EA 2010 Sch.9 para.1(2)(b).
[250] *Allonby v Accrington and Rossendale College* [2001] I.C.R. 1189 (CA) at 1202.
[251] ibid.
[252] *Leeds City Council v Woodhouse* [2010] I.R.L.R. 625 (CA), [11], [22].
[253] [1997] I.R.L.R. 583 (CA).
[254] [2010] I.R.L.R. 625 (CA).

8–091   There is no need for the employer to have a *direct* contractual relationship with the principal. In *Abbey Life v Tansell*[255] the Court of Appeal held that a worker, who was employed by a company wholly owned by him, which in turn supplied him to an agency, which in turn supplied him to Abbey Life, was a "contract worker".[256] This was even though there was no contract between the company employing the worker (that is, his own company) and Abbey Life. It was enough that the worker was supplied to the principal (Abbey Life) under a contract. This case was codified and s.41(5) now demands only that the worker was supplied "in furtherance of a contract" to which the principal is a party (whether or not the main employer is a party to it).

Discrimination by the principal is not limited to when the contract worker is actually doing work for the principal. It includes decisions on selection. In *BP Chemicals v Gillick*[257] the EAT held that a principal could be liable for sex discrimination for refusing to allow a contract worker to return to the same job following her maternity leave.

The GOR general defence and defence afforded to employers with an ethos based on a religion or belief[258] apply *only* where the principal discriminates by "not allowing the worker to do, or continue to do, the work" (s.41(1)(b)). The "child care" defence[259] applies *only* to access to opportunities for receiving benefits, facilities or services (s.41(1)(c)).

(2) Employment Service Providers

8–092   Section 55 of the EA 2010 covers employment agencies and bodies providing vocational training, or assisting persons to obtain employment. It makes it unlawful for these "employment service-providers" to discriminate, harass or victimise, when providing an employment service.

These services would include: providing CV writing classes; English or Maths classes to help adults into work; training in IT/keyboard skills; or providing work placements.[260] The Explanatory Notes (189) provide these examples:

> "A company which provides courses to train people to be plumbers refuses to enrol women because its directors assume

---

[255] *Abbey Life Assurance Co Ltd v Tansell (MHC Consulting Services Ltd v Tansell)* [2000] I.C.R. 789 (CA), at 798–799.
[256] For the now repealed DDA 1995 s.12
[257] *BP Chemicals v Gillick and Roevin Management Services* [1995] I.R.L.R. 128 (EAT), applied *Patefield v Belfast CC* [2000] I.R.L.R. 664 (NICA).
[258] EA 2010 Sch.9 paras 1 and 3, discussed above, paras 8–019, 8–058.
[259] ibid. Sch.9 para.15, see above, para.8–080.
[260] EA 2010, Explanatory Note (190).

that very few people want to employ female plumbers. This would be direct discrimination."

"An agency which finds employment opportunities for teachers in schools offers placements only to white teachers based on the assumption that this is what parents in a particular area would prefer. This would be direct discrimination."

The GOR and "organised religion" defences, the defence afforded to employers with an ethos based on a religion or belief, or for the armed forces[261] apply in relation to discrimination in recruitment and during the service provision.[262]

(3) Partnerships

Under ss.44 and 45 EA 2010, partnerships and limited liability **8–093** partnerships are covered in parallel terms to the employment provisions.

The GOR general defence and defence afforded to employers with an ethos based on a religion or belief[263] apply to the arrangements for recruitment, rejections, access to opportunities for receiving benefits, facilities or services, or expulsion.[264] The "child care" defence[265] applies to access to opportunities to benefits, facilities or services.

(4) Personal and Public Offices

Sections 49–51 EA 2010 cover workers who technically are not in **8–094** employment, but whose position may be similar to that of employees. These workers are either personal, or public, office holders. They include a person appointed or recommended by a Minister or government department (paid or unpaid), or a person appointed to discharge functions personally for pay (not just expenses or compensation) and could be subject to the direction of another person. Government appointments covered include the chairs/members of some non-departmental public bodies, judges, members of tribunals or special advisory committees. Other office holders will include some ministers of religion. Politically elected positions, such as local councillors are not covered.[266] The provisions account for the situation where a person may be recommended by one party (e.g. a government minister), appointed by another (a tribunal appointment body), and employed by another (the tribunal body). Each must not

---

[261] EA 2010 Sch.9 paras 1–4, discussed above, respectively, paras 8–030, 8–058, 8–031.
[262] EA 2010 Sch.9 para.5. The armed forces exception does not apply to dismissal.
[263] EA 2010 Sch.9 paras 1 and 3, discussed above, paras 8–019, 8–058.
[264] ibid. respectively, s.44(1)(a), (c), (2)(b), (c); or (for LLPs), s.45(1)(a), (c), 2(b), (c).
[265] ibid. Sch.9 para.15, see above, para.8–080.
[266] EA 2010 s.52(5).

discriminate against, harass, nor victimise, the office holder at the relevant stages.

The GOR and "organised religion" defences, and the defence afforded to employers with an ethos based on a religion or belief,[267] apply to discrimination in the arrangements for making an appointment, rejection, access to opportunities for receiving benefits, facilities, or services, or termination of the appointment,[268] or in the recommendation for appointments.[269]

(5) Local Authority Members

8–095   Section 58 of the EA 2010 prohibits discrimination, harassment, or victimisation, by local authorities. It protects "members" (i.e. councillors when carrying out official business) of locally-electable authorities, which include local authorities in England, Wales and Scotland and the Greater London Authority. It does not protect members' actual appointment or election.

The "child care" defence[270] applies to access to opportunities for training or receiving any other facility (s.58(3)(a)).

(6) Barristers and Advocates

8–096   Sections 47 and 48 of the EA 2010 cover barristers (including squatters and door tenants), advocates and pupils in the normal way. For example, it is unlawful for a barrister or barrister's clerk to discriminate against, harass or victimise, a pupil or tenant in the arrangements for recruitment, or by "pressure to leave chambers" or by any other detriment. It also is unlawful, in relation to instructing a barrister, for any person to discriminate against, harass or victimise the barrister. The "child care" defence[271] applies to access to opportunities to training, gaining experience or receiving any other benefit, service or facility.[272] The employment GORs do *not* apply here.

(7) The Police

8–097   Section 42 of the EA 2010 identifies the "employer" as the "chief officer" and the police authority, for employment-related claims under the Act by police officers.

---

[267] EA 2010 Sch.9 paras 1–3, discussed above, respectively, paras 8–019, 8–030, 8–058.
[268] ibid. respectively, s.49(3)(a) or (c) or (6)(b) or (c); or (public office holders) s.50(3)(a) or (c) or (6)(b) or (c).
[269] ibid. s.51(1).
[270] ibid. Sch.9 para.15, see above, para.8–080.
[271] ibid.
[272] ibid. s.47(2)(b), or (Advocates) s.48(2)(b).

(8) Trade Organisations

Section 57 of the EA 2010 prohibits discrimination, harassment and **8–098** victimisation by trade organisations in access to and conditions of membership—as opposed to employment—as well as benefits, facilities and services conditional upon such membership, and expulsion and the imposition of any other detriment.

Trade organisations are defined in the legislation as "an organisation of workers, an organisation of employers, or any other organisation whose members carry on a particular trade or profession for the purposes of which the organisation exists."[273] This would include, respectively, a trade union; a Chambers of Commerce; or the British Medical Association, the Institute of Civil Engineers and the Law Society.[274]

The phrase "organisation of workers" includes an organisation of "professionals", as the label "profession" does not prevent an occupation from being work for these provisions. Hence, an indemnity and advice society for the medical profession was an "organisation of workers".[275] These provisions also apply to employers' organisations, even though these may have a far looser relationship with their members than trade unions. In *National Federation of Self-Employed and Small Businesses Ltd v Philpott*,[276] it was held that the Federation was "an organisation of employers", even though it was partly a campaigning group and not all its members were employers. As a result, the tribunal had jurisdiction to hear a claim by a person who was expelled from the organisation.

Trade unions may face a dilemma where an allegation of harassment or discrimination is made by one union member against another. This occurred in *Fire Brigades Union v Fraser*.[277] The union's policy was to support the claimant (of whichever sex) and not the accused. Accordingly, it supported a woman who had complained of harassment and gave the accused, Mr Fraser, no assistance or representation in the disciplinary hearing. The Court of Session held that as the policy was conduct-related, rather than gender-related, it did not infringe what is now s.57, and so the accused lost his claim against the union for sex discrimination.

The "child care" defence[278] applies to access to opportunities for receiving any other benefit, service or facility (s.57(2(a)).

---

[273] EA 2010 s.57(7).
[274] EA 2010, Explanatory Note 192.
[275] *Sadek v Medical Protection Society* [2004] I.C.R. 1263 (CA).
[276] [1997] I.C.R. 518 (EAT).
[277] [1998] I.R.L.R. 697 (CS).
[278] EA 2010 Sch.9 para.15, see above, para.8–080.

(9) Qualifications Bodies

8–099   Section 53 of the EA 2010 prohibits discrimination, harassment and victimisation by bodies which confer authorisation or qualification necessary for entry into employment. In parallel with the basic employment provisions, the sections cover the grant of the relevant qualification, its terms and its withdrawal.

It defines a qualifications body as a body that can confer any academic, medical, technical, or other standard which is required to carry out a particular trade or profession, or which better enables a person to do so by, for example, determining whether the person has a particular level of competence or ability. This covers bodies as wide ranging as the Council for Legal Education[279] and the Law Society to sporting bodies such as the British Boxing Board of Control.[280] In *British Judo Association v Petty*[281] the Association refused to grant Ms Petty a certificate to referee in men's judo competitions. It argued it was not a qualifications body because its job was to uphold refereeing standards rather than to award a qualification. The EAT held that the matter was one of substance and not form. The issue was whether the Association's activities in fact controlled entry into refereeing. In *Patterson v Legal Services Commission*,[282] the Court of Appeal held that the provision of a legal aid franchise to a sole practitioner solicitor "facilitated" her entry into, and continuing, practice, and so came within what is now s.53. However, in *Tattari v Private Patients Plan Ltd*[283] the Court of Appeal held that the rejection by the defendant, who underwrites private health care, of the plaintiff's application to be added to their list of accredited specialists, fell outside of what is now s.53. The defendant was not authorising her to practise in her profession. It simply required that those wishing to enter commercial agreements with them should have a recognised UK qualification.

The nomination of candidates by political parties for elections does not fall within this section, although it would come under Part 7 "Associations".[284]

Qualifications bodies may not use the standard GOR defence, but may invoke the "religious organisation" defence in Sch.9, para.2 in the arrangements, terms, for conferring a qualification, or not conferring one, or by its withdrawal or variation.[285]

---

[279] *Bohon-Mitchell v Common Professional Examination Board* [1978] I.R.L.R. 525, IT. See further Ch.6, para.6–039.

[280] Refusing a woman a licence to box professionally was held to be unlawful in *Couch v British Boxing Board of Control*, unreported, IT, (1998) *The Guardian*, March 31, 1998.

[281] [1981] I.C.R. 660 (EAT).

[282] [2004] I.C.R. 312 (CA), [63]–[79].

[283] [1998] I.C.R. 106 (CA).

[284] *Watt (formerly Carter) v Ahsan* [2008] 1 A.C. 696 (HL), [18]–[19].

[285] EA 2010, respectively, s.53(1) or (2)(a) or (b). The defence is discussed above, para.8–030.

5. EMPLOYER AND INDIVIDUAL LIABILITY

(1) Liability of Employers and Principals

Section 109 of the EA 2010 makes liable an employer for anything **8–100** done by its workers in the course of their employment, and a principal for anything done by his agent within his (actual or subsequent) authority. An employer can be liable even if the act was done without its knowledge or approval, although it has a defence if it "took all reasonable steps" to prevent the worker from acting as he did. Generally, employers and principals cannot be held liable for any criminal offences under the Act committed by their employees or agents[286] and are not liable for the acts of third parties, save in certain cases of harassment (see below).

The phrase "in the course of their employment" suggests that the more serious the discrimination or harassment, the less likely it is that the employer could be held liable, because it becomes less likely that such serious conduct could fall within the course of a worker's employment. The courts have avoided this paradox with a generous and purposive approach. In *Jones v Tower Boot Co*,[287] the claimant was of mixed race, 16 years old, and in his first job. His co-workers subjected him to serious racial harassment. Among other incidents, they burnt his arm with a hot screwdriver, threw metal bolts at his head, and repeatedly called him derogatory names such as "chimp", "monkey" and "baboon". The claimant resigned and sued the employer for racial discrimination. The EAT applied the existing test of vicarious liability in tort and concluded, predictably, that the employers were not liable, as the acts of harassment were committed outside the course of employment. The Court of Appeal reversed, holding that the phrase "in the course of employment" (in the Race Relations Act 1976) should be given a broad interpretation, regardless of the then common law doctrine of vicarious liability. Otherwise, "the more heinous the act of discrimination, the less likely it will be that the employer is liable."[288]

References to *principal* and *agent* in the provisions should bear their common law meaning. In *Yearwood v Commissioner of Police of the Metropolis*,[289] the EAT noted that at common law an agent may be appointed to do any act on behalf of the principal which the

---

[286] EA 2010 s.109(5), except for those in the provisions on transport services for disabled people in EA 2010 Pt 12. For an example, see making false statements, below, para.8–104.

[287] [1997] I.C.R. 254 (CA).

[288] ibid, at 264. See R. Townshend-Smith, "Case note" (1996) 2 I.J.D.L. 137, pp.139–40. For development of the argument, see R. Townshend-Smith, "Harassment as a tort in English law: the boundaries of *Wilkinson v Downton*" (1995) 24 Anglo-Am LR 299; J. Dine and B. Watt, "Sexual harassment: moving away from discrimination" (1995) 58 MLR 343, fn.3.

[289] [2004] I.C.R. 660 (EAT). See also, *May & Baker Ltd (t/a Sanofi-Aventis Pharma) v Okerago* [2010] I.R.L.R. 394 (EAT) [36]–[38].

principal might do himself, and held that an investigating officer appointed to carry out disciplinary hearings was not an agent of the chief of police because his task, by its nature, was independent of any control by the chief.

8–101   Employers (but not principals) have a defence if they prove that they "took all reasonable steps to prevent" the employee from doing that act, or acts of that description.[290] In *Canniffe v East Riding of Yorkshire Council*,[291] the EAT appeared to suggest that employers should take all reasonably practicable steps to prevent the discriminatory act, even where these steps would not have prevented the act. In this case the claimant was sexually assaulted by a colleague, and argued that their employer had not responded adequately to her prior complaints about the colleague's sexual harassment. The employment tribunal found that a better implementation of its personal harassment policy would not have prevented this serious criminal behaviour, any more than widespread advice about honesty would not prevent theft. On that basis the tribunal dismissed the complaint. The EAT held that this was the wrong approach: whether reasonably practicable further steps would have made a difference should not be "determinative either way". The case was remanded for a rehearing. However, the Court of Appeal in *Croft v Royal Mail*[292] preferred the approach at first instance:

> "In considering what steps are reasonable in the circumstances, it is legitimate to consider the effect they are likely to have. Steps which require time, trouble and expense, and which may be counterproductive given an agreed low-key approach, may not be reasonable steps if, on an assessment, they are likely to achieve little or nothing."[293]

In *Croft* the claimant, a victim of sexual harassment by colleagues, argued that her employer failed to respond properly to her complaints. The employment tribunal noted the employer's existing policy and practice, and found that further actions would not "have had more than at most a marginal effect" on the harassment.[294] The Court of Appeal upheld this approach.

8–102   The existence of the defence suggests that it is possible for an act of discrimination by a co-worker to take place while the employer has taken "all reasonable steps" to prevent it. The approach in *Croft*

---

[290] EA 2010 s.109(4).
[291] [2000] I.R.L.R. 555.
[292] [2003] I.C.R. 1425, [61].
[293] ibid. [63].
[294] Reported ibid., [59].

suggests that the more heinous the discrimination (such as a serious sexual assault) the less likely it is that the employer will be liable, which conflicts with the spirit adopted in *Jones v Tower Boot Co* (above).[295] The statutory phrase considered in these cases was in fact "such steps as were reasonably practicable". In the Equality Act, the word *such* was replaced with *all*, while *practicable* was dropped, to read "took all reasonable steps". It is thus arguable that *Canniffe* (EAT) has been restored. However, the Court in *Croft* used the phrase *reasonable steps* interchangeably with the (then) statutory phrase when coming to its decision, and the Equality Act 2010 did not expressly abolish this "no difference" rule.[296] Further, the *Draft Code of Practice* suggests that "In deciding whether a step is reasonable, an employer should consider its likely effect and whether an alternative step could be more effective."[297] This suggests that this part of *Croft* remains good law.

(a) Harassment by Third Parties

The traditional rule is that employers are not liable for discrimina- **8–103** tion, harassment or victimisation by third parties.[298] This caused notable problems with harassment, as illustrated by the next two cases. In *Burton and Rhule v de Vere Hotels*[299] two black waitresses were subjected to racist and sexist jibes by a guest speaker at an all-male private dinner party. The speaker, Bernard Manning, was well-known for his sexist and racist comments. The EAT held that a "reasonable" employer would have foreseen the problem and withdrawn the two waitresses, and so found the defendant employer liable to the waitresses for the harassment. However, in *Pearce v Governing Body of Mayfield Secondary School*,[300] the House of Lords disapproved of *Burton*. In *Pearce*, pupils at a school regularly taunted a schoolteacher, who was a lesbian, with names such as "lesbian", "dyke", "lesbian shit", "lemon", "lezzie" or "lez". The teacher sued her employer for sexual harassment. The House stated obiter that the employer could not be liable for the acts of the (third party) pupils. The basis of this approach was twofold. First, the legislation outlaws specific forms of discrimination, committed either by a worker, for which his employer may be liable, or by the employer itself. In this

---

[295] An argument was raised, but not considered, in *Canniffe*, that the whole defence is incompatible with the parent Directives, which do not specify such a defence: [2000] I.R.L.R. 555 [24]. See also *UP and GS v N and RJ*, unreported, IT, Case No: 10781/95, see 35 DCLD 11 (Equal Opportunities Review and Discrimination Case Law Digest).

[296] cf. Employment Rights Act 1996, which expressly codified (s.98A(2)), and then repealed (Employment Act 2008, s.2), the "no difference" rule for unfair dismissal procedure.

[297] EHRC *Draft* Code of Practice on Employment, para.10.51.

[298] *Pearce v Governing Body of Mayfield Secondary School* [2003] I.C.R. 937 (HL). Discussed in Ch.5, para.5–023 above.

[299] [1997] I.C.R. 1, EAT.

[300] [2003] I.C.R. 937, at [29]–[37], [96]–[103], [105], [120]–[124] and [200]–[205]. see further, Ch.5, para.5–023.

case, neither the employer nor the staff had harassed the teacher. In particular, whether the employer acted unreasonably is irrelevant. What matters is whether it committed an unlawful act of discrimination. Second, where it is lawful for a third party to discriminate (as with pupils harassing a teacher, or an entertainer harassing a waitress), the employer of the victims should not be put in a worse position than the perpetrator and be made liable for something which was otherwise lawful.

The situation has been retrieved, in part at least, by EA 2010 s.40. Where the employer (1) knows that the its worker has been harassed by *any* third party on at least two other occasions, and (2) the employer failed to take such steps as would have been reasonably practicable to prevent the third party from doing so, the employer will be liable for a further act of third party harassment against that worker. This means that, say, the three acts of harassment could each have been inflicted by a different person, so long as none of them were fellow employees or the employer. This would probably resolve the problem in *Pearce*, but not in *Burton*, unless either waitress had the misfortune of suffering Mr Manning's abuse in previous jobs, *and* her employer knew of this.

This court's attitude here is in contrast to the approach in the United States, where the law of agency is used to impose tortuous liability on employers for their own negligence.[301] Thus, where an employer *ought* to know a third party would harass a worker (as in *Burton*), it should take preventative steps.[302]

(2) Individual Liability

8–104 Section 110 of the EA 2010, makes an employee *personally* liable for unlawful acts committed in the course of employment. This arises where the employer is liable because of s.109 (above), or would be but for the defence of having taken all reasonable steps. By parallel logic, an agent is personally liable for any unlawful acts committed under his principal's authority.

Neither employee nor agent will be liable if told, respectively, by their employer or principal, that the act is lawful and they reasonably believe this to be true. It is an offence for employers or principals knowingly or recklessly makes a false statement about the lawfulness of doing something under the Act.

---

[301] See *Faragher v City of Boca Raton* 524 US 775, at 799–800 (Sup Ct 1998); D. Oppenheimer, "Exacerbating the exasperating: Title VII liability of employers for sexual harassment committed by their supervisors", 81 Cornell L Rev 66 (1995).

[302] See EEOC guidelines 29 CFR s.1604.11(e) (*www.eeoc.gov*; click "Laws, Regulations", click "Regulations", scroll down to 1604) and e.g. *Lockard v Pizza Hut* 162 F 3d 848 (10th Cir 1998).

CHAPTER 9

EQUAL PAY

INTRODUCTION

The gender pay gap has remained notoriously high. There are many **9–001** and varied methods of measuring the pay gap. Just a few statistics will indicate the problem. For the period 2004–2007, the *overall* gap, measuring the difference between all working men and all working women's hourly earnings, was 19 per cent. Between full-timers, it was 15 per cent. Between full-time men and part-time women, it was 31 per cent. Given that the part-time workforce is predominantly female, this represents a particular area for concern. Meanwhile, 10 per cent of the overall pay gap can be attributed to occupational sex segregation. Women tend to cluster in fewer occupations. Of the gap, 21 percent is caused by length of service in full-time work, again women suffering because of an interrupted career. However, when work histories, education, institutional factors, sector of employment and occupational segregation are accounted for, 36 per cent of the gender pay gap remains unexplained.[1] This means that even a woman with the same work history and education, and working in the same type of organisation and occupation as the average man, would still be likely to be paid significantly less. Clearly, equal pay and sex discrimination law cannot present a complete resolution of the pay gap, but as we shall see, it is arguable it could do more.

The law addresses unequal pay in the following way. Part 5, Chapter 3, of the Equality Act 2010 (EA 2010), enables a woman to claim equality with a man where she is engaged on "like work," work "rated as equivalent" under a job evaluation study, or where her work is of equal value with that of her male comparator.[2] This is achieved by implying a "sex equality clause" into every contract of employment. The employer has a defence where the difference is not due to sex discrimination, or if it is objectively justified. Chapter 3 covers the same broad range of workers as the employment provisions,[3] including the self-employed, Crown employment, House of Commons and House of Lords staff,[4] the armed forces,[5] plus personal and public office holders.[6]

Article 157, TFEU (ex 141, ex 119 TEC), guarantees the application of "the principle of equal pay for male and female workers for equal work or work of equal value." This is directly effective and so public and private employers are bound.[7] Article 157 is amplified in the Recast Directive 2006/54/EC, art.4. It is possible to mount a claim based on art.157, even if the claim falls outside the provisions of Chapter 3, and vice versa. Both the Equality and Human Rights

---

[1] See "The Gender Pay Gap in the UK 1995–2007 Research Reports Parts 1 and 2" (2010), Wendy Olsen, Vanessa Gash, Leen Vandecasteele, Pierre Walthery and Hein Heuvelman, Cathie Marsh Centre for Census and Survey Research, University of Manchester, published by the Government Equalities Office (2010) JN301113S. *http://www.equalities.gov.uk/default.aspx?page=1524*
[2] EA 2010 s.65
[3] EA 2010 s.64(1)(a). See Ch.8, para.8–002.
[4] ibid. s.83(1).
[5] ibid. s.83(3).
[6] ibid. s.64(1)(b).
[7] *Defrenne v Sabena* Case 43/75, [1976] I.C.R. 547 (ECJ); *Jenkins v Kingsgate (Clothing Productions) Ltd* Case 96/80, [1981] I.C.R. 592 (ECJ).

Commission and the European Commission have issued Codes of Practice on equal pay.[8] Both domestic and European schemes apply equally to men and women.

1. The Relationship between Equal Pay and Sex Discrimination

Of course, sex-discriminatory pay amounts to sex discrimination. But pay is dealt with separately, by Part 5, Chapter 3, which in fact covers all contractual terms, be they for the wages or other benefits, such as sick pay, holiday entitlement, and so on.[9] The Equality Act 2010 s.70 maintains this distinction by disapplying the sex discrimination provisions in relation to the terms of the employment contract (s.39(2)).

9–002

The sex discrimination provisions[10] prohibit sex discrimination in relation to job offers, but once the offer is accepted, the pay offer becomes a contractual term and Chapter 3 takes over. The sex discrimination provisions continue to cover non-contractual pay and benefits such as promotion, transfer and training.

The chief distinction between Chapters 1 (Discrimination) and 3 are that under Chapter 3 the comparator cannot be hypothetical; he must be a real worker, although there are some exceptions.[11] In time, this difference may dissolve, as the Recast Directive 2006/54/EC includes pay in its definition of discrimination, which includes the standard definitions of direct and indirect sex discrimination.[12]

What follows are discussions of the meaning of pay, the choice of comparator, the meaning of equal work, the employer's defence, and the effect of the equality clause.

2. The Meaning of Pay

The Equality Act 2010 Pt.5 Chapter 3, covers all contractual benefits, whereas art.57 TFEU covers just pay, although this is broadly defined:

9–003

---

[8] Respectively, *Equality Act 2010 Code of Practice on Equal Pay*, *Draft* issued by the Equality and Human Rights Commission, under EA 2006 s.14. See *equalityhumanrights.com/legal-and-policy/equality-act/equality-act-codes-of-practice/*; *A Code of Practice on the Implementation of Equal Pay for Work of Equal Value for Women and Men*, Commission of the European Communities COM(96) 336 final, see (1996) 70 EOR 43.

[9] See below, "The Meaning of Pay", para.9–003.

[10] EA 2010 s.39(2)(b), or s.49(6) (appointment to personal office), or 50(6) (appointment to public office). See above Ch.8, paras 8–008 and 8–094.

[11] See below, para.9–005, p.290.

[12] arts 1 and 2(1).

"... the ordinary basic or minimum wage or salary and any other consideration, whether in cash or in kind, which the worker receives directly or indirectly, in respect of his employment, from his employer."

This broad definition has been given its full potential by the case law. Thus, it covers future pay,[13] overtime,[14] performance-related pay and piece rates,[15] sick pay[16] and maternity pay.[17] Payment for time off to attend training courses is covered, even if the employer may not benefit from the training (such as obligatory trade union activities).[18] This is particularly relevant to part-time workers (predominantly women), who may be paid only up to their normal working hours (say 20 per week), even though they spend more time (say 30 hours) on the training course. All fringe benefits are covered, including removal expenses,[19] mortgage interest allowance[20] and voluntary Christmas bonuses.[21] Further, pay covers these benefits where they are given to third parties, such as travel concessions for the whole family.[22] This shows that even non-contractual benefits are covered. Where benefits such as concessions may not be "pay" under Chapter 3, a claim will fall instead under Chapter 1 (sex discrimination).

Occupational pensions and contracted out non-contributory pensions (that, in part, replace the state scheme) also fall within art.157,[23] but the position is somewhat complicated. The ECJ ruled, in *Barber v Guardian Royal Exchange*,[24] that what is now art.157 applied to discriminatory pension *payments*. The ECJ accepted that this decision was unexpected, so to avoid an enormous upset to the pension industry it further held that no claims (bar existing ones) could be made relating to pension payments attributable to service before the

---

[13] *Arbeiterwohlfahrt der Stadt Berlin Ev v Botel* Case C-360/90, [1992] I.R.L.R. 423 (ECJ), [12].
[14] ibid. [27].
[15] *Handels-og Kontorfunktionaerernes Forbund i Danmark v Dansk Arbejdsgiverforening (acting for Danfoss)* Case 109/88, [1991] I.C.R. 74 (ECJ); *Royal Copenhagen* Case C-400/93 [1996] I.C.R. 51 (ECJ).
[16] *Rinner-Kuhn v FWW Spezial-Gebäudereinigung*, Case 171/88, [1989] ECR 2743.
[17] Although this is largely theoretical, as the ECJ in *Gillespie v Northern Health and Social Services Board* Case C-342/93 [1996] I.C.R. 498, and *Boyle v EOC* Case C411/96 [1998] I.R.L.R. 717, held respectively, that no comparison could be made with either a man at work, or a man on sick leave. Hence it is not discriminatory to cease paying normal salary, or to provide benefits inferior to sick pay, to a woman on maternity leave. But see also *Alabaster v Woolwich plc* Case C-147/02, [2004] ECR I-0000 (below, para.9–005). (See generally, Ch.4, para.4–054).
[18] *Arbeiterwohlfahrt der Stadt Berlin Ev v Botel* Case C-360/90 [1992] I.R.L.R. 423 (ECJ); *Davies v Neath Port Talbot BC* [1999] I.R.L.R. 769 (EAT).
[19] *Durrant v North Yorkshire HA* [1979] I.R.L.R. 401 (EAT).
[20] *Sun Alliance and London Insurance Ltd v Dudman* [1978] I.C.R. 551 (EAT).
[21] *Lewen v Denda* Case C-333/97, [2000] I.C.R. 648 (ECJ).
[22] *Garland v British Rail Engineering* Case C-12/81 [1983] 2 A.C. 751 (ECJ).
[23] *Bilka-Kaufhaus v Weber von Hartz* Case C-170/84, [1987] I.C.R. 110 (ECJ); *Barber v Guardian Royal Exchange* Case C-262/88, [1991] 1 Q.B. 344 (ECJ).
[24] Case C-262/88, [1991] 1 Q.B. 344 (ECJ).

date of its judgment, May 17, 1990.[25] This does not affect an earlier ruling, in *Bilka*,[26] that a discriminatory exclusion from *membership* of an occupational pension falls under what is now art.157.[27] Typically, low paid and part-time workers have been excluded from pension schemes. Where these were predominantly women, a retrospective claim may be made under art.157.[28]

Article 157 also covers statutory and contractual redundancy payments,[29] as well as compensation and awards for statutory unfair dismissal.[30]

3. CHOOSING A COMPARATOR

(1) Who Chooses the Comparator(s)?

The general rule is that the claimant chooses her comparator, and the tribunal cannot substitute another it considers more appropriate. In *Pickstone v Freemans*,[31] Mrs Pickstone was one of many "warehouse operatives"; all but one were women. They were paid £77.66 per week. However, a *"checker* warehouse operative"—a Mr Phillips— was paid £81.88 per week. Mrs Pickstone's work was of equal value to Mr Phillips' and so she chose him as her comparator. Freemans argued that as Mrs Pickstone was paid same as the lone male warehouse operative (who did "like work") she could not "have it both ways" and make an alternative "equal value" claim. The House of Lords held that the claimant was entitled to use any appropriate comparator, and so Mrs Pickstone prevailed. The benefit of this approach is that prevents an employer using a token male worker in a predominantly female occupation to avoid equal-value claims, for instance, a supermarket employing a lone male on the checkouts, while paying more to the predominantly male shelf-stackers who are doing work of equal value.[32]

9–004

[25] This temporal rule is now contained in the Recast Directive 2006/54/EC, art.12.
[26] *Bilka-Kaufhaus v Weber von Hartz* Case 170/84, [1987] I.C.R. 110 (ECJ).
[27] See *Vroege v NCIV Institut voor Volkshuisvesting BV and Stichting Pensioenfonds NCIV* Case C-57/93, [1995] I.C.R. 635 (ECJ).
[28] See below, Ch.12, para.12–022.
[29] *Barber v Guardian Royal Exchange* Case C-262/88, [1991] 1 Q.B. 344 (ECJ), at [13].
[30] *R. v Secretary of State for Employment ex p. Seymour-Smith* Case C-167/97, [1999] I.C.R. 447 (ECJ), [27]–[29]. See further Ch.6, paras 6–027 and 6–050.
[31] [1988] I.C.R. 697 (HL).
[32] In *North Cumbria Acute Hospitals NHS Trust v Potter* [2009] I.R.L.R. 176, [47]–[50], [57] the EAT rejected the employer's "wrecking" argument that as there were two workers on different terms, a comparison with others on "common terms and conditions" at associated employer could not be made.

However, doubt has been raised over this as an absolute rule where there is no sex discrimination and the claimant chooses an anomalous comparator. In *McPherson v Rathgael Centre for Children*[33] five out of six instructors were male. All six were paid the same. The lone female brought an equal pay claim using as a comparator a newly recruited (seventh) male instructor, who was put on higher pay by mistake.[34] While her appeal succeeded on the point that a mistake is no justification, Hutton L.C.J. doubted that *Pickstone* should be applied in cases such as this, where clearly there was no sex discrimination (the majority of the lower-paid instructors were men). There is support for this sentiment in the ECJ, which has stated art.157 only prohibits different pay exclusively based on the difference in sex of the employees concerned.[35] In *Glasgow City Council v Marshall*[36] the claim was by special-school instructors who were doing the same work as teachers for less pay. Seven female instructors compared themselves with a male teacher. At the same time, a *male* instructor compared himself with a female teacher. However, there was no sex disparity between the two groups (females made up about 96 per cent instructors and 97 per cent teachers).[37] The quandary was expressed by Lord Nicholls: "It is a curious result in a sex discrimination case that, on the same facts, claims by women and a claim by a man all succeed."[38] The House of Lords rejected the claim, but rather than disturbing *Pickstone*, it resolved the matter under the material factor defence: as the difference in pay "is not the difference of sex", no further justification was necessary.[39] Thus, where there is no sex discrimination, an anomalous choice of comparator will be allowed (the *Pickstone* rules survives), but the claim will fail on the "material factor defence" element. Accordingly, there is nothing to prevent a claimant bringing several (appropriate) comparators into court.[40] In *Hayward v Cammell Laird Shipbuilders Ltd (No.2)*,[41] Ms Hayward, a canteen cook in a shipyard, used a painter, a decorator and a thermal insulation engineer as comparators.

[33] [1991] I.R.L.R. 206 (NICA).
[34] ibid. [40]. The House of Lords stated that the mistake point was wrongly decided: *Strathclyde Regional Council v Wallace* [1998] I.C.R. 205, at 214–215. See further below, para.9–041.
[35] *Brunnhofer v Bank der Österreichischen Postsparkasse* Case C-381/99, [2001] I.R.L.R. 571, [40]; *Jenkins v Kingsgate* Case 96/80, [1981] I.C.R. 592, [10].
[36] [2000] I.C.R. 196. See also *Strathclyde Regional Council v Wallace* [1998] I.C.R. 205 (HL).
[37] A separate argument comparing instructors and teachers from *all* schools was not taken up for being introduced too late.
[38] [2000] I.C.R. 196, at 203.
[39] Discussed further below, para.9–030.
[40] But note the House of Lords' caution against this as abuse in equal value claims: *Leverton v Clwyd CC* [1989] A.C. 706, at 751–752. See further below, n.128 and accompanying text.
[41] [1988] A.C. 894 (HL).

(2) Real and Hypothetical Comparators

Both art.157 and EA 2010 Pt 5, Chapter 3, with some exceptions, **9–005**
appear to demand that the comparator must be a real person. This
restriction can limit the ability of the law to address (at least) two
scenarios. The first can arise in segregated occupations, typically
portrayed in all-female sweatshops. As the law stands, female cooks
in a shipyard may compare their jobs to painters, while cleaners at a
coal mine may compare themselves to clerical staff, and seamstresses
in a motor factory compare themselves to repair workers.[42] But where
these occupations are segregated, a comparison for equal pay is
impossible. So the cook or the cleaner working for an outside contractor,[43] or the seamstress in a sweatshop, cannot use comparators in
other higher paid occupations of equal value. The sweatshop's
seamstress may see her neighbour working for Vauxhall or Ford,
being paid a lot more for the same work. As such, the National
Minimum Wage legislation did more for these workers than the equal
pay legislation.[44]

The second scenario arose with pregnancy and pay. Although
pregnancy discrimination has been held to amount to *sex* discrimination,[45] discrimination in *pay* on the ground of pregnancy may
escape liability because the female claimant can find no male comparator. In *Alabaster v Woolwich Plc*[46] the claimant's maternity pay
was related to her salary. However, the formula pinned maternity
pay to the salary some time before her leave began. Accordingly, a
pay rise awarded after this time was not reflected in her maternity
pay. The ECJ ruled that this was sex discrimination under art.157, as
pregnant women did not receive the benefit of the pay rise because
they were pregnant. When the case returned to the UK, the Court of
Appeal implemented this ruling by disapplying the requirement for a
comparator (then in EPA 1970 s.1), so that Alabaster's claim could
proceed without the need for a comparator.[47] "Pregnancy pay" is now
dealt with by EA 2010 s.73.[48]

---

[42] See, respectively, *Hayward v Cammell Laird Shipbuilders (No.2)* [1988] A.C. 894 (HL);
British Coal v Smith [1996] I.C.R. 515 (HL); *Neil v Ford* [1984] I.R.L.R. 339 (IT) (unsuc-
cessfully), but successfully after arbitration: *The Independent* May 14, 1991, *The Guardian*
March 11, 1991.

[43] *Lawrence v Regent Office Care* Case C-320/00, [2003] I.C.R. 1092 (ECJ) discussed below,
para.9–016; see also *Allonby v Accrington & Rossendale College* Case C-256/01, [2004] I.C.R.
1328 (ECJ), (college lecturers) see below para.9–016.

[44] In 1998, the government calculated that the proposed minimum wage rate of £3.60 would
benefit 1.4 million women and 1.3 million part-time workers. (Department of Trade and
Industry Press Release, P/98/489, 18 June 1998, London: DTI.) See further, M. Connolly,
Townshend-Smith Discrimination Law: Text, Cases and Materials (London: Cavendish, 2004)
pp.40–41.

[45] *Dekker v Stichting Vormingscentrum voor Jonge Volwassen (VJV-Centrum) Plus* Case C-
177/88, [1990] E.C.R. I-3941. See further Ch.4, para.4–040.

[46] Case C-147/02, [2004] E.C.R. I-3101 (ECJ).

[47] *Alabaster v Barclays Bank (No.2)* [2005] EWCA 508.

[48] Discussed in the section on direct discrimination and pregnancy, in Ch.4, para.4–052.

However, s.71 of the EA 2010 provides a new exception to the demand for a real comparator. Where the equality clause "has no effect", it permits the woman to invoke the sex discrimination provisions if her discriminatory "pay" arose from *direct* discrimination because of sex (s.13), or sex and one other protected characteristic, under s.14.[49] This codifies *Alabaster*, and resolves some other cases in need of a hypothetical comparator, such as those arising from segregated occupations. The Explanatory Note (246) offers a crude example of an employer telling a black female worker: "I would pay you more if you were a white man". Of course, few employers are likely to be as self-destructive. Otherwise, evidence may prove more difficult to collect, and be more nuanced in nature, such as revealing conversations between employers, the explanation behind the employer's hiring patterns that seem to exclude men from the low paid segregated jobs, and the difference between the wages and those paid elsewhere for like, or equal-value, work. Bearing in mind that s.71 extends only to direct discrimination, an interesting question arises of whether statistics alone could be enough to prove a case. This could arise where, say, a large undertaking, over several years, has employed only women in its low paid jobs. Could proof of such a pattern be enough to establish a prima facia case of direct discrimination? The US Supreme Court has held that:

> "Statistics showing a racial or ethnic imbalance are probative ... only because such imbalance is often a telltale sign of purposeful discrimination ... it is ordinarily expected that non-discriminatory hiring practices will in time result in a workforce more or less representative ...".[50]

This logic could apply, with necessary adjustments, to direct sex discrimination.

(3) Predecessors and Successors as Comparators

9–006 Section 64(2) of the Equality Act 2010 provides that the comparator's work "is not restricted to work done contemporaneously". This codifies *Macarthys Ltd v Smith*,[51] where the ECJ held that it was possible to use a predecessor in the same job as a comparator, under what is now art.157. That decision suggests it was possible to use a

---

[49] That is either age; disability; gender reassignment; race; religion or belief; sexual orientation. Note though, that s.14 (Combined (or dual) discrimination) may not yet be in force. See *http://www.equalities.gov.uk/equality_act_2010.aspx* (accessed January 1, 2011).
[50] *International Brotherhood of Teamsters v US* 431 US 324, 329, n.20 (Sup Ct 1977)
[51] Case 129/79, [1980] I.C.R. 672 (ECJ).

successor as a comparator. In *Diocese of Hallam Trustee v Connaughton*,[52] an organist was paid £11,138 per annum at her time of leaving in September 1994. Her male successor was paid £20,000 per annum from January 1995. The EAT held that while using a successor as a comparator posed evidential problems it did not preclude Miss Connaughton's equal pay claim. Although the successor was appointed some four months later, it was on near double her salary. However, *Connaughton* was not followed in *Walton Centre for Neurology & Neuro Surgery NHS Trust v Bewley*,[53] where the EAT pointed out (1) (at the time of the of the pay in question) using a successor as a comparator was in fact using a hypothetical comparator, and (2) the ECJ in *Macarthys* and subsequent cases set itself against the use of hypothetical comparators, demanding a "concrete appraisal".[54] Therefore, successors should not be used in equal pay claims. Thus, it would seem, the new s.64(2) (coming into force after *Bewley*), does not codify *Connaughton* nor question *Bewley's* logic, which is likely to prevail as long as courts demand a real comparison.

Three question marks hang over *Bewley*. First, the *Bewley* logic, that a successor-comparator is a hypothetical one, and that a hypothetical comparator cannot provide a "concrete appraisal", is flawed and artificial, as the facts of *Connaughton* and *Bewley* illustrate. Although Ms Connaughton's successor was appointed some four months later, it was on near double her salary. In *Bewley,* the claimant worked alongside her comparators. But for the period before their appointment, they were treated as hypothetical. Hence her claim for equal pay for the period she worked *before* their appointment was barred, despite the obvious evidence that their appointment presented of the pre-existing discriminatory pay. Both claims presented a "concrete" appraisal of how much men doing equal work would have been paid, and shows the *Bewley* reasoning to be somewhat artificial. These comparisons were no less concrete than, say, that of a predecessor from several years" past. Predicting what this man would have been earning at the time of the claim would be, if anything, more speculative. This would be especially so if the job were the only one of its kind within the undertaking, such as firm's only surveyor or cook or typist, and so on. Moreover, if the law were serious about combating the notorious gender pay gap (above, para.9–001), it would not cling to an inflexible rule against successors as comparators, and instead treat each case on the merits of the evidence presented,

---

[52] [1996] I.C.R. 860 (EAT).
[53] [2008] I.C.R. 1047. The EAT also noted (at [13]) that *Connaughton* was decided per incuriam because it relied on a Commission argument that was rejected by the EJC.
[54] [2008] I.C.R. 1047, [36] and [47] citing *Macarthys* Case 129/79, [1980] I.C.R. 672, [15]; *Coloroll Pension Trustees Ltd v Russell* Case C-200/91 [1995] I.C.R. 179 (ECJ), [101].

without some notional distinction between real and hypothetical, or predecessor and successor.[55]

9–007   Second, the new s.71 permits claims to proceed as direct sex discrimination where there is no comparator (see above, para.9–005, p.290). Thus, if *Bewley* is good law, *some* claims (such as *Connaughton*) could succeed via this route. However, cases of indirect discrimination (such as *Bewley*) remain stranded without a remedy.

Third, in any case, the ECJ rule against hypothetical comparators is not absolute. It has been argued that *Macarthys*, the principal case behind the *Bewley* logic, applied only for the purpose of the direct effect of art.157. It did not question the legality of other instruments, made under art.157, implementing the principle of equal pay.[56] Accordingly, the Recast Directive 2006/54/EC includes pay in its definition of discrimination, which embraces the standard definitions of direct and indirect discrimination (which permit hypothetical comparators).[57]

Given limited effect of s.71, it would be better for tribunals to abandon the fragile reasoning of *Bewley*, and take a more flexible approach, with the purpose of remedying discriminatory pay.

(4) "Proportionate" Comparators

9–008   The legislation limits comparisons to those doing "equal work". Yet discriminatory pay exists beyond the simplistic equal-pay-for-equal-work mantra. For instance, a woman may be doing superior work to a man and receive inferior, or at best, equal pay. Although she can compare herself to a man doing *inferior* work, and achieve the *same* level of pay as him,[58] she cannot claim for proportionally *more* pay than he receives.[59] Alternatively, men doing *superior* work may receive disproportionately more pay. In the US case *County of Washington v Gunther*,[60] male prison officers had more onerous duties than female prison officers. However, a job evaluation study recommended that the women's pay should be 95 per cent of the

---

[55] For a flexible approach see the US cases *Gandy v Sullivan County* 24 F 3d 861 (6th Cir 1994), and *Brinkley-Obu v Hughes Training* 36 F.3d 336 (4th Cir 1994).

[56] S. Fredman, "Reforming Equal Pay Laws" (2008) 37 ILJ 193, at 201.

[57] arts.1 and 2(1). This model was first introduced by the Equal Treatment (Amendment) Directive 2002/73/EC and should have been implemented by the UK by October 1, 2005. In *Bewley*, at [65], Elias J. considered that a Directive made under art.157 (such as the Recast Directive) "cannot expand the scope or effect of the Treaty Article". This view falls away if indeed the scope of art.157 is not as limited by *Macarthys* as he thought.

[58] *Murphy v Bord Telecom Eireann* Case 157/86, [1988] I.C.R. 445 (ECJ), [10]; contrast *Waddington v Leicester Council for Voluntary Service* [1977] I.C.R. 266, at 270–271 EAT. See also para.9–020, below.

[59] *Evesham v North Hertfordshire Health Authority* [2000] I.C.R. 612 (CA); *Redcar & Cleveland Borough Council v Bainbridge (No.1)* [2007] I.R.L.R. 984 (CA).

[60] 452 US 161 (Sup Ct 1981). See also *Ledbetter v Goodyear* 560 US 618, where the US Supreme Court acknowledged an equal pay claim under Title VII of the Civil Rights Act 1964. The issue was the time limits. (The decision to time-bar the claim was reversed by the Lily Ledbetter Equal Pay Act 2009.)

men's. The men were paid their worth in full, while the women were paid just 70 per cent of the men's pay. In the United States, just as in the UK, the Equal Pay Act 1963 demands a real comparator. The Supreme Court bypassed this restriction ruling that the female prison officers could make a claim using conventional sex discrimination law,[61] which does not demand a real comparator.[62]

As things stand, the exception provided by s.71 EA 2010 (above, para.9–005, p.290), cannot address this problem, as normally these "disproportionate differentials" are caused by *indirect* discrimination. Further, it is arguable that s.71 has no application in the sub-class of "inferior work" cases, because Chapter 3 has *some* effect (of equalising the pay).[63] Thus, s.71 does little to address the problem of disproportionate differentials.

The ideal solution would be an addition (to "Like Work" etc.) to Chapter 3 of a "proportionate comparator", i.e. someone doing different work but earning *disproportionate* pay. In the absence of this, *Gunther* provides a hint at a practical solution. The Recast Directive 2006/54/EC includes pay in its definition of discrimination, which includes the standard definitions of direct and indirect discrimination.[64] Thus, it should be possible in these cases to invoke the Directive and present the claim under the conventional definitions of direct or (more likely) indirect discrimination.[65]

(5) Comparing Part-time to Full-time Workers

As noted above, part-time work tends to be occupied predominantly by women. Hence, an apparently neutral practice disfavouring part-time workers may adversely affect women. Under equal pay legislation (predominantly female) part-time workers can compare themselves to full-time workers, as long as otherwise they are doing equal work.[66]

In *Elsner-Lakeberg*[67] both part- and full-time teachers were obliged to work three hours per month in excess of their normal working

9–009

---

[61] Civil Rights Act 1964, Title VII, the loose equivalent of EA 2010 Pt. 5, Chapter 1.

[62] In fact, the claimants used this path because, at the time, the Equal Pay Act did not cover municipal workers: but the point (that Title VII can be used without a comparator) stands. It has been argued that discrimination in collective bargaining and in resulting collective agreements is unlawful as sex discrimination (under the old SDA 1975) irrespective of the position under equal pay law: A. Lester and D. Rose, "Equal value claims and sex bias in collective bargaining" (1991) 20 ILJ 163. See also S. Fredman, "Reforming Equal Pay Laws" (2008) 37 ILJ 193, 208–211.

[63] s.71 applies if the equality clause has "no effect".

[64] arts.1 and 2(1). This model was first introduced by the Equal Treatment (Amendment) Directive 2002/73/EC and should have been implemented by the UK by October 1, 2005.

[65] For a summary of ways to measure disproportionate differences, see S. Fredman "Reforming Equal Pay Laws" (2008) 37 ILJ 193, 199–200.

[66] *Bilka-Kaufhaus v Weber von Hartz* Case C-170/84, [1987] I.C.R. 110 (ECJ). See further paras 9–034 and 9–035. On choosing the pool for the comparison, see Ch.6, para.6–015.

[67] *Elsner-Lakeberg v Land Nordrhein-Westfalen* Case C-285/02, ECR [2004] I-05861. See also *Kowalska v Freie und Hansestadt Hamburg* Case C-33/89, [1992] I.C.R. 29, at [19] (ECJ).

week, to qualify for overtime pay. The ECJ held that this placed an unequal burden on the part-timers. Where, say, the normal part-time obligation was 15 hours per week, the part-timer who worked 17½ hours would receive less pay than a full-timer working 17½ hours. This raised a prima facie case under art.157. Similarly, in a variation on this theme, where overtime pay is *less* than normal pay, and awarded for hours worked in excess of the worker's normal working week, a prima facie case will arise. A part-time teacher whose normal weekly obligation is 23 hours per week, and who works 3 hours overtime receives less pay for 26 hours than that received by a full-time teacher.[68]

Part-time workers cannot compare their overtime pay to that of full-time workers, until the part-time overtime hours reaches a threshold, say, the normal full time obligation of 38 hours per week. So, while a full-time worker may be paid at double rates for hours worked in excess of 38 per week, a part-time worker may be paid at her standard rate for her extra hours up to 38 per week.[69] Here, part-time workers receive the same overall pay as full-time workers for the same number of hours worked, so there is no discriminatory effect. However, where the full-timers are paid a bonus for some of their contractually obliged hours, then a comparison can be made.[70]

Note that where the practice does not adversely affect women, it may be challenged under the Part-time Workers (Prevention of Less Favourable Treatment) Regulations 2000,[71] which provides that less favourable treatment, including pay, of part-time workers is unlawful unless objectively justified. Regulation 1(2) provides that comparisons can be made on a pro rata basis, so that the level of pay for part-time worker should be proportionally the same as the full-time worker's. The regulations demand a real comparator, so claimants cannot use these regulations to bypass the requirement for a real comparator by Chapter 3 (of Pt 5 of the Equality Act 2010).

(6) The Scope of the Comparison

9–010 Chapter 3, Part 5 of the Equality Act 2010 requires that the comparator must be in the "same employment", however, s.79 provides an expansive definition of this, allowing a claimant to chose a comparator who works for an "associated employer". Article 157, TFEU, goes further than that in some respects. In *Defrenne v Sabena*

---

[68] Case C-300/06 *Voss v Land Berlin* [2008] 1 C.M.L.R. 49 (ECJ), [34]–[38].

[69] *Stadt Lengerich v Helmig* Case C-399/92 [1994] ECR I-5725; [1996] I.C.R. 35 (ECJ), codified by Part-Time Workers (Prevention of Less Favourable Treatment) Regulations 2000, SI 2000/1551, reg.5(4)).

[70] *James v Great North Eastern Railways* Unreported, (2004) UKEAT/0496/04/SM (Transcript), (available at www.employmentappeals.gov.uk). Decided under Part-Time Workers Regulations 2000, ibid.

[71] SI 2000/1551, implementing Directive 97/81/EC. See further Ch.6, para.6–043.

(No.2),[72] the ECJ stated that it allowed a comparator who is in the same establishment or "service", whether public or private, and whose terms originate from the same legislative provisions or collective agreement.[73] The direct effect of art.157 allows claimants to argue either route in domestic tribunals.

(a) Equality Act 2010

Under Chapter 3 s.79, a comparator (i) must work for the same or an "associated" employer *and* (ii) be employed at the same establishment, or if at a different establishment, on terms and conditions common to both establishments or between the claimant and her comparator.

9–011

(i) "Associated employer"

Under s.79(9), two employers are to be treated as "associated" if one is a company of which the other (not necessarily a company) has control, or where both employers are companies under the control of a third person (not necessarily a company). The control can be direct of indirect. Local authorities and public bodies, as statutory bodies corporate, are not "companies" within this definition.[74]

9–012

(ii) Cross-establishment comparisons

If the comparator works at the same establishment, there is no need for him to work under common terms and conditions.[75] If the comparator works (for the same or associated employer) at another establishment, then s.79(4)(b) stipulates that he must do so on terms and conditions common to both establishments either generally or as between the claimant and her comparator.

In *Leverton v Clwyd County Council*[76] Lord Bridge explained the purpose of this formula:

9–013

> "An employer operates factory A where he has a long standing collective agreement with the ABC union. The same employer takes over a company operating factory X and becomes an 'associated employer' of the persons working there. The previous owner of factory X had a long standing collective agreement

---

[72] Case C-43/75, [1976] I.C.R. 547, [40 (ECJ).

[73] These limits cannot be used to restrict Chapter 3 claims: *North Cumbria Acute Hospital NHS Trust v Potter* [2009] I.R.L.R. 176 (EAT), [86]–[87], approved *Wilson v Health and Safety Executive* [2010] I.C.R. 302 (CA), [86]–[87].

[74] *Merton LBC v Gardiner* [1981] Q.B. 269 (CA), at 287; *Hasley v Fair Employment Agency* [1989] I.R.L.R. 106, (NICA), [12].

[75] *Lawson v Britfish Ltd* [1987] I.C.R. 726 (EAT), approved *North Cumbria Acute Hospitals NHS Trust v Potter* [2009] I.R.L.R. 176 (EAT), [75].

[76] [1989] A.C. 706 (CA and HL), at 746.

with the XYZ union which the new employer continues to operate. The two collective agreements have produced quite different structures governing pay and other terms and conditions of employment at the two factories. Here ... [what is now s.79] will operate to prevent women in factory A claiming equality with men in factory X and vice versa."

Of course, if the interpretation were too strict and only comparators who worked on identical terms could be used, the result would be paradoxical: a claimant on identical terms to her comparator would have no need for an equal pay claim. Thus "the terms and conditions do not have to be identical, but on a broad basis to be substantially comparable."[77] In *Leverton* a nursery nurse compared her pay with 11 male clerical officers employed in other establishments by the County Council on terms derived from the same collective agreement, although the comparators worked longer hours and had shorter holidays. In *British Coal Corporation v Smith*[78] canteen workers and cleaners compared themselves with surface mineworkers and one clerical worker. The claimants were employed at 47 different establishments, while their comparators were at 14. Both the claimants and comparators worked under a single national agreement, but with some variations, such as concessionary coal and locally operated incentive bonuses. In both *Leverton* and *Smith* the House of Lords applied the "broad" comparison and held that the comparators worked under common terms and conditions.

9–014 One line of argument fleetingly embraced is that the claimant has to show that her comparator *would have* been employed in her establishment. This would unduly restrict the legislation. For instance, a clerical worker "on the fifth floor of an office block without so much as a window box"[79] comparing her work to a gardener's, or a classroom assistant comparing her work to a gravedigger's (each pair being employed by the same local authority) would find it impossible to show that her comparator would have been employed at her establishment. This argument was actually adopted in one EAT judgment,[80] but subsequently rejected by the Court of Appeal,[81] and indeed a little later by the same EAT judge.[82]

As *Leverton* and *Smith* demonstrate, where there is a centralised agreement, some variations will not prevent a claim. However, where there is plant bargaining, or a fragmented management structure, or no collective bargaining at all, cross-establishment comparisons may

[77] *British Coal v Smith* [1996] I.C.R. 515 (HL), at 531 (Lord Slynn).
[78] [1996] I.C.R. 515 (HL).
[79] *Dumfries and Galloway Council v North* [2009] I.R.L.R. 915 (EAT Sc), [40].
[80] ibid. [59]. (Lady Smith)
[81] *South Tyneside Metropolitan Borough Council v Anderson* [2007] I.R.L.R. 715 (CA), [26]–[27].
[82] *City Of Edinburgh Council v Wilkinson* [2010] I.R.L.R. 756 (EAT Sc), [77] (Lady Smith).

not be possible under the Chapter 3. In these cases, claimants may instead try to claim under art.157 TFEU (discussed below).

(b) Article 157 TFEU

Article 157, as interpreted in *Defrenne v Sabena*,[83] has in some ways a broader application than s.79 EA 2010. First, there is no restriction that one of the associated employers must be a "company". Unlike s.79, art.157 covers the situation where both the claimant's and comparator's employers are *not* companies. This facilitates public sector claims, as *Morton* (below) illustrates. But art.157 only applies where the claimant and comparator are in the "same service" and share a single source of pay (e.g. provided by legislation or collective agreement), which limits its impact on contracted-out workers, and by extension, "departmentalised" workers.

9–015

The broad application of art.157 was illustrated in *South Ayrshire Council v Morton*,[84] a case of two separate public sector employers, operating under the same collective agreement. In Scotland, the salary scale for primary school head teachers (75 per cent women) was lower than for secondary school head teachers (25 per cent women). Both salary scales were set by the Scottish Joint Negotiating Committee, a quasi-autonomous body set up by the Education (Scotland) Act 1980 under the general control of the Secretary of State. There were 32 local authorities in Scotland and each was obliged to implement the salary scale, but each had autonomy, as an employer, on how to do this. It was held that Ms Morton, a primary school head teacher, employed by South Ayrshire Council, could use as a comparator a male secondary school head teacher, employed by Highland Council.

In *North Cumbria Acute Hospitals NHS Trust v Potter*,[85] a newly formed NHS trust adopted the Whitley Council terms of employment. The Whitley Councils were established to develop and govern pay in the NHS, although the Trust was not bound to abide by it. The EAT held that the single source of pay was the Trust itself, as it alone was responsible for the pay and remedying any inequality in pay. The Whitley Councils were "merely the process by which pay and conditions are determined".[86] The EAT reversed the employment tribunal's decision that both the Trust and Whitley Council were the sources of pay, as there could not be two single sources of pay.

The limit of art.157 was demonstrated when contracted-out workers tried to compare their pay with a male worker of the principal employer. In *Lawrence v Regent Office Care*,[87] North Yorkshire

9–016

---

[83] Case C-43/75, [1976] I.C.R. 547 (ECJ).
[84] [2002] I.C.R. 956 (CS).
[85] [2009] I.RL.R. 176 (EAT).
[86] ibid. [125].
[87] Case C-320/00, [2003] I.C.R. 1092 (ECJ).

County Council, in some districts, contracted out its school cleaning and catering services. In other districts, the council carried on providing the service itself. The workers affected by the contracting-out were made redundant and re-employed by Regent, who paid them less than the Council's rates. These workers brought a claim of equal pay, using an existing Council worker as a comparator. The ECJ held that such a claim was not possible because the pay could not be attributed to a single source, and so there was no single body responsible for the inequality and which could restore equal pay. A similar situation arose in *Allonby v Accrington and Rossendale College*,[88] where the college dismissed all its part-time lecturers and rehired them through an agency, for less pay. Ms Allonby tried to compare herself with a full-time male lecturer (who earned more pro rata). The ECJ again rejected her claim.[89]

A perhaps logical extension of these ECJ decisions suggests that art.157 has no application where a single employer has a fragmented management structure, leaving its workers "departmentalised". In *Robertson v DEFRA*[90] civil servants working in the Department for Environment Food and Rural Affairs brought equal pay claims using comparators from the Department of the Environment, Transport and the Regions. The claimants and comparators shared the same employer, the Crown. However, since 1995 the terms of employment had been individually negotiated within each civil service department, with the result that claimants worked under different terms from their comparators (a reason why they could not use what is now Chapter 3, s.79). The Court of Appeal rejected their claim under what is now art.157 because the difference in pay could not be attributed to a single source.

The decisions in *Lawrence, Allonby*, and *Robertson* have been criticised on a number grounds, but *Robertson* requires special attention. First, the decisions essentially are fault based. As the ECJ in *Lawrence* noted, there was no one body responsible for disparity in pay. This may be a practical and even laudable sentiment, but as Fredman has observed, it does not explain why the loss should fall on those least at fault.[91] In *Robertson,* Mummery L.J. suggested a further dimension to the fault-based notion in these cases when observing that the change from central to departmental pay negotiations and agreements was "genuine" and not made in order to avoid the equal pay legislation.[92] If this stands as a reason for the decision, it will compel tribunals to determine the motive behind the fragmentation, a process loaded with problems of proof, causation and the definition

---

[88] Case C-256/01, [2004] I.C.R. 1328 (ECJ).
[89] See now, the Temporary Agency Work Directive 2008/104/EC, which must be implemented by December 5, 2011.
[90] [2005] I.C.R. 750 (CA). Followed in *Armstrong v Newcastle* [2006] I.R.L.R. 124 (CA).
[91] S. Fredman, "Marginalising Equal Pay Laws", (2004) 33(3) ILJ 281, at 283.
[92] [2005] I.C.R. 750, [35].

of intent: it may have been *one* of the motives, or a "background" motive, or an inevitable though unintended consequence. In *Robertson*, one motive was to value workers according to the needs of particular departments. Yet the fragmentation had the obvious consequence of avoiding the harmonising effects of equal pay, and so the distinction between the declared motive and a discriminatory motive is substantially one without a difference.[93] The declared motive should only become relevant at the objective justification stage, where inter alia it can be weighed against its discriminatory effect. Employers should be aware though that where there is sex discrimination in pay, it cannot be justified on the ground that the inequality was the result of separate collective bargaining.[94]

Another apparent reason for the decision in *Robertson* was the **9–017** "flood-gates" argument. Mummery L.J. noted that there were about half a million civil servants and that if the departmental barriers were ignored, to reveal a single employer (the Crown), the "the extravagant consequence" would be "that every civil servant would be entitled to compare himself or herself with any other civil servant of the opposite sex, subject only to objective justification by the employer of differences in pay." This was not "sensible or practical".[95] That reason carries two problems. First, the enthusiasm to avoid the "extravagant" spectacle of numerous "fair pay" claims (where men and women doing equal work use anomalous non-typical comparators to achieve a pay rise) is misplaced, because the matter was addressed some time before in *Glasgow City Council v Marshall*,[96] when the House of Lords ruled that such claims should founder at the "genuine material factor" defence stage because any difference in pay was not due to sex. Second, it ignores the possibility that there may be large scale sex discrimination across departmental pay, as shown in *Morton*. Mummery L.J.'s reasoning erects a barrier to *both* "fair-pay" and genuine claimants, when *Marshall* had already produced a refined solution of allowing the comparison, and then sifting out the "fair-pay" claims at a later stage.

The strongest part of the decision in *Robertson* is its reliance on the "same source" tenet from *Lawrence*. But even that is not watertight. *Lawrence* and *Allonby* were cases with separate employers. The ECJ did not speculate on the position where there is a single employer. Further, the concept of "single source" becomes somewhat blurred where there is separate bargaining but undoubtedly a single ultimate source of the payment, the employer. In the context of *Robertson*, it

---

[93] This point was made by I. Steele, "Tracing the Single Source: Choice of Comparators in Equal Pay Claims", (2005) 34(4) ILJ 338, at 343.

[94] *Enderby v Frenchay HA* Case C-127/92, [1994] I.C.R. 112, [23] (ECJ). See further below, para.9–031.

[95] [2005] I.C.R. 750, [29].

[96] [2000] I.C.R. 196. See below, para.9–030. See also *Strathclyde Regional Council v Wallace* [1998] I.C.R. 205 (HL).

was observed that there is a "trend encouraged by the current government of movement of civil servants between departments, which
reinforces the view of the Civil Service as a single amorphous
entity."[97] Where private sector employers do this, but retain some
control over its workers, by say, the use of mobility clauses, the
distinction between the autonomous establishment and the ultimate
employer becomes even more blurred. The ECJ in *Lawrence* was
concerned that it could not identify a body responsible for the
inequality which could restore equal pay. No such problem exists in
single-employer cases.

   Robertson is an encouragement to private employers to follow their
Government's lead and create separate establishments, each with
autonomous management, with the consequence of avoiding the
equal pay legislation operating across those establishments.[98] As
noted above, after many battles, female cooks in a shipyard could
compare their jobs to painters, while cleaners at a coal mine may
compare themselves to clerical staff, and motor factory seamstresses
may compare themselves to repair workers.[99] At its worst, *Robertson*
suggests that an employer may locate its cooks, cleaners and
seamstresses in separate establishments with separate bargaining, and
then restore these predominantly female occupations to inferior pay,
turning back the clock some 35 years and frustrating the harmonising
ambition of art.157.

4. EQUAL WORK

9–018   Under the Equality Act 2010 Pt 5, Chapter 3 s.65(1), "equal work"
means "like work", work "rated as equivalent" under a job evaluation study, or work of equal value.

(1) Like Work—Section 65(1)(a)
9–019   Under s.65 of the EA 2010 work is "like work" if it is "the same or
broadly similar", and any differences "are not of practical importance
in relation to the terms of their work". It is necessary to have regard
to (a) "the frequency with which differences between their work occur
in practice", and (b) "the nature and extent of the differences."

   Tribunals should approach this question in two stages. First, they
should decide if the comparator's work is the same, or of a "broadly

---

[97] I. Steele, "Tracing the Single Source: Choice of Comparators in Equal Pay Claims", (2005)
34(4) ILJ 338, at 343.
[98] Steele suggests that *Robertson* may be distinguished on the ground that the departmentali-
sation in the civil service was created by statute. See above fn.78, (2005) 34 ILJ 338, at 344.
[99] See n.42 above.

similar nature". Second, they should consider if any differences are of "practical importance".

(a) "Broadly Similar"

"Broadly similar" simply means that a tribunal "should not be   **9–020**
required to undertake a too minute an examination"[100] of the
respective jobs. In *Capper Pass v Lawton*,[101] Ms Lawton cooked 10 to
20 lunches per day for managers and directors and worked a 40-hour
week. Her comparator cooked 350 meals per day in the staff canteen
and worked a 45½ hour week. The EAT held that Ms Lawton did
like work to her comparator.

Back in 1977, the EAT suggested that was not possible for a
woman to compare herself to man doing *inferior* work for more
pay.[102] However, the ECJ, in *Murphy v Bord Telecom Eireann*[103]
stated (in an equal value case), that such logic should not prevail,
because otherwise it would "be tantamount to rendering the principle
of equal pay ineffective and nugatory ... an employer would easily be
able to circumvent the principle by assigning additional or more
onerous duties to workers of a particular sex, who could then be paid
a lower wage." This logic applies equally to like-work cases, and so
s.65 should be given a purposive interpretation.[104]

(b) Differences of "Practical Importance"

The point of this question is to remove spurious or theoretical dif-   **9–021**
ferences, when the jobs are, in reality, broadly the same. In *Shields v
Coomes Holdings*,[105] male workers in a betting shop were paid more
because they had special responsibility for security in shops considered particularly vulnerable to robbery, aggravation and hassle.
The Court of Appeal held that this difference was of no practical
importance. First, in fact no such problems ever arose, so the men's
extra duties were theoretical. Second, the men had no special qualifications to deal with trouble. They were given these responsibilities
simply because they were men. As Lord Denning M.R. observed,
women could be just as capable of dealing with trouble, rather as a
barmaid might deal with trouble differently from a barman.

---

[100] *Capper Pass v Lawton* [1977] Q.B. 852 (EAT), at 857 (Phillips J.).
[101] ibid.
[102] Unless the difference is of no practical importance: *Waddington v Leicester Council for Voluntary Service* [1977] I.C.R. 266, at 270–271.
[103] Case 157/86, [1988] I.C.R. 445, [10].
[104] See e.g. *Redcar & Cleveland BC v Bainbridge (No.1)* [2007] I.R.L.R. 984 (CA).
[105] [1978] I.C.R. 1159 (CA).

Alternatively, a woman may carry a strong physical presence, while "a small nervous man ... could not say 'boo to a goose' ".[106]

Under art.157 the ECJ—in the Vienna Area Health Fund case[107]—has taken a perhaps slightly narrower approach, apparently suggesting that persons doing similar tasks, but with different qualifications, were not comparable. The persons were qualified doctors or qualified psychologists working alongside each other as psychotherapists, save that the doctors could be called upon to perform other tasks in an emergency. It was not clear from the case whether the Court considered this "emergency" duty real or theoretical. If theoretical, then Chapter 3 (according to *Shields v Coomes*) goes further than art.157.

Where the difference is real, there is a practical difference for the purpose of Chapter 3. The difference may be one of supervision, responsibility or skills. In *Eaton v Nuttall*,[108] Phillips J. gave the example of "two book-keepers working side by side doing, so far as actions were concerned, almost identical work, where on an examination of the importance of the work done it could be seen that one was a senior book-keeper and another a junior book-keeper." In *Eaton v Nuttall*, the claimant was a production scheduler responsible for ordering supplies of 2,400 items up to a value of £2.50 each. Her male comparator was also a production scheduler who looked after 1,200 items worth between £5 and £1,000. The EAT held that that as a mistake by the man could prove more expensive, he had more responsibility, and this practical difference meant that he was not doing like work.

9–022 The time when work is performed is not relevant to the comparison. In *Dugdale v Kraft Foods*[109] female quality control inspectors compared themselves with male quality control inspectors from another department, who were paid a higher basic wage. Unlike the women, these men worked night shifts every third Sunday, (and received a separate premium for doing so). The EAT held that the men were doing like work, the only difference being the time at which it was done, which was not a practical difference.[110] It may be that the nature of the night work carries extra burdens and so is not like work to its daytime counterpart. In *Thomas v National Coal Board*[111] female daytime canteen workers used a male night-time canteen worker as a comparator. Here it was found that the night work inherently carried extra responsibility because with fewer people on duty, the night staff would have to deal with emergencies.

---

[106] ibid. at 1172.
[107] *Angestelltenbetriebsrat der Wiener Gebietskrankenhasse v Wiener Gebietskrankenkasse* Case C-309/97, [1999] I.R.L.R. 804.
[108] [1977] I.C.R. 272, at 277 (EAT).
[109] [1977] I.C.R. 48.
[110] Approved by Lord Denning M.R. in *Shields v Coomes Holdings* [1978] I.C.R. 1159 (CA), who also noted that this was required by what is now art.157 TFEU (at 1171).
[111] [1987] I.C.R. 757 (EAT).

Of course, it will be more difficult to recruit for unsocial hours and nightshifts, and if the law prevented a pay difference, recruitment would be near to impossible. Thus, the law allows employers to pay a separate premium to account for the undesirable hours, but this premium must be objectively justified (discussed below, at para.9–038).

(2) Work Rated as Equivalent—Section 65(1)(b)

Where an employer has carried out a job evaluation study, a woman may use the results of that study to bring claim of equal pay. So where her job was rated as equivalent to the job of a male employee, she may use that employee as her comparator. He does not have to be doing like work, so long as the work was rated as equivalent under the study, for instance, a shipyard cook could be rated as doing equivalent work to a shipyard painter. The comparator may be doing work of *less* value.[112] A study may also be used by employers when defending an equal pay claim.[113] The study can be relied on for a claim even if it has not been implemented,[114] but the parties who agreed to carry out the study must have accepted its validity.[115] A study does not have retroactive effect. Nor does it automatically prove equivalence for an equal value claim relating to a period before the study was concluded, although the study "will in no doubt assist in proving equivalence" for this purpose.[116]

9–023

(a) Validity of the Study

Section 65(4) provides that work is rated as equivalent if the study "gives an equal value to [the jobs] ... in terms of the demands made on a worker". No part of the study should be "sex-specific", that is setting "values for men different from those it sets for women." If, after disregarding the sex-specific parts, the study shows equivalence, the claim should proceed.

9–024

The key guidance throughout is objectivity. This means that the jobs of each worker should be valued in terms of the demand made on the worker under various headings, such as training, responsibility and skill. A more expansive definition was given in *Eaton v Nuttall*[117] where the EAT stated that the study should be:

---

[112] *Murphy v Bord Telecom Eireann* Case 157/86, [1988] I.C.R. 445 (ECJ), [10], applied *Redcar & Cleveland BC v Bainbridge (No.1)* [2007] I.R.L.R. 984 (CA).

[113] EA 2010 s.131(5), (6). See below, para.9–027, p.307.

[114] *O'Brien v Sim-Chem Ltd* [1980] I.C.R. 573 (HL), (study not implemented because of Government pay policy).

[115] *Arnold v Beecham Group* [1982] I.C.R. 744, at 752 (EAT).

[116] *Redcar & Cleveland Borough Council v Bainbridge (No.2)* [2008] I.R.L.R. 776, [279]; *Hovell v Ashford and St Peter's Hospital NHS Trust* [2009] I.R.L.R. 734 (CA), [4]–[8].

[117] [1977] I.C.R. 272, at 278–279.

"... thorough in analysis and capable of impartial application. It should be possible by applying the study to arrive at the position of a particular employee at a particular point in a particular salary grade without taking other matters into account except those unconnected with the nature of the work. It will be in order to take into account such matters as merit or seniority, etc.,[118] but any matters concerning the work (e.g. responsibility) one would expect to find taken care of in the evaluation study. One which does not satisfy that test, and requires the management to make a subjective judgment concerning the nature of the work before the employee can be fitted into the appropriate place in the appropriate salary grade, would seem to us not to be a valid study for the purpose of [what is now s.65]."

In *Bromley v Quick*[119] a job evaluation study measured some of the jobs by the demands on the worker, and attributing a value (or weighting) to each demand. The factors used were: skill/training/ experience (43 per cent); mental demands (37 per cent); responsibility (10 per cent); physical environment (7 per cent); and external contacts (3 per cent). After the calculations were done, these jobs were ranked. Then other jobs not covered by the study were "slotted in" using a subjective judgment of how the job, *as a whole*, compared with those ranked in by the study. The Court of Appeal held that the study was analytical and objective but for the last stage ("slotting in"), which was a fatal flaw, and for that reason it did not comply with what is now s.65. Further, it was not saved by a right to appeal given by the employer. However, the court appreciated that any objective study inherently will involve some subjective, or value, judgments, such as the weightings accorded to the job factors.[120]

9–025   In *Rummler v Dato-Druck GmbH*,[121] the ECJ stated that so far as the nature of the work allows, factors should be attributed to it which do not discriminate on the ground of sex. So factors generally favouring women or men can be used where the nature of the job demands it. In *Rummler*, the pay scale in the printing industry was divided into seven grades. The factors used were previous knowledge required, concentration, effort and exertion, and responsibility. According to the study, Grade II jobs could be performed with little previous knowledge and a short training period, a low level of precision, a slight to medium muscular effort, and a slight to medium level of responsibility. Grade III jobs could be performed with a medium previous knowledge and training period, a medium level of precision, a medium to high muscular effort, and a low to medium level of responsibility. Grade IV jobs required previous knowledge

---

[118] For justifying length of service benefits, see below, para.9–039.
[119] [1988] I.C.R. 623 (CA).
[120] ibid. at 632.
[121] Case 237/85, [1987] I.C.R. 774.

gained through task-specific training or, on occasion, lengthy experience on the job, a medium level of precision, medium to high levels of exertion of various kinds, and a medium level of responsibility.

The case centred on the use of physical exertion as a factor. The claimant, a woman classified as Grade II, was required to pack parcels weighing in excess of 20 kg, which *for her* was heavy (rather than medium to heavy) physical work. Accordingly she argued that she should be placed on (a higher) Grade VI. The ECJ rejected this argument, as it would in effect introduce a subjective factor (the strength of the individual, rather than that required by the job). Given that generally men have more physical strength, this would amount to (unlawful) positive sex discrimination.

The general principle of proportionality means that in addition, each factor should be given a proportionate weighting in the overall study. If say, a job required tactful customer relations (favouring females) and physical strength (favouring males), the study should not give a disproportionate weighting to either factor.

(b) Assessing the Study for Equivalence
In *Hovell v Ashford and St Peter's Hospital NHS Trust*[122] the Court of Appeal stated that where the study presented a small difference between the claimant's and her comparator's job, a tribunal was not obliged to treat them as equal: "equal value does not mean nearly equal value". On the other hand, "a slavish attachment to the marks scored suggests a degree of precision which the assessment of job value cannot bear." The difference may be caused by a number of reasons:

9–026

> "Jobs may be equal in value even though not precisely equal in the points scored. It may be, for example, that a particular factor is given a weighting in the job evaluation study which would not normally be provided for in a simple one-on-one job comparison. Or the employee might be able to show that her tasks have in the past differed, perhaps only in minor ways, from the typical job profile which is measured in the JES, but nonetheless sufficient to bridge any small gap. Perhaps in the JES certain jobs were not the subject of very detailed scrutiny because it was clear that they would fall within a particular grade boundary, and no one was too concerned precisely where they fell."[123]

---

[122] [2009] I.R.L.R. 734 (CA).
[123] ibid. [35].

This shows that assessment of the study could be fact-sensitive, and bearing in mind the onus is on the claimant, using a study for an equal pay claim may not be straightforward.

3. Work of Equal Value—Section 65(1)(c)

9–027   Section 65(1)(c) entitles a woman to compare herself with a man doing a different job, so long as it is work of equal value (rather than just "like work"). In *Hayward v Cammell Laird Shipbuilders Ltd (No.2)*,[124] Ms Hayward, a canteen cook in a shipyard, was able to compare her work to that of a painter, a decorator and a thermal insulation engineer. The claimant may also compare herself to a man doing work of a lesser value.[125] More recently, there has been a raft of equal value claims following the negotiation of a Single Status Agreement between local authorities and trade unions. This has led to claims by women in predominantly female occupations, such as catering and care work, comparing their work with men in predominantly male occupations, such as road cleaning and gardening.[126]

A claimant is *reasonably* free to choose her comparator. In *Pickstone v Freemans*[127] the House of Lords held that a woman could use a comparator doing different work (of the same value) for more money, even though there was another man doing the same work, for the same money (see above, para.9–004). This also makes sense in more complex cases. Equal value claims can be fraught with evidential difficulties and, at an early stage, a woman may suspect that she is doing work of equal value to several men, each in a different job on different pay. The quandary for the claimant is that if she plumps for a comparator very obviously doing work of equal or lesser value, the resulting pay increase is likely to be minimal. If she opts for the man on the highest pay, her chances of proving that he is doing work of equal value are likely to be reduced. To achieve an optimal result, a claimant may bring several comparators into court. But she may face hostility from the tribunal, inspired by this observation made by the Lord Bridge:

> "I think that industrial tribunals should, so far as possible, be alert to prevent abuse of the equal value claims procedure by applicants who cast their net over too wide a spread of comparators. To take an extreme case, an applicant who claimed equality with A who earns £X and also with B who earns £2X

---

[124] [1988] A.C. 894 (HL).
[125] *Murphy v Bord Telecom Eireann* Case 157/86, [1988] I.C.R. 445 (ECJ), see further above para.9–020.
[126] See e.g. *Gibson v Sheffield CC* [2010] I.R.L.R. 311 (CA); *Redcar & Cleveland Borough Council v Bainbridge (No.2)* [2008] I.R.L.R. 776 (CA).
[127] [1988] I.C.R. 697 (HL).

could hardly complain if an industrial tribunal concluded that her claim of equality with A itself demonstrated that there were no reasonable grounds for her claim of equality with B."[128]

This "extreme case" is not a helpful guide for tribunals when deciding if claimants have "cast their net too wide". All that can be taken from this dictum is that too many comparators may amount to an abuse of process. Tribunals are well familiar with abuse of process principles and should have no trouble applying them in this context.

The most obvious obstacle to a claim at the early stage is the existence of a job evaluation study already carried out by the employer, which places the claimant below the value of her comparator(s). This will defeat a claim unless the tribunal has reasonable grounds for suspecting that it is discriminatory or otherwise unreliable.[129]

5. Defending Equal Pay Claims

The Equality Act 2010 introduced a new formula for defending equal pay claims:

9–028

69 Defence of material factor

(1) The sex equality clause in A's terms has no effect in relation to a difference between A's terms and B's terms if the responsible person shows that the difference is because of a material factor reliance on which—

    (a) does not involve treating A less favourably because of A's sex than the responsible person treats B, and

    (b) if the factor is within subsection (2), is a proportionate means of achieving a legitimate aim.

(2) A factor is within this subsection if A shows that, as a result of the factor, A and persons of the same sex doing work equal to A's are put at a particular disadvantage when compared with persons of the opposite sex doing work equal to A's.

This provides, potentially, two defences, one to direct discrimination and one to indirect discrimination. This is because the new formula adopts the conventional concepts of direct and indirect discrimination. It envisages the following process. First, the claimant raises a

---

[128] *Leverton v Clwyd CC* [1989] A.C. 706 (HL), at 751–752. The House concurred in Lord Bridge's speech.
[129] See ER 2010 s.131(5), (6). Discussed above, para.9–024.

presumption that the difference in pay is because of the claimant's sex. The employer then may show that the inferior pay is not because of the claimant's sex. If the employer fails to do this, it is liable. (There is no defence to direct discrimination.) Otherwise, the claimant may now prove[130] the disparity was caused by indirect discrimination. If she achieves this, the burden switches to the employer to show that the cause is a material factor that "is a proportionate means of achieving a legitimate aim", in other words it must objectively justify the difference.

(1) Transparency

9–029 Some pay structures and levels have often developed piecemeal and it may be difficult or impossible for the employer to show the extent to which particular factors contribute to overall pay. Nonetheless, the employer carries the onus of explaining any pay difference. In *Danfoss*,[131] the ECJ held that if a female worker establishes, in relation to a relatively large number of employees, that the average pay for women is less than that for men, and the employer's system of pay is "totally lacking in transparency", it is for the employer to prove that its pay system is not discriminatory.

(2) Fair Pay and Equal Pay

9–030 In *Glasgow CC v Marshall*[132] special-school instructors were doing the same work as teachers for less pay. Seven female instructors compared themselves with a male teacher. At the same time, a *male* instructor compared himself with a female teacher. However, there was no sex disparity between the two groups (females made up about 96 per cent instructors and 97 per cent teachers). The House of Lords held that by showing a difference in pay, the claimants raised a rebuttable presumption of sex discrimination.[133] The House then applied the "material factor" defence (in the previous Equal Pay Act 1970), and held simply that as the employer had shown there "is not

---

[130] The burden is on the claimant: *Nelson v Carrilion* [2003] I.R.L.R. 428 (CA). Subsequently, the Court of Appeal, in *Gibson v Sheffield CC* [2010] I.R.L.R. 311 (CA), [67], doubted this: "there are powerful arguments for saying that *Nelson* was wrongly decided". However, s.69(2) endorses *Nelson*.

[131] *Handels-og Kontorfunktionaerernes Forbund i Danmark v Dansk Arbejdsgiverforening (acting for Danfoss)* Case 109/88, [1989] I.R.L.R. 532, [16]. See also *Barton v Investec* [2003] I.C.R. 1205 (EAT), below para.9–037.

[132] [2000] I.C.R. 196 (HL).

[133] ibid. at p.203.

the difference of sex", it was not required to objectively justify the difference in pay. Otherwise it would be:

> "... a curious result in a sex discrimination case that, on the same facts, claims by women and a claim by a man all succeed."[134]

Marshall seems to have been understood by some to mean that employers are only obliged to objectively justify a difference in pay in cases of indirect discrimination where a facially neutral practice, criterion or provision is applied that adversely affects a higher proportion of women than men, and not in an "*Enderby*-type" situation where statistics alone are enough to oblige the employer to justify the disparity (see below). For instance, in *Armstrong v Newcastle upon Tyne NHS Hospital Trust*,[135] Buxton L.J. said:

> "Once disparate adverse impact has been established, the burden passes to the employer in respect of two issues. First, that the difference between the man's and the woman's contract is not discriminatory, in the sense of being attributable to a difference of gender. Second, if the employer cannot show that the difference in treatment was not attributable to a difference of gender he must then demonstrate that there was nonetheless an objective justification for the difference ...".[136]

On the face of it, this may not appear controversial. But consider the following two discussions in the context of the gender pay gap.

(a) Fair Pay and "Enderby-type" Indirect Discrimination— Section 69(2)

The phrase "a difference in gender" (from *Armstrong*, above) is key **9–031** here, and rather ambiguous. It could be doing no more than excluding from further scrutiny the "facade" type of case that arose in *Marshall* (the narrow view). Some commentators fear it goes further: that there is no need to objectively justify certain cases of indirect discrimination (the wide view).[137] These are equal pay claims based solely on statistics showing, say, one occupation (predominantly female) being paid more than another (predominantly or exclusively male), where the occupations are of equal value. Here, the employer

---

[134] ibid. at p.202 (Lord Nicholls, giving the unanimous judgment).
[135] [2006] I.R.L.R. 124, see also [32]–[33] (Arden L.J.). Approved with caveats, in *Gibson v Sheffield CC* [2010] I.R.L.R. 311 (CA), [59]–[72] (Smith L.J.), [73]–[74] (Maurice Kay L.J.) but doubted [49] (Pill L.J.), and doubted in *Villalba v Merrill Lynch* [2007] I.C.R. 469 (EAT), [131] (Elias J.).
[136] ibid. [110]. See also Arden L.J. at [32]–[33].
[137] See I. Steele, "Sex Discrimination and the Material Factor Defence under the Equal Pay Act 1970 and the Equality Act 2010" (2010) 39 ILJ 264.

points to an innocent cause of the disparity, and is then freed from
having to objectively justify it (in other words showing a "good"
reason[138] for the disparity). Such a case arose in *Enderby v Frenchay
Health Authority*[139] where the employer paid pharmacists (63 per cent
female) 40 per cent more than speech therapists (98 per cent female).
An industrial tribunal found that the collective bargaining agreements that had led to respective different pay structures for the these
occupations were in no way sex-tainted and rejected the claim.[140] But
the ECJ held that the statistics alone were enough to oblige the
employer to objectively justify the disparity. The wide view of *Armstrong* holds that such an employer would not now have the justify
the disparity. If this is correct, *Armstrong* must be wrong. This is
because simply *every* case of indirect discrimination involves, by its
nature, facially neutral or "innocent" behaviour. The reason it comes
up for legal scrutiny is its discriminatory *effect*. Proving that the *cause*
is not tainted by sex is meaningless in the context of indirect discrimination. Further, the *Marshall* decision was concerned primarily
with distinguishing "fair pay" claims from sex discrimination.
Enderby-type claims are rooted in sex discrimination, and any doubts
over this were laid to rest by the ECJ's decision. Whatever the merits
of that debate, the wide view of *Armstrong* cannot stand for the bald
fact it contradicts the ECJ authority of *Enderby*.[141] In spite of this, the
new s.69(2) does little to clarify the matter. For objective justification
to apply, the claimant must show that women "are put at a particular
disadvantage" as a result of the material factor. Take this variation of
Enderby-type case. Suppose a historic event, such as the implementation of a collective agreement, afforded less pay to one occupation. At the time it had no discriminatory impact because each
occupation comprised similar proportions of men and women.
However, over the years the lesser paid occupation became predominantly female and statistics now show overwhelmingly that
women are disadvantaged by the pay structure.[142] It is arguable that
at the time it was implemented, the collective agreement had no
adverse impact on women, and that a strained interpretation is
required to comply with *Enderby*. The "innocent" factor (the collective agreement) which would have been put forward to escape
liability for direct discrimination under s.69(1)(a), is what *now* causes

---

[138] *Glasgow CC v Marshall* [2000] I.C.R. 196 at p.203 (Lord Nicholls, giving the unanimous
    judgment).
[139] Case C-127/92, [1994] I.C.R. 112 (ECJ). See further, below, para.9–034. See also *Brunnhofer*,
    discussed below. For the problem of presenting discrimination cases based on statistics in the
    United States, see *Wards Cove v Atonio* 490 US 642 (Sup Ct 1989) and its part-codification,
    part-reversal, by the Civil Rights Act 1991. Discussed, M. Connolly "Discrimination law
    and the quota fear in Britain and the United States" (2005) 6 I.J.D.L. 325.
[140] Paras 10.1–10.5, reported [1991] EAT 382 (EAT), at p.396.
[141] See *Villalba v Merrill Lynch* [2007] I.C.R. 469 (EAT), [131] (Elias J.)
[142] See *Middlesbrough BC v Surtees (No.1)* [2007] I.R.L.R. 869 (EAT), [54] (Elias J.). Reversed
    on other grounds: [2008] I.R.L.R. 776 (CA).

the adverse impact.[143] It is also arguable (more simply) that the collective agreement presently dictates or influences the pay, and so women *are* put a disadvantage by it.

Section 69(2) places the burden on the claimant to identify the factor that caused the adverse impact. In *Enderby*-type cases, the prima case has no such factor. The bald statistics establish the case. This should not (normally, at least) defeat the claim, because the employer would have identified the factor when defending direct discrimination at the first stage.

(b) Fair Pay and Direct Discrimination—Section 69(1)(a)
The use of the word "because" in s.69(1)(a) (which also is used for   **9–032**
direct discrimination, s.13) effectively states that the employer must prove the pay difference was not caused by direct discrimination. It has to: (1) identify the whole reason(s) for the disparity, and (2) prove that the reason(s) was not sex-related.

This will be a straightforward task in some cases, such as the "facade" scenario in *Marshall*. Other cases will be fact-sensitive, with a tribunal having to draw inferences of discrimination from much indirect evidence.[144]

Section 69, confining claims to direct or indirect discrimination, entrenches the notion that Chapter 3 is about sex discrimination, rather than eliminating all sex inequality in pay. There are many cases where the disparity in pay is not the result of sex discrimination, but neither is the disparity there for a "good" business-related reason.[145] Thus, a woman remains on less pay than a comparable man for no good reason, because Chapter 3 does not reach that far. For instance, in *Parliamentary Commissioner for Administration v Fernandez*,[146] the claimant, a barrister, was employed as a case worker with the Parliamentary Ombudsman. The comparator was a case worker for the Health Service Ombudsman, a different department within the same overall office. The disparity comprised: (1) a difference in starting salary (£423); (2) a payment of an allowance only to the comparator (£1,500); (3) a difference in the performance-related salary increase following the annual appraisal (£1,520). The first two differences arose because the claimant had asked for a higher starting salary before accepting the post, and had then later pressed for a pay rise. The EAT, following *Marshall* (above, para.9–030) held that as the employer had showed that the differences were not because of sex

---

[143] See I. Steele, "Sex Discrimination and the Material Factor Defence under the Equal Pay Act 1970 and the Equality Act 2010" 39 ILJ 264, 273–274, who also finds support for this view in the legislative history.

[144] See Ch.12, para.12–008.

[145] *Glasgow CC v Marshall* [2000] I.C.R. 196 at p.203 (Lord Nicholls, giving the unanimous judgment).

[146] [2004] I.C.R. 123. Followed, *Villalba v Merrill Lynch & Co* [2007] I.C.R. 469 (EAT).

discrimination, it did not have to objectively justify them. There will be variations of this type of case. The employer may have given a pay rise because it enjoyed the working relationship, and/or did not want to lose the worker and go to the trouble of rehiring, or simply wanted to reward a pleasant working relationship with a goodwill gesture. If these reasons accounted for the whole of the disparity, the woman remains on less pay, and the gender pay gap is not addressed fully. The decision in *Fernandez* was perhaps more palatable because the claimant was a man.

This more ambitious approach was expressed by the ECJ in *Brunnhofer*.[147] Here, a female bank worker was paid less than a male doing the same work, ostensibly because his work was of a higher standard. The ECJ held that the pay difference had to be objectively justified, stating that the principle of equal pay "prohibits comparable situations from being treated differently unless the difference is objectively justified."[148]

9–033   *Brunnhofer* was followed by the EAT in *Sharp v Caledonia Group Services Ltd.*[149] Here, the claimant was a managing accountant, while her comparator was a personal assistant to Lord Cayzer, and later an office manager. The EAT accepted that the (non-discriminatory) reason for the comparator's better pay was his personal relationship with Lord Cayzer and that this was a material factor that was not based on sex. Nonetheless, applying *Brunnhofer*, the employer still was obliged to objectively justify the difference.

Brunnhofer is a major obstacle to even the narrow view of *Armstrong*. As such, British courts have tended to ignore it,[150] sheltering under the lengthy and detailed analysis provided by Elias J. which concluded that "objectively" as expressed in *Brunnhofer* was used in the "causative and not the justificatory sense". In other words, if objective factors showed the cause of difference was not sex, then there would be no liability.[151] Consequently, Elias J. disapproved of *Sharp*.

The debate comes to this. Should the equal pay legislation be limited to sex discrimination, or go further and address any situation where a woman is being paid less than a comparable man (or vice versa). If the latter, "equal pay has broken loose from its moorings in

---

[147] *Brunnhofer v Bank der Österreichischen Postsparkasse* Case C-381/99, [2001] I.R.L.R. 571.
[148] ibid. [28]. See also *Lawrence v Regent Office Care* Case C-320/00, [2003] I.C.R. 1092 (ECJ), [12]
[149] [2006] I.C.R. 218 (EAT).
[150] *Brunnhofer* was not discussed in *Armstrong v Newcastle Upon Tyne NHS Hospital Trust* [2006] I.R.L.R. 124 (CA) nor *Gibson v Sheffield CC* [2010] I.R.L.R. 311 (CA).
[151] *Villalba v Merrill Lynch & Co* [2007] I.C.R. 469 (EAT), [149], see also [152]. Elias J. dedicated some 15 pages to the matter (paras 124–185). He also considered the wide view of *Armstrong* was wrong [131] (see above, para.9–030). The EAT has deferred to this opinion when dismissing *Brunnhofer*: *Middlesbrough BC v Surtees (No.1)* [2007] I.R.L.R. 869 (EAT), [23]. Reversed on other grounds: [2008] I.R.L.R. 776 (CA).

discrimination law."[152] This would bring practical difficulties, such as men making "fair pay" claims (*Fernandez* or *Marshall*). On the other hand, this would help close the gender pay gap and "be a price worth paying for the elimination of inequality in pay which was a key foundation" of the EU.[153] British courts generally, and s.69 in particular, has plumped for the former "discrimination" model. It is now for the ECJ either to reinforce *Brunnhofer*, or reinterpret it.

(3) Objective Justification

Section 69 maintains that only cases of indirect discrimination need be objectively justified. The formula for objective justification was provided by the ECJ in *Bilka-Kaufhaus v Weber von Hartz*,[154] which itself is rooted in the Community law principle of proportionality,[155] and is generally known as the "*Bilka* test". The employer must show (1) there was a legitimate aim, and that the means of achieving the legitimate aim were (2) appropriate, and (3) necessary. This formula is restated in the UK legislation, and for equal pay by s.69(1)(b), as "a proportionate means of achieving a legitimate aim", with "proportionate means" encapsulating stages (2) and (3) of *Bilka*.

"Necessity" encapsulates two further stages. The defence should not succeed where there exists a less discriminatory alternative. For instance, in *Enderby v Frenchay Health Authority*[156] the employer paid pharmacists (63 per cent female) 40 per cent more than speech therapists (98 per cent female). There was a need to attract a sufficient number of pharmacists (the "legitimate aim"), so they were paid more (an appropriate means), but only a 10 per cent premium was *necessary* to achieve that aim, so only 10 per cent of the pay difference could be justified. In other words, there existed a less discriminatory alternative of paying pharmacists a 10 per cent premium. In addition, a court may have to balance any discriminatory effect of the challenged practice against the benefits of achieving the legitimate aim. For instance, in *R. v Secretary of State, ex parte Equal Opportunities Commission*[157] Lord Keith held that Regulations that afforded inferior benefits to part-time workers constituted a "gross breach of the principle of equal pay and could not be possibly regarded as a suitable means of achieving an increase in part-time employment."

9–034

---

[152] *Middlesbrough BC v Surtees* [2007] I.R.L.R. 869 (EAT), [23] (Elias J.). Reversed on other grounds: [2008] I.R.L.R. 776 (CA).

[153] An argument put forward by Robin Allen QC in *Villalba v Merrill Lynch & Co* [2007] I.C.R. 469 (EAT), [50].

[154] Case 170/84, [1987] I.C.R. 110, [36].

[155] See the *Cassis de Dijon* case, C-120/78 (*Rewe-Zentral AG v Bundesmonopolverwaltung für Branntwein*) [1979] E.C.R. 649.

[156] Case C-127/92, [1994] I.C.R. 112 (ECJ). See above, para.9–031. Applied *Cumbria CC v Dow* [2008] I.R.L.R. 91 [105] (Elias J.): "It is not enough to establish that some differential is justified without giving the tribunal a proper evidential basis for determining whether it is the whole amount or something short of it."

[157] [1995] 1 A.C. 1 (HL) at p.30.

It seems that factors considered and discounted from the equal work question may used again in the objective justification defence. In *Christie v Haith*[158] the EAT held that factors used in the job evaluation could also be relied on as factors for the objective justification. The comparators' work was slightly more heavy and dirty. Nonetheless, the tribunal found their work to be of equal value. But then it held the pay difference was justified because the comparators were doing slightly heavier and more dirty work. Rubenstein commented:

> "It is illogical that a difference in effort (or skill or responsibility) should not be sufficiently important to make two jobs of unequal value and yet the same difference should be treated as sufficient to negate the equal pay claim of applicants employed on work of equal value."[159]

The decision also clouds this already difficult process. All litigants would benefit if they knew there were clear boundaries between the factors available to the comparison and the defence.

What follows are number of examples of the defence in operation.

(a) Economic Reasons

9–035   In *Jenkins v Kingsgate (Clothing Productions) Ltd,*[160] the ECJ held that lower pay (measured pro-rata) for (predominantly female) part-time workers could be justified by economic factors, which were in this case encouraging full-time work to achieve better utilisation of the employer's machinery and to discourage absenteeism. An "economic reason" was also approved in *Bilka,*[161] where a department store wanted to discourage part-time work (by excluding part-time workers from its pension scheme), because part-time workers generally refuse to work late afternoons and Saturdays. In *Cumbria CC v Dow (No.1)*[162] the EAT accepted that productivity bonuses for one (predominantly male) group of workers could justify a pay disparity. In the event, they did not, because the bonus arrangements were no longer properly enforced and made no difference to productivity.

---

[158] [2003] I.R.L.R. 670, applying *Davies v McCartneys* [1989] I.C.R. 707 (EAT).
[159] [2003] I.R.L.R. Highlights, October.
[160] Case 96/80, [1981] ECR 911, [12] (ECJ), applied by the EAT [1981] I.C.R. 715, esp. at pp.723–724.
[161] *Bilka-Kaufhaus v Weber von Hartz* Case 170/84, [1987] I.C.R. 110, [36] (ECJ).
[162] [2008] I.R.L.R. 91 (EAT), [129]–[136]. See further below, para.9–036.

(b) Market Forces

In *Rainey v Greater Glasgow Health Board*,[163] in order to establish a new NHS prosthetic service, 20 existing private-sector prosthetists were recruited on their private-sector wage. All 20 were men. Subsequent recruits were paid on the lower Whitley scale, a national agreement for ancillary health service staff. A newly recruited female prosthetist claimed equal pay with the higher paid men. The House of Lords held that the pay difference was justified by the need to attract from the private sector in order to establish the service. The law was refined in *Enderby v Frenchay Health Authority*[164] where the employer paid pharmacists (63 per cent female) 40 per cent more than speech therapists (98 per cent female), apparently to attract a sufficient number of pharmacists. But the evidence was that only a 10 per cent premium was necessary to achieve that aim, so only a 10 per cent pay difference was justified. Thus, employers must be able to show with some precision that *all* the difference can be attributed to the market forces.

9–036

A lack of precision, to say the least, was apparent in *Cumbria CC v Dow (No.1)*.[165] The council paid road workers (overwhelmingly male) a productivity bonus because inter alia it would otherwise lose them to the private sector. Carers (overwhelmingly female) doing equal work were paid no such bonus. The EAT held that evidence that the council had no recruitment problem with the road workers did not necessarily justify the bonuses: it may have been because "the council was paying over the odds".[166] The case was remitted to an employment tribunal to decide if the bonus was necessary, and if so to what extent.

In principle, a defence of market forces is questionable. As Lord Denning M.R. observed in *Clay Cross (Quarry Services) Ltd v Fletcher*:[167]

> "An employer cannot avoid his obligations under the Act by saying: "I paid him more because he asked for more," or "I paid her less because she was willing to come for less." If any such excuse were permitted, the Act would be a dead letter. Those are the very reasons why there was unequal pay before the statute."

In *Clay Cross* the claimant sales clerk sought equal pay with a male sales clerk appointed on higher pay, to match his previous wage. The Court of Appeal held that this market forces factor fell outside of the "personal equation" between the claimant and the comparator. The

---

[163] [1987] A.C. 224. See "Market forces and the equal value material factor defence" (1986) 5 EOR 5.
[164] Case C-127/92, [1994] I.C.R. 112 (ECJ).
[165] [2008] I.R.L.R. 91 (EAT). See also *Gibson v Sheffield CC* [2010] I.C.R. 708 (CA).
[166] ibid. [106] (Elias J.).
[167] [1979] I.C.R. 1 (CA), at 6.

House of Lords in *Rainey* stated that this was "unduly restrictive",[168] but at the same time approved of Browne-Wilkinson J.'s observation in *Jenkins v Kingsgate* that market forces reasons should not include obtaining "cheap female labour".[169] This suggests that not all market forces factors can be used, and the *decision* of *Clay Cross* has survived *Rainey*. In *Ratcliffe v North Yorkshire County Council*,[170] school catering assistants claimed equal pay with men in jobs such as road sweepers and gardeners, with whom they had been rated as equivalent under the local government revaluation scheme. Their pay was lower to compete with private contractors for the supply of school meals. The House of Lords rejected this defence. The feature of *Ratcliffe* was lower wages for a predominantly female occupation, and whatever the technical difficulties with the decision, it is supportable on policy grounds.

(c) Merit and Bonus Payments

9–037   In principle these are permissible, as long as the system is transparent, and the payments are proportionate. In *Danfoss*,[171] a collective agreement allowed the employer to make additional payments to individuals within a grade on the basis of the employee's "flexibility", which was defined as including an assessment of their capacity, quality of work, autonomy of work and responsibilities. In addition, pay could be increased on the basis of the employee's vocational training and seniority. But the workers were only informed of the amount of their increased wages. They could not determine the relationship of any particular criterion to the increases. Thus, workers were unable to compare their additional payments even against workers within the same grade. The average pay of women was 6.85 per cent less than that of men. The ECJ held that once the claimant had shown lower average wage for women, the "total lack of transparency" meant that it was for the employer to show that the system was not discriminatory. The Court further noted first, that payments for higher quality work were gender-neutral, but at the same time it was "inconceivable" that the women's work was of generally lower quality. So if the difference in pay shows that a gender neutral criterion had been *applied* in a discriminatory manner, it was not justifiable. Second, that a criterion of "flexibility" in the sense of being able to work various times, or at different locations, may operate to the disadvantage of women who will generally find it more difficult to organise their working time in a flexible manner. This, of course, will prove much more difficult to justify. Third, employers

---

[168] [1987] A.C. 224, at 235.
[169] ibid. at 237, citing [1981] I.C.R. 715, at 727 (EAT).
[170] [1995] I.C.R. 837. See also *Cumbria CC v Dow (No.1)* [2008] I.R.L.R. 91 (EAT).
[171] *Handels-og Kontorfunktionaerernes Forbund i Danmark v Dansk Arbejdsgiverforening (acting for Danfoss)* Case 109/88, [1989] I.R.L.R. 532 (ECJ). See also para.9–029.

may justify rewarding specific vocational training by demonstrating that that training is of importance for the performance of the specific duties entrusted to the worker.

This approach was taken up by the EAT in *Barton v Investec Henderson Crosthwaite Securities*.[172] The claimant was a City fund manager. She earned the same basic salary (£105,000) as her comparator, and was awarded 7,500 share options. Other firms tried to poach the comparator, and to avoid the prospect of him being headhunted, his salary was raised to £150,000, he was given a "long-term incentive" payment of £75,000, and awarded 12,000 share options. The employer produced no evidence as to the basis upon which bonuses could be paid, disclosing only the payments made to the claimant and her comparator. The employment tribunal found that the difference in pay was justified, stating that "it is a vital component of the City bonus culture that bonuses are discretionary, scheme rules are unwritten and individuals' bonuses are not revealed," and that "the cultural reason for this is that invidious comparisons would become inevitable. If such comparisons were generally possible the bonus system would collapse."[173] The EAT held that the tribunal was in error to endorse this lack of transparency and that it was for the employer to prove that sex was not a reason for difference in pay.

Where the bonus or premium is unrealistic, disproportionate or **9–038** even a sham, the tribunal should adjust the wages so that the premium does no more than properly reflect its legitimate aim. Most litigation on this issue has arisen with premiums paid for working undesirable hours. In *National Coal Board v Sherwin*[174] the industrial tribunal heard evidence that inconvenient hours should attract a 20 per cent premium and adjusted the wage structure accordingly. The EAT approved. The difficulty with this is that it resembles wage-setting, a task beyond a tribunal's jurisdiction. Nonetheless, in *Enderby v Frenchay AHA*,[175] the ECJ took a similar line, but with the rider that where it is not possible to determine how much of the pay difference is due to market forces, it must decide if market forces can justify the whole difference. This rider appears to encourage a lack of transparency in premiums. However, as the ECJ stated in *Danfoss*,[176] a prima facie case of equal pay will force an employer to make its wage structure transparent, otherwise it will not be able to show that the difference is not due to sex. Thus, if an employer comes to court stating that premiums are paid to recruit night workers, but without any evidence of how much extra is required for this recruitment, it runs the risk of the whole premium being ruled as discriminatory.

---

[172] [2003] I.C.R. 1205 (EAT).
[173] Reported ibid. [10].
[174] [1978] I.C.R. 700.
[175] Case C-127/92, [1994] I.C.R. 112. See further paras 9–031 and 9–036.
[176] *Handels-og Kontorfunktionaerernes Forbund i Danmark v Dansk Arbejdsgiverforening (acting for Danfoss)* Case C-109/88, [1989] I.R.L.R. 532, at [11]–[16]. See further above para.9–029.

Where the claimants prove that they are doing equal work, despite doing it at a different time, the employer may still escape liability by justifying the extra pay for unsocial hours. In *Blackburn v Chief Constable of West Midlands Police*,[177] the Force paid a supplement for night work. The women claimants were unable to do night work because of their childcare responsibilities, and thus were not paid the supplement. The employment tribunal found that although the need for a 24/7 service was a legitimate aim, paying the supplement to those women would have cost relatively little (less than £20,000 on the annual wage bill), and this cost was outweighed by the discriminatory impact of the policy. Further, it had been shown to work in other forces. The EAT and Court of Appeal reversed. The EAT said that, if the legitimate aim is to reward 24/7 working, it is "difficult to see how that objective is achieved if those who do not work nights are also paid the same amount."[178]

(d) Seniority and Length of Service Benefits[179]

9–039   As a rule, length of service benefits will disadvantage women, who are more likely to have an interrupted career and/or start a career late, because of child bearing and child rearing. The general rule is that employers *do not* have to justify these benefits. In *Cadman v Health & Safety Executive*,[180] the ECJ departed from its familiar strict approach to equal pay. Mrs Cadman was employed by the HSA as head of a Field Management Unit. While she was paid around £35,000 pa, four male colleagues on the same grade were paid anything from £39,000 to £44,000, a pay gap ranging from £4,000 to £9,000. This difference was the result of a length of service criterion in the pay structure, which had a disparate impact on women. The ECJ held first, that "rewarding experience acquired which enables the worker to perform his duties better" is a legitimate objective. The general rule was that the "employer does not have to establish specifically that [a length of service criterion] ... is appropriate to attain that objective as regards a particular job." The qualification arises only "where the worker provides evidence ... giving rise to serious doubts as to whether recourse to the criterion of length of service is, in the circumstances, appropriate to attain the ... objective".[181] Once the duty to justify has been triggered, the Court made clear that the employer's justification need only relate to the job, and not any particular individual. This objective approach means that there is no need to show that "an individual worker has acquired experience

---

[177] [2009] I.R.L.R. 135 (CA).
[178] ibid. [40].
[179] For a detailed exploration, see D. Rowbottom, "Justifying Service-Related Pay in the Context of Sex Discrimination Law" (2010) 39 ILJ 382.
[180] Case C-17/05, [2006] I.C.R. 1623 (ECJ).
[181] ibid. [38].

during the relevant period which has enabled him to perform his duties better."[182] While the decision, signalling a light touch to length of service benefits, would have been welcomed by some, it did little for legal certainty. If it means that the claimant has to show that the benefit is *not* appropriate, then it goes against the established rules on the burden of proof, which state it is for the employer to prove an otherwise discriminatory practice is appropriate (and necessary) to achieve the legitimate aim, presumably better job performance.[183]

The situation was rescued somewhat by the Court of Appeal's subsequent decision in *Wilson v Health and Safety Executive*[184] (a case related to *Cadman*). It held that the "serious doubts" mantra was merely a "filter" at the preliminary stage, and not at trial. It did not shift the burden to the claimant of showing the practice was *not* justified. That squares it with the burden of proof rules.[185] Once the "serious doubts" test has been satisfied, the general rule falls away and the employer must objectively justify the scheme in the normal way. Even if this were not the position in EU law, domestic legislation carried no exception for length of service benefits, and workers could rely on this. EU law did not reduce workers' rights in this regard.[186]

(e) Pay Protection or "Red-circling"

A person who is unable to continue with a job because of illness or redundancy, may be able to take an alternative job in the workplace. He may be retained and paid at his existing rate, and in some cases, continue to receive the customary pay rises due under his old job. This practice is called "red-circling", or more often nowadays "pay-protection". Where the difference comes about by direct discrimination, it cannot be justified.[187]

9–040

However, where the higher pay is rooted in *indirect* sex discrimination, the employer may be able to objectively justify the difference. Section 69(3) of the EA 2010, confirms (for the first time) that "the long-term objective of reducing inequality between men's and women's terms of work is always to be regarded as a legitimate aim." Thus, the employer must show that the pay protection scheme is appropriate and necessary to achieve that aim. Section 69(3) has roots in the Court of Appeal's opinion in *Redcar v Bainbridge*.[188]

---

[182] ibid. [38]. See especially in this regard *Rummler* Case 237/85 [1987] I.C.R. 774 (ECJ).
[183] See now, Recast Directive 2006/54/EC, art.19. (See also EA 2010, s.136.)
[184] [2010] I.C.R. 302.
[185] ibid. [47]–[50].
[186] ibid. [69]–[71].
[187] Case C-408/92 *Smith v Avdel* [1994] I.R.L.R. 602 (ECJ), [25]–[27]; *Snoxell v Vauxhall Motors*; *Charles Early and Marriott (Witney) Ltd v Smith and Ball* [1978] 1 Q.B. 11, approved in *Redcar* [2009] I.C.R. 133 (CA), [104].
[188] *Redcar and Cleveland BC v Bainbridge; Middlesbrough Borough Council v Surtees, Redcar and Cleveland Borough Council v Bainbridge (No.2)* [2009] I.C.R. 133 (CA).

Here, after reclassifying a range of jobs (including road cleaners, gardeners and carers) to ensure equal pay, local authorities negotiated transitional pay protection for some workers whose pay was due to drop. It meant that male-dominated jobs such as road cleaning and gardening (which were to lose their bonuses) were paid temporarily a supplement to ensure a "soft landing". Meanwhile, the female-dominated carers (who were never entitled to a bonus) were given no such payment. The Court of Appeal stated it was possible to objectively justify transitional pay protection, but warned that where the employer is knowingly trying to correct past discrimination and continues it through the pay protection arrangement, by analogy to the rule on direct discrimination, it "will have great difficulty" in justifying it. On the other hand, where it has "no reason to think" that the old arrangements were indirectly discriminatory, it will be easier to justify.[189] Given that they are now obliged to make an equality impact assessment any transitional arrangements, justification seems a remote possibility for local authorities.[190]

In this conjoined case, the Court of Appeal upheld the employment tribunals' decisions, that in one case the pay protection was not justified because the authority was aware of any discriminatory impact. In the second case, it was not justified because the authority had not calculated the size of the disadvantaged group nor the cost of including or excluding it from the scheme.[191]

Any goal of equality which is *long term* seems counter-intuitive or even offensive to a discrimination lawyer. Yet, in *Bainbridge*, even the Equality and Human Rights Commission petitioned for justification, presumably in a pragmatic move to encourage unions and employers alike to embark upon reclassifying jobs where inferior pay structures had become entrenched in typically female occupations. In a different context (length of service benefits) the Court of Appeal has asserted:

> "The right to equal pay, and the right not to be discriminated against on the grounds of sex, are both aspects of a wider principle of equal treatment. ... It is not ... simply a right to be achieved progressively. ... It has immediacy. It expresses an ideal of social progress and human dignity. It is an immediate right of equality. ... The employer has defences, but not excuses."[192]

(f) Mistakes

9–041　Where the comparator is paid more because of a genuine mistake, it seems that the employer is not obliged to justify the difference. In

---

[189] ibid. [133].
[190] See Ch.10 for the public authority equality duties.
[191] [2009] I.C.R. 133, respectively [139], [149].
[192] *Wilson v Health and Safety Executive* [2010] I.C.R. 302, [64].

Yorkshire Blood Transfusion Service v Plaskitt,[193] a male laboratory officer was appointed on point 23 of the Whitley wage scale by mistake (the rules allowed appointments up to point 21). An existing female laboratory officer on point 19 brought an equal pay claim. The EAT held that the mistake was genuine and not tainted with discrimination and so the employer was not obliged to justify the pay difference. It came to this result by holding that only in cases of indirect discrimination did the employer have to justify a pay difference.[194] Conversely, in *McPherson v Rathgael Centre for Children*[195] a female instructor brought an equal pay claim using as a comparator a newly recruited male instructor, who was put on higher pay by mistake. The Northern Ireland Court of Appeal held that any difference in pay had to be objectively justified, noting that it is not enough for the employer to show that it had no discriminatory intent.[196] However, the House of Lords in *Strathclyde Regional Council v Wallace*[197] stated that *McPherson* was wrongly decided, and approved of the *Plaskitt* decision.

(g) Social Policy

Social policy justifications for equal pay and other discrimination claims are considered together in Chapter 6, para.6–048.   **9–042**

(h) Collective Bargaining

In *Enderby v Frenchay AHA* (see above),[198] the pay difference between   **9–043**
the speech therapists and the pharmacists came about (in part, at least) as a result of separate collective agreements, neither of which taken in isolation was tainted with sex. The ECJ held that an employer could not justify a discriminatory pay difference on the basis it resulted from separate collective bargaining. Otherwise, an employer could "easily circumvent the principle of equal pay by using separate bargaining processes."[199]

However, just two years later, in the *Royal Copenhagen*[200] case, the ECJ appeared to depart from this. Here, a single collective agreement for a producer of ceramics afforded better pay to turners (exclusively male) than to painters (almost exclusively female). The ECJ held that the fact that these rates had been negotiated under a collective agreement may be taken into account as a factor when deciding if the

---

[193] [1994] I.C.R. 74.
[194] ibid. at 81.
[195] [1991] I.R.L.R. 206, NICA.
[196] ibid. [25].
[197] [1998] I.C.R. 205, at 214–215.
[198] Case C-127/92, [1994] I.C.R. 112. See further para.9–031 and para.9–036.
[199] Case C-127/92, [1994] I.C.R. 112 (ECJ), [22].
[200] Case C-400/93 *Specialarbejderforbundet i Danmark v Dansk Industri (Royal Copenhagen)* [1996] I.C.R. 51 (ECJ).

pay disparity is "due to objective factors unrelated to any discrimination on grounds of sex."[201] In coming to this conclusion, the
Court gave no apparent reason, nor did it refer to *Enderby*.[202]

The Court of Appeal in *Redcar v Bainbridge*,[203] cited both *Royal
Copenhagen* and *Enderby* when stating that collective bargaining
"*could* constitute a genuine reason, other than sex, which explained
the difference in pay". This could occur for instance, "where two
different groups are of similar proportions by gender, but one of the
groups earns less than the other."[204] The Court noted that this was
"an important defence for large employers ... which have separate
bargaining groups with separate bargaining histories." And that the
"differences may be unfair, but may have nothing to do with discrimination on the prohibited ground of sex."[205]

The day before *Redcar v Bainbridge* was decided, a differently
constituted Court of Appeal handed down its judgment in *British
Airways v Grundy (No.2)*.[206] It set itself against the use of collective
bargaining in the justification defence. Sedley L.J. (speaking for the
Court) said:

> "... there may be many reasons why, in the give and take of
> collective bargaining, one group of employees does worse than
> another. But one of the important messages sent out by the
> Equal Pay Act has been that attention must be paid by nego-
> tiators to the possibility that such differentials will have a dis-
> parate impact on employees of one gender."[207]

9–044   These cases present a rather confusing picture. To make sense of it, it
is worth bearing mind that the Equality Act 2010 s.145(1) provides
that, "A term of a collective agreement is void in so far as it constitutes, promotes or provides for" discriminatory treatment.[208]
Where, say, a (single) agreement contains terms affording better pay
to one occupation than another, and those occupations are of equal
value (*Royal Copenhagen* and *Grundy*), those terms would be void if
one of those occupations were predominantly female and the other
predominantly male. Here, recourse to the collective agreement to
justify the disparity would be meaningless as the relevant terms were

---

[201] ibid. [46].
[202] The judgment ignored the Opinion of the Advocate General (ibid. [56]), who, in addition to
    Enderby, cited *Stadt Lengerich v Helmig* [1996] I.C.R. 35, [12]; *Kowalska* [1992] I.C.R. 29
    [12], [18]; *Nimz* [1991] E.C.R. I-297, [11].
[203] *Redcar and Cleveland BC v Bainbridge; Middlesbrough Borough Council v Surtees, Redcar
    and Cleveland Borough Council v Bainbridge (No.2)* [2009] I.C.R. 133 (CA).
[204] ibid. [198] emphasis original. In the event the Court held that as the agreement was tainted
    with discrimination, it could not be used as a defence.
[205] ibid. [181].
[206] [2008] I.R.L.R. 7815. *BA v Grundy (No.1)* is discussed in Ch.6, para.6–024.
[207] ibid. [11].
[208] The word "treatment" is this context is not expressed to refer only to direct discrimination.
    See also, Recast Directive 2006/54/EC, art.23(b).

void. Where the pay for each occupation was negotiated by respective (separate) agreements (*Enderby* and *Redcar*), it is more difficult to hold that any particular term "constitutes, promotes or provides for" discrimination and is thus void. But once it is shown the agreements *combined*, cause an adverse impact on women (as in *Enderby*), it becomes logical to hold that they, at the least, "promote or provide for" discrimination. As such, those terms must be void also, at least as far as they cause discrimination. Finally, it may be that when negotiated, the single, or separate, agreements may not have had an adverse impact because the respective occupations were evenly balanced by gender. But over time, this balance changed and women became disadvantaged by the agreed pay structure(s). If and when this occurs, the relevant terms should become void.

This means that recourse to a collective agreement to justify a disparity in pay can only occur when it neither "constitutes, promotes or provides" for discrimination. This is likely to occur where is no gender imbalance between the two groups and the employer wishes to show the reason why a female claimant is paid less than her male comparator (or vice versa). If the employer does this, under EA 2010 s.69, it does not have to objectively justify the difference.

6. THE EFFECT OF THE EQUALITY CLAUSE

If not already in the workers' employment contract, s.66(1) of the EA **9–045** 2010 implies an equality clause. Section 66(2) provides that any term of the contract which is less favourable than the man's is modified to provide equivalence, and where there is no such equivalent term, the contract is "modified so as to include such a term". A new or modified term introduced to accord with the equality clause remains part of the contract in the normal way. So, for example, it cannot be "undone", should the comparator cease to do like work.[209]

This means that the comparison must be on a term-by-term basis. So, for example, basic pay, cash bonuses, perks (such as company car) and sickness benefits, are not lumped together, so as to compare the overall package each worker receives. Differences between pay packages occur more often in equal value claims, where the comparator, doing different work, is likely to have been recruited on different terms. The criticism of this approach is that it could lead to mutual enhancement, or "piggy-backing". The woman without a car, gets one because the man has one. Then the man, with inferior holiday rights, gets them improved to match the woman's. She in

---

[209] *Sorbie v Trust House Forte Hotels* [1976] 371 (EAT), approved *Sodexo Ltd v Gutridge* [2009] I.C.R. 1486 (CA).

turn, claims an improved bonus scheme, to match the man's, and so on and so forth. This argument was raised and firmly rejected in *Hayward v Cammell Laird Shipbuilders Ltd,*[210] where a female canteen cook in a shipyard was doing work of equal value to a painter, a joiner and a thermal insulation engineer. While conceding that Ms Hayward received less basic pay than her comparators, the employer argued that there was no obligation to raise her basic pay to match the men's, because she had a paid meal break, additional holidays and better sickness benefits which resulted in her being *better* off than her comparators. Lord Goff rejected this argument, reasoning that first, the genuine material factor defence would prevent some mutual enhancement and, second, the wording of the Act demanded a term-by-term approach, thus it was for Parliament to make any amendment.[211] The same approach was taken by the ECJ in *Landsting,*[212] wherein the comparison was between the basic salaries of midwives and a clinical technician, the "unsocial-hours" payment to the midwives was excluded.

9–046   At one level, piggy-back claims will appear palatable. For instance, in *Hartlepool v Llewellyn,*[213] the claimants were the few men working in predominantly female occupations. The women in those jobs sought equal pay with those doing equal work in predominantly male occupations. The claimants were allowed to make a subsequent, or "piggy-back", claim using their female colleagues (now on enhanced terms) as comparators, in order to bring their pay up to that level.

    At another level, the term-by-term approach can raise difficulties. In *Degnan v Redcar and Cleveland BC*[214] several women claimants from predominantly female occupations, such as carers and cleaners, compared their work to predominantly male occupations: refuse collectors, gardeners and road workers. Although the hourly basic pay was equal, gardeners were paid a fixed 40 per cent bonus, while the refuse collectors were paid a 36 per cent bonus plus an "attendance allowance". In one example, a claimant compared her pay to the gardeners' bonus, and then to the refuse collectors' attendance allowance, with the end result of *more* pay than any of the male workers. (Of course, the males may have then brought equal pay claims using this claimant as their comparator.) The EAT and Court of Appeal sidestepped the problem by holding that the comparators' pay arose from one single term: "Provision for monetary payment for the performance of the contract by employees during normal working hours."[215] As such, the claimants could not achieve more pay than

---

[210] [1988] A.C. 894 (HL). See E. Ellis, "A Welcome Victory for Equality" (1988) 51 M.L.R. 781.
[211] ibid. at 908–909.
[212] *Jämställdhetsombudsmannen v Örebro Läns Landsting* Case C-236/98, [2001] I.C.R. 249. See also *Brunnhofer v Bank der Österreichischen Postsparkasse* Case C-381/99, [2001] I.R.L.R. 571 (ECJ).
[213] [2009] I.C.R. 1426 (EAT).
[214] [2005] I.R.L.R. 615 (CA).
[215] ibid. [10].

any particular comparator. The reasoning is somewhat artificial. Although a *fixed* bonus could be equated with basic pay, attendance allowance was different. For instance, a worker could lose a week's pay for one day's unauthorised absence. As such, it is artificial to hold that basic pay and attendance allowance were parts of one single term.

Degnan was distinguished by the EAT in *Brownbill v St Helens and Knowsley Hospital NHS Trust*,[216] where basic salary and payments for unsocial hours were treated as separate terms.

[216] (2010) 107(33) L.S.G. 14 (EAT).

CHAPTER 10

PUBLIC SECTOR EQUALITY DUTY

1. HISTORY

In general, this duty requires public authorities to have "due regard" **10–001** to certain equality aspirations when carrying out their functions. The legislation developed piecemeal, beginning with the race equality duty in 2001,[1] which was passed in the wake of the Stephen Lawrence Inquiry.[2] A parallel disability duty was added in December 2006,[3] and a gender equality duty came into force in April 2007.[4]

All three used the common phrase "due regard", but the aspirations varied slightly. In addition to these general duties, statutory instruments imposed many specific duties, such as the preparation, publication, and implementation of an "equality scheme" for race, disability, or gender,[5] or a duty to "monitor" the racial profile of its workforce.[6]

---

[1] RRA 1976 s.71 (SI 2001/566, art.2(1)). For a history and comment, see C. O'Cinneide, "Legislative Comment" [2001] P.L. 220.

[2] The Stephen Lawrence Inquiry, Report of an Inquiry by Sir William Macpherson, advised by Tom Cook, The Right Reverend Dr John Sentamu, Dr Richard Stone. February 1999. Presented to Parliament by the Home Secretary. Cm 4262-I, London: TSO. See Ch.1, para.1–002.

[3] DDA 1995 s.49A. For certain purposes, June 30, 2005 (SI 2005/1676) and December 5, 2005 (SI 2005/2774, art.3) and for remaining purposes December 4, 2006 (SI 2005/2774).

[4] SDA 1975 s.76A. (SI 2006/1082.)

[5] Respectively, SI 2001/3458; 2005/2966; SI 2006/2930.

[6] SI 2006/2471.

The variation of aspirations, and a lack of coverage for other protected characteristics, prompted a new regime for the Equality Act 2010, which provides a common theme of aspirations, and adds sexual orientation, age, religion or belief, pregnancy and maternity, and (more fully) gender reassignment.[7] However, the Coalition Government deferred implementation until (at least) April 2011, principally because it wanted to reformulate the specific duties.[8]

The new formula retains the phrase "due regard". Many cases under the old regime turned on this phrase, and so they are a useful pointer to its meaning under the Equality Act 2010. The cases are very fact sensitive, and so their value beyond providing general principles is limited.

2. THE GENERAL DUTY

10–002 Section 149 of the Equality Act 2010 imposes three duties on public authorities:

"(1) A public authority must, in the exercise of its functions, have due regard to the need to—

(a) eliminate discrimination, harassment, victimisation and any other conduct that is prohibited by or under this Act;

(b) advance equality of opportunity between persons who share a relevant protected characteristic and persons who do not share it;

(c) foster good relations between persons who share a relevant protected characteristic and persons who do not share it."

---

[7] Outside of England and Wales, the duties are not always confined to the Equality Act's protected characteristics. The Scottish Parliament may (by Scotland Act 1998) impose an equal opportunities duty local authorities. "Equal Opportunities" means: "the prevention, elimination or regulation of discrimination between persons on grounds of sex or marital status, on racial grounds, or on grounds of disability, age, sexual orientation, language or social origin, or of other personal attributes, including beliefs or opinions, such as religious beliefs or political opinions." (Sch.5 Pt II s.L2). (See e.g. Housing (Scotland) Act 2001 s.106.) Northern Ireland Act 1998 s.75(1) provides: "A public authority shall in carrying out its functions relating to Northern Ireland have due regard to the need to promote equality of opportunity—(a) between persons of different religious belief, political opinion, racial group, age, marital status or sexual orientation; (b) between men and women generally; (c) between persons with a disability and persons without; and (d) between persons with dependants and persons without."

[8] "Equality Act 2010: The public sector Equality Duty" (2010) JN402461, Ch.4. *http:// www.equalities.gov.uk/pdf/402461_GEO_EqualityAct2010ThePublicSectorEqualityDuty_acc.pdf* (accessed December 23, 2010).

This applies to all the protected characteristics, save that paragraphs (b) and (c) do not apply to marriage and civil partnership.[9] An extensive list of "public authorities" covered by this duty is provided in Sch.19. There are two classes. For the most part, the public authorities owe this duty whether or not the particular function is private or public. But authorities may be listed in respect of just some of their functions.[10] The Minister can, and plans to,[11] add to this list.[12] Those listed when the Act was passed included: national, devolved and local government; education authorities; the armed forces; the NHS; and the police. Three broad categories are excluded from the duty. First, for the protected characteristic of age only, education and benefits to school pupils and children's accommodation. Second, for age, religion or belief, nationality, or ethnic or national origins, immigration matters. Third, for all protected characteristics, judicial functions.[13]

Any private body carrying out a public function[14] is bound by the duty.[15] (Hence, the phrase "public authority" is a little misleading.) This will cover, among others, businesses which provide public services contracted out by local, devolved, or central, government.

3. SPECIFIC DUTIES

Section 153 of the Equality Act 2010 authorises a Minister of the **10–003** Crown, Welsh Minister or Scottish Minister to impose specific duties on a relevant public authority specified in sch.19 "for the purpose of enabling the better performance by the authority" of the equality duty. This must be done by making regulations, and before doing so, the Minister must consult the Equality and Human Rights Commission.

As noted above, the Coalition Government announced that it wanted to reformulate the specific duties. It wants to move away from what it considered a process-driven top-down model, to a localised

---

[9] EA 2010 s.149(7).
[10] EA 2010 s.150(3) and (4).
[11] "Equality Act 2010: The public sector Equality Duty", (n.8, above), para.7.7.
[12] EA 2010 s.151.
[13] EA 2010 Sch.18 paras (1)–(3).
[14] As defined under the Human Rights Act 1998: EA 2010 s.150(5). See Ch.2, paras 2–022 et seq.
[15] EA 2010 s.149(2). The exception here is in relation to the functions of the House of Commons or House of Lords, the Scottish Parliament and the Welsh Assembly: the House of Commons, the House of Lords, the Scottish Parliament, the Welsh Assembly, the General Synod of the Church of England; the Security Service, the Secret Intelligence Service, and the Government Communications Headquarters (including any armed forces assisting) (Sch.18(4)).

and transparent one.[16] Those authorities covered will set their own targets, rather than have them set by central government. One particularly effective way for local and devolved government to advance its equality goals is by insisting that businesses comply with certain equality requirements in order to win contracts (procurement). In line with its general approach, the Coalition Government announced it would not impose procurement requirements. This would be a matter for each authority, who "will be judged on the outcomes they deliver".[17]

The Government proposed that an authority must publish: (1) assessments of the impact of its policies and practices; (2) the information upon which it took into account in making that assessment; (3) for those employing 150 or more persons, information about the protected characteristics of the workforce. Further, within a year of the specific duties coming into force, it must prepare and publish one or more objectives which it reasonably thinks that it should achieve in order to further one or more of the aims of the equality duty.[18] Finally, the Coalition Government stated that although local authorities should "engage with" those with protected characteristics from time to time in order to carry out their general duties, it did not think that these duties should be specified by central government: "public bodies should have the flexibility to decide for themselves when and how to engage with citizens." However, details of any engagement should be published.[19]

4. THE "DUE REGARD" DUTY

10–004 Sub-sections (3), (4) and (5) of s.149 of the EA 2010, set out in a little more detail matters to which "due regard" should be given. For the duty of "advancement of equality of opportunity" (s.149(1)(b), above), due regard should be given to removing or minimising disadvantages, and taking steps to meet the needs of those who share a protected characteristic. Where participation is disproportionately low, those who share a protected characteristic should be encouraged to participate in public life or any other activity.[20] On the duty to "foster good relations" (s.149(1)(c), above), due regard should be had to tackling prejudice and promoting understanding.[21]

---

[16] See n.8, above.
[17] "Equality Act 2010: The public sector Equality Duty" (n.8, above), para.5.21.
[18] ibid., p.31.
[19] ibid. para.5.7.
[20] EA 2010 s.149(3).
[21] EA 2010 s.149(5).

When the equality duties were first introduced, starting in 2001, there were fears that they may amount to no more than a bureaucratic tick-box exercise. These fears were allayed by the case law.[22] The tone was set in *Secretary of State for Defence v Elias*:[23]

> "It is the clear purpose of [the equality duty] to require public bodies ... to give advance consideration to issues of ... discrimination before making any policy decision that may be affected by them. This is a salutary requirement, and this provision must be seen as an integral and important part of the mechanisms for ensuring the fulfilment of the aims of anti-discrimination legislation. ... In the context of the wider objectives of anti-discrimination legislation, [the equality duty] has a significant role to play."[24]

This means that an authority should *consider* the impact of any policy decision on those with protected characteristics. When doing this, the authority should assess the risk and extent of any adverse impact and the ways in which such a risk may be eliminated.[25] On the other hand, if it is clear "even after a cursory consideration" that the equality duty is not engaged, there is no need to "enter into time consuming and potentially expensive consultation exercises or monitoring when discrimination issues are plainly not in point."[26]

The duty is non-delegable, in sense that the public authority will remain responsible, even if a third party carries out the practical steps to fulfil the duty on behalf of the authority.[27] It has been suggested that authorities are under no duty when merely enforcing the law.[28] This goes too far. It might be, for instance, that an authority enforces a law unevenly, say with parking restrictions in a district populated predominantly by Asians.

If an impact assessment is required, it must be carried out *before* the policy decision is made. Compliance with the duty should be "not as rearguard action following a concluded decision" but rather "an essential preliminary to any such decision. Inattention to it is both unlawful and bad government."[29] Further, it would send out "quite

---

[22] See e.g. K. Monaghan, *Equality Law* (Oxford: OUP, 2008), pp.625–629.

[23] [2006] 1 W.L.R. 3213 (CA). Heard under the equality duty imposed by RRA 1976 s.71. On other issues raised in this case, see further, Ch.6, para.6–042.

[24] ibid. [274].

[25] *R. (Kaur) v Ealing LBC* [2008] EWHC 2062 (Admin), [23] (Moses L.J.).

[26] *Elias v Secretary of State for Defence* [2005] I.R.L.R. 788 (HC) [96] (Elias J.), affirmed [2006] 1 W.L.R. 3213 (CA).

[27] *R. (Brown) v Secretary of State for Work and Pensions* [2008] EWHC 3158 (Admin), [94].

[28] *Brent v Corcoran* [2010] EWCA Civ 774, [19] (Jacob L.J.): It would be "far-fetched" to impose a duty on an authority evicting Romany travellers for "severe" breaches of their licence agreement, including criminality. See also *R. (Ghai) v Newcastle CC* [2010] 3 W.L.R. 737 (HC and CA), [158] (Cranston J.) reversed on other grounds.

[29] *R. (BAPIO) v Secretary of State for the Home Department* [2007] EWCA Civ 1139, [3] (Sedley L.J.).

the wrong message", to allow a deficit to be cured by a review taken sometime later, which also would be wrong as a matter of principle.[30] It should be noted though, that the equality duty is also a "continuing duty", and so the effects of any policy should be monitored.[31]

10–005 It would seem that the s.149(1) duties (above) are aspirations, rather than goals that must be achieved. In *R. (Baker) v Secretary of State for Communities and Local Government*,[32] the Court of Appeal stated that the race equality duty was not a duty to achieve a result (i.e. the elimination of discrimination, promotion of equality of opportunity, and fostering good relations). Rather, it was a duty "to *have due regard to the need* to achieve these goals." And "due regard" meant:

> "... the regard that is appropriate in all the circumstances. These include on the one hand the importance of the areas of life of the members of the disadvantaged racial group that are affected by the inequality of opportunity and the extent of the inequality; and on the other hand, such countervailing factors as are relevant to the function which the decision-maker is performing."[33]

5. POSITIVE ACTION

10–006 The Act reminds authorities that complying with the duties may involve treating some persons more favourably than others, which is permissible so far as it is not otherwise prohibited by the Act.[34] This suggests that any positive action must comply with either s.158, or (for recruitment and promotion in employment) s.159 (discussed Chapter 11, paras 11–008 et seq). The general tenet reflects a case decided under the Race Relations Act 1976. In *R. (Kaur) v Ealing LBC*[35] the local authority decided to reallocate funding to an organisation which could provide support to victims of domestic violence, irrespective of their protected characteristic. This would mean the withdrawal of the funding from the "Southall Black Sisters", who provided support and advice for Asian and black victims only. The decision was challenged as not complying with the authority's race equality duty, as it did not account for the impact on the black and Asian recipients of the service. The authority maintained that the

---

[30] *R. v (C (A Minor) v Secretary of State for Justice* [2009] Q.B. 657 (CA), [49]. See also *Elias v Secretary of State for Defence* [2005] I.R.L.R. 788 (HC), [98].
[31] *R. (Brown) v Secretary of State for Work and Pensions* [2008] EWHC 3158 (Admin), [95].
[32] [2008] EWCA Civ 141.
[33] ibid. [31]. Emphasis original.
[34] EA 2010 s.149(6).
[35] [2008] EWHC 2062 (Admin).

1976 Act did not permit funding of an organisation providing support for particular racial groups to the exclusion of others. In other words, it did not permit preferential treatment for some racial groups, or positive discrimination. Further, exclusive services did not accord with the authority's goal of social cohesion. These arguments were rejected. First, the "important principle of anti-discrimination and equality measures" is that "not only must like cases be treated alike but that unlike cases but must be treated differently".[36] Thus, preferential treatment was not necessarily unlawful. Second, the Court accepted that "Cohesion is achieved by overcoming barriers", which may require that the needs of ethnic minorities are "met in a particular and focussed way". The proposed general service may be reluctant to intervene in the cultural and religious affairs of a minority for fear of causing offence, whereas a specialist service such as the Southall Black Sisters avoids those traps.[37] Such funding could now be justified under EA 2010 s.158(1)(b), which permits positive action where: "persons who share a protected characteristic have needs that are different".

6. Form and Substance

A major aspect of the proposed specific duties is transparency. This **10–007** entails the publication of impact assessments. If this is to be done, public authorities must engage in detailed record-keeping. Previous case-law has produced mixed signals on this issue. In *R. (Kaur) v Ealing LBC*[38] (above), Moses L.J. asserted that the process of assessments should be recorded. This was because records contribute to transparency, demonstrate that a genuine assessment was made in good time, and "discipline the policy maker to undertake the conscientious assessment". However, the process was not satisfied by ticking boxes; it should be undertaken as "a matter of substance and with rigor".[39]

In some cases, the latter demand for substance has prevailed at the expense of any weight afforded to the need for record-keeping. In *R. (MS) v Oldham MBC*,[40] Langstaffe J.—without apparent reference to *Kaur*—stated that there was no duty to minute and record every assessment. He applied this in *R. (Broster) v Wirral MBC*,[41] holding

[36] ibid. [52] (Moses L.J.).
[37] ibid. [54].
[38] [2008] EWHC 2062 (Admin).
[39] ibid. [24].
[40] *R. (MS) (by his mother and litigation friend SS) v Oldham MBC* [2010] EWHC 802 (Admin), [20].
[41] [2010] EWHC 3086 (Admin).

that if the duty was inherent in the actions of the defendant, the duty was discharged, even in the absence of specific record-keeping.[42] In *R. (McCarthy) v Basildon DC*,[43] the local authority, when evicting Romany and Irish travellers from land, recorded its race impact assessment, but not its disability one (the evictions raised some health care issues). The authority was not in breach of its disability equality duty because "the balancing exercise" relevant to the race equality duty was the same as that for the disability equality duty.[44] It would seem that under the Coalition Government's proposals, the need for transparency and publication would reverse this aspect of these three cases.

7. The Commission's Role

10–008   The Equality and Human Rights Commission has two roles in relation to the equality duty. First, it may issue Codes of Practice.[45]

Under the original race equality duty, the Commission for Racial equality issued a Code of Practice and four non-statutory guides.[46] In *R. (Kaur) v Ealing LBC*[47] (above), Moses L.J. stated that an authority could only depart from the Code for "clear and cogent reasons" and suggested it would have to justify any departure from the guide. The Code for the race equality duty suggested a four step process:

> "a. Identify which of their functions and policies are relevant to the duty, or, in other words, affect most people.
>
> b. Put the functions and policies in order of priority, based on how relevant they are to race equality.
>
> c. Assess whether the way these 'relevant' functions and policies are being carried out meets the three parts of the duty.
>
> d. Consider whether any changes need to be made to meet the duty, and make the changes."[48]

---

[42] ibid. [67].
[43] [2009] EWCA Civ 13. See also *R. (Baker) v Secretary of State for Communities and Local Government* [2008] EWCA Civ 141, [36]–[38].
[44] ibid. [57] and [67].
[45] EA 2006 s.14. At the time of writing, no code hade been issued for the equality duty under the EA 2010.
[46] See "Code of Practice on the duty to promote racial equality." (2002) London: CRE (ISBN 1 85442 430 0), issued by the CRE. For a commentary, see (2002) 102 EOR 28.
[47] [2008] EWHC 2062 (Admin), [22].
[48] "Code of Practice on the duty to promote racial equality" (above, n.46), para.3.11.

The second role of the Commission begins with a power to carry out an "assessment" of a public authority's compliance with its equality duty.[49] If, following an assessment, the Commission "thinks" that a public authority has failed in its duties in relation to a general or specific duty, the Commission may issue a notice requiring compliance.[50] If the Commission "thinks" that the public authority is not complying with the notice, the Commission may apply for an order requiring compliance.[51] In the case of a general duty, it should apply to the High Court or Court of Session, and in the case of a specific duty, it should apply to the county court or the sheriff.

Alternatively, the Commission can make a statutory agreement with a public authority in respect of a breach of any of a public sector duty in lieu of issuing a public sector duty compliance notice.[52]

---

[49] EA 2006, s.31. Details are provided by EA 2006 Sch.2.
[50] EA 2006 s.32(2).
[51] EA 2006 s.32(8).
[52] EA 2006 s.23(5).

CHAPTER 11

POSITIVE ACTION

INTRODUCTION

Positive action (or in the US, "affirmative action") has been defined **11–001** as "any measure, beyond simple termination of a discriminatory practice, adopted to correct or compensate for past or present discrimination or to prevent discrimination recurring in the future."[1]

McCrudden identified five classes of positive action used in "common parlance":[2]

> *Eradicating discrimination.* This involves employers taking steps (e.g. monitoring, regular reviews) to ensure that they are not discriminating.

> *Facially neutral but purposefully inclusionary polices.* Examples would be recruitment from the unemployed, or from particular geographical areas, where say, ethnic minorities may be

---

[1] US Commission on Civil Rights, Statement on Affirmative Action 2 (1977). See generally, *www.usccr.gov.*

[2] C. McCrudden, "Rethinking positive action" (1986) 15 ILJ 219, pp. 223–225. See also C. McCrudden, "The Constitututionality of Affirmative Action in the United States: a Note on *Adarand Constructors Inc v Pena"* (1996) 1 I.J.D.L. 369 where the author identifies "at least" three types of affirmative action; D. Oppenheimer, "Discrimination and affirmative action: an analysis of competing theories of equality and *Weber"* 59 NCL Rev 531, who identifies a similar five models (at 534); R. Jenkins, "Equal opportunity in the private sector: the limits of voluntarism", in R. Jenkins and J. Solomos (eds), *Racism and Equal Opportunity Policies in the 1980s* (Cambridge: CUP, 1987), pp. 113–115. The whole of one issue of the *Journal of Law and Society* is dedicated to positive action: (2006) 33(1) JLS 1.

overrepresented. The danger here, theoretically at least, is that the majority groups could bring an action of indirect discrimination.[3]

Outreach programmes. These are designed to attract qualified candidates from underrepresented groups, by bringing job opportunities to the attention of these groups and providing training to help them compete with other applicants. This is to combat what is sometimes called the "pool problem", or more colloquially, the "old boy" or "school tie" network, formed of persons from a close cultural and social background. The typical pool consists of white middle class males. In many occupations, recruits are drawn from these informal pools.

Preferential treatment in employment. This is reverse discrimination in hiring, promotion or redundancy. Membership of the targeted group may a partial, or the sole, factor in the decision.

Redefining "merit". This alters the qualifications which are necessary to do the job, by including race, gender, sexual orientation or religion as a relevant factor for doing the job properly.

11–002   The irony of the discrimination legislation is that (save for disability) the equal treatment model it employs *prevents* more favourable treatment of those whose disadvantages it seeks to redress. The symmetrical nature of the equal treatment model means that it protects men as well as women, white and black, straight and gay, Christian and Muslim, young and old, even though protecting the former of each of these pairs is not the principal goal of the legislation. The consequence is that an act to favour a principal protected group will disfavour another group. Once this produces a victim, it becomes unlawful discrimination. A benign motive will not save it.[4] This means, save for the specified exceptions noted below, positive action is in principle unlawful.

Yet, a common theme of the protected groups is that the cause of their present disadvantage is past discrimination. Just as prosperity can tumble down the family heirs, the negative consequences of inferior housing, education, career opportunities and (particularly in the US) slavery, can spill down the generations. Indeed, a history of prejudice has been the main driving force behind the enactments. Any attempt to redress the effects of past discrimination will breach the equality principle, because it will discriminate against the dominant

---

[3] See *United States v City of Warren, Michigan* 138 F 3d 1083 (6th Cir 1998), where, conversely, an employer advertised in predominantly white areas.
[4] *R. (E) v Governing Body of JFS* [2009] UKSC 15.

group, such as men or whites. Further, positive action is received by the media and public (largely uninformed of this history) as *unfair* or *unequal* treatment.[5] Accordingly, politicians and judges have allowed very few exceptions for positive discrimination.

The problem is well illustrated by the British Labour Party's attempts to get more women elected to Parliament. One only had to look, or listen, to proceedings at the Westminster House of Commons, especially a few years ago, to appreciate its overwhelmingly dominant male culture, and how unrepresentative this was.[6] Yet, in *Jepson and Dyas-Elliott v The Labour Party*,[7] the Labour Party's policy of all-women short-lists for parliamentary candidates was held to be unlawful under the Sex Discrimination Act 1975. The effect of the decision was reversed by dedicated legislation, providing a non-symmetrical exception to the equality principle.[8]

The unforgiving nature of the symmetrical rule was emphasised by Balcombe L.J. in *Lambeth LBC v Commission for Racial Equality*[9] who was "wholly unpersuaded that one of the two main purposes of the [Race Relations Act 1976] is to promote positive action to benefit racial groups." It was illustrated in *ACAS v Taylor*,[10] where ACAS invited its staff to apply for 31 Senior Executive Officer (SEO) posts. This was a nationwide exercise and the first stage was for regional managers to rank the applicants. In Mr Taylor's region, four applicants, three of whom were male, were ranked "B" grade. Mr Taylor was one of these. However, only the female was selected for interview. Nationally, eight out of eight of the "B" grade females, and just six from 16 "B" grade males, were selected for interview. This selection procedure was influenced by the following guidance:

"Please remember that more needs to be done to ensure the reality of the claim that ACAS is an equal opportunity employer. For example women make up only 17% of those at SEO level at present and ethnic minorities staff less than 1%. All staff should be considered on their merits as individuals. Where you have any

---

[5] In the 2004 general election, Peter Law resigned from the Labour Party in protest at the selection of a candidate from an all-women short-list. He stood as an independent and overturned the Labour majority of 19,000 votes, winning with a majority of 9,000 (*The Times*, April 6, 2004).

[6] The UN Committee on the Elimination of Discrimination against Women reported in 2008 (40th and 41st Sessions) that: "women continue to be underrepresented in political and public life, especially in leadership and decisionmaking positions. ... women's representation currently stands at 19.3 per cent in the House of Commons and 19.7 per cent in the House of Lords. ... figures are higher, however, in Scotland (34.1 per cent) and Wales (46.7 per cent). *http://daccess-dds-ny.un.org/doc/UNDOC/GEN/N08/458/40/PDF/N0845840.pdf?OpenElement* (accessed December 5, 2010).

[7] [1996] I.R.L.R. 116, IT.

[8] SDA 1975 s.42A, inserted by the Sex Discrimination (Election Candidates) Act 2002 s.1. See now, EA 2010 s.104.

[9] [1990] I.C.R. 768 (CA), at p.774.

[10] EAT/788/97 (Transcript).

doubts about the fairness of the Annual Reports you should not hesitate to take appropriate action."

The EAT held that Mr Taylor had been a victim of a policy of positive discrimination and as such had suffered direct sex discrimination. Morison J. noted that the opening sentence of the guidance was "readily capable of being misconstrued" and "capable of leading the unwary into positive discrimination".

11–003   More recently though, speaking in the High Court, and without reference to the *Lambeth* or *Taylor* cases, Moses L.J. stated that the positive action provisions in the Race Relations Act 1976 were *not* exceptions to the Act. Instead, they were:

> "... a manifestation of the important principle of anti-discrimination and equality measures that not only must like cases be treated alike but that unlike cases but must be treated differently".[11]

This less dogmatic but rather isolated view is reflected in the Equality Act 2010. Otherwise, before the Act, save for the general position of the disability discrimination law permitting,[12] and in some cases mandating,[13] preferable treatment, the legislation of Great Britain provided only very limited and specific forms of positive action.

The Equality Act 2010 introduced new, general, and simpler, provisions on positive action. The mainstay is the general *permissive* s.158, applying to all fields. This is complimented by s.159, which permits "tie-breaks" in recruitment and promotion. Section 104 continues and expands the permissive exception for the selection of candidates by political parties. Finally, it is arguable that an extended remedy for employment tribunals encompasses positive action.

As positive action always risks being challenged as unlawful discrimination, these provisions must comply with the European Convention on Human Rights[14] (where engaged) and EU law. The European Court of Human Rights has sanctioned, and at times, *mandated*, positive action:

> "Article 14 [discrimination] does not prohibit a Member State from treating groups differently in order to correct 'factual inequalities' between them; indeed in certain circumstances a

---

[11] *R. (Kaur) v Ealing LBC* [2008] EWHC 2062 (Admin), [52].
[12] Direct disability discrimination, see Ch.13, para.13–021.
[13] Duty to make reasonable adjustments, ibid. para.13–032.
[14] See Ch.2, para.2–007.

failure to attempt to correct inequality through different treatment may in itself give rise to a breach of the Article."[15]

The EU legislation *permits* positive action and under it, the ECJ has developed some fairly detailed parameters. Sections 158 and 159 were drafted with these parameters in mind.[16] And so, before discussing the Equality Act's provisions, a brief account of the ECJ principles is required.

1. EC Law[17]

The European discrimination legislation permits some positive action. Most challenges arriving in the ECJ are to state-run schemes deemed permissible under domestic law, the issue being whether they are permissible under Community law. The Treaty on the Functioning of European Union (TFEU), art.157(4) provides: **11–004**

"With a view to ensuring full equality in practice between men and women in working life, the principle of equal treatment shall not prevent any Member State from maintaining or adopting measures providing for specific advantages in order to make it easier for the underrepresented sex to pursue a vocational activity or to prevent or compensate for disadvantages in professional careers."

The Recast Directive 2006/54/EC art.3 implements this formula, while the Race and Framework Directives substantially restate it,[18] save that the Race Directive it is not limited to employment matters.

The case law so far has concerned only sex discrimination. At first, in *Kalanke*, the ECJ demonstrated a notable lack of enthusiasm for the notion of positive action. In subsequent cases, however, the ECJ

[15] *Stec v United Kingdom* (2006) 43 E.H.R.R. 47, [51]–[66]; See also *DH v Czech Republic* (2008) 47 E.H.R.R. 3, [175], *Runkee v United Kingdom* [2007] 2 F.C.R. 178, [40]. See C. Van de Heyning, "Is it still a sin to kill a mockingbird? Remedying factual inequalities through positive action—what can be learned from the US Supreme Court and the European Court of Human Rights case law?" (2008) 3 E.H.R.L.R. 376.
[16] EA 2010, Explanatory Notes, (512) (520).
[17] For a discussion of EC positive action law and substantive equality, see C. Barnard and B. Hepple, "Substantive equality", (2000) 59(3) CLJ 562, at pp.576–579.
[18] Respectively, Council Directive 2000/43/EC art.5; Council Directive 2000/78 art.7(1), and in addition art.7(2) provides: "With regard to disabled persons, the principle of equal treatment shall be without prejudice to the right of Member States to maintain or adopt provisions on the protection of health and safety at work or to measures aimed at creating or maintaining provisions or facilities for safeguarding or promoting their integration into the working environment".

has taken a less strict line and endorsed a number of positive action programmes, although there are still boundaries.

In *Kalanke v Freie Hansestadt Bremen*,[19] a case originating from Germany, the practice was that whenever two candidates were equally qualified, the employer gave preference to the woman (the "tie-break"). This implemented the Bremen public service law, which required this preference where (a) the candidates were equally qualified, and (b) where women were underrepresented in the relevant post, defined as where women do not make up at least half the staff in the "relevant personnel group". The ECJ held that that this public service law breached the Equal Treatment Directive (now Recast Directive), stating that the exception for positive action is limited to advantages that improve women's ability to compete in the labour market. The Directive did not permit "an unconditional priority for appointment".[20] Another problem with this programme was that the trigger of underrepresentation was rather crude. It presumed that as many women as men were economically active, which, because of domestic responsibilities (among other factors) clearly is not the case. There was no attempt to measure the proportion of women in the job market.[21]

11–005   *Kalanke* was distinguished in *Marschall v Land Nordrhein-Westfalen*.[22] The positive action under challenge here stated that where "there are fewer women than men in the particular higher grade post in the career bracket, women are to be given priority for promotion in the event of equal suitability, competence and professional performance, unless reasons specific to an individual [male] candidate tilt the balance in his favour." This last phrase has become known as a "savings clause". Like *Kalanke*, this is a "tie-break" rule, but with the added savings clause. This distinction allowed the ECJ to hold that this positive action was permissible under the Directive, despite the clause being rather vague. Otherwise, the rule in *Marschall* was just as crude as the one in *Kalanke*, and that the main objection to *Kalanke* (the crudeness of the rule) is now irrelevant.[23]

In *Re Badeck*[24] the ECJ ruled that all five of the following particular systems provided by German local legislation were permissible under the Directive. In the first, *flexible result quota*, sectors and departments set binding targets. A woman will be preferred in any appointment if (a) she is equally qualified as the man, (b) it is necessary to achieve the target, and (c) there are no "reasons of greater legal weight". These "reasons" favoured former employees

---

[19] Case C-450/93, [1996] I.C.R. 314. For comment, see E. Szyszczak, "Positive action after *Kalanke*" (1996) 59 MLR 876.
[20] ibid. [19]–[22].
[21] These points were made in (1996) 65 EOR 31.
[22] Case C-409/95, [1988] I.R.L.R. 39.
[23] See "Limited positive action allowed" (1998) 77 EOR 38, pp. 39–40.
[24] Case C-158/97, [2000] I.R.L.R. 432. See K. Küchhold, "*Badeck*—the third German reference on positive action" (2001) 30 ILJ 116.

who left because for family reasons, employees who went part-time for family reasons, former temporary soldiers, seriously disabled persons, and the long-term unemployed. The ECJ approved this because of the "greater legal weight" rule, a savings clause. Unlike *Kalanke*, the preference for women was not "absolute and unconditional".[25]

By the second, *academic flexible result quota*, quotas were applied as above because women were underrepresented among universities' temporary research assistants and academic assistants. These quotas reflected the proportion of women among respectively, graduates, or students, in the particular discipline. The ECJ held this to be permissible because there was some relationship between the quota and the "actual fact" of those qualified to do the job, and so there was no fixed "absolute ceiling".[26]

Under the third, *strict training quota,* where women were under-represented on training programmes, half of the places were reserved for women, if enough women applied. The ECJ permitted this because (a) it did not entail "totally inflexibility" because if not enough women applied, more than half the places would go to men; (b) there was no monopoly, other training places were available in the private sector; and (c) this rule only applied to training (as opposed to employment).[27]

11–006

The fourth, *interview quota*, provided that for sectors where women are underrepresented, at least as many women as men, or all the women applicants, should be called for interview for a job or training position. Those called had to be suitably qualified for the job. If, for example, only three from seven qualified female applicants are called for interview, then only three men can be called, no matter how many qualified men apply. If, however, all the female applicants are qualified and called, then there is no limit on the number of qualified men who may be called. This was permissible because (a) it was not an "attempt to achieve a final result—appointment or promotion—but afforded qualified women additional opportunities to facilitate their entry into working life and their career", and (b) only qualified candidates could be called to interview.[28]

By the fifth, *quota for collective bodies*, in making appointments to commissions, advisory boards, boards of directors and supervisory boards and other collective bodies, at least half the members should be women. This was permissible because (a) these were non-elected

---

[25] ibid. [26]–[38].
[26] ibid. [39]–[44].
[27] ibid. [45]–[55].
[28] ibid. [56]–[63].

bodies, and (b) since the provision was not mandatory it allowed, to some extent, other criteria to be taken into account.[29]

11–007   In *Lommers*[30] the challenged scheme was one set up by a Minister to tackle extensive underrepresentation of women within his Ministry. The scheme provided a limited number of subsidised nursery places only for women, although male workers could use it in emergencies. The ECJ held that this scheme was permissible under the Directive, again the ("emergencies") savings clause being central to the decision.

The limit of the ECJ's post-*Kalanke* tolerance was found in *Abrahamsson and Anderson v Fogelqvist.*[31] In the Swedish university sector just 10 per cent of professors were women. In response legislation was passed to the effect that a woman possessing sufficient qualifications for the post *must* be chosen in preference to a male candidate who would otherwise have been chosen, provided that the difference between their qualifications was not so great that the appointment would be contrary to the requirement of objectivity in the making of appointments. There are two features to this system. First, it is mandatory, with no savings clause. Second, a *lesser-* (rather than just *equally-*) qualified candidate could be selected. The ECJ held that this legislation breached the Directive, holding that the ("objectivity") condition could not be "precisely determined" and could not prevent the mandatory appointment of a lesser- or equally-qualified woman.[32] In other words, the condition did not amount to a savings clause. In answer to a further question the Court stated it would be permissible if "substantially" equally-qualified women could be preferred if there was a savings clause, such as one that took "account of the specific personal situations of all the candidates".[33]

It is clear from these cases that the ECJ has abandoned its strict approach taken in *Kalanke*. From *Marschall and Badeck*, three requirements emerge for positive action to be lawful. First, there must be underrepresentation in the particular sector, department or profession. Second, the woman being preferred must be *equally* qualified to the man.[34] Third, there must be a "savings clause". This third ingredient is what the ECJ used to distinguish *Kalanke*. It seems a

---

[29] ibid. [64]–[66].
[30] *Lommers v Minister Van Landbouw, Natuurbeheer en Visserij* Case C-476/99, [2002] I.R.L.R. 430.
[31] Case C-407/98 [2000] I.R.L.R. 732. Applied, Case C-319/03 *Briheche v Ministre de l'Interieur* [2004] E.C.R. I-8807 (ECJ). See A. Numhauser-Henning, "Swedish Sex Equality Law before the ECJ" (2001) 30 ILJ 121.
[32] ibid. [44]–[56].
[33] ibid. [62].
[34] Quaere did the ECJ in *Abrahamsson* (ibid.) imply it is permissible to give priority to a *lesser*-qualified candidate when suggesting that the candidates could possess "*substantially* equivalent merits"? (Emphasis supplied.) cf. *Johnson v Transportation Agency, Santa Clara County* 480 US 616 (Sup Ct 1987), where the US Supreme Court held it permissible to favour the (underrepresented) female candidate who scored 73 in a job test when two men scored 75.

savings clause may be vague (as in *Marschall*) so long as it prevents a *mandatory* appointment (*Abrahamsson*).

2. EQUALITY ACT 2010

(1) Positive Action—Section 158

Section 158 applies to all fields within the Act, such as education, the **11–008** provision of services, and some aspects of employment, save that it does *not* apply where s.104 (election candidates) or s.159 (work recruitment and promotion) apply.[35]

Section 158(1) provides three triggers and corresponding aims that may be pursued. If a person "reasonably thinks" that either:

(a) persons who share a protected characteristic suffer a disadvantage connected to the characteristic ("disadvantaged"),

(b) persons who share a protected characteristic have needs that are different from the needs of persons who do not share it ("different needs"), or

(c) participation in an activity by persons who share a protected characteristic is disproportionately low ("underrepresented").

Accordingly, s.158(2) permits action which is a proportionate means of achieving the aim of:

(a) enabling or encouraging persons who share the protected characteristic to overcome or minimise that disadvantage,

(b) meeting those needs, or

(c) enabling or encouraging persons who share the protected characteristic to participate in that activity.

During the passage of the Equality Bill, the Government resisted an amendment substituting the phrase "reasonably thinks" with "can demonstrate" (rather curiously, suggested only for s.159, below). The argument could be just as relevant here. The Government stated that this "higher threshold" would deter employers from using it. Employers could "make clear identifications from their day-to-day business, from the evidence surrounding them, from their own understanding of the market and from the need to redress any imbalance in their work force". Otherwise, they might have to get

[35] EA 2010 s.158(4).

"some presumably rather expensive consultant to obtain statistical evidence [of] what they could see before their very eyes ...".[36]

11–009   Nonetheless, the aim must be "legitimate" where it falls under EC law, and so presumably it must be evidence-based, and as the wording demands, the action must be proportionate. The Explanatory Notes (517) provided the following examples:

> "Having identified that its white male pupils are underperforming at maths, a school could run supplementary maths classes exclusively for them."

> "An NHS Primary Care Trust identifies that lesbians are less likely to be aware that they are at risk of cervical cancer and less likely to access health services such as national screening programmes. It is also aware that those who do not have children do not know that they are at an increased risk of breast cancer. Knowing this it could decide to establish local awareness campaigns for lesbians on the importance of cancer screening."

As noted above, s.158 does not extend to any employer-related action that falls within s.159, and so the scope for employment-related positive action is limited. Nevertheless, there remains some scope for employment positive action under s.158. The Government suggested, for example, that it could enable a construction firm wishing to diversify its male-dominated workforce to add a statement to its job advertisement inviting women to apply.[37]

Finally, note that s.158(3) empowers the Minister to issue regulations specifying certain actions to which s.158 does not apply.

(2) Positive Action—Section 159

11–010   Section 159 is a "tie-break" provision. It was due to come into force in April 2011, a little later than the rest of the Act.[38] It applies at the point of recruitment or promotion. "Recruitment" covers: employment, contract workers, partnerships in firms and LLPs, pupillages or tenancies in barristers' chambers, advocate's devils or a person membership of an advocate's stable, personal offices, public offices (including recommendations and approvals), and employment services (the offering of a service for finding employment).[39]

---

[36] Solicitor-General, Official Report, Commons, Equality Bill Committee, 30/6/09; cols 608–609.

[37] Baroness Royall, Hansard, Official Report HL Vol.717, No.41, p.657 (Feb 9, 2010).

[38] This was because of some hesitation by the Coalition Government which inherited the Act from the previous Labour administration. It put most of the Act into force in October 2010. See *http://www.equalities.gov.uk/equality_act_2010.aspx* (accessed December 4, 2010).

[39] EA 2010 s.159(5).

Section 159(1) provides two triggers and corresponding aims that may be pursued. If the employer "reasonably thinks" that either:

(a) persons who share a protected characteristic suffer a dis-advantage connected to the characteristic ("disadvantage"), or

(b) participation in an activity by persons who share a protected characteristic is disproportionately low ("underrepresentation").

Accordingly, s.159(2) permits employers to take *specified* action with the aim of enabling or encouraging disadvantaged or under-represented candidates to:

(a) overcome or minimise that disadvantage, or

(b) participate in that activity.

The specified action is treating the disadvantaged or under-represented candidate more favourably in connection with recruit-ment, *but only* where: (1) that candidate "is as qualified as" another, and (2) there is no policy of automatic favouring, and (3) the favourable treatment is proportionate.[40] If these conditions are met, the "tie break" may be resolved in favour of this candidate.

The phrase "reasonably thinks" is considered above, para.11–008. **11–011** The Government resisted an amendment substituting "as qualified as" with "equally qualified to". According to the Government, this could be "misinterpreted" to mean that both candidates should have identical qualifications: "Formal qualifications are only one way in which a candidate's overall suitability may be assessed."[41] Thus, the phrase envisages a broad range of factors in this question, such as experience, aptitude, physical ability or performance during an interview or assessment. Where one candidate may have a better aptitude, another may be "as qualified as" him because she has superior experience. Where both candidates meet the job criteria, but the other candidate is better qualified, the section does not apply. That would be favouring a *lesser* qualified candidate and in breach of EU law.[42]

The employer must have no policy of automatically preferring the candidate from the group. This rather awkwardly phrased require-ment alludes to the savings clause absent from *Kalanke* and seemingly

---

[40] EA 2010 s.159(4).
[41] Baroness Royall, *Hansard*, Official Report HL Vol.717, No.41, p.659 (Feb 9, 2010).
[42] Case C-407/98 *Abrahamsson and Anderson v Fogelqvist*. [2000] I.R.L.R. 732.

required by the ECJ.[43] Thus, employers must include some sort of savings clause to accompany any positive action.

(3) Election Candidates—Section 104

11–012 Section 104 continues the approval of favouring women when selecting election candidates,[44] and extends this to the other protected characteristics. It applies to "registered political parties", where persons who share a protected characteristic are underrepresented in either the Scottish, European, or Westminster Parliaments, the Welsh National Assembly or local government. This section does not (yet) apply to age.[45]

There is "underrepresentation" if there is "inequality" between the *numbers* of the existing elected candidates in one particular parliament, assembly or council. Presumably, this means less than 50 per cent. Of course, it is not possible for every group with a protected characteristic to form half of the political party's elected body. As such it seems that all groups (save perhaps for men, whites, heterosexuals or Christians) could take advantage of s.104.

For the purpose of this calculation, those with disabilities share a single characteristic, rather than sharing their particular disability.[46] So there is no need, say, to show that those with depression are underrepresented in order to favour selecting a candidate with depression under s.104. So long as those with disabilities are underrepresented, then a candidate with *any* disability may be preferred under s.104.

Once s.104 is triggered the party may favour the underrepresented group in its selection of candidates. However, apart from single-sex shortlists which are permitted by exception, the proportionality principle means that shortlists cannot be filled exclusively by persons sharing a protected characteristic. So, it not permissible, for instance, to use s.104 to create an all-black, all-gay or all-Muslim shortlist. The exception for single-sex shortlists will expire in 2030, unless expressly extended by the Minister.[47] Section 106 would permit regulations to made requiring parties to publish information regarding the protected characteristics of those nominated and elected, although this does not extend to pregnancy or maternity, nor marriage or civil partnership.[48] These regulations would be enforced by the Equality and Human Rights Commission.

---

[43] Case C-450/93 *Kalanke v Freie Hansestadt Bremen* [1996] I.C.R. 314. See generally, above, para.11–004.
[44] See above, para.11–012.
[45] Age was excluded from the commencement instrument: SI 2010/2317 art.2(7)(a).
[46] EA 2010 s.104(5), disapplying s.6(3)(b).
[47] EA 2010 s.105.
[48] At the time of writing, this section had not been brought into force.

(4) Remedies—Section 124

For employment cases only, where an individual wins a claim under **11–013** the Act, the tribunal is empowered to make a declaration, order compensation and make a recommendation. The recommendation is the key here. The tribunal can order that the employer "takes specified steps for the purpose of obviating or reducing the adverse effect of any matter to which the proceedings relate (a) on the complainant; (b) on any other person."[49] Both have potential for positive action, although it has been held under the old legislation that what is now paragraph (a) could not be used to order that a rejected claimant "jump the queue" for the next vacancy, as this would amount to positive discrimination.[50]

Paragraph (b) is new, and permits the tribunal to order an employer to change its practices *generally*, rather than just in relation to the claimant.[51] This has potential going beyond facially neutral recommendations (say, requiring the employer to adopt an anti-harassment policy). Take the case of *King v Great Britain-China Centre*.[52] If were heard now under s.124, a tribunal *could* recommend that the Centre adopt positive action similar to the "tie-break" policy permitted under s.159 (above), until such a time as, say, the representation of ethnic Chinese workers reflected that of its catchment area.

This has long been the approach of Federal Courts in the United States under Title VII of the Civil Rights Act 1964, which prohibits employment discrimination. Title VII authorises courts to remedy unlawful discrimination by ordering: "such affirmative action as may be appropriate, which may include, but is not limited to, reinstatement or hiring of employees, with or without back pay ... or any other equitable relief as the court deems appropriate."[53] In *United States v Paradise*[54] the Supreme Court (by a majority of 6 to 3) upheld an order that the Alabama Department of Public Safety hire whites and blacks on a one-to-one ratio until the proportion of black troopers reached 25 per cent, which was roughly the proportion of qualified blacks in the area. Of course, Title VII *expressly* authorises "affirmative action", unlike s.124. But nothing in s.124 expressly prevents positive action. The limits may lie elsewhere.

There are three potential limits to tribunals ordering positive action **11–014** under s.124. The first is the attitude of the judiciary. If it remains rooted in the approach adopted in *Lambeth LBC v Commission For*

---

[49] EA 2010 s.124(3).
[50] *British Gas v Sharma* [1991] I.C.R. 19 (EAT).
[51] See Ch.12, para.12–034.
[52] [1992] I.C.R. 516 (CA). See Ch.4, para.4–006, and Ch.12 para.12–008.
[53] Section 706(g)(1), USC s.2000e–5(g)(1).
[54] 480 US 149 (1987).

Racial Equality,[55] then tribunals are unlikely even to consider such recommendations. This is in marked contrast to the US Federal Courts, who do not see the symmetrical anti-discrimination formula in Title VII as a barrier to positive action:

> "... the very statutory words intended as a spur or catalyst to cause 'employers and unions to self-examine and to self-evaluate their employment practices and to endeavor to eliminate, so far as possible, the last vestiges of an unfortunate and ignominious page in this country's history,' ... cannot be interpreted as an absolute prohibition against all private, voluntary, race-conscious affirmative action efforts to hasten the elimination of such vestiges."[56]

Federal Courts went on to sanction voluntary positive schemes not only for race but for sex as well.[57]

The second limitation is squaring such a recommendation with other sections of the Act. The obvious one here is the symmetrical prohibition of direct discrimination provided by s.13. It is well established that s.13 will not tolerate a benign motive defence.[58] It is arguable also that as ss.158 and 159 cover positive action, no other section, unless expressly stated, should be taken to provide for it. But s.124 is open enough to include positive action, and as such, it is arguable that it operates as (another) exception to s.13. It is also arguable that s.124 operates independently of ss.158 and 159, which are confined to voluntary action.

The third limitation is that any recommendation should fall with the parameters set by the ECJ (above).

---

[55] [1990] I.C.R. 768 (CA), at p.774. Balcombe L.J. was "wholly unpersuaded that one of the two main purposes of the Race Relations Act 1976 was to promote positive action to benefit racial groups."

[56] *United Steelworkers of America v Weber* 443 US 193, at 201–203 (Sup Ct 1979), citing *Albemarle Paper v Moody*, 422 US 405, at 418 (Sup Ct 1975).

[57] *Johnson v Transportation Agency, Santa Clara County* 480 US 616 (Sup Ct 1987). See n.34, above.

[58] *R. (E) v Governing Body of JFS* [2009] UKSC 15. For argument, pre-*JFS*, that the direct discrimination model could accommodate positive action, see L. Barnes, "Proving Diversity and the Definition of Direct Discrimination" (2003) 32 ILJ 200.

CHAPTER 12

ENFORCEMENT OF THE EQUALITY ACT

INTRODUCTION

The Equality Act 2010 provides two forms of enforcement: individual **12–001** and strategic. The strategic enforcement is entrusted to Equality and Human Rights Commission.

Most actions will be brought in employment tribunals. Those outside employment are brought before the county court or (for Scotland) the sheriff. These may grant remedies which could be granted by the High Court in tort, or (for Scotland) by the Court of Session in reparation.

Employment tribunals—once known as industrial tribunals—are statutory bodies established to resolve disputes concerning the individual employment relationship.[1] They were established in 1964 and dealt with, inter alia, disputes under the Redundancy Payments Act 1965 and claims of unfair dismissal under the Industrial Relations Act 1971 (redundancy and unfair dismissal are now consolidated in the Employment Rights Act 1996). They also hear employment discrimination claims. This makes sense for no better reason than the facts of many cases give rise to both discrimination and unfair dismissal claims.

There was little planning or forethought as to the way in which the tribunals would operate.[2] In particular, they were established on the assumption that the normal "judicial" accusatorial approach would operate, rather than an "administrative" inquisitorial approach.[3] The tribunals were intended to be a cheap, informal and speedy resolution of employment disputes. Yet cases proceed by the traditional process of examination and cross-examination of witnesses, so legal and evidential skills are necessary. Of course, a tribunal panel is limited in the assistance it may give to unrepresented litigants, as it needs to be seen as impartial in the accusatorial arena. This is particularly problematic in discrimination cases because this law is highly technical and the facts giving rise to claims are, more often than not, complex and difficult to analyse, thus presenting a significant drawback for the unrepresented litigant. Nonetheless, the Court of Appeal has made it clear that that employment tribunals should be neither inquisitorial nor proactive.[4]

1. Individual Claims

(1) The Burden of Proof

12–002   The shifting burden of proof in cases of indirect discrimination has always been clear from the statutory definition: once the claimant proves a prima facie case, the burden shifts to the defendant to justify the challenged practice.[5] In practice, direct discrimination has presented more challenging issues of proof. This is because "Very little direct discrimination is today overt or even deliberate."[6] It may be

---

[1] For a brief history and discussion of employment tribunals, see S. Deacon, and G. Morris, *Labour Law* (4th edn, Oxford: Hart, 2005), pp.74–82.

[2] P. Davies and M. Freedland, *Labour Legislation and Public Policy* (Oxford: Clarendon, 1993) pp.161–64.

[3] See J. Clark, "Adversarial and Investigative Approaches to the Arbitral Resolution of Dismissal Disputes: A Comparison of South Africa and the UK" (1999) 28 ILJ 319.

[4] *McNicol v Balfour Beatty Rail Maintenance* [2002] I.C.R. 1498, [26].

[5] See further, Ch.9.

[6] *Anya v University of Oxford* [2001] I.C.R. 847 (CA), [11] (Sedley L.J.).

based upon stereotypes, cultural nuances and values, or sub-conscious assumptions or bias.[7]

As discrimination is a civil matter, the traditional rule was that the burden was on the claimant to prove the case on a balance of probabilities.[8] But, starting with the Burden of Proof Directive 97/80/EC, a shifting burden process has become the norm, and now covers virtually all matters heard under the Equality Act 2010. The specific rule will shift the burden to the defendant once the claimant has proved a prima facie case. This loosely replicates the approach developed by the US Supreme Court in *McDonnell Douglas Corp v Green*.[9] Here, there is three-stage procedure for disparate treatment (direct discrimination) claims. First, the plaintiff must show that: (a) he belongs to a protected group, (b) he applied and was qualified for a job for which the employer was seeking applicants, (c) he was rejected, and (d) that after the rejection the position remained open. The burden then shifts to the employer to articulate some legitimate non-discriminatory reason for the employer's rejection. The third stage arises where the plaintiff tries to show that the employer's stated reason for rejection was a pretext. The formula is varied for dismissal claims.[10] A pretext could be revealed if the employer's reason had never been utilised before, where say, a black worker is disciplined for a minor transgression, where in the past no white workers had been disciplined for similar transgressions. Statistics of say, the prior hiring practice, may debunk the stated reason.[11]

(a) Legislation and Guidelines
Statutory rules on the burden of proof in discrimination cases began with the Burden of Proof Directive 97/80/EC and are now the norm in the equality Directives.[12] In essence, it provides:

12–003

> "... when persons ... establish ... facts from which it may be presumed that there has been direct or indirect discrimination, it

---

[7] In *Deman v AUT* [2003] EWCA 329, the Court of Appeal reversed the employment tribunal and EAT (EAT/746/99) decisions because the employment tribunal failed to look for sub-conscious discrimination.

[8] "It is sometimes suggested that tribunals see an allegation of discrimination as very serious, almost quasi-criminal in nature, and as a result may, consciously or subconsciously, demand a rather higher standard than the normal balance of probabilities test. See C. Bourn and J. Whitmore, *Anti-Discrimination Law in Britain* (3rd edn, London: Sweet & Maxwell, 1996), p.116.

[9] 411 US 792 (1973).

[10] See e.g. *McKnight v Kimberly Clark Corporation* 149 F 3d 1125, at 1129 (10th Cir 1998), where the first part requires: (1) the plaintiff belonged to a protected group (say aged over 50), (2) and was doing satisfactory work; (3) and was discharged, and (4) his position was filled by a person from a different group (say a younger person).

[11] See *King v Great Britain-China Centre* [1992] I.C.R. 516 (CA), below, para.12–008.

[12] Recast Directive 2006/54/EC art.19; Framework Directive 2000/78/EC art.10; Race Directive 2000/43/EC art.8.

shall be for the respondent to prove that there has been no breach of the principle of equal treatment."

The Equality Act 2010 s.136 provides:

"(2) If there are facts from which the court could decide, in the absence of any other explanation, that a person (A) contravened the provision concerned, the court must hold that the contravention occurred.

(3) But subsection (2) does not apply if A shows that A did not contravene the provision."

The EC derived rule on the burden of proof applies to any contravention of the Act (save for criminal offences) and so will include direct and indirect discrimination, harassment and victimisation, although, as seen below, most of the litigation centres on direct discrimination.[13] The reference to "court" includes: an employment tribunal; the Asylum and Immigration Tribunal; the Special Immigration Appeals Commission; the First-tier Tribunal; the Special Educational Needs Tribunal for Wales; an Additional Support Needs Tribunal for Scotland.[14] The formula reproduces the various provisions previously in force. So there is case law on its precise meaning.

12–004   The starting point is the extensive guidance provided by the Court of Appeal in *Igen (formally Leeds Careers Guidance) v Wong*:[15]

"(1) [I]t is for the claimant who complains of sex discrimination to prove on the balance of probabilities facts from which the tribunal could conclude, in the absence of an adequate explanation, that the employer has committed an act of discrimination against the claimant which is unlawful . . ..

(2) If the claimant does not prove such facts he or she will fail.

(3) It is important to bear in mind in deciding whether the claimant has proved such facts that it is unusual to find direct evidence of sex discrimination. Few employers would be prepared to admit such discrimination, even to themselves. In some cases the discrimination will not be an intention but merely based on the assumption that 'he or she would not have fitted in'.

(4) In deciding whether the claimant has proved such facts, it is important to remember that the outcome at this stage of the analysis by the tribunal will therefore usually depend on what inferences it is proper to draw from the primary facts found by the tribunal.

---

[13] EA 2010 s.136(6).
[14] EA 2010 s.136(6).
[15] [2005] I.C.R. 931, annexed to the judgment. This revised the guidance given in *Barton v Investec* [2003] I.C.R. 1205 (EAT), [25].

(5) It is important to note the word 'could' in [the formula]. ...
At this stage the tribunal does not have to reach a definitive
determination that such facts would lead it to the conclusion that
there was an act of unlawful discrimination. At this stage a tribunal is looking at the primary facts before it to see what
inferences of secondary fact could be drawn from them.

(6) In considering what inferences or conclusions can be
drawn from the primary facts, the tribunal must assume that
there is no adequate explanation for those facts.

(7) These inferences can include, in appropriate cases, any
inferences that it is just and equitable to draw ... from an evasive
or equivocal reply to a questionnaire. ... [16]

(8) Likewise, the tribunal must decide whether any provision
of any relevant code of practice is relevant and, if so, take it into
account. ... This means that inferences may also be drawn from
any failure to comply with any relevant code of practice.[17]

(9) Where the claimant has proved facts from which conclusions could be drawn that the employer has treated the claimant
less favourably on the ground of sex, then the burden of proof
moves to the employer.

(10) It is then for the employer to prove that he did not
commit, or as the case may be, is not to be treated as having
committed, that act.

(11) To discharge that burden it is necessary for the employer
to prove, on the balance of probabilities, that the treatment was
in no sense whatsoever on the grounds of sex, since 'no discrimination whatsoever' is compatible with the Burden of Proof
Directive 97/80/EC.[18]

(12) That requires a tribunal to assess not merely whether the
employer has proved an explanation for the facts from which
such inferences can be drawn, but further that it is adequate to
discharge the burden of proof on the balance of probabilities
that sex was not a ground for the treatment in question.

(13) Since the facts necessary to prove an explanation would
normally be in the possession of the respondent, a tribunal
would normally expect cogent evidence to discharge that burden
of proof. In particular, the tribunal will need to examine carefully explanations for failure to deal with the questionnaire
procedure and/or code of practice."

There are two notable features here, both of which favour the claimant. The first is that once a prima facie case has been established by

---

[16] See now EA 2010 s.138.
[17] A breach of the Code does not in itself make a person liable: EA 2006 s.14(4).
[18] This Directive introduced the burden of proof rule into sex discrimination law, now
absorbed into the Recast Directive 2006/54/EC. Of the current equality Directives, only the
Framework Directive 2000/78/EC carries the qualifier "whatsoever" (art.2(1)).

the claimant, tribunals are *compelled* to find liability, unless the defendant proves otherwise. Second, the defendant's burden is onerous, requiring "cogent" evidence to prove no discrimination *whatsoever*.

12–005   The *Igen* judgment and guidelines have since been approved as "authoritative" and "helpful" by the Court of Appeal,[19] although this was not without some qualification on "how the burden of proof should work".[20] This was because there still seemed to be "much confusion" created by *Igen*.[21] Thus, in three consecutive cases in 2007,[22] the Court of Appeal revisited the *Igen* guidelines. In general, the judgments suggest that tribunals should be afforded some flexibility on how to apply s.136: "Could decide" in s.136 "must mean that 'a reasonable tribunal could properly conclude' from all the evidence before it."[23] The question addressed in these judgments was which evidence should be assessed at which stage. Two particular points emerged.

The first is that although s.136 sets out a two-stage process, tribunals would have heard all the evidence before embarking on this process, and so it would be "absurd" to assess all the evidence in isolation.[24] Accordingly, Mummery L.J. found that what is now s.136:

"... does not expressly or impliedly prevent the tribunal at the first stage from hearing, accepting or drawing inferences from evidence adduced by the respondent disputing and rebutting the complainant's evidence of discrimination."[25]

Thus, he continued, at the first stage, a tribunal could consider the defendant's evidence on (1) the truth of the facts alleged, (2) whether the treatment was less favourable, (3) the correctness of the comparison, and (4) the reasons for the treatment.

A concern here is that if a tribunal considers at the first stage the defendant's evidence, especially on the reason for the treatment, the defendant can destroy the prima facie case there and then. This means that the employer's burden does not arise, and with this disappears the employer's obligation to produce "cogent evidence", and the tribunal's obligation to "examine carefully explanations for failure to deal with the questionnaire procedure and/or code of practice" (*Igen*, guidelines, above). This blurring of the first and second stages

---

[19] *Madarassy v Nomura International* [2007] I.C.R. 867 (CA), [7].
[20] ibid. [13].
[21] ibid. [7], citing *Laing v Manchester CC* [2006] I.C.R. 1519 (EAT), [71] (Elias J.).
[22] *Madarassy v Nomura* [2007] I.C.R. 867; *Appiah v Governing Body of Bishop Douglass Roman Catholic High School* [2007] I.C.R. 897; *Brown v Croydon LB* [2007] I.C.R. 909.
[23] ibid. [57].
[24] *Appiah v Governing Body of Bishop Douglass Roman Catholic High School* [2007] I.R.L.R. 264 (CA), [43]. See also *Madarassy* [2007] I.C.R. 867 (CA), [70].
[25] *Madarassy v Nomura* [2007] I.C.R. 867 (CA), [71].

is facilitated by a discrepancy between the parent Directives and the Equality Act 2010. The Directives stipulate that "... when persons ... establish ... facts from which it may be presumed ...". Whereas, s.136 provides: "If there are facts from which the court could decide ...".[26] The difference is that the Directives confine the first stage to the claimant's evidence, whereas s.136 suggests that the facts could come from either party. The process envisaged by the Directives may be an artificial one,[27] but it accords with the purpose of the two-stage process.

The Court of Appeal stated that tribunals should not "presume" an "absence of any other explanation" at the first stage, as the word "presume" does not appear in what is now s.136.[28] This overlooks a second discrepancy with the Directives, which state that the burden shifts if it could be *presumed* there was discrimination, whereas for s.136, it is if a court *could decide*. The use of different phraseology in the transposition is no reason to erase the original from the process.

The second feature was that where the claimant presents a **12–006** hypothetical comparator, tribunals may[29] go straight to the second stage. This builds on Lord Nicholls' speech in *Shamoon v Chief Constable of the RUC*,[30] which pointed out that the proper identity of the hypothetical comparator could be resolved only when the reason for the treatment was identified. Thus, tribunals are free, where appropriate, to go straight to the second stage and establish the reason for the treatment. In *Madarassy v Nomura*,[31] Mummery L.J. observed that this should not prejudice claimants. In fact, it prejudices the defendant "if the burden of proof ought not to have moved to him in the first place."[32] This is rather patronising, implying that a claimant is "lucky" not to have to establish a prima facie case. First, if it prejudices the defendant, it should not happen. Second, in such a move, the claimant's evidence could be reduced to evidence merely rebutting the defendant's case, a bizarre conclusion, bearing in mind the wording and purpose of s.136, which envisages the defendant rebutting the claimant's case. Worst still, the claimant's evidence could be overlooked altogether. The defendant's case may sound perfectly plausible in isolation. Suppose a variation on *Shamoon*:[33]

---

[26] Above, para.12–003.
[27] Acknowledged as necessary for the process in *Igen* [2005] I.C.R. 931 (CA), [22] ("it may be contrary to reality") and guideline (6), above, para.12–004, but condemned in *Madarassy v Nomura* [2007] I.C.R. 867 (CA), [70] ("there is an air of unreality about all of this").
[28] *Madarassy v Nomura* [2007] I.C.R. 867 (CA), [77].
[29] They are not compelled. It will depend on the circumstances: *Madarassy v Nomura* [2007] I.C.R. 867 (CA), [83].
[30] [2003] I.C.R. 337 (HL), [10]–[12].
[31] [2007] I.C.R. 867 (CA).
[32] ibid. [82], citing *Brown v Croydon LB* [2007] I.C.R. 909 (CA), [33]–[40], in turn citing *Laing v Manchester CC* [2006] I.C.R. 1519 (EAT), [76] (Elias J.).
[33] The facts are set out in Ch.4, para.4–006.

Following complaints from officers, the sole female police inspector is suspended from carrying out appraisals of them. As there have never been such complaints against male inspectors, the claimant presents a hypothetical comparator. The tribunal goes straight to stage two, where the employer explains that it would have suspended *any* inspector if he were the subject of complaints from officers. Meanwhile, the evidence of the inspector is that the exclusively male cohort of officers resent being appraised by a woman, and that (sex) is real reason behind their complaints. This evidence is overlooked, never rebutted, and yet the employer prevails.

The underlying problem with this approach is confusing substantive law (*Shamoon*) with procedure. *Shamoon* suggests that a hypothetical comparator cannot be identified before identifying the reason for the treatment. This does confine the burden to one party or another. Both sides almost certainly will have a view on the identity of the comparator and reason for the treatment. And it is well established that a prima facie case of direct discrimination cannot be established without some evidence of a discriminatory reason (see immediately below).

(b) Proving Direct Discrimination

12–007 It is clear from case law both before and after the statutory burden of proof rules, that showing that the claimant had a protected characteristic and was badly treated is not enough to establish even a prime facie case. Some evidence of a connection between the treatment and the protected characteristic is necessary.

In *Glasgow CC v Zafar*[34] an employment tribunal found that the claimant had been unfairly dismissed because the dismissal procedure had fallen far below that of the reasonable employer, and been discriminated against on grounds of race. Giving judgment for the House of Lords, Lord Browne-Wilkinson held that tribunals should ask two questions: (1) was there less favourable treatment? And (2) if so, was it on grounds of race? The House of Lords reversed the tribunal decision. There had been no racial discrimination: the employer's unreasonable behaviour did not bind a tribunal to make a finding of racial discrimination.

In *University of Huddersfield v Wolff*[35] a female lecturer complained that she was rejected for promotion in favour of a male colleague. The EAT held that these facts alone were not enough to raise a prima facie case and shift the burden to the University to explain the difference in treatment on a non-discriminatory basis. In *St*

---

[34] [1998] I.C.R. 120 (HL).
[35] [2004] I.C.R. 828, EAT.

Christopher's Fellowship v Walters-Ennis,[36] the claimant, who was black, was removed from recruitment responsibilities and her preferred candidate was not appointed. This was because the management mistakenly thought that the candidate was the claimant's friend. The Chief Executive, HR Director, Head of Services and the claimant's line manager were white. These facts were not enough to establish a prima facie case.

It has been held in Northern Ireland that no inference of any kind is raised by the mere fact that the members of the appointing panel were all of a different religion from a candidate.[37] (But the profile of an interview panel cannot always be excluded as irrelevant to a claim,[38] especially where the panel's membership was manipulated.[39])

All that said, it should not take much more to raise the inference of discrimination. In *King v Great Britain-China Centre*,[40] the defendant was an organisation dedicated to fostering closer ties with China. It advertised for a deputy director of the centre, requiring fluent spoken Chinese and personal knowledge of China. Ms King was of Chinese origin, educated in Britain, and met the requirements. She applied but did not even make the short list. All eight short-listed candidates were white and the successful candidate was an English graduate in Chinese. None of the five ethnically Chinese applicants had been short-listed. Further, no ethnically Chinese person had ever been employed by the Centre. King brought a claim of direct race discrimination. The industrial tribunal drew an inference that the defendant had discriminated against King because she did not come from the "same, essentially British, academic background" as the existing staff. The Court of Appeal upheld this finding, observing:

12–008

> "Though there will be some cases where, for example, the non-selection of the applicant for a post or for promotion is clearly not on racial grounds, a finding of discrimination and a finding of a difference in race will often point to the possibility of racial discrimination. In such circumstances, the tribunal will look to the employer for an explanation. If no explanation is then put forward or if the tribunal considers the explanation to be inadequate or unsatisfactory it will be legitimate for the tribunal to infer that the discrimination was on racial grounds. This is not

---

[36] [2010] EWCA Civ. See also *Fox v Rangecroft* [2006] EWCA Civ 1112, where the claimant detailed 19 instances of treatment which breached the employer's procedure, none of which suggested discrimination.

[37] *Armagh DC v Fair Employment Agency* [1994] I.R.L.R. 234 (NICA).

[38] See *Short v Greater London Unison*, Case No.2301192/98 [2000] DCLD 46, referred to in the previous "Code of practice on racial equality in employment", 2006, CRE, at para.5.7 (ISBN 1 85442 570 6).

[39] See the US case, *Domingo v New England Fish Company* 727 F 2d 1429 at 1435-36 (9th Cir 1984).

[40] [1992] I.C.R. 516 (CA).

a matter of law, but, as May L.J. put it in *Noone*,[41] 'almost common sense'."[42]

In *Igen v Wong*,[43] a black worker was treated unreasonably by three supervisors, each white, in disciplinary proceedings. While cautioning against a finding discrimination merely on unreasonable treatment, the Court of Appeal upheld the tribunal's finding of a prima facie case of racial discrimination on these facts.

12–009   What *King* and *Zafar* have in common is that there was unfavourable treatment and each victim had a protected characteristic. In *Zafar*, Lord Browne-Wilkinson is saying that alone this is not enough for a finding of discrimination on one of the protected characteristics. That was the sum of the evidence in *Zafar*. The additional evidence in *King* was the racial origin of the Centre's staff and those short-listed for interview. This pointed to the rejection being on the grounds of race. The Centre's failure to explain the less favourable treatment on grounds other than race confirmed this. Combined with the less favourable treatment and the racial origin of the claimant, this was enough to draw an inference of racial discrimination. This demonstrates *Igen's* fourth guideline (above), that in absence of direct evidence of unlawful discrimination, inferences may be made from circumstantial evidence and the defendant has the burden to refute those inferences with contrary evidence.

Both *Walters-Ennis* and *Igen* go further than *Zafar*, because of the racial make-up of the management, but that alone does not explain the different outcomes. It seems that the distinctive feature of *Igen* was the close involvement of the three white supervisors in the treatment of the black worker.[44] However, it shows that cases are illustrative and that the process is very fact sensitive. It might also demonstrate that since *Madarassy* et al. (above, para.12–006), tribunals are more willing to consider the *defendant's* evidence at the first stage, which alone could destroy the prima facie case.

An exception to this general approach appears to be where there is a lack of transparency in equal pay claims. In *Barton v Investec Henderson Crosthwaite Securities*,[45] a City worker's male comparator was paid more and the employer produced no evidence as to the basis for the extra pay. The employment tribunal gave deference to the "vital" culture of discretionary and "unwritten" bonuses, and found that the difference in pay was justified.[46] The EAT held that the tribunal was in error to condone this lack of transparency and that it

---

[41] *Noone v North West Thames RHA* [1988] I.C.R. 813 (CA).
[42] [1992] I.C.R. 516 (CA), at p.529.
[43] [2005] I.C.R. 931 (CA).
[44] [2005] I.C.R. 931, [39]–[51].
[45] [2003] I.C.R. 1205, EAT. See also *Handels-og Kontorfunktionaerernes Forbund i Danmark v Dansk Arbejdsgiverforening (acting for Danfoss)* Case 109/88 [1989] I.R.L.R. 532.
[46] Reported ibid. [10].

was for the employer to prove that sex was not a reason for difference in pay. It remains to be seen if this approach spreads beyond equal pay claims, for instance to discretionary and unwritten promotion and recruitment practices.[47]

(2) Commission Assistance

Legal assistance may be provided by the Equality and Human Rights Commission. See further below, para.12–044.

12–010

(3) Time Limits

The normal rule for employment tribunals is that an application must be presented within three months of the commission of the acts of discrimination alleged. The normal rule for the county court or sheriff is six months.[48] Different rules apply to equal pay claims (see below) and there a number of extensions in specific cases.[49]

12–011

If a claim is out of time, the employment tribunal or county court (or sheriff) has discretion to extend the time to "such other period as [it] thinks just and equitable"[50] There are two connected issues with the limitation period. First, identifying when the act of discrimination occurs so to start time running, and second, when it is "just and equitable" to permit a claim to proceed, despite the standard period having elapsed.

(a) When Time Starts Running

For establishing when time begins to run, the Equality Act 2010 s.118(6) provides that (a) "conduct extending over a period is to be treated as done at the end of the period"; and (b) a "failure to do something is to be treated as occurring when the person in question decided on it".[51]

12–012

(i) Continuing act

Where the discrimination is by a contractual term, the time does not begin to run until the term is removed or the contract ends. So where, for example, an Asian man is employed with an inferior pension

12–013

---

[47] For a discussion on nepotism and word-of-mouth hiring as indirect discrimination, see Ch.6, para.6–013.

[48] EA 2010, respectively ss.118(1), 123(1).

[49] e.g., For the armed forces, the time limit is six months (EA 2010 s.121(2)); for conciliation under EA 2006 s.27 (inter alia complaints in higher education, and claims to county court or sheriff), it is nine months (EA 2010 118(2)).

[50] EA 2010, respectively ss.118(1)(b), 123(1)(b).

[51] For the county court or sheriff. Section 123(3) repeats this for employment tribunals.

entitlement to his white colleagues, the discrimination extends to the duration of the employment contract.[52]

The main area of dispute here falls under paragraph (a). The issue is whether a series of separate acts can amount to a single continuing act "extending over a period". If not, only those acts falling within the time limit can be included in the claim (subject to the "just and equitable" discretion, see below). But if a series of acts can be treated as a single continuing act, they become part of the claim so long as the final act fell within the time limit.

In *Hendricks v Metropolitan Police Commissioner*[53] the Court of Appeal offered some guidance on this question. First, the phrase in the legislation *act extending over a period* is legally "more precise" than expressions such as "institutionalised racism", "a prevailing way of life", a "generalised policy of discrimination", or "climate" or "culture" of unlawful discrimination. But it is not confined to something so formal as a policy, rule, practice, scheme or regime. What is required is that "the numerous alleged incidents of discrimination are linked to one another and that they are evidence of a continuing discriminatory state of affairs covered by the concept of 'an act extending over a period.'" These acts may continue into a period of absence from work. In addition, evidence of long-past less favourable treatment may still be used to reinforce the current claim. In this case, Joy Hendricks, a black woman police constable, specified nearly 100 acts of sex and race discrimination committed by her employer spanning the whole of her 11-year career. Most were committed in the first five years of service. Her final year of service was spent on long-term stress-related sick leave. The Court of Appeal upheld the employment tribunal's finding that the behaviour over the whole 11 years amounted to a continuing act. There was no need to show that the behaviour amounted to a policy of discrimination.

12–014   In *Barclays Bank v Kapur*[54] the claimants, East African Asians, had worked in banks in Kenya and Tanzania, before moving to the UK in the early 1970s, where they were employed by Barclays. In contrast to its normal policy, Barclays refused to credit the claimant's previous service with the East African banks when calculating their pension entitlement. The claimants could not argue that this was *contractual* discrimination, because the refusal was made before the Race Relations Act 1976 came into force. However, the House of Lords held that the refusal was continuing discrimination, rather than a one-off act at the start of their employment, which effectively extended to the duration of their employment. Hence their claim of racial discrimination was not time-barred.

---

[52] *Barclays Bank v Kapur* [1991] 2 A.C. 355 (HL), obiter, at p.367. Contractual terms unlawful under the Act are unenforceable against the victim: EA 2010 s.142.

[53] [2003] I.C.R. 530, [48]–[52].

[54] [1991] 2 A.C. 355.

In *Calder v James Finlay Corporation*,[55] Mrs Calder requested a mortgage subsidy twice, in March and May 1981. Each time she was refused. She resigned in October and presented a claim of sex discrimination (all male staff had been given mortgage subsidies). The EAT held that the refusal amounted to continuing discrimination as long as she remained in this employment, and so time did not begin to run until her resignation. In *Cast v Croydon College*[56] the claimant, after becoming pregnant, was refused permission to return to work part-time after the birth. Further requests to transfer to a part-time contract were refused and eventually she resigned one month after returning from her maternity leave, and then two months later made a claim of sex discrimination. The Court of Appeal held that the application of a discriminatory policy here amounted to an act extending over a period, so that the effects of the first decision (made before the birth) were continuing. Finally, in *Aziz v FDA*,[57] the Court of Appeal confirmed that one relevant but not necessarily conclusive factor is whether the same, or different, individuals were involved in the discriminatory conduct.

There appear to be two circumstances where the courts take a less generous view of "continuing act". The first is where a single act causes continuing *effects*, such as re-grading a worker to a lower grade. This occurred in *Sougrin v Haringey HA*[58] where the Court of Appeal held that as this was not a case where there was a discriminatory "policy" of paying less on racial grounds, the only acts were the re-grading (and rejection of subsequent appeal), which occurred some six months before the claim was submitted. Thus it was out of time. Similarly, in *Amies v ILEA*[59] the failure to promote a woman was a one-off act, and its continuing effects did not establish a continuing act. Such a delicate distinction between a continuing act and continuing *effects* is extremely difficult to reconcile with *Barclays Bank v Kapur* (above), yet the House of Lords in *Kapur* approved of both *Calder* and *Amies*, thus endorsing this distinction.[60]

The second restriction applies to job applicants who are not **12–015** employees. In *Tyagi v BBC World Service*[61] an existing worker was refused a promotion in April 1997. In relation to this, he presented a claim of racial discrimination in July 1998, after having left the BBC in July 1997. He argued that the BBC had a discriminatory recruitment policy and so he could never get the position he had applied for, whether he applied as an existing worker or as an outsider, and so the alleged discrimination was continuing into the period when he was no

---

[55] [1989] I.C.R. 157.
[56] [1998] I.C.R. 500 (CA).
[57] [2010] EWCA Civ 304, [33], [43].
[58] [1992] I.C.R. 650.
[59] [1977] I.C.R. 308 (EAT).
[60] [1991] 2 A.C. 355, at p.369. The House of Lords considered that discriminatory pension rights were no different from discriminatory pay.
[61] [2001] I.R.L.R. 465 (CA).

longer an employee. The Court of Appeal held that there was no continuing act of discrimination and so his claim was out of time. This restriction is based on the employment provisions of the legislation.[62] The equivalent nowadays, EA 2010 s.39(1), applies to the "arrangements" for deciding to whom to offer employment, or the terms of the offer, or not offering the employment. None of these, according to the Court of Appeal, can be continuing acts. By contrast, s.39(2) applies to *employees* and the way they are afforded access to opportunities for promotion, transfer or training, or to any other benefits, facilities or services, or any other detriment. Any of these can amount to continuing acts.

(ii) Deliberate omission

12–016   The Act states that a "failure to do something is to be treated as occurring when the person in question decided on it."[63] This suggests that an employer's deliberate omission to do something is fixed in time and so cannot be a continuing act. This may be so, but the House of Lords in *Barclays Bank v Kapur*[64] afforded paragraph (b) such a limited scope, that this should matter little. The bank argued that its failure to credit the claimant's previous service was a "deliberate omission" which had to be attributed to the time when the bank "decided upon it", which was when the claimants were first employed. The House of Lords rejected this interpretation, as it could not be squared with the notion that an unlawful contractual term continued to have effect for the duration of the contract.[65] Further, this was a "very artificial way" of looking at the facts: "Whenever terms of employment are less favourable it is possible to dress up the complaint as a deliberate omission by saying that the employer 'deliberately omitted' to include the more favourable term in the contract of employment". The House suggested that "deliberate omission" in this context "was included by the draftsman as a sweeping-up provision intended for the protection of employees and addressed to activities peripheral to the employment rather than to the terms of the employment itself, and intended to cover a one-off rather than a continuing situation: for example, a deliberate failure to notify a [black] employee of a vacancy for a better job in the company when all his white comparators were invited to apply for the job."[66]

---

[62] See Ch.8.
[63] EA 2010 ss.118(3)(b), 123(6)(b). In the absence of evidence to the contrary, this is either when the person does something which conflicts with doing the act in question; or at the end of the time when it would have been reasonable for them to do the thing. (EA 2010 ss.118(4), 123(7), and Explanatory Notes (387)).
[64] [1991] 2 A.C. 355. See above, para.12–014.
[65] See above, para.8–007.
[66] [1991] 2 A.C. 355, at pp.367–368 (Lord Griffiths, delivering the judgment of the House).

(b) The Meaning of "Just and Equitable"

In *British Coal Corporation v Keeble*[67] the EAT stated that tribunals **12–017**
should adopt as a checklist the factors mentioned in s.33 of the
Limitation Act 1980, which provides a broad discretion to extend the
limitation period of three years in cases of personal injury and death.
Paraphrased, the factors are: (a) the length of and reasons for the
delay; (b) the extent to which the cogency of the evidence is likely to
be affected by the delay; (c) the extent to which the party sued had
cooperated with any requests for information; (d) the promptness
with which the claimant had acted once he had known of the facts
giving rise to the cause of action; and (e) the steps taken by the
claimant to obtain appropriate professional advice once he had
known of the possibility of taking action.

In *London Borough of Southwark v Afolabi*,[68] Peter Gibson L.J., in
the Court of Appeal, said that a failure to adopt such a checklist was
not necessarily an error in law, although it had "utility" in many
cases.[69] In *Department of Constitutional Affairs v Jones*,[70] a worker
who had developed a depressive illness was dismissed for gross misconduct. At first, he denied his illness was severe enough to amount
to a disability. As a result, he submitted his claim for disability discrimination five weeks' late. This case centred on the state of mind of
the claimant, and so it was appropriate to disregard the "promptness" guideline ((d), above), and extend the time. Giving judgment for
the Court, Pill L.J. cautioned: "I am far from stating any general
principle that a person with mental health problems is entitled to
delay as a matter of course in bringing a claim." But to this he added
the point may arise: "when there is a physical injury which is on the
margin of being disabling as perceived, or where a mental condition
arises."[71]

The wide discretion afforded to a tribunal in discrimination cases
was emphasised by the Court of Appeal in *Robertson v Bexley
Community Centre (t/a Leisure Link)*,[72] stating that a decision should
not be reversed unless it was plainly wrong in law. This cuts both
ways though, as it prevents an appeal by *either* side unless there was
an error in law.

In *Robertson* the claimant trainee was racially abused by his **12–018**
supervisor in April 1999. He complained and the supervisor was
disciplined and then went off sick for several months. Upon his
return, in October, the supervisor again racially abused the claimant,
who resigned the following the day. The employment tribunal held

---

[67] [1997] I.R.L.R. 336.
[68] [2003] EWCA Civ 15.
[69] ibid. [33]. Peter Gibson L.J. dissented on a separate issue.
[70] [2008] I.R.L.R. 128 (CA). See also *Chief Constable of Lincolnshire v Cashton* [2010] I.R.L.R.
327 (CA).
[71] ibid. [51].
[72] [2003] I.R.L.R. 434 (CA), [25].

that the claim relating to the abuse in April was out of time and in light of the disciplinary action taken for that, it would not be just and equitable to hear that claim. The Court of Appeal upheld that decision as it was not wrong in law.

Time may be extended when incorrect legal advice delays the claim. In *British Coal v Keeble*,[73] the claimant was made redundant and paid according to a scheme which was more favourable to men. Her union advised her, incorrectly, that the scheme was lawful, but later, counsel's opinion advised her to claim. As a result, her claim was made 22 months after she was made redundant. The EAT allowed her to pursue her claim. In *Hawkins v Ball and Barclays Bank*,[74] a worker presented a claim of sexual harassment five months after the incident, having been advised originally by a solicitor that the incident was trivial. The EAT held that in the circumstances it was just and equitable to permit the claim to proceed. Of course, where the advice comes after the normal time limit, it cannot cause the delay.[75]

In *Afolabi*, the claimant was interviewed in 1990 for the post of auditor. He was rejected but offered a job at a lower grade, which he took. Nine years later he brought proceedings in relation to a re-grading. For these proceedings he inspected his personnel file, which revealed that in his original interview he been given a very high score. Within three months of inspecting the file, he brought proceedings for racial discrimination in relation to that original interview. The Court of Appeal held, in this "wholly exceptional" case, it was just and equitable to allow the claim to proceed. The Court noted that Mr Afolabi had no reason to inspect his file at an earlier time and no reason to think he had an arguable case before he had seen it. Further, extending the time was equally prejudicial to the claimant, who had to prove discrimination.

12–019   The question of extending time arises commonly where the worker awaits the outcome of a grievance or disciplinary procedure before issuing proceedings. In *Aniagwu v London Borough of Hackney*,[76] Morison J. suggested time should always be extended in this circumstance, saying:

> "... it seems to us that every industrial tribunal, unless there was some particular feature about the case, or some particular piece of prejudice which the employers could show, would inevitably take the view that that was a responsible and proper attitude for someone to take ...".[77]

[73] [1997] I.R.L.R. 336.
[74] [1996] I.R.L.R. 258 (EAT). See also *Verdi v Commissioner of Police of The Metropolis* [2007] I.R.L.R. 24 (EAT).
[75] *Hunwicks v Royal Mail* (2007) UKEAT/0003/07/ZT, [14]–[15].
[76] [1999] I.R.L.R. 303, EAT.
[77] ibid. [19].

However, in *Robinson v Post Office*[78] Lindsay J., in a response later approved by the Court of Appeal,[79] made it clear that delay because of an internal, or "domestic", process, was just one factor in the question. This was applied in *Hunwicks v Royal Mail*,[80] where the claimant (upon her trade union's advice) exhausted the grievance procedure, which took five months, before issuing proceedings. The EAT refused to extend time, as "the claimant is a person of some intelligence and some education with access to legal advice".[81]

(4) Time Limits—Equal Pay Claims

During 1999-2000, two procedural rules for equal pay claims were challenged as being contrary to art.119 TEC (now art.157, TFEU). The cases were *Levez v Jennings*[82] and *Preston v Wolverhampton Healthcare NHS Trust*.[83] The first rule, by s.2(4) of the Equal Pay Act 1970 (EPA 1970), required that claims are brought, at the latest, within six months of the termination of employment ("the qualifying date"). The second rule, by s.2(5), was that arrears or damages in respect of unequal pay could only be awarded in respect of the period of two years before the proceedings were instituted; tribunals had no discretion. These rules were amended[84] to accord with the judgments of the two cases, and have been updated for the Equality Act 2010. Accordingly, it is appropriate to refer to those judgments when interpreting the rules.

12–020

(a) The Qualifying Date—Equality Act 2010 Section 129(3)

The general[85] rule requires that claims are brought within six months of the termination of employment ("the qualifying date"). There are three exceptions. The first exception is where a worker is employed on a series of temporary contracts. Where the series of contracts could be defined as a "stable work case", the time limit will not begin to run until the end of the stable working relationship. A stable work case can arise with a series of fixed- or short-term contracts, irrespective if there are significant gaps in between, or whether the terms significantly change (but the nature of the work is the same).[86] However, it has been held that where the worker changes jobs with the same

12–021

---

[78] [2000] I.R.L.R. 804, at [29]–[31], EAT.
[79] *Apelogun-Gabriels v Lambeth LBC* [2002] I.C.R. 713, [16] and [24].
[80] *Hunwicks v Royal Mail* (2007) UKEAT/0003/07/ZT.
[81] ibid. [9] (Underhill J.).
[82] Case C-326/96, [1999] I.R.L.R. 36.
[83] Case C-78/98, [2000] I.C.R. 961.
[84] SI 2003/1656.
[85] The periods for armed forces cases are generally 3 months longer: EA 2010 s.129(4).
[86] *North Cumbria University Hospitals NHS Trust v Fox* [2010] I.R.L.R. 804 (CA), following *Slack v Cumbria CC* [2009] I.R.L.R. 463 (CA), holding that *Preston* (above, n.83) should not be confined to its facts [24]–[33].

employer, each job should be treated separately.[87] The second exception arises where, for instance, the employer lies about the pay of a comparator (a "concealment case"). The qualifying date is six months after the claimant discovered ("or could with reasonable diligence have discovered") the truth. This scenario occurred in *Levez* (see below). The third exception arises with incapacity[88] during the six-month period following employment.[89] The qualifying date is six months after the claimant ceased to have the incapacity. In a case of both concealment *and* incapacity, the qualifying date is the later of the two.

(b) Award of Arrears or Damages

12–022   The general purpose of these rules is to align claims with breach of contract. So, the arrears date is now six years before the day proceedings were instituted (England and Wales).[90] For Scotland it is five years before the day proceedings were commenced.[91] In concealment or disability cases, arrears can be claimed from the day on which the breach first occurred,[92] although, for Scotland, this is limited to a 20-year maximum.[93]

There are separate rules for pension cases. There are three types. First, where damages are payable for breach of an equality clause or rule, the same time limits apply.[94] Second, where a person has been excluded from a scheme a tribunal or court may declare the claimant be admitted to the scheme. This can be backdated, but not beyond April 8, 1976 (the date when the ECJ held[95] that art.119 (now art.157 TFEU) had direct effect).[96] Third, for those with membership, where there is a breach of the scheme, the claimant is entitled to have any rights which would have accrued under the scheme secured from a date specified by the tribunal, although the date cannot be earlier than May 17, 1990 (the date when the ECJ established[97] that occupational pensions were pay for the purposes of art.119).[98]

---

[87] *Newcastle upon Tyne CC v Allan* [2005] I.C.R. 1170 (EAT), [28]–[39].

[88] That is, being under 18, or lacking capacity under the Mental Capacity Act 2005 (England and Wales); or under 16 or incapable according to the Adults with Incapacity (Scotland) Act 2000 (EA 2010 s.141(6)–(7)).

[89] EA 2010 s.130(7).

[90] EA 2010 s.132(4).

[91] EA 2010 s.132(5).

[92] EA 2010 s.132(4).

[93] EA 2010 s.135(6).

[94] EA 2010 s.134.

[95] *Defrenne v Sabena* Case C-43/75, [1976] I.C.R. 547.

[96] EA 2010 s.133(2)(a), (4), (5). This was subject to an employee paying contributions owing for the period for which retroactive membership is claimed: see *Fisscher v Voorhuis Hengelo BV and Stichting Bedrijfspensioenfonds voor de Detailhandel* Case C-128/93, [1995] I.C.R. 635 (ECJ), [37].

[97] *Barber v Guardian Royal Exchange* C 262/88, [1990] E.C.R. I-1889.

[98] EA 2010 s.133(2)(a), (6), (7).

In *Levez*, Mrs Levez began work as betting shop manager in February 1991, at £10,000 per annum. In December, her employer falsely told her that another manager (male), doing like work, earned £10,800 pa, and raised her salary accordingly. In fact the male manager had earned £11,400 pa. On leaving her job in March 1993, Mrs Levez discovered the truth. In September she began proceedings for equal pay, claiming arrears from February 1991. The employer argued that by the then EPA 1970 s.2(5), it was only liable for arrears going back two years from the date the claim was made, that is September 1991. The ECJ held that the general two-year limit imposed by s.2(5) was not of itself incompatible with Community law. However, this limit, as far as it was inflexible and so allowing an employer to profit from its deceit, was incompatible with Community law. Under the new rule, Levez could claim equal pay from the time "when the breach first occurred",[99] which was the first day of her employment with the defendant in February 1991.

In *Preston,* the ECJ held that the then EPA 1970 s.2(5), in preventing pensionable service to be credited before the two years preceding an initial claim of equal pay, contravened Community Law. When the case returned to the House of Lords,[100] it was held that credit should be backdated to April 8, 1976.

(5) Remedies

Generally, a county court can order remedies available to the High Court in tort and judicial review; in Scotland, the sheriff can order remedies available to the Court of Session in reparation and judicial review.[101] Employment tribunals can provide compensation, a declaration, and recommendations.[102]   **12–023**

(a) Compensation

As the basis for remedies is tort, compensation should put successful claimants in the position in which they have been but for the unlawful discrimination. As with tort generally, claimants are under a duty to mitigate their loss. However, compensation is not restricted to foreseeable losses. It should be awarded for losses flowing naturally and directly from the wrong.[103] Further, compensation can be awarded for non-pecuniary losses of psychiatric damage, aggravated damage   **12–024**

---

[99] EA 2010 s.132(4)
[100] *Preston v Wolverhampton Healthcare NHS Trust (No.2)*[2001] 2 A.C. 455, [10]–[12].
[101] EA 2010 s.119.
[102] EA 2010 s.124.
[103] *Essa v Laing Ltd* [2004] I.C.R. 746 (CA) [37] (Pill L.J.), [44] (Clark L.J.), approved *Chagger v Abbey National* [2010] I.C.R. (CA), [12]. See also *Sheriff v Klyne Tugs (Lowestoft) Ltd* [1999] I.C.R. 1170 (CA), [17]–[22] (Stuart-Smith L.J.).

and injury to feelings. It is now probable that exemplary damages are available, albeit only in exceptional circumstances.

Unlike unfair dismissal, there is no upper limit for compensation in discrimination cases in employment tribunals.[104] In some cases, compensation will not be available for "unintentional" indirect discrimination.

(i) Pecuniary loss

12–025   Some of calculations necessary were illustrated in *Ministry of Defence v Cannock*,[105] a case concerning many women dismissed from the armed forces because of pregnancy, which was brought under the Equal Treatment Directive 76/207/EEC (at the time the armed forces were excluded from the Sex Discrimination Act 1975). The first feature of the case is that the EAT applied the relevant principles of tort to a claim under EC law. Second, the EAT observed that there was a distinction between these claims and ones for serious personal injury, where there might be loss of a chance ever to work again.[106] The EAT stated that the approach to calculating losses should be neither a finding of fact of what would have happened, nor based simply on what facts are known. The claimants in this case took an "all-or-nothing" strategy, arguing that a tribunal should award compensation based upon for instance (i) whether or not a claimant would have returned to service after the birth; (ii) if so, for how long; and (iii) to what ranks, if any, she would have been promoted during her future service. The MOD argued that the award should be restricted to the known fact of the length of each claimant's commission, which in effect, is a contractual measure. The EAT stated that the correct approach was assess the "chance" of each the events occurring, and compensate for the loss of chance.[107] It is permissible to use statistics in this assessment. In *Vento v Chief Constable of West Yorkshire*[108] statistics were used showing the percentage of women who in the past had continued to serve in the police force until the age of retirement.

It was held in *Chagger v Abbey National*[109] that in a case of discriminatory dismissal, the chances of being dismissed without discrimination must be factored into the calculation. In *Chagger*, the claimant was one of just two persons vulnerable to redundancy. He

---

[104] In *Marshall v Southampton and South West Hampshire AHA (No.2)* Case C-271/91 [1993] I.R.L.R. 445, the ECJ ruled that the (then £11,000) cap breached the Equal Treatment Directive 76/207/EEC (now Recast 2006/54/EC). It was lifted by SI 1993/2798. The cap for other protected characteristics was lifted to avoid an anomaly. The cap for unfair dismissal claims stands at £68,400 on February 13, 2011: SI 2010/2926. It is normally adjusted each February in line with retail prices.
[105] [1994] I.C.R. 918 (EAT). Approved *Chagger v Abbey National* [2010] I.C.R. (CA), [76]. See A. Arnull, "EC law and the dismissal of pregnant servicewomen" (1995) 24 ILJ 215.
[106] ibid. at 929.
[107] ibid. at 935–938.
[108] [2003] I.C.R. 318 (CA), [32]–[44].
[109] [2010] I.C.R. (CA), [57].

was chosen and race played a part in that decision. But had it not done, he may well have been made redundant anyway. By the same reasoning, when a job applicant is rejected because of discrimination, the chances of being rejected without discrimination should be factored into the calculation.

Claimants are expected to mitigate their loss in the normal way.[110] So, a victim of a discriminatory dismissal is likely to be under a duty to seek work. In *Cannock*, this may have been reapplying to the services once the "no-pregnancy" rule had been abandoned.[111] In other cases it may mean accepting an offer of reinstatement. A failure to mitigate entitles the tribunal to reduce the award. For the Court of Appeal in *Ministry of Defence v Wheeler*[112] (another armed forces "pregnancy dismissal" case), it came to this: first, take the sum that the victim would have earned but for the unlawful dismissal, second, deduct from that sum the amount that (in mitigation) she had, or should have, earned elsewhere, and third, apply to that net loss the percentage chance that she would have remained in her pre-dismissal employment. In other words, mitigation should be considered before the question of chance is applied.

It might be that that the stigma of suing for discriminatory dismissal prevents the claimant from obtaining work elsewhere. Prospective employers may perceive this person as a troublemaker. This is more likely in a particularly narrow field where there are relatively few employers.[113] Examples could be the police force, the private security sector, the legal profession and academia. In *Chagger v Abbey National*[114] the Court of Appeal held that damages were recoverable for such a stigma. The theoretical difficulty is that a employer who refuses to appoint because that person's previous discrimination claim is liable for unlawful victimisation. This would appear to be the direct cause of the claimant's loss, rather than the prior dismissal. Nonetheless, the Court rejected that notion, and held that a prospective employer's rejection could be caused by the dismissal. Even if that rejection is unlawful (victimisation) it does not break the chain of causation. The Court invoked an analogy with

12–026

---

[110] Note that in employment unfair dismissal cases, TULRCA 1992 s.207A provides that any award can be increased by 25 per cent where employer unreasonably failed to comply with the ACAS Code of Practice on Disciplinary and Grievance Procedures, and *decreased* by 25 per cent where *employee* unreasonably failed to comply with the Code. For the Code, see *www.acas.org.uk/dgcode2009* (accessed December 13, 2010).

[111] [1994] I.C.R. 918, at 938–940.

[112] [1998] I.C.R. 242 (CA), at 246–254, 257.

[113] For a case where the employer with dominant position in the market effectively blacklisted the dismissed worker, see *Khanum v IBC Vehicles* (1999) EAT/685/98.

[114] [2010] I.C.R. (CA).

Malik v BCCI[115] where the House of Lords recognised stigma loss where the employer had run its business so badly to ruin the reputation of its workers.[116]

On the difficult matter of proving stigma loss, the Court said that a mere assertion by the claimant would not be enough: if the claimant was unwilling to "make good his suspicions" by suing the prospective employer for victimisation, little weight should be afforded to a mere assertion.[117] This is odd, because a claimant suing prospective employers for victimisation would have no need to claim against the employer who dismissed him. Further, the stigma is likely to extend beyond the time of the dismissal litigation. The best that can be made of this statement is evidence over and above a presumption is required. A stronger body of evidence is likely to emerge from the claimant's attempts at mitigation in trying to find other employment.[118] In *Chagger*, the claimant was a chartered accountant specialising in market risk control. He had applied unsuccessfully for 111 jobs. This, said the Court, was good evidence of his stigma claim.

The calculation of the stigma loss would not normally be as a separate head of loss. It will normally "be one of the features which impacts on the question how long it will be before a job can be found."[119]

(ii) Non-pecuniary loss

12–027 Where appropriate, damages may be awarded for psychiatric damage, aggravated damage and (provided specifically by the Equality Act 2010) injured feelings.[120] Injured feelings includes subjective feelings of upset, frustration, worry, anxiety, mental distress, fear, grief, anguish, humiliation, unhappiness, stress and depression. Compensation for injury to feelings cannot be fixed with any degree of precision. "Translating hurt feelings into hard currency is bound to be an artificial exercise."[121] Or, as Dickson J. said in the Canadian Supreme Court:

---

[115] [1998] A.C. 20 (HL). It is conceivable that the stigma caused by the dismissal itself (discriminatory or otherwise) prevents the person obtaining work in a chosen field and so breach her right to privacy: *Sidibras v Lithuania* (2006) 42 E.H.R.R. 6, [49]; *L v Metropolitan Police* [2009] UKSC 3, [24]; generally M. Connolly, "Victimising third parties: the Equality Directives, the European Convention on Human Rights, and EU General Principles", (2010) 35(6) E.L. Rev 822, at 830–832.

[116] [2010] I.C.R. (CA), [88]–[91].

[117] ibid. [97]. See *Leeds Rhinos Rugby Club v Sterling* (2002) EAT/267/01, where the EAT reversed the ET's presumption that the claimant would not find other work because, having sued for racial discrimination, he would be known as a troublemaker.

[118] ibid. [98].

[119] ibid. [95].

[120] EA 2010 s.119(4): "An award of damages may include compensation for injured feelings (whether or not it includes compensation on any other basis)". This applies to employment tribunals as well (s.124(6)).

[121] *Vento v Chief Constable of West Yorkshire Police* [2003] I.C.R. 318, [50] (Mummery L.J.).

"There is no medium of exchange for happiness. ... The monetary evaluation of non-pecuniary losses is a philosophical and policy exercise more than a legal or logical one."[122]

In *Vento v Chief Constable of West Yorkshire Police*[123] Mummery L.J. offered extensive guidance on calculating the award. He first noted that older cases were decided before the ceiling on damages was removed, in 1993,[124] implying that their usefulness as a guide was limited. Since *Vento* was decided, in 2002, the EAT has uplifted the sums, which are ones given below.[125] The guidance divided cases into three bands. The first, for the "most serious cases", (such as a lengthy campaign of discriminatory harassment) should attract awards of £18,000 to £30,000. Only in "the most exceptional case" should it exceed £30,000. The middle band, for "serious cases" should be between £6,000 and £18,000. The lowest band, for "less serious cases" should be between £500 and £6,000. Generally awards of less than £500 should not be made as they risk not indicating a proper recognition of the injury.

In this case, Ms Vento won her claim for sex discrimination following a series of bullying which ended with her dismissal for alleged dishonesty. The employment tribunal found that she had "been put through four traumatic years by the conduct of the respondent's officers." It further found that Ms Vento's employer and colleagues acted in a "high-handed manner" by raising questions about her honesty and private life, even after the appeal was decided. The employer made "a cynical offer of reinstatement principally designed to limit the financial damage". None of the relevant officers ever apologised, and when the Deputy Chief Constable eventually attempted to apologise he did so unaware of the decisions against him and so spoke "not really knowing for what he was apologising". Overall, the employer and its officers were in "institutional denial". For her non-pecuniary loss, the Court of Appeal awarded Ms Vento £18,000 for injury to feelings, £5,000 aggravated damages and £9,000 for psychiatric damage.

Where the victim suffers two (or more) forms of discrimination (say, disability and race) arising from the same facts, it would be "artificial" to assess each discrete head of discrimination. In *Khanum v IBC Vehicles*[126] a Muslim woman was dismissed suffering both racial and sexual harassment. The EAT held there was no error in law in calculating a single award for her injured feelings. However:

---

[122] *Andrews v Grand & Toy Alberta Ltd* (1978) 83 DLR (3d) 452, at 475, cited in *Vento*, ibid. [50].

[123] [2003] I.C.R. 318, at §§ 52 and 65.

[124] In 1993.

[125] *Da'Bell v NSPCC* [2010] I.R.L.R. 19 (EAT), [44]. The original *Vento* limits were £25,000, £15,000, and £5,000.

[126] (1999) EAT/685/98.

"... where ... certain acts of discrimination fall only into one category or another, then the injury to feelings should be considered separately with respect to those acts. Each is a separate wrong for which damages should be provided."[127]

12–028 In *Al Jumard v Clywd Leisure*,[128] the claimant suffered race and disability discrimination, plus victimisation. He was of Iraqi origin and had a hip problem. The racial discrimination comprised: being disciplined for setting off the alarm and two other incidents; and subjecting him to surveillance. The disability discrimination comprised: being disciplined for setting off the alarm; two failures to make reasonable adjustments; and subjecting him to surveillance. The victimisation was the surveillance. The "alarm problem" arose from the claimant's inability to walk fast enough out of the building after setting the alarm. The surveillance, it seems, was to check if the disability was genuine. So here, there were some overlapping (the alarm and surveillance incidents), and some discrete, heads of discrimination. The EAT ruled that the direct disability and reasonable adjustments heads could be calculated together, but the victimisation incident should be calculated separately.

Note that it has been held that damages for injury to feelings are not available for equal pay claims, which are essentially contractual rather than tortuous.[129]

(iii) Exemplary damages

12–029 Exemplary damages for unlawful discrimination (including harassment and victimisation) presents a rather confusing story, which shows that the courts have inched towards recognition for discrimination cases. Unlike the pecuniary and non-pecuniary awards discussed above, exemplary damages are not compensatory, but instead are to deter and punish the defendant. Three categories were identified in *Rookes v Barnard* in 1964.[130] The first is oppressive, arbitrary or unconstitutional behaviour by government servants, who include the police.[131] The second category arises where the defendant calculated that his conduct would make him a profit exceeding any compensation he would have to pay. This is not confined to "moneymaking", but extends to seeking a gain of some object at the expense of the claimant. It can apply to private defendants. The third is where exemplary damages are expressly authorised by statute. The Equality Act 2010 does not do this, so only the first two categories are relevant here.

---

[127] *Al Jumard v Clywd Leisure* [2008] I.R.L.R. 345 (EAT), [50].
[128] [2008] I.R.L.R. 345 (EAT).
[129] *Newcastle upon Tyne CC v Allan* [2005] I.C.R. 1170 (EAT).
[130] [1964] A.C. 1129 (HL), at 1226–1227.
[131] *Cassell v Broome* [1972] A.C. 1027 (HL), at 1077–1078, 1130, 1134.

In 1991, in *City of Bradford Metropolitan Council v Arora*,[132] the Court of Appeal upheld an award (under the first category) for £1,000 exemplary damages for a sex and race discrimination claim by an unsuccessful job applicant because of the conduct of the interview process, which included "entirely unnecessary" questions designed "for the purpose of making suggestive, insidious and prejudicial remarks against her". However, in 1993, in *AB v South West Water Services*,[133] the Court of Appeal held that exemplary damages were only available if they had been awarded for the tort in question before *Rookes v Barnard* (the "cause of action" test). Inevitably, this excluded discrimination.[134] Then, in 2001, the House of Lords, in *Kuddus v Chief Constable of Leicestershire Constabulary*,[135] overruled *AB v South West Water Services* and held that exemplary damages depend on the conduct of the public authority (the "conduct" test), rather than the cause of action. This resurrected the possibility of exemplary damages for discrimination, although the House of Lords in *Kuddus* offered no certainty on the issue. Of those who commented, Lords Hutton and Nicholls said that such awards have a role to play in "outrageous behaviour" (by public authorities) in civil liberties cases.[136] Lord Mackay stated that exemplary damages should not be awarded in discrimination cases unless expressly authorised by statute.[137] Lord Hutton preferred to reserve his opinion on discrimination until the matter came before him.[138] It seems, at the least (Lord Mackay's opinion notwithstanding), that exemplary damages in principle (the "conduct" test) should be available against public authorities in discrimination cases.

Two separate developments support this view. The Law Commission has recommended that exemplary damages are appropriate in some cases of discrimination, where there is "deliberate and outrageous disregard" of the victim's rights, and where "the other remedies awarded would be inadequate to punish the defendant." An example would be an employer ignoring, and effectively conniving in, a campaign of racial harassment.[139] Second, the parent discrimination Directives also suggest that exemplary damages should be available: "The sanctions, which may comprise the payment of compensation to the victim, must be effective, proportionate and *dissuasive*."[140]

---

[132] [1991] 2 Q.B. 507.
[133] [1993] Q.B. 507.
[134] *Ministry of Defence v Meredith* [1995] I.R.L.R. 539 (EAT), *McConnell v Police Authority of Northern Ireland* [1997] I.R.L.R. 625 (NICA).
[135] [2002] 2 A.C. 122.
[136] ibid. respectively [63] and [75].
[137] ibid. [46].
[138] ibid. [92].
[139] *Aggravated, Exemplary and Restitutionary Damages*, Law Commission Report No. 247, 1997, London: TSO, at pp.4–8. This was a general survey into their appropriateness as tort remedies. *www.lawcom.gov.uk/lc_reports.htm#1997* (accessed January 1, 2011).
[140] Emphasis supplied. 2006/54/EC art.18; 2000/43/EC art.15; 2000/78/EC art.7.

12–030   As the Court of Appeal once pointed out, in light of *Rookes v Barnard* there is no reason why exemplary damages *should not* be awarded in discrimination cases.[141] This logic applies to both the first and second categories ("public authority" and "profit" cases).

In the wake of all this, case law now suggests exemplary damages are available for discrimination, harassment and victimisation, but not equal pay. The suggestions remain obiter, and so some doubt still hangs over this issue.

In *Newcastle upon Tyne CC v Allan*,[142] the President of the EAT, Burton J., suggested obiter, that the decision in *Kuddus* "could found an argument" for recovering exemplary damages under the Sex Discrimination Act 1975. The Court of Appeal in 2006 appeared to accept they were available for racial discrimination.[143] This was the position taken most recently by the EAT, in *Ministry of Defence v Fletcher*.[144] In this army case, Ms Fletcher, a lesbian, was sexually harassed by her sergeant. Quite deliberately, her life was made a misery. Disciplinary procedures and sanctions were used to victimise her. For Ms Fletcher, there was a "systemic failure of mechanisms of redress". Finally, in the employment tribunal hearing, the MoD tried to procure evidence defending the sexual harassment claim even though previously it had accepted its truth in an internal hearing, and it subjected Ms Fletcher to a "particularly unpleasant" cross-examination. The employment tribunal awarded her £50,000 exemplary damages.

The EAT felt bound by *Arora* (above) that exemplary damages were available in discrimination cases, but on the facts reversed the tribunal's decision. There were three features to this decision. First, the EAT noted that the "the exercise by those of sufficient seniority within the Army of its functions under statutory procedures for the redress of complaints are activities which ... are capable of falling within the scope of Lord Devlin's first category". However, the Army's conduct of the employment tribunal hearing was not, because it used no special power to conduct those proceedings.[145]

12–031   Second, the threshold for an award was "conscious and contumelious"[146] conduct,[147] and the Army's failure to provide a proper procedure of redress, deplorable though it was, did not cross this high threshold.[148] The EAT added though, had the it been shown that the Army had victimised Ms Fletcher to prevent her bringing a claim, an

---

[141] *Alexander v Home Office* [1988] 1 W.L.R. 968 (CA), p.976.
[142] [2005] I.C.R. 1170 (EAT), [12].
[143] *Elias v Secretary of State for Defence* [2006] I.R.L.R. 934 (CA) [245] (Mummery L.J.), [262] (Arden L.J.), citing *Alexander v Home Office* [1988] 1 W.L.R. 968 (CA), at p.976.
[144] [2010] I.R.L.R. 210 (EAT).
[145] ibid. [99]–[100].
[146] "Reproachful and tending to convey disgrace and humiliation; despiteful" (OED).
[147] ibid. [104].
[148] ibid. [115].

award would have been appropriate.[149] Such a case might fall more appropriately under the *Rookes v Barnard* second category, as seeking to make a profit (or avoid a loss), as the ultimate purpose of victimising claimants or witnesses often will be to save money (e.g. paying compensation and costs). In such a case though, damages for victimisation—which, in part at least, should be dissuasive—may fulfil the purpose of exemplary damages.

Third, even if an award were appropriate, £50,000 was too high. An appropriate figure would have been no more than £7,500.[150]

It has been held that exemplary damages are not available in equal pay claims, because they are essentially contractual rather than tortious.[151] The statement does not account for the parent Directives' requirement that "sanctions ... must be effective, proportionate and *dissuasive*"[152] which suggests that exemplary damages should be payable where appropriate. The obvious candidate for such payments is a "concealment case", where the employer seeks to profit by deceiving a worker about the pay of her comparator (see above, para.12–022, p.369). Such practices require a deterrent, otherwise the risk is worth taking. The sanction of compensation alone leaves the employer paying no more than it owed in any case. This could fall into *Rookes v Barnard* second category.

If it were found appropriate to award exemplary damages, a further uncertainty is the calculation, which is not subject to "nice legal principles"[153] or "weighed in nice scales".[154] In *Fletcher,* the EAT was influenced by the maximum of £50,000 for wrongful arrest and false imprisonment.[155] The only other guise is that it should not matter if the defendant's wrongful act did not produce the desired effect, because the main purpose is to deter future wrongful conduct. The award must be "moderate", and not "excessive". Otherwise, the award is calculated "to mark the displeasure of the court".[156]

(iv) Compensation for indirect discrimination

In cases of indirect discrimination, if the defendant proves that there was no intention to discriminate against the claimant (or pursuer), a tribunal or court (or the sheriff) cannot award damages unless it has first "considered" other remedies (e.g. an injunction, or in employment cases, making a declaration or recommendation).[157]   **12–032**

---

[149] ibid. [116].
[150] ibid. [117]–[118].
[151] *Newcastle upon Tyne CC v Allan* [2005] I.C.R. 1170 (EAT), [12].
[152] Emphasis supplied. 2006/54/EC art.18; 2000/43/EC art.15; 2000/78/EC art.17.
[153] *Design Progression v Thurloe* [2005] 1 W.L.R. 1 (Ch D), [148] (Peter Smith J.).
[154] *Drane v Evangelou* [1978] 1 W.L.R. 455 (CA), at p.459 (Lord Denning M.R.).
[155] [2010] I.R.L.R. 210 (EAT), [118] citing *Thompson v Commissioner of Police for the Metropolis*[1998] Q.B. 498 (CA), [13] (Lord Woolf).
[156] *Design Progression v Thurloe* [2005] 1 W.L.R. 1 (Ch D) [146]–[148].
[157] EA 2010 ss.119(6), 124(5).

The "other remedies" rider was added in deference to the ECJ judgment in *Draehmpaehl v Urania Immobilien Service ohg*,[158] which held that compensation could not be made dependant on proving fault. Also in deference to this case is the requirement that the defendant *disproves* intent, rather than the claimant proves it. Nonetheless, it is a somewhat hollow response. If another remedy, such as a declaration, was adequate, then no damages would be awardable in any case, intentional or not. On the other hand, withholding damages where otherwise they would be appropriate, again becomes dependant on fault liability, and so runs contrary to *Draehmpaehl*.

The issue will rarely, or never, arise because the EAT has given the word *intention* in this context a particularly wide meaning, making it difficult for defendants to disprove intent. In *JH Walker Ltd v Hussain*[159] the EAT held that these provisions were not concerned with the motive or reason behind the defendant's act, but rather with his awareness of the consequences of his act:

> " '[I]ntention' in this context signifies the state of mind of a person who, at the time when he does the relevant act ...
>
> (a) *wants* to bring about the state of affairs which constitutes the prohibited act of unfavourable treatment on racial grounds; and
> (b) *knows* that the prohibited act will follow from his acts."

In *Hussain*, 18 employees were disciplined for taking a day off work to celebrate Eid, a Muslim holy day, in breach of a new rule that holidays could not be taken during the during the company's busiest time. The workers brought a claim of indirect discrimination. The EAT upheld the award of £1,000 compensation to each applicant for injury to feelings. The company was aware that Eid was important to its Muslim workers and the effect of the new rule upon them. The company's motive of promoting business efficiency could not "displace" its knowledge of the consequences of the new rule.

(b) Declaration

12–033   Employment tribunals may "make a declaration as to the rights of the complainant and the respondent in relation to the matters to

---

[158] Case C-180/95 [1997] I.R.L.R. 538. See A. McColgan, "Remedies for discrimination" (1994) 23 ILJ 226; A. Arnull, "EC law and the dismissal of pregnant servicewomen" (1995) 24 ILJ 215.

[159] [1996] I.C.R. 291, at 299–300. See also Ch.6. Similarly, in *London Underground Ltd v Edwards* [1995] I.C.R. 574, the EAT held that compensation was payable for indirect discrimination as the employers were aware of the adverse impact of the new rostering arrangements even though they had not been drawn up with the purpose of treating women unfavourably.

which the proceedings relate".[160] This follows a finding in the claimant's favour, but in most cases is accompanied by one or both of the other available remedies, which normally are of more practical significance. They can be of more practical use in collective actions, where, say, the Equality and Human Rights Commission, a trade union, pensions supplier, or employer, wishes to clarify the law.[161]

(c) Recommendations
Employment tribunals may make a recommendation,[162] which can require: **12-034**

"that within a specified period the respondent takes specified steps for the purpose of obviating or reducing the adverse effect of any matter to which the proceedings relate—

(a) on the complainant;
(b) on any other person".[163]

If the employer fails to comply with the recommendation, the tribunal may order compensation.[164]

Paragraph (b) is new, and will be discussed below. On paragraph (a), in *Chief Constable of West Yorkshire v Vento*,[165] speaking in the EAT, Wall J. considered the power to make recommendations was "extremely wide". It has been argued that where the victim *would have* got the job but for the discrimination, the victim should be able jump ahead of the next queue.[166] The case law so far is less ambitious. It was suggested by the EAT that under paragraph (a) it was possible to order that a worker with a disability, who would otherwise be dismissed, be retained on full benefits until his retirement, provided that the worker complies with reasonable requests to submit to medicals for the employer's insurance.[167] Otherwise, the story is of recommendations being overturned on appeal for being too wide.

In *Noone v North West Thames RHA (No.2)*,[168] the defendant rejected on racial grounds Dr Noone's job application for the post of consultant microbiologist. The industrial tribunal found in her favour and made a recommendation to the effect that the Health Authority

---

[160] EA 2010 s.124(2)(a).
[161] See e.g. *Rolls Royce v Unite* [2010] I.C.R. (CA), where an employer applied (unsuccessfully) for a length-of-service redundancy factor in a collective agreement to be declared unlawful on the basis it was age-discriminatory.
[162] EA 2010 s.124(2)(c).
[163] EA 2010 s.124(3).
[164] EA 2010 s.124(7).
[165] [2002] I.R.L.R. 177 (EAT), [49].
[166] See A. McColgan, *Discrimination Law, Text Cases and Materials* (2nd edn, Oxford: Hart, 2005) p.339.
[167] *Atos Origin IT Services v Haddock* [2005] I.R.L.R. (EAT) 20, [33].
[168] [1988] I.C.R. 813 (CA).

dispense with the statutory procedure of advertising the next consultant microbiologist post, so the field would be narrowed, thus
favouring Dr Noone. The Court of Appeal held this was too wide
under what is now paragraph (a), because it "set at nought" the
statutory hiring procedure. Instead, the recommendation should be
that if Dr Noone applied again, the authority should draw to the
attention of the appointment committee the relevant requirements of
the race relations legislation, and that Dr Noone's previous application had failed because of racial discrimination.[169]

12–035   In *British Gas v Sharma*,[170] the claimant had been wrongly
excluded from a post on racial grounds. An industrial tribunal
recommended that the claimant be promoted the next time a suitable
vacancy arose. The EAT held that this (i) amounted to positive discrimination and (ii) as it was not known when such a vacancy would
arise, it could not indicate a "specified period", as required by what is
now paragraph (a). In *Leeds Rhinos Rugby Club v Sterling*[171] the EAT
held that a tribunal could not recommend that a rugby player's
contract was renewed simply on the reasoning (no evidence was
offered) that following his successful claim for racial discrimination
other clubs would view him as a troublemaker, making him less
employable. Finally, in *Irvine v Prestcold*[172] the Court of Appeal held
that a recommendation could not include an increase in wages (to
compensate for lost promotion) as such matters should be accounted
for by compensation.

Paragraph (a) epitomises the individualistic historical basis of the
discrimination legislation. It is limited to making a recommendation
affecting the claimant, but not those in the same position. This
restriction is now cured by the introduction of paragraph (b), which
allows the recommendation to apply to "any other person" affected
by matters in the proceedings. This brings the legislation into line
with the Northern Ireland[173] and the United States.[174] For paragraph
(b), the Explanatory Notes (406) suggest a tribunal could recommend
that an employer:

"introduces an equal opportunities policy;

ensures its harassment policy is more effectively implemented;

sets up a review panel to deal with equal opportunities and
harassment/grievance procedures;

re-trains staff; or

---

[169] ibid. at pp.840D–F, 841C–F.
[170] [1991] I.C.R. 19 (EAT).
[171] (2002) EAT/267/01.
[172] [1981] I.C.R. 777 (CA).
[173] Fair Employment and Treatment Order, 1998, SI 1998/3162, art.39(1)(d).
[174] Civil Rights Act 1964 s.706(g)(1), USC § 2000e–5(g)(1). This is the principal employment
discrimination federal legislation.

makes public the selection criteria used for transfer or promotion of staff."

For a discussion on the potential of recommendations for positive action, see Chapter 11, para.11–013.

2. STRATEGIC ENFORCEMENT

Prior to the new regime introduced by the Equality Act 2010, the **12–036** Equality Act *2006* (EA 2006) established the Commission for Equality and Human Rights,[175] a new single strategic enforcement body, which absorbed the three existing bodies, the Equal Opportunities Commission, the Disability Rights Commission, and the Commission for Racial Equality. It is broader in scope than those commissions, as it embraced the other protected characteristics of religion or belief, sexual orientation and age. As its title suggests, its remit goes beyond discrimination and equality, extending to human rights, defined principally, but not exclusively, by the European Convention on Human Rights through the Human Rights Act 1998.[176] According to the Convention, its rights must be secured without discrimination. This means that discrimination is relevant to the Commission's human rights brief as well.

(1) The Commission for Equality and Human Rights
The Equality Act 2006 states that the general duties of Commission **12–037** for Equality and Human Rights (CEHR) are to exercise its functions:

"... with a view to encouraging and supporting the development of a society in which—(a) people's ability to achieve their potential is not limited by prejudice or discrimination, (b) there is respect for and protection of each individual's human rights, (c) there is respect for the dignity and worth of each individual, (d) each individual has an equal opportunity to participate in society, and (e) there is mutual respect between groups based on understanding and valuing of diversity and on shared respect for equality and human rights."[177]

Its duties specific to "equality and diversity" are that the Commission "shall" (a) promote understanding of the importance of

---

[175] See C. O'Cinneide, "The Commission for Equality and Human Rights: a new institution for new and uncertain times" (2007) 36 ILJ 141.
[176] EA 2006 s.9(2). On the Convention and Human Rights Act, see Ch.2.
[177] EA 2006 s.3.

equality and diversity, (b) encourage good practice in relation to equality and diversity, (c) promote equality of opportunity, (d) promote awareness and understanding of rights under the Equality Act 2010, (e) enforce the Equality Act 2010, (f) work towards the elimination of unlawful discrimination and (g) harassment.[178] In addition, the Commission "shall" promote and encourage "understanding of the importance of good relations" and "good practice in relation to relations" between members of different groups, and between members of groups and others. "Groups" can be defined by age, disability, gender, gender reassignment, race, religion or belief, and sexual orientation.[179] Its other specific duty is to promote human rights.[180]

The Commission has the power to issue Codes of Practice,[181] conduct formal Inquiries and Investigations, enforce the Equality Act 2010 and in some cases Community discrimination law,[182] and provide legal assistance to individuals.[183] For these purposes, and the discussion below, an "unlawful act" is an act contrary to the Equality Act 2010.[184]

(a) Inquiries and Investigations

12–038   The Act provides the Commission with two forms of investigatory power: Inquiries and Investigations. Inquiries are less serious and cannot, in themselves, lead to legal action by the Commission. By contrast, Investigations can have legal consequences.

Under EA 2006 s.16, the Commission can launch an Inquiry simply in pursuit of its duties.[185] "These could be thematic (for example into the causes of unequal outcomes), sectoral (looking at inequality in, for example, the uptake of health screening services or at the employment of disabled people in particular sectors, e.g. the retail sector), or relate to one or more named parties."[186] A "named party" includes individuals, companies and organisations. Before the Inquiry, the Commission must publish its Terms of Reference.[187] Afterwards, it may publish a report, but it cannot state or imply that

---

[178] EA 2006 s.8.
[179] EA 2006 s.10.
[180] EA 2006 s.9.
[181] EA 2006 s.14.
[182] EA 2006 s.25.
[183] EA 2006 s.28.
[184] Except for (a) socio-economic inequalities public sector duty (s.1); (b) public sector equality duties (ss.149, 153 or 154); (c) disabled persons: transport (Part 12); or (d) disability: improvements to let dwelling houses (s.90): EA 2006 s.34.
[185] For details of each of the Commission's Inquiries, see *http://www.equalityhumanrights.com/ legal-and-policy/formal-inquiries/* (accessed December 21, 2010).
[186] Explanatory Notes to the Equality Act 2006, para.56. Available at *www.legislation.gov.uk/ ukpga/2006/3/notes/contents*.
[187] EA 2006 Sch.2, para.2.

a person has committed an unlawful act, unless it relates to human rights (even if this has implications under the Equality Act 2010).[188]

If, during the Inquiry, the Commission suspects that person has committed an unlawful act, the Inquiry must *not* pursue that suspicion. Instead, the Commission may pursue it using an Investigation.

The Equality Act 2006 s.20 provides for Investigations, which involve formal and intrusive scrutiny of a named person, with potential legal consequences. Three possible triggers allow the Commission to embark on an Investigation. The first is where the Commission has a suspicion that a named person has committed an unlawful act. Under the previous regime the House of Lords held that this suspicion had to be a reasonable one (i.e. objective, not subjective) as a matter of public law principle.[189] The White Paper suggested "Suspicion that unlawful acts may have occurred could be formed by reports to the CEHR from victims of discrimination or harassment, by reports from third parties, or from cases ruled on by courts or tribunals."[190] The Act itself suggests that the suspicion may be based on the results of, or a matter arising during the course of, an Inquiry under s.16.[191] The Commission must draw up and publish terms of reference for the Investigation, and these must accord with its suspicion.[192]

The second and third possibilities for a named Investigation are where the Commission decides to ascertain if a person has complied with a requirement imposed by an Unlawful Act Notice, or with an undertaking given under a statutory Binding Agreement[193] (see both below).

(b) Unlawful Act Notices

If, following an Investigation, the Commission concludes that **12–039**
unlawful discrimination has taken place, it may serve a notice on the named person requiring the discrimination to stop. This may also require the person to draft an action plan designed to avoid repetition or continuation of the unlawful act, which for a period of five years the Commission may monitor and enforce. Named persons subject to an Unlawful Act Notice may appeal within six weeks to an employment tribunal if the allegations fall within its jurisdiction, or to a county court or sheriff for any other acts.[194]

[188] EA 2006 s.16(3) and (4).
[189] *Re Prestige Group Plc* [1984] I.C.R. 473 (HL).
[190] White Paper, "Fairness For All: A New Commission for Equality and Human Rights", 2004, URN 04/1072, London: TSO, para.4.25.
[191] EA 2006 s.20(3).
[192] This was established under the original regime in *Hillingdon London BC v CRE* [1982] A.C. 779 (HL).
[193] EA 2006 s.20(1)(b) and (c).
[194] EA 2006 ss.21-22.

(c) Binding Agreements

12–040   Section 23 of the Equality 2006 allows the Commission to enter an Agreement with a person who undertakes to refrain from committing any discrimination and to take (or refrain from taking) any specified act, including drafting an action plan. In exchange, the Commission promises not to pursue an Investigation nor issue an Unlawful Act Notice. The trigger for this power is where the Commission "thinks" unlawful discrimination has been committed by the person.[195] The Explanatory Notes (83) to the Equality Act 2006 assume that this means "reason to suspect".[196]

The Agreement itself is enforceable. Where the Commission "thinks" that a party to an Agreement has failed to comply, or is likely not to comply, with the Agreement, it may apply to a county court or sheriff for an order of compliance or for the person to take "such other action as the court of sheriff may specify".[197]

(d) Application for Injunction

12–041   If the Commission "thinks" that a person is likely to commit an unlawful act, it may apply to the county court (or sheriff) for an injunction (or interdict) restraining the person from committing the act.[198]

(e) Enforcement

12–042   Section 24A of the Equality Act 2006 provides that the Commission can use its powers set out above (Investigations, Unlawful Act Notices, Binding Agreements, and Injunctions) whether or not it "knows or suspects that a person has been or may be affected by the unlawful act or application."[199] This section was inserted by the Equality Act 2010,[200] and it replaces the Commission's previous powers which were more limited, regarding, for instance, advertisements and discriminatory practices.

This power now applies to: direct and indirect discrimination, including the making of arrangements which would result in direct discrimination; combined discrimination;[201] pregnancy and maternity discrimination;[202] discrimination arising from disability;[203] asking job

---

[195] EA 2006 s.23(2).
[196] Available at *www.legislation.gov.uk/ukpga/2006/3/notes/contents*.
[197] EA 2006 s.24(2) and (3).
[198] EA 2006 s.24(1).
[199] EA 2006 s.24A(2).
[200] Inserted by EA 2010 Sch.26, para.68. (Originally by para.13; Sch.26 has since been restructured: SI 2010/2279.)
[201] EA 2010 s.14.
[202] EA 2010 ss.18, 19.
[203] EA 2010 s.15.

applicants about disability and health;[204] where the relationship between the parties has ended;[205] and any diversity reporting requirements imposed on political parties.[206]

(f) Judicial Review and other Legal Proceedings

Section 30 of the Equality Act 2006 provides that the Commission may institute, or intervene in,[207] proceedings "if it appears to the Commission that the proceedings are relevant to a matter in connection with which the Commission has a function." This applies to the Human Rights Act 1998 as well as the Equality Act 2010.

12–043

(g) Legal Assistance

Section 28 of the Equality Act 2006 authorises the Commission to provide legal assistance where the proceedings may relate (wholly or partly) to the Equality Act 2010,[208] and "the individual alleges that he has been the victim of behaviour contrary to a provision of that Act." If the Equality Act 2010 ceases to be relevant to the proceedings, the assistance must stop. However, if the Human Rights Act 1998 remains relevant to the proceedings, the Lord Chancellor may by order enable the Commission to continue the assistance;[209] or, if the person relies on a matter relating to his disability, the Secretary of State may by order enable the Commission to provide assistance.[210]

12–044

This power to give assistance also applies where an individual alleges he is disadvantaged by legislation[211] which is contrary to Community law, or by a failure to implement Community law. This operates so far as the Community law *relates to* discrimination (on grounds of sex, gender reassignment, racial origin, ethnic origin, religion, belief, disability, age or sexual orientation), and confers rights on individuals.[212]

Under this section the Commission may provide legal advice and representation; facilities for the settlement of a dispute; and any other form of assistance.[213]

---

[204] EA 2010 s.60.
[205] EA 2010 s.108.
[206] EA 2010 s.106.
[207] A Charity Tribunal hearing may permit a Commission intervention: *Father Hudson's Society v Charity Commission* [2009] P.T.S.R. 1125 (Charity Tribunal), [40]–[42]. For an equal pay case where the Commission was permitted "exceptionally" to intervene at a late stage, raising new points, see *Slack v Cumbria CC* [2009] I.C.R. 1217 (CA), [20]–[32]. For an unsuccessful challenge to the Commission intervening, see *McCarthy v Basildon DC* [2008] EWCA Civ 1586.
[208] Except for Pt 12 (disabled persons: transport) EA 2006 s.28(5).
[209] EA 2006 s.28(6)(b).
[210] EA 2006 s.28(8), except for EA 2010 Pt 12 (disabled persons: transport).
[211] "including an enactment in or under an Act of the Scottish Parliament": EA 2006 s.28(13)(a).
[212] EA 2006 s.28(12)–(13).
[213] EA 2006 s.28(4).

(h) Rejected Proposals—Class Actions and Hypothetical Cases

12–045   The Government expressly rejected some proposals for other strategic enforcement.[214] The first was that the Commission should be able to bring class actions on behalf of similarly placed "victims". The Government considered that as these were generally not used in Great Britain, the matter went beyond the introduction of the Commission. Class actions play a considerable role in the United States.[215] For instance, the US Federal enforcement agency, EEOC, has reported settlements in discrimination class actions of $170 million and $192.5 million,[216] while the ongoing Wal-Mart litigation involves some 1.5 million female workers from 3,500 stores nationwide.[217]

The second proposal was that the new Commission should be able to bring hypothetical cases to clarify points of law. This was rejected because "it is very difficult for a court to reach a useful decision in the absence of particular facts" and it is not the practice of the European Court of Justice, the European Court of Human Rights, or the domestic courts.

---

[214] White Paper, "Fairness For All: A New Commission for Equality and Human Rights" 2004, URN 04/1072, London: TSO, at paras 4.40–4.43.

[215] Rule 23, Fed R Civ Proc. The requirements are: (i) *numerosity*, claimants so numerous as to make individual claims unruly and impracticable; (ii) *Commonality*, there must common questions of law and fact; (iii) *Typicality*, claims or defences must be typical of the class; (iv) *Representation*, named petitioner can fairly represent the class with competent counsel and no conflict of interest. For other restrictions see *General Telephone Company of the Southwest v Falcon* 457 US 147 (Sup Ct 1982) and D. Piar, "The uncertain future of Title VII class action cases after the Civil Rights Act of 1991", 2001 BYU L Rev 305. See also D. Panicky, *Sex Discrimination Law* (Oxford: OUP, 1985), pp.284–301.

[216] Respectively *Roberts v Texaco* (racial discrimination), noted 979 F. Supp. 185, n.6 (S.D.NY. 1997), see generally B. Roberts and J.E. White, *Roberts Vs Texaco: A True Story of Race and Corporate America* (New York: Avon Books, 1998 ISBN 0-380-79639-2); *Ingram v The Coca-Cola Company* 200 F.R.D. 685 (N.D. Ga. 2001) (systematic discrimination against 2,200 African-Americans). *www.eeoc.gov/eeoc/meetings/archive/5-16-07/mehri_bio.html* (accessed December 21, 2010).

[217] See e.g. *Dukes v Wal-Mart* 603 F.3d 571(9th Cir 2010).

CHAPTER 13

DISABILITY DISCRIMINATION

INTRODUCTION

The anti-discrimination principle was extended to disability through **13–001** the Disability Discrimination Act 1995 (DDA 1995).[1] It is now integrated into the Equality Act 2010 (EA 2010). Its distinctive features are the complex rules for identifying those protected under the Act (the definition of disability), and the conceptually different definitions of discrimination. Here, the anti-discrimination principle is not rooted in symmetry. While the conventional direct/indirect discrimination framework plays a part, the substantial and tailored concepts are "discrimination arising from disability" and positive duties to make reasonable adjustments. Underlying this exceptional

---

[1] See B. Doyle, "Enabling legislation or dissembling law? The Disability Discrimination Act 1995" (1997) 60 MLR 64.

approach is the simple reality that there is no point in identifying the protected group as a single class because disabilities vary in form and severity. When this is coupled with the need of most persons with a disability for *different* (rather than *equal*) treatment, it becomes easy to appreciate why the equal treatment model plays only a minor role. The many forms of disability make it difficult to deal with all cases through primary legislation. So much of the law is given in Regulations or Guidance.

The result is technical and complex legislation. Commenting on the original DDA 1995, Mummery L.J. stated:[2]

> "[I]t is without doubt an unusually complex piece of legislation which poses novel questions of interpretation. It is not surprising that different conclusions have been reached at different levels of decision.
>
> This state of affairs should not be taken as a criticism of the legislation or of its drafting or of the judicial disagreements about its interpretation. The whole subject presents unique challenges to legislators and to tribunals and courts, as well as to those responsible for the day-to-day operation of the Act in the workplace."

For disability, the Equality Act 2010 prohibits direct discrimination, discrimination arising from disability, indirect discrimination, and a failure to make reasonable adjustments. These four forms of discrimination are covered in this chapter, as well as the definition of disability. The parent Directive here (for work matters) is the Employment Equality Directive 2000/78/EC. What follows is the definition of disability, and the four types of disability discrimination.

1. THE DEFINITION OF DISABILITY

13–002   In general, the legislation adopts the "medical" model of disability. This contrasts with the "social" model, which identifies the infrastructure of society and social barriers as the cause of disability, rather than a condition or impairment of the claimant. Whatever the model chosen, the task of drawing the line is not easy. "The definition of disability must be both inclusive and exclusive: embracing individuals outside the limited popular perception of 'disability', yet excluding idiosyncrasies, human traits and transient illness. A

---

[2] *Clark v TGD t/a Novacold* [1999] I.C.R. 951 (CA), at p.954.

distinction must be drawn between chronic or handicapping conditions and temporary or minor maladies."[3]

At a European level, under the Framework Directive 2000/78/EC, the ECJ held in *Chacón Navas*[4] that:

> "... the concept of "disability" must be understood as referring to a limitation which results in particular from physical, mental or psychological impairments and which hinders the participation of the person concerned in professional life".[5]

It did not cover persons "as soon as they develop any type of sickness".[6] Of this definition, one commentator observed:

> "Failing to recognise that disability is a complex relationship between impairment and the social environment, the Court's decision will have the effect of reinforcing the application of the medical model in the domestic disability policies of the Member States."[7]

The domestic definition is provided by the Equality Act 2010 s.6, amplified by Sch.1, Pt 1, *and* by Regulations,[8] *and* further, by Guidance.[9] The Guidance is not law, but tribunals, courts and school authorities[10] *must* take it into account.[11] A new Guidance was published in 2010, and at the time of writing was due in force in April 2011. Until it is in force, the previous Guidance—which was substantially the same—should be used.[12] However, all references below are to the new Guidance.

Some conditions are "deemed" as disabilities under the Act, irrespective of whether they cause the person an impairment. The deemed conditions are certified blindness or partial sightedness,[13] HIV infection, multiple sclerosis or cancer.[14]

Otherwise, a claimant must fall within the definition provided by s.6, which requires that the person has "a physical or mental impairment, and the impairment has a substantial and long-term

---

[3] B. Doyle, "Employment rights, equal opportunities and disabled persons: the ingredients of reform" (1993) 22 ILJ 89, p.91.
[4] Case C-13/05 *Chacón Navas v Eurest Colectividades SA* [2006] 3 C.M.L.R. 1123 (ECJ).
[5] ibid. [43].
[6] ibid. [43].
[7] D. Hoskin, "A high bar for EU disability rights", (2007) 36 ILJ 228, at p.237
[8] Equality Act (Disability) Regulations 2010 SI 2010/2128.
[9] "Guidance on matters to be taken into account in determining questions relating to the definition of disability". Made under EA 2010 s.6(5). See *www.odi.gov.uk/docs/wor/new/eaguide.pdf* (accessed January 1, 2011).
[10] See EA 2010 s.85(9), defining "responsible bodies" for schools as either local or education authorities, managers, or proprietors.
[11] EA 2010 Sch.1, para.12.
[12] SI 2010/2317 art.13. The previous Guidance came into force on May 1, 2006 (SI 2006/1005).
[13] Equality Act (Disability) Regulations 2010, SI 2010/2128 reg.7.
[14] EA 2010 Sch.1, para.6.

adverse effect on P's ability to carry out normal day-to-day activities". There are four requirements: (a) a physical or mental impairment, which (b) affects the ability to carry out everyday activities, and such effect is both (c) long-term and (d) substantial.[15]

13–003   Before looking each in turn, it is worth appreciating the general approach adopted by the courts. First, in *J v DLA Piper*,[16] Underhill J. observed that it was not always necessary to decide the elements in "rigid consecutive stages". This could be the case where the effects of a mainly physical nature *could* stem from an underlying mental impairment, and vice versa; or where it is suggested that the impairment was not clinically recognised; or not readily identifiable or immediately obvious.[17] In such cases it might prove easier to assess the *effects* first. From these, it might be possible to infer that there was an impairment.

Second, the Rules of Procedure state that the employment judge "shall make such enquiries of persons appearing before ... it and of witnesses as ... it considers appropriate and shall otherwise conduct the hearing in such manner as ... it considers most appropriate for the clarification of the issues and generally for the just handling of the proceedings."[18] In *Goodwin v The Patent Office*[19] Morison J. emphasised the inquisitorial element, which he said should used to avoid a "Catch-22" situation in disability discrimination claims: "Some disabled persons may be unable or unwilling to accept that they suffer from any disability; indeed, it may be symptomatic of their condition that they deny it." In such cases, he suggested, the tribunal should offer claimants "direct assistance". However, Morison J.'s enthusiasm was quelled by the Court of Appeal, which has made it clear that that employment tribunals should be neither inquisitorial nor proactive.[20] Morison J.'s suggestion was developed into another strand of argument by counsel in *Woodrup v London Borough of Southwark*.[21] He argued that, in providing a service to the public, tribunals were obliged under what is now EA 2010 Pt 3 (provision of services to the public), to make "reasonable adjustments" when dealing with disabled people. However, the Court of Appeal called this notion "far fetched".

---

[15] These should be considered in the context of *Chacon Navas* Case C-13/05 [2006] 3 C.M.L.R. 1123, [43], [46] (above). See e.g. below, para.13–009.
[16] [2010] I.R.L.R. 936 (EAT), [40].
[17] Guidance 2010 (above, n.9), para.A5.
[18] Employment Tribunals (Constitution and Rules of Procedure) Regulations 2004, SI 2004/1861 Sch.1, reg.14(3).
[19] [1999] I.C.R. 302, at 307 (EAT). The facts are set out below, para.13–014, p.401.
[20] *McNicol v Balfour Beatty Rail Maintenance* [2002] I.C.R. 1498, [26], citing *Morgan v Staffordshire University* [2002] I.C.R. 475 (EAT), [20].
[21] [2002] EWCA Civ 1716, [16].

(1) Impairment

"Impairment" must be given its ordinary meaning[22] and so it is not   **13–004**
necessary that the impairment is a clinically recognised disability.
Accordingly, tribunals need not assess the question by reference to a
recognised "illness": an amputee, for example, does not have an
"illness" but clearly has an impairment.[23] In *Millar v Inland Revenue*,[24] the claimant, after a fall, experienced drooping of his left
eyelid, which he associated with sensitivity to bright light, and
headaches. The Court of Session held that these conditions could
amount to an impairment, even though a consultant neurologist and
a consultant ophthalmologist could find no abnormalities or cause of
the conditions. In *College of Ripon & York St John v Hobbs*[25] it was
held that a claimant with muscle-twitching and cramps, and who
could walk only with the aid of a stick, had an impairment, even
though expert evidence showed no underlying organic disease. At one
time the Act took a more restrictive approach to mental impairments,
requiring any mental illness to be a "clinically well-recognised illness". This requirement was repealed on December 5, 2005,[26] and
since then the same approach applies to mental and physical
impairments.

The Guidance offers a non-exhaustive list of impairments,[27] but
cautions that not all impairments are readily identifiable, there being
many which are not immediately obvious.[28] Further, there may be
adverse effects which are both physical and mental in nature and the
effects of a mainly physical nature may stem from an underlying
mental impairment, and vice versa.[29]

Addictions, save those resulting from medical treatment, are
excluded from the Act.[30] So addictions to alcohol, tobacco or other
drugs are excluded. Where a person suffers such a condition, its

---

[22] Guidance 2010 (above, n.9), para.A3. *McNicol v Balfour Beatty Rail Maintenance* [2002] I.R.L.R. 711, (CA), [17] (Mummery L.J.).

[23] *Millar v Inland Revenue Commissioners* [2005] I.R.L.R. 112 (CS), [23] (Lord Penrose). See also *J v DLA Piper* [2010] I.R.L.R. 936 (EAT), where the employment tribunal erroneously distinguished depression from *clinical* depression when rejecting as claim.

[24] [2005] I.R.L.R. 112 (CS).

[25] [2002] I.R.L.R. 185 (EAT).

[26] Disability Discrimination Act 2005 Sch.2, para.1 (in force SI 2005/2774).

[27] Above n.9, para.A6: "A disability can arise from a wide range of impairments which can be: sensory impairments, such as those affecting sight or hearing; impairments with fluctuating or recurring effects such as rheumatoid arthritis, myalgic encephalitis (ME)/chronic fatigue syndrome (CFS), fibromyalgia, depression and epilepsy; progressive, such as motor neurone disease, muscular dystrophy, forms of dementia and lupus (SLE); organ specific, including respiratory conditions, such as asthma, and cardiovascular diseases, including thrombosis, stroke and heart disease; developmental, such as autistic spectrum disorders (ASD), dyslexia and dyspraxia; learning difficulties; mental health conditions and mental illnesses, such as depression, schizophrenia, eating disorders, bipolar affective disorders, obsessive compulsive disorders, as well as personality disorders and some self-harming behaviour; produced by injury to the body or brain."

[28] Above n.9, para.A5.

[29] Above n.9, para.A7.

[30] Equality Act (Disability) Regulations 2010, SI 2010/2128 reg.3.

effects may amount to an impairment under the Act. So liver disease can be an impairment under the Act, even if it arose from alcoholism.[31] Accordingly, where an impairment (say depression) is accompanied by an addiction (say alcoholism), the correct approach is to assess the depression irrespective of the alcoholism, and decide if amounts to an impairment.[32] Other excluded conditions are: (a) a tendency to set fires; (b) a tendency to steal; (c) a tendency to physical or sexual abuse of other persons; (d) exhibitionism; and (e) voyeurism.[33]

13–005 A problem that has arisen here is where the excluded condition is caused by a legitimate impairment, say a tendency to violence caused by schizophrenia, or indecent exposure caused by depression. In *Murray v Newham Citizens Advice Bureau*,[34] the EAT held that for an impairment to be an excluded condition, it had to be "free-standing", in the sense that it was not caused by a legitimate impairment. This was criticised because (a) the more severe the tendency, the more likely it is to be caused by a legitimate impairment, and (b) it means that employers are under a duty to make reasonable adjustments for those with a tendency to setting fires, theft, or physical or sexual abuse.[35] In *Nuttall v Butterfield*,[36] the EAT commented that the "free-standing" approach was "not helpful" and ruled that the proper approach was to identify the cause of the less favourable treatment: if it were the legitimate impairment, there is a prima facie case, if it were the excluded condition, there is not.[37]

In *Butterfield*, the employer discovered that the claimant had two convictions for indecent exposure, and subsequently dismissed him, on the ground that such behaviour could bring the company's reputation into disrepute. The claimant's exhibitionism was caused by his depression, which was an impairment. The EAT's approach meant that the cause of the dismissal was the claimant's exhibitionism, and not his impairment, which was irrelevant.

The claim in *Butterfield* was for disability-related discrimination (now "discrimination arising from disability").[38] Nonetheless, it

---

[31] Guidance, above n.9, para.A8.

[32] *Power v Panasonic* [2003] I.R.L.R. 151 (EAT), at [12]. See also *Hutchison 3G UK Ltd v Mason* (2003) unreported, EAT/0369/03/MAA: depression accompanied by cocaine addiction.

[33] Equality Act (Disability) Regulations 2010, SI 2010/2128 reg.4(1). Note also that "seasonal allergic rhinitis" (e.g. hay fever) is not an "impairment", although it can be taken into account where it aggravates the effect of another condition: ibid. reg.4(2) and (3).

[34] [2003] I.C.R. 643.

[35] I.R.L.R. "Highlights" June 2003.

[36] [2006] I.C.R. 77 (EAT).

[37] ibid. [29]. For a similar approach in Australia, see *Purvis (on behalf of Hoggan) v New South Wales (Department of Education and Training)* 202 ALR 133 (2003) High Ct of Australia.

[38] See below, para.13–024.

provided "powerful support" for the defendant in a reasonable adjustments claim in *Governors of X Endowed Primary School v SENDT*.[39] Here, a child with Attention Deficit and Hyperactivity Disorder (ADHD) was excluded from his school after assaulting a member of staff. The tendency to violence was a manifestation of his ADHD. The child's parents claimed that the school had failed to make reasonable adjustments.[40] The High Court held that the protection of the legislation did not extend *at all* to excluded conditions "whether or not they are manifestations of an underlying protected impairment".[41] However, before the assault, the school had failed to engage any de-escalation and calming measures normally provided for pupils with ADHD, and so it *was* liable for failing to make reasonable adjustments for the pupil.

The criticism of *Murray* is rather alarmist, as it overlooks the utility in these cases of the justification defence[42] or assessing the reasonableness of making no adjustments,[43] which affords a more flexible approach. For instance, where the tendency last manifested some time ago, and appears to be under control, a dismissal for a reason "arising from" the disability will be harder to justify. On the other hand, where the tendency is severe, and not apparently under control, dismissal becomes much easier to justify. Accordingly, the approaches in *Butterfield* or *Governors of X* gets no nearer to a solution. In *Butterfield,* the EAT leapt from the statutory question, was the treatment "because of something arising in consequence of" the claimant's disability to a new one, what was the reason for the treatment?[44] Quite clearly the dismissal was because of something arising from the legitimate impairment (depression), although not for that immediate reason, which was the excluded condition (exhibitionism). *Governors of X* gives an exception to the general rule the broadest possible interpretation, which is not the normal practice where derogating from a fundamental principle. If Parliament wanted excluded conditions completely detached from the causes of action, it would have expressed this. Instead, it outlawed discrimination because of "something arising from" the disability, and confined its excluded conditions to the matter of "impairments".[45]

There are two ways by which the impact of *Butterfield* could be curtailed. First, where the duty to make adjustments arises

13–006

---

[39] *Governing Body of X Endowed Primary School v Special Educational Needs and Disability Tribunal* [2009] I.R.L.R. 1007 (HC, QBD), [31]. At the time, in the wake of *Lewisham LBC v Malcolm* [2008] I..R.L.R. 700 (HL), disability-related discrimination was not a viable cause of action, see below, para.13–024.

[40] Discussed below, para.13–032.

[41] [2009] I.R.L.R. 1007, [48].

[42] For discrimination arising from disability, s.15.

[43] For the reasonable adjustments duty, ss.21 and 85.

[44] At the time, the cause of action characterised as "disability-related discrimination", which poses substantially the same question: was the treatment *related to* the disability?

[45] Equality Act (Disability) Regulations 2010, SI 2010/2128 reg.4.

independently of the excluded condition, the defendant's response can be assessed (*Governing Body of X*). The second, and less likely, is by *Butterfield's* causation question. If say, the tendency arose some time ago and was now under control, it would be harder for a defendant to argue that it was the tendency, rather than the underlying disability, which caused it the treat the claimant less favourably. These are only partial solutions and would arise only in some cases.

(2) Ability to Carry Out Normal Day-to-Day Activities

13–007 The impairment must have an adverse effect on the claimant's ability to carry out normal day-to-day activities. This is otherwise known as the *functional requirement*. The previous legislation provided an *exhaustive* list of eight capacities that could adversely affect day-to-day activities: (a) mobility; (b) manual dexterity; (c) physical co-ordination; (d) continence; (e) ability to lift, carry out or otherwise move everyday objects; (f) speech, hearing or eyesight; (g) memory or ability to concentrate, learn or understand; or (h) perception of the risk of physical danger.[46] The Equality Act 2010 no longer provides an exhaustive list, making it easier for claimants to prove they have a disability. The list is now useful for illustrative purposes only.

Each of these capacities should be considered in relation to both physical and mental impairments. Mental impairments are not confined to the obvious "memory and ability to concentrate" capacity. For instance, a mental impairment may affect a person's mobility, because of a fear of travelling in cars or buses. Conversely, a physical impairment, such as pain or fatigue, may affect a person's ability to concentrate.[47]

The Guidance provides examples of day-to-day activities corresponding to each of these capacities, and suggests which examples it would be reasonable to regard as having a substantial adverse effect, and which it would not. For instance, under "Mobility", the Guidance suggests that a "total inability to walk, or difficulty walking other than at a slow pace or with unsteady or jerky movements", or "difficulty in travelling a short journey as a passenger in a vehicle, because, for example, it would be painful getting in and out of a car, or sitting in a car for even a short time" would be substantial enough. On the other hand, "experiencing some tiredness or minor discomfort as a result of walking unaided for a distance of about 1.5 kilometres or one mile", or "experiencing some discomfort as a result of travelling in a car for a journey lasting more than two hours", if *considered alone,* would not be.[48] These are examples, not a definitive list. As Morison J. stated in *Goodwin v The Patent Office*,[49] "What is a

[46] DDA 1995 Sch.1, para.4 (now repealed).
[47] Guidance 2010 (above, n.9), para.D17–18.
[48] Guidance 2010 (above, n.9), Appendix, pp.47–51.
[49] [1999] I.C.R. 302, at 309 EAT. See further below, para.13–14, p.401.

day-to-day activity is best left unspecified: easily recognised, but defined with difficulty."

An impairment also may indirectly affect how a person carries out **13–008** day-to-activities. For instance, a man with chronic fatigue syndrome may have the physical capability to walk and to stand, but find these very difficult to sustain for any length of time because of the overwhelming fatigue he experiences. Or a person, on medical advice, may refrain from an activity that otherwise he could do.[50]

A particular problem in assessing this question was highlighted by Morison J. in *Goodwin*. He observed that persons with a disability will often adjust their lives to cope. "Thus a person whose capacity to communicate through normal speech was obviously impaired might well choose, more or less voluntarily, to live on their own. If one asked such a person whether they managed to carry on their daily lives without undue problems, the answer might well be 'yes', yet their ability to lead a 'normal' life had obviously been impaired."[51]

The activities affected should be assessed as a whole, and not in isolation. In *Ekpe v Commissioner of Police of the Metropolis*,[52] Mrs Ekpe was moved by her employer to a job which involved keyboard duties. She felt that she could not do such a job because she had a physical impairment, which consisted of a wasting of the intrinsic muscles of her right hand. The evidence was that Mrs Ekpe could not carry heavy shopping, scrub pans, peel, grate, sew or put rollers in her hair. She said that sometimes she had to apply her make-up, and feed herself, with her left hand. The employment tribunal concluded that the Mrs Ekpe's impairment did not have a substantial adverse effect on her ability to carry out normal day-to-day activities because, inter alia, she was only unable to cope with heavy shopping; she could cook normally and could still apply make-up with her left hand. Further, applying make-up and putting in hair-rollers were not normal day-to-day activities because "they are activities carried out almost exclusively by women".[53] The EAT allowed Mrs Ekpe's appeal because the tribunal had erred in law by focusing on each activity, rather than making an overall assessment.

The focus should not be on what a claimant *can* do. In *Leonard v Southern Derbyshire Chamber of Commerce*[54] the EAT criticised an employment tribunal for concentrating on what the claimant (with clinical depression) could do—such as being able to eat, drink and catch a ball—and weighed them against what she could not do—such

---

[50] Guidance 2010, above n.9, para.D9.
[51] [1999] I.C.R. 302 (EAT), at 309.
[52] [2001] I.C.R. 1084 (EAT).
[53] The Guidance 2010 (above, n.9), paras D3–D4, state that although an activity cannot be one which is normal only for a small group of people, it need not be one carried out by the majority of population, especially so to exclude activities carried out predominantly by one sex.
[54] [2001] I.R.L.R. 19, [27]. Applied *R. (Mr and Mrs H) v Chair of The Special Educational Needs Tribunal and R School* [2004] EWHC 981, [33].

as negotiate a pavement edge safely. The EAT stated that while tribunals should consider matters "in the round", it "must concentrate on what the applicant cannot do or can only do with difficulty rather than on the things that they can do."

(a) Work as a Day-to-Day Activity

13–009 The impairment must affect a person's capacity to carry out *normal* day-to-day activities. This implies that particular work activities are excluded, because they are not normal for most people. Thus, the Guidance suggests, a concert pianist with carpal tunnel syndrome in her wrists may still be able to play the piano to an ordinary standard, if not a concert standard. However, the impairment will affect her normal day-to-day activities if also it affects her ability to use a computer keyboard to send emails. Likewise, a man with a back condition may still be able to lift ordinary objects, if not heavy ones for his job. However, his condition will affect his normal day-to-day activities if it also affects his ability to lift ordinary objects at home.[55] However, this perhaps runs contrary to the definition of disability handed down by the ECJ. In *Chacón Navas*,[56] the ECJ stated that the impairment must hinder the participation of the person in *professional* life,[57] suggesting that the definition is less to do with day-to-day activities, and more to do with work life. The mismatch was highlighted but sidestepped in *Paterson v Commissioner of Police for the Metropolis*.[58] Here, Patterson suffered "mild" dyslexia; it only affected his performance in promotion exams. The employer argued that as this was a work activity, it was not "normal". The EAT held that it was neither abnormal nor unusual for someone to take high pressure examinations, in some cases for the purposes of gaining promotion. On the contrary, it is a usual, if irregular, everyday activity. This was enough to avoid a head-on conflict. In any case, the EAT continued, it would be bound by *Chacón Navas* to include "professional life" in the definition.[59]

A particular problem arises where a person's capacity to carry out normal day-to-day activities occurs only when at work. In *Cruickshank v VAW Motorcast*,[60] the claimant suffered severe breathing difficulties ("occupational asthma") at work because of the fumes in

---

[55] Guidance 2010 (above, n.9), para.D7.
[56] Case C-13/05 *Chacón Navas v Eurest Colectividades SA* [2006] 3 C.M.L.R. 1123 (ECJ). See above, para.13–002.
[57] ibid. [43].
[58] [2007] I.R.L.R. 763 (EAT).
[59] Applied, *Chief Constable of Dumfries and Galloway v Adams* [2009] I.C.R. 1034 (EAT, Sc) (Night shift working "normal"); distinguished *Chief Constable of Lothian and Borders v Cumming* [2010] I.R.L.R. 109 (EAT, Sc).
[60] [2002] I.C.R. 729 (EAT), [28]. In *Law Hospital NHS Trust v Rush* [2001] I.R.L.R. 611, the Court of Session held that a nurse's back condition was a disability, despite her being able to perform her work duties.

the works foundry. When away from work, on sick leave, and at the tribunal hearing following his dismissal, the symptoms cleared up. And so, when not at work, he could carry out normal day-to-day activities. The EAT held that so long as the symptoms were sufficient to affect day-to-day tasks, it did not matter where this occurred, at work or at home. Thus, the claimant had a disability. Accordingly, the Guidance now states: "The effects experienced by a person as a result of environmental conditions, either in the workplace or in another location where a specialised activity is being carried out, should not be discounted simply because there may be a work-related or other specialised activity involved."[61]

(b) Babies and Young Children

Young children are too young to have developed the capacities (such as mobility, dexterity, co-ordination, and continence) to carry out normal day-to-day activities. Hence, those under six years of age with an impairment are treated as if that impairment has the requisite effect, where normally it would have such an effect on the ability of an older person to carry out normal day-to-day activities.[62]   **13–010**

This is relevant for two reasons. First, in employment, it is possible to discriminate because of *another's* disability. So although young children themselves will not be considered workers under the Act, an employer can be liable for discriminating against, or harassing, a worker, on the ground that the worker has a child with a disability.[63] Second, the Act will apply to babies and young children when coving the provision of services, access to premises and education.[64]

(c) Disfigurements

There is an exception under the Equality Act 2010 where the impairment is a "severe disfigurement". Here, the disfigurement need not adversely affect the person's day-to-day activities. It will "be treated as having a substantial adverse effect on the ability of the person concerned to carry out normal day-to-day activities".[65] This exception does not include tattoos or decorative or other (non-medical) piercings.[66] The Guidance suggested severe disfigurements   **13–011**

---

[61] Guidance 2010 (above, n.9), para.D8.
[62] Equality Act (Disability) Regulations 2010, SI 2010/2128 reg.6.
[63] See Case C-303/06 *Coleman v Attridge Law* [1998] 3 C.M.L.R. 27 (ECJ) and now, EA 2010, ss.13 and 26. See paras 4–027 and 5–006.
[64] EA 2010, respectively, Pts, 3, 4, and 6.
[65] EA 2010 Sch.1, para.3.
[66] Equality Act (Disability) Regulations 2010, SI 2010/2128 reg.5. EA, 2010 Sch.1. para.3(3) also empowers the Minister to exclude, "in particular", deliberately acquired disfigurements, although, at the time of writing, this had not been done.

may include: "scars, birthmarks, limb or postural deformation (including restricted bodily development), or diseases of the skin".[67]

It also suggested that when assessing whether the disfigurement is "severe", account should be taken of where it is, (e.g. on the back as opposed to the face).[68] This exception is based on the social rather than functional model.[69] Disfigurements may not cause any functional impairment, but instead may lead to disadvantage or discrimination because of other people's reaction to the disfigurement.

(3) Long-Term Effects

13–012 The effect of the impairment must be long term. According to the Equality Act 2010 Sch.1, para.2(1), the effect of an impairment has a long-term effect if: (a) it has lasted at least 12 months; or (b) the period for which it lasts is likely to be at least 12 months; or (c) it is likely to last for the rest of the life of the person affected. Sub-paragraph (b) provides for the situation where the effects began less than a year ago, but are likely to continue for at least a year after they began. Sub-paragraph (c) provides for the situation where a person's life expectancy may be shorter than the requisite 12-month period.

The Act also caters for recurring or fluctuating effects. Paragraph 2(2) provides that "Where an impairment ceases to have a substantial adverse effect ... it is to be treated as continuing to have that effect if that effect is likely to recur." Primarily, this means that intermittent effects will be treated as if they were continuing effects. However, the "12-month rule" must still be met. For instance, where the first episode of a recurring form of depression (bipolar affective disorder) occurred in months one and two of a 13-month period, and the second episode took place in month 13, the effects are treated as having continued for the whole period of 13 months, and would be "long-term" because they recurred beyond 12 months after the first occurrence. On the other hand, where a person suffers two discrete episodes of depression within a ten-month period, triggered by a loss of job and a bereavement respectively, the effects, at this stage, are not "long-term", because they have not yet lasted more than 12 months after the first occurrence, and there is no evidence that these episodes are part of an underlying condition of depression which is likely to recur.[70] Some other impairments with effects which can recur, or where effects can be sporadic, include rheumatoid arthritis, Menières disease and epilepsy as well as mental health conditions such as schizophrenia, bipolar affective disorder and certain types of depression.[71]

[67] Guidance 2010 (above, n.9), para.B22
[68] ibid.
[69] See above, para.13–002.
[70] Guidance 2010 (above, n.9), para.C6.
[71] ibid.

Things become more complex when trying to meet the 12-month rule by predicting if the effects will recur. Sub-paragraph (b) includes the situation where the effects began, then ceased, but are likely to recur beyond a year from when they first occurred. Any likely recurring effects must again have a *substantial* adverse effect on the person's ability to carry out day-to-day activities. In *Swift v Chief Constable of Wiltshire Constabulary*[72] the claimant's depression caused her substantial concentration and memory problems for an 18-month period. The evidence was that some effects of the depression were likely to recur, such as an occasional panic attack and consequential sleepless night, but these would not have a *substantial* adverse effect, and so the effects were held not to be long-term.

The phrase in paragraph 2(2) *if that effect is likely to recur* suggests the recurring effects must be the same effects as the previous one. This was the view of the EAT in *Swift*, which appeared to base its decision also on the fact the "recurring" effects were different from the original ones. However, the Guidance suggests otherwise. Under the heading "Recurring or fluctuating effects", it states that it is "not necessary for the effect to be the same throughout the period which is being considered ... other effects on the ability to carry out normal day-to-day activities may develop and the initial effect may disappear altogether."[73] This discrepancy, which existed under the old regime, has been repeated under the Equality Act 2010 and the new Guidance. To square this Guidance with the wording of Sch.1, para.2(2), *that effect*, should be taken not to refer to the type of effect previously experienced (say concentration or memory problems), but only to the effect being "substantial". Thus the ratio decidendi in *Swift* should be confined to a rule that any recurring adverse effects must be substantial.

13–013

The likelihood of recurrence should be assessed at the time of the discriminatory act, and not at a later date, such as the tribunal hearing, with the benefit of hindsight. This excludes from the Act the situation where the effects were unlikely to recur at the time of the discriminatory act, but in fact did recur before the tribunal hearing. In *Richmond Adult Community College v McDougall*[74] the claimant had a history of mental health problems. From November 2001 to February 2002 she was sectioned under the Mental Health Act 1983. In April 2005 she was offered a job as a database assistant at the Richmond College, subject to satisfactory medical clearance and references. The claimant accepted. But the College withdrew the offer after seeing the medical report. At this time, her condition was unlikely to recur. However, in August she had a relapse and in December was readmitted to hospital. One issue for the Court of

---

[72] [2004] I.C.R. 909, [49]–[52] (EAT).
[73] Guidance 2010 (above, n.9), para.C7. The similarly worded original Guidance was available to EAT in *Swift*.
[74] [2008] I.C.R. 431 (CA).

Appeal was at what time should the assessment be made of a likely recurrence: at the time of the employer's withdrawal of the offer, or at the tribunal hearing. Only if it was at the later time, could the claimant be considered to have had a disability for the purpose of suing the College. The Court held it should be at the earlier time, the time of the alleged discriminatory act:

> "... it is fallacious to assume that the occurrence of an event in month six proves that, viewing the matter exclusively as at month one, that occurrence was likely. It does not. It merely proves that the event happened, but by itself leaves unanswered whether, looking at the matter six months earlier, it was *likely* to happen, a question which has to be answered exclusively by reference to the evidence then available."[75]

In *SCA Packaging v Boyle*[76] the House of Lords has held that word "likely", as used in Sch.1, means "could well happen", rather than the higher threshold of "more probably than not".[77] This overruled *Latchman v Reed Business Information*,[78] where the risk of the effects (that had lasted about nine months) of depression recurring were assessed at 50 per cent, and the EAT ruled they were *not* likely to recur because it was *not* more probable than not that they would recur.

(4) Substantial

13–014   *Substantial* means "more than minor or trivial".[79] In *Vicary v British Telecommunications*,[80] Morison J. stated that it was not for medical experts to decide whether the effects are substantial: this was a matter for the tribunal.

The Guidance provides some factors that may help decide if the effect is substantial. First, the time taken to carry out an activity. Second, the effects of the impairment should be considered

---

[75] ibid. [33], (Rimer L.J.). Following *Latchman v Reed Business Information* [2002] I.C.R. 1453 (EAT) [17], disapproving the contrary view expressed obiter in *Greenwood v British Airways* [1999] I.C.R. 969, at p.977; *Collet v Diocese of Hallam Trustee* (2001) EAT/1400/00; *Cruickshank v VAW Motorcast* [2002] I.C.R. 729, [22]–[25]. Distinguished in *Ministry of Defence v Hay* [2008] I.C.R. 1247 (EAT) [49] where the issue was whether at the time of his dismissal, the claimant's continuing effects were likely to last 12 months, rather than deciding the likelihood of recurrence. See James E. Petts, "Prognosis for Disability Discrimination Following *McDougall*", [2008] 37 ILJ 268, who makes the point that knowledge is required for liability (at p.273).

[76] [2009] UKHL 37.

[77] ibid. The case centred on the effect of medical treatment (now para.5, see below, para.13–015), but the House included long term effects in its reasoning: ibid. [52], [78], (Lady Hale), [81] (Lord Neuberger), [78] (Lord Brown). See also, Guidance 2010, above, n.9, para.C3.

[78] [2002] I.C.R. 1453 (EAT).

[79] EA 2010 s.212(1). See also *Goodwin v The Patent Office* [1999] I.C.R. 302 (EAT), at 310 (Morison J.).

[80] [1999] I.R.L.R. 680, at 682 (EAT). Applied *Abadeh v BT* [2001] I.C.R. 156 (EAT).

cumulatively, and not in isolation. So several effects, in themselves minor, could cumulate into a substantial effect. Similarly, where a person has more than one impairment, account should be taken of whether the impairments together have a substantial effect overall on the person's ability to carry out normal day-to-day activities.[81] Persons are expected, within reason, to modify their behaviour to prevent or reduce the effects of an impairment, for example, someone with a back problem should avoid extreme activities, such as parachuting. Otherwise, such persons may not be considered as having a disability for the Act. Account should be taken of environmental conditions that may exacerbate the effect of an impairment. "Factors such as temperature, humidity, lighting, the time of day or night, how tired the person is, or how much stress he or she is under, may have an impact on the effects." For example, rheumatoid arthritis produces particularly bad effects during cold and damp weather.[82]

In *Goodwin*, the claimant had paranoid schizophrenia and suffered auditory hallucinations (he heard voices) which interrupted his concentration. He brought this claim of disability discrimination after being dismissed from his post as a patent examiner following complaints from female staff of disturbing behaviour. The employment tribunal found that he had no disability because he was able to "perform his domestic activities without the need for assistance, to get to work efficiently and to carry out his work to a satisfactory standard." The EAT reversed that decision, holding that the tribunal's analysis was too narrow, as it ignored the claimant's capacity to concentrate and communicate, which meant, for instance, he was unable to carry out day-to-day conversation with colleagues. In *Vicary v British Telecommunications*,[83] the claimant had an impairment in her right arm and hand. She suffered pain when doing repetitive light work, for example typing or cutting vegetables, or when she was doing more physical work on a one-off basis, such as shifting a chair at home when sitting down or getting up from a table. The EAT held that these were normal day-to-day activities and that an inability to carry out those functions would "obviously be regarded as a substantial impairment of an ability to carry out normal day-to-day activities."[84]

---

[81] In *M v SW School* [2004] EWHC 2586, [13]–[14], the Special Educational Needs and Disability Tribunal analysed the each of the claimant's vision, mobility and speech difficulties in isolation, and concluded that the effects of each were not substantial. The High Court reversed, holding that the effects of the impairments should be considered as a whole.

[82] Guidance 2010 (above, n.9), paras.B2–B10.

[83] [1999] I.R.L.R. 680, at 682 (EAT). Applied *Abadeh v BT* [2001] I.C.R. 156 (EAT).

[84] Contrast the US case *Carr v Publix Super Markets* No 05-12611 (2006 11th Cir) (US App LEXIS 2845), at p.7, where it was held that the plaintiff, who found it impossible, or difficult, to perform certain tasks with his right arm (lifting and operating a cash register), was not limited substantially in his ability to perform manual tasks central to his daily life or otherwise to care for himself.

There are three situations for which the Act makes specific provision on the issue of "substantial".

(a) The Effect of Medical Treatment

13–015 The Act (Sch.1, para.5) stipulates that an impairment is to be treated as having the substantial adverse effect if "(a) measures are being taken to treat or correct it, and (b) but for that, it would be likely to have that effect." In other words, tribunals must assess the likely effects *as if* there were no treatment. This does not apply to the correction by glasses or contact lenses of sight impairments.

In this context, "likely", means "could well happen", rather than the higher threshold of "more probably than not".[85] The reasoning behind the Lords' decision is that the *more probable than not* rubric is used in civil law by courts looking back at events, and treating some as facts. In the context of Sch.1, the exercise is different. It requires a *prediction*:

> "The prediction of medical outcomes is something which is frequently difficult. There are many quiescent conditions which are subject to medical treatment or drug regimes and which can give rise to serious consequences if the treatment or the drugs are stopped. These serious consequences may not inevitably happen and in any given case it may be impossible to say whether it is more probable than not that this will occur. This being so, it seems highly likely that in the context of para.[5] in the disability legislation the word 'likely' is used in the sense of 'could well happen'."[86]

In *Goodwin v The Patent Office*[87] Morison J. suggested that when approaching the question, "The tribunal will wish to examine how the applicant's abilities had actually been affected at the material time, whilst on medication, and then to address their minds to the difficult question as to the effects which they think there would have been but for the medication: the *deduced* effects. The question is then whether the actual and deduced effects on the applicant's abilities to carry out normal day-to-day activities is *clearly more than trivial*." This "deduced effects" doctrine applies even where the effects are not at all apparent, or completely under control.[88]

---

[85] *SCA Packaging v Boyle* [2009] UKHL 37. See also, above, para.13–013, and Guidance 2010, above, n.9, para.B11.
[86] [2009] UKHL 37, [69]–[70], citing [2009] I.R.L.R. 54 (NICA), [19] (Girvan L.J.).
[87] [1999] I.C.R. 302, at 310 (EAT).
[88] Guidance 2010, above, n.9, para.B12.

"Measures" include medical treatment and the use of a prosthesis **13–016** (e.g. an artificial leg) or other aid.[89] In *Kapadia v Lambeth LBC*[90] the EAT held that counselling sessions for a man with depression constituted "medical treatment". In *Carden v Pickerings Europe*[91] the EAT held that plates and pins used for a broken ankle could be an "other aid", even some 20 years after they were inserted, provided that they still corrected or treated what would otherwise be a disability. In *SCA Packaging v Boyle*, the measure was a voice training regime for a woman who had suffered hoarseness and vocal nodes.[92]

The Act is concerned with measures that "are being taken" and, accordingly, where treatment has ceased, a tribunal can no longer disregard the treatment.[93] It must judge the effects of the impairment as they are presented. Where the effect of the continuing treatment creates a permanent improvement, that improvement should be taken into account. If the improvement reduces the effects to below being substantial, then the person does not have a disability.[94] The tribunal should take account of any permanent improvement. A person treated for pneumonia may make a permanent recovery.[95] However, if the improvement is temporary, or it cannot be ascertained whether it is permanent, then the treatment must be disregarded. For instance, a person's depression may improve with psychotherapy, but that person may suffer a relapse should the treatment cease.[96]

(b) Progressive Conditions

By Sch.1, para.8, the Act protects a person with a progressive con- **13–017** dition that results in an impairment that has *some* adverse effect (i.e. not substantial), but which is likely to become substantial. Progressive conditions include cancer, systemic lupus erythematosis (SLE), various types of dementia, rheumatoid arthritis, and motor neurone disease. Note that some specified conditions are "deemed" as disabilities under the Act, from the moment they arise (effectively from the point of diagnosis) irrespective of whether there is any adverse effect. These conditions include HIV, multiple sclerosis or cancer.[97]

Under para.8, a person is protected not from the point of diagnosis, but from when the effects of the condition arise. In *Mowat-Brown v University of Surrey*, the EAT held that "likely" in para.8

---

[89] EA 2010 Sch.1, para.5(2).
[90] [2000] I.R.L.R. 14, affirmed [2000] I.R.L.R. 699 (CA).
[91] [2005] I.R.L.R. 720 (EAT).
[92] [2009] UKHL 37.
[93] *Abadeh v BT* [2001] I.C.R. 156 (EAT), [30].
[94] ibid. [31].
[95] Guidance 2010 (above, n.9), para.B15.
[96] *Abadeh v BT* [2001] I.C.R. 156, at [33] (EAT)
[97] Guidance 2010 (above, n.9), paras B17–B18.

meant "more likely than not".[98] Of course, in the later case of *SCA Packaging v Boyle* (above, para.13–015), the House of Lords held that for the purpose of Sch.1, paras 2 and 5, "likely" meant *could well happen* rather than the higher threshold of *more likely than not*. None of the judgments cited *Mowat-Brown*, although Lady Hale suggested than para.8 was included in her reasoning (with which Lords Hope, Brown, Neuberger agreed).[99] After referring to para.8, she said: "it is usual for the same word to mean the same thing when used in the same group of statutory provisions".[100] Given this, and the reasoning behind the *Boyle* decision (that "likely" means *could well happen* because of its predictive nature), there seems every reason to abandon *Mowat-Brown* in favour of *Boyle*.

The effect need not be continuous.[101] Any effect can be directly or indirectly caused by the condition, and the predicted effect does not have to be the same as the current effect. In *Kirton v Tetrosyl*[102] the claimant was diagnosed with prostate cancer. Surgery to treat the cancer resulted in a sphincter deficiency which gave the claimant infrequent (i.e. not substantial) incontinence. The Court of Appeal held that the claimant had now a progressive condition, even though the current impairment was only indirectly caused by the cancer (and its treatment) and is different from the likely substantial effects of the cancer.

The requirement for the effects to be "long-term" apply in the normal way.[103] Of course, for some progressive conditions where death is likely to result quickly, the 12-month rule may not apply. In less serious cases the 12-month rule applies, although the period begins when the first effects arise. In *Grimley v Turner & Jarvis Ltd*[104] the claimant was diagnosed with cancer that had an insubstantial adverse effect. About a year later he underwent surgery for this on his kidney, which resulted in a predicted two-month period of substantial adverse effects. The EAT held that the claimant had a progressive condition under para.8, as the effects had lasted over 12 months. It did not matter that the predicted substantial effect was only two months.

(c) Disfigurements

13–018 Severe disfigurements may be considered without more as substantial. See above, para.13–011.

[98] [2002] I.R.L.R. 235 (EAT), [21].
[99] [2009] UKHL 37, respectively, [1], [76], [81].
[100] ibid. [52]. See also [40 (Lord Roger). The new Guidance 2010 is neutral on this matter.
[101] Guidance 2010 (above, n.9), para.B16.
[102] [2003] I.C.R. 1237. See Guidance, ibid, B19.
[103] See above, para.13–012.
[104] (2004) UKEAT/0967/03/ILB.

(5) Past Disabilities

Section 6(4) of the EA 2010 extends the Act's coverage to those who **13–019** have had a disability in the past. The question of whether or not somebody had a disability is determined under the Act in the normal way, which applies even to those who claim to have had a disability before the Act came into force.[105]

Without this, someone who has recovered from a past disability would not be protected. This is particularly important for disabilities that carry a stigma, such as a mental illness. And so, for instance, an employer who dismisses a worker upon discovering that she once had a mental illness can be liable under the Act. Case law and the Guidance suggest that where the effects are fluctuating, they are treated as continuing if effects cease and if in fact recur (rather than were *likely* to recur).[106]

2. DISABILITY DISCRIMINATION GENERALLY

For some purposes, the disability provisions are similar to those for **13–020** other protected characteristics. This is so for Work coverage (Chapter 8), harassment, (Chapter 5), victimisation (Chapter 7), individual and strategic enforcement (Chapter 12), the single equality duty (Chapter 10) and positive action (Chapter 11).

The essential difference is in the meaning of discrimination. Most discrimination legislation is symmetrical in nature.[107] This means that a white person may claim for racial discrimination, and a man may claim for sex discrimination. Disability discrimination law aspires to its goal of equality by other (non-symmetrical) means. Rather than giving formal equal rights to persons with or without a disability, it identifies persons with a disability for protection, and (in the case of the duty to make reasonable adjustments) affords persons with a disability *different* treatment, which can be *more* favourable. For instance, a person confined to a wheelchair is in no need of equal treatment in the sense of sharing a staircase. She requires equal *access*, which is achieved by *different* treatment. This approach means that persons without disabilities cannot bring claims under the Act where they consider that they have been treated less favourably than a person with a disability.

In the context of employment note that, for disability, the armed forces are not bound by the Work provisions (Pt 5).[108] A *draft* Code

---

[105] EA 2010 Sch.1, para.9.
[106] See *Greenwood v British Airways* [1999] I.C.R. 969 (EAT); Guidance 2010 (above, n.9), para.C5.
[107] See further Ch.1, para.1–005 and Ch.11, para.11–002.
[108] EA 2010 Sch.9, para.4(3).

of Practice for Employment was issued in 2010.[109] At the time of writing it was awaiting Parliamentary approval. References below are to this *draft* Code. The Act defines four types of employment discrimination: direct discrimination, discrimination arising from disability, indirect discrimination, and a failure to make reasonable adjustments.

3. DIRECT DISCRIMINATION

13–021 The standard definition of direct discrimination (EA 2010 s.13) applies here, with the qualification that a person cannot sue for less favourable treatment because he does *not* have a disability.[110] This could arise say, where a worker with mobility problems is permitted to carry out some duties at home, and a colleague complains that *he* is not afforded this benefit. This distinguishes direct disability discrimination from conventional direct discrimination, where the symmetrical format permits say, men, whites, atheists and heterosexuals, to complain of discrimination because of, respectively, sex, race, religion and sexual orientation.

Bearing in mind that it is unlawful also to discriminate for a reason arising from a disability, direct discrimination covers a particularly narrow range of facially discriminatory conduct. The drafting draws a line between the person's disability and the consequences of that disability. Apart from the impairment in question, the comparator must have the same abilities as the claimant (EA 2010 s.23(2)(a)). For instance, an employer may refuse to hire a woman with epilepsy because he considers that she cannot drive safely. The comparator will be someone who he considers cannot drive safely, but does not have epilepsy. The refusal to hire was because of her driving capability, and not because of her disability. It could of course amount to "discrimination arsing from disability" under s.15, where the employer has the opportunity to justify the treatment (discussed below). In *High Quality Lifestyles v Watts*,[111] the claimant worked with persons with learning difficulties. Occasionally he could be bitten or scratched by the "service users". The claimant was HIV positive, but had not disclosed this to his employer. When his employer discovered his HIV status, it fired him. The EAT held that the claimant was fired because of the risk of infection, and not because of his HIV. The correct (hypothetical) comparator was a person without HIV, but with an equally communicable disease. However, the employer

---

[109] *www.equalityhumanrights.com/legal-and-policy/equality-act/equality-act-codes-of-practice/* (accessed January 1, 2011).
[110] EA 2010 s.13(3).
[111] [2006] I.R.L.R. 850 (EAT).

was liable for what is now discrimination arising from disability (discussed below).

When direct discrimination was introduced into disability law, the Government envisaged it covering the following instances:[112]

(a) an employer, on learning that a job applicant has diabetes, summarily rejects the application without giving any consideration of the applicant's circumstances or whether the person concerned would be competent to do the job (with or without a reasonable adjustment);

(b) a disabled employee is refused access to the employer's sports and social club simply on the basis that the club does not allow disabled members, and without any consideration of whether the employee might benefit from membership, and even though they could access the club with a reasonable adjustment;

(c) without any consideration of whether he will be able to work for as many years as other employees, a newly recruited disabled person is required to pay the same contributions to an occupational pension scheme even though he is denied access to ill health retirement benefits available to other members of the scheme.

Despite this narrow approach mandated by s.23(2)(a), *Watts*, and the Government guidance, the Court of Appeal signalled a relaxed approach to the comparison in *Stockton on Tees BC v Aylott*.[113] Here, Mr Aylott had bipolar affective disorder. He had a number of sickness absences from work. Following a length of absence, and concerns about his behaviour and performance, he was moved to another post, where deadlines were set, and his performance was closely monitored. Eventually he was dismissed on grounds of capability (ill-health). For his claim of direct discrimination, the employment tribunal compared his treatment to that of a worker returning to work after a complicated broken bone, and found the reason for the treatment was the employer's "stereotypical view of mental illness". The EAT reversed, holding that the comparison should have included the concerns about his behaviour and performance, and the move. The Court of Appeal restored the original decision, holding it was wrong to include the additional factors because they arose from the claimant's disability.[114] Invoking *Shamoon v Chief Constable of the RUC*,[115] Mummery L.J. said: "the real question is not so much about the hypothetical comparator, as whether the employment tribunal's

13–022

---

[112] Explanatory Notes to the *pre-consultation draft* Regulations (SI 2003/1673), para.32.
[113] [2010] I.C.R. 1278 (CA).
[114] ibid. [47].
[115] [2003] I.C.R. 337 (HL). See above, Ch.4, para.4–006.

finding on the ground of dismissal was supported by evidence."[116] This was not to say that the comparison should be abandoned, it was part of the process and good practice as a cross check.[117] With respect, concerns over a worker's job performance relate more directly to his *abilities*, than his disability. Discrimination based on job performance is more readily analysed as discrimination arising from disability, under s.15 (discussed below).

In line with other protected characteristics, stereotyping can amount to direct discrimination. This was seen in *Aylott*. A more simplistic example would be an employer rejecting an application from a blind person because he wrongly assumed that blind people cannot use a computer.[118] It is possible to directly discriminate without knowledge of the victim's disability. For instance, the employer may advertise internally for a promotion, stating that the post is not suitable for anyone with a history of mental illness and exclude, unknowingly, a member of staff with a history of schizophrenia.[119] It is conceivable also to directly discriminate by acting on discriminatory factors of which it is unaware. In *Williams v YKK*[120] Elias J. suggested obiter that an unprejudiced manager's decision may be affected, or tainted, by a report made by a prejudiced supervisor. So for instance, a manager who is unaware that a worker's absenteeism was due to her disability, may be influenced to dismiss her by unfavourable opinions delivered by prejudiced colleagues who were aware of her disability. This is direct discrimination because the reason for the treatment is the victim's disability: the basis of the prejudiced opinions was disability, rather than absenteeism.[121]

13–023   In line with other protected characteristics, direct discrimination because of a third party's disability is actionable,[122] as is (in principle) "perceived discrimination". Perceived discrimination can occur when the discriminator acts on a mistaken belief that a person has a protected characteristic, say, an Islamaphobe mistaking a Sikh to be Muslim. But cases of perceived disability discrimination may not be so straightforward because of the unusually complex definition of disability in comparison to other protected characteristics. In *J v Piper*,[123] Underhill J. observed:

---

[116] ibid. [44] (giving judgment for the Court).
[117] ibid. [45].
[118] Suggested by the previous Code of practice: *Code of Practice Employment and Occupation* (2004) London: TSO (ISBN 0 11 703419 3), para.4.8.
[119] ibid. para.4.11.
[120] (2002) EAT/0408/01 AM (see *employmentappeals.gov.uk*).
[121] ibid. [23]. In the US, this is known as the "Cat's Paw" theory. See further Ch.4, para.4–022. For knowledge and discrimination arising from disability, see para.13–028, below.
[122] As a result of the decision in Case C-303/06 *Coleman v Attridge Law* [2008] C.M.L.R. 27 (ECJ), discussed above, Ch.5, para.5–006.
[123] [2010] I.C.R. 1052 (EAT).

"If a manager discriminates against an employee because he believes her to have a broken leg, or ... to be "depressed", the question whether the effects of the perceived injury, or of the perceived depression, are likely to last more or less than 12 months may never enter his thinking ...".[124]

Of course, such a manager may not have considered if the effects adversely affected day-to-day activities, or did so substantially. In the event, the issue did not arise in that case, and so the problem remains.

Finally, the Genuine Occupational Requirement defence provided by the Equality Act 2010 Sch.9, para.1, applies to disability discrimination in the normal way. The text, and general points relating to this exemption, are at Chapter 8, para.8–019. Note that Sch.9, para.1, applies to "a requirement to have a particular protected characteristic". It does not permit the inverse requirement, not to have a particular protected characteristic, and so, on the face of it, permits employers to require a worker with a disability, but not a worker without one. Curiously (and unusually) here, the domestic version was drafted in slightly narrower terms than the corresponding defence in its parent Framework Directive 2000/78/EC art.4(1), which permits a difference of treatment "which is based on" disability. The Explanatory Notes (789) provide this example:

"An organisation for deaf people might legitimately employ a deaf person who uses British Sign Language to work as a counsellor to other deaf people whose first or preferred language is BSL."

4. DISCRIMINATION ARISING FROM DISABILITY

This differs from direct discrimination in two essential ways. First, it **13–024** targets treatment related to the *consequences* of a disability, rather than the disability itself. Second, it carries a general justification defence. Section 15 of the EA 2010, provides:

"(1) A person (A) discriminates against a disabled person (B) if—

  (a) A treats B unfavourably because of something arising in consequence of B's disability, and

  (b) A cannot show that the treatment is a proportionate means of achieving a legitimate aim.

[124] ibid. [62].

(2) Subsection (1) does not apply if A shows that A did not know, and could not reasonably have been expected to know, that B had the disability."

This cause of action has a chequered history. It was known first as "disability-related discrimination"[125] and was given its full potential by the judgment in *Clark v TGD Ltd t/a Novacold*.[126] In this case Mr Clark suffered a back injury at work in August 1996 and was diagnosed as having soft tissue injuries around the spine. He was unable to work and absent from September 1996 until his dismissal, in January 1997. In response to Clark's claim for disability-related discrimination Novacold argued that it would have dismissed any person unable to work for that long. The Court of Appeal held that this was using the wrong comparator. The reason for Clark's dismissal was his inability to work, which was related to his disability. Clark should have been compared with a person without his disability who was able to work (the "reason"). Thus, the reason for the less favourable treatment need only be *related to* the disability. Thus if a cafe has a "no dogs" rule, the reason for refusing entry to a blind man with his guide dog related to his disability.[127] Similarly, a disabled customer who is told to leave the restaurant because she has difficulty eating as a result of her disability is so treated for a reason *related to* her disability. Accordingly, the choice of comparator differed from that under direct discrimination. In these examples the comparator was a person *without* a dog, or *without* an eating difficulty. If it were otherwise, and the comparator were a sighted man *with* a dog, or a person who had difficulty eating for a reason unrelated to a disability (say a coughing fit, or because the food tasted off), this cause of action would be reduced to direct discrimination.

13–025   However, this approach was overturned by the House of Lords in *Lewisham LBC v Malcolm*.[128] In this case, Mr Malcolm suffered from schizophrenia. In 2002, he exercised his right to buy his (rented) flat from Lewisham Council, but completion was delayed for some time. Then, in May 2004, he lost his job. In June he moved out, and (in breach of the lease) sub-let the flat. Just after that, he informed the council he wished to complete the transfer on July 26. By sub-letting before completion, he had "jumped the gun", because (it was alleged) his judgment was impaired by his schizophrenia. On July 6, the council discovered the sub-letting, and gave Malcolm notice to quit. Malcolm claimed his eviction was for a reason related to his

---

[125] DDA 1995 s.3A(1), now repealed.
[126] [1999] I.C.R. 951 (CA) at pp.964–966.
[127] Minister of State for Social Security and Disabled People, 253 HC Official Report (6th series) col.150, Jan 24, 1995.
[128] [2008] I..R.L.R. 700 (HL). See R. Horton "The End of Disability-Related Discrimination in Employment?" (2008) 37 ILJ 376; M. Connolly "Equal Treatment, Fault-Based Liability, And Disability-Related-Discrimination" (2008) 9 I.J.D.L. 251.

schizophrenia, and so amounted to disability-related discrimination. The case centred on the identity of the comparator: (1) a person without schizophrenia who *had not* sub-let (*Novacold*); or (2) a person without schizophrenia who *had* sub-let. The majority went for the second option and, of course, found the council not liable, as it would have evicted any tenant caught sub-letting. Thus, *Novacold* was overruled and the proverbial blind man with a dog should be compared with sighted man *with* a dog.[129] The decision reduced disability-related discrimination to no more than direct discrimination, and effectively destroyed it as a separate cause of action.

Parliament responded with the reformulated "discrimination arising from disability" (s.15 EA 2010, above) which abolished altogether the requirement for a comparison. All that is required now for the prima facie case is unfavourable treatment because of something arising in consequence of the claimant's disability. Under s.15, the worker with the back problem was unfavourably treated because of his absenteeism (*Novacold*);[130] the blind man was unfavourably treated because of his dog, and the customer because of her eating difficulties. In each of these examples, the defendant would have to justify its treatment. However, the *result* of the *Malcolm* case may survive under s.15, for the reason given below (para.13–028).

A consequence of this saga was that for a period between *Malcolm* (June 25, 2008) and the coming into force of s.15 (October 1, 2010), it was not worth pleading disability-related discrimination because, as it was as narrow as (or narrower than) direct discrimination, but permitted the defendant a defence, it was a pointless exercise. In the wake of *Malcolm* claimants shifted their focus to exploiting the full potential of the duty to make reasonable adjustments.[131]

(1) Something Arising from the Disability

In many cases this will be obvious, such as the absenteeism, the dog   **13–026**
or the eating disorder in the examples above. In other cases it will be less obvious. The Code of Practice on Employment suggests that this could be having to follow a restricted diet, or a loss of temper as a result of severe pain from cancer.[132]

(2) Unfavourable Treatment

This is a fresh concept in discrimination law. The nearest comparison   **13–027**
comes from cases deciding—irrespective of the comparative aspect—if the treatment was *less* favourable enough for liability. Here,

---

[129] Lady Hale dissented on this point. See [2008] I.L.I.R. 700, [78]–[81].
[130] See also *Draft Equality Act 2010 Code of Practice on Employment* (see above, n.109), paras 5.3 and 5.6.
[131] See e.g. *Stockton on Tees BC v Aylott* [2010] I.C.R. 1278 (CA), [68]–[70].
[132] *Draft Equality Act 2010 Code of Practice on Employment* (see above, n.109), para.5.9.

although *different* treatment is not in itself actionable, it is enough
that the victim perceived—reasonably—that he had been treated less
favourably.[133] The same approach is likely to be taken under s.15.

(3) Knowledge of the Disability

13–028   Section 15(2) states that there is no liability if the defendant "did not
know, and could not reasonably have been expected to know", that
the claimant had the disability. This effectively codifies the second
part of *Lewisham LBC v Malcolm*[134] (above, para.13–025). The second issue in that case was whether the council could have been liable
if it was unaware of Malcolm's schizophrenia. The answer was "no".
A unanimous House held that for the treatment to be "related" to the
claimant's disability, the defendant must have known, or ought to
have known, of the disability at the time of the treatment.

Before *Malcolm*, it was suggested that where the treatment was for
a reason related to the disability, there was no need for the defendant
to have had knowledge of that disability. Two vivid examples were
provided by Lindsay J. in *Heinz v Kendrick*.[135] First, a postman with a
concealed artificial leg may be dismissed for being too slow. Second, a
secretary with undeclared dyslexia may be dismissed for "typing
hopelessly misspelt letters". The Code of Practice in force at the time
supported this view, giving an example of a woman dismissed for
persistent absenteeism (as any worker would be) where the employer
was unaware that the reason for her absence was her multiple
sclerosis.[136] In all these examples, the employer's act amounted to
treatment related to the worker's disability (which may or may not be
justified). However, this was rejected by the House in *Malcolm*.

This reduced the reach of disability-related discrimination to less
than direct discrimination, where knowledge of a claimant's protected characteristic is not necessary for liability.[137] Lord Bingham
and Lady Hale considered that as disability-related discrimination
carried a justification defence, knowledge must be an element,
otherwise the defendant would be in no position to justify the challenged treatment.[138] This is not entirely true. Knowledge of the claimant's protected characteristic is unnecessary for liability for *indirect*
discrimination, which carries also a justification defence. And, in the
context of housing, for instance, a landlord without knowledge of his
tenants' mental illness could justify evicting them for causing a

---

[133] See e.g. *R. v Birmingham City Council, ex parte EOC* [1989] A.C. 1155 (HL), discussed Ch.4,
para.4–015, p.91.
[134] [2008] I.R.L.R. 700 (HL).
[135] [2000] I.C.R. 491 (EAT) [5]. See also Lord Johnston in *Callaghan v Glasgow CC* [2001]
I.R.L.R. 724 (EAT), at p.726.
[136] Code of practice: *Code of Practice Employment and Occupation* (2004) London: TSO (ISBN
0 11 703419 3), para.4.31.
[137] Case C-54/07 *Feryn* [2008] I.R.L.R. 732 (ECJ). See Ch.4, para.4–024, p.101.
[138] [2008] I.R.L.R. 700 (HL), [18] (Lord Bingham), [86] (Lady Hale).

nuisance to their neighbours, even though their behaviour was caused by the mental illness.[139] Nonetheless, this part of the *Malcolm* decision is now represented by s.15(2). As such, if *Malcolm* were heard today under s.15, it is likely that the claim would still fail.

A lot may turn on how the courts interpret *reasonably expected to*   **13–029**
know. The Code of Practice on Employment suggests that employers should be proactive and—within reason—do all to find out if any workers have a disability, and bear in mind that "not all workers who meet the definition of disability may think of themselves as a 'disabled person'." For example, a person with a good work record suddenly becomes emotional and upset and less reliable. This should alert the employer of a possible disability, and it should explore with the worker the reasons for the change in conduct. When making enquiries, employers should also consider the worker's dignity and privacy,[140] and the restrictions on asking applicants about disability and health.[141]

In "no knowledge" cases, claimants may find more success pleading direct or indirect discrimination.

(4) Objective Justification

The defendant can avoid liability by showing that "the treatment was   **13–030**
a proportionate means of achieving a legitimate aim" (s.15(1)(b)). This is the standard formula for justification used throughout the Act. The principles are set out in Chapter 6, para.6–035. This defence replaces a less strict defence used for disability-related discrimination,[142] and as such the case law on this is of little value now as a guide.

Note, that where a duty to make reasonable adjustments also arises (see below), it is most unlikely that a defendant could justify discrimination arising from disability if it had not discharged its reasonable adjustments duty. Conversely, a defendant who had discharged this duty has not necessarily justified discrimination arising from disability. It may be that the adjustment is unrelated to the unfavourable treatment. For example, an employer may adjust the working hours of a worker with multiple sclerosis, so that she starts at 9.30am instead of 9.00am. But later it fires her for absenteeism arising from her disability. The reasonable adjustment does not necessarily justify the dismissal.[143]

---

[139] *Manchester City Council v Romano* [2005] 1 W.L.R. 2775 (CA).
[140] *Draft Equality Act 2010 Code of Practice on Employment* (see above, n.109), paras 5.14–5.16.
[141] EA 2010 s.60. See below, para.13–037.
[142] *Jones v Post Office* [2001] I.C.R. 805 (CA).
[143] *Draft Equality Act 2010 Code of Practice on Employment* (see above, n.109), paras 5.20–5.22.

5. INDIRECT DISCRIMINATION

13–031   Indirect discrimination applies to disability for the first time under the Equality Act 2010.[144] Conventional indirect discrimination theory,[145] being rooted in group disadvantage (defined e.g. by race, sex, a sexual orientation, religion), is not the best way to address disability discrimination because disabilities are so many and so varied. Section 6(3)(b) tries to cope with this by declaring that: "a reference to persons who share a protected characteristic is a reference to persons who have the same disability." Thus, under s.19 (defining indirect discrimination for the whole Act), it must be shown that a provision, criterion or practice, puts at a particular disadvantage those with the same disability as the claimant. Such a group may be less easy to define than groups defined by sex, or race, etc. especially where the impairment is not clinically recognised. It is also likely to be much smaller, giving rise to problems in some cases with statistical proof. As well as difficulties of proof, the relatively small impact (by numbers) on the claimant's group may make any prima facie case easier to justify.

In some cases, the victim will be the only person with his particular disability adversely affected by the challenged practice. Here, as s.19 is confined to *group* disadvantage,[146] it will not apply at all. Such cases should be pleaded as discrimination arising from disability under s.15 (above).

If a claimant can present a prima facie case, then the advantage over discrimination arising from disability is that there is no need for the defendant to have had knowledge (real or constructive) of the disability.

6. THE DUTY TO MAKE ADJUSTMENTS—WORK

13–032   A failure to make a reasonable adjustment amounts to discrimination (s.21, EA 2010). This is the most obvious expression that disability discrimination is different from other grounds. It entails a degree of positive discrimination.[147]

Employers are bound to consider three ways to make reasonable adjustments. They may change a provision, criterion or practice, or

---

[144] Another consequence of *Lewisham LBC v Malcolm* [2008] I.R.L.R. 700 (HL). Discussed above, para.13–025. See also Explanatory Notes (81).

[145] Discussed Ch.6, para.6–003.

[146] See *Eweida v BA* [2010] I.C.R. 890 (CA), [15]–[19], discussed Ch.3, para.3–022.

[147] *Archibald v Fife Council* [2004] I.C.R. 954 (HL), [57] (Lady Hale), see below, para.13–033.

overcome a physical feature, or provide auxiliary aids. Apart from the express requirement regarding auxiliary aids,[148] the Act reproduces the existing duties from the Disability Discrimination Act 1995.

There are three corresponding triggers for a duty to arise. Section 20 imposes a duty to take such steps as it is reasonable to have to take to avoid the disadvantage where either:

> "... a provision, criterion or practice of [the employer's] puts a disabled person at a substantial disadvantage in relation to a relevant matter in comparison with persons who are not disabled," or
>
> "a physical feature puts a disabled person at a substantial disadvantage in relation to a relevant matter in comparison with persons who are not disabled".

Third, s.20(5) imposes a duty to take such steps as it is reasonable to have to take to provide the auxiliary aid, where:

> "... a disabled person would, but for the provision of an auxiliary aid, be put at a substantial disadvantage in relation to a relevant matter in comparison with persons who are not disabled".

Auxiliary aids include specialist equipment such as an adapted keyboard or text to speech software, and auxiliary *services*, for example, provision of a sign language interpreter or a support worker.[149] Where the first or third duty relates to the provision of information, the duty includes ensuring that the information is provided in an accessible format,[150] for example "providing letters, training materials or recruitment forms in Braille or on audio-tape."[151]

Unlike the duty to adjust in some other fields, such as the supply of services, this duty is not anticipatory. It only arises (the "relevant matter") when "triggered" by an existing employee or (for the first and third triggers) a job applicant (Sch.8).

(1) "Provision, Criterion or Practice"

Prior to October 2004, the duty arose when the employer's "arrangements" (or the physical features of its premises) placed a disabled person at a "substantial disadvantage". The definition of "arrangements" was limited to job offers and "any term, condition or

13–033

---

[148] EA 2010 Sch.8, para.2(1).
[149] *Draft Equality Act 2010 Code of Practice on Employment* (see above, n.109), para.6.13.
[150] EA 2010 s.20(6).
[151] *Draft Equality Act 2010 Code of Practice on Employment* (see above, n.109), para.6.6.

arrangements" on which the employment was afforded.[152] This produced perhaps unforeseen technical difficulties in *Archibald v Fife Council*.[153] Here, the claimant road-sweeper underwent a routine operation on her back. There was a complication leaving her virtually unable to walk and of course unable to do her job. The council offered her the chance to do office-work, but only through competitive interviews. She failed over 100 and eventually was dismissed. She claimed that the council had failed to make reasonable adjustments. The employment tribunal held that the duty did not arise because the "arrangements" only encompassed the office-work arrangements, which did not place Ms Archibald at any disadvantage because of her disability. The Court of Session upheld that decision, but on the different ground that "arrangements" could not include the "fundamental essence of the job". The logic here is that where no adjustments can be made to enable the person to do job in question (road-sweeping), a duty cannot arise.[154] Of course, the outcome defeats the purpose of the Act, which envisages a transfer to other work as a reasonable adjustment.[155] However, the House of Lords, giving a purposive interpretation, stated that the "arrangements" were the job description and the liability to dismissal for a worker who was unable to do the job. Here, the job description was to walk and use a broom, and Ms Archibald was dismissed for not being able to do that.[156] Accordingly the House held that the duty was triggered in this case. The more recent definition "provision, criterion or practice", should if necessary be given an equally generous construction. In *Fareham College Corporation v Walters* the EAT held that "a dismissal can ... itself be an unlawful act of discrimination by reason of a failure to make reasonable adjustments."[157]

(2) When the Duty is Triggered

13–034   The employer's duty is triggered when its provision, criterion or practice, or physical feature of its premises, or failure to provide an auxiliary aid, places the person at a "substantial disadvantage ... in comparison with persons who are not disabled". *Substantial* means simply "more than minor or trivial".[158]

The comparison will be relatively straightforward in most cases. However, difficulties have arisen in some cases. These are overcome with a liberal approach to the comparison. Although the Act demands a like-for-like comparison for direct and indirect

---

[152] DDA 1995 s.6(2), prior to October 2004 (now repealed).
[153] [2004] I.C.R. 954 (HL).
[154] See [2004] I.R.L.R. 197, [27] and [44] (CS).
[155] *Draft Equality Act 2010 Code of Practice on Employment* (see above, n.109), para.6.33.
[156] [2004] I.C.R. 954, [11], [42] and [62].
[157] [2009] I.R.L.R. 991 (EAT), [70]. See also, [69], [73] (Cox J.).
[158] EA 2010 s.212(1).

discrimination (s.23(1)), it makes no such demand for the reasonable adjustments duty. This can be seen in the three cases below.

In *Archibald v Fife Council*[159] (the facts are given above) the council argued that as she could not do the job at all, a proper comparison could not be made: "it was impossible to compare in terms of advantage in a running race a runner and a non-runner".[160] The House of Lords found that she was placed at a disadvantage when compared to others, but the reasoning was not straightforward or unanimous. Lord Rodger found that the comparators should be a limited class of persons that would vary from case to case, reflecting the variety of scenarios envisaged by the legislation. Further, this class of persons was flexible. For instance, a job applicant may be compared with existing workers (rather than other applicants), or a candidate for promotion may be compared with other candidates who at the time were doing different jobs. In the instant case the comparators should be other road sweepers who were not disabled.[161] In apparent contrast, Lady Hale stipulated that the comparators were *not* Ms Archibald's fellow road-sweepers, because that merely decides that her disadvantage was caused by her disability. (Her concern here appears to be that upon such an interpretation, no duty on the council to adjust could arise, because there was nothing the council could do to enable Ms Archibald to do the job: it was the disability, and not the council, that caused the disadvantage.) Lady Hale noted that the Act does not require a like-for-like comparison used for direct and indirect discrimination legislation and then virtually abandoned the notion of a comparison, preferring simply to rule that "the duty is triggered where an employee becomes so disabled that she can no longer meet the requirements of her job description."[162]

In the second case, even some able-bodied persons could not do the job. In *Smith v Churchills Stairlifts*,[163] Mr Smith had lumbar spondylosis, which prevented him from lifting heavy objects. He was offered a place on a training course, along with nine other candidates, with a view to being appointed to sell radiator cabinets. Between the offer and the start of the training course Churchills decided that their sales team should carry a full-sized radiator cabinet weighing 25 kilograms as a sales aid. Mr Smith was unable to lift the cabinet and his offer was withdrawn. The employment tribunal compared him to members of the population generally and concluded that as most of the population were unable to lift the cabinet, Mr Smith had not been placed at a substantial disadvantage. (In fact one person on the training course dropped out because he could not carry the cabinet.) The Court of Appeal disagreed, echoing Lady Hale's opinion from

13–035

---

[159] [2004] I.C.R. 954 (HL).
[160] See [2004] I.R.L.R. 197 (CS), [16].
[161] [2004] I.C.R. 954, [42].
[162] ibid. [64].
[163] [2006] I.R.L.R. 41 (CA). See further below, para.13–040.

Archibald, stating that "the proper comparator is readily identified by reference to the disadvantage caused by the relevant arrangements."[164] Here, the proper comparators were the other nine candidates offered the training course.

This approach was articulated by Cox J. in *Fareham College v Waters*,[165] the third case. She stated that the like-for-like comparison required for direct discrimination had no place in a reasonable adjustments complaint. To hold otherwise "would defeat the purpose of the disability discrimination legislation." In this case the employer refused a phased return to work for a employee who had been absent for eight months with fibromyalgia. As she would not return full-time, her employer dismissed her. Cox J. rejected the employer's argument that the comparator should be a worker absent for a similar time, who would have been dismissed. It was "quite clear" that the comparator group was "other employees ... who are not disabled and who are able forthwith to attend work and to carry out the essential tasks required of them in their post."[166] Unlike the claimant, these workers were not under the threat of dismissal.

This general approach reflects the "positive discrimination" aspect of the duty. It does not require *equal* treatment, but particular treatment, or "adjustments" for those with disabilities.

(3) Knowledge of the Disability

(a) Applicants

13–036   Schedule 8, para.20(a) of the EA 2010, provides that no duty arises if the employer does not know, and could not reasonably be expected to know, that a person with a disability is an applicant or potential applicant. Bear in mind the restrictions on asking applicants about disability and health.[167]

Some guidance was provided in *Ridout v TC Group*.[168] Here a job applicant declared that she suffered from "photosensitive epilepsy controlled by Epilim" (a rare form of epilepsy). Before her interview she complained about the bright unscreened lighting in the room, and wore sunglasses around her neck. The employer thought that this complaint merely explained her sunglasses and proceeded with the interview, during which Ms Ridout neither used her sunglasses nor stated that she was at a disadvantage. The EAT held that no duty arose. Morison J. stated that what is now para.20(1)(a) required tribunals to "measure the extent of the duty if any, against the actual or assumed knowledge of the employer both as to the disability and

---

[164] ibid. [39].
[165] [2009] I.R.L.R. 991 (EAT).
[166] ibid. [58]–[59].
[167] EA 2010 s.60. See immediately below, para.13–037.
[168] [1998] I.R.L.R. 628 (EAT).

its likelihood of causing the individual a substantial disadvantage."[169] On the facts of this case, especially Ms Ridout's condition being "very rare", the employer could not be expected to make adjustments without being told in terms that the lighting would disadvantage her.[170]

More generally, Morison J. commented that it was undesirable that applicants should be forced to "harp on" about their disability during an interview (which will be, of course, before any appointment decided upon), while at the same time it was equally undesirable for employers to ask a number of intrusive questions of the applicant about his or her disability: "People must be taken very much on the basis of how they present themselves."[171] Morison J.'s caution has been formalised by EA 2010 s.60, discussed next.

(i) Enquiries about disability and health—section 60
The purpose of s.60 is to prevent any *unnecessary* questions relating **13–037** to disability and health. Section 60 achieves this with a general rule that an employer may not make enquiries of an applicant's disability or health, until that person has been either offered a job (on a conditional or unconditional basis) or been included in a pool of successful candidates to be offered a job when a suitable position arises. It is qualified by a number of exceptions. The first exception permits questions to be asked where they are needed in the context of national security vetting.[172] The other five are provided by s.60(6)(a)–(e):

(a) Making reasonable adjustments to enable the disabled person to participate in the recruitment process.
This applies only to the recruitment process, not to any requirements to do the job itself. This is to allow, for example, people with a speech impairment more time for interview.[173] It could go further to see whether an applicant would be able to participate in an assessment to test his or her suitability for the work.

The Code of Practice suggests:

"An employer is recruiting play workers for an outdoor activity centre and wants to hold a practical test for applicants as part of the recruitment process. He asks a question about health in order to ensure that applicants who are not able to undertake the test (for example, because they have a particular mobility

[169] ibid. [23].
[170] ibid. [4].
[171] ibid. [25]–[26].
[172] EA 2010 s.60(14).
[173] Explanatory Note (202).

impairment or have an injury) are not required to take the test. This would be lawful under the Act."[174]

(b) *Establishing whether a job applicant would be able to undertake a function that is intrinsic to the job, with reasonable adjustments in place as required.*
An applicant applies for a job in a warehouse, which requires the manual lifting and handling of heavy items. As manual handling is a function which is intrinsic to the job, the employer is permitted to ask the applicant questions about his health to establish whether he is able to do the job (with reasonable adjustments for a disabled applicant, if required). The employer would not be permitted to ask the applicant other health questions until he or she offered the candidate a job.[175]

(c) *Monitoring diversity in applications for jobs.*

(d) *Supporting positive action in employment for disabled people.*
The employer can ask if a person is disabled so they can benefit from any measures aimed at improving disabled people's employment rates (under s.158, see above, Chapter 11, para.11–008). This could include the guaranteed interview scheme whereby any disabled person who meets the essential requirements of the job is offered an interview. The employer should make the clear the purpose of the question.[176]

(e) *If the employer applies in relation to the work a requirement to have a particular disability, establishing whether the applicant has that disability.*
This could arise where the job determines that the person has a particular disability and falls within a GOR exception provided in Sch.9, para.1.[177]

Only the Equality and Human Rights Commission can bring action for a breach of s.60, in itself. However, where reliance on the information given leads to an act of discrimination by the employer, such as a rejection, the applicant may sue for disability discrimination. In a case of rejection this will be for direct discrimination, and "the particulars of the complaint" are enough to establish a prima facie case.[178]

[174] *Draft Equality Act 2010 Code of Practice on Employment* (see above, n.109), para.10.31.
[175] Explanatory Note (202).
[176] *Draft Equality Act 2010 Code of Practice on Employment* (see above, n.109), para.10.33
[177] See Ch.8, para.8–019.
[178] EA 2010 s.60(5). See further, Ch.12, para.12–002.

(b) Cases other than Applicants

For cases other than applicants, such as existing workers, the test is **13–038** slightly different. An employer is under no duty if it does not know, and could not reasonably be expected to know that the person has a disability and is likely to be placed at the disadvantage (Sch.8, para.20(1)(b)).

This question is better understood asked in the positive. If the employer knows, or ought to know, that the worker has a disability *and* the disability puts her at the substantial disadvantage, the duty arises. Otherwise it does not. So no duty arises where the employer knows, or ought to know, of the disability, but not that it puts her at the disadvantage. In *Secretary of State for Work and Pensions v Alam*,[179] the claimant expressed symptoms of depression with sudden losses of temper, a loss of concentration, and severe headaches. On one occasion, he left work early without permission. This was to attend an interview for second job, which he desperately needed. He was disciplined and for this and claimed that his employer was under a duty to make reasonable adjustments. The EAT held that the symptoms expressed meant that the employer ought to have known that he had a disability, but the employer had no reason to believe that this would lead to him having to leave work early. Thus, no duty arose.

However, the Code of Practice on Employment suggests that an employer alerted to the existence of a disability should make reasonable enquiries about the disability and what adjustments could be made, bearing mind matters of dignity and privacy.

> "A worker who deals with customers by phone at a call centre has depression which sometimes causes her to cry at work. She has difficulty dealing with customer enquiries when the symptoms of her depression are severe. It is likely to be reasonable for the employer to discuss with the worker whether her crying is connected to a disability and whether a reasonable adjustment could be made to her working arrangements."[180]

(4) The Reasonable Adjustment Duty[181]

Once the duty is triggered, the employer's duty definitely becomes **13–039** proactive. In *Cosgrove v Caesar and Howie*,[182] Ms Cosgrove, a secretary with a firm of solicitors, went off work for a year with

---

[179] [2010] I.C.R. 665 (EAT), [21].

[180] *Draft Equality Act 2010 Code of Practice on Employment* (see above, n.109), para.6.19. See also, in the context of discrimination arising from disability, para.13–029, above.

[181] For a criticism of the application of the parallel duty in the United States, see M. Weber, "Unreasonable Accommodation and Due Hardship" (2010) 62 Florida Law 1119, or *papers.ssrn.com/sol3/papers.cfm?abstract_id=1559899* (accessed January 1, 2010).

[182] [2001] I.R.L.R. 653 (EAT), [7]–[8].

depression. Neither she nor her doctor could suggest any steps that her employer could take to help her back into work. Nonetheless, the EAT held that her employer remained under a duty to take reasonable steps. The duty to make adjustments was on the employer, not the worker. If the employer had turned his mind to the question, he may have considered an alteration of hours, or a gradual return to work, or a transfer to another (less stressful) office.

The word "reasonable" means that the duty will be judged objectively. In *Mid-Staffordshire General Hospital NHS Trust v Cambridge*,[183] the EAT suggested that where the employer does not know what to do, it should make a proper inquiry. The previous Code of Practice (published after *Mid-Staffordshire* decision) built on this, suggesting that "it might be reasonable" to conduct "a proper assessment of what reasonable adjustments may be required".[184] This has been criticised for going too far. An objective test means that a person who unknowingly makes a reasonable adjustment is not liable, even though he failed to make a proper inquiry.[185] This could occur where, say, a hotelier installs a lift to make his hotel more attractive to the general public. Conversely, where nothing could be done, the employer is under no duty to make an inquiry or consider adjustments.[186] It follows that defendants who fail to make reasonable adjustments cannot hide behind a "proper inquiry". Nevertheless, the new Code of Practice suggests that "It is a good starting point for an employer to conduct a proper assessment, in consultation with the disabled person concerned ...".[187]

The most notable feature of this duty is that it permits employers to treat a person with a disability *more* favourably.[188] This contrasts with the symmetrical model of used in discrimination law elsewhere, which tries to achieve *equal* treatment. In *Archibald v Fife Council*[189] an employment tribunal held that an employer did not breach its duty to make adjustments when failing to waive the "well-established" competitive interview for a transfer to other work. This was because inter alia the tribunal incorrectly understood that the Act did not permit more favourable treatment. The House of Lords reversed, holding that in some cases, the duty to make reasonable adjustments not only permits, but obliges employers to treat a claimant more favourably.[190] In *Archibald*, that could be waiving the normal requirement for a competitive interview.

---

[183] [2003] I.R.L.R. 566, (EAT).
[184] *Code of Practice Employment and Occupation* (2004) London: TSO (ISBN 0 11 703419 3), para.5.20.
[185] See K. Monaghan "Equality Law" (Oxford: OUP, 2008), 6.209; *Tarbuck v Sainsbury* [2006] I.R.L.R. 664 (EAT), [65]–[74] (Elias J.).
[186] *British Gas v McCaull* [2001] I.R.L.R. 60 (EAT).
[187] *Draft Equality Act 2010 Code of Practice on Employment* (see above, n.109), para.6.32.
[188] EA 2010 s.13(3).
[189] (2003) EATS/0025/02; [2004] I.C.R. 954 (HL). See further above, para.13–033.
[190] [2004] I.C.R. 954, [19] (Lord Hope), [30] (Lord Roger), [47] (Lady Hale).

As seen in *Archibald*, possible adjustments are not confined to the **13–040** job being done by the worker in question. Where reasonable, a different job could be offered, or a job-swap.[191] Although the onus falls on the employer, the employer should consider any reasonable suggestions by the worker. This allows for more imaginative solutions. In *Smith v Churchills Stairlifts*[192] (see above) Mr Smith suggested a trial period of selling without the using the heavy radiator cabinet. The employer acted unreasonably when rejecting this suggestion.

The Code of Practice suggests that it may sometimes be necessary for an employer to take a combination of steps.[193] In *Gibson Shipbrokers v Staples*,[194] the claimant worked as broker, earning around £280,000 pa. He had a heart condition and suffered occasional dizzy spells and blackouts. Consequently, he went off sick for 18 months. His employer dismissed him on the ground of ill-health, despite his doctor suggesting: a phased return to work; additional support to enable the claimant to get up to speed on market conditions; a reduction in his working hours or duties; some home working and reduced travel. The employer argued that each adjustment in itself would not have prevented the dismissal. The EAT rejected this, holding that it was not necessary for each adjustment to prevent the substantial disadvantage. They could be assessed cumulatively.[195] The EAT cited the Code of Practice in force at the time:

> "[A]n adjustment which, taken alone, is of marginal benefit, may be one of several adjustments which, when looked at together, would be effective. In that case, it is likely to be reasonable to have to make it."[196]

The Act does not specify any particular factors that should be taken into account. The new Code emphasises that all depends on the circumstances of each individual case,[197] but it provides the following guidelines:[198]

> *(a) Whether taking any particular steps would be effective in preventing the substantial disadvantage;*
>
> *(b) the practicality of the step;*

---

[191] *Chief Constable of South Yorkshire Police v Jelic* [2010] I.R.L.R. 744 (EAT).
[192] [2006] I.R.L.R. 41 (CA). See further above, para.13–035.
[193] *Draft Equality Act 2010 Code of Practice on Employment* (see above, n.109), para.6.34.
[194] (2008) UKEAT/0178/08/RN.
[195] ibid. [44].
[196] *Code of Practice Employment and Occupation* (2004) London: TSO (ISBN 0 11 703419 3), para.5.29. This extract was not repeated in the new *draft* Code.
[197] *Draft Equality Act 2010 Code of Practice on Employment* (see above, n.109), para.6.23, echoing the EAT in *Chief Constable of South Yorkshire Police v Jelic* [2010] I.R.L.R. 744 (EAT) [52] (Cox J.).
[198] ibid. para.6.28.

(c) *the financial and other costs of making the adjustment and the extent of any disruption caused.* The Code of Practice suggests:

> "Even if an adjustment has a significant cost associated with it, it may still be cost-effective in overall terms—for example, compared with the costs of recruiting and training a new member of staff – and so may still be a reasonable adjustment to have to make."[199]

(d) *the extent of the employer's financial and other resources.*

(e) *the availability to the employer of financial or other assistance to help make an adjustment.*
Section 20(7), EA 2010, states that, (subject to express provision), an employer cannot pass on any costs to the person of making the adjustment.

(f) *the type and size of the employer*
Small businesses are not exempt, however, a small business is less likely, for instance, to have cover for absences enforced by a worker's disability, or to be able to offer alternative employment.

13–041   The Code of Practice provides the following examples of steps that may have to be taken:[200]

- Making adjustments to premises;
- Providing information in accessible formats
- Allocating some of the person's duties to another worker
- Transferring the person to fill an existing vacancy
- Altering the person's hours of working or training
- Assigning the person to a different place of work or training, or arrangement home working
- Allowing the person to be absent during working or training hours for rehabilitation, assessment or treatment
- Giving, or arranging for, training or mentoring (whether for the disabled person or any other person)
- Acquiring or modifying equipment
- Modifying procedures for testing or assessment
- Providing a reader or interpreter

[199] ibid. para.6.25
[200] ibid. para.6.33.

- Providing supervision or other support.

- Allowing the person to take a period of disability leave

- Participating in supported employment schemes, such as Workstep

- Employing a support worker to assist a disabled worker

- Modifying disciplinary or grievance procedures for a disabled worker

- Adjusting redundancy selection criteria for a disabled worker

- Modifying performance-related pay arrangements for a disabled worker

This is an illustrative non-exhaustible list, and other steps may have to be taken. In *Chief Constable of South Yorkshire v Jelic*,[201] it was held that the employer was obliged to consider in the circumstances a job swap, even though this adjustment did not appear in the (previous) list, which was then provided in the legislation.

INDEX

LEGAL TAXONOMY
FROM SWEET & MAXWELL

This index has been prepared using Sweet and Maxwell's Legal Taxonomy. Main index entries conform to keywords provided by the Legal Taxonomy except where references to specific documents or non-standard terms (denoted by quotation marks) have been included. These keywords provide a means of identifying similar concepts in other Sweet & Maxwell publications and online services to which keywords from the Legal Taxonomy have been applied. Readers may find some minor differences between terms used in the text and those which appear in the index. Suggestions to: **sweetandmaxwell.taxonomy@thomson.com**

427